C# Annotated Standard

C# Annotated Standard

Jon Jagger
Software Consultant/Trainer
United Kingdom

Nigel Perry
Computer Scientist
New Zealand

Peter Sestoft
IT University of Copenhagen
Denmark

ELSEVIER

AMSTERDAM · BOSTON · HEIDELBERG · LONDON
NEW YORK · OXFORD · PARIS · SAN DIEGO
SAN FRANCISCO · SINGAPORE · SYDNEY · TOKYO

Morgan Kaufmann Publishers is an imprint of Elsevier

MORGAN KAUFMANN PUBLISHERS

Publishing Director	Joanne Tracy
Acquisitions Editor	Tiffany Gasbarrini
Publishing Services Manager	George Morrison
Senior Production Manager	Paul Gottehrer
Assistant Editor	Michele Cronin
Marketing Manager	Ian Seager
Cover Design	Joanne Blank
Text Design	Dennis Schaefer
Composition	SPI
Interior printer	Sheridan Books
Cover printer	Phoenix

Morgan Kaufmann Publishers is an imprint of Elsevier
30 Corporate Drive, Suite 400, Burlington, MA 01803, USA

This book is printed on acid-free paper

Library of Congress Cataloging-in-Publication Data
Jagger, Jon.
  Annotated C# standard / by Jon Jagger, Nigel Perry, Peter Sestoft.
      p. cm.
  Includes bibliographical references and index.
  ISBN 978-0-12-372511-0 (alk. paper)
  1. C# (Computer program language)   I. Perry, Nigel. II. Sestoft, Peter. III. Title.
QA76.73.C154J35 2007
005.13'3–dc22

ISBN: 978-0-12-372511-0

For information on all Morgan Kaufmann publications,
visit our Web site at www.mkp.com or www.books.elsevier.com

Printed in the United States of America
07 08 09 10 11   5 4 3 2 1

Dedications

To my beautiful wife, Natalie, and to our three beautiful children—Ellie, Penny, and Patrick. *Jon*

To Janet and Sam; Dad, for striving to keep the young numerate literate; and my students, who've made teaching a privilege. *Nigel*

To Lone, who is both my dear wife and an exemplary scientist. *Peter*

Contents

Foreword to the Annotated Standard

Why is this thus? What is the reason of this thusness?

— Artemus
Ward

Why does my program work the way it does? For many programmers, all they need to figure this out is some experimentation with the compiler and debugger, along with a tutorial description of the language. By observing what the compiler does, and using a little trial and error, they can make their programs run (mostly) correctly, which is enough to get their job done.

But some programmers want to understand their programs and their language at a deeper level. *Why* does the compiler give this error message? *Why* is this method called, instead of that one? To fully understand exactly how every program should behave, you need a formal language specification. This specification describes, in exacting detail, what programs are valid or invalid (and why), and how the valid programs should behave.

Unlike many languages, the formal specification for C# was not written after the first compiler was written, but together with it, in simultaneous but always distinct efforts. The language team, led by Anders Hejlsberg and guided by his vision, always had as its goal the production of a formal language specification, which eventually became the base document that the Ecma committee continued to refine. The compiler team, led by myself, had to quickly develop a compiler that implemented the evolving spec, and could also be used to do real work.

This dual arrangement worked surprisingly well. The language specification kept the compiler honest, while the compiler kept the language specification honest. And most importantly, the users of C# kept us both honest. (The Windows Forms team deserves a special commendation for bravery in being the first to irrevocably port their entire code base to C#.) These early users let us know in no uncertain terms when the language hindered them rather than helped!

But *why* is the spec written the way it is? As we were developing the language specification, we always knew that the reasoning behind our decisions was also important. However, between creating the compiler and writing the spec, we never had the time to write down this history and rationale in any formal way. As the refinement of the language moved into the Ecma committee, more changes were made, and the committee grappled with issues both old and new, but again no formal history of these discussions was written.

At long last, this book fills that gap. The annotations provided in this book (alongside the complete language specification) provide the *why* that is often missing from the spec itself, as well as useful perspective on the language and implications that might not be obvious on first (or second, or third…) reading. If you really want to know all there is to know about the *why* behind C#, this is the book for you.

Peter Golde
Original C# Design Team

Preface to the Annotated Standard

This book is an annotated version of the C# Language Standard, created by adding around 400 separate annotations to the complete text of the Standard. The Standard was formally adopted as ISO Standard 23270:2006 in April 2006 and published in August 2006, and adopted as Ecma International Standard 334 version 4 in June 2006. Microsoft Visual Studio 2005 (released November 2005) and Novell Mono 1.2 (released fall 2006) implement this version of the Standard, commonly referred to as C# 2.0.

Like any programming language, the C# language does not exist in isolation. Most C# compilers target implementations of the Common Language Infrastructure (CLI, Ecma International Standard 335, ISO Standard 23271). Indeed, the design of the language itself has been influenced by, though is not reliant upon, the CLI, and in particular the C# Standard Library (Annex D) is defined in terms of the CLI Standard Library. Specific C# systems add further to the environment in which C# programs execute, such as Microsoft's System.Windows.Forms and Novell's Mono. Math.Prime.

This rich environment surrounding C# and its necessary interaction with it raises the question of what topics annotations may cover. Most annotations concern the C# language itself or the C# Standard Library, but some annotations highlight unusual interactions between C# and the CLI or even the behavior of specific implementations. The annotations range from short illuminating comments over (hopefully) interesting anecdotes to larger code samples designed to highlight some of the new features of C# 2.0. Deciding what could be included and what should be omitted was often difficult, a task kept in check by the publisher's page limits!

This is a book about the language and its purpose does not include reporting "features" in compiler versions current at the time of writing. However, we have included a few annotations that report on such features where we felt the impact was significant enough. Compilers change, and it is more than likely that the reader will be using more recent versions than were available during the writing of the book.

Readers will note that the three of us live in different countries and timezones. While Jon fished local rivers in early summer, Nigel was sitting out a snowstorm. Technology, which worked most of the time, made this book possible. The main text was created by distributed collaborative authoring and editing using a special-purpose XML-based Wiki implemented by Jon in Britain and hosted on a web server by Peter in Copenhagen, Denmark, with backup done to a system in New Zealand by Nigel. Annotations were contributed from homes, offices, hotels and airports worldwide; one (§12.3) was even added in-flight over Greenland using wireless from a Scandinavian Airlines flight. The initial text for the Wiki was created by importing the Word source document into OpenOffice, exporting it in XML format, and then cleaning up and regularizing the XML using XSLT (and good text editors!).

Acknowledgments

For the Standard itself, the text of the original submission to Ecma that formed the basis of Ecma version 2 and ISO version 1 was written by Anders Hejlsberg, Scott Wiltamuth, and Peter Golde. Major submissions which formed the basis of Ecma version 4 and ISO version 2 were written by Andrew Kennedy, Don Syme and Shon Katzenberger. Further contributions to all versions came from the Ecma TC39 TG2 (C#) standardization committee, and other employees of Microsoft and the other companies represented at Ecma. The committee's editor, Rex Jaeschke, maintained the Standard text for all versions over the long process of gradual extensions and refinements.

International Standards, by convention, do not acknowledge by name those who gave their time to produce them, though in this version we did manage to list the companies and institutions for whom they worked. So we'd like to take this opportunity to publicly thank the main members of the C# committee: Michal Cierniak, Andrew Clinick, Jeff Dyer, Carol Thompson Eidt, Erik Eidt, Peter Golde, Peter Hallam, Waldemar Horwat, Mike Iarrobino, Miguel de Icaza, Jon Jagger, Rex Jaeschke, Kazuyoshi Korosue, Toshiaki Kurakawa, Steven Lees, Joel Marcey, Nigel Perry, Thomas Plum, Sam Ruby, Peter Sestoft, Scott Smith, Danny Thorpe and Satoshi Yajima; and also the myriad of others who worked from the sidelines or came along as guests to meetings.

Some annotations in this book were written by people other than the primary authors. Many guest annotators from the committee, the language teams at Microsoft and Novell, and others from the wider community contributed annotations and suggestions for us to review and include. Each annotation written by a guest is acknowledged, whereas those by the primary authors are uncredited.

In a number of cases annotations were merged with others or so heavily edited/destroyed by us that the original contributor could no longer be held responsible for the contents; these too go uncredited. In particular, we are indebted to Jon Skeet who contributed far more time and effort than will be apparent from browsing this book, and to Peter Hallam and Shon Katzenberger from Microsoft who replied to countless questions about subtleties in the Standard and in Microsoft's implementation.

Those who have contributed annotations to the book are as follows:

- *Martin Baulig* implemented many of the new C# 2.0 features, in particular, generics, in the Mono C# compiler and runtime system. He has also contributed to GNOME and other open source projects. Martin lives in Trier, Germany, and joined Novell three years ago.
- *Mike Cowlishaw* has worked in both hardware and software design and is the leader of the IBM decimal arithmetic initiative. Mike is an IBM Fellow, a Fellow of the Royal Academy of Engineering, and a Visiting Professor in Computer Science at the University of Warwick.
- *Nicu Georgian Fruja* is a PhD candidate at ETH Zurich working on the dissertation "Type Safety in C# and .NET CLR." He obtained his bachelors in applied mathematics and masters in applied statistics and operations research from the University of Bucharest.
- *Peter Golde* was a member of the original C# design team and the development lead for the initial implementation of the Microsoft C# compiler. Peter is also the author of the *Power Collections* framework, which is available for download via his blog at www.wintellect.com/Weblogs.
- *Peter Hallam* is a Tech Lead at Microsoft responsible for the C# compiler and is a member of the C# language design team. He holds a B.Math in Computer Science from the University of Waterloo.
- *Raja Harinath* is from Novell and a maintainer of Mono's C# compiler. He obtained a PhD on "QoS-aware Multimedia Middleware Frameworks" in November 2003 from the University of Minnesota; he previously obtained a BE from the BMS College of Engineering (Bangalore).
- *Miguel de Icaza* is a free software programmer from Mexico, best known for starting the GNOME and Mono projects. He was one of the founders of Ximian, a Linux Desktop company that was acquired in 2003 by Novell and is now Mono project manager at Novell.
- *Paolo Molaro* led the development of the Mono virtual machine as part of Novell and was in charge of designing the new portable just-in-time compiler as well as the compacting garbage collector in Mono. Paolo lives in Padova, Italy.
- *Marek Safar* is from the Czech Republic and has worked in the software field for the last decade. He currently works as an IT Consultant for a company in London. He has been

involved in C#/CLI development since 2001, and he has been a Mono contributor since 2004.

- *Jon Skeet* is a software engineer in Reading, UK and self described "amateur language lawyer." He is well known for answering community questions in the C# newsgroups. Jon has been a C# Microsoft Most Valuable Professional since 2003.

Finally we wish to thank Jan van den Beld, secretary general of Ecma International, for permission to use the entire text of the Standard as the basis for this book; and the publisher's three reviewers, Nigel Dickens, Derek Jones, and Matthew Strawbridge for their comments on the draft text.

Jon Jagger
Nigel Perry
Peter Sestoft
August 2006

About The Authors

Jon Jagger runs a software consultancy, JSL (http://www.jaggersoft.com), in the United Kingdom. Jon is a consultant, developer, and a trainer with wide experience of C# (as well as C++, Java, C, OO, and Patterns). He was the Principal UK Expert for the ISO Ballot Meeting on the First Edition of the C# Standard and took over convenorship of the Ecma TC39 TG2 (C#) working on the Second Edition shortly afterwards. Jon is also a member of TG3 (CLI). He likes to while away his spare time fishing on a riverbank.

Dr. Nigel Perry is a computer scientist from New Zealand with particular research interests in programming languages, recently including expanding the range of languages that can be supported on the CLI. Nigel has acted in an advisory role with Microsoft's CLR team for a number of years. A member of the Ecma TC39 TG2 (C#) and TG3 (CLI) for four years, he took over the convenorship of TG2 (C#) in late 2004. Nigel likes to use a cycle for transport and, when he has time, for recreation. He combines his professional expertise and recreational interest through involvement in road safety and cycle advocacy.

Dr. Peter Sestoft is a professor at the IT University of Copenhagen and the Royal Veterinary and Agricultural University, Denmark, and a member of the Ecma TC39 TG2 (C#) and TG3 (CLI). His research interests include programming languages and their implementation. He has recently been working on an advanced collection library called C5 for C#. Peter is an author of a number of books, including *C# Precisely* at the MIT Press (2004, revised 2006).

Errata To The International Standard

During the course of writing this book, a number of minor errors in the Standard were discovered. A number of errata were also found by the Japanese JIS (Japanese Industrial Standards) translation committee chaired by Toshiaki Kurokawa. The following table contains all known errata:

Clause	Location	Errata
3	2nd para	Correct "23271:2005" to "23271:2006"
8.5	table	Replace reference to §14.5.14 with §14.6
8.7.12	1st para	Correct "typeof" to "`typeof`"
8.7.13	code example	Remove comment (`//`) preceding ellipsis.
8.16.2	3rd para	Correct "an runtime" to "a runtime"
9.1	last 2 paras	Remove indentation, they are not part of the list.
9.4.2	1st Note	Correct "verson" to "version"
11.1.5	1st para after 2nd list	Replace reference to §14.5.12 with §14.5.13
11.1.6	1st bullet	Replace reference to §14.7.2 with §14.7
12.3.3.20	1st para	Replace reference to §14.5.12 with §14.5.13
13.1.5	1st para, 2nd sent	Correct "copying the *value-type* value" to "copying the value"
13.2.1	1st & 3rd bullets of 2nd list	Replace reference to §14.5.12 with §14.5.13
13.7.2	3rd para	Replace reference for "standard implicit conversions" §13.1.1 with §13.3.1
14.2.3	2nd bullet	Replace reference to §14.5.14 with §14.6
14.5.2	2nd bullet of 2nd bullet of 4th bullet	Correct "*namespace-or-type-name*" to "*simple-name*"
14.5.12	1st para	Correct "sizeof" to "`sizeof`", twice
14.6.6	3rd para	Remove indentation.
14.6.6	last 2 paras	Remove indentation.
14.7.4	table, 2nd row, 4th column	Correct "X" to "x"
14.7.5	table, 2nd row, 2nd thru 4th columns	Remove "+" signs
14.9.6	3rd bullet	This bullet is wrong, not matching statements later in same clause. See annotation on clause for details.
14.9.9	title	Replace "Equality operators and null" with "Equality operators and nullable types"
14.12	3rd para	Replace "E1 ?? E2 ?? ... ?? EN" with "E_1 ?? E_2 ?? ... ?? E_N"
14.12	3rd para	Correct "[Example: ... end example]" to "*[Example*: ... *end example]*"
14.16	code sample	Correct double quotation marks (",") surrounding "hello" to straight double quotation marks (")
14.16	3rd para from end	Replace reference to §14.5.12 with §14.5.13
15.7.2	1st para	Correct "switch" to "`switch`"
15.11	last para	Replace reference to §14.5.12 with §14.5.13

16.4.1	10th code block	Comment misaligned
17.1	2nd para	Replace reference to §17.1.1.3 with §17.1.2
17.4.5	1st para after 1st example	Replace reference to §17.4.3 with §17.4.4
17.4.5.1	both examples	Replace method name "f" with "F"
17.5.1.4	1st para before 3rd example	Correct "expended" to "expanded"
17.9.1	2nd bullet	Correct "type that same type" to "the same type"
17.12	2nd code sample	Correct "B's" and "A's" to "B's" and "A's" respectively
18.2	last para	Replace reference to §17.1.4 with §17.2
19.2	1st para	Replace reference to §19.6 with §19.7
19.6	code block	Comments misaligned
20.4.2	1st para after 1st example	Replace "class" with "class or struct"
21.1	last note	Replace reference to §19.6 with §19.7
23.1	1st para	Replace "Exception" with "Exceptions"
23.1	2nd bullet	Replace "expression" with "expressions"
24.2	1st para	Replace reference to §17.1.4 with §17.2
24.2	1st para	Replace reference to §21.1 with §21.3
24.2	1st note	Replace reference to §19.6 with §19.7
24.4.2.1	after 2nd bullet	Insert omitted bullet "The conditional method shall not have out parameters."
24.4.2.1	1st code example	Remove comment (//) preceding ellipsis.
24.4.2.2	2nd code sample	Correct double quotation marks (", ") surrounding "DEBUG" to straight double quotation marks (")
25.3.1	Last code example	Correct new X to new Derived
25.5.5	1st para	Insert space before 1st T_N
25.7.1	1st inner bullet of 4th outer bullet	The 2nd sentence should be a separate bullet
25.7.2	1st para	Correct "theses types" to "these types"
27.2	3rd bullet from end	Correct operator => to >=
27.5	3rd para	Replace reference to §14.5.14 with §14.6
27.5.7	1st para	Correct operator => to >=
27.5.8	2nd para	Correct "sizeof" to "sizeof"
27.6	1st bullet	Replace reference to §12.3.3.27 with §12.4
27.8	last para	Format 3 occurrences of "byte" as byte
D	1st para	Correct "23271:2005" to "23271:2006"
E.1	2nd bullet	Correct "refered" to "referred", twice
E.2	last row of table	Replace reference to §E.2.15 with §E.2.17
E.2.4	list, 1st item	Correct cref="member" to member
E.2.6	example	Correct "non-trvial" to "non-trivial"
E.2.16	example	Correct MakeArray<t> to MakeArray<T>
E.2.16	example	Correct <typeparamref name="T"/> to <typeparamref name="T"/>
E.3.1	last bullet	Correct "typs" to "types"

E.3.1	last bullet	Insert space before followed in: grave accent character "'"followed
E.4.1	code sample	Correct "non-trvial" to "non-trivial"
E.4.2	XML sample	Correct "non-trvial" to "non-trivial"
G	Index	Correct "movable" to "moveable", twice

Rather than adding an intrusive annotation for each of these minor errors, we have fixed them in the text, thus deviating very slightly from the "full text" of the Standard. We have not changed the Standard's words in any other way.

The C# International Standard

Annotation

Foreword

This fourth edition cancels and replaces the third edition. Changes from the previous edition were made to align this Standard with ISO/IEC 23270:2006.

Introduction

This International Standard is based on a submission from Hewlett-Packard, Intel, and Microsoft, that described a language called C#, which was developed within Microsoft. The principal inventors of this language were Anders Hejlsberg, Scott Wiltamuth, and Peter Golde. The first widely distributed implementation of C# was released by Microsoft in July 2000, as part of its .NET Framework initiative.

Ecma Technical Committee 39 (TC39) Task Group 2 (TG2) was formed in September 2000 to produce a standard for C#. Another Task Group, TG3, was also formed at that time to produce a standard for a library and execution environment called Common Language Infrastructure (CLI). (CLI is based on a subset of the .NET Framework.) Although Microsoft's implementation of C# relies on CLI for library and runtime support, other implementations of C# need not, provided they support an alternate way of getting at the minimum CLI features required by this C# standard (see Annex D).

CLI not required

The last sentence above does not imply there must be a CLI implementation available so that its minimum features can be accessed; a better wording might have been:

Although the current Microsoft and Mono implementations of C# rely on the CLI for library and runtime support, other implementations of C# need not. They must, however, provide the library and runtime features (Annex D) required by this International Standard.

As the definition of C# evolved, the goals used in its design were as follows:

- C# is intended to be a simple, modern, general-purpose, object-oriented programming language.
- The language, and implementations thereof, should provide support for software engineering principles such as strong type checking, array bounds checking, detection of attempts to use uninitialized variables, and automatic garbage collection. Software robustness, durability, and programmer productivity are important.
- The language is intended for use in developing software components suitable for deployment in distributed environments.
- Source code portability is very important, as is programmer portability, especially for those programmers already familiar with C and C++.
- Support for internationalization is very important.
- C# is intended to be suitable for writing applications for both hosted and embedded systems, ranging from the very large that use sophisticated operating systems, down to the very small having dedicated functions.
- Although C# applications are intended to be economical with regard to memory and processing power requirements, the language was not intended to compete directly on performance and size with C or assembly language.

The following companies and organizations have participated in the development of this standard, and their contributions are gratefully acknowledged: ActiveState, Borland, CSK Corp., Hewlett-Packard, IBM, Intel, IT University of Copenhagen, Jaggersoft (UK), Microsoft, Mountain View Compiler, Monash University (AUS), Netscape, Novell, Pixo, Plum Hall, Sun, and the University of Canterbury (NZ).

The development of this version of the standard started in January 2003.

This Ecma Standard has been adopted by the General Assembly of June 2006.

1 Scope

This International Standard specifies the form and establishes the interpretation of programs written in the C# programming language. It specifies

- The representation of C# programs;
- The syntax and constraints of the C# language;
- The semantic rules for interpreting C# programs;
- The restrictions and limits imposed by a conforming implementation of C#.

This International Standard does not specify

- The mechanism by which C# programs are transformed for use by a data-processing system;
- The mechanism by which C# applications are invoked for use by a data-processing system;
- The mechanism by which input data are transformed for use by a C# application;
- The mechanism by which output data are transformed after being produced by a C# application;
- The size or complexity of a program and its data that will exceed the capacity of any specific data-processing system or the capacity of a particular processor;
- All minimal requirements of a data-processing system that is capable of supporting a conforming implementation.

2 Conformance

Conformance is of interest to the following audiences:

- Those designing, implementing, or maintaining C# implementations.
- Governmental or commercial entities wishing to procure C# implementations.
- Testing organizations wishing to provide a C# conformance test suite.
- Programmers wishing to port code from one C# implementation to another.
- Educators wishing to teach Standard C#.
- Authors wanting to write about Standard C#.

As such, conformance is most important, and the bulk of this International Standard is aimed at specifying the characteristics that make C# implementations and C# programs conforming ones.

The text in this International Standard that specifies requirements is considered **normative**. All other text in this specification is **informative**; that is, for information purposes only. Unless stated otherwise, all text is normative. Normative text is further broken into **required** and **conditional** categories. **Conditionally normative** text specifies a feature and its requirements where the feature is optional. However, if that feature is provided, its syntax and semantics must be exactly as specified.

Undefined behavior is indicated in this International Standard only by the words "undefined behavior."

A **strictly conforming program** shall use only those features of the language specified in this International Standard as being required. (This means that a strictly conforming program cannot use any conditionally normative feature.) It shall not produce output dependent on any unspecified, undefined, or implementation-defined behavior.

A **conforming implementation** of C# must accept any strictly conforming program.

A conforming implementation of C# must provide and support all the types, values, objects, properties, methods, and program syntax and semantics described in the normative (but not the conditionally normative) parts in this International Standard.

A conforming implementation of C# shall interpret characters in conformance with the Unicode Standard, Version 4.0, and ISO/IEC 10646-1. Conforming implementations must accept Unicode source files encoded with the UTF-8 encoding form.

A conforming implementation of C# shall not successfully translate source containing a `#error` preprocessing directive unless it is part of a group skipped by conditional compilation.

A conforming implementation of C# shall produce at least one diagnostic message if the source program violates any rule of syntax, or any negative requirement (defined as a "shall" or "shall not" or "error" or "warning" requirement), unless that requirement is marked with the words "no diagnostic is required".

A conforming implementation of C# is permitted to provide additional types, values, objects, properties, and methods beyond those described in this International Standard, provided they do not alter the behavior of any strictly conforming program. Conforming implementations are required to diagnose programs that use extensions that are ill formed according to this International Standard. Having done so, however; they can compile and execute such programs. (The ability to have extensions implies that a conforming implementation reserves no identifiers other than those explicitly reserved in this International Standard.)

A conforming implementation of C# shall be accompanied by a document that defines all implementation-defined characteristics, and all extensions.

A conforming implementation of C# shall support the class library documented in Annex D. This library is included by reference in this International Standard.

A **conforming program** is one that is acceptable to a conforming implementation. (Such a program is permitted to contain extensions or conditionally normative features.)

Interpreters

The Standard is written as though a C# implementation consists of a compiler and separate runtime phase, and uses terms such as: compiler, compilation, compile-time, run-time. This should not be taken to imply that a conforming implementation may not be *interpreter* based.

To correctly support the semantics specified in this Standard in an interpreter may be challenging, but should an interpreter do so, then it can be said to be a conforming implementation.

For example, constant expressions (§14.16) require that certain exceptions are thrown at compile-time even if the code causing the exception is unreachable at run-time. If an interpreter-based implementation throws these exceptions and does so before any effect of executing the code is visible, then it can be said to be conforming.

3 Normative references

The following normative documents contain provisions, which, through reference in this text, constitute provisions of this International Standard. For dated references, subsequent amendments to, or revisions of, any of these publications do not apply. However, parties to agreements based on this International Standard are encouraged to investigate the possibility of applying the most recent editions of the normative documents indicated below. For undated references, the latest edition of the normative document referred to applies. Members of ISO and IEC maintain registers of currently valid International Standards.

ISO/IEC 23271:2006, *Common Language Infrastructure (CLI), Partition IV: Base Class Library (BCL), Extended Numerics Library, and Extended Array Library.*

ISO 31.11:1992, *Quantities and units — Part 11: Mathematical signs and symbols for use in the physical sciences and technology.*

ISO/IEC 2382.1:1993, *Information technology — Vocabulary — Part 1: Fundamental terms.*

ISO/IEC 10646 (all parts), *Information technology — Universal Multiple-Octet Coded Character Set (UCS).*

IEC 60559:1989, *Binary floating-point arithmetic for microprocessor systems* (previously designated IEC 559:1989). (This standard is widely known by its U.S. national designation, ANSI/IEEE Standard 754-1985, *IEEE Standard for Binary Floating-Point Arithmetic.*)

The Unicode Consortium. The Unicode Standard, Version 4.0, defined by: *The Unicode Standard, Version 4.0* (Boston, MA, Addison-Wesley, 2003. ISBN 0-321-18578-1).

4 Definitions

For the purposes of this International Standard, the following definitions apply. Other terms are defined where they appear in *italic* type or on the left side of a syntax rule. Terms explicitly defined in this International Standard are not to be presumed to refer implicitly to similar terms defined elsewhere. Terms not defined in this International Standard are to be interpreted according to ISO/IEC 2382.1. Mathematical symbols not defined in this International Standard are to be interpreted according to ISO 31.11.

Application — refers to an assembly that has an entry point (§10.1). When an application is run, a new application domain is created. Several different instantiations of an application can exist on the same machine at the same time, and each has its own application domain.

Application vs. program

Note that an application is *just* an assembly with an entry point, and an application may be used as a *class library* by another application.

Common usage often has the terms *application* and *program* interchangeable, but there is a defined difference in C#; see the definition of program in the following text.

Application domain — an entity that enables application isolation by acting as a container for application state. An application domain acts as a container and boundary for the types defined in the application and the class libraries it uses. Types loaded into one application domain are distinct from the same type loaded into another application domain, and instances of objects are not directly shared between application domains. For instance, each application domain has its own copy of static variables for these types, and a static constructor for a type is run at most once per application domain. Implementations are free to provide implementation-specific policy or mechanisms for the creation and destruction of application domains.

Argument — an expression in the comma-separated list bounded by the parentheses in a method or instance constructor call expression or bounded by the square brackets in an element access expression. It is also known as an *actual argument*.

Assembly — refers to one or more files that are output by the compiler as a result of program compilation. An assembly is a configured set of loadable code modules and other resources that together implement a unit of functionality. An assembly can contain types, the executable code used to implement these types, and references to other assemblies. The physical representation of an assembly is not defined by this specification. Essentially, an assembly is the output of the compiler.

Assembly vs. class files

It is interesting to compare the granularity of Java and C# compiler outputs. A C# compiler will probably emit an assembly, a Java compiler a collection of class files. This emphasizes an important C# design goal—to support components rather than individual types.

Behavior — external appearance or action.

Behavior, implementation-defined — unspecified behavior where each implementation documents how the choice is made.

Behavior, undefined — behavior, upon use of a non-portable or erroneous construct or of erroneous data, for which this International Standard imposes no requirements. [Possible handling of undefined behavior ranges from ignoring the situation completely with unpredictable results, to behaving during translation or execution in a documented manner characteristic of the environment (with or without the issuance of a diagnostic message), to terminating a translation or execution (with the issuance of a diagnostic message)].

Behavior, unspecified — behavior where this International Standard provides two or more possibilities and imposes no further requirements on which is chosen in any instance.

Class library — refers to an assembly that can be used by other assemblies. Use of a class library does not cause the creation of a new application domain. Instead, a class library is loaded into the application domain that uses it. For instance, when an application uses a class library, that class library is loaded into the application domain for that application. If an application uses a class library A that itself uses a class library B, then both A and B are loaded into the application domain for the application.

Accessing class libraries

The mechanism by which class libraries are made available to the current compilation is not defined by this specification.

See the annotation on §16.1 for additional details on class libraries.

Diagnostic message — a message belonging to an implementation-defined subset of the implementation's output messages.

Error, compile-time — an error reported during program translation.

Exception — an error condition that is outside the ordinary expected behavior.

Implementation — particular set of software (running in a particular translation environment under particular control options) that performs translation of programs for, and supports execution of methods in, a particular execution environment.

Namespace — a logical organizational system that provides a way of presenting program elements that are exposed to other programs.

Parameter — a variable declared as part of a method, instance constructor, operator, or indexer definition, which acquires a value on entry to that function member. It is also known as a *formal parameter*.

Program — refers to one or more source files that are presented to the compiler. Essentially, a program is the input to the compiler.

Programs, assemblies, applications and class libraries

This definition of program differs from common usage. In C#, a program is just the *input* to the compiler. The *output* of the compiler is an *assembly*, which is either an *application* or a *class library*.

Program, valid — a C# program constructed according to the syntax rules and diagnosable semantic rules.

Program instantiation — the execution of an application.

Recommended practice — specification that is strongly recommended as being aligned with the intent of the standard, but that might be impractical for some implementations.

Source file — an ordered sequence of Unicode characters. Source files typically have a one-to-one correspondence with files in a file system, but this correspondence is not required.

Unsafe code — code that is permitted to perform such lower-level operations as declaring and operating on pointers, performing conversions between pointers and integral types, and taking the address of variables. Such operations provide functionality such as permitting interfacing with the underlying operating system, accessing a memory-mapped device, or implementing a time-critical algorithm.

Warning, compile-time — an informational message reported during program translation, that is intended to identify a potentially questionable usage of a program element.

5 Notational conventions

Lexical and syntactic grammars for C# are interspersed throughout this specification. The lexical grammar defines how characters can be combined to form **tokens** (§9.4), the minimal lexical elements of the language. The syntactic grammar defines how tokens can be combined to make valid C# programs.

Grammar productions include both non-terminal and terminal symbols. In grammar productions, *non-terminal* symbols are shown in italic type, and `terminal` symbols are shown in a fixed-width font. Each non-terminal is defined by a set of productions. The first line of a set of productions is the name of the non-terminal, followed by one or two colons. One colon is used for a production in the syntactic grammar, two colons for a production in the lexical grammar. Each successive indented line contains the right-hand side for a production that has the non-terminal symbol as the left-hand side. For example:

class-modifier:
```
new
public
protected
internal
private
abstract
sealed
static
```

defines the *class-modifier* non-terminal as having seven productions.

Alternatives are normally listed on separate lines, as shown above, though in cases where there are many alternatives, the phrase "one of" precedes a list of the options. This is simply shorthand for listing each of the alternatives on a separate line. For example:

decimal-digit: *one of*
```
0   1   2   3   4   5   6   7   8   9
```

is equivalent to:

decimal-digit:
```
0
1
2
3
4
5
6
7
8
9
```

A subscripted suffix "$_{opt}$", as in *identifier*$_{opt}$, is used as shorthand to indicate an optional symbol. The example:

for-statement:
    `for` `(` *for-initializer*$_{opt}$ `;` *for-condition*$_{opt}$ `;` *for-iterator*$_{opt}$ `)` *embedded-statement*

is equivalent to:

for-statement:
```
for ( ; ; )
```
     embedded-statement
```
for ( for-initializer ; ; )
```
     embedded-statement
```
for ( ; for-condition ;)
```
     embedded-statement
```
for ( ; ; for-iterator )
```
     embedded-statement
```
for ( for-initializer ; for-condition ;)
```
     embedded-statement
```
for ( ; for-condition ; for-iterator )
```
     embedded-statement
```
for ( for-initializer ; ; for-iterator )
```
     embedded-statement
```
for ( for-initializer ; for-condition ; for-iterator )
```
     embedded-statement

All terminal characters are to be understood as the appropriate Unicode character from the range U+0020 to U+007F, as opposed to any similar-looking characters from other Unicode character ranges.

6 Acronyms and abbreviations

This clause is informative.

The following acronyms and abbreviations are used throughout this International Standard:

BCL — Base Class Library, which provides types to represent the built-in data types of the CLI, simple file access, custom attributes, security attributes, string manipulation, formatting, streams, and collections.

CLI — Common Language Infrastructure

CLS — Common Language Specification

IEC — the International Electrotechnical Commission

IEEE — the Institute of Electrical and Electronics Engineers

ISO — the International Organization for Standardization

The name C# is pronounced "C Sharp".

The name C# is written as the LATIN CAPITAL LETTER C (U+0043) followed by the NUMBER SIGN # (U+0023).

ASCII Rules!

Note that despite being pronounced "C Sharp," and despite C# supporting Unicode, the name is not written using the MUSIC SHARP SIGN (U+266F), that is, as C♯. Further, the second character is not superscripted, as in C$^{\#}$ or C$^{\sharp}$.

The C# name

The story behind the name "C#" is not very deep. The powers that be wanted a name that connected with the "C" language heritage. "C Sharp" was the best option that was free of trademark encumbrances and so forth. (Believe it or not, "Cesium" was briefly considered....)

Note: While "Visual C#®" is a registered trademark of Microsoft Corporation and is used by them to refer to one of their C# compiler implementations, the term "C#" itself is not a trademark.

End of informative text.

7 General description

This text is informative.

This International Standard is intended to be used by implementers, academics, and application programmers. As such, it contains a considerable amount of explanatory material that, strictly speaking, is not necessary in a formal language specification.

This standard is divided into the following subdivisions:

1. Front matter (clauses 1–7);
2. Language overview (clause 8);
3. The language syntax, constraints, and semantics (clauses 9–27);
4. Annexes

Examples are provided to illustrate possible forms of the constructions described. References are used to refer to related clauses. Notes are provided to give advice or guidance to implementers or programmers. Annexes provide additional information and summarize the information contained in this International Standard.

Clauses 1–5, part of 7, 9–26, the beginning of 27, and most of annex D form a normative part of this standard; all of clause 27 with the exception of the beginning is conditionally normative; and Foreword, Introduction, clause 6, part of 7, 8, annexes A, B, C, part of D, E, and F, notes, examples, and the index are informative.

Where to look for requirements on unsafe constructs

The C# standard is deliberately organized so that normative requirements rarely mention unsafe constructs; requirements on unsafe constructs (such as pointers) are conditionally normative and are specified in §27. For example, §12.3 describes definite assignment and does not mention pointer types. However, this does *not* mean that pointers do not affect definite assignment—it means that if they do, it will be specified somewhere in clause 27 (which it is, in §27.5.4, because they do).

End of informative text.

Informative text is indicated in the following ways:

1. Whole or partial clauses or annexes delimited by "**This clause/text is informative**" and "**End of informative text**".
2. [*Example*: The following example … code fragment, possibly with some narrative … *end example*]
3. [*Note*: narrative … *end note*]

All text not marked as being informative is normative.

8 Language overview

This clause is informative.

C# (pronounced "C Sharp") is a simple, modern, object oriented, and type-safe programming language. It will immediately be familiar to C and C++ programmers. C# combines the high productivity of Rapid Application Development (RAD) languages and the raw power of C++.

The rest of this clause describes the essential features of the language. While later clauses describe rules and exceptions in a detail-oriented and sometimes mathematical manner, this clause strives for clarity and brevity at the expense of completeness. The intent is to provide the reader with an introduction to the language that will facilitate the writing of early programs and the reading of later clauses.

> **Annotation free zone**
>
> This entire clause is informative and intended to be an informal introduction to C#, so we have left it as is, unannotated. All the material in this clause is covered in more depth in later normative clauses, and any relevant annotations have been placed in those clauses instead. This clause does round a few corners, and tells a small white lie or two, but such an approach is common in informal overviews and annotating them would disrupt the flow.

8.1 Getting started

The canonical "hello, world" program can be written as follows:

```
using System;

class Hello
{
  static void Main()
  {
    Console.WriteLine("hello, world");
  }
}
```

The source code for a C# program is typically stored in one or more text files with a file extension of `.cs`, as in `hello.cs`. Using a command-line compiler, such a program can be compiled with a command line like

```
csc hello.cs
```

which produces an application named `hello.exe`. The output produced by this application when it is run is:

```
hello, world
```

Close examination of this program is illuminating:

- The `using System;` directive references a namespace called `System` that is provided by the Common Language Infrastructure (CLI) class library. This namespace contains the `Console` class referred to in the `Main` method. Namespaces provide a hierarchical means of organizing the elements of one or more programs. A using directive enables unqualified use of the types that are members of the namespace. The "hello, world" program uses `Console.WriteLine` as shorthand for `System.Console.WriteLine`.

- The `Main` method is a member of the class `Hello`. It has the `static` modifier, and so it is a method on the class `Hello` rather than on instances of this class.
- The entry point for an application—the method that is called to begin execution—is always a static method named `Main`.
- The "hello, world" output is produced using a class library. This standard does not include a class library. Instead, it references the class library provided by CLI.

For C and C++ developers, it is interesting to note a few things that do *not* appear in the "hello, world" program.

- The program does not use a global method for `Main`. Methods and variables are not supported at the global level; such elements are always contained within type declarations (e.g., class and struct declarations).
- The program does not use either "`::`" or "`->`" operators. The "`::`" token is used only to separate a namespace alias from a member of the namespace, and the "`->`" operator is used in only a small fraction of programs (which involve unsafe code). The separator "`.`" is used in compound names such as `Console.WriteLine`.
- The program does not contain forward declarations. Forward declarations are never needed, as declaration order is not significant.
- The program does not use `#include` to import program text. Dependencies among programs are handled symbolically rather than textually. This approach eliminates barriers between applications written using multiple languages. For example, the `Console` class need not be written in C#.

8.2 Types

C# supports two kinds of types: ***value types*** and ***reference types***. Value types include simple types (e.g., `char`, `int`, and `float`), enum types, and struct types. Reference types include class types, interface types, delegate types, and array types.

Value types differ from reference types in that variables of the value types directly contain their data, whereas variables of the reference types store references to objects. With reference types, it is possible for two variables to reference the same object, and thus possible for operations on one variable to affect the object referenced by the other variable. With value types, the variables each have their own copy of the data, and it is not possible for operations on one to affect the other.

The example

```
using System;

struct Struct1
{
    public int Value;
}

class Class1
{
    public int Value = 0;
}

class Test
{
    static void Main()
```

```
  {
    Struct1 val1 = new Struct1();
    Struct1 val2 = val1;
    val2.Value = 123;

    Class1 ref1 = new Class1();
    Class1 ref2 = ref1;
    ref2.Value = 123;

    Console.WriteLine("Values: {0} , {1} ", val1.Value, val2.Value);
    Console.WriteLine("Refs: {0} , {1} ", ref1.Value, ref2.Value);
  }
}
```

shows this difference. The output produced is

```
Values: 0, 123
Refs: 123, 123
```

The assignment to a field of the local variable `val2` does not impact the local variable `val1` because both local variables are of a value type (the type `Struct1`) and each local variable of a value type has its own storage. In contrast, the assignment `ref2.Value = 123;` affects the object that both `ref1` and `ref2` reference.

The lines

```
Console.WriteLine("Values: {0} , [1] ", val1.Value, val2.Value);
Console.WriteLine("Refs: {0} , {1} ", ref1.Value, ref2.Value);
```

deserve further comment, as they demonstrate some of the string formatting behavior of `Console.WriteLine`, which, in fact, takes a variable number of arguments. The first argument is a string, which can contain numbered placeholders like {0} and {1} . Each placeholder refers to a trailing argument with {0} referring to the second argument, {1} referring to the third argument, and so on. Before the output is sent to the console, each placeholder is replaced with the formatted value of its corresponding argument.

Developers can define new value types through enum and struct declarations, and can define new reference types via class, interface, and delegate declarations. The example

```
using System;

public enum Color
{
   Red, Blue, Green
}

public struct Point
{
   public int x, y;
}

public interface IBase
{
   void F();
}

public interface IDerived: IBase
```

```
{
  void G();
}

public class A
{
  protected virtual void H()
  {
    Console.WriteLine("A.H");
  }
}

public class B: A, IDerived
{
  public void F()
  {
    Console.WriteLine("B.F, implementation of IDerived.F");
  }

  public void G()
  {
    Console.WriteLine("B.G, implementation of IDerived.G");
  }

  override protected void H()
  {
    Console.WriteLine("B.H, override of A.H");
  }
}

public delegate void EmptyDelegate();
```

shows an example of each kind of type declaration. Later clauses describe type declarations in detail.

8.2.1 Predefined types

C# provides a set of predefined types, most of which will be familiar to C and C++ developers.

The predefined reference types are `object` and `string`. The type `object` is the ultimate base type of all other types. The type `string` is used to represent Unicode string values. Values of type `string` are immutable.

The predefined value types include signed and unsigned integral types, floating-point types, and the types `bool`, `char`, and `decimal`. The signed integral types are `sbyte`, `short`, `int`, and `long`; the unsigned integral types are `byte`, `ushort`, `uint`, and `ulong`; and the floating-point types are `float` and `double`.

The `bool` type is used to represent Boolean values: values that are either true or false. The inclusion of `bool` makes it easier to write self-documenting code; it also helps eliminate the all-too-common C++ coding error in which a developer mistakenly uses "=" when "==" should have been used. In C#, the example

```
int i = ...;
F(i);
if (i = 0)  // Bug: the test should be (i == 0)
  G();
```

results in a compile-time error because the expression i = 0 is of type int, and if statements require an expression of type bool.

The char type is used to represent Unicode code units. A variable of type char represents a single 16-bit Unicode code unit.

The decimal type is appropriate for calculations in which rounding errors caused by floating point representations are unacceptable. Common examples include financial calculations such as tax computations and currency conversions. The decimal type provides for at least 28 significant digits.

The table below lists the predefined types, and shows how to write literal values for each of them.

Type	Description	Example
object	The ultimate base type of all other types	object o = null;
string	String type; a string is a sequence of Unicode code units	string s = "hello";
sbyte	8-bit signed integral type	sbyte val = 12;
short	16-bit signed integral type	short val = 12;
int	32-bit signed integral type	int val = 12;
long	64-bit signed integral type	long val1 = 12; long val2 = 34L;
byte	8-bit unsigned integral type	byte val1 = 12;
ushort	16-bit unsigned integral type	ushort val1 = 12;
uint	32-bit unsigned integral type	uint val1 = 12; uint val2 = 34U;

ulong	64-bit unsigned integral type	ulong val1 = 12;
		 ulong val2 = 34U;
		 ulong val3 = 56L;
		 ulong val4 = 78UL;

float	Single-precision floating point type	float val = 1.23F;
double	Double-precision floating point type	double val1 = 1.23; double val2 = 4.56D;
bool	Boolean type; a bool value is either true or false	bool val1 = true; bool val2 = false;
char	Character type; a char value is a Unicode code unit	char val = 'h';
decimal	Precise decimal type with at least 28 significant digits	decimal val = 1.23M;

Each of the predefined types is shorthand for a system-provided type. For example, the keyword int refers to the struct System.Int32. As a matter of style, use of the keyword is favored over use of the complete system type name.

Predefined value types such as int are treated specially in a few ways but are for the most part treated exactly like other structs. Operator overloading enables developers to define new struct types that behave much like the predefined value types. For instance, a Digit struct can support the same mathematical operations as the predefined integral types, and can define conversions between Digit and predefined types.

The predefined types employ operator overloading themselves. For example, the comparison operators == and != have different semantics for different predefined types:

- Two expressions of type `int` are considered equal if they represent the same integer value.
- Two expressions of type `object` are considered equal if both refer to the same object, or if both are `null`.
- Two expressions of type `string` are considered equal if the string instances have identical lengths and identical characters in each character position, or if both are `null`.

The example

```
using System;

class Test
{
  static void Main()
  {
    string s = "Test";
    string t = string.Copy(s);
    Console.WriteLine(s == t);
    Console.WriteLine((object)s == (object)t);
  }
}
```

produces the output

```
True
False
```

because the first comparison compares two expressions of type `string`, and the second comparison compares two expressions of type `object`. (Note that when the Standard Library produces a string representation of a Boolean value, as is the case with `System.WriteLine` above, it uses "True" and "False", while the corresponding C# language Boolean literals are spelled `true` and `false`.)

8.2.2 Conversions

The predefined types also have predefined conversions. For instance, conversions exist between the predefined types `int` and `long`. C# differentiates between two kinds of conversions: ***implicit conversions*** and ***explicit conversions***. Implicit conversions are supplied for conversions that can safely be performed without careful scrutiny. For instance, the conversion from `int` to `long` is an implicit conversion. This conversion always succeeds, and never results in a loss of information. The following example

```
using System;

class Test
{
  static void Main()
  {
    int intValue = 123;
    long longValue = intValue;
    Console.WriteLine("{0} , {1} ", intValue, longValue);
  }
}
```

implicitly converts an `int` to a `long`.

In contrast, explicit conversions are performed with a cast expression. The example

```
using System;

class Test
{
  static void Main()
  {
    long longValue = Int64.MaxValue;
    int intValue = (int) longValue;
    Console.WriteLine("(int) {0} = {1} ", longValue, intValue);
  }
}
```

uses an explicit conversion to convert a `long` to an `int`. The output is:

```
(int) 9223372036854775807 = -1
```

because an overflow occurs. Cast expressions permit the use of both implicit and explicit conversions.

8.2.3 Array types

Arrays can be single-dimensional or multi-dimensional. Both "rectangular" and "jagged" arrays are supported.

Single-dimensional arrays are the most common type. The example

```
using System;

class Test
{
  static void Main()
  {
    int[ ] arr = new int[5] ;

    for (int i = 0; i < arr.Length; i++)
      arr[i] = i * i;

    for (int i = 0; i < arr.Length; i++)
      Console.WriteLine("arr[{0}] = {1} ", i, arr[i] );
  }
}
```

creates a single-dimensional array of `int` values, initializes the array elements, and then prints each of them out. The output produced is:

```
arr[0] = 0
arr[1] = 1
arr[2] = 4
arr[3] = 9
arr[4] = 16
```

The type `int[ ]` used in the previous example is an array type. Array types are written using a *non-array-type* followed by one or more rank specifiers. The example

```
class Test
{
  static void Main()
  {
    int[ ] a1;       // single-dimensional array of int
```

```
    int[,] a2;      // 2-dimensional array of int
    int[,,] a3;     // 3-dimensional array of int

    int[][] j2;     // "jagged" array: array of (array of int)
    int[][][] j3;   // array of (array of (array of int))
  }
}
```

shows a variety of local variable declarations that use array types with int as the element
type.

Array types are reference types, and so the declaration of an array variable merely sets aside
space for the reference to the array. Array instances are actually created via array initializers
and array creation expressions. The example

```
class Test
{
  static void Main()
  {
    int[] a1 = new int[] {1, 2, 3};
    int[,] a2 = new int[,] {{1, 2, 3}, {4, 5, 6}};
    int[,,] a3 = new int[10, 20, 30];

    int[][] j2 = new int[3][];
    j2[0] = new int[] {1, 2, 3};
    j2[1] = new int[] {1, 2, 3, 4, 5, 6};
    j2[2] = new int[] {1, 2, 3, 4, 5, 6, 7, 8, 9};
  }
}
```

shows a variety of array creation expressions. The variables a1, a2 and a3 denote **rectangular
arrays**, and the variable j2 denotes a **jagged array**. It should be no surprise that these terms
are based on the shapes of the arrays. Rectangular arrays always have a rectangular shape. Given
the length of each dimension of the array, its rectangular shape is clear. For example, the lengths
of a3's three dimensions are 10, 20, and 30, respectively, and it is easy to see that this array contains 10* 20* 30 elements.

In contrast, the variable j2 denotes a "jagged" array, or an "array of arrays". Specifically, j2
denotes an array of an array of int, or a single-dimensional array of type int[]. Each of these
int[] variables can be initialized individually, and this allows the array to take on a jagged shape.
The example gives each of the int[] arrays a different length. Specifically, the length of j2[0] is
3, the length of j2[1] is 6, and the length of j2[2] is 9.

[*Note*: In C++, an array declared as int x[3][5][7] would be considered a three dimensional
rectangular array, while in C#, the declaration int[][][] declares a jagged array type.
end note]

The element type and shape of an array—including whether it is jagged or rectangular, and the
number of dimensions it has—are part of its type. On the other hand, the size of the array—as
represented by the length of each of its dimensions—is not part of an array's type. This split is
made clear in the language syntax, as the length of each dimension is specified in the array creation expression rather than in the array type. For instance the declaration

```
    int[,,] a3 = new int[10, 20, 30];
```

has an array type of int[,,] and an array creation expression of new int[10, 20, 30].

For local variable and field declarations, a shorthand form is permitted so that it is not necessary to re-state the array type. For instance, the example

```
int[] a1 = new int[] {1, 2, 3};
```

can be shortened to

```
int[] a1 = {1, 2, 3};
```

without any change in program semantics.

The context in which an array initializer such as {1, 2, 3} is used determines the type of the array being initialized. The example

```
class Test
{
  static void Main()
  {
    short[] a = {1, 2, 3};
    int[] b = {1, 2, 3};
    long[] c = {1, 2, 3};
  }
}
```

shows that the same array initializer syntax can be used for several different array types. Because context is required to determine the type of an array initializer, it is not possible to use an array initializer in an expression context without explicitly stating the type of the array.

8.2.4 Type system unification

C# provides a "unified type system". All types—including value types—derive from the type object. It is possible to call object methods on any value, even values of "primitive" types such as int. The example

```
using System;

class Test
{
  static void Main()
  {
    Console.WriteLine(3.ToString());
  }
}
```

calls the object-defined ToString method on an integer literal, resulting in the output "3".

The example

```
class Test
{
  static void Main()
  {
    int i = 123;
    object o = i;    // boxing
    int j = (int) o; // unboxing
  }
}
```

is more interesting. An `int` value can be converted to `object` and back again to `int`. This example shows both **boxing** and **unboxing**. When a variable of a value type needs to be converted to a reference type, an object **box** is allocated to hold the value, and the value is copied into the box. **Unboxing** is just the opposite. When an object box is cast back to its original value type, the value is copied out of the box and into the appropriate storage location.

This type system unification provides value types with the benefits of object-ness without introducing unnecessary overhead. For programs that don't need `int` values to act like objects, `int` values are simply 32-bit values. For programs that need `int` values to behave like objects, this capability is available on demand. This ability to treat value types as objects bridges the gap between value types and reference types that exists in most languages. For example, a `Stack` class can provide `Push` and `Pop` methods that take and return `object` values.

```
public class Stack
{
  public object Pop() {...}

  public void Push(object o) {...}
}
```

Because C# has a unified type system, the `Stack` class can be used with elements of any type, including value types like `int`.

8.3 Variables and parameters

Variables represent storage locations. Every variable has a type that determines what values can be stored in the variable. **Local variables** are variables that are declared in function members such as methods, properties, and indexers. A local variable is defined by specifying a type name and a declarator that specifies the variable name and an optional initial value, as in:

```
int a;
int b = 1;
```

but it is also possible for a local variable declaration to include multiple declarators. The declarations of `a` and `b` can be rewritten as:

```
int a, b = 1;
```

A variable shall be assigned before its value can be obtained. The example

```
class Test
{
  static void Main()
  {
    int a;
    int b = 1;
    int c = a + b; // error, a not yet assigned
    ...
  }
}
```

results in a compile-time error because it attempts to use the variable `a` before it is assigned a value. The rules governing definite assignment are defined in §12.3.

A **field** (§17.4) is a variable that is associated with a class or struct, or an instance of a class or struct. A field declared with the `static` modifier defines a **static variable**, and a field declared without this modifier defines an ***instance variable***. A static variable is associated with a type, whereas an instance variable is associated with an instance. The example

```
using Personnel.Data;
class Employee
{
  private static DataSet ds;

  public string Name;
  public decimal Salary;

  ...
}
```

shows an `Employee` class that has a private static variable and two public instance variables.

Formal parameter declarations also define variables. There are four kinds of parameters: value parameters, reference parameters, output parameters, and parameter arrays.

A ***value parameter*** is used for "in" parameter passing, in which the value of an argument is passed into a method, and modifications of the parameter do not impact the original argument. A value parameter refers to its own variable, one that is distinct from the corresponding argument. This variable is initialized by copying the value of the corresponding argument. The example

```
using System;

class Test
{
  static void F(int p)
  {
    Console.WriteLine("p = {0} ", p);
    p++;
  }

  static void Main()
  {
    int a = 1;
    Console.WriteLine("pre:  a = {0} ", a);
    F(a);
    Console.WriteLine("post: a = {0} ", a);
  }
}
```

shows a method `F` that has a value parameter named `p`. The example produces the output:

```
pre:  a = 1
p = 1
post: a = 1
```

even though the value parameter `p` is modified.

A ***reference parameter*** is used for "by reference" parameter passing, in which the parameter acts as an alias for a caller-provided argument. A reference parameter does not itself define a variable, but rather refers to the variable of the corresponding argument. Modifications of a reference parameter impact the corresponding argument. A reference parameter is declared with a `ref` modifier. The example

```
using System;

class Test
{
  static void Swap(ref int a, ref int b)
  {
    int t = a;
    a = b;
    b = t;
  }

  static void Main()
  {
    int x = 1;
    int y = 2;

    Console.WriteLine("pre:  x = {0} , y = {1} ", x, y);
    Swap(ref x, ref y);
    Console.WriteLine("post: x = {0} , y = {1} ", x, y);
  }
}
```

shows a Swap method that has two reference parameters. The output produced is:

```
pre:  x = 1, y = 2
post: x = 2, y = 1
```

The ref keyword shall be used in both the declaration of the formal parameter and in uses of it. The use of ref at the call site calls special attention to the parameter, so that a developer reading the code will understand that the value of the argument could change as a result of the call.

An ***output parameter*** is similar to a reference parameter, except that the initial value of the caller-provided argument is unimportant. An output parameter is declared with an out modifier. The example

```
using System;

class Test
{
  static void Divide(int a, int b, out int result, out int remainder)
  {
    result = a / b;
    remainder = a % b;
  }

  static void Main()
  {
    for (int i = 1; i < 10; i++)
      for (int j = 1; j < 10; j++)
      {
        int ans, r;
        Divide(i, j, out ans, out r);
        Console.WriteLine("{0}  / {1}  = {2} r{3} ", i, j, ans, r);
      }
  }
}
```

shows a `Divide` method that includes two output parameters—one for the result of the division and another for the remainder.

For value, reference, and output parameters, there is a one-to-one correspondence between caller-provided arguments and the parameters used to represent them. A ***parameter array*** enables a many-to-one relationship: many arguments can be represented by a single parameter array. In other words, parameter arrays enable variable length argument lists.

A parameter array is declared with a `params` modifier. There can be only one parameter array for a given method, and it shall always be the last parameter specified. The type of a parameter array is always a single dimensional array type. A caller can either pass a single argument of this array type, or any number of arguments of the element type of this array type. For instance, the example

```
using System;

class Test
{
  static void F (params int[ ] args)
  {
    Console.WriteLine ("# of arguments: {0} ", args.Length);
    for (int i = 0; i < args.Length; i++)
      Console.WriteLine ("\targs[{0}] = {1} ", i, args[i] );
  }

  static void Main ()
  {
    F ();
    F (1);
    F (1, 2);
    F (1, 2, 3);
    F (new int[ ] {1, 2, 3, 4} );
  }
}
```

shows a method `F` that takes a variable number of `int` arguments, and several invocations of this method. The output is:

```
# of arguments: 0
# of arguments: 1
  args[0] = 1
# of arguments: 2
  args[0] = 1
  args[1] = 2
# of arguments: 3
  args[0] = 1
  args[1] = 2
  args[2] = 3
# of arguments: 4
  args[0] = 1
  args[1] = 2
  args[2] = 3
  args[3] = 4
```

Most of the examples presented in this introduction use the `WriteLine` method of the `Console` class. The argument substitution behavior of this method, as exhibited in the example

```
int a = 1, b = 2;
Console.WriteLine("a = {0} , b = {1} ", a, b);
```

is accomplished using a parameter array. The `WriteLine` method provides several overloaded methods for the common cases in which a small number of arguments are passed, and one method that uses a parameter array.

```
namespace System
{
  public class Console
  {
    public static void WriteLine(string s) {...}
    public static void WriteLine(string s, object a) {...}
    public static void WriteLine(string s, object a, object b) {...}
    ...
    public static void WriteLine(string s, params object[] args) {...}
  }
}
```

8.4 Automatic memory management

Manual memory management requires developers to manage the allocation and de-allocation of blocks of memory. Manual memory management can be both time-consuming and difficult. In C#, *automatic memory management* is provided so that developers are freed from this burdensome task. In the vast majority of cases, automatic memory management increases code quality and enhances developer productivity without negatively impacting either expressiveness or performance.

The example

```
using System;

public class Stack
{
  private Node first = null;

  public bool Empty
  {
    get
    {
      return (first == null);
    }
  }

  public object Pop()
  {
    if (first == null)
      throw new Exception("Can't Pop from an empty Stack.");
    else
    {
      object temp = first.Value;
      first = first.Next;
      return temp;
    }
  }
```

```
public void Push(object o)
{
  first = new Node(o, first);
}

class Node
{
  public Node Next;
  public object Value;
  public Node(object value): this(value, null) {}
  public Node(object value, Node next)
  {
    Next = next;
    Value = value;
  }
}
}
}
```

shows a `Stack` class implemented as a linked list of `Node` instances. Node instances are created in the `Push` method and are garbage collected when no longer needed. A `Node` instance becomes eligible for garbage collection when it is no longer possible for any code to access it. For instance, when an item is removed from the `Stack`, the associated `Node` instance becomes eligible for garbage collection.

The example

```
class Test
{
  static void Main()
  {
    Stack s = new Stack();
    for (int i = 0; i < 10; i++)
      s.Push(i);
    s = null;
  }
}
```

shows code that uses the `Stack` class. A `Stack` is created and initialized with 10 elements, and then assigned the value `null`. Once the variable `s` is assigned null, the `Stack` and the associated 10 `Node` instances become eligible for garbage collection. The garbage collector is permitted to clean up immediately, but is not required to do so.

The garbage collector underlying C# might work by moving objects around in memory, but this motion is invisible to most C# developers. For developers who are generally content with automatic memory management but sometimes need fine-grained control or that extra bit of performance, C# provides the ability to write "unsafe" code. Such code can deal directly with pointer types and object addresses; however, C# requires the programmer to *fix* objects to temporarily prevent the garbage collector from moving them.

This "unsafe" code feature is in fact a "safe" feature from the perspective of both developers and users. Unsafe code shall be clearly marked in the code with the modifier `unsafe`, so developers can't possibly use unsafe language features accidentally, and the compiler and the execution engine work together to ensure that unsafe code cannot masquerade as safe code. These restrictions limit the use of unsafe code to situations in which the code is trusted.

The example

```
using System;

class Test
{
  static void WriteLocations(byte[] arr)
  {
    unsafe
    {
      fixed (byte* pArray = arr)
      {
        byte* pElem = pArray;
        for (int i = 0; i < arr.Length; i++)
        {
          byte value = *pElem;
          Console.WriteLine("arr[{0}] at 0x{1:X} is {2} ",
            i, (uint)pElem, value);
          pElem++;
        }
      }
    }
  }

  static void Main()
  {
    byte[] arr = new byte[] {1, 2, 3, 4, 5};
    WriteLocations(arr);
  }
}
```

shows an unsafe block in a method named `WriteLocations` that fixes an array instance and uses pointer manipulation to iterate over the elements. The index, value, and location of each array element are written to the console. One possible example of output is:

```
arr[0] at 0x8E0360 is 1
arr[1] at 0x8E0361 is 2
arr[2] at 0x8E0362 is 3
arr[3] at 0x8E0363 is 4
arr[4] at 0x8E0364 is 5
```

but, of course, the exact memory locations can be different in different executions of the application.

8.5 Expressions

C# includes unary operators, binary operators, and one ternary operator. The following table summarizes the operators, listing them in order of precedence from highest to lowest:

Subclause	Category	Operators
§14.5	Primary	x.y f(x) a[x] x++ x-- new typeof checked unchecked
§14.6	Unary	+ - ! ~ ++x --x (T)x
§14.7	Multiplicative	* / %

§14.7	Additive	+ -
§14.8	Shift	<< >>
§14.9	Relational and type-testing	< > <= >= is as
§14.9	Equality	== !=
§14.10	Logical AND	&
§14.10	Logical XOR	^
§14.10	Logical OR	|
§14.11	Conditional AND	&&
§14.11	Conditional OR	||
§14.13	Conditional	? :
§14.14	Assignment	= *= /= %= += -= <<= >>= &= ^= |=

When an expression contains multiple operators, the **precedence** of the operators controls the order in which the individual operators are evaluated. For example, the expression x + y * z is evaluated as x + (y * z) because the * operator has higher precedence than the + operator.

When an operand occurs between two operators with the same precedence, the **associativity** of the operators controls the order in which the operations are performed:

- Except for the assignment operators, all binary operators are **left-associative**, meaning that operations are performed from left to right. For example, x + y + z is evaluated as (x + y) + z.
- The assignment operators and the conditional operator (? :) are **right-associative**, meaning that operations are performed from right to left. For example, x = y = z is evaluated as x = (y = z).

Precedence and associativity can be controlled using parentheses. For example, x + y * z first multiplies y by z and then adds the result to x, but (x + y) * z first adds x and y and then multiplies the result by z.

8.6 Statements

C# borrows most of its statements directly from C and C++, though there are some noteworthy additions and modifications. The table below lists the kinds of statements that can be used, and provides an example for each.

Statement	Example
Statement lists and block statements	```static void Main()\n{\n F();\n G();\n {\n H();\n I();\n }\n}```
Labeled statements and goto statements	```static void Main(string[] args)\n{\n if (args.Length == 0)\n goto done;\n Console.WriteLine(args.Length);```

| | ```
done:
  Console.WriteLine("Done");
}
``` |
| Local constant declarations | ```
static void Main()
{
  const float pi = 3.14f;
  const int r = 123;
  Console.WriteLine(pi * r * r);
}
``` |
| Local variable declarations | ```
static void Main()
{
  int a;
  int b = 2, c = 3;
  a = 1;
  Console.WriteLine(a + b + c);
}
``` |
| Expression statements | ```
static int F(int a, int b)
{
  return a + b;
}
static void Main()
{
  F(1, 2);  // Expression statement
}
``` |
| if statements | ```
static void Main(string[] args)
{
  if (args.Length == 0)
    Console.WriteLine("No args");
  else
    Console.WriteLine("Args");
}
``` |
| switch statements | ```
static void Main(string[] args)
{
  switch (args.Length)
  {
    case 0:
      Console.WriteLine("No args");
      break;
    case 1:
      Console.WriteLine("One arg ");
      break;
    default:
      int n = args.Length;
      Console.WriteLine("{0} args", n);
      break;
  }
}
``` |
| while statements | ```
static void Main(string[] args)
{
  int i = 0;
  while (i < args.Length)
  {
    Console.WriteLine(args[i]);
    i++;
  }
}
``` |
| do statements | ```
static void Main()
{
  string s;
``` |

| | ```c#
do
{
  s = Console.ReadLine();
}
while (s != "Exit");
}
``` |
| for **statements** | ```c#
static void Main(string[] args)
{
  for (int i = 0; i < args.Length; i++)
    Console.WriteLine(args[i]);
}
``` |
| foreach **statements** | ```c#
static void Main(string[] args)
{
  foreach (string s in args)
    Console.WriteLine(s);
}
``` |
| break **statements** | ```c#
static void Main(string[] args)
{
  int i = 0;
  while (true)
  {
    if (i == args.Length)
      break;
    Console.WriteLine(args[i++]);
  }
}
``` |
| continue **statements** | ```c#
static void Main(string[] args)
{
  int i = 0;
  while (true)
  {
    Console.WriteLine(args[i++]);
    if (i < args.Length)
      continue;
    break;
  }
}
``` |
| return **statements** | ```c#
static int F(int a, int b)
{
  return a + b;
}
static void Main()
{
  Console.WriteLine(F(1, 2));
  return;
}
``` |
| yield **statements** | ```c#
static IEnumerable<int> FromTo(int a, int b)
{
  if (a > b)
    yield break;
  for ( ; ; a++)
  {
    yield return a;
    if (a == b)
      break;
  }
}
``` |
| throw **statements and** try **statements** | ```c#
static int F(int a, int b)
{
  if (b == 0)
``` |

| | ```
      throw new Exception("Divide by zero");
      return a / b;
}
static void Main()
{
   try
   {
      Console.WriteLine(F(5, 0));
   }
   catch(Exception e)
   {
      Console.WriteLine("Error");
   }
}
``` |
| `checked` and `unchecked` **statements** | ```
static void Main()
{
   int x = Int32.MaxValue;
   Console.WriteLine(x + 1);    // Overflow
   checked
   {
      Console.WriteLine(x + 1); // Exception
   }
   unchecked
   {
      Console.WriteLine(x + 1); // Overflow
   }
}
``` |
| `lock` **statements** | ```
static void Main()
{
   A a = ...;
   lock(a)
   {
      a.P = a.P + 1;
   }
}
``` |
| `using` **statements** | ```
static void Main()
{
   using (Resource r = new Resource())
   {
      r.F();
   }
}
``` |

8.7 Classes

Class declarations define new reference types. A class can inherit from another class, and can implement interfaces. Generic class declarations (§25.1) have one or more type parameters.

Class members can include constants, fields, methods, properties, events, indexers, operators, instance constructors, finalizers, static constructors, and nested type declarations. Each member has an associated accessibility (§10.5), which controls the regions of program text that are able to access the member. There are five possible forms of accessibility. These are summarized in the table below.

Form	Intuitive meaning
`public`	Access not limited
`protected`	Access limited to the containing class or types derived from the containing class

internal	Access limited to this program
protected internal	Access limited to this program or types derived from the containing class
private	Access limited to the containing type

The example

```
using System;

class MyClass
{
  public const int MyConst = 12;

  public int MyField = 34;

  public static int MyStaticField = 34;

  public void MyMethod()
  {
    Console.WriteLine("MyClass.MyMethod");
  }

  public int MyProperty
  {
    get
    {
      return MyField;
    }

    set
    {
      MyField = value;
    }
  }

  public event EventHandler MyEvent;

  public int this[int index]
  {
    get
    {
      return 0;
    }

    set
    {
      Console.WriteLine("this[{0}] = {1} ", index, value);
    }
  }

  public static MyClass operator+(MyClass a, MyClass b)
  {
    return new MyClass(a.MyField + b.MyField);
  }
```

```
public MyClass()
{
  Console.WriteLine("Instance constructor");
}

public MyClass(int value)
{
  MyField = value;
  Console.WriteLine("Instance constructor");
}

~MyClass()
{
  Console.WriteLine("Finalizer");
}

static MyClass()
{
  MyStaticField *= 2;
  Console.WriteLine("Static constructor");
}

internal class MyNestedClass {}
}
```

shows a class that contains each kind of member. The example

```
class Test
{
  static void Main()
  {
    // Instance constructor usage
    MyClass a = new MyClass();
    MyClass b = new MyClass(123);

    // Constant usage
    Console.WriteLine("MyConst = {0} ", MyClass.MyConst);

    // Field usage
    a.MyField++;
    Console.WriteLine("a.MyField = {0} ", a.MyField);

    // Method usage
    a.MyMethod();

    // Property usage
    a.MyProperty++;
    Console.WriteLine("a.MyProperty = {0} ", a.MyProperty);

    // Indexer usage
    a[3] = a[1] = a[2];
    Console.WriteLine("a[3] = {0} ", a[3]);
```

```
   // Event usage
   a.MyEvent += new EventHandler(MyHandler);

   // Overloaded operator usage
   MyClass c = a + b;

   // Nested type usage
   MyClass.MyNestedClass d = new MyClass.MyNestedClass();
 }

 static void MyHandler(object sender, EventArgs e)
 {
   Console.WriteLine("Test.MyHandler");
 }
}
```

shows uses of these members.

8.7.1 Constants

A *constant* is a class member that represents a constant value: a value that can be computed at compile-time. Constants are permitted to depend on other constants within the same program as long as there are no circular dependencies. The rules governing constant expressions are defined in §14.16. The example

```
class Constants
{
  public const int A = 1;
  public const int B = A + 1;
}
```

shows a class named `Constants` that has two public constants.

Even though constants are considered static members, a constant declaration neither requires nor allows the modifier `static`. Constants can be accessed through the class, as in

```
using System;

class Test
{
  static void Main()
  {
    Console.WriteLine("{0} , {1} ", Constants.A, Constants.B);
  }
}
```

which prints out the values of `Constants.A` and `Constants.B`, respectively.

8.7.2 Fields

A *field* is a member that represents a variable associated with an object or class. The example

```
class Color
{
  internal ushort redPart;
  internal ushort bluePart;
  internal ushort greenPart;
```

```
public Color(ushort red, ushort blue, ushort green)
{
  redPart = red;
  bluePart = blue;
  greenPart = green;
}

public static Color Red = new Color(0xFF, 0, 0);
public static Color Blue = new Color(0, 0xFF, 0);
public static Color Green = new Color(0, 0, 0xFF);
public static Color White = new Color(0xFF, 0xFF, 0xFF);
}
```

shows a `Color` class that has internal instance fields named `redPart`, `bluePart`, and `green-Part`, and static fields named `Red`, `Blue`, `Green`, and `White`

The use of static fields in this manner is not ideal. The fields are initialized at some point before they are used, but after this initialization, there is nothing to stop a client from changing them. Such a modification could cause unpredictable errors in other programs that use `Color` and assume that the values do not change. ***Readonly fields*** can be used to prevent such problems. Assignments to a readonly field can only occur as part of the declaration, or in an instance constructor or static constructor in the same class. A static readonly field can be assigned in a static constructor, and a non-static readonly field can be assigned in an instance constructor. Thus, the `Color` class can be enhanced by adding the modifier `readonly` to the static fields:

```
class Color
{
  internal ushort redPart;
  internal ushort bluePart;
  internal ushort greenPart;

  public Color(ushort red, ushort blue, ushort green)
  {
    redPart = red;
    bluePart = blue;
    greenPart = green;
  }

  public static readonly Color Red = new Color(0xFF, 0, 0);
  public static readonly Color Blue = new Color(0, 0xFF, 0);
  public static readonly Color Green = new Color(0, 0, 0xFF);
  public static readonly Color White = new Color(0xFF, 0xFF, 0xFF);
}
```

8.7.3 Methods

A ***method*** is a member that implements a computation or action that can be performed by an object, or class. Methods have a (possibly empty) list of formal parameters, a return value (unless the method's *return-type* is `void`), and are either static or non-static. ***Static methods*** are accessed through the class. ***Non-static methods***, which are also called ***instance methods***, are accessed through instances of the class. A ***generic method*** (§25.6) has a list of one or more type parameters. The example

```
using System;

public class Stack
{
  public static Stack Clone(Stack s) {...}

  public static Stack Flip(Stack s) {...}

  public object Pop() {...}

  public void Push(object o) {...}

  public void PushMultiple<T>(T[] a) {...}

  public override string ToString() {...}
  ...
}

class Test
{
  static void Main()
  {
    Stack s = new Stack();
    for (int i = 1; i < 10; i++)
      s.Push(i);

    Stack flipped = Stack.Flip(s);

    Stack cloned = Stack.Clone(s);

    Console.WriteLine("Original stack: " + s.ToString());
    Console.WriteLine("Flipped stack: " + flipped.ToString());
    Console.WriteLine("Cloned stack: " + cloned.ToString());
  }
}
```

shows a `Stack` that has several static methods (`Clone` and `Flip`) and several instance methods (`Pop`, `Push`, and `ToString`) and a generic method (`PushMultiple<T>`).

Methods can be overloaded, which means that multiple methods can have the same name so long as they have unique signatures. The signature of a method consists of the name of the method and the number, modifiers, and types of its formal parameters, and the number of generic type parameters. The signature of a method does not include the return type or the names of the formal parameters or type parameters. The example

```
using System;

class Test
{
  static void F()
  {
    Console.WriteLine("F()");
  }

  static void F(object o)
```

```
  {
    Console.WriteLine("F(object)");
  }

  static void F(int value)
  {
    Console.WriteLine("F(int)");
  }

  static void F(ref int value)
  {
    Console.WriteLine("F(ref int)");
  }

  static void F(int a, int b)
  {
    Console.WriteLine("F(int, int)");
  }

  static void F(int[] values)
  {
    Console.WriteLine("F(int[])");
  }

  static void F<T>(T t)
  {
    Console.WriteLine("F<T>(T)");
  }

  static void Main()
  {
    F();
    F(1);
    int i = 10;
    F(ref i);
    F((object)1);
    F(1, 2);
    F(new int[] {1, 2, 3} );
    F("Hello");
    F<string>("World");
  }
}
```

shows a class with a number of methods called F. The output produced is

```
F()
F(int)
F(ref int)
F(object)
F(int, int)
F(int[])
F<T>(T)
F<T>(T)
```

8.7.4 Properties

A *property* is a member that provides access to a characteristic of an object or a class. Examples of properties include the length of a string, the size of a font, the caption of a window, the name of a customer, and so on. Properties are a natural extension of fields. Both are named members with associated types, and the syntax for accessing fields and properties is the same. However, unlike fields, properties do not denote storage locations. Instead, properties have accessors that specify the statements to be executed when their values are read or written.

Properties are defined with property declarations. The first part of a property declaration looks quite similar to a field declaration. The second part includes a get accessor and/or a set accessor. In the example below, the `Button` class defines a `Caption` property.

```
public class Button
{
  private string caption;

  public string Caption
  {
    get
    {
      return caption;
    }

    set
    {
      caption = value;
      Repaint();
    }
  }
  ...
}
```

Properties that can be both read and written, such as `Caption`, include both get and set accessors. The get accessor is called when the property's value is read; the set accessor is called when the property's value is written. In a set accessor, the new value for the property is made available via an implicit parameter named `value`.

The declaration of properties is relatively straightforward, but the real value of properties is seen when they are used. For example, the `Caption` property can be read and written in the same way that fields can be read and written:

```
Button b = new Button();
b.Caption = "ABC";      // set; causes repaint
string s = b.Caption;   // get
b.Caption += "DEF";     // get & set; causes repaint
```

8.7.5 Events

An *event* is a member that enables an object or class to provide notifications. A class defines an event by providing an event declaration (which resembles a field declaration, though with an added `event` keyword) and an optional set of event accessors. The type of this declaration shall be a delegate type.

An instance of a delegate type encapsulates one or more callable entities. For instance methods, a callable entity consists of an instance and a method on that instance. For static methods, a callable entity consists of just a method. Given a delegate instance and an appropriate set of arguments, one can invoke all of that delegate instance's methods with that set of arguments.

In the example

```
public delegate void EventHandler(object sender, System.EventArgs e);

public class Button
{
  public event EventHandler Click;
  public void Reset()
  {
    Click = null;
  }
}
```

the `Button` class defines a `Click` event of type `EventHandler`. Inside the `Button` class, the `Click` member is exactly like a private field of type `EventHandler`. However, outside the `Button` class, the `Click` member can only be used on the left-hand side of the += and −= operators. The += operator adds a handler for the event, and the −= operator removes a handler for the event. The example

```
using System;

public class Form1
{
  public Form1()
  {
    // Add Button1_Click as an event handler for Button1's Click event
    Button1.Click += new EventHandler(Button1_Click);
  }

  Button Button1 = new Button();

  void Button1_Click(object sender, EventArgs e)
  {
    Console.WriteLine("Button1 was clicked!");
  }

  public void Disconnect()
  {
    Button1.Click -= new EventHandler(Button1_Click);
  }
}
```

shows a `Form1` class that adds `Button1_Click` as an event handler for `Button1`'s `Click` event. In the `Disconnect` method, that event handler is removed.

For a simple event declaration such as

```
public event EventHandler Click;
```

the compiler automatically provides the implementation underlying the += and −= operators.

An implementer who wants more control can get it by explicitly providing add and remove accessors. For example, the `Button` class could be rewritten as follows:

```
public class Button
{
    private EventHandler handler;
    public event EventHandler Click
```

```
        {
          add { handler += value; }
          remove { handler -= value; }
        }
    }
```

This change has no effect on client code, but allows the `Button` class more implementation flexibility. For example, the event handler for `Click` need not be represented by a field.

8.7.6 Operators

An *operator* is a member that defines the meaning of an expression operator that can be applied to instances of the class. Three kinds of operators can be defined: unary, binary, and conversion.

The following example defines a `Digit` type that represents decimal digits—integral values between 0 and 9.

```csharp
using System;

public struct Digit
{
  byte value;

  public Digit(int value)
  {
    if (value < 0 || value > 9) throw new ArgumentException();
    this.value = (byte)value;
  }

  public static implicit operator byte(Digit d)
  {
    return d.value;
  }

  public static explicit operator Digit(int value)
  {
    return new Digit(value);
  }

  public static Digit operator+(Digit a, Digit b)
  {
    return new Digit(a.value + b.value);
  }

  public static Digit operator-(Digit a, Digit b)
  {
    return new Digit(a.value - b.value);
  }

  public static bool operator==(Digit a, Digit b)
  {
    return a.value == b.value;
  }

  public static bool operator!=(Digit a, Digit b)
```

```
    {
      return a.value != b.value;
    }

    public override bool Equals(object value)
    {
      if (value == null) return false;
      if (GetType() == value.GetType()) return this == (Digit)value;
      return false;
    }

    public override int GetHashCode()
    {
      return value.GetHashCode();
    }

    public override string ToString()
    {
      return value.ToString();
    }
  }

  class Test
  {
    static void Main()
    {
      Digit a = (Digit) 5;
      Digit b = (Digit) 3;
      Digit plus = a + b;
      Digit minus = a - b;
      bool equals = (a == b);
      Console.WriteLine("{0} + {1} = {2} ", a, b, plus);
      Console.WriteLine("{0} - {1} = {2} ", a, b, minus);
      Console.WriteLine("{0} == {1} = {2} ", a, b, equals);
    }
  }
```

The `Digit` type defines the following operators:

- An implicit conversion operator from `Digit` to `byte`.
- An explicit conversion operator from `int` to `Digit`.
- An addition operator that adds two `Digit` values and returns a `Digit` value.
- A subtraction operator that subtracts one `Digit` value from another, and returns a `Digit` value.
- The equality (`==`) and inequality (`!=`) operators, which compare two `Digit` values.

8.7.7 Indexers

An **indexer** is a member that enables an object to be indexed in the same way as an array. Whereas properties enable field-like access, indexers enable array-like access.

As an example, consider the `Stack` class presented earlier. The designer of this class might want to expose array-like access so that it is possible to inspect or alter the items on the stack without performing unnecessary `Push` and `Pop` operations. That is, class `Stack` is implemented as a linked list, but it also provides the convenience of array access.

Indexer declarations are similar to property declarations, with the main differences being that indexers are nameless (the "name" used in the declaration is this, since this is being indexed) and that indexers include indexing parameters. The indexing parameters are provided between square brackets. The example

```csharp
using System;

public class Stack
{
  private Node GetNode(int index)
  {
    Node temp = first;
    while (true)
    {
      if (temp == null || index < 0)
        throw new Exception("Index out of range.");
      if (index == 0)
        return temp;
      temp = temp.Next;
      index--;
    }
  }

  public object this[int index]
  {
    get
    {
      return GetNode(index).Value;
    }

    set
    {
      GetNode(index).Value = value;
    }
  }
  ...
}

class Test
{
  static void Main()
  {
    Stack s = new Stack();

    s.Push(1);
    s.Push(2);
    s.Push(3);

    s[0] = 33;  // Changes the top item from 3 to 33
    s[1] = 22;  // Changes the middle item from 2 to 22
    s[2] = 11;  // Changes the bottom item from 1 to 11
  }
}
```

shows an indexer for the Stack class.

8.7.8 Instance constructors

An **instance constructor** is a member that implements the actions required to initialize an instance of a class.

The example

```
using System;

class Point
{
  public double x, y;

  public Point()
  {
    this.x = 0;
    this.y = 0;
  }

  public Point(double x, double y)
  {
    this.x = x;
    this.y = y;
  }

  public static double Distance(Point a, Point b)
  {
    double xdiff = a.x - b.x;
    double ydiff = a.y - b.y;
    return Math.Sqrt(xdiff * xdiff + ydiff * ydiff);
  }

  public override string ToString()
  {
    return string.Format("({0} , {1} )", x, y);
  }
}

class Test
{
  static void Main()
  {
    Point a = new Point();
    Point b = new Point(3, 4);
    double d = Point.Distance(a, b);
    Console.WriteLine("Distance from {0} to {1} is {2} ", a, b, d);
  }
}
```

shows a `Point` class that provides two public instance constructors, one of which takes no arguments, while the other takes two `double` arguments.

If no instance constructor is supplied for a class, then one having no parameters is automatically provided, which simply invokes the parameterless constructor of the direct base class.

8.7.9 Finalizers

A *finalizer* is a member that implements the actions required to finalize an instance of a class. Finalizers cannot have parameters, they cannot have accessibility modifiers, and they cannot be called explicitly. The finalizer for an instance is called automatically during garbage collection.

The example

```csharp
using System;

class Point
{
  public double x, y;

  public Point(double x, double y)
  {
    this.x = x;
    this.y = y;
  }

  ~Point()
  {
    Console.WriteLine("Finalized {0} ", this);
  }

  public override string ToString()
  {
    return string.Format("({0} , {1} )", x, y);
  }
}
```

shows a `Point` class with a finalizer.

8.7.10 Static constructors

A *static constructor* is a member that implements the actions required to initialize a class. Static constructors cannot have parameters, they cannot have accessibility modifiers, and they cannot be called explicitly. The static constructor for a class is called automatically.

The example

```csharp
using Personnel.Data;
class Employee
{
  private static DataSet ds;

  static Employee()
  {
    ds = new DataSet(...);
  }

  public string Name;
  public decimal Salary;
  ...
}
```

shows an `Employee` class with a static constructor that initializes a static field.

8.7.11 Inheritance

Classes support single inheritance, and the type object is the ultimate base class for all classes. The classes shown in earlier examples all implicitly derive from object. The example

```
using System;

class A
{
  public void F() { Console.WriteLine("A.F"); }
}
```

shows a class A that implicitly derives from object. The example

```
class B: A
{
  public void G() { Console.WriteLine("B.G"); }
}

class Test
{
  static void Main()
  {
    B b = new B();
    b.F();        // Inherited from A
    b.G();        // Introduced in B

    A a = b;      // Treat a B as an A
    a.F();
  }
}
```

shows a class B that derives from A. The class B inherits A's F method, and introduces a G method of its own.

Methods, properties, and indexers can be ***virtual***, which means that their implementation can be overridden in derived classes. The example

```
using System;

class A
{
  public virtual void F() { Console.WriteLine("A.F"); }
}

class B: A
{
  public override void F() {
    base.F();
    Console.WriteLine("B.F");
  }
}

class Test
{
  static void Main()
  {
```

```
      B b = new B();
      b.F();

      A a = b;
      a.F();
   }
}
```

shows a class A with a virtual method F, and a class B that overrides F. The overriding method in B contains a call, `base.F()`, which calls the overridden method in A.

A class can indicate that it is incomplete, and is intended only as a base class for other classes, by including the modifier `abstract`. Such a class is called an **abstract class**. An abstract class can specify **abstract members**—members that a non-abstract derived class shall implement. The example

```
using System;

abstract class A
{
   public abstract void F();
}

class B: A
{
   public override void F() { Console.WriteLine("B.F"); }
}

class Test
{
   static void Main()
   {
      B b = new B();
      b.F();

      A a = b;
      a.F();
   }
}
```

introduces an abstract method F in the abstract class A. The non-abstract class B provides an implementation for this method.

8.7.12 Static classes

Classes that are not intended to be instantiated, and which contain only static members should be declared as static classes. Examples of such classes are `System.Console` and `System.Environment`. Static classes are implicitly sealed and have no instance constructors. Static classes can be used only with the `typeof` operator and to access elements of the class. In particular, a static class cannot be used as the type of a variable or be used as a type argument.

```
public static class Months
{
   static Months() {...}
   private static readonly string[] monthName = {...}
   public static string GetMonthName(int mm) {...}
```

```
    private static readonly int[,] daysInMonth = {...}
    public static int GetDaysInMonth(bool isLeapYear, int mm) {...}
    public static bool IsLeapYear(int yy) {...}
}
```

8.7.13 Partial type declarations

In certain situations, the declaration of a type may grow so large that keeping it in a single source file becomes impractical or difficult. In such cases, it is often desirable to split that class declaration into multiple source files, with each source file focusing on one or more semi-independent concerns.

Another common situation occurs when code is generated from a program rather than written by a person. In rich frameworks and development environments, it is often most efficient to have parts of a project's source code generated automatically from visual form designers, database schemas, RPC descriptions, etc. While these kinds of tools produce huge productivity gains, they suffer from problems when we wish to customize the output, possibly by adding members to generated classes. If we directly modify the output of the code generator, then those changes will be lost if the code generator needs to be run again. By placing the customized additions in a different source file, lost modifications can be greatly reduced or eliminated.

Partial type declarations allow greater flexibility in these situations by allowing the definition of a class, struct, or interface to be split into as many different pieces as needed. For example, when the following source files are compiled together:

```
// machine-generated code in file #1
partial class Widget
{
  private int[] counts;
  public string ToString()
  {
    ...
  }
}

// programmer-generated code in file #2
partial class Widget
{
  private int value;
  private void Helper()
  {
    ...
  }

  public int Process(object obj)
  {
    ...
  }
}
```

Widget's members are the union of all the members in all its parts.

8.8 Structs

The list of similarities between classes and structs is long—structs can implement interfaces, and can have the same kinds of members as classes. Structs differ from classes in several important ways, however: structs are value types rather than reference types, and inheritance is not supported for structs. Struct values are stored "on the stack" or "in-line". Careful programmers can sometimes enhance performance through judicious use of structs.

For example, the use of a struct rather than a class for a `Point` can make a large difference in the number of memory allocations performed at run time. The program below creates and initializes an array of 100 points. With `Point` implemented as a class, 101 separate objects are instantiated—one for the array and one each for the 100 elements.

```
class Point
{
  public int x, y;

  public Point(int x, int y)
  {
    this.x = x;
    this.y = y;
  }
}

class Test
{
  static void Main()
  {
    Point[] points = new Point[100];
    for (int i = 0; i < 100; i++)
      points[i] = new Point(i, i*i);
  }
}
```

If `Point` is instead implemented as a struct, as in

```
struct Point
{
  public int x, y;

  public Point(int x, int y)
  {
    this.x = x;
    this.y = y;
  }
}
```

only one object is instantiated—the one for the array. The `Point` instances are allocated in-line within the array. This optimization can be misused. Using structs instead of classes can also make an application run slower or take up more memory, as passing a struct instance by value causes a copy of that struct to be created.

8.9 Interfaces

An interface defines a contract. A class or struct that implements an interface shall adhere to its contract. Interfaces can contain methods, properties, events, and indexers as members.

The example

```
interface IExample
{
  string this[int index] { get; set; }
  event EventHandler E;
  void F(int value);
  string P { get; set; }
}

public delegate void EventHandler(object sender, EventArgs e);
```

shows an interface that contains an indexer, an event E, a method F, and a property P.

Interfaces can employ multiple inheritance. In the example

```
interface IControl
{
  void Paint();
}

interface ITextBox: IControl
{
  void SetText(string text);
}

interface IListBox: IControl
{
  void SetItems(string[] items);
}

interface IComboBox: ITextBox, IListBox {}
```

the interface IComboBox inherits from both ITextBox and IListBox.

Classes and structs can implement multiple interfaces. In the example

```
interface IDataBound
{
  void Bind(Binder b);
}

public class EditBox: Control, IControl, IDataBound
{
  public void Paint() {...}
  public void Bind(Binder b) {...}
}
```

the class EditBox derives from the class Control and implements both IControl and IDataBound.

In the previous example, the Paint method from the IControl interface and the Bind method from IDataBound interface are implemented using public members on the EditBox class. C# provides an alternative way of implementing these methods that allows the implementing class to avoid having these members be public. Interface members can be implemented using a qualified name. For example, the `EditBox` class could instead be implemented by providing `IControl.Paint` and `IDataBound.Bind` methods.

```
public class EditBox: IControl, IDataBound
{
  void IControl.Paint() {...}
  void IDataBound.Bind(Binder b) {...}
}
```

Interface members implemented in this way are called ***explicit interface members*** because each member explicitly designates the interface member being implemented. Explicit interface members can only be called via the interface. For example, the `EditBox`'s implementation of the `Paint` method can be called only by casting to the `IControl` interface.

```
class Test
{
  static void Main()
  {
    EditBox editbox = new EditBox();
    editbox.Paint(); // error: no such method
    IControl control = editbox;
    control.Paint(); // calls EditBox' s Paint implementation
  }
}
```

8.10 Delegates

Delegates enable scenarios that some other languages have addressed with function pointers. However, unlike function pointers, delegates are object-oriented and type-safe.

A delegate declaration defines a class that is derived from the class `System.Delegate`. A delegate instance encapsulates one or more methods, each of which is referred to as a ***callable entity***. For instance methods, a callable entity consists of an instance and a method on that instance. For static methods, a callable entity consists of just a method. Given a delegate instance and an appropriate set of arguments, one can invoke all of that delegate instance's methods with that set of arguments.

An interesting and useful property of a delegate instance is that it does not know or care about the classes of the methods it encapsulates; all that matters is that those methods be consistent (§22.1) with the delegate's type. This makes delegates perfectly suited for "anonymous" invocation. This is a powerful capability.

There are three steps in defining and using delegates: declaration, instantiation, and invocation. Delegates are declared using delegate declaration syntax. The example

```
delegate void SimpleDelegate();
```

declares a delegate named `SimpleDelegate` that takes no arguments and returns no result.

The example

```
class Test
{
  static void F()
  {
```

```
      System.Console.WriteLine("Test.F");
   }

   static void Main()
   {
      SimpleDelegate d = new SimpleDelegate(F);
      d();
   }
}
```

creates a `SimpleDelegate` instance and then immediately calls it.

There is not much point in instantiating a delegate for a method and then immediately calling that method via the delegate, as it would be simpler to call the method directly. Delegates really show their usefulness when their anonymity is used. The example

```
void MultiCall(SimpleDelegate d, int count)
{
   for (int i = 0; i < count; i++)
   {
      d();
   }
}
```

shows a `MultiCall` method that repeatedly calls a `SimpleDelegate`. The `MultiCall` method doesn't know or care about the type of the target method for the `SimpleDelegate`, what accessibility that method has, or whether or not that method is static. All that matters is that the target method is consistent (§22.1) with `SimpleDelegate`.

8.11 Enums

An enum type declaration defines a type name for a related group of symbolic constants. Enums are used for "multiple choice" scenarios, in which a runtime decision is made from a fixed number of choices that are known at compile-time.

The example

```
enum Color
{
   Red,
   Blue,
   Green
}

class Shape
{
   public void Fill(Color color)
   {
      switch(color)
      {
         case Color.Red:
            ...
            break;

         case Color.Blue:
            ...
```

```
      break;

    case Color.Green:
      ...
      break;

    default:
      break;
    }
  }
}
```

shows a `Color` enum and a method that uses this enum. The signature of the `Fill` method makes it clear that the shape can be filled with one of the given colors.

The use of enums is superior to the use of integer constants—as is common in languages without enums—because the use of enums makes the code more readable and self-documenting. The self-documenting nature of the code also makes it possible for the development tool to assist with code writing and other "designer" activities. For example, the use of `Color` rather than `int` for a parameter type enables smart code editors to suggest `Color` values.

8.12 Namespaces and assemblies

The programs presented so far have stood on their own except for dependence on a few system-provided classes such as `System.Console`. It is far more common, however, for real-world applications to consist of several different pieces, each compiled separately. For example, a corporate application might depend on several different components, including some developed internally and some purchased from independent software vendors.

Namespaces and *assemblies* enable this component-based system. Namespaces provide a logical organizational system. Namespaces are used both as an "internal" organization system for a program, and as an "external" organization system—a way of presenting program elements that are exposed to other programs.

Assemblies are used for physical packaging and deployment. An assembly can contain types, the executable code used to implement these types, and references to other assemblies.

To demonstrate the use of namespaces and assemblies, this subclause revisits the "hello, world" program presented earlier, and splits it into two pieces: a class library that provides messages and a console application that displays them.

The class library will contain a single class named `HelloMessage`. The example

```
// HelloLibrary.cs

namespace CSharp.Introduction
{
  public class HelloMessage
  {
    public string Message
    {
      get
      {
        return "hello, world";
      }
    }
```

```
  }
}
```

shows the `HelloMessage` class in a namespace named `CSharp.Introduction`. The `Hello-Message` class provides a read-only property named `Message`. Namespaces can nest, and the declaration

```
namespace CSharp.Introduction
{...}
```

is shorthand for two levels of namespace nesting:

```
namespace CSharp
{
  namespace Introduction
  {...}
}
```

The next step in the componentization of "hello, world" is to write a console application that uses the `HelloMessage` class. The fully qualified name (§10.8.2) for the class—`CSharp.Introduction.HelloMessage`—could be used, but this name is quite long and unwieldy. An easier way is to use a ***using namespace directive***, which makes it possible to use all of the types in a namespace without qualification. The example

```
// HelloApp.cs

using CSharp.Introduction;

class HelloApp
{
  static void Main()
  {
    HelloMessage m = new HelloMessage();
    System.Console.WriteLine(m.Message);
  }
}
```

shows a using namespace directive that refers to the `CSharp.Introduction` namespace. The occurrences of `HelloMessage` are shorthand for `CSharp.Introduction.HelloMessage`.

C# also enables the definition and use of aliases. A ***using alias directive*** defines an alias for a type or namespace. Such aliases can be useful in situation in which name collisions occur between two class libraries, or when a small number of types from a much larger namespace are being used. The example

```
using MessageSource = CSharp.Introduction.HelloMessage;
```

shows a using alias directive that defines `MessageSource` as an alias for the `HelloMessage` class.

The code we have written can be compiled into a class library containing the class `HelloMessage` and an application containing the class `HelloApp`. The details of this compilation step might differ based on the compiler or tool being used. A command-line compiler might enable compilation of a class library and an application that uses that library with the following command-line invocations:

```
csc /target:library HelloLibrary.cs
```

```
csc /reference:HelloLibrary.dll HelloApp.cs
```

which produce a class library named `HelloLibrary.dll` and an application named `HelloApp.exe`.

8.13 Versioning

Versioning is the process of evolving a component over time in a compatible manner. A new version of a component is ***source compatible*** with a previous version if code that depends on the previous version can, when recompiled, work with the new version. In contrast, a new version of a component is ***binary-compatible*** if an application that depended on the old version can, without recompilation, work with the new version.

Most languages do not support binary compatibility at all, and many do little to facilitate source compatibility. In fact, some languages contain flaws that make it impossible, in general, to evolve a class over time without breaking at least some client code.

As an example, consider the situation of a base class author who ships a class named `Base`. In the first version, `Base` contains no method F. A component named `Derived` derives from `Base`, and introduces an F. This `Derived` class, along with the class `Base` on which it depends, is released to customers, who deploy to numerous clients and servers.

```
// Author A
namespace A
{
  public class Base   // version 1
  {
  }
}

// Author B
namespace B
{
  class Derived: A.Base
  {
    public virtual void F()
    {
      System.Console.WriteLine("Derived.F");
    }
  }
}
```

So far, so good, but now the versioning trouble begins. The author of `Base` produces a new version, giving it its own method F.

```
// Author A
namespace A
{
  public class Base        // version 2
  {
    public virtual void F()  // added in version 2
    {
      System.Console.WriteLine("Base.F");
    }
  }
}
```

This new version of `Base` should be both source and binary compatible with the initial version. (If it weren't possible to simply add a method then a base class could never evolve.) Unfortunately, the new `F` in `Base` makes the meaning of `Derived`'s `F` unclear. Did `Derived` mean to override `Base`'s `F`? This seems unlikely, since when `Derived` was compiled, `Base` did not even have an `F`! Further, if `Derived`'s `F` does override `Base`'s `F`, then it shall adhere to the contract specified by `Base`—a contract that was unspecified when `Derived` was written. In some cases, this is impossible. For example, `Base`'s `F` might require that overrides of it always call the base. `Derived`'s `F` could not possibly adhere to such a contract.

C# addresses this versioning problem by requiring developers to state their intent clearly. In the original code example, the code was clear, since `Base` did not even have an `F`. Clearly, `Derived`'s `F` is intended as a new method rather than an override of a base method, since no base method named `F` exists.

If `Base` adds an `F` and ships a new version, then the intent of a binary version of `Derived` is still clear—`Derived`'s `F` is semantically unrelated, and should not be treated as an override.

However, when `Derived` is recompiled, the meaning is unclear—the author of `Derived` might intend its `F` to override `Base`'s `F`, or to hide it. Since the intent is unclear, the compiler produces a warning, and by default makes `Derived`'s `F` hide `Base`'s `F`. This course of action duplicates the semantics for the case in which `Derived` is not recompiled. The warning that is generated alerts `Derived`'s author to the presence of the `F` method in `Base`.

If `Derived`'s `F` is semantically unrelated to `Base`'s `F`, then `Derived`'s author can express this intent—and, in effect, turn off the warning—by using the `new` keyword in the declaration of `F`.

```
// Author A
namespace A
{
  public class Base        // version 2
  {
    public virtual void F()  // added in version 2
    {
      System.Console.WriteLine("Base.F");
    }
  }
}

// Author B
namespace B
{
  class Derived: A.Base  // version 2a: new
  {
    new public virtual void F()
    {
      System.Console.WriteLine("Derived.F");
    }
  }
}
```

On the other hand, `Derived`'s author might investigate further, and decide that `Derived`'s `F` should override `Base`'s `F`. This intent can be specified by using the `override` keyword, as shown below.

```
// Author A
namespace A
{
  public class Base        // version 2
  {
    public virtual void F()  // added in version 2
    {
      System.Console.WriteLine("Base.F");
    }
  }
}

// Author B
namespace B
{
  class Derived: A.Base   // version 2b: override
  {
    public override void F()
    {
      base.F();
      System.Console.WriteLine("Derived.F");
    }
  }
}
```

The author of Derived has one other option, and that is to change the name of F, thus comple-tely avoiding the name collision. Although this change would break source and binary compat-ibility for Derived, the importance of this compatibility varies depending on the scenario. If Derived is not exposed to other programs, then changing the name of F is likely a good idea, as it would improve the readability of the program—there would no longer be any confusion about the meaning of F.

8.14 Extern aliases

By default types from all referenced assemblies and the current program are placed into a single namespace hierarchy. With only a single namespace hierarchy, it is not possible to reference types with the same fully qualified name from different assemblies, a situation that arises when types are independently given the same name, or when a program needs to reference several ver-sions of the same assembly. *Extern aliases* make it possible to create and reference separate namespace hierarchies in such situations.

Consider the following two assemblies:

```
// Assembly a1.dll:

namespace N
{
  public class A {}

  public class B {}
}

// Assembly a2.dll:

namespace N
```

```
  {
    public class B {}

    public class C {}
  }
```

and the following program:

```
class Test
{
  N.A a;      // Ok
  N.B b;      // Error
  N.C c;      // Ok
}
```

A command-line compiler might allow compilation of this program with a command-line something like this:

```
csc /r:a1.dll /r:a2.dll test.cs
```

where the types contained in a1.dll and a2.dll are all placed in the ***global namespace hierarchy***, and an error occurs because the type N.B exists in both assemblies. With extern aliases, it becomes possible to place the types contained in a1.dll and a2.dll into separate namespace hierarchies.

The following program declares and uses two extern aliases, X and Y, each of which represent the root of a distinct namespace hierarchy created from the types contained in one or more assemblies.

```
extern alias X;
extern alias Y;

class Test
{
  X::N.A a;
  X::N.B b1;
  Y::N.B b2;
  Y::N.C c;
}
```

The program declares the existence of the extern aliases X and Y, but the actual definitions of the aliases are external to the program. A command line compiler can enable the definition of the extern aliases X and Y such that the extern alias X is the root of a namespace hierarchy formed by the types in a1.dll and Y is the root of a namespace hierarchy formed by the types in a2.dll. A compiler might enable the above example with a command-line like:

```
csc /r:X=a1.dll /r:Y=a2.dll test.cs
```

The identically named N.B classes can now be referenced as X.N.B and Y.N.B, or, using the namespace alias qualifier, X::N.B and Y::N.B. An error occurs if a program declares an extern alias for which no external definition is provided.

An extern alias can include multiple assemblies, and a particular assembly can be included in multiple extern aliases. For example, given the assembly

```
// Assembly a3.dll:

namespace N
{
```

```
        public class D{}

        public class E{}
    }
```

a command line like

```
    csc /r:X=a1.dll /r:X=a3.dll /r:Y=a2.dll /r:Y=a3.dll test.cs
```

might define the extern alias X to be the root of a namespace hierarchy formed by the types in
a1.dll and a3.dll and Y to be the root of a namespace hierarchy formed by the types in
a2.dll and a3.dll. Because of this definition, it is possible to refer to the class N.D in a3.dll
as both X::N.D and Y::N.D.

An assembly can be placed in the global namespace hierarchy even if it is also included in one or
more extern aliases. For example, the command line

```
    csc /r:a1.dll /r:X=a1.dll /r:Y=a2.dll test.cs
```

places the assembly a1.dll in both the global namespace hierarchy and the namespace hierarchy rooted by the extern alias X. Consequently, the class N.A can be referred to as N.A or X::N.A.

It is possible to ensure that a lookup always starts at the root of the global namespace hierarchy
by using the identifier global with the namespace alias qualifier, such as global::System.IO.
Stream.

A using directive may reference an extern alias that was defined in the same immediately enclosing namespace declaration or compilation unit. For example:

```
    extern alias X;

    using X::N;

    class Test
    {
      A a;        // X::N.A
      B b;        // X::N.B
    }
```

8.15 Attributes

C# is an imperative language, but like all imperative languages, it does have some declarative elements. For example, the accessibility of a method in a class is specified by declaring it public,
protected, internal, protected internal, or private. C# generalizes this capability, so
that programmers can invent new kinds of declarative information, attach this declarative information to various program entities, and retrieve this declarative information at run-time. Programs specify this additional declarative information by defining and using attributes (§24).

For instance, a framework might define a HelpAttribute attribute that can be placed on program elements such as classes and methods, enabling developers to provide a mapping from program elements to documentation for them. The example

```
    using System;

    [AttributeUsage(AttributeTargets.All)]
    public class HelpAttribute: Attribute
```

```
  {
    public HelpAttribute(string url)
    {
      this.url = url;
    }

    public string Topic = null;

    private string url;

    public string Url
    {
      get { return url; }
    }
  }
```

defines an attribute class named `HelpAttribute`, or `Help` for short, that has one positional parameter (`string url`) and one named parameter (`string Topic`). Positional parameters are defined by the formal parameters for public instance constructors of the attribute class, and named parameters are defined by public non-static read-write fields and properties of the attribute class.

The example

```
[Help("http://www.mycompany.com/.../Class1.htm")]
public class Class1
{
  [Help("http://www.mycompany.com/.../Class1.htm", Topic = "F")]
  public void F() {}
}
```

shows several uses of the attribute `Help`.

Attribute information for a given program element can be retrieved at run-time by using reflection support. The example

```
using System;

class Test
{
  static void Main()
  {
    Type type = typeof(Class1);
    object[] arr = type.GetCustomAttributes(
              typeof(HelpAttribute), true);
    if (arr.Length == 0)
      Console.WriteLine("Class1 has no Help attribute.");
    else
    {
      HelpAttribute ha = (HelpAttribute) arr[0];
      Console.WriteLine("Url = {0} , Topic = {1} ", ha.Url, ha.Topic);
    }
  }
}
```

checks to see if `Class1` has a `Help` attribute, and writes out the associated `Url` and `Topic` values if the attribute is present.

8.16 Generics

C# allows classes, structs, interfaces, and methods to be parameterized by the types of data they store and manipulate. This feature is really a set of features known collectively as **generics**. C# generics will immediately be familiar to users of generics in Eiffel or Ada, or to users of templates in C++.

Many common classes and structs can be parameterized by the types of data being stored and manipulated—these are called **generic class declarations** and **generic struct declarations**, respectively. Similarly, many interfaces define contracts that can be parameterized by the types of data they handle—these are called **generic interface declarations**. In order to implement "generic algorithms," methods can also be parameterized by type; such methods are known as **generic methods**.

8.16.1 Why generics?

Without generics, programmers can store data of any type in variables of the base type `object`. To illustrate, let's create a simple `Stack` type with two actions, "Push" and "Pop". The `Stack` class stores its data in an array of `object`, and the `Push` and `Pop` methods use the `object` type to accept and return data, respectively:

```
public class Stack
{
  private object[ ] items = new object[100] ;
  public void Push(object data) {...}
  public object Pop() {...}
}
```

We can then push a value of any type, such as a `Customer` type, for example, onto the stack. However, when we wanted to retrieve that value, we would need to cast explicitly the result of the `Pop` method, an `object`, into a `Customer` type, which is tedious to write, and carries a performance penalty for run-time type checking:

```
Stack s = new Stack();
s.Push(new Customer());
Customer c = (Customer)s.Pop();
```

If we pass to the `Push` method a value type, such as an `int`, it will automatically be boxed. Similarly, if we want to retrieve an `int` from the stack, we would need to unbox explicitly the `object` type we obtain from the `Pop` method:

```
Stack s = new Stack();
s.Push(3);
int i = (int)s.Pop();
```

Such boxing and unboxing operations can affect performance.

Furthermore, in the implementation shown, it is not possible to enforce the kind of data placed in the stack. Indeed, we could create a stack and push a `Customer` type onto it. However, later, we could use the same stack and try to pop data off of it and cast it into an incompatible type:

```
Stack s = new Stack();
s.Push(new Customer());
Employee e = (Employee)s.Pop();  // runtime error
```

While the code above is an improper use of the `Stack` class we presumably intended to implement, and *should* be a compile-time error, it is actually valid code. However, at run-time, the application will fail because we have performed an invalid cast operation.

8.16.2 Creating and consuming generics

Generics provide a facility for creating high-performance data structures that are specialized by the compiler and/or execution engine based on the types that they use. These so-called **generic type declarations** are created so that their internal algorithms remain the same, yet the types of their external interface and internal data can vary based on user preference.

In order to minimize the learning curve for developers, generics are used in much the same way as C++ templates. Programmers can create classes and structures just as they normally have, and by using the angle bracket notation (< and >) they can specify type parameters. When the generic class declaration is used, each type parameter shall be replaced by a type argument that the user of the class supplies.

In the example below, we create a `Stack` generic class declaration where we specify a **type parameter**, called `ItemType`, declared in angle brackets after the declaration. Rather than forcing conversions to and from `object`, instances of the generic `Stack` class will accept the type for which they are created and store data of that type without conversion. The type parameter `ItemType` acts as a placeholder until a runtime type is specified at use. Note that `ItemType` is used as the element type for the internal items array, the type for the parameter to the `Push` method, and the return type for the `Pop` method:

```
public class Stack<ItemType>
{
  private ItemType[] items = new ItemType[100];
  public void Push(ItemType data) {...}
  public ItemType Pop() {...}
}
```

When we use the generic class declaration `Stack`, as in the short example below, we can specify the runtime type to be used by the generic class. In this case, we instruct the `Stack` to use an `int` type by specifying it as a **type argument** using the angle brackets after the name:

```
Stack<int> s = new Stack<int>();
s.Push(3);
int x = s.Pop();
```

In so doing, we have created a new **constructed type**, `Stack<int>`, for which every `ItemType` inside the declaration of `Stack` is replaced with the supplied type argument `int`. Indeed, when we create our new instance of `Stack<int>`, the native storage of the items array is now an `int[]` rather than `object[]`, providing substantial storage efficiency. Additionally, we have eliminated the boxing penalty associated with pushing an `int` onto the stack. Further, when we pop an item off the stack, we no longer need to cast it explicitly to the appropriate type because this particular kind of `Stack` class natively stores an `int` in its data structure.

If we wanted to store items other than an `int` into a `Stack`, we would have to create a different constructed type from `Stack`, specifying a new type argument. Suppose we had a simple `Customer` type and we wanted to use a `Stack` to store it. To do so, we simply use the `Customer` class as the type argument to `Stack` and easily reuse our code:

```
Stack<Customer> s = new Stack<Customer>();
s.Push(new Customer());
Customer c = s.Pop();
```

Of course, once we've created a `Stack` with a `Customer` type as its type argument, we are now limited to storing only `Customer` objects (or objects of a class derived from `Customer`). Generics provide strong typing, meaning we can no longer improperly store an integer into the stack, like so:

```
Stack<Customer> s = new Stack<Customer>();
s.Push(new Customer());
s.Push(3);              // compile-time error
Customer c = s.Pop();   // no cast required
```

8.16.3 Multiple type parameters

Generic type declarations can have any number of type parameters. In our `Stack` example, we used only one type parameter. Suppose we created a simple `Dictionary` generic class declaration that stored values alongside keys. We could define a generic version of a `Dictionary` by declaring two type parameters, separated by commas within the angle brackets of the declaration:

```
public class Dictionary<KeyType, ElementType>
{
  public void Add(KeyType key, ElementType val) {...}
  public ElementType this[KeyType key] {...}
}
```

When we use `Dictionary`, we need to supply two type arguments within the angle brackets. Then when we call the `Add` function or use the indexer, the compiler checks that we supplied the right types:

```
Dictionary<string, Customer> dict = new Dictionary<string, Customer>();
dict.Add("Peter", new Customer());
Customer c = dict["Peter"];
```

8.16.4 Constraints

In many cases, we will do more than store data based on a given type parameter. Often, we will also want to use members of the type parameter to execute statements within our generic type declaration.

For example, suppose in the `Add` method of our `Dictionary` we wanted to compare items using the `CompareTo` method of the supplied key, like so:

```
public class Dictionary<KeyType, ElementType>
{
  public void Add(KeyType key, ElementType val)
  {
    ...

    if (key.CompareTo(x) < 0) {...}  // compile-time error
    ...
  }
}
```

Unfortunately, at compile-time the type parameter `KeyType` is, as expected, generic. As written, the compiler will assume that only the operations available to `object`, such as `ToString`, are available on the variable `key` of type `KeyType`. As a result, the compiler will display an error because the `CompareTo` method would not be found. However, we can cast the `key` variable to a type that does contain a `CompareTo` method, such as an `IComparable` interface, allowing the program to compile:

```
public class Dictionary<KeyType, ElementType>
{
  public void Add(KeyType key, ElementType val)
  {
    ...
```

```
      if (((IComparable)key).CompareTo(x) < 0) {...}
      ...
   }
}
```

However, if we now construct a type from `Dictionary` and supply a type argument, which does not implement `IComparable`, we will encounter a run-time error, specifically an `InvalidCastException`. Since one of the objectives of generics is to provide strong typing and to reduce the need for casts, a more elegant solution is needed.

We can supply an optional list of **constraints** for each type parameter. A constraint indicates a requirement that a type shall fulfill in order to be accepted as a type argument. (For example, it might have to implement a given interface or be derived from a given base class.) A constraint is declared using the word `where`, followed by a type parameter and colon (`:`), followed by a comma-separated list of constraints, which can include a class type, interface types, other type parameters, the reference type constraint "`class`", the value type constraint "`struct`", and the constructor constraint "`new()`".

In order to satisfy our need to use the `CompareTo` method inside `Dictionary`, we can impose a constraint on `KeyType`, requiring any type passed as the first argument to `Dictionary` to implement `IComparable`, like so:

```
public class Dictionary<KeyType, ElementType> where KeyType:
 IComparable
{
  public void Add(KeyType key, ElementType val)
  {
    ...
    if (key.CompareTo(x) < 0) {...}
    ...
  }
}
```

When compiled, this code will now be checked to ensure that each time we construct a `Dictionary` type we are passing a first type argument that implements `IComparable`. Further, we no longer have to cast variable `key` to `IComparable` explicitly before calling the `CompareTo` method.

Constraints are most useful when they are used in the context of defining a *framework*, i.e. a collection of related classes, where it is advantageous to ensure that a number of types support some common signatures and/or base types. Constraints can be used to help define "generic algorithms" that plug together functionality provided by different types. This can also be achieved by subclassing and runtime polymorphism, but static, constrained polymorphism can, in many cases, result in more efficient code, more flexible specifications of generic algorithms, and more errors being caught at compile-time rather than run-time. However, constraints need to be used with care and taste. Types that do not implement the constraints will not easily be usable in conjunction with generic code.

For any given type parameter, we can specify any number of interfaces and type parameters as constraints, but no more than one class. Each constrained type parameter has a separate `where` clause. In the example below, the `KeyType` type parameter has two interface constraints, while the `ElementType` type parameter has one class type constraint:

```
public class Dictionary<KeyType, ElementType >
   where KeyType: IComparable, IEnumerable
   where ElementType: Customer
```

```
{
  public void Add(KeyType key, ElementType val)
  {
    ...

    if (key.CompareTo(x) < 0) {...}
    ...
  }
}
```

8.16.5 Generic methods

In some cases, a type parameter is not needed for an entire class, but only when calling a particular method. Often, this occurs when creating a method that takes a generic type as a parameter. For example, when using the Stack described earlier, we might often find ourselves pushing multiple values in a row onto a stack, and decide to write a method to do so in a single call. If we are only using a single kind of Stack, say Stack<int>, writing such a method is easy:

```
static void PushMultiple(Stack<int> s, params int[] values)
{
  foreach (int v in values)
  {
    s.Push(v);
  }
}
```

We can use this method to push multiple int values onto a Stack<int>:

```
Stack<int> s = new Stack<int>();
PushMultiple(s, 1, 2, 3, 4);
```

However, the method above only works with one particular constructed type: Stack<int>. While we can easily write similar code for other constructed Stack types, we would like to write a single method that can work with any Stack, no matter what type argument was used.

We do this by writing a ***generic method***. Like a generic class declaration, a generic method is written with type parameters enclosed in angle brackets. With a generic method, the type parameters are written immediately after the method name, and can be used within the parameter list, return type, and body of the method. A generic PushMultiple method would look like this:

```
static void PushMultiple<ItemType>(Stack<ItemType> s,
    params ItemType[] values)
{
  foreach (ItemType v in values)
  {
    s.Push(v);
  }
}
```

Using this generic method, we can now push multiple items onto a Stack of any kind. Furthermore, the compiler type checking will ensure that the pushed items have the correct type for the kind of Stack being used. When calling a generic method, we place type arguments to the method in angle brackets. The generic PushMultiple method can be called this way:

```
Stack<int> s = new Stack<int>();
PushMultiple<int>(s, 1, 2, 3, 4);
```

This generic `PushMultiple` method is much better than the previous version, since it works on any kind of `Stack`. However, it appears to be less convenient to call, since the desired `ItemType` shall be supplied as a type argument to the method. In many cases, however, the compiler can deduce the correct type argument from the other arguments passed to the method, using a process called **type inferencing**. In the example above, since the first regular argument is of type `Stack<int>`, and the subsequent arguments are of type `int`, the compiler can reason that the type parameter shall also be `int`. Thus, the generic `PushMultiple` method can be called without specifying the type parameter:

```
Stack<int> s = new Stack<int>();
PushMultiple(s, 1, 2, 3, 4);
```

8.17 Anonymous methods

In C# code, a callback method is often invoked strictly through a delegate and not invoked directly. The purpose of such a method is obscured by the necessary separation of the method declaration from the delegate instantiation. In contrast, the body of an **anonymous method** is written "in-line" where the delegate is used, conveniently tying the method source code to the delegate instance. Besides this convenience, anonymous methods have shared access to the local state of the containing function member. To achieve the same state sharing using named methods requires "lifting" local variables into fields of some object, further obscuring the source code.

An anonymous method is declared using an *anonymous-method-expression*:

> *anonymous-method-expression:*
>   `delegate`   *anonymous-method-signature$_{opt}$*   *block*

The optional *anonymous-method-signature* defines the names and types of the formal parameters for the anonymous method. If the *anonymous-method-signature* is omitted, the *block* does not use any formal parameters. The *block* defines the body of the anonymous method.

An *anonymous-method-expression* is classified as a special kind of value that references the anonymous method. This value has no intrinsic type, but is implicitly convertible to any delegate type that has parameter types and a return type compatible with the anonymous method. If an anonymous method is declared without a signature, any delegate parameter types that do not include an `out` parameter are compatible with the anonymous method. If an anonymous method is declared with a signature, only delegate parameter types that exactly match in type and order are compatible. The return type of a delegate is compatible with an anonymous method if the expressions associated with all `return` statements in the anonymous method can be implicitly converted to the return type of the delegate. A `void` delegate return type is compatible with an anonymous method that has no `return` statements, or only has `return` statements with no expression.

Local variables and value parameters (including `this`) whose scope contains an anonymous method declaration are called **outer variables** of the anonymous method.

In the absence of anonymous methods, the lifetime of a local variable or value parameter ends when execution of its scope ends, as described in §12.1.7. However, an anonymous method can access an outer variable instance after execution has left the scope of the outer variable. In this case, the lifetime of the outer variable extends until all referencing anonymous method delegates are eligible for garbage collection, as described in §10.9.

An anonymous method cannot access `ref` or `out` parameters of an outer scope. The reason for this is that the caller of a function member allocates the storage for such parameters, so their lifetimes cannot be extended arbitrarily by the called function member. Consequently, since the this value of an instance method of a struct is equivalent to a ref parameter, an anonymous method in a struct is not allowed to access this.

Semantically, an anonymous method contained in a class or struct T is considered a method of T. If T is a class type, the anonymous method is considered an instance method or static method according to whether the containing function member is instance or static, respectively. In contrast, if T is a struct type, the anonymous method is always considered static and, as indicated above, cannot access this.

The following code defines an Action delegate type and a Walk method. The Walk method invokes an action sequentially on nodes in a linked list until either the action returns false or the end of the list is encountered.

```
delegate bool Action(Node n);

static void Walk(Node n, Action a)
{
   while (n != null && a(n)) n = n.Next;
}
```

The following invocation of Walk employs an anonymous method to display the names of the nodes in a list:

```
Walk(list,
   delegate(Node n)
   {
      Console.WriteLine(n.Name);
      return true;
   }
);
```

This code could easily be implemented using a named method, but doing so would require separating the method declaration from the invocation, obscuring the purpose of the method and the result of the invocation:

```
Walk(list, new Action(DisplayNodeName));
...

bool DisplayNodeName(Node n)
{
   Console.WriteLine(n.Name);
   return true;
}
```

The following code uses an outer local variable c to display the ordinal position of each node:

```
int c = 0;

Walk(list,
   delegate(Node n)
   {
      Console.WriteLine("{0} : {1} ", ++c, n.Name);
      return true;
   }
);

Console.WriteLine("Processed {0} nodes", c);
```

Implementing this example using a named method would require "lifting" the outer local variable c into a field, which would further obscure the code, would introduce additional overhead in the type, and could introduce concurrency issues.

The following code uses an outer local variable c and an instance field max to restrict the number of items displayed:

```
class A
{
  int max;
  ...

  void F(Node list)
  {
    int c = 0;

    Walk(list,
      delegate(Node n)
      {
        if (c >= max)
        {
          Console.WriteLine("... display truncated");
          return false;
        }
        Console.WriteLine("{0} : {1} ", ++c, n.Name);
        return true;
      }
    );

    Console.WriteLine("Processed {0} nodes", c);
  }
}
```

Since F is an instance method of class A, the anonymous method is considered to be an instance method of A, and the field max is accessed through the anonymous method's this variable (which is the same as F's this variable). That is, max is a field, *not* an outer variable, and the anonymous method can access max just as any other instance method does.

Implementing this example in a safe way (considering the possibility of concurrency) without an anonymous method requires a significant amount of work and decreases clarity:

```
class A
{
  int max;
  ...

  void F(Node list)
  {
    NodeNameDisplayer nnd = new NodeNameDisplayer(this);
    nnd.c = 0;

    Walk(list, new Action(nnd.DisplayNodeName));

    Console.WriteLine("Processed {0} nodes", nnd.c);
  }

  internal class NodeNameDisplayer
```

```
    {
      A outer;
      internal int c;

      public NodeNameDisplayer(A outer)
      {
        this.outer = outer;
      }

      bool DisplayNodeName(Node n)
      {
        if (c >= outer.max)
        {
          Console.WriteLine("... display truncated");
          return false;
        }
        Console.WriteLine("{0} : {1} ", ++c, n.Name);
        return true;
      }
    }
  }
}
```

8.18 Iterators

The `foreach` statement is used to iterate over the elements of an ***enumerable*** collection. In order to be enumerable, a collection shall have a parameterless `GetEnumerator` method that returns an ***enumerator***. Generally, enumerators are difficult to implement, but the task is significantly simplified with iterators.

An ***iterator*** is a statement block that ***yields*** an ordered sequence of values. An iterator is distinguished from a normal statement block by the presence of one or more `yield` statements:

- The `yield return` statement produces the next value of the iteration.
- The `yield break` statement indicates that the iteration is complete.

An iterator can be used as the body of a function member as long as the return type of the function member is one of the ***enumerator interfaces*** or one of the ***enumerable interfaces***:

- The enumerator interfaces are `System.Collections.IEnumerator` and types constructed from `System.Collections.Generic.IEnumerator<T>`.
- The enumerable interfaces are `System.Collections.IEnumerable` and types constructed from `System.Collections.Generic.IEnumerable<T>`.

It is important to understand that an iterator is not a kind of member, but is a means of implementing a function member. A member implemented via an iterator can be overridden or overloaded by other members, which may or may not be implemented with iterators.

The following `Stack<T>` class implements its `GetEnumerator` method using an iterator, which enumerates the elements of the stack in top-to-bottom order.

```
using System.Collections.Generic;

public class Stack<T>: IEnumerable<T>
{
  T[] items;
  int count;
```

```
  public void Push(T data) {...}

  public T Pop() {...}

  public IEnumerator<T> GetEnumerator()
  {
    for (int i = count - 1; i >= 0; --i)
    {
      yield return items[i];
    }
  }
}
```

The presence of the `GetEnumerator` method makes `Stack<T>` an enumerable type, allowing instances of `Stack<T>` to be used in a `foreach` statement. The following example pushes the values 0 through 9 onto an integer stack and then uses a `foreach` loop to display the values in top-to-bottom order.

```
using System;

class Test
{
  static void Main()
  {
    Stack<int> s = new Stack<int>();
    for (int i = 0; i < 10; i++) s.Push(i);
    foreach (int i in s) Console.Write("{0} ", i);
    Console.WriteLine();
  }
}
```

The output of the example is:

```
9 8 7 6 5 4 3 2 1 0
```

The `foreach` statement implicitly calls a collection's parameterless `GetEnumerator` method to obtain an enumerator. There can only be one such parameterless `GetEnumerator` method defined by a collection, yet it is often appropriate to have multiple ways of enumerating, and ways of controlling the enumeration through parameters. In such cases, a collection can use iterators to implement properties or methods that return one of the enumerable interfaces. For example, `Stack<T>` might introduce two new properties, `TopToBottom` and `BottomToTop`, of type `IEnumerable<T>`:

```
using System.Collections.Generic;

public class Stack<T>: IEnumerable<T>
{
  T[] items;
  int count;

  public void Push(T data) {...}

  public T Pop() {...}

  public IEnumerator<T> GetEnumerator()
```

```
      {
        for (int i = count - 1; i >= 0; --i)
        {
          yield return items[i];
        }
      }

      public IEnumerable<T> TopToBottom
      {
        get
        {
          return this;
        }
      }

      public IEnumerable<T> BottomToTop
      {
        get
        {
          for (int i = 0; i < count; i++)
          {
            yield return items[i];
          }
        }
      }
    }
```

The `get` accessor for the `TopToBottom` property just returns `this` since the stack itself is an enumerable. The `BottomToTop` property returns an enumerable implemented with an iterator. The following example shows how the properties can be used to enumerate stack elements in either order:

```
using System;

class Test
{
  static void Main()
  {
    Stack<int> s = new Stack<int>();
    for (int i = 0; i < 10; i++) s.Push(i);

    foreach (int i in s.TopToBottom) Console.Write("{0} ", i);
    Console.WriteLine();

    foreach (int i in s.BottomToTop) Console.Write("{0} ", i);
    Console.WriteLine();
  }
}
```

Of course, these properties can be used outside of a `foreach` statement as well. The following example passes the results of invoking the properties to a separate `Print` method. The example also shows an iterator used as the body of a `FromToBy` method that takes parameters:

```
using System;
using System.Collections.Generic;

class Test
{
  static void Print(IEnumerable<int> collection)
  {
    foreach (int i in collection) Console.Write("{0} ", i);
    Console.WriteLine();
  }

  static IEnumerable<int> FromToBy(int from, int to, int by)
  {
    for (int i = from; i <= to; i += by)
    {
      yield return i;
    }
  }

  static void Main()
  {
    Stack<int> s = new Stack<int>();
    for (int i = 0; i < 10; i++) s.Push(i);
    Print(s.TopToBottom);
    Print(s.BottomToTop);
    Print(FromToBy(10, 20, 2));
  }
}
```

The output of the example is:

```
9 8 7 6 5 4 3 2 1 0
0 1 2 3 4 5 6 7 8 9
10 12 14 16 18 20
```

The generic and non-generic enumerable interfaces contain a single member, a `GetEnumerator` method that takes no arguments and returns an enumerator interface. An enumerable acts as an *enumerator factory*. Properly implemented enumerables generate independent enumerators each time their `GetEnumerator` method is called. Assuming the internal state of the enumerable has not changed between two calls to `GetEnumerator`, the two enumerators returned should produce the same set of values in the same order. This should hold even if the lifetimes of the enumerators overlap as in the following code sample:

```
using System;
using System.Collections.Generic;

class Test
{
  static IEnumerable<int> FromTo(int from, int to)
  {
    while (from <= to) yield return from++;
  }

  static void Main()
  {
```

```
       IEnumerable<int> e = FromTo(1, 10);
       foreach (int x in e)
       {
         foreach (int y in e)
         {
           Console.Write("{0,3} ", x * y);
         }
         Console.WriteLine();
       }
     }
   }
```

The code above prints a simple multiplication table of the integers 1 through 10. Note that the `FromTo` method is invoked only once to generate the enumerable e. However, `e.GetEnumerator()` is invoked multiple times (by the `foreach` statements) to generate multiple equivalent enumerators. These enumerators all encapsulate the iterator code specified in the declaration of `FromTo`. Note that the iterator code modifies the `from` parameter. Nevertheless, the enumerators act independently because each enumerator is given *its own copy* of the `from` and `to` parameters. The sharing of transient state between enumerators is one of several common subtle flaws that should be avoided when implementing enumerables and enumerators. Iterators are designed to help avoid these problems and to implement robust enumerables and enumerators in a simple intuitive way.

8.19 Nullable types

Support for nullability across all types, including value types, is essential when interacting with databases; yet, historically, general-purpose programming languages have provided little or no support in this area. Many approaches exist for handling nulls and value types without direct language support, but all have shortcomings. For example, one approach is to use a "special" value (such as –1 for integers) to indicate null, but this only works when an unused value can be identified. Another approach is to maintain Boolean null indicators in separate fields or variables, but this doesn't work well for parameters and return values. A third approach is to use a set of user-defined nullable types, but this only works for a closed set of types. C#'s *nullable types* solve this long-standing problem by providing complete and integrated support for nullable forms of all value types.

Nullable types are constructed using the `?` type modifier. For example, `int?` is the nullable form of the predefined type `int`. A nullable type's underlying type must be a non-nullable value type.

A nullable type is a structure that combines a value of the underlying type with a Boolean null indicator. An instance of a nullable type has two public read-only properties: `HasValue`, of type `bool`, and `Value`, of the nullable type's underlying type. `HasValue` is true for a non-null instance and false for a null instance. When `HasValue` is true, the `Value` property returns the contained value. When `HasValue` is false, an attempt to access the `Value` property throws an exception.

An implicit conversion exists from any non-nullable value type to a nullable form of that type. Furthermore, an implicit conversion exists from the `null` type (§11.2.7) to any nullable type. In the example

```
   int? x = 123;
   int? y = null;

   if (x.HasValue) Console.WriteLine(x.Value);
   if (y.HasValue) Console.WriteLine(y.Value);
```

the `int` value `123` and the `null` literal are implicitly converted to the nullable type `int?`. The example outputs `123` for `x`, but the second `Console.WriteLine` isn't executed because `y.HasValue` is false.

Nullable conversions and ***lifted conversions*** permit predefined and user-defined conversions that operate on non-nullable value types also to be used with nullable forms of those types. Likewise, ***lifted operators*** permit predefined and user-defined operators that work for non-nullable value types also to work for nullable forms of those types.

For every predefined conversion from a non-nullable value type `S` to a non-nullable value type `T`, a predefined nullable conversion automatically exists from `S?` to `T?`. This nullable conversion is a ***null propagating*** form of the underlying conversion: It converts a null source value directly to a null target value, but otherwise performs the underlying non-nullable conversion. Nullable conversions are furthermore provided from `S` to `T?` and from `S?` to `T`, the latter as an explicit conversion that throws an exception if the source value is null.

Some examples of nullable conversions are shown in the following.

```
int i = 123;
int? x = i;          // int --> int?
double? y = x;       // int? --> double?
int? z = (int?)y;    // double? --> int?
int j = (int)z;      // int? --> int
```

A user-defined conversion operator has a lifted form when the source and target types are both non-nullable value types. A `?` modifier is added to the source and target types to create the lifted form. Similar to predefined nullable conversions, lifted conversion operators propagate nulls.

A non-comparison operator has a lifted form when the operand types and result type are all non-nullable value types. For non-comparison operators, a `?` modifier is added to each operand type and the result type to create the lifted form. For example, the lifted form of the predefined `+` operator that takes two `int` operands and returns an `int`, is an operator that takes two `int?` operands and returns an `int?`. Similar to lifted conversions, lifted non-comparison operators are null-propagating: If either operand of a lifted operator is null, the result is null.

The following example uses a lifted `+` operator to add two `int?` values:

```
int? x = GetNullableInt();
int? y = GetNullableInt();
int? z = x + y;
```

the assignment to `z` effectively corresponds to:

```
int? z = x.HasValue && y.HasValue ? x.Value + y.Value : (int?)null;
```

Because an implicit conversion exists from a non-nullable value type to its nullable form, a lifted operator is applicable when just one operand is of a nullable type. The following example uses the same lifted `+` operator as the example above:

```
int? x = GetNullableInt();
int? y = x + 1;
```

If `x` is null, `y` is assigned null. Otherwise, `y` is assigned the value of `x` plus one.

The null-propagating semantics of C#'s nullable conversions, lifted conversions, and lifted non-comparison operators are very similar to the corresponding conversions and operators in SQL. However, C#'s lifted comparison operators produce regular Boolean results rather than introducing SQL's three-valued Boolean logic.

A comparison operator (==, !=, <, >, <=, >=) has a lifted form when the operand types are both non-nullable value types and the result type is bool. The lifted form of a comparison operator is formed by adding a ? modifier to each operand type (but not to the result type). Lifted forms of the == and != operators consider two null values equal, and a null value unequal to a non-null value. Lifted forms of the <, >, <=, and >= operators return false if one or both operands are null.

When one of the operands of the == or != operator has the null type (§11.2.7), the other operand may be of any nullable type regardless of whether the underlying value type actually declares that operator. In cases where no operator == or != implementation is available, a check of the operand's HasValue property is substituted. The effect of this rule is that statements such as

```
if (x == null) Console.WriteLine ("x is null");
```

```
if (x != null) Console.WriteLine ("x is non-null");
```

are permitted for an x of any nullable type or reference type, thus providing a common way of performing null checks for all types that can be null.

A new **null coalescing operator**, ??, is provided. The result of a ?? b is a if a is non-null; otherwise, the result is b. Intuitively, b supplies the value to use when a is null.

When a is of a nullable type and b is of a non-nullable type, a ?? b returns a non-nullable value, provided the appropriate implicit conversions exist between the operand types. In the example

```
int? x = GetNullableInt();
int? y = GetNullableInt();
int? z = x ?? y;
int i = z ?? -1;
```

the type of x ?? y is int?, but the type of z ?? -1 is int. The latter operation is particularly convenient because it removes the ? from the type and at the same time supplies the default value to use in the null case.

The null coalescing operator also works for reference types. The example

```
string s = GetStringValue();
Console.WriteLine(s ?? "Unspecified");
```

outputs the value of s, or outputs Unspecified if s is null.

End of informative text.

9 Lexical structure

9.1 Programs

A C# **program** consists of one or more source files, known formally as **compilation units** (§16.1). A source file is an ordered sequence of Unicode characters. Source files typically have a one-to-one correspondence with files in a file system, but this correspondence is not required.

Conceptually speaking, a program is compiled using three steps:

1. Transformation, which converts a file from a particular character repertoire and encoding scheme into a sequence of Unicode characters.
2. Lexical analysis, which translates a stream of Unicode input characters into a stream of tokens.
3. Syntactic analysis, which translates the stream of tokens into executable code.

Conforming implementations shall accept Unicode source files encoded with the UTF-8 encoding form (as defined by the Unicode standard), and transform them into a sequence of Unicode characters. Implementations can choose to accept and transform additional character encoding schemes (such as UTF-16, UTF-32, or non-Unicode character mappings).

[*Note*: It is beyond the scope of this standard to define how a file using a character representation other than Unicode might be transformed into a sequence of Unicode characters. During such transformation, however, it is recommended that the usual line-separating character (or sequence) in the other character set be translated to the two-character sequence consisting of the Unicode carriage-return character followed by Unicode line-feed character. For the most part this transformation will have no visible effects; however, it will affect the interpretation of verbatim string literal tokens (§9.4.4.5). The purpose of this recommendation is to allow a verbatim string literal to produce the same character sequence when its source file is moved between systems that support differing non-Unicode character sets, in particular, those using differing character sequences for line-separation. *end note*]

Much ado about nothing

The null character is valid in Unicode and may occur in C# programs in places such as string literals. For example, consider:

```
class NullLiteral
{
  public static void Main()
  {
    System.Console.WriteLine("A null >^@<");
  }
}
```

where the sequence "^@" represents the null character. This is a perfectly valid C# program.

However, at the time of writing, the Microsoft compiler fails to accept the preceding program and reports an unexpected end-of-file in the string literal. The current Mono compiler accepts the program and outputs the null correctly when executed.

The Microsoft behavior can result in code being missed. For example, consider ("^@" represents null as before):

```
class AccidentalNull
{
  public static void Main()
  {
    System.Console.WriteLine("Should fail to compile");
  }
}
^@
class Missed
{
  public void NeverReached() {}
}
```

The null character is not valid whitespace so this example is erroneous. The Mono compiler correctly reports the, (presumably accidental), null character as an error and aborts compilation. However, the Microsoft compiler simply skips the remainder of the input without warning and produces an assembly without the `Missed` class. This error will presumably be confusingly discovered later when another compilation attempts to reference the `Missed` class and finds it missing despite its apparent successful compilation.

This Microsoft behavior is unfortunate, but is probably rarely a problem unless your text editor allows the easy accidental typing of nulls.

Marek Safar

9.2 Grammars

This specification presents the syntax of the C# programming language using two grammars. The *lexical grammar* (§9.2.1) defines how Unicode characters are combined to form line terminators, white space, comments, tokens, and pre-processing directives. The *syntactic grammar* (§9.2.2) defines how the tokens resulting from the lexical grammar are combined to form C# programs.

9.2.1 Lexical grammar

The lexical grammar of C# is presented in §9.3, §9.4, and §9.5. The terminal symbols of the lexical grammar are the characters of the Unicode character set, and the lexical grammar specifies how characters are combined to form tokens (§9.4), white space (§9.3.3), comments (§9.3.2), and pre-processing directives (§9.5).

Every source file in a C# program shall conform to the *input* production of the lexical grammar (§9.3).

9.2.2 Syntactic grammar

The syntactic grammar of C# is presented in the clauses, subclauses, and appendices that follow this subclause. The terminal symbols of the syntactic grammar are the tokens defined by the lexical grammar, and the syntactic grammar specifies how tokens are combined to form C# programs.

Every source file in a C# program shall conform to the *compilation-unit* production (§16.1) of the syntactic grammar.

9.2.3 Grammar ambiguities

The productions for *simple-name* (§14.5.2) and *member-access* (§14.5.4) can give rise to ambiguities in the grammar for expressions. [*Example*: The statement:

```
F(G<A, B>(7));
```

could be interpreted as a call to F with two arguments, G < A and B > (7). Alternatively, it could be interpreted as a call to F with one argument, which is a call to a generic method G with two type arguments and one regular argument. *end example*]

If a sequence of tokens can be parsed (in context) as a *simple-name* (§14.5.2), *member-access* (§14.5.4), or *pointer-member-access* (§27.5.2) ending with a *type-argument-list* (§25.5.1), the token immediately following the closing > token is examined. If it is one of

```
( ) ]  :  ; ,  . ?  ==  !=
```

then the *type-argument-list* is retained as part of the *simple-name, member-access* or *pointer-member-access* and any other possible parse of the sequence of tokens is discarded. Otherwise, the *type-argument-list* is not considered part of the *simple-name, member-access* or *pointer-member-access*, even if there is no other possible parse of the sequence of tokens. [*Note*: These rules are not applied when parsing a *type-argument-list* in a *namespace-or-type-name* (§10.8). *end note*] [*Example*: The statement:

```
F(G <A, B> (7));
```

will, according to this rule, be interpreted as a call to F with one argument, which is a call to a generic method G with two type arguments and one regular argument. The statements

```
F(G <A, B>7);
F(G <A, B>>7);
```

will each be interpreted as a call to F with two arguments. The statement

```
x = F<A> + y;
```

will be interpreted as a less-than operator, greater-than operator and unary-plus operator, as if the statement had been written x = (F < A) > (+y), instead of as a *simple-name* with a *type-argument-list* followed by a binary-plus operator. In the statement

```
x = y is C<T> + z;
```

the tokens C<T> are interpreted as a *namespace-or-type-name* with a *type-argument-list*. *end example*]

Rationale: the "following token" set

The set of tokens considered in resolving the preceding ambiguity is given as:

```
( ) ]  :  ; ,  . ?  ==  !=
```

Why were these tokens chosen?

An expression should be recognized as a generic method call if it can be parsed as a simple-name with a type parameter list followed by a '(' token. This is the reason for the token '(' appearing in the set. This is a breaking change in the grammar relative to C# version 1, but the actual code example shown earlier is obscure at best.

Likewise, to support access to a member of a generic type, the '.' token is included in the set. This allows List<string>.Sort(...) to be parsed as expected. Since '.' could not be found at the start of an expression, this does not break any version 1 code.

To support the standard conversion from a method name to a delegate, tokens that can be found immediately after an expression, but cannot start an expression, are included in the set. This includes ‘)’, ‘]’, ‘:’, ‘;’, ‘,’, and ‘?’. This gives the expected parse of an expression such as `F(G <string>)`, where `G` is a generic method taking one argument and `F` is a method taking a single argument of delegate type to which `(G <string>)` is convertible.

To avoid unnecessary breaking changes, ‘>’ should continue to parse as a binary operator whenever possible, so that no other token that can start an expression is included in the set. Tokens that can start expressions include literals, unary operators (‘+’, ‘++’, the unsafe unary pointer dereferencing operator ‘*’, and for consistency, binary multiplicative operators as well), and some keywords (`new`, `base`, ...). Tokens that cannot end or start an expression are not included either. This accounts for most remaining keywords. The `is` and `as` keywords could be used in an expression of the form `if (G <string> as MyDelegateType)`. However, this can never compile successfully, so those keywords are not included in the set either.

The only binary operators included are ‘==’ and ‘!=’. This allows for code fragments like: `if (G <string> == myDelegate) {...}`. These are the only binary operators that can reasonably take a delegate as a first argument.

The compound assignment operators (‘+=’, ‘-=’, ...) and remaining binary operators (‘<<’) can never produce a valid expression when found after a ‘>’ so are not included in the set.

Peter Hallam

Similar cast expression ambiguity

A similar ambiguity and disambiguation rule with cast expressions is discussed in (§14.6.6).

Peter Golde

F(G<A, B>>7)

At the time of writing both the Mono and the Microsoft C# compilers fail to parse the F(G<A, B>>7) example:

```
public class ShouldCompile
{
  public static void Main()
  {
    int G = 1, A = 2, B = 2;
    int blah = F(G<A, B>>7);
  }

  public static int F(bool a, int b)
  {
    return 42;
  }
}
```

9.3 Lexical analysis

The *input* production defines the lexical structure of a C# source file. Each source file in a C# program shall conform to this lexical grammar production.

input::
   input-section$_{opt}$

input-section::
  input-section-part
  input-section   input-section-part

input-section-part::
  input-elements$_{opt}$ *new-line*
  pp-directive

input-elements::
  input-element
  input-elements   input-element

input-element::
  whitespace
  comment
  token

Five basic elements make up the lexical structure of a C# source file: Line terminators (§9.3.1), white space (§9.3.3), comments (§9.3.2), tokens (§9.4), and pre-processing directives (§9.5). Of these basic elements, only tokens are significant in the syntactic grammar of a C# program (§9.2.2), except in the case of a > token being combined with another token to form a single operator (§9.4.5).

The lexical processing of a C# source file consists of reducing the file into a sequence of tokens which becomes the input to the syntactic analysis. Line terminators, white space, and comments can serve to separate tokens, and pre-processing directives can cause sections of the source file to be skipped, but otherwise these lexical elements have no impact on the syntactic structure of a C# program.

When several lexical grammar productions match a sequence of characters in a source file, the lexical processing always forms the longest possible lexical element. [*Example*: The character sequence // is processed as the beginning of a single-line comment because that lexical element is longer than a single / token. *end example*]

9.3.1 Line terminators
Line terminators divide the characters of a C# source file into lines.

new-line::
  Carriage return character (U+000D)
  Line feed character (U+000A)
  Carriage return character (U+000D) followed by line feed character (U+000A)
  Next line character (U+2085)
  Line separator character (U+2028)
  Paragraph separator character (U+2029)

For compatibility with source code editing tools that add end-of-file markers, and to enable a source file to be viewed as a sequence of properly terminated lines, the following transformations are applied, in order, to every source file in a C# program:

- If the last character of the source file is a Control-Z character (U+001A), this character is deleted.
- A carriage-return character (U+000D) is added to the end of the source file if that source file is non-empty and if the last character of the source file is not a carriage return (U+000D), a line feed (U+000A), a next line character (U+2085), a line separator (U+2028), or a para-graph separator (U+2029). [*Note*: The additional carriage-return allows a program to end in a *pp-directive* (§9.5) that does not have a terminating *new-line*. *end note*]

9.3.2 Comments

Two forms of comments are supported: delimited comments and single-line comments.

A **delimited comment** begins with the characters /* and ends with the characters * /. Delimited comments can occupy a portion of a line, a single line, or multiple lines. [*Example*: The example

```
/* Hello, world program
   This program writes "hello, world" to the console
*/
class Hello
{
  static void Main()
  {
    System.Console.WriteLine("hello, world");
  }
}
```

includes a delimited comment. *end example*]

A **single-line comment** begins with the characters // and extends to the end of the line. [*Example*: The example

```
// Hello, world program
// This program writes "hello, world" to the console
//
class Hello  // any name will do for this class
{
  static void Main()  // this method must be named "Main"
  {
    System.Console.WriteLine("hello, world");
  }
}
```

shows several single-line comments. *end example*]

comment::
  single-line-comment
  delimited-comment

single-line-comment::
  //   *input-characters$_{opt}$*

input-characters::
  input-character
  input-characters   *input-character*

input-character::
  Any Unicode character except a *new-line-character*

new-line-character::
  Carriage return character (U+000D)
  Line feed character (U+000A)
  Next line character (U+0085)
  Line separator character (U+2028)
  Paragraph separator character (U+2029)

delimited-comment::
    /*   *delimited-comment-text$_{opt}$*   *asterisks*   /

delimited-comment-text::
  delimited-comment-section
  delimited-comment-text   *delimited-comment-section*

delimited-comment-section::
  not-asterisk
  asterisks   *not-slash*

asterisks::
  *
  asterisks   *

not-asterisk::
  Any Unicode character except *

not-slash::
  Any Unicode character except /

Comments do not nest. The character sequences /* and */ have no special meaning within a single-line comment, and the character sequences // and /* have no special meaning within a delimited comment.

Comments are not processed within character and string literals.

9.3.3 White space

White space is defined as any character with Unicode class Zs (which includes the space character) as well as the horizontal tab character, the vertical tab character, and the form feed character.

whitespace::
  whitespace-characters

whitespace-characters::
  whitespace-character
  whitespace-characters   *whitespace-character*

whitespace-character::
  Any character with Unicode class Zs
  Horizontal tab character (U+0009)
  Vertical tab character (U+000B)
  Form feed character (U+000C)

9.4 Tokens

There are several kinds of **tokens**: identifiers, keywords, literals, operators, and punctuators. White space and comments are not tokens, though they act as separators for tokens.

token::
  identifier
  keyword
  integer-literal
  real-literal

character-literal
string-literal
operator-or-punctuator

9.4.1 Unicode escape sequences

A Unicode escape sequence represents a Unicode character. Unicode escape sequences are processed in identifiers (§9.4.2), regular string literals (§9.4.4.5), and character literals (§9.4.4.4). A Unicode character escape is not processed in any other location (for example, to form an operator, punctuator, or keyword).

No escapes in verbatim strings

This is decidedly different from Java, which processes Unicode escape sequences in all locations. In particular, note that Unicode escape sequences are not processed within verbatim string literals (§9.4.4.5).

Peter Golde

No escapes in comments

The lack of Unicode processing within comments can prevent errors and surprises. For example, it means that the following single line comment does not give an error message (it does in Java):

```
// Note that \u000a is a line feed
```

Jon Skeet

---

unicode-escape-sequence::
  \u *hex-digit* *hex-digit* *hex-digit* *hex-digit*
  \U *hex-digit* *hex-digit* *hex-digit* *hex-digit* *hex-digit* *hex-digit* *hex-digit*
     hex-digit

A Unicode escape sequence represents the single Unicode character formed by the hexadecimal number following the "\u" or "\U" characters. Since C# uses a 16-bit encoding of Unicode characters in characters and string values, a Unicode code point in the range U+10000 to U+10FFFF is represented using two Unicode surrogate code units. Unicode code points above 0x10FFFF are invalid and are not supported.

Multiple translations are not performed. For instance, the string literal "\u005Cu005C" is equivalent to "\u005C" rather than "\". [*Note*: The Unicode value \u005C is the character "\". *end note*]

[*Example*: The example

```
class Class1
{
  static void Test(bool \u0066)
  {
    char c = '\u0066';
    if (\u0066)
      System.Console.WriteLine(c.ToString());
  }
}
```

shows several uses of \u0066, which is the escape sequence for the letter "f". The program is equivalent to

```
class Class1
{
  static void Test(bool f)
  {
    char c = 'f';
    if (f)
      System.Console.WriteLine(c.ToString());
  }
}
```

end example]

9.4.2 Identifiers

The rules for identifiers given in this subclause correspond exactly to those recommended by the Unicode Standard Annex 15 except that underscore is allowed as an initial character (as is traditional in the C programming language), Unicode escape sequences are permitted in identifiers, and the "@" character is allowed as a prefix to enable keywords to be used as identifiers.

identifier::
  available-identifier
  @ *identifier-or-keyword*

available-identifier::
  An *identifier-or-keyword* that is not a *keyword*

identifier-or-keyword::
  identifier-start-character *identifier-part-characters$_{opt}$*

identifier-start-character::
  letter-character
  _(the underscore character U+005F)

identifier-part-characters::
  identifier-part-character
  identifier-part-characters *identifier-part-character*

identifier-part-character::
  letter-character
  decimal-digit-character
  connecting-character
  combining-character
  formatting-character

letter-character::
  A Unicode character of classes Lu, Ll, Lt, Lm, Lo, or Nl
  A *unicode-escape-sequence* representing a character of classes Lu, Ll, Lt, Lm, Lo, or Nl

combining-character::
  A Unicode character of classes Mn or Mc
  A *unicode-escape-sequence* representing a character of classes Mn or Mc

decimal-digit-character::
    A Unicode character of the class Nd
    A *unicode-escape-sequence* representing a character of the class Nd

connecting-character::
    A Unicode character of the class Pc
    A *unicode-escape-sequence* representing a character of the class Pc

formatting-character::
    A Unicode character of the class Cf
    A *unicode-escape-sequence* representing a character of the class Cf

[*Note*: For information on the Unicode character classes mentioned above, see *The Unicode Standard, Version 3.0*, §4.5. *end note*]

[*Example*: Examples of valid identifiers include "`identifier1`", "`_identifier2`", and "`@if`". *end example*]

An identifier in a conforming program shall be in the canonical format defined by Unicode Normalization Form C, as defined by Unicode Standard Annex 15. The behavior when encountering an identifier not in Normalization Form C is implementation-defined; however, a diagnostic is not required.

Identifier normalization

The wording about normalization form C is a compromise. The issue arises as some characters (such as ü — that is, the letter u with a diaeresis) can be represented in Unicode in both a combined form as a single character (LATIN SMALL LETTER U WITH DIAERESIS, U+00FC), or as two characters: a plain one (LATIN SMALL LETTER U, U+0075) followed by a combining one (COMBINING DIAERESIS, U+0308). The Unicode Standard recommends that identifiers be canonicalized so that equivalent Unicode code sequences are recognized as denoting the same identifier. However, many people on the committee felt that it was excessively burdensome on compilers to have to implement the (fairly complex) Unicode normalization rules. Hence, it is left up to the implementation whether to normalize or not.

Peter Golde

The humble underscore

The production *identifier-start-character* allows an *identifier* to start with a *unicode-escape-sequence* for any valid identifier start character *except* an underscore. This was not intended and a *unicode-escape-sequence* for the underscore may appear at the start of an *identifier*. For example, both "_kahu" and "\u005Fkahu" are valid, and equivalent, identifiers.

Furthermore, while an underscore is explicitly allowed as the first character in an *identifier* (by *identifier-start-character*), less obviously it is also allowed in any subsequent position because it is also a *connecting-character*, as it is a Unicode character of class Pc.

The prefix "@" enables the use of keywords as identifiers, which is useful when interfacing with other programming languages. The character @ is not actually part of the identifier, so the identifier might be seen in other languages as a normal identifier, without the prefix. An identifier with an @ prefix is called a **verbatim identifier**. [*Note*: Use of the @ prefix for identifiers that are not keywords is permitted, but strongly discouraged as a matter of style. *end note*]

[*Example*: The example:

```
class @class
{
  public static void @static(bool @bool)
  {
    if (@bool)
      System.Console.WriteLine("true");
    else
      System.Console.WriteLine("false");
  }
}

class Class1
{
  static void M()
  {
    cl\u0061ss.st\u0061tic(true);
  }
}
```

defines a class named "class" with a static method named "static" that takes a parameter named "bool". Note that since Unicode escapes are not permitted in keywords, the token "cl \u0061ss" is an identifier, and is the same identifier as "@class". *end example*]

Two identifiers are considered the same if they are identical after the following transformations are applied, in order:

- The prefix "@", if used, is removed.
- Each *unicode-escape-sequence* is transformed into its corresponding Unicode character.
- Any *formatting-character*s are removed.

Identifiers containing two consecutive underscore characters (U+005F) are reserved for use by the implementation; however, no diagnostic is required if such an identifier is defined. [*Note*: For example, an implementation might provide extended keywords that begin with two underscores. *end note*]

Keyword escape mechanism

The C# language is designed to operate in a multilanguage environment. This creates a problem when a public identifier in a class library authored in a different language is the same as a C# keyword. For example, "lock" is a valid VB.NET identifier but a keyword in C#. Programs written in C# would have a problem referencing this VB.NET identifier. This raises two issues:

- Any language designed for interoperability should have a way of escaping keywords to handle this situation. C# uses the @ prefix on identifiers.
- In the context of language interoperability, the naming guidelines (such as always naming public methods using the PascalCase style) become more than just stylistic issues.

Note that Java does not have a mechanism for escaping keywords.

Code generation

Any tool that produces C# code in an automated way may benefit from judicious use of verbatim identifiers. For example, object-relational mapping tools may need to create C# identifiers that match arbitrary external identifiers. Using verbatim identifiers when such identifiers conflict with keywords can resolve an otherwise thorny problem.

Peter Golde

9.4.3 Keywords

A *keyword* is an identifier-like sequence of characters that is reserved, and cannot be used as an identifier except when prefaced by the @ character.

keyword:: one of

abstract	as	base	bool	break
byte	case	catch	char	checked
class	const	continue	decimal	default
delegate	do	double	else	enum
event	explicit	extern	false	finally
fixed	float	for	foreach	goto
if	implicit	in	int	interface
internal	is	lock	long	namespace
new	null	object	operator	out
override	params	private	protected	public
readonly	ref	return	sbyte	sealed
short	sizeof	stackalloc	static	string
struct	switch	this	throw	true
try	typeof	uint	ulong	unchecked
unsafe	ushort	using	virtual	void
volatile	while			

The following identifiers have special meaning in the syntactic grammar, but they are not keywords: add (§17.7), alias (§16.3), get (§17.6.2), global (§16.7), partial (§17.1.4), remove (§17.7), set (§17.6.2), value (§17.6.2, §17.7.2), where (§25.7), and yield (§15.14). For convenience and clarity, these identifiers appear as terminals in the syntactic grammar; however, they are identifiers. [*Note*: As a result, unlike keywords, these identifiers can be written with a @ prefix and can contain *unicode-escape-sequence*s. *end note*]

Language evolution

As the C# language evolves and new features are added, there is inevitable pressure to add new keywords. Using new keywords for new features is a problem since any new keyword has very likely already been used as an identifier in some existing program. C# solves this problem by introducing only new *contextual keywords*, such as where. Unlike standard keywords, a contextual keyword can be used as an identifier. For example, in this fragment where is used as an identifier:

```
struct Info
{ ...
    private string where;
}
```

and in this fragment where is used as a contextual keyword:

```
class Printer<T> where T: IPrintable
{   ...
}
```

By design, contextual keywords are used only in contexts where an identifier would be invalid, so no ambiguity arises in existing programs. Interestingly, the 1960s programming language PL/I had no reserved words, so all its keywords were contextual.

9.4.4 Literals

A literal (§14.5.1) is a source code representation of a value.

9.4.4.1 Boolean literals

There are two Boolean literal values: `true` and `false`.

boolean-literal::
    `true`
    `false`

The type of a *boolean-literal* is `bool`.

Boolean arguments considered harmful?

Consider the last statement of the following C# fragment:

```
using System.Reflection;

class ObscureFalseArgument
{
  static void Main(string[] args)
  {
    Assembly loaded = Assembly.Load(args[0]);
    foreach (Type type in loaded.GetTypes())
    {
      object[] attributes = type.GetCustomAttributes(
        typeof (SomeAttribute), false);
      ...
    }
  }
}
```

Here `GetCustomAttributes` is from Microsoft's CLR, not Standard CLI.

A possible problem with true/false arguments is that they may offer no clue to *what* is true or false (in this case, the false means not to consider base classes when gathering custom attributes). This lack of readability leads some coding guidelines to suggest using enum types instead. For example:

```
enum InBaseClasses { No, Yes }
...
object[] attributes = type.GetCustomAttributes(
                      typeof(SomeAttribute), InBaseClass.No);
```

However, there is a potential drawback. While Booleans in C# are strong types and have exactly 2 possible values, the preceding enum type has 2^{32} possible values, most of which are meaningless. For example:

```
object[] attributes = type.GetCustomAttributes(
              typeof(SomeAttribute), ~InBaseClass.Yes); // ???
```
Which is more robust in C#, Boolean parameters or enum type parameters? Another option is to simply define two functions without the Boolean parameter; one naming the true case, one naming the false case.

9.4.4.2 Integer literals

Integer literals are used to write values of types `int`, `uint`, `long`, and `ulong`. Integer literals have two possible forms: decimal and hexadecimal.

integer-literal::
  decimal-integer-literal
  hexadecimal-integer-literal

decimal-integer-literal::
  decimal-digits   integer-type-suffix$_{opt}$

decimal-digits::
  decimal-digit
  decimal-digits   decimal-digit

decimal-digit::   one of
    0   1   2   3   4   5   6   7   8   9

integer-type-suffix::   one of
    U   u   L   l   UL   Ul   uL   ul   LU   Lu   lU   lu

hexadecimal-integer-literal::
  0x   *hex-digits   integer-type-suffix$_{opt}$*
  0X   *hex-digits   integer-type-suffix$_{opt}$*

hex-digits::
  hex-digit
  hex-digits   hex-digit

hex-digit::   one of
    0   1   2   3   4   5   6   7   8   9   A   B   C   D   E   F   a   b   c   d   e   f

The type of an integer literal is determined as follows:

- If the literal has no suffix, it has the first of these types in which its value can be represented: `int`, `uint`, `long`, `ulong`.
- If the literal is suffixed by `U` or `u`, it has the first of these types in which its value can be represented: `uint`, `ulong`.
- If the literal is suffixed by `L` or `l`, it has the first of these types in which its value can be represented: `long`, `ulong`.
- If the literal is suffixed by `UL`, `Ul`, `uL`, `ul`, `LU`, `Lu`, `lU`, or `lu`, it is of type `ulong`.

If the value represented by an integer literal is outside the range of the `ulong` type, a compile-time error occurs.

Historical note

Early versions of C# included a "Y" suffix for byte literals and an "S" suffix for short literals. In the end, however, it was felt that they had such limited utility that they were dropped.

Peter Golde

[*Note*: As a matter of style, it is suggested that "L" be used instead of "l" when writing literals of type `long`, since it is easy to confuse the letter "l" with the digit "1". *end note*]

To permit the smallest possible `int` and `long` values to be written as decimal integer literals, the following two rules exist:

- When a *decimal-integer-literal* with the value 2147483648 (2^{31}) and no *integer-type-suffix* appears as the token immediately following a unary minus operator token (§14.6.2), the result (of both tokens) is a constant of type `int` with the value –2147483648 (–2^{31}). In all other situations, such a *decimal-integer-literal* is of type `uint`.
- When a *decimal-integer-literal* with the value 9223372036854775808 (2^{63}) and no *integer-type-suffix* or the *integer-type-suffix* L or l appears as the token immediately following a unary minus operator token (§14.6.2), the result (of both tokens) is a constant of type `long` with the value –9223372036854775808 (–2^{63}). In all other situations, such a *decimal-integer-literal* is of type `ulong`.

Boundary differences

The boundary where decimal integer literals change type is different in C# and C/C++. In both camps, all decimal integer literals are positive. However, in C# the previous rules combine a preceding minus sign with the literal in two specific cases. Consider the following constant expression fragments:

```
-2147483647-1   // type int in both C# and C/C++
-2147483648     // type int in C#, long in C/C++
-2147483649     // type long in both C# and C/C++
```

In C#, the `long` value –2147483648 is written as:

```
-2147483648L   // type long in C#
```

9.4.4.3 Real literals

Real literals are used to write values of types `float`, `double`, and `decimal`.

real-literal::
  decimal-digits **.** *decimal-digits exponent-part$_{opt}$ real-type-suffix$_{opt}$*
  . *decimal-digits exponent-part$_{opt}$ real-type-suffix$_{opt}$*
  decimal-digits exponent-part real-type-suffix$_{opt}$
  decimal-digits real-type-suffix

exponent-part::
  e *sign$_{opt}$ decimal-digits*
  E *sign$_{opt}$ decimal-digits*

sign:: one of
  + –

real-type-suffix:: one of
    F f D d M m

If no *real-type-suffix* is specified, the type of the real literal is `double`. Otherwise, the *real-type-suffix* determines the type of the real literal, as follows:

- A real literal suffixed by F or f is of type `float`. [*Example*: The literals `1f`, `1.5f`, `1e10f`, and `123.456F` are all of type `float`. *end example*]
- A real literal suffixed by D or d is of type `double`. [*Example*: The literals `1d`, `1.5d`, `1e10d`, and `123.456D` are all of type `double`. *end example*]
- A real literal suffixed by M or m is of type `decimal`. [*Example*: The literals `1m`, `1.5m`, `1e10m`, and `123.456M` are all of type `decimal`. *end example*] This literal is converted to a `decimal` value by taking the exact value, and, if necessary, rounding to the nearest representable value using banker's rounding (§11.1.7). Any scale apparent in the literal is preserved unless the value is rounded. [*Note*: Hence, the literal `2.900m` will be parsed to form the `decimal` with sign 0, coefficient 2900, and scale 3. *end note*]

If the specified literal is too large to be represented in the indicated type, a compile-time error occurs. [*Note*: In particular, a *real-literal* will never produce a floating-point infinity. A non-zero *real-literal* may, however, be rounded to zero. *end note*]

The value of a real literal having type `float` or `double` is determined by using the IEC 60559 "round to nearest" mode.

What is 1.D?

C# allows members to be accessed directly from literals. For example, you can call the ToString() method directly on an integer literal:

```
string s = 1.ToString();
```

This makes expressions such as `1.D` potentially ambiguous:

```
double eg = 1.D;  // ?
```

Is this

- 1. (a double literal) followed by D (a double-type-suffix confirming 1. as a double)? or
- 1 (an int literal) followed by . (the member access operator) followed by D (a field/property member of int)?

C# avoids this problem by disallowing a trailing period on real literals (C, C++, and Java allow it).

```
double eg1 = 1D;     // ok
double eg2 = 1.D;    // compile time error - nothing called D in int
double eg3 = 1.0D;   // ok
double eg4 = 1.0.D;  // compile time error - nothing called D in double
```

Money or deciMal?

The `decimal` suffix is M/m since D/d was already taken by `double`. Although it has been suggested that M stands for money, Peter Golde recalls that M was chosen simply as the next best letter in `decimal`.

9.4.4.4 Character literals

A character literal represents a single character, and usually consists of a character in quotes, as in `'a'`.

> *character-literal::*
>   '   *character*   '
>
> *character::*
>   *single-character*
>   *simple-escape-sequence*
>   *hexadecimal-escape-sequence*
>   *unicode-escape-sequence*
>
> *single-character::*
>   *Any character except' (U+0027),\ (U+005C), and new-line-character*
>
> *simple-escape-sequence::*   one of
>   \' \" \\ \0 \a \b \f \n \r \t \v
>
> *hexadecimal-escape-sequence::*
>   \x *hex-digit hex-digit$_{opt}$ hex-digit$_{opt}$ hex-digit$_{opt}$*

[*Note*: A character that follows a backslash character (\) in a *character* shall be one of the following characters: ', ", \, 0, a, b, f, n, r, t, u, U, x, v. Otherwise, a compile-time error occurs. *end note*]

A hexadecimal escape sequence represents a single Unicode character, with the value formed by the hexadecimal number following "\x".

If the value represented by a character literal is greater than U+FFFF, a compile-time error occurs.

A Unicode character escape sequence (§9.4.1) in a character literal shall be in the range U+0000 to U+FFFF.

A simple escape sequence represents a Unicode character encoding, as described in the table below.

Escape sequence	Character name	Unicode code point
\'	Single quote	0x0027
\"	Double quote	0x0022
\\	Backslash	0x005C
\0	Null	0x0000
\a	Alert	0x0007
\b	Backspace	0x0008
\f	Form feed	0x000C
\n	New line	0x000A
\r	Carriage return	0x000D
\t	Horizontal tab	0x0009
\v	Vertical tab	0x000B

The type of a *character-literal* is char.

> **No octal character escapes**
>
> C# breaks from C in that it does not have octal character escapes. However, it does preserve \0 as an escape for the NUL character. Octal is somewhat the Betamax of number bases; everyone uses hexadecimal now.
>
> *Peter Golde*

9.4.4.5 String literals

C# supports two forms of string literals: ***regular string literals*** and ***verbatim string literals***. A regular string literal consists of zero or more characters enclosed in double quotes, as in `"hello, world"`, and can include both simple escape sequences (such as `\t` for the tab character), and hexadecimal and Unicode escape sequences.

A verbatim string literal consists of an `@` character followed by a double-quote character, zero or more characters, and a closing double-quote character. [*Example*: A simple example is `@"hello, world"`. *end example*] In a verbatim string literal, the characters between the delimiters are interpreted verbatim, with the only exception being a *quote-escape-sequence*, which represents one double-quote character. In particular, simple escape sequences, and hexadecimal and Unicode escape sequences are not processed in verbatim string literals. A verbatim string literal can span multiple lines.

> *string-literal::*
>   *regular-string-literal*
>   *verbatim-string-literal*
>
> *regular-string-literal::*
>   `"`   *regular-string-literal-characters_{opt}*   `"`

regular-string-literal::
   `"`   *regular-string-literal-characters*$_{opt}$ `"`

regular-string-literal-characters::
   regular-string-literal-character
   regular-string-literal-characters   *regular-string-literal-character*

regular-string-literal-character::
   single-regular-string-literal-character
   simple-escape-sequence
   hexadecimal-escape-sequence
   unicode-escape-sequence

single-regular-string-literal-character::
   Any character except `"` (U+0022), `\` (U+005C), and *new-line-character*

verbatim-string-literal::
   `@"`   *verbatim-string-literal-characters*$_{opt}$ `"`

verbatim-string-literal-characters::
   verbatim-string-literal-character
   verbatim-string-literal-characters   *verbatim-string-literal-character*

verbatim-string-literal-character::
   single-verbatim-string-literal-character
   quote-escape-sequence

single-verbatim-string-literal-character::
　　Any character except"

quote-escape-sequence::
　　" "

[*Note*: A character that follows a backslash character (\) in a *regular-string-literal-character* shall be one of the following characters: ', ", \, 0, a, b, f, n, r, t, u, U, x, v. Otherwise, a compile-time error occurs. *end note*]

[*Example*: The example

```
string a = "Happy birthday, Joel";            // Happy birthday, Joel
string b = @"Happy birthday, Joel";           // Happy birthday, Joel

string c = "hello \t world";                  // hello    world
string d = @"hello \t world";                 // hello \t world

string e = "Joe said \"Hello\" to me";        // Joe said "Hello" to me
string f = @"Joe said ""Hello"" to me";       // Joe said "Hello" to me

string g = "\\\\server\\share\\file.txt"; // \\server\share\file.txt
string h = @"\\server\share\file.txt";     // \\server\share\file.txt

string i = "one\r\ntwo\r\nthree";
string j = @"one
 two
 three";
```

shows a variety of string literals. The last string literal, j, is a verbatim string literal that spans multiple lines. The characters between the quotation marks, including white space such as new line characters, are preserved verbatim, and each pair of double-quote characters is replaced by one such character. *end example*]

Platform independent newlines

The preceding example is the only place in the entire standard where a newline is hard-coded inside a string literal. Unfortunately, the Standard provides no way to avoid the well known platform variations for newline, a surprising omission.

Java provides `java.lang.System.getProperty("line.separator")` to obtain the line separator appropriate to the underlying platform. On C# implementations running on the CLI you may use its `System.Environment.NewLine` property, but C# need not be implemented on the CLI.

Historical note

Verbatim string literals were originally introduced because using regular expressions was so painful. Regular expressions themselves use backslash as an escape character, so matching a true backslash required *four* consecutive backslashes in a C# string literal!

Although the need for them was recognized early on, the syntax of verbatim string literals was subject to much debate and went through many changes; finally, the @ prefix was settled on as being similar to the @ prefix for verbatim identifiers.

Peter Golde

Happy birthday, Joel

At each Ecma meeting the TG2 (C#) and TG3 (CLI) members often spent the evenings together in a local restaurant. It became a long running joke that someone would mention to the staff that it was Joel Marcey's birthday (Joel is the convenor for TG3) and we would all sing "Happy Birthday" to him. In meetings he was often asked if he had had a good birthday. The TG2 committee decided to immortalize Joel in the preceding string literals.

[*Note*: Since a hexadecimal escape sequence can have a variable number of hex digits, the string literal "\x123" contains a single character with hex value 123. To create a string containing the character with hex value 12 followed by the character 3, one could write "\x00123" or "\x12" + "3" instead. *end note*]

The type of a *string-literal* is string.

Each string literal does not necessarily result in a new string instance. When two or more string literals that are equivalent according to the string equality operator (§14.9.7), appear in the same assembly, these string literals refer to the same string instance. [*Example*: For instance, the output produced by

```
class Test
{
  static void Main()
  {
    object a = "hello";
    object b = "hello";
    System.Console.WriteLine(a == b);
  }
}
```

is True because the two literals refer to the same string instance. *end example*]

Overspecification...

To require that two equivalent string literals occurring in the same assembly must refer to the same instance is overspecification, and is an unfortunate example of where the behavior of a particular implementation has been included in the Standard. The requirement provides no benefit to the C# user, and cannot, for instance, be used to define string equality.

Furthermore, there is no prohibition against string literals from different assemblies being represented by the same instance. Indeed one of the current implementations of C# behaves this way under certain circumstances. Thus, if the preceding example returns True when applied to two string values that refer to literals, it *does not* mean that the literals are in the same assembly.

In summary: This requirement provides zero benefit to the C# user but imposes a cost on the C# implementation. Oops.

Hexadecimal escape character pitfalls

Escape sequences are considered on individual string literals before any concatenation takes place. A string created from a concatenation can be different from the "same" single string literal. For example:

```
string s1 = "\x0" + "000";
Debug.Assert(s1.Length == 4);
string s2 = "\x0000";
Debug.Assert(s2.Length == 1);
```

The *hexadecimal-escape-sequence* should be used with care due to its variable length. In particular, two string literals that appear to contain the same number of source characters may actually define string values of different lengths. For example:

```
string s1 = "\x7Germany"; // BEL followed by "Germany" because '\x7' is BEL
string s2 = "\x7Austria"; // "zustria" because '\7A' is 'z'
```

Because of the potential pitfalls, it would have been better for the hexadecimal escape sequence to have fixed width, as in:

hexadecimal-escape-sequence::
  \x *hex-digit hex-digit*

The simplest way to avoid these potential pitfalls is to always use the *unicode-escape-sequence*.

9.4.4.6 The null literal

null-literal::
```
null
```

The type of a *null-literal* is the null type (§11.2.7).

9.4.5 Operators and punctuators

There are several kinds of operators and punctuators. Operators are used in expressions to describe operations involving one or more operands. [*Example*: The expression a + b uses the + operator to add the two operands a and b. *end example*] Punctuators are for grouping and separating.

operator-or-punctuator::   one of

{	}	[	]	(	)	.	,	:	;
+	–	*	/	%	&	|	^	!	~
=	<	>	?	??	::	++	– –	&&	||
->	==	!=	<=	>=	+=	-=	*=	/=	%=
&=	|=	^=	<<	<<=					

right-shift::
  > >

right-shift-assignment::
  > >=

right-shift is made up of the two tokens > and >. Similarly, *right-shift-assignment* is made up of the two tokens > and >=. Unlike other productions in the syntactic grammar, no characters of any kind (not even whitespace) are allowed between the two tokens in each of these productions. [*Note*: Prior to the addition of generics to C#, >> and >>= were both single tokens. However, the syntax for generics uses the < and > characters to delimit type parameters and type arguments. It is often desirable to use nested constructed types, such as List<Dictionary<string, int>>. Rather than requiring the programmer to separate the > and > by a space, the definition of the two *operator-or-punctuator*s was changed. *end note*]

>>== tokenization oddity

The >> and >>= operators are "split" but the >= operator is not. This means the sequence of characters >>== must tokenize as > (because >> is split), then >= (the longest possible lexical element at this point; see §9.3), then =. This sequence is rare but can occur. For example:

```
delegate void D();
class C
{
  static void F<T>()
  {
    ...
  }

  static D d = F<F<int>>;

  static void Main()
  {
    bool b = F<F<int>> == d;
  }
}
```

In this example, a space is required *after* the >> and before the ==. The committee considered also splitting the >= operator. However, since >>== is rare (outside C# test suites) the committee decided against this.

Note that C# (like C, C++, and Java) already has a whitespace dependency in delimited comments: you cannot put a space between the / and the * that start a delimited comment.

Tokenization anecdote

When the original rules for the tokenizer were presented by Microsoft, an obvious choice was to allow a space in the middle of ">" and "=". This would have made the compiler simpler to implement; in particular, I supported this as it would have been trivial to add to Mono's C# compiler.

In the end, good reason prevailed (I believe it was Jon Jagger who was the most vocal in the group) that rejected this hack in favor of a properly implemented tokenizer that could assist in the disambiguation. It was slightly harder to implement, but it gave developers the semantics they expected.

Miguel de Icaza

9.5 Pre-processing directives

The pre-processing directives provide the ability to skip conditionally sections of source files, to report error and warning conditions, and to delineate distinct regions of source code. [*Note*: The term "pre-processing directives" is used only for consistency with the C and C++ programming languages. In C#, there is no separate pre-processing step; pre-processing directives are processed as part of the lexical analysis phase. *end note*]

To pre-process, or not pre-process?

Readers are reminded that a *Note* in the Standard is informative. A C# compiler may choose to handle pre-processing directives in a separate phase, just as a C compiler can choose not to do so.

The important point is that the source is compiled *after* all pre-processing directives have been handled; apart from this it is not important *when* a particular C# compiler processes the directives.

Pre-processing directives have their own sublanguage (*pp-directive*), which includes expressions (*pp-expression*) that can reference symbols (*conditional-symbol*)—none of these can reference anything defined in C#, such as constants or variables.

pp-directive::
   pp-declaration
   pp-conditional
   pp-line
   pp-diagnostic
   pp-region
   pp-pragma

The following pre-processing directives are available:

- `#define` and `#undef`, which are used to define and undefine, respectively, conditional compilation symbols (§9.5.3).
- `#if`, `#elif`, `#else`, and `#endif`, which are used to skip conditionally sections of source code (§9.5.4).
- `#line`, which is used to control line numbers emitted for errors and warnings (§9.5.7).
- `#error` and `#warning`, which are used to issue errors and warnings, respectively (§9.5.5).
- `#region` and `#endregion`, which are used to explicitly mark sections of source code (§9.5.6).
- `#pragma`, which is used to provide contextual information to a compiler (§9.5.8).

A pre-processing directive always occupies a separate line of source code and always begins with a # character and a pre-processing directive name. White space can occur before the # character and between the # character and the directive name.

A source line containing a `#define`, `#undef`, `#if`, `#elif`, `#else`, `#endif`, or `#line` directive can end with a single-line comment. Delimited comments (the `/* */` style of comments) are not permitted on source lines containing pre-processing directives.

Why no delimited comments in #directives?

The reason that only single-line comments are permitted is that, otherwise, directives might span multiple lines. This would be confusing, and also cause problems for tools. Directives like this seem problematic:

```
#if /* hello,
world */ true
#endif
```

Peter Golde

Pre-processing directives are not tokens and are not part of the syntactic grammar of C#. However, pre-processing directives can be used to include or exclude sequences of tokens and in that way can affect the meaning of a C# program. [*Example*: When compiled, the program

```
#define A
#undef B

class C
{
#if A
  void F() {}
#else
  void G() {}
#endif

#if B
  void H() {}
#else
  void I() {}
#endif
}
```

results in the exact same sequence of tokens as the program

```
class C
{
  void F() {}
  void I() {}
}
```

Thus, whereas lexically, the two programs are quite different, syntactically, they are identical. *end example*]

Why no macros?

The pre-processor is notable by virtue of what it omits—macros. You can define a pre-processor token:

```
// ok
#define Debug
```

but you cannot define a token that gets replaced by something else (as you can in C and C++):

```
// compile time error
#define Begin {
```

Why is this? To quote Bjarne Stroustrup:

> *Maybe the worst aspect of Cpp [the C pre-processor] is that it has stifled the development of programming environments for C. The anarchic and character-level operation of Cpp makes nontrivial tools for C and C++ larger, slower, less elegant, and less efficient than one would have thought possible.*

In other words, ensuring the program you see is the same as the program the compiler sees is a Good Thing.

9.5.1 Conditional compilation symbols

The conditional compilation functionality provided by the #if, #elif, #else, and #endif directives is controlled through pre-processing expressions (§9.5.2) and conditional compilation symbols.

> *conditional-symbol::*
>   *identifier*
>   *Any keyword except* `true` *or* `false`

Conditional symbol oddity

The non-terminal for conditional-symbol relies on the identifier non-terminal, which allows a leading @ character and embedded unicode-escape-sequences. This means that the following #defines are both conforming and both define a conditional-symbol whose normalized name is `true` (since \u0065 == e), yet it is *not* a keyword!

```
#define @true
#define tru\u0065
```

The @ keyword escape mechanism has important applications in multilanguage environments (§9.4.2). However, as the example shows, its use in defining conditional symbols would obfuscate the code without any benefit, and similarly for unicode escapes. Using either of these is definitely not recommended (except inside compiler test suites!).

A conditional compilation symbol has two possible states: ***defined*** or ***undefined***. At the beginning of the lexical processing of a source file, a conditional compilation symbol is undefined unless it has been explicitly defined by an external mechanism (such as a command-line compiler option). When a `#define` directive is processed, the conditional compilation symbol named in that directive becomes defined in that source file. The symbol remains defined until a `#undef` directive for that same symbol is processed, or until the end of the source file is reached. An implication of this is that `#define` and `#undef` directives in one source file have no effect on other source files in the same program.

No program-wide pre-processing symbols

It is unfortunate that there is no standardized place that can be used to define pre-processing symbols for an entire program consisting of many source files. Instead, implementation specific compiler options must be used, if provided at all.

Peter Golde

The name space for conditional compilation symbols is distinct and separate from all other named entities in a C# program. Conditional compilation symbols can only be referenced in `#define` and `#undef` directives and in pre-processing expressions.

9.5.2 Pre-processing expressions

Pre-processing expressions can occur in `#if` and `#elif` directives. The operators `!`, `==`, `!=`, `&&` and `||` are permitted in pre-processing expressions, and parentheses can be used for grouping.

> *pp-expression::*
>   *whitespace$_{opt}$* *pp-or-expression* *whitespace$_{opt}$*
>
> *pp-or-expression::*
>   *pp-and-expression*
>   *pp-or-expression* *whitespace$_{opt}$* `||` *whitespace$_{opt}$* *pp-and-expression*
>
> *pp-and-expression::*
>   *pp-equality-expression*
>   *pp-and-expression* *whitespace$_{opt}$* `&&` *whitespace$_{opt}$* *pp-equality-expression*

pp-equality-expression::
  pp-unary-expression
  pp-equality-expression   *whitespace$_{opt}$*   ==   *whitespace$_{opt}$*   *pp-unary-expression*
  pp-equality-expression   *whitespace$_{opt}$*   !=   *whitespace$_{opt}$*   *pp-unary-expression*

pp-unary-expression::
  pp-primary-expression
  !   *whitespace$_{opt}$*   *pp-unary-expression*

pp-primary-expression::
  true
  false
  conditional-symbol
  (*whitespace$_{opt}$*   *pp-expression*   *whitespace$_{opt}$*   )

When referenced in a pre-processing expression, a defined conditional compilation symbol has the Boolean value true, and an undefined conditional compilation symbol has the Boolean value false.

Inequality is xor; equality is not-xor

Because a *pp-primary-expression* is Boolean valued, the inequality and equality operators != and == perform the xor and not-xor functions, respectively. For example:

    #if ALPHA == BETA

is true when either:

  - both ALPHA and BETA are defined
  - both ALPHA and BETA are undefined

We suggest that such code is rare outside test suites. In contrast, code such as this:

    #if GAMMA == true

is more common but stylistically better as:

    #if GAMMA

Evaluation of a pre-processing expression always yields a Boolean value. The rules of evaluation for a pre-processing expression are the same as those for a constant expression (§14.16), except that the only user-defined entities that can be referenced are conditional compilation symbols.

9.5.3 Declaration directives

The declaration directives are used to define or undefine conditional compilation symbols.

pp-declaration::
  whitespace$_{opt}$ #   *whitespace$_{opt}$*   define   *whitespace*   *conditional-symbol*
  pp-new-line
  whitespace$_{opt}$ #   *whitespace$_{opt}$*   undef   *whitespace*   *conditional-symbol*
  pp-new-line

pp-new-line::
  whitespace$_{opt}$ *single-line-comment$_{opt}$*   *new-line*

The processing of a #define directive causes the given conditional compilation symbol to become defined, starting with the source line that follows the directive. Likewise, the processing of a #undef directive causes the given conditional compilation symbol to become undefined, starting with the source line that follows the directive.

Any #define and #undef directives in a source file shall occur before the first *token* (§9.4) in the source file; otherwise a compile-time error occurs. In intuitive terms, #define and #undef directives shall precede any "real code" in the source file.

Rationale: pp-declaration placement

Allowing #define and #undef only at the beginning of the file serves two useful purposes. First, it is good programming style because there is a single fixed place to find such directives. Secondly, it greatly simplifies the implementation of tools such as code-coloring editors, since they only need to track state for each file, rather than each line.

Peter Golde

[*Example*: The example:

```
#define Enterprise

#if Professional || Enterprise
  #define Advanced
#endif

namespace Megacorp.Data
{
  #if Advanced
  class PivotTable {...}
  #endif
}
```

is valid because the #define directives precede the first token (the namespace keyword) in the source file.

end example]

[*Example*: The following example results in a compile-time error because a #define follows real code:

```
#define A
namespace N
{
  #define B
  #if B
  class Class1 {}
  #endif
}
```

end example]

A #define can define a conditional compilation symbol that is already defined, without there being any intervening #undef for that symbol. [*Example*: The example below defines a conditional compilation symbol A and then defines it again.

```
#define A
#define A
```

For compilers that allow conditional compilation symbols to be defined as compilation options, an alternative way for such redefinition to occur is to define the symbol as a compiler option as well as in the source. *end example*]

A #undef can "undefine" a conditional compilation symbol that is not defined. [*Example*: The example below defines a conditional compilation symbol A and then undefines it twice; although the second #undef has no effect, it is still valid.

```
#define A
#undef A
#undef A
```

end example]

Conditional symbol style

Unfortunately, many naming guidelines, including the one in this Standard (Annex C), are silent about conditional symbol naming. The two most common pre-processor symbols are probably DEBUG and TRACE, suggesting an uppercase style. However, the PascalCase style is also quite common (and occurs in several places in this Standard).

In C/C++ there is a strong convention: Write pre-processor symbols in uppercase so that they are stylistically distinct from program text. However, this rationale is less compelling in C# since its pre-processor symbols control, but never generate, program text (as they can in C/C++). Nevertheless, the authors recommend the ALL_UPPERCASE style.

9.5.4 Conditional compilation directives

The conditional compilation directives are used to conditionally include or exclude portions of a source file.

> *pp-conditional::*
>   *pp-if-section*   *pp-elif-sections$_{opt}$*   *pp-else-section$_{opt}$*   *pp-endif*
>
> *pp-if-section::*
>   *whitespace$_{opt}$*   #   *whitespace$_{opt}$*   if   *whitespace*   *pp-expression*   *pp-new-line*
>   *conditional-section$_{opt}$*
>
> *pp-elif-sections::*
>   *pp-elif-section*
>   *pp-elif-sections*   *pp-elif-section*
>
> *pp-elif-section::*
>   *whitespace$_{opt}$*   #   *whitespace$_{opt}$*   elif   *whitespace*   *pp-expression*   *pp-new-line*
>   *conditional-section$_{opt}$*
>
> *pp-else-section::*
>   *whitespace$_{opt}$*   #   *whitespace$_{opt}$*   else   *pp-new-line*   *conditional-section$_{opt}$*
>
> *pp-endif::*
>   *whitespace$_{opt}$*   #   *whitespace$_{opt}$*   endif   *pp-new-line*

conditional-section::
  input-section
  skipped-section

skipped-section::
  skipped-section-part
  skipped-section   skipped-section-part

skipped-section-part::
  whitespace_{opt}   skipped-characters_{opt}   new-line
  pp-directive

skipped-characters::
  not-number-sign   input-characters_{opt}

not-number-sign::
  Any input-character except#

[*Note*: As indicated by the syntax, conditional compilation directives shall be written as sets consisting of, in order, a `#if` directive, zero or more `#elif` directives, zero or one `#else` directive, and a `#endif` directive. Between the directives are conditional sections of source code. Each section is controlled by the immediately preceding directive. A conditional section can itself contain nested conditional compilation directives provided these directives form complete sets. *end note*]

A *pp-conditional* selects at most one of the contained *conditional-section*s for normal lexical processing:

- The *pp-expression*s of the `#if` and `#elif` directives are evaluated in order until one yields `true`. If an expression yields `true`, the *conditional-section* of the corresponding directive is selected.
- If all *pp-expression*s yield `false`, and if a `#else` directive is present, the *conditional-section* of the `#else` directive is selected.
- Otherwise, no *conditional-section* is selected.

The selected *conditional-section*, if any, is processed as a normal *input-section*: the source code contained in the section shall adhere to the lexical grammar; tokens are generated from the source code in the section; and pre-processing directives in the section have the prescribed effects.

The remaining *conditional-section*s, if any, are processed as *skipped-section*s: except for pre-processing directives, the source code in the section need not adhere to the lexical grammar; no tokens are generated from the source code in the section; and pre-processing directives in the section shall be lexically correct but are not otherwise processed. Within a *conditional-section* that is being processed as a *skipped-section*, any nested *conditional-section*s (contained in nested `#if...#endif` and `#region...#endregion` constructs) are also processed as *skipped-section*s.

[*Example*: The following example illustrates how conditional compilation directives can nest:

```
#define Debug    // Debugging on
#undef Trace     // Tracing off

class PurchaseTransaction
{
  void Commit()
  {
    #if Debug
```

```
            CheckConsistency();
            #if Trace
              WriteToLog(this.ToString());
            #endif
        #endif
        CommitHelper();
    }
    ...
}
```

Except for pre-processing directives, skipped source code is not subject to lexical analysis. For example, the following is valid despite the unterminated comment in the #else section:

```
#define Debug     // Debugging on

class PurchaseTransaction
{
  void Commit()
  {
    #if Debug
      CheckConsistency();
    #else
      /* Do something else
    #endif
  }
  ...
}
```

Note, however, that pre-processing directives are required to be lexically correct even in skipped sections of source code.

Pre-processing directives are not processed when they appear inside multi-line input elements. For example, the program:

```
class Hello
{
  static void Main()
  {
    System.Console.WriteLine(@"hello,
#if Debug
    world
#else
    Nebraska
#endif
    ");
  }
}
```

results in the output:

```
hello,
#if Debug
    world
#else
    Nebraska
#endif
```

In peculiar cases, the set of pre-processing directives that is processed might depend on the evaluation of the *pp-expression*. The example:

```
#if X
  /*
#else
  /* */ class Q { }
#endif
```

always produces the same token stream (`class Q { }`), regardless of whether or not `X` is defined. If `X` is defined, the only processed directives are `#if` and `#endif`, due to the multi-line comment. If `X` is undefined, then three directives (`#if`, `#else`, `#endif`) are part of the directive set. *end example*

Another issue with comments and #if

Source code that is valid when being processed normally, or when being conditionally included (for instance, as part of an *input-section*), can be invalid when it is being conditionally excluded (i.e., as part of a *skipped-section*). For example, consider:

```
/* The format of the config file is like this:

   # Hash starts a comment line
   name=value
*/
```

This compiles without error; the "# Hash" is not treated specially as it is part of a comment. However, put the whole thing in an ignored `#if` section and the situation changes:

```
#if false
/* The format of the config file is like this:

   # Hash starts a comment line
   name=value
*/
#endif
```

The compiler will complain when it encounters "# Hash", as it is not a valid *pp-directive* and within a *skipped-section* comments are not recognized as such.

The issue can only occur if a "#" is the first non-whitespace character on a line within a comment. The preceding can be rewritten to avoid the problem:

```
#if false
/* The format of the config file is like this:
 *
 *  # Hash starts a comment line
 *  name=value
 */
#endif
```

Jon Skeet

Carbuncle

C# is beautiful in terms of how straightforward all of its keywords are. The `#elif` directive is an eyesore on this otherwise tranquil vista; `#elseif` would have been preferable. It may have made the specification or compilers harder to write (in terms of lexical analysis), although I doubt it would have been a significant problem. Fortunately, this blemish is rarely seen in real code.

Jon Skeet

9.5.5 Diagnostic directives

The diagnostic directives are used to generate explicitly error and warning messages that are reported in the same way as other compile-time errors and warnings.

pp-diagnostic::
   *whitespace*opt   #   *whitespace*opt   error   *pp-message*
   *whitespace*opt   #   *whitespace*opt   warning   *pp-message*

pp-message::
   new-line
   *whitespace   input-characters*opt   *new-line*

[*Example*: The example

```
#warning Code review needed before check-in

#if Debug && Retail
  #error A build can't be both debug and retail
#endif

class Test {...}
```

always produces a warning ("Code review needed before check-in"), and produces a compile-time error if the pre-processing identifiers Debug and Retail are both defined. Note that a *pp-message* can contain arbitrary text; specifically, it need not contain well-formed tokens, as shown by the single quote in the word can't. *end example*]

Diagnostic directive example

One use of these directives is to check on conditional attribute specifications (§24.4.2.2). For example:

```
using System;
using System.Diagnostics;

[Conditional("DEBUG")]
class TestAttribute : Attribute
{
}
```

and then

```
#if !DEBUG
#warning Test attribute _not_ specified on class C
#endif
[Test]
class C
{
}
```

If DEBUG is undefined, class C will not have the Test attribute. A compile-time warning is issued to that effect but compilation proceeds.

9.5.6 Region control

The region directives are used to mark explicitly regions of source code.

> *pp-region::*
>> *pp-start-region   conditional-section$_{opt}$ pp-end-region*
>
> *pp-start-region::*
>> *whitespace$_{opt}$ #   whitespace$_{opt}$*   region   *pp-message*
>
> *pp-end-region::*
>> *whitespace$_{opt}$ #   whitespace$_{opt}$*   endregion   *pp-message*

No semantic meaning is attached to a region; regions are intended for use by the programmer or by automated tools to mark a section of source code. The message specified in a #region or #endregion directive likewise has no semantic meaning; it merely serves to identify the region. Matching #region and #endregion directives can have different *pp-messages*.

The lexical processing of a region:

```
#region
...
#endregion
```

corresponds exactly to the lexical processing of a conditional compilation directive of the form:

```
#if true
...
#endif
```

Historical note

To my knowledge, the #region concept is not present in any other language. It was originally invented to provide a place for the form designer to place automatically generated code that the user should not edit or even usually look at. Editors and integrated development environments may support selective hiding and viewing of regions of source code. In practice, this feature has proved quite useful beyond the narrow use in the form designer, both for automatically generated code and for organizing large source files of human-written code.

It is recommended to use the same *pp-message* on a #region directive and on its matching #endregion directive, so as to make the matching more obvious to human readers.

Peter Golde

9.5.7 Line directives

Line directives can be used to alter the line numbers and source file names that are reported by the compiler in output such as warnings and errors.

[*Note*: Line directives are most commonly used in meta-programming tools that generate C# source code from some other text input. *end note*]

> *pp-line::*
>> *whitespace$_{opt}$ #   whitespace$_{opt}$*   line   *whitespace   line-indicator   pp-new-line*

line-indicator::
   decimal-digits   whitespace   file-name
   decimal-digits
   identifier-or-keyword

file-name::
   " *file-name-characters*   "

file-name-characters::
   file-name-character
   file-name-characters   file-name-character

file-name-character::
   Any character except"(U+0022), and new-line-character

When no `#line` directives are present, the compiler reports true line numbers and source file names in its output. When processing a `#line` directive that includes a *line-indicator* that is not *identifier-or-keyword*, the compiler treats the line *after* the directive as having the given line number (and file name, if specified).

A `#line` directive in which the *line-indicator* is an *identifier-or-keyword* whose value equals `default` (using equality as specified in §9.4.2) reverses the effect of all preceding `#line` directives. The compiler reports true line information for subsequent lines, precisely as if no `#line` directives had been processed.

The purpose of a *line-indicator* with an *identifier-or-keyword* whose value does not equal `default` is implementation-defined. An implementation that does not recognize such an *identifier-or-keyword* in a line-indicator shall issue a warning.

[*Note*: Note that a *file-name* differs from a regular string literal in that escape characters are not processed; the '\' character simply designates an ordinary back-slash character within a *file-name*. *end note*]

Historical note

Most of the syntax of the `#line` directive is taken directly from the C preprocessor, whereas "`#line default`" was a new invention.

Peter Golde

#line example

Attempting to compile the following program:

```
class Test
{
  static void Main()
  {
#line 50 "unlikely\filename.cs"
    Foo();
#line default
    Bar();
  }
}
```

results in errors such as (the exact wording will be compiler dependent):

- unlikely\filename.cs(50,7): error CS0103: The name 'Foo' does not exist in the class or namespace 'Test'
- Test.cs(8,7): error CS0103: The name 'Bar' does not exist in the class or namespace 'Test'

where Test.cs is the genuine name of the file being compiled and the first number within the parentheses is the line number.

Note: The phrase "precisely as if no `#line` directives had been processed" in the clause does not mean that lines containing the directives themselves are not counted, so the second error above reports the true line number within the file (8).

Jon Skeet

9.5.8 Pragma directives

The `#pragma` directive is a preprocessing directive used to specify contextual information to a compiler. [*Note*: For example, a compiler might provide `#pragma` directives that

- Enable or disable particular warning messages when compiling subsequent code.
- Specify which optimizations to apply to subsequent code.
- Specify information to be used by a debugger.

end note]

pp-pragma:
    whitespace$_{opt}$ # *whitespace$_{opt}$* pragma *pp-pragma-text*

pp-pragma-text:
    new-line
    whitespace input-characters$_{opt}$ new-line

The *input-characters* in the *pp-pragma-text* are interpreted by the compiler in an implementation-defined manner. The information supplied in a `#pragma` directive shall not change program semantics. A `#pragma` directive shall only change compiler behavior that is outside the scope of this language specification. If the compiler cannot interpret the *input-characters*, the compiler can produce a warning; however, it shall not produce a compile-time error.

[*Note*: *pp-pragma-text* can contain arbitrary text; specifically, it need not contain well-formed tokens. *end note*]

10 Basic concepts

The emperor has no threads!

Threads are clearly a basic concept in C#, as hinted at several places in the Standard:

- Garbage collection may run a finalizer on another thread (§10.9).
- Execution proceeds such that the side effects of each executing thread are preserved at critical execution points (§10.10). This in turn leads to the introduction of volatile fields (§17.4.3) and the `lock` statement (§15.12).
- The `throw` statement (§15.9.5) might terminate the current thread. How exception handling interacts with threads is further covered in §23.3.
- The clause on field-like events (§17.7.1) discusses thread safety.
- Iterators (§26.4) are implemented so as to ensure thread safety.

Despite this, there is no section describing them in §10, *Basic Concepts*, and no methods to create and control them are listed in Annex D. This is a little surprising.

The types in Annex D are based on those of the CLI Standard Library and were kept to a minimum so as not to create undue dependency on the CLI. Here we present a core set of types and methods drawn in a similar way from the CLI Standard Library. It is likely that the C# Committee would have made a similar selection, had it chosen to include types for threads in this Standard; certainly it is most likely that such types would have been based on those of the CLI Standard Library.

We present the types and methods along with a brief description. The text of the remainder of this annotation is drawn largely from the CLI Standard library description itself.

Some of these types are used in informative examples in other parts of this Standard.

The Thread Class

An instance of the class:

```
public sealed class System.Threading.Thread
```

represents a running thread. Even if no threads are created by the user, the application itself runs in a thread and the `Thread` instance for that can be obtained using the static method `Thread.CurrentThread`. An application terminates only when all its *foreground* threads have terminated; see `Thread.IsBackground`. The following members exist:

`public Thread(ThreadStart start)`

Constructs and initializes a new instance of the `Thread` class.

`public void Abort()`

Raises a `ThreadAbortException` in the thread on which it is invoked, to begin the process of terminating the thread. In most situations, calling this method will terminate that thread.

`public void Join()`

Blocks the calling thread until the thread on which this method is invoked terminates.

`public bool Join(int millisecondsTimeout)`

Blocks the calling thread until the thread on which this method is invoked terminates or the specified time elapses.

`public static void ResetAbort()`

Cancels an `Abort` requested for the current thread.

`public static void Sleep(int millisecondsTimeout)`

Blocks the current thread for the specified number of milliseconds.

```
public void Start()
```
Causes the operating system to consider the thread ready to be scheduled for execution.
```
public static Thread CurrentThread{ get; }
```
Gets a `Thread` instance that represents the currently executing thread.
```
public bool IsAlive{ get; }
```
Gets a `bool` value indicating the execution status of the thread.
```
public bool IsBackground{ get; set; }
```
Gets or sets a `bool` value indicating whether the thread is a *background* one or not. An application terminates after all *foreground* threads have terminated; at this point any background threads are stopped and do not complete. This property is initially `false` for a new thread.
```
public ThreadState ThreadState{ get; }
```
Gets a value that is a combination of one or more `ThreadState` values, which indicate the state of the current thread.

The ThreadStart delegate

An instance of the `ThreadStart` delegate must be given when a `Thread` is created and becomes the "main method" of the resultant thread.

```
public delegate void System.Threading.ThreadStart();
```

The existence of method group conversions (§13.6) means that it is often not necessary to create `ThreadStart` instances explicitly.

The ThreadState enum

This enumeration describes the state of a thread:

```
public enum ThreadState
{
   Aborted = 0x100,
   AbortRequested = 0x80,
   Running = 0x0,
   Stopped = 0x10,
   Unstarted = 0x8,
   WaitSleepJoin = 0x20
}
```

Once a thread is created, it is in one or more of these states until it terminates. Not all combinations of `ThreadState` values are valid. For example, a thread cannot simultaneously be in the `ThreadState.Stopped` and `ThreadState.Unstarted` states.

The Monitor Class

The class:

```
public sealed class System.Threading.Monitor
```

contains a number of static methods for object level locks. Two methods, `Monitor.Enter` and `Monitor.Exit`, are used by the lock statement (§15.12) and are already included in Annex D. Locks by themselves provide mutually exclusive access but are less essential when non-busy-waiting conditional acquire and release methods are available, and these are provided by `Wait`, `Pulse` and `PulseAll`. Associated with these methods is:

```
public class System.Threading.SynchronizationLockException
                                            : SystemException
```

The following members are specified in `Monitor`:

```
public static void Enter(object obj)
```

Acquire an exclusive lock on `obj`. The current thread will be blocked until the lock is acquired. Used by the lock statement (§15.12) and specified in Annex D.

```
public static bool Wait(object obj)
```

Release the lock on `obj` and block until the lock is reacquired. Multiple threads can be blocked waiting to reacquire the lock. A thread reacquires the lock and is released only as a consequence of calls to `Pulse` or `PulseAll`. The return value can be ignored; it is specified for CLI compatibility where it is defined to always be `true`. Throws `Synchronization-LockException` if the lock is not currently held.

```
public static void Pulse(object obj)
```

Releases one thread in the waiting queue of `obj` to enable it to reacquire the lock. This will occur sometime after the current thread relinquishes the lock and once the released thread gains the lock it becomes runnable again. If no threads are in the waiting queue nothing happens. Throws `SynchronizationLockException` if the lock is not currently held.

```
public static void PulseAll(object obj)
```

Releases all threads in the waiting queue of `obj` to reacquire the lock. This will occur sometime after the current thread relinquishes the lock. Only one thread at a time can acquire the lock, but each released thread will eventually do so and then become runnable. If no threads are in the waiting queue nothing happens. Throws `SynchronizationLock-Exception` if the lock if not currently held.

```
public static void Exit(object obj)
```

Releases an exclusive lock on `obj`. Used by the lock statement (§15.12) and specified in Annex D. Throws `SynchronizationLockException` if the lock is not currently held.

The ThreadAbortException class

```
public sealed class System.Threading.ThreadAbortException
                                        : SystemException
```

This exception is thrown as a result of calling `Thread.Abort`. When a thread receives this exception the thread abort proceeds as follows:

1. An abort begins as soon as the thread is running C# code outside any catch handler, finally clause, or type initializer (class constructor). An abort may begin earlier than this if a thread is running non-C# code if an implementation allows; the CLI does support other places an abort may begin.
2. When an outermost catch handler finishes execution, the `ThreadAbortException` is rethrown unless the thread being aborted has called `ResetAbort` since the call to `Abort`.

Unexecuted finally blocks are executed before the thread is aborted; this includes any finally block that is executing when the exception is thrown. The thread is not guaranteed to abort immediately, or at all. This situation can occur if a thread does an unbounded amount of computation in the finally blocks that are called as part of the abort procedure, thereby indefinitely delaying the abort. To ensure a thread has aborted, invoke `Join` on the thread after calling `Abort`.

If `Abort` is called on a thread that has not been started, the thread aborts when `Start` is called. If the target thread is blocked or sleeping in managed code and is not inside any of the code blocks that are required to delay an abort, the thread is resumed and immediately aborted.

After `Abort` is invoked on a thread, the thread includes `ThreadState.AbortRequested`. After the thread has terminated as a result of a successful call to `Abort`, the state of the thread includes `ThreadState.Stopped` and `ThreadState.Aborted`.

For another annotation dealing with `ThreadAbortException` see §15.10.

Example: Synchronization and Threads

As threading is not well covered in the Standard (see previous annotation) we include this small, but complete, example. Readers familiar with threading in Java will find the C# approach familiar; those coming from Ada 95 will find it less so. The example is a simple one-place buffer with multiple producer and consumer threads.

A Thread-Safe Buffer

Thread safety and interthread synchronization are based around locks (lock statement, Monitor.Enter() and Monitor.Exit()) and the ability to queue for a lock (Monitor. Wait()) until notified (Monitor.Pulse() and Monitor.PulseAll()).

The following is a simple one-place buffer built using these facilities:

```
public class Buffer<Kind>
{
  private readonly object getQueue = new object();
  private readonly object putQueue = new object();

  private bool empty = true;
  private Kind store;

  public void PutItem(Kind item)
  {
    lock (putQueue)
    {
      while (!empty)
        Monitor.Wait(putQueue);
      lock (getQueue)
      {
        store = item;
        empty = false;
        Monitor.Pulse(getQueue);
      }
    }
  }

  public Kind GetItem()
  {
    Kind item;
    lock (getQueue)
    {
      while (empty)
        Monitor.Wait(getQueue);

      lock (putQueue)
      {
        item = store;
        empty = true;
        Monitor.Pulse(putQueue);
      }
    }
    return item;
  }
}
```

The algorithm for `PutItem` is:

1. Acquire the lock for putting (`putQueue`); the code design ensures only one thread can be active in `PutItem` by doing this. If the lock is currently held, the calling thread will be blocked until it becomes available.

2. Check whether an item can be placed in the buffer (`!empty`). If not, release the lock and enter the wait queue (`Monitor.Wait`). Threads are removed from the wait queue in response to `Pulse/PulseAll` calls; when this happens they queue up to reacquire the lock. When the lock is reacquired, the call to `Wait` returns. As other threads that are not yet in the wait queue may attempt to use the buffer after `Wait` returns, the buffer status must be checked again, hence the `while` loop.

3. When the while loop exits, the put lock is held and the buffer is empty. Now the get lock must be obtained (`getQueue`) before the item is placed in the buffer, the status updated, and, at most one, waiting getter notified using `Monitor.Pulse`.

The algorithm for `GetItem` mirrors this. Note that though both methods require both locks, and acquire them in opposite order—a classic condition for deadlock—the use of the `empty` flag, which can only be changed when both locks are held, prevents deadlock from occurring.

A Simple Thread

A thread is similar to the main C# program. The main C# program is represented by the `Main()` method and any code called from that method. The main program is started by the system and terminates when `Main()` returns. To create a thread, a delegate for a `void` method is passed to the `Thread` class constructor. The thread is started by calling `Thread.Start()` and terminates when the supplied delegate returns.

Though not required, it is common to create a class instance per thread. However the method used for the thread body can come from any type, instance or static, and indeed multiple threads can be executing based on the same object. Continuing our example, the following is a simple producer class that creates items and places them into a `Buffer`:

```
public class Producer
{
  private uint current, inc;
  private Buffer<uint> buf;
  private int doze;
  private string name;

  public Producer(string id, uint step, Buffer<uint> exch, int pause)
  {
    current = inc = step;
    buf = exch;
    doze = pause;
    name = id;
  }

  // The main method for the thread
  public void Run()
  {
    while (true)
    {
      Console.WriteLine("{0} trying to put {1} ", name, current);
      buf.PutItem(current);
      Console.WriteLine("{0} placed {1} ", name, current);
      current += inc;
```

```
        if (current > int.MaxValue)
          current = inc;
        Thread.Sleep(doze);
      }
    }
  }
```

Note that there is nothing special about this class that makes it a thread; creating the thread is a separate operation. Instances of this class may be created and the `Run` method called just as for any other class; however, as it is intended to be used as a thread, the `Run` method never terminates, so invoking it as anything other than a thread body is probably not advised in this case.

The class is simply an infinite loop generating a sequence of `uint` values. The call to `Thread.Sleep` causes the calling thread's execution to stop for the specified number of milliseconds. For completeness, here is a matching consumer class:

```
public class Consumer
{
  private Buffer<uint> buf;
  private int doze;
  private string name;

  public Consumer(string id, Buffer<uint> exch, int pause)
  {
    buf = exch;
    doze = pause;
    name = id;
  }

  public void Run()
  {
    while (true)
    {
      Console.WriteLine("{0} trying to get", name);
      uint item = buf.GetItem();
      Console.WriteLine("{0} got {1} ", name, item);
      Thread.Sleep(doze);
    }
  }
}
```

Putting it all together

The following is a simple main program to exercise the above:

```
class ProducerConsumerDemo
{
  // Exercise the buffer and producer/consumer threads
  static void Main()
  {
    Buffer<uint> buf = new Buffer<uint>();

    // Create objects and threads
    Thread p1 = new Thread(new Producer("p1", 3, buf, 500).Run);
    Thread p2 = new Thread(new Producer("p2", 5, buf, 600).Run);
    Thread p3 = new Thread(new Producer("p3", 7, buf, 400).Run);
```

```
    Thread c1 = new Thread(new Consumer("c1", buf, 200).Run);
    Thread c2 = new Thread(new Consumer("c2", buf, 300).Run);

    // Start everything going
    c1.Start();
    p1.Start();
    c2.Start();
    p2.Start();
    p3.Start();
  }
}
```

The act of creating a thread consists of three distinct actions:

1. First an object to hold the state of the thread is created:

    ```
    new Producer("p1", 3, buf, 500)
    ```

    Call this `obj`.

2. Second, a thread is created based on a method (delegate) from the object:

    ```
    Thread p1 = new Thread(obj.Run);
    ```

    Note: The expression `obj.Run` is a method group conversion (§13.6) that creates a delegate instance referencing the `Run` method.

3. Finally, the thread is started:

    ```
    p1.Start();
    ```

This simple example does not store the references to the objects on which the threads are based. In real-world situations they typically would be, as the objects provide a way to communicate with the thread—provided appropriate thread-safe design is used, of course.

10.1 Application startup

Application startup occurs when the execution environment calls a designated method, which is referred to as the application's *entry point*. This entry point method is always named `Main`, and shall have one of the following signatures:

```
static void Main() {...}
static void Main(string[] args) {...}
static int Main() {...}
static int Main(string[] args) {...}
```

As shown, the entry point can optionally return an `int` value. This return value is used in application termination (§10.2).

The entry point can optionally have one formal parameter, and this formal parameter can have any name. If such a parameter is declared, it shall obey the following constraints:

- The implementation shall ensure that the value of this parameter is not `null`.
- Let `args` be the name of the parameter. If the length of the array designated by `args` is greater than zero, the array members `args[0]` through `args[args.Length-1]`, inclusive, shall refer to strings, called *application parameters*, which are given implementation-defined values by the host environment prior to application startup. The intent is to supply to the application information determined prior to application startup from elsewhere in the hosted environment. If the host environment is not capable of supplying

strings with letters in both uppercase and lowercase, the implementation shall ensure that the strings are received in lowercase. [*Note*: On systems supporting a command line, application parameters correspond to what are generally known as command-line arguments. *end note*]

Since C# supports method overloading, a class or struct can contain multiple definitions of some method, provided each has a different signature. However, within a single program, no class or struct shall contain more than one method called `Main` whose definition qualifies it to be used as an application entry point. Other overloaded versions of `Main` are permitted, however, provided they have more than one parameter, or their only parameter is other than type `string[]`.

An application can be made up of multiple classes or structs. It is possible for more than one of these classes or structs to contain a method called `Main` whose definition qualifies it to be used as an application entry point. In such cases, one of these `Main` methods shall be chosen as the entry point so that application startup can occur. This choice of an entry point is beyond the scope of this specification—no mechanism for specifying or determining an entry point is provided.

In C#, every method shall be defined as a member of a class or struct. Ordinarily, the declared accessibility (§10.5.1) of a method is determined by the access modifiers (§17.2.3) specified in its declaration, and similarly the declared accessibility of a type is determined by the access modifiers specified in its declaration. In order for a given method of a given type to be callable, both the type and the member shall be accessible. However, the application entry point is a special case. Specifically, the execution environment can access the application's entry point regardless of its declared accessibility and regardless of the declared accessibility of its enclosing type declarations.

The entry point method shall not be defined in a generic class declaration (§25.1) or a generic struct declaration (§25.2).

In all other respects, entry point methods behave like those that are not entry points.

Main is callable

This clause does not forbid user code calling `Main`. In this respect, C# is similar to Java and C. The C++ specification, on the other hand, says (clause 3.6.1), "The function `main` shall not be used (3.2) within a program."

The absence in C# of this restriction means that the `Main(string[] args)` method should not assume that `args` and all `args[i]` are non-null, despite the two bullets at the top of this clause, *unless* it is known that user code does not call `Main` directly. One way to reduce opportunities for `Main` to be called directly is to declare it with `private` accessibility.

10.2 Application termination

Application termination returns control to the execution environment.

If the return type of the application's entry point method is `int`, the value returned serves as the application's **termination status code**. The purpose of this code is to allow communication of success or failure to the execution environment.

If the return type of the entry point method is `void`, reaching the right brace (}) which terminates that method, or executing a `return` statement that has no expression, results in a termination status code of 0.

Prior to an application's termination, finalizers for all of its objects that have not yet been garbage collected are called, unless such cleanup has been suppressed (by a call to the library method `GC.SuppressFinalize`, for example).

Suppression of finalizers

Other methods of cleanup suppression are implementation specific. For example, some environments may allocate a fixed amount of time for all finalizers to run in just before application termination. If that time is exceeded, the environment may decide not to run any further finalizers. The current Microsoft implementation behaves this way.

Jon Skeet

No infanticide

Note that the application will not necessarily terminate when the `Main` method finishes if other threads are executing in the application. See the annotations on §10.1 for further details.

Jon Skeet

10.3 Declarations

Declarations in a C# program define the constituent elements of the program. C# programs are organized using namespace declarations (§16), which can contain type declarations and nested namespace declarations. Type declarations (§16.6) are used to define classes (§17), structs (§18), interfaces (§20), enums (§21), and delegates (§22). The kinds of members permitted in a type declaration depend on the form of the type declaration. For instance, class declarations can contain declarations for constants (§17.3), fields (§17.4), methods (§17.5), properties (§17.6), events (§17.7), indexers (§17.8), operators (§17.9), instance constructors (§17.10), finalizers (§17.12), static constructors (§17.11), and nested types.

A declaration defines a name in the **declaration space** to which the declaration belongs. It is a compile-time error to have two or more declarations that introduce members with the same name in a declaration space, except in the following cases:

- Two or more namespace declarations with the same name are allowed in the same declaration space. Such namespace declarations are aggregated to form a single logical namespace and share a single declaration space.
- Declarations in separate programs but in the same namespace declaration space are allowed to share the same name.
- Two or more methods with the same name but distinct signatures are allowed in the same declaration space (§10.6).
- Two or more type declarations with the same name but distinct numbers of type parameters are allowed in the same declaration space (§10.8.2).
- Two or more type declarations with the `partial` modifier in the same declaration space may share the same name, same number of type parameters and same classification (`class`, `struct` or `interface`). In this case, the type declarations contribute to a single type and are themselves aggregated to form a single declaration space (§17.1.4).

- A namespace declaration and a type declaration in the same declaration space can share the same name as long as the type declaration has at least one type parameter (§10.8.2).

It is never possible for a type declaration space to contain different kinds of members with the same name. [*Example*: A type declaration space can never contain a field and a method by the same name. *end example*]

There are several different types of declaration spaces, as described in the following.

- Within all source files of a program, *namespace-member-declaration*s with no enclosing *namespace-declaration* are members of a single combined declaration space called the **global declaration space**.
- Within all source files of a program, *namespace-member-declaration*s within *namespace-declaration*s that have the same fully qualified namespace name are members of a single combined declaration space.
- Each *compilation-unit* and *namespace-body* has an **alias declaration space**. Each *extern-alias-directive* and *using-alias-directive* of the *compilation-unit* or *namespace-body* contributes a member to the alias declaration space (§16.4.1).
- Each non-partial class, struct, or interface declaration creates a new declaration space. Each partial class, struct, or interface declaration contributes to a declaration space shared by all matching parts in the same program (§17.1.4). Names are introduced into this declaration space through the *type-parameter-list* and *class-member-declaration*s, *struct-member-declaration*s, or *interface-member-declaration*s. Except for overloaded instance constructor declarations and static constructor declarations, a class or struct member declaration cannot introduce a member by the same name as the class or struct. A class, struct, or interface permits the declaration of overloaded methods and indexers. Furthermore, a class or struct permits the declaration of overloaded instance constructors, operators, and types. [*Example*: A class, struct, or interface can contain multiple method declarations with the same name, provided these method declarations differ in their signature (§10.6). A class or struct can contain multiple nested types with the same name provided the types differ in the number of type parameters. *end example*] Base classes do not contribute to the declaration space of a class, and base interfaces do not contribute to the declaration space of an interface. Thus, a derived class or interface is allowed to declare a member with the same name as an inherited member.
- Each enumeration declaration creates a new declaration space. Names are introduced into this declaration space through *enum-member-declaration*s.
- Each *block,switch-block*, *for-statement*, *foreach-statement*, or *using-statement* creates a declaration space for local variables and local constants called the **local variable declaration space**. Names are introduced into this declaration space through *local-variable-declaration*s and *local-constant-declaration*s. If a block is the body of an instance constructor, method, or operator declaration, or a get or set accessor for an indexer declaration, the parameters declared in such a declaration are members of the block's local variable declaration space. If a block is the body of a generic method, the type parameters declared in such a declaration are members of the block's local variable declaration space. It is an error for two members of a local variable declaration space to have the same name. It is an error for a local variable declaration space and a nested local variable declaration space to contain elements with the same name. [*Note*: Thus, within a nested block it is not possible to declare a local variable or constant with the same name as a local variable or constant in an enclosing block. It is possible for two nested blocks to contain elements with the same name as long as neither block contains the other. *end note*]

- Each *block* or *switch-block* creates a separate declaration space for labels called the **label declaration space** of the block. Names are introduced into this declaration space through *labeled-statement*s, and the names are referenced through *goto-statement*s. It is an error for the label declaration space of a block and the label declaration space of a nested block to contain elements with the same name. Thus, within a nested block it is not possible to declare a label with the same name as a label in an enclosing block. [*Note*: It is possible for two nested blocks to contain elements with the same name as long as neither block contains the other. *end note*]

Declaration spaces and anonymous methods

The introduction of anonymous methods (§14.5.15) means that one (anonymous) method may now be nested inside another method. That is, the *block* that defines a method in an *anonymous-method-expression* is nested inside the *block* of a *method-body* or another *anonymous-method-expression* (see annotation example in §14.5.15.5).

Parameters declared in an *anonymous-method-parameter-list* are members of the local variable declaration space of the *block* of that *anonymous-method-expression*.

These rules are implicit above. Anonymous methods also impact scoping (§10.7) in a similar way.

The textual order in which names are declared is generally of no significance. In particular, textual order is not significant for the declaration and use of namespaces, constants, methods, properties, events, indexers, operators, instance constructors, finalizers, static constructors, and types. Declaration order is significant in the following ways:

- Declaration order for field declarations and local variable declarations determines the order in which their initializers (if any) are executed. When there are field declarations in multiple partial type declarations for the same type, the order of the parts is unspecified. However, within each part the field initializers are executed in order.
- Local variables and local constants shall be defined before they are used (§10.7).
- Declaration order for enum member declarations (§21.3) is significant when *constant-expression* values are omitted.

[*Example*: The declaration space of a namespace is "open ended", and two namespace declarations with the same fully qualified name contribute to the same declaration space. For example

```
namespace Megacorp.Data
{
  class Customer
  {
    ...
  }
}

namespace Megacorp.Data
{
  class Order
  {
    ...
  }
}
```

The two namespace declarations above contribute to the same declaration space, in this case declaring two classes with the fully qualified names `Megacorp.Data.Customer` and `Megacorp.Data.Order`. Because the two declarations contribute to the same declaration space, it would have caused a compile-time error if each contained a declaration of a class with the same name.

All declarations of a partial type contribute to the same declaration space:

```
partial class C
{
  int F;
  partial struct N1 {...}
  partial class N2 {...}
  partial class N3 {...}
}

partial class C
{
  void F() {...}              // Error: conflicts with field F
  partial class N1 {...}      // Error: conflicts with struct N1
  class N2 {...}              // Error: conflicts with other N2
  partial class N3 {...}      // Ok
}
```

The two partial declarations for `C` combine to form a single declaration space and a single type. The field named `F` in the first part conflicts with the method named `F` in the second part. The struct named `N1` in the first part conflicts with the class named `N1` in the second part. The non-partial class `N2` in the second part conflicts with the partial class `N2` in the first part. The two partial declarations for `N3` combine to form a single type `C.N3`. *end example*]

[*Note*: As specified above, the declaration space of a block cannot share names with the declaration spaces of any nested blocks. Thus, in the following example, the `F` and `G` methods result in a compile-time error because the name `i` is declared in the outer block and cannot be redeclared in the inner block. However, the `H` and `I` methods are valid since the two `i`'s are declared in separate non-nested blocks.

```
class A
{
  void F()
  {
    int i = 0;
    if (true)
    {
      int i = 1;
    }
  }

  void G()
  {
    if (true)
    {
      int i = 0;
    }
    int i = 1;
  }
```

```
    void H()
    {
      if (true)
      {
        int i = 0;
      }
      if (true)
      {
        int i = 1;
      }
    }

    void I()
    {
      for (int i = 0; i < 10; i++)
        H();
      for (int i = 0; i < 10; i++)
        H();
    }
  }
```

end note]

10.4 Members

Namespaces and types have **members**. [*Note*: The members of an entity are generally available through the use of a qualified name that starts with a reference to the entity, followed by a "." token, followed by the name of the member. *end note*]

Members of a type are either declared in the type or **inherited** from the base class of the type. When a type inherits from a base class, all members of the base class, except instance constructors, finalizers, and static constructors become members of the derived type. The declared accessibility of a base class member does not control whether the member is inherited—inheritance extends to any member that isn't an instance constructor, static constructor, or finalizer. However, an inherited member might not be accessible in a derived type, either because of its declared accessibility (§10.5.1) or because it is hidden by a declaration in the type itself (§10.7.1.2).

10.4.1 Namespace members

Namespaces and types that have no enclosing namespace are members of the **global namespace**. This corresponds directly to the names declared in the global declaration space.

Namespaces and types declared within a namespace are members of that namespace. This corresponds directly to the names declared in the declaration space of the namespace.

Namespaces have no access restrictions. It is not possible to declare private, protected, or internal namespaces, and namespace names are always publicly accessible.

10.4.2 Struct members

The members of a struct are the members declared in the struct and the members inherited from the struct's direct base class `System.ValueType` and the indirect base class `object`.

The members of a simple type are the members of the struct type aliased by the simple type (§11.1.4).

10.4.3 Enumeration members

The members of an enumeration are the constants declared in the enumeration and the members inherited from the enumeration's direct base class `System.Enum` and the indirect base classes `System.ValueType` and `object`.

10.4.4 Class members

The members of a class are the members declared in the class and the members inherited from the base class (except for class `object` which has no base class). The members inherited from the base class include the constants, fields, methods, properties, events, indexers, operators, and types of the base class, but not the instance constructors, finalizers, and static constructors of the base class. Base class members are inherited without regard to their accessibility.

A class declaration can contain declarations of constants, fields, methods, properties, events, indexers, operators, instance constructors, finalizers, static constructors, and types.

The members of `object` and `string` correspond directly to the members of the class types they alias:

- The members of `object` are the members of the `System.Object` class.
- The members of `string` are the members of the `System.String` class.

10.4.5 Interface members

The members of an interface are the members declared in the interface and in all base interfaces of the interface. [*Note*: The members in class `object` are not, strictly speaking, members of any interface (§20.2). However, the members in class `object` are available via member lookup in any interface type (§14.3). *end note*]

10.4.6 Array members

The members of an array are the members inherited from class `System.Array`.

10.4.7 Delegate members

The members of a delegate are the members inherited from class `System.Delegate`.

10.5 Member access

Declarations of members allow control over member access. The accessibility of a member is established by the declared accessibility (§10.5.1) of the member combined with the accessibility of the immediately containing type, if any.

When access to a particular member is allowed, the member is said to be ***accessible.*** Conversely, when access to a particular member is disallowed, the member is said to be ***inaccessible***. Access to a member is permitted when the textual location in which the access takes place is included in the accessibility domain (§10.5.2) of the member.

10.5.1 Declared accessibility

The ***declared accessibility*** of a member can be one of the following:

- Public, which is selected by including a `public` modifier in the member declaration. The intuitive meaning of `public` is "access not limited".
- Protected, which is selected by including a `protected` modifier in the member declaration. The intuitive meaning of `protected` is "access limited to the containing class or types derived from the containing class".

- Internal, which is selected by including an `internal` modifier in the member declaration. The intuitive meaning of `internal` is "access limited to this program".

> **Clarification of internal**
>
> Recall that the definition of *program* in C# is the *input* to the compiler (§4) and includes class libraries.
>
> The precise meaning of `internal` is "access limited to this assembly." An assembly is the output of the compiler and might be a *class library* or an *application*.
>
> The normal use of `internal` is to limit access to the containing class library.

- Protected internal, which is selected by including both a `protected` and an `internal` modifier in the member declaration. The intuitive meaning of `protected internal` is "access limited to this program or types derived from the containing class".

> **Clarification of protected internal**
>
> Following `internal`, the precise meaning of `protected internal` is "access limited to this assembly or to types derived from the containing type." Again, in normal use the assembly is a class library.
>
> Note also that `internal protected` means the same as `protected internal`, but the former is more commonly used.

- Private, which is selected by including a `private` modifier in the member declaration. The intuitive meaning of `private` is "access limited to the containing type".

Depending on the context in which a member declaration takes place, only certain types of declared accessibility are permitted. Furthermore, when a member declaration does not include any access modifiers, the context in which the declaration takes place determines the default declared accessibility.

- Namespaces implicitly have `public` declared accessibility. No access modifiers are allowed on namespace declarations.
- Types declared in compilation units or namespaces can have `public` or `internal` declared accessibility and default to `internal` declared accessibility.
- Class members can have any of the five kinds of declared accessibility and default to `private` declared accessibility. [*Note*: A type declared as a member of a class can have any of the five kinds of declared accessibility, whereas a type declared as a member of a namespace can have only `public` or `internal` declared accessibility. *end note*]
- Struct members can have `public`, `internal`, or `private` declared accessibility and default to `private` declared accessibility because structs are implicitly sealed. Struct members introduced in a struct (that is, not inherited by that struct) cannot have `protected` or `protected internal` declared accessibility. [*Note*: A type declared as a member of a struct can have `public`, `internal`, or `private` declared accessibility, whereas a type declared as a member of a namespace can have only `public` or `internal` declared accessibility. *end note*]
- Interface members implicitly have `public` declared accessibility. No access modifiers are allowed on interface member declarations.
- Enumeration members implicitly have `public` declared accessibility. No access modifiers are allowed on enumeration member declarations.

Accessibility vs. visibility

C# uses the term *accessibility* for both top-level types (types, possibly in a namespace, not declared inside another type) and nested types (types, possibly in a namespace, declared inside another type). C# also uses the term *visibility* as an opposite to the term *hidden* (a declaration in an outer scope is said to be hidden when an entity with the same name is declared in an inner scope). The CLI, on the other hand, tends to describe nested types as (in)accessible and top-level types as (in)visible.

Default considered harmful?

Some would argue that having any default accessibility is a bad thing—that accessibility should always be explicitly declared. Regardless of that point, if there *is* to be a default accessibility, C#'s stance of "the default accessibility is always the most restrictive one that could be explicitly declared" is a very good one. It is easy to remember, and it errs on the side of privacy.

Jon Skeet

Default class accessibility pitfall

Consider this code fragment, which uses the NUnit test framework (http://www.nunit.org/):

```
using NUnit.Framework;

namespace Company.WidgetLibTests
{
  [TestFixture]          // Mark as a test class
  class WidgetTests
  {
    [Test]               // Mark as a test method
    public void SomeTest()
    {
      ...
    }
  }
}
```

The attributes mark `WidgetTests.SomeTest` as a method NUnit should run. Compile this code and no errors are produced; load the resulting assembly into NUnit and it might easily appear to be passing all its tests. But beware, the tests are *not* being run!

The `WidgetTests` class, having default internal accessibility, is not accessible and is silently ignored by NUnit. In a large project with many tests it might be difficult to spot that some tests are not being included, especially if the tester and coder are not the same person. This is one reason to always write test cases so that they initially fail.

One way to solve this is to write a test that looks for tests that NUnit ignores! Such a test would use reflection to load its own assembly and look for any nonpublic [TestFixture]'d classes. For example:

```
[TestFixture]
public class MetaTest
{
  [Test]
  public void AccidentalNonPublicTestFixture()
  {
```

```
      Type tf = typeof(TestFixtureAssembly);
      Assembly self = this.GetType().Module.Assembly;
      foreach (Type type in self.GetTypes())
      {
        object[] attributes = type.GetCustomAttributes(tf, false);
        if (attributes != null
            && attributes.Length > 0 && type.IsNotPublic)
        {
          Assert.Fail(type.ToString()
                 + " is a non-public [TestFixture] 'd class.");
        }
      }
    }
  }
```

Then make sure this *sourcefile* is included when building any test assembly.

10.5.2 Accessibility domains

The ***accessibility domain*** of a member consists of the (possibly disjoint) sections of program text in which access to the member is permitted. For purposes of defining the accessibility domain of a member, a member is said to be ***top-level*** if it is not declared within a type, and a member is said to be ***nested*** if it is declared within another type. Furthermore, the text of a program is defined as all source text contained in all source files of that program, and the source text of a type is defined as all source text contained between the opening and closing "{ " and "} " tokens in the *class-body*, *struct-body*, *interface-body*, or *enum-body* of all declarations for the type (including, possibly, multiple partial declarations and all types that are nested within the type).

The accessibility domain of a predefined type (such as `object`, `int`, or `double`) is unlimited.

The accessibility domain of a top-level type `T` that is declared in a program `P` is defined as follows:

- If the declared accessibility of `T` is `public`, the accessibility domain of `T` is the program text of `P` and any program that references `P`.
- If the declared accessibility of `T` is `internal`, the accessibility domain of `T` is the program text of `P`.

[*Note*: From these definitions, it follows that the accessibility domain of a top-level type is always at least the program text of the program in which that type is declared. *end note*]

The accessibility domain of a nested member `M` declared in a type `T` within a program `P`, is defined as follows (noting that `M` itself might possibly be a type):

- If the declared accessibility of `M` is `public`, the accessibility domain of `M` is the accessibility domain of `T`.
- If the declared accessibility of `M` is `protected internal`, let `D` be the union of the program text of `P` and the program text of any type derived from `T`, which is declared outside `P`. The accessibility domain of `M` is the intersection of the accessibility domain of `T` with `D`.
- If the declared accessibility of `M` is `protected`, let `D` be the union of the program text of `T` and the program text of any type derived from `T`. The accessibility domain of `M` is the intersection of the accessibility domain of `T` with `D`.
- If the declared accessibility of `M` is `internal`, the accessibility domain of `M` is the intersection of the accessibility domain of `T` with the program text of `P`.
- If the declared accessibility of `M` is `private`, the accessibility domain of `M` is the program text of `T`.

[*Note*: From these definitions, it follows that the accessibility domain of a nested member is always at least the program text of the type in which the member is declared. Furthermore, it follows that the accessibility domain of a member is never more inclusive than the accessibility domain of the type in which the member is declared. *end note*]

[*Note*: In intuitive terms, when a type or member M is accessed, the following steps are evaluated to ensure that the access is permitted:

- First, if M is declared within a type (as opposed to a compilation unit or a namespace), a compile-time error occurs if that type is not accessible.
- Then, if M is public, the access is permitted.
- Otherwise, if M is protected internal, the access is permitted if it occurs within the program in which M is declared, or if it occurs within a class derived from the class in which M is declared and takes place through the derived class type (§10.5.3).
- Otherwise, if M is protected, the access is permitted if it occurs within the class in which M is declared, or if it occurs within a class derived from the class in which M is declared and takes place through the derived class type (§10.5.3).
- Otherwise, if M is internal, the access is permitted if it occurs within the program in which M is declared.
- Otherwise, if M is private, the access is permitted if it occurs within the type in which M is declared.
- Otherwise, the type or member is inaccessible, and a compile-time error occurs.

end note]

[*Example*: In the following code

```
public class A
{
  public static int X;
  internal static int Y;
  private static int Z;
}

internal class B
{
  public static int X;
  internal static int Y;
  private static int Z;

  public class C
  {
    public static int X;
    internal static int Y;
    private static int Z;
  }

  private class D
  {
    public static int X;
    internal static int Y;
    private static int Z;
  }
}
```

the classes and members have the following accessibility domains:

- The accessibility domain of A and A.X is unlimited.
- The accessibility domain of A.Y, B, B.X, B.Y, B.C, B.C.X, and B.C.Y is the program text of the containing program.
- The accessibility domain of A.Z is the program text of A.
- The accessibility domain of B.Z and B.D is the program text of B, including the program text of B.C and B.D.
- The accessibility domain of B.C.Z is the program text of B.C.
- The accessibility domain of B.D.X and B.D.Y is the program text of B, including the program text of B.C and B.D.
- The accessibility domain of B.D.Z is the program text of B.D.

As the example illustrates, the accessibility domain of a member is never larger than that of a containing type. For example, even though all X members have public declared accessibility, all but A.X have accessibility domains that are constrained by a containing type. *end example*]

As described in §10.4, all members of a base class, except for instance constructors, finalizers, and static constructors are inherited by derived types. This includes even private members of a base class. However, the accessibility domain of a private member includes only the program text of the type in which the member is declared. [*Example*: In the following code

```
class A
{
  int x;
  static void F(B b)
  {
    b.x = 1;   // Ok
  }
}

class B: A
{
  static void F(B b)
  {
    b.x = 1;   // Error, x not accessible
  }
}
```

the B class inherits the private member x from the A class. Because the member is private, it is only accessible within the *class-body* of A. Thus, the access to b.x succeeds in the A.F method, but fails in the B.F method. *end example*]

10.5.3 Protected access for instance members

When a protected instance member is accessed outside the program text of the class in which it is declared, and when a protected internal instance member is accessed outside the program text of the program in which it is declared, the access is required to take place *through* an instance of the derived class type in which the access occurs. Let B be a base class that declares a protected instance member M, and let D be a class that derives from B. Within the *class-body* of D, access to M can take one of the following forms:

- An unqualified *type-name* or *primary-expression* of the form M.
- A *primary-expression* of the form E.M, provided the type of E is D or a class derived from D.
- A *primary-expression* of the form base.M.

In addition to these forms of access, a derived class can access a protected instance constructor of a base class in a *constructor-initializer* (§17.10.1).

[*Example*: In the following code

```
public class A
{
  protected int x;

  static void F(A a, B b)
  {
    a.x = 1;   // Ok
    b.x = 1;   // Ok
  }
}

public class B: A
{
  static void F(A a, B b)
  {
    a.x = 1;   // Error, must access through instance of B
    b.x = 1;   // Ok
  }
}
```

within A, it is possible to access x through instances of both A and B, since in either case the access takes place *through* an instance of A or a class derived from A. However, within B, it is not possible to access x through an instance of A, since A does not derive from B. *end example*]

Rationale: access to protected members

The reasoning behind the special instance member rule is that, without it, protected access would not actually provide any data encapsulation at all. Protected members would be accessible to anyone that could access public members. Protected access could be circumvented using code following the pattern:

```
public class Malicious : Base
{
  public static void ByPassProtectedAccess(Base b)
  {
    b.ProtectedInstanceMethod();
  }
}
```

If this were allowed, then for any class derived from Base the protected members it inherits from Base would be accessible to code such as Malicious. With the "protected access for instance members" rule, bypassing protected access is not possible in this way.

Programmers use the protected access modifier to control access to the state of their objects to trusted sources. Allowing a way to circumvent access to protected members could result in security vulnerabilities in your code. We have caught security issues very similar to this in the .Net framework code.

Astute readers will notice that this still leaves protected static members as accessible as public static members. So with that in mind, I recommend never declaring static members to be protected. Always decide if they should be public, private, or internal so that there is no confusion.

Peter Hallam

In the context of generics (§25.1.6), the rules for accessing `protected` and `protected internal` instance members are augmented by the following:

- Within a generic class `G`, access to an inherited protected instance member `M` using a *primary-expression* of the form `E.M` is permitted if the type of `E` is a class type constructed from `G` or a class type derived from a class type constructed from `G`.

Access to other instantiations

The preceding rule means that within a class that derives from a generic class `G<T>`, access to protected instance members of type instances of `G<S>` may be possible. For example, consider:

```
public class A<R>
{
  protected R x;

  public void F<S, T>(A<S> a, B<T> b)
  {
    a.x = default(S);  // OK, can access A<S> even in A<R>
    b.x = default(T);  // OK, can access through B<T> which extends  A<T>
  }
}

public class B<J> : A<J>
{
  public void F<K, L>(A<K> a, B<L> b)
  {
    a.x = default(K); // Error, cannot access through A<K>
    b.x = default(L); // OK, can access through B<L> even in B<J>
  }
}
```

Here the last assignment is within the class `B<J>` and to a field inherited from `A<L>` by an instance of `B<L>`—so the base class is `A<J>`, while the access is to class `A<L>`.

Twin or just sibling?

During the Standardization process there was some discussion about whether one type instantiation of a generic type should be able to access the nonpublic members of a different type instantiation of the same generic type. The debate centers on whether instantiation is seen as similar to derivation or not. If two types `N` and `O` are siblings, both deriving from `M`, then they *cannot* access each other's nonpublic members. So should two types `E<P>` and `E<Q>`, which might also be thought of as siblings with parent `E`, be able to access each other's nonpublic members? The decision was to follow Java and Visual Basic and allow such access. For example, consider:

```
public class B<J>
{
  private J y;
```

```
    public void F<L> (B<L> b)
    {
      b.y = default(L); // OK, can access non-public members
                        //  of "twin" B<L> from B<J>
    }
  }
```
Note that different instantiations do not share static fields; see §25.1.4.

10.5.4 Accessibility constraints

Several constructs in the C# language require a type to be ***at least as accessible as*** a member or another type. A type T is said to be at least as accessible as a member or type M if the accessibility domain of T is a superset of the accessibility domain of M. In other words, T is at least as accessible as M if T is accessible in all contexts in which M is accessible.

The following accessibility constraints exist:

- The direct base class of a class type shall be at least as accessible as the class type itself.
- The explicit base interfaces of an interface type shall be at least as accessible as the interface type itself.
- The return type and parameter types of a delegate type shall be at least as accessible as the delegate type itself.
- The type of a constant shall be at least as accessible as the constant itself.
- The type of a field shall be at least as accessible as the field itself.
- The return type and parameter types of a method shall be at least as accessible as the method itself.
- The type of a property shall be at least as accessible as the property itself.
- The type of an event shall be at least as accessible as the event itself.
- The type and parameter types of an indexer shall be at least as accessible as the indexer itself.
- The return type and parameter types of an operator shall be at least as accessible as the operator itself.
- The parameter types of an instance constructor shall be at least as accessible as the instance constructor itself.

[*Example*: In the following code

```
class A {...}

public class B: A {...}
```

the B class results in a compile-time error because A is not at least as accessible as B. *end example*]

[*Example*: Likewise, in the following code

```
class A {...}

public class B
{
  A F() {...}
```

```
        internal A G() {...}

        public A H() {...}
    }
```

the H method in B results in a compile-time error because the return type A is not at least as accessible as the method. *end example*]

Declaration accessibility consistency

These restrictions prevent inconsistent declarations. For example, consider a class with internal accessibility:

```
    internal class Detail
    {
       ...
    }
```

and a public method accepting this class as a parameter:

```
    public class Example
    {
      public void DoSomething(Detail parameter)
      {
         ...
      }
    }
```

These two declarations are illegal and cannot be compiled:

- If they are compiled into different assemblies, the assembly containing Example will not be able to access Detail (since it is internal to the other assembly).
- If they are compiled into the same assembly, there is *still* a problem; the method is apparently callable from a different assembly (since the method is public), yet it cannot be callable from a different assembly because the parameter's type is internal.

Note that one may present an internal class to another assembly through a public interface. For example:

```
    public interface IDetail
    {
       ...
    }

    internal class Detail: IDetail
    {
       ...
    }

    public class Example
    {
      public void DoSomething(IDetail parameter)
      {
         ...
      }
    }
```

Constrained object creation

These constraints do not prevent you from declaring a public class with only internal constructors:

```
public class Example
{
    ...
    internal Example()
    {
    }
}
```

Using this combination, instances of the class can be created, but only by code within the same assembly, and can be passed to and used by code outside the assembly. (Inheritance is similarly constrained.)

10.6 Signatures and overloading

Methods, instance constructors, indexers, and operators are characterized by their *signatures*:

- The signature of a method consists of the name of the method, the number of type parameters, and the type and kind (value, reference, or output) of each of its formal parameters, considered in the order left to right. The signature of a method specifically does not include the return type, parameter names, or type parameter names, nor does it include the `params` modifier that can be specified for the right-most parameter. When a parameter type includes a type parameter of the method, the ordinal position of the type parameter is used for type equivalence, not the name of the type parameter.

  ### Explicit interface implementation

  The name of a method is defined by the *method-name*; see §17.5. In the case of explicit interface implementation (§20.4.1), the method-name includes the interface name and thus is part of the signature.

- The signature of an instance constructor consists of the type and kind (value, reference, or output) of each of its formal parameters, considered in the order left to right. The signature of an instance constructor specifically does not include the parameter names or the `params` modifier that can be specified for the right-most parameter.
- The signature of an indexer consists of the type of each of its formal parameters, considered in the order left to right. The signature of an indexer specifically does not include the element type or parameter names, nor does it include the `params` modifier that can be specified for the right-most parameter.
- The signature of an operator consists of the name of the operator and the type of each of its formal parameters, considered in the order left to right. The signature of an operator specifically does not include the result type or parameter names.

Signatures are the enabling mechanism for *overloading* of members in classes, structs, and interfaces:

- Overloading of methods permits a class, struct, or interface to declare multiple methods with the same name, provided their signatures are unique within that class, struct, or interface.
- Overloading of instance constructors permits a class or struct to declare multiple instance constructors, provided their signatures are unique within that class or struct.
- Overloading of indexers permits a class, struct, or interface to declare multiple indexers, provided their signatures are unique within that class, struct, or interface.
- Overloading of operators permits a class or struct to declare multiple operators with the same name, provided their signatures are unique within that class or struct.

Although `out` and `ref` parameter modifiers are considered part of a signature, members declared in a single type cannot differ in signature solely by `ref` and `out`. A compile-time error occurs if two members are declared in the same type with signatures that would be the same if all parameters in both methods with `out` modifiers were changed to `ref` modifiers. For other purposes of signature matching (e.g., hiding or overriding), `ref` and `out` are considered part of the signature and do not match each other. [*Note*: This restriction is to allow C# programs to be easily translated to run on the Common Language Infrastructure (CLI), which does not provide a way to define methods that differ solely in `ref` and `out`. *end note*]

Pitfall of overloading on ref or out

Overloading solely on a ref parameter or solely on an out parameter is possible but generally to be avoided.

```
class EasyToMisuse
{
  public void Method(int value) { ...}
  public void Method(ref int value) { ...}
}
```

In this case, if you forget the ref keyword, your mistake will go unreported. A possible alternative is:

```
class HarderToMisuse
{
  public void Method(int value) { ...}
  public void RefMethod(ref int value) { ...}
}
```

Why no ref and out overloading?

The following is illegal:

```
class Allowed
{
  public void Method(ref int value) { ...}
  public void Method(out int value) { ...}
}
```

The reason is that the CLI does not support out parameters, so a C# compiler targeting the CLI must use a CLI ref parameter to implement a C# out parameter. If the overloading were allowed, the CLI signatures of the two methods would be identical.

[*Example*: The following example shows a set of overloaded method declarations along with their signatures.

```
interface ITest
{
  void F();                      // F()
  void F(int x);                 // F(int)
  void F(ref int x);             // F(ref int)
  void F(out int x);             // F(out int)  error

  void F(int x, int y);          // F(int, int)
  int F(string s);               // F(string)
  int F(int x);                  // F(int)     error

  void F(string[] a);            // F(string[])
  void F(params string[] a);     // F(string[]) error

  void F<S>(S s);                // F<`0>(`0)
  void F<T>(T t);                // F<`0>(`0)   error

  void F<S,T>(S s);              // F<`0,`1>(`0)
  void F<T,S>(S s);              // F<`0,`1>(`1)  ok
}
```

Note that any `ref` and `out` parameter modifiers (§17.5.1) are part of a signature. Thus, `F(int)`, `F (ref int)`, and `F(out int)` are all unique signatures. However, `F(ref int)` and `F(out int)` cannot be declared within the same interface because their signatures differ solely by `ref` and `out`. Also, note that the return type and the `params` modifier are not part of a signature, so it is not possible to overload solely based on return type or on the inclusion or exclusion of the `params` modifier. As such, the declarations of the methods `F(int)` and `F(params string[])` identified above, result in a compile-time error. *end example*]

10.7 Scopes

The ***scope*** of a name is the region of program text within which it is possible to refer to the entity declared by the name without qualification of the name. Scopes can be ***nested***, and an inner scope can redeclare the meaning of a name from an outer scope. [*Note*: This does not, however, remove the restriction imposed by §10.3 that within a nested block it is not possible to declare a local variable or local constant with the same name as a local variable or local constant in an enclosing block. *end note*] The name from the outer scope is then said to be ***hidden*** in the region of program text covered by the inner scope, and access to the outer name is only possible by qualifying the name.

- The scope of a namespace member declared by a *namespace-member-declaration* (§16.5) with no enclosing *namespace-declaration* is the entire program text.
- The scope of a namespace member declared by a *namespace-member-declaration* within a *namespace-declaration* whose fully qualified name is N, is the *namespace-body* of every *namespace-declaration* whose fully qualified name is N or starts with N, followed by a period.
- The scope of a name defined by an *extern-alias-directive* (§16.3) extends over the *using-directives*, *global-attributes* and *namespace-member-declarations* of the *compilation-unit* or *namespace-body* in which the *extern-alias-directive* occurs. An *extern-alias-directive*

does not contribute any new members to the underlying declaration space. In other words, an *extern-alias-directive* is not transitive, but, rather, affects only the *compilation-unit* or *namespace-body* in which it occurs.

- The scope of a name defined or imported by a *using-directive* (§16.4) extends over the *global-attributes* and *namespace-member-declarations* of the *compilation-unit* or *namespace-body* in which the *using-directive* occurs. A *using-directive* can make zero or more namespace or type names available within a particular *compilation-unit* or *namespace-body*, but does not contribute any new members to the underlying declaration space. In other words, a *using-directive* is not transitive, but, rather, affects only the *compilation-unit* or *namespace-body* in which it occurs.

- The scope of a member declared by a *class-member-declaration* (§17.2) is the *class-body* in which the declaration occurs. In addition, the scope of a class member extends to the *class-body* of those derived classes that are included in the accessibility domain (§10.5.2) of the member.

- The scope of a member declared by a *struct-member-declaration* (§18.2) is the *struct-body* in which the declaration occurs.

- The scope of a member declared by an *enum-member-declaration* (§21.3) is the *enum-body* in which the declaration occurs.

- The scope of a parameter declared in a *method-declaration* (§17.5) is the *method-body* of that *method-declaration*.

- The scope of a parameter declared in an *indexer-declaration* (§17.8) is the *accessor-declarations* of that *indexer-declaration*.

- The scope of a parameter declared in an *operator-declaration* (§17.9) is the *block* of that *operator-declaration*.

- The scope of a parameter declared in a *constructor-declaration* (§17.10) is the *constructor-initializer* and *block* of that *constructor-declaration*.

- The scope of a label declared in a *labeled-statement* (§15.4) is the *block* in which the declaration occurs.

- The scope of a local variable declared in a *local-variable-declaration* (§15.5.1) is the *block* in which the declaration occurs.

- The scope of a local variable declared in a *switch-block* of a `switch` statement (§15.7.2) is the *switch-block*.

Declaration scope within switch statements

The C# scope rule follows the same model as used, for example, in Java and C++, where *switch-labels* are semantically similar to ordinary labels (§15.4) and denote places within a block where control may be transferred.

It could be argued that this rule is counter-intuitive, as it might be reasonably assumed that declaring a variable in a *switch-section* would limit its scope to that *switch-section* rather than the enclosing *switch-block*.

To limit the scope of declarations to a single *switch-section*, you may enclose the statements within a *block* (§15.2).

- The scope of a local variable declared in a *for-initializer* of a `for` statement (§15.8.3) is the *for-initializer*, the *for-condition*, the *for-iterator*, and the contained *statement* of the `for` statement.

- The scope of a local constant declared in a *local-constant-declaration* (§15.5.2) is the *block* in which the declaration occurs. It is a compile-time error to refer to a local constant in a textual position that precedes its *constant-declarator*.

Anonymous methods impact scope and lifetime

The introduction of anonymous methods (§14.5.15) means that one method may now be nested inside another method; see the annotation in §10.3 for details. This can have a significant impact on the scope and lifetime of parameters and local variables declared in a *method-body* or *anonymous-method-expression* that *contains* a nested *anonymous-method-expression*. Such changes to the lifetime of variables can impact runtime performance.

This topic and its potential implications are explained in §14.5.15.3.1 and associated annotations.

Within the scope of a namespace, class, struct, or enumeration member it is possible to refer to the member in a textual position that precedes the declaration of the member. [*Example*:

```
class A
{
  void F()
  {
    i = 1;
  }
  int i = 0;
}
```

Here, it is valid for F to refer to i before it is declared. *end example*]

Within the scope of a local variable, it is a compile-time error to refer to the local variable in a textual position that precedes the *local-variable-declarator* of the local variable. [*Example*:

```
class A
{
  int i = 0;

  void F()
  {
    i = 1;          // Error, use precedes declaration
    int i;
    i = 2;
  }

  void G()
  {
    int j = (j = 1);     // Valid
  }

  void H()
  {
    int a = 1, b = ++a;  // Valid
  }
}
```

In the F method above, the first assignment to i specifically does not refer to the field declared in the outer scope. Rather, it refers to the local variable and it results in a compile-time error because it textually precedes the declaration of the variable. In the G method, the use of j in the initializer for the declaration of j is valid because the use does not precede the *local-variable-declarator*. In the H method, a subsequent *local-variable-declarator* correctly refers to a local variable declared in an earlier *local-variable-declarator* within the same *local-variable-declaration*. *end example*]

[*Note*: The scoping rules for local variables and local constants are designed to guarantee that the meaning of a name used in an expression context is always the same within a block. If the scope of a local variable were to extend only from its declaration to the end of the block, then in the example above, the first assignment would assign to the instance variable and the second assignment would assign to the local variable. (In certain situations, but not in the example above, this could lead to a compile-time error if the statements of the block were later to be rearranged.)

The meaning of a name within a block can differ based on the context in which the name is used. In the example

```
using System;

class A {}

class Test
{
   static void Main()
   {
      string A = "hello, world";        // declarator context
      string s = A;                      // expression context

      Type t = typeof(A);                // type context

      Console.WriteLine(s);              // writes "hello, world"
      Console.WriteLine(t.ToString());   // writes "Type: A"
   }
}
```

the name A is used in an expression context to refer to the local variable A and in a type context to refer to the class A. *end note*]

In scope but not referable

Despite the opening statement that the "scope of a name is the region of program text within which it is possible to refer to the entity declared by the name without qualification of the name," the previous paragraph makes it clear that it is an error to refer to a local variable in that part of its scope that textually precedes the declaration of the variable. However, note that as no two declarations can introduce the same name into the same declaration space, then the declaration of a name (but not any initial assignment) can be moved to the start of its scope without affecting the meaning of the program.

Further, within the scope of a name, it is possible for it to be hidden (§10.7.1) and hence it cannot be referred to directly.

Therefore, the scope of a name is the region in which it is *potentially* possible to refer to the name without qualification, provided it is not hidden and the declaration point is taken to coincide with the start of the immediately enclosing block. Note this differs from Java, where the scope of a local name starts at its declaration point and continues to the end of the block.

Additional restrictions apply to the declaration/scope/visibility of names; see §14.5.2.1 and associated annotation.

10.7.1 Name hiding

The scope of an entity typically encompasses more program text than the declaration space of the entity. In particular, the scope of an entity can include declarations that introduce new declaration spaces containing entities of the same name. Such declarations cause the original entity to become **hidden**. Conversely, an entity is said to be **visible** when it is not hidden.

Name hiding occurs when scopes overlap through nesting and when scopes overlap through inheritance. The characteristics of the two types of hiding are described in the following subclauses.

Local variables, local constants, parameters, and method type parameters cannot hide other local variables, local constants, parameters, or method type parameters (§10.3).

Context-sensitive name resolution

Many constructs in C# require a type to be specified; among the many are, for example, the new operator (§14.5.10) and local variable declarations (§15.5.1). In such constructs only types are considered and so other kinds of declaration, such as fields and methods, do *not* hide type declarations. For example, consider:

```
public enum Color { ... }
public class Control
{
   public Color Color   // OK, context resolves each identifier correctly
   {
     get { ... }
     set { ... }
   }
}
```

Here the property Control.Color is of type Color and the context allows each use of Color to be resolved. This example is drawn from the naming guidelines referenced by Annex C, which include the suggestion that properties should be named after their underlying type in cases such as this one.

The one location where there might be ambiguity between whether a name represents a type or not is for member accesses (§14.5.4) and in this situation special resolution rules exist (§14.5.4.1).

10.7.1.1 Hiding through nesting

Name hiding through nesting can occur as a result of nesting namespaces or types within namespaces, as a result of nesting types within classes or structs, and as a result of parameter, local variable, and local constant declarations. [*Example*: In the following code

```
class A
{
  int i = 0;

  void F()
  {
    int i = 1;
  }

  void G()
  {
    i = 1;
  }
}
```

within the F method, the instance variable i is hidden by the local variable i, but within the G method, i still refers to the instance variable. *end example*]

When a name in an inner scope hides a name in an outer scope, it hides all overloaded occurrences of that name. [*Example*: In the following code

```
class Outer
{
  static void F(int i) {}

  static void F(string s) {}

  class Inner
  {
    void G()
    {
      F(1);           // Invokes Outer.Inner.F
      F("Hello");     // Error
    }

    static void F(long l) {}
  }
}
```

the call F(1) invokes the F declared in Inner because all outer occurrences of F are hidden by the inner declaration. For the same reason, the call F("Hello") results in a compile-time error. *end example*]

Name hiding in a constructor

In general, name hiding should be discouraged as a matter of style; it should be used only where necessary, or in highly stylized code. A common use of name hiding is where a constructor's parameters are named after the fields which they initialize:

```
public class Person
{
  public Person (string name)
  {
    this.name = name; // Note the qualification here
  }
  ...
  private string name;
}
```

This style is not without its pitfalls. Consider these two buggy versions:

```
public Person(string name)
{
  name = name;
}

public Person (string theName)
{
  this.name = name;
}
```

You will hopefully get warnings in both cases (the first saying the field is unassigned, the second saying the parameter is unused). Note that both mistakes would be a compile time error if `Person` was a struct.

Jon Skeet

10.7.1.2 Hiding through inheritance

Name hiding through inheritance occurs when classes or structs redeclare names that were inherited from base classes. This type of name hiding takes one of the following forms:

- A constant, field, property, or event introduced in a class or struct hides all base class members with the same name and no type parameters.
- A type introduced in a class or struct hides all base class members with the same name and same number of type parameters.
- A method introduced in a class or struct hides all non-method base class members with the same name and either, the same number of type parameters or no type parameters, and all base class methods with the same signature.
- An indexer introduced in a class or struct hides all base class indexers with the same signature (parameter count and types).

Contrary to hiding a name from an outer scope, hiding an accessible name from an inherited scope causes a warning to be reported. [*Example*: In the following code

```
class Base
{
   public void F() {}
}

class Derived: Base
{
   public void F() {}     // Warning, hiding an inherited name
}
```

the declaration of F in Derived causes a warning to be reported. Hiding an inherited name is specifically not an error, since that would preclude separate evolution of base classes. For example, the above situation might have come about because a later version of Base introduced an F method that wasn't present in an earlier version of the class. Had the above situation been an error, then *any* change made to a base class in a separately versioned class library could potentially cause derived classes to become invalid. *end example*]

The warning caused by hiding an inherited name can be eliminated through use of the new modifier: [*Example*:

```
class Base
{
   public void F() {}
}

class Derived: Base
{
   new public void F() {}
}
```

The `new` modifier indicates that the `F` in `Derived` is "new", and that it is indeed intended to hide the inherited member. *end example*]

A declaration of a new member hides an inherited member only within the scope of the new member. [*Example*:

```
class Base
{
  public static void F() {}
}

class Derived: Base
{
  new private static void F() {}   // Hides Base.F in Derived only
}

class MoreDerived: Derived
{
  static void G() { F(); }          // Invokes Base.F
}
```

In the example above, the declaration of `F` in `Derived` hides the `F` that was inherited from `Base`, but since the new `F` in `Derived` has private access, its scope does not extend to `MoreDerived`. Thus, the call `F()` in `MoreDerived.G` is valid and will invoke `Base.F`. *end example*]

Abstract cannot be hidden

Though the Standard does not explicitly specify that hiding an inherited abstract member is disallowed, it is a direct consequence of the rule that an abstract member must be implemented (§17.5.6).

When a derived class inherits an abstract member it must either provide an implementation for it or, if the derived class is itself abstract, the first more derived non-abstract class must do so. If the derived class introduces a new member that hides the inherited abstract one, then it cannot also provide an implementation and, if the derived class is abstract, a more derived class cannot either as it is now hidden. Therefore, the requirements cannot be met and the derived class is erroneous, resulting in a compile time error.

For example consider:

```
abstract class B
{
  public abstract void M();
}

class C : B
{
  new public void M() {} // compile-time error,
                         // cannot hide an abstract method
}
```

The declaration of `C.M` makes it impossible to provide an implementation for inherited method `B.M` in class `C`.

10.8 Namespace and type names

Several contexts in a C# program require a *namespace-name* or a *type-name* to be specified.

> *namespace-name:*
>   *namespace-or-type-name*
>
> *type-name:*
>   *namespace-or-type-name*
>
> *namespace-or-type-name:*
>   *identifier   type-argument-list$_{opt}$*
>   *qualified-alias-member*
>   *namespace-or-type-name   .   identifier   type-argument-list$_{opt}$*

A *namespace-name* is a *namespace-or-type-name* that refers to a namespace.

Following resolution as described below, the *namespace-or-type-name* of a *namespace-name* shall refer to a namespace, or otherwise a compile-time error occurs. Type arguments (§25.5.1) shall not be present in a *namespace-name* (only types can have type arguments).

A *type-name* is a *namespace-or-type-name* that refers to a type. Following resolution as described below, the *namespace-or-type-name* of a *type-name* shall refer to a type, or otherwise a compile-time error occurs.

The syntax and semantics of *qualified-alias-member* are defined in §16.7.

A *namespace-or-type-name* that is not a *qualified-alias-member* has one of four forms:

- I
- I<A_1, ..., A_K>
- N.I
- N.I<A_1, ..., A_K>

where I is a single identifier, N is a *namespace-or-type-name* and <A_1, ..., A_K> is an optional *type-argument-list*. When no *type-argument-list* is specified, consider K to be zero.

The meaning of a *namespace-or-type-name* is determined as follows:

- If the *namespace-or-type-name* is a *qualified-alias-member*, the meaning is as specified in §16.7.
- Otherwise, if the *namespace-or-type-name* is of the form I or of the form I<A_1, ..., A_K>:
    - If K is zero and the *namespace-or-type-name* appears within the body of a generic method declaration (§25.6) and if that declaration includes a type parameter (§25.1.1) with name I, then the *namespace-or-type-name* refers to that type parameter.
    - Otherwise, if the *namespace-or-type-name* appears within the body of a type declaration, then for each instance type T (§25.1.2), starting with the instance type of that type declaration and continuing with the instance type of each enclosing class or struct declaration (if any):
        - If K is zero and the declaration of T includes a type parameter with name I, then the *namespace-or-type-name* refers to that type parameter.
        - Otherwise, if T contains a nested accessible type having name I and K type parameters, then the *namespace-or-type-name* refers to that type constructed with the given type arguments. If there is more than one such type, the type declared within the more derived type is selected. [*Note*: Non-type

members (constants, fields, methods, properties, indexers, operators, instance constructors, finalizers, and static constructors) and type members with a different number of type parameters are ignored when determining the meaning of the *namespace-or-type-name. end note*]

○ Otherwise, for each namespace N, starting with the namespace in which the *namespace-or-type-name* occurs, continuing with each enclosing namespace (if any), and ending with the global namespace, the following steps are evaluated until an entity is located:

- If K is zero and I is the name of a namespace in N, then:
  - ○ If the location where the *namespace-or-type-name* occurs is enclosed by a namespace declaration for N and the namespace declaration contains an *extern-alias-directive* or *using-alias-directive* that associates the name I with a namespace or type, then the *namespace-or-type-name* is ambiguous and a compile-time error occurs.
  - ○ Otherwise, the *namespace-or-type-name* refers to the namespace named I in N.
- Otherwise, if N contains an accessible type having name I and K type parameters, then:
  - ○ If K is zero and the location where the *namespace-or-type-name* occurs is enclosed by a namespace declaration for N and the namespace declaration contains an *extern-alias-directive* or *using-alias-directive* that associates the name I with a namespace or type, then the *namespace-or-type-name* is ambiguous and a compile-time error occurs.
  - ○ Otherwise, the *namespace-or-type-name* refers to the type constructed with the given type arguments.
- Otherwise, if the location where the *namespace-or-type-name* occurs is enclosed by a namespace declaration for N:
  - ○ If K is zero and the namespace declaration contains an *extern-alias-directive* or *using-alias-directive* that associates the name I with an imported namespace or type, then the *namespace-or-type-name* refers to that namespace or type.
  - ○ Otherwise, if the namespaces imported by the *using-namespace-directive*s of the namespace declaration contain exactly one type having name I and K type parameters, then the *namespace-or-type-name* refers to that type constructed with the given type arguments.
  - ○ Otherwise, if the namespaces imported by the *using-namespace-directive*s of the namespace declaration contain more than one type having name I and K type parameters, then the *namespace-or-type-name* is ambiguous and an error occurs.

○ Otherwise, the *namespace-or-type-name* is undefined and a compile-time error occurs.

• Otherwise, the *namespace-or-type-name* is of the form N.I or of the form N.I<A_1, ..., A_K>. N is first resolved as a *namespace-or-type-name*. If the resolution of N is not successful, a compile-time error occurs. Otherwise, N.I or N.I<A_1, ..., A_K> is resolved as follows:

     o If K is zero and N refers to a namespace and N contains a nested namespace with name I, then the *namespace-or-type-name* refers to that nested namespace.

     o Otherwise, if N refers to a namespace and N contains an accessible type having name I and K type parameters, then the *namespace-or-type-name* refers to that type constructed with the given type arguments.

     o Otherwise, if N refers to a (possibly constructed) class or struct type and N contains a nested accessible type having name I and K type parameters, then the *namespace-or-type-name* refers to that type constructed with the given type arguments. If there is more than one such type, the type declared within the more derived type is selected.

     o Otherwise, N.I is an invalid *namespace-or-type-name*, and a compile-time error occurs.

A *namespace-or-type-name* is permitted to reference a static class (§17.1.1.3) if

- The *namespace-or-type-name* is the T in a *namespace-or-type-name* of the form T.I, or
- The *namespace-or-type-name* is the T in a *typeof-expression* (§14.5.11) of the form typeof(T)

An extended example

This is a long, important clause that, unfortunately, has no examples.

The following source file contains a class whose name coincides with one of the namespaces it is declared inside (this is not recommended but it does make for a useful example). All subsequent code fragments reference the assembly generated from this when compiled.

```
namespace Company.Widget.Framework
{
  public class Widget
  {
  }
}
```

Here is our first attempt. It fails to compile since the compiler cannot resolve Widget.

```
namespace Company.Other.Framework.Tests
{
  public class FubarTests
  {
    public void SomeTest()
    {
      Widget w = new Widget(); // compile-time error
    }
  }
}
```

Suppose we try to fix this by adding a using directive as follows:

```
using Company.Widget.Framework;

namespace Company.Other.Framework.Tests
{
  public class FubarTests
  {
```

```
      public void SomeTest()
      {
        Widget w = new Widget(); // still a compile-time error
      }
    }
  }
}
```

This does *not* solve the problem. Why? Because the compiler attempts to resolve `Widget` by looking from the innermost namespace outwards:

- There is nothing called `Widget` in the `Company.Other.Framework.Tests` namespace.
- There is nothing called `Widget` in the `Company.Other.Framework` namespace.
- There is nothing called `Widget` in the `Company.Other` namespace.
- There *is* something called `Widget` in the `Company` namespace. `Widget` is the name of a namespace inside the `Company` namespace (see the first source file). The compiler stops here and so never even tries our using directive.

What if we place the using directive *inside* the namespace?

```
namespace Company.Other.Framework.Tests
{
  using Company.Widget.Framework;

  public class FubarTests
  {
    public void SomeTest()
    {
      Widget w = new Widget(); // ok
    }
  }
}
```

This works because the using directive is now associated with the innermost namespace (`Company.Other.Framework.Tests`) and so is found straightaway, before unwinding to the outermost `Company` namespace.

Suppose the using directive occurs as follows, where the full namespace name is split in two parts to allow the using directive to be placed between the namespace declarations:

```
namespace Company.Other
{
  using Company.Widget.Framework;

  namespace Framework.Tests
  {
    public class FubarTests
    {
      public void SomeTest()
      {
        Widget w = new Widget(); // ok
      }
    }
  }
}
```

This works for the same reason; the using directive is used before unwinding to the outermost Company namespace.

Here is a similar example:

```
namespace Company
{
  using Company.Widget.Framework;

  namespace Other.Framework.Tests
  {
    public class FubarTests
    {
      public void SomeTest()
      {
        Widget w = new Widget(); // compile-time error
      }
    }
  }
}
```

Now we get a compile time error. This is because the namespace Company contains a nested *namespace* called Widget but it *also* contains a using directive that makes the Company.Widget.Framework.Widget *type* available. In this situation there is effectively a tie, but the namespace wins, so the compile time error says Widget resolves to Company.Widget, which is a namespace. Note that you cannot solve this problem by writing a using alias directive. If you try (as in the following example) you still get a compile time error (probably saying there is an ambiguity/conflict).

```
namespace Company
{
  using Widget = Company.Widget.Framework.Widget;

  namespace Other.Framework.Tests
  {
    public class FubarTests
    {
      public void SomeTest()
      {
        Widget w = new Widget(); // compile-time error
      }
    }
  }
}
```

Suppose we start again and change the name of the namespace (note that Tests is now a prefix rather than a suffix and we have our using directive outside the namespace again).

```
using Company.Widget.Framework;

namespace Tests.Company.Other.Framework
{
  public class FubarTests
```

```
  {
    public void SomeTest()
    {
      Widget w = new Widget(); // ok
    }
  }
}
```

This works. Once again the compiler tries to resolve `Widget` by looking from the innermost namespace outwards:

- There is nothing called `Widget` in the `Tests.Company.Other.Framework` namespace.
- There is nothing called `Widget` in the `Tests.Company.Other` namespace.
- There is nothing called `Widget` in the `Tests.Company` namespace.
- There is nothing called `Widget` in the `Tests` namespace.
- We have reached the global namespace containing our using directive.

What happens if we try to place the using directive inside the namespace?

```
namespace Tests.Company.Other.Framework
{
  using Company.Widget.Framework; // compile-time error

  public class FubarTests
  {
    public void SomeTest()
    {
      Widget w = new Widget();
    }
  }
}
```

This time you get a compile time error on the using directive itself (rather than on the line trying to declare a `Widget` local variable). This is because `Company.Widget.Framework` (in the using directive) has an outermost namespace of `Company`. The problem is that `Company` is resolving to `Tests.Company` (and not the "global" `Company`) because the using directive occurs inside the namespace that begins `Tests.Company`. In other words, it is as if you had written:

```
namespace Tests.Company.Other.Framework
{
  // presumed to be a non-existent namespace
  using Tests.Company.Widget.Framework;
  ...
}
```

Note that we can fix this problem with `global::` qualified alias member.

```
namespace Tests.Company.Other.Framework
{
  using global::Company.Widget.Framework; // ok

  public class FubarTests
  {
    public void SomeTest()
```

```
    {
       Widget w = new Widget(); // ok
    }
  }
}
```

In summary, the best option is to avoid namespace/type-name clashes. For example:

```
namespace Company.WidgetFramework
{
  public class Widget
  {
    ...
  }
}


using Company.WidgetFramework;

namespace Company.WidgetFrameworkTests
{
  public class WidgetTests
  {
    ...
  }
}
```

See also the annotation on §16.4.2.

10.8.1 Unqualified name

Every namespace declaration and type declaration has an ***unqualified name*** determined as follows:

- For a namespace declaration, the unqualified name is the *qualified-identifier* specified in the declaration.
- For a type declaration with no *type-parameter-list*, the unqualified name is the *identifier* specified in the declaration.
- For a type declaration with K type parameters, the unqualified name is the *identifier* specified in the declaration, followed by the *generic-dimension-specifier* (§14.5.11).

10.8.2 Fully qualified names

Every namespace declaration and type declaration has a ***fully qualified name,*** which uniquely identifies the namespace or type amongst all others. The fully qualified name of a namespace or type declaration with unqualified name N is determined as follows:

- If the declaration is contained directly in a compilation unit and not nested in any other declaration, its fully qualified name is N.
- Otherwise, its fully qualified name is S.N, where S is the fully qualified name of the immediately enclosing namespace or type declaration.

In other words, the fully qualified name of a declaration is the complete hierarchical path of identifiers (and *generic-dimension-specifier* (§14.5.11)) that lead to the type or namespace, starting from the global namespace. The fully qualified name of a declaration shall uniquely identify the namespace, non-generic type or generic instance type (§25.1.2) associated with the declaration. It is a compile-time error for the same fully qualified name to refer to two distinct entities. In particular:

- It is an error for both a namespace declaration and a type declaration to have the same fully qualified name.
- It is an error for two different kinds of type declarations to have the same fully qualified name (for example, if both a struct and class declaration have the same fully qualified name).
- It is an error for a type declaration without the `partial` modifier to have the same fully qualified name as another type declaration (§17.1.4).

[*Example*: The example below shows several namespace and type declarations along with their associated fully qualified names.

```
class A {}          // A

namespace X         // X
{
  class B           // X.B
  {
    class C {}      // X.B.C
  }

  namespace Y       // X.Y
  {
    class D {}      // X.Y.D
  }
}

namespace X.Y       // X.Y
{
  class E {}        // X.Y.E

  class G<T>        // X.Y.G<>
  {
    class H {}      // X.Y.G<>.H
  }

  class G<S,T>      // X.Y.G<,>
  {
    class H<U> {}   // X.Y.G<,>.H<>
  }
}
```

end example]

10.9 Automatic memory management

C# employs automatic memory management, which frees developers from manually allocating and freeing the memory occupied by objects. Automatic memory management policies are implemented by a garbage collector. The memory management life cycle of an object is as follows:

1. When the object is created, memory is allocated for it, the constructor is run, and the object is considered ***live***.

Constructors, exceptions, and finalizers: a volatile combination

The preceding statement is rather vague. What happens, for example, if the constructor throws an exception? Does the object exist? It might be hoped that an implementation would clean up and no object would be left, *but this is not required*. Indeed, the statement allows an object to be considered ***live*** even if the constructor throws, which in turn means the object is eligible for finalization. This might be surprising should an implementation choose to allow this.

Consider the following (written by Jeffrey Richter):

```
using System;

class App
{
  static void Main()
  {
    try
    {
      new App();
    }
    catch
    {
      Console.WriteLine("in catch");
    }
    GC.Collect();
    GC.WaitForPendingFinalizers();
  }

  App()
  {
    throw new InvalidOperationException("Hi Jeff");
  }

  ~App()
  {
    Console.WriteLine("in Finalize");
  }
}
```

In testing this on various systems at the time of writing, some appeared to consistently execute the finalizer, while others did so *nondeterministically*, sometimes doing it and sometimes not!

The recommendation is to avoid throwing exceptions from constructors. When this cannot be avoided, then the object under construction must be put into a safe state before the exception is thrown, so that the execution of a finalizer will not generate further errors. But what if the constructor invokes an operation that may throw an exception that cannot meaningfully be handled by the constructor itself? In this case the constructor should include a general catch statement that puts the object into a safe state and then rethrows the exception. When an object does not have a finalizer, such stringent measures may not be required.

2. If no part of the object can be accessed by any possible continuation of execution, other than the running of finalizers, the object is considered *no longer in use* and it becomes eligible for finalization. [*Note*: Implementations might choose to analyze code to determine which references to an object can be used in the future. For instance, if a local variable that is in scope is the only existing reference to an object, but that local variable is never referred to in any possible continuation of execution from the current execution point in the procedure, an implementation might (but is not required to) treat the object as no longer in use. *end note*]

One implementation's garbage is another's treasure

Any object that can be determined to be *no longer in use* is eligible for garbage collection, including those objects referenced by local variables. Consider the contrived program fragment:

```
class Waste
{
  int[ ] hold;

  public Waste()
  {
    hold = new int[ 1000000] ;          // a lot of waste
  }
}

class KeepAround
{
  public static int Count = 0;

  ~KeepAround()
  {
    Console.WriteLine("Garbage collected: {0} ", Count);
  }
}

void Test()
{
  KeepAround ka = new KeepAround(); // assign to local

  for (int i = 0; i < 100; i++)        // generate garbage
  {
    Waste two = new Waste();
    KeepAround.Count++;
  }
  Console.WriteLine("Done: {0} ", KeepAround.Count);
}
```

Here the method `Test` creates an instance of `KeepAround` followed by enough instances of `Waste` to trigger garbage collection. Since the local variable `ka` is not used after the loop, the `KeepAround` object that it references will probably be collected, and its finalizer run, after some iterations. Depending on the C# implementation, this program may print:

```
Garbage collected: 22
Done: 100
```

In test runs the number of Waste allocations before the KeepAround object was collected ranged from 3 to 86; the number will likely be different on other systems. However, if the C# implementation does not determine that ka is unused after allocation, the output will always be:

```
Done: 100
Garbage collected: 100
```

Both behaviors are completely correct. There is no time-specific requirement to reclaim items that are no longer in use. However if one lapses into assuming that the lifetime of a local variable and the period it is in use coincide, then a surprise might result. This issue is covered in an annotation on §15.13.

3. Once the object is eligible for finalization, at some unspecified later time the finalizer (§17.12) (if any) for the object is run. Unless overridden by explicit calls, the finalizer for the object is run once only.
4. Once the finalizer for an object is run, if that object, or any part of it, cannot be accessed by any possible continuation of execution, including the running of finalizers, the object is considered ***inaccessible*** and the object becomes eligible for collection.
5. Finally, at some time after the object becomes eligible for collection, the garbage collector frees the memory associated with that object.

The garbage collector maintains information about object usage, and uses this information to make memory management decisions, such as where in memory to locate a newly created object, when to relocate an object, and when an object is no longer in use or inaccessible.

Like other languages that assume the existence of a garbage collector, C# is designed so that the garbage collector can implement a wide range of memory management policies. For instance, C# does not require that finalizers be run or that objects be collected as soon as they are eligible, or that finalizers be run in any particular order, or on any particular thread.

The behavior of the garbage collector can be controlled, to some degree, via static methods on the class System.GC.

[*Example*: Since the garbage collector is allowed wide latitude in deciding when to collect objects and run finalizers, a conforming implementation might produce output that differs from that shown by the following code. The program

```
using System;

class A
{
  ~A()
  {
    Console.WriteLine("Finalize instance of A");
  }
}
```

```csharp
class B
{
  object Ref;
  public B(object o)
  {
    Ref = o;
  }
  ~B()
  {
    Console.WriteLine("Finalize instance of B");
  }
}

class Test
{
  static void Main()
  {
    B b = new B(new A());
    b = null;
    GC.Collect();
    GC.WaitForPendingFinalizers();
  }
}
```

creates an instance of class A and an instance of class B. These objects become eligible for garbage collection when the variable b is assigned the value null, since after this time it is impossible for any user-written code to access them. The output could be either

```
Finalize instance of A
Finalize instance of B
```

or

```
Finalize instance of B
Finalize instance of A
```

because the language imposes no constraints on the order in which objects are garbage collected.

In subtle cases, the distinction between "eligible for finalization" and "eligible for collection" can be important. For example,

```csharp
using System;

class A
{
  ~A()
  {
    Console.WriteLine("Finalize instance of A");
  }
  public void F()
  {
    Console.WriteLine("A.F");
    Test.RefA = this;
  }
}
```

```
class B
{
  public A Ref;
  ~B()
  {
    Console.WriteLine("Finalize instance of B");
    Ref.F();
  }
}

class Test
{
  public static A RefA;
  public static B RefB;
  static void Main()
  {
    RefB = new B();
    RefA = new A();
    RefB.Ref = RefA;
    RefB = null;
    RefA = null;

    // A and B now eligible for finalization
    GC.Collect();
    GC.WaitForPendingFinalizers();
    // B now eligible for collection, but A is not
    if (RefA != null)
      Console.WriteLine("RefA is not null");
  }
}
```

In the above program, if the garbage collector chooses to run the finalizer of A before the finalizer of B, then the output of this program might be:

```
Finalize instance of A
Finalize instance of B
A.F
RefA is not null
```

Note that although the instance of A was not in use and A's finalizer was run, it is still possible for methods of A (in this case, F) to be called from another finalizer. Also, note that running of a finalizer might cause an object to become usable from the mainline program again. In this case, the running of B's finalizer caused an instance of A that was previously not in use, to become accessible from the live reference RefA. After the call to WaitForPendingFinalizers, the instance of B is eligible for collection, but the instance of A is not, because of the reference RefA.

To avoid confusion and unexpected behavior, it is generally a good idea for finalizers to perform cleanup only on data stored in their object's own fields, and not to perform any actions on referenced objects or static fields. *end example*]

10.10 Execution order

Execution shall proceed such that the side effects of each executing thread are preserved at critical execution points. A **side effect** is defined as a read or write of a volatile field, a write to a non-volatile variable, a write to an external resource, and the throwing of an exception. The critical execution points at which the order of these side effects shall be preserved are references to volatile fields (§17.4.3), `lock` statements (§15.12), and thread creation and termination. An implementation is free to change the order of execution of a C# program, subject to the following constraints:

- Data dependence is preserved within a thread of execution. That is, the value of each variable is computed as if all statements in the thread were executed in original program order.
- Initialization ordering rules are preserved (§17.4.4, §17.4.5).
- The ordering of side effects is preserved with respect to volatile reads and writes (§17.4.3). Additionally, an implementation need not evaluate part of an expression if it can deduce that that expression's value is not used and that no needed side effects are produced (including any caused by calling a method or accessing a volatile field). When program execution is interrupted by an asynchronous event (such as an exception thrown by another thread), it is not guaranteed that the observable side effects are visible in the original program order.

Synchronous order, asynchronous chaos

The preceding statements allow the execution order to be rearranged, or even parts of the code never to be executed, provided that there is no observable change from doing so, with the single exception that an asynchronous event might make such alterations visible. The exception `ThreadAbortException` (see annotation in §10.1) thrown by another thread is an asynchronous event. Consider the following code fragment:

```
int a, b, c;
...
a = b = c = 0;
try
{
   a = 3;
   b = 4;
   c = 5;
}
catch (ThreadAbortException)
{
   // Possible that a = 3 and c = 5 but b = 0
   // or any other permutation
   ...
}
```

Here if execution ends up in the `catch` block *any* permutation of the assignments may have been executed. However, consider the similar fragment:

```
try
{
   Console.WriteLine('a');
   Console.WriteLine('b');
   Console.WriteLine('c');
}
```

```
catch (ThreadAbortException)
{
  // What output might have occurred?
  ...
}
```

In this case the output will be nothing, "a", "ab", or "abc"—the three calls cannot be executed in any order. Any method call may alter the state of an object, and the first bullet in the list before this annotation requires that data dependencies are preserved.

11 Types

The types of the C# language are divided into three main categories: Value types, reference types, and type-parameter types.

> *type:*
> > *value-type*
> > *reference-type*
> > *type-parameter*

Type parameters are part of generics, and are discussed in §25.1.1. A fourth category of types, pointers, is available only in unsafe code. This is discussed further in §27.2.

Value types differ from reference types in that variables of the value types directly contain their data, whereas variables of the reference types store **references** to their data, the latter being known as **objects**. With reference types, it is possible for two variables to reference the same object, and thus possible for operations on one variable to affect the object referenced by the other variable. With value types, the variables each have their own copy of the data, and it is not possible for operations on one to affect the other. [*Note*: When a variable is a `ref` or `out` parameter, it does not have its own storage but references the storage of another variable. In this case, the `ref` or `out` variable is effectively an alias for another variable and not a distinct variable. *end note*]

Shallow copying of value types

Instances of value types are copied using a bitwise (shallow) copy. Therefore, if a value type contains a variable whose type is a reference type, then after copying an instance, both copies refer to the same object. Modifications to that object would then be visible through both copies.

Jon Skeet

C#'s type system is unified such that *a value of any type can be treated as an object*. Every type in C# directly or indirectly derives from the `object` class type, and `object` is the ultimate base class of all types. Values of reference types are treated as objects simply by viewing the values as type `object`. Values of value types are treated as objects by performing boxing and unboxing operations (§11.3).

Uniformity and hidden costs

C#'s type system is based upon that of the CLI[†], which also has a "unified" type system. However, the unification in the CLI type system only goes so far; while a value type *V* is derived from `System.ValueType`, or more precisely from an anonymous reference type "*boxed V*," which in turn derives from `System.ValueType`, an instance of *V* is **not** convertible to a value of type `System.ValueType`. As described previously, the value must first be boxed to produce a value of anonymous type "*boxed V*," which can then be converted to `System.ValueType`. The boxing operation in the CLI is explicit, resulting in the lack of uniformity in its type system.

C# makes the boxing operation implicit, producing a more unified type system. However, in some cases it was decided implicit representation changes were not appropriate, so the system is still not fully unified. The following code demonstrates this:

```
class A{}      //A derives from object    struct C{}
class B : A{}  // B derives from A                  // C derives from <boxed C>
B b_inst = new B();                                 // & <boxed C> derives from
A a_inst = b_inst;                                  // ValueType implicitly
              // b_inst & a_inst         C c_inst = new C();
              // refer to same object    ValueType vt_inst = c_inst;
                                                    // instance of <boxed C>
                                                    // created which contains
B[] b_arr = new B[1];                               // a *copy* of c_inst
A[] a_arr = b_arr;
              // b_arr & a_arr           C[] c_arr = new C[1];
              // refer to same object        // ValueType[] vt_arr = c_arr;
                                                    // invalid...
```

In a fully unified system both the left and right code fragments would compile; B derives from A, which derives from object, and C derives from *boxed C*, which derives from ValueType. However, in C# array assignments the two behave differently. Also, when both value and reference types are involved, there is a hidden representation conversion, which is not free.

Recommendations:

- When mixing value and reference types keep the cost of the hidden representation changes in mind.
- When possible avoid passing values as objects. Many of the cases can be replaced by the use of generics, which can often avoid the representation changes.

[†*Note: This does not imply a dependency between C# and the CLI anymore than stating Ada's type system is derived from Pascal's makes Ada dependent on Pascal.*]

11.1 Value types

A value type is either a struct type or an enumeration type. C# provides a set of predefined struct types called the ***simple types***. The simple types are identified through reserved words.

> *value-type:*
>   *struct-type*
>   *enum-type*
>
> *struct-type:*
>   *type-name*
>   *simple-type*
>   *nullable-type*
>
> *simple-type:*
>   *numeric-type*
>   bool
>
> *numeric-type:*
>   *integral-type*
>   *floating-point-type*
>   decimal

integral-type:
  sbyte
  byte
  short
  ushort
  int
  uint
  long
  ulong
  char

floating-point-type:
  float
  double

enum-type:
  type-name

nullable-type:
  non-nullable-value-type   ?

non-nullable-value-type:
  enum-type
  type-name
  simple-type

All value types implicitly inherit from class `object`. It is not possible for any type to derive from a value type, and value types are thus implicitly sealed (§17.1.1.2).

The immediate base class of value types

All value types derive *indirectly* from `object`. Enumeration types derive from `System.Enum`, which derives from `System.ValueType`. All other value types derive from `System.ValueType`.

Jon Skeet

A variable of a value type always contains a value of that type. Unlike reference types, it is not possible for a value of a value type to be `null`, or to reference an object of a more derived type.

Assignment to a variable of a value type creates a *copy* of the value being assigned. This differs from assignment to a variable of a reference type, which copies the reference but not the object identified by the reference.

11.1.1 The System.ValueType type

All value types implicitly inherit from the class `System.ValueType`, which, in turn, inherits from class `object`.

Note that `System.ValueType` is not itself a *value-type*. Rather, it is a *class-type* from which all *value-type*s are automatically derived.

11.1.2 Default constructors

All value types implicitly declare a public parameterless instance constructor called the ***default constructor***. The default constructor returns a zero-initialized instance known as the ***default value*** for the value type:

- For all *simple-types*, the default value is the value produced by a bit pattern of all zeros:
  - For sbyte, byte, short, ushort, int, uint, long, and ulong, the default value is 0.
  - For char, the default value is '\x0000'.
  - For float, the default value is 0.0f.
  - For double, the default value is 0.0d.
  - For decimal, the default value is 0m.
  - For bool, the default value is false.
- For an *enum-type* E, the default value is 0.
- For a *struct-type*, the default value is the value produced by setting all value type fields to their default value and all reference type fields to null.
- For a nullable type, the default value is one for which HasValue returns false.

Like any other instance constructor, the default constructor of a value type is invoked using the new operator. [*Note*: For efficiency reasons, this requirement is not intended to actually have the implementation generate a constructor call. For value types, the default value expression (§14.5.14) produces the same result as using the default constructor. *end note*] [*Example*: In the code below, variables i, j and k are all initialized to zero.

```
class A
{
  void F()
  {
    int i = 0;
    int j = new int();
    int k = default(int);
  }
}
```

end example]

Because every value type implicitly has a public parameterless instance constructor, it is not possible for a struct type to contain an explicit declaration of a parameterless constructor. A struct type is however permitted to declare parameterized instance constructors (§18.3.8).

11.1.3 Struct types

A struct type is a value type that can declare constants, fields, methods, properties, indexers, operators, instance constructors, static constructors, and nested types. Struct types are described in §18.

11.1.4 Simple types

C# provides a set of predefined struct types called the simple types. The simple types are identified through reserved words, but these reserved words are simply aliases for predefined struct types in the System namespace, as described in the table below.

Reserved word	Aliased type
sbyte	System.SByte
byte	System.Byte

short	System.Int16
ushort	System.UInt16
int	System.Int32
uint	System.UInt32
long	System.Int64
ulong	System.UInt64
char	System.Char
float	System.Single
double	System.Double
bool	System.Boolean
decimal	System.Decimal

Because a simple type aliases a struct type, every simple type has members. [*Example*: int has the members declared in System.Int32 and the members inherited from System.Object, and the following statements are permitted:

```
int i = int.MaxValue;       // System.Int32.MaxValue constant
string s = i.ToString();    // System.Int32.ToString() instance method
string t = 123.ToString();  // System.Int32.ToString() instance method
```

end example] The simple types differ from other struct types in that they permit certain additional operations:

- Most simple types permit values to be created by writing *literals* (§9.4.4). [*Example*: 123 is a literal of type int and 'a' is a literal of type char. *end example*] C# makes no provision for literals of struct types in general.
- When the operands of an expression are all simple type constants, the compiler evaluates the expression at compile-time. Such an expression is known as a *constant-expression* (§14.16). Expressions involving operators defined by other struct types are not considered constant expressions.
- Through const declarations, it is possible to declare constants of the simple types (§17.3). It is not possible to have constants of other struct types, but a similar effect is provided by static readonly fields.
- Conversions involving simple types can participate in evaluation of conversion operators defined by other struct types, but a user-defined conversion operator can never participate in evaluation of another user-defined conversion operator (§13.4.2).

Use the keywords!

Some writers have suggested that you should write C# with a bias towards the CLI Standard Library it probably rests upon (e.g., that you write Int32 rather than int, String rather than string, Object rather than object, etc.). This is not considered good style. If you are writing C# then write C#! Use the keywords! This is consistent, keywords are usually color highlighted, and avoids needless subtle uppercase–lowercase differences.

```
using System;

public delegate Int32 DontWriteThis(String s);
public delegate int DoWriteThis(string s);
```

Keywords not allowed!

Very occasionally, you cannot use a keyword:

- In a using alias:

```
using Integer = System.Int32; // ok
using Integer = int;          // compile-time error
```

- In a string during reflection:

```
Type t1 = Type.GetType("System.Int32"); // ok
Type t2 = Type.GetType("int");          // runtime failure
```

Do not use the keywords

While it makes sense to use the C# keywords when writing code, it may sometimes be better to use the CLI Standard Library names when naming publicly available members. Consider `Convert.ToSingle`, for example; if that were `Convert.ToFloat`, it might be confusing to users of other languages that may not use "float" as a keyword (or may even use it for the `Double` type).

The underlying library names (rather than the keywords) can also usefully document required type sizes in interop method signatures:

```
public unsafe extern static void Process(Int32 length, Int32 * array);
```

Jon Skeet

11.1.5 Integral types

C# supports nine integral types: `sbyte`, `byte`, `short`, `ushort`, `int`, `uint`, `long`, `ulong`, and `char`. The integral types have the following sizes and ranges of values:

- The `sbyte` type represents signed 8-bit integers with values from –128 to 127, inclusive.
- The `byte` type represents unsigned 8-bit integers with values from 0 to 255, inclusive.
- The `short` type represents signed 16-bit integers with values from –32768 to 32767, inclusive.
- The `ushort` type represents unsigned 16-bit integers with values from 0 to 65535, inclusive.
- The `int` type represents signed 32-bit integers with values from –2147483648 to 2147483647, inclusive.
- The `uint` type represents unsigned 32-bit integers with values from 0 to 4294967295, inclusive.
- The `long` type represents signed 64-bit integers with values from –9223372036854775808 to 9223372036854775807, inclusive.
- The `ulong` type represents unsigned 64-bit integers with values from 0 to 18446744073709551615, inclusive.
- The `char` type represents unsigned 16-bit integers with values from 0 to 65535, inclusive. The set of possible values for the `char` type corresponds to the Unicode character set. [*Note*: Although `char` has the same representation as `ushort`, not all operations permitted on one type are permitted on the other. *end note*]

The integral-type unary and binary operators always operate with signed 32-bit precision, unsigned 32-bit precision, signed 64-bit precision, or unsigned 64-bit precision, as detailed in clause §14.

The `char` type is classified as an integral type, but it differs from the other integral types in two ways:

- There are no implicit conversions from other types to the `char` type. In particular, even though the `sbyte`, `byte`, and `ushort` types have ranges of values that are fully representable using the `char` type, implicit conversions from `sbyte`, `byte`, or `ushort` to `char` do not exist.
- Constants of the `char` type shall be written as *character-literals* or as *integer-literals* in combination with a cast to type `char`. [*Example*: `(char)10` is the same as `'\x000A'`. *end example*]

The `checked` and `unchecked` operators and statements are used to control overflow checking for integral-type arithmetic operations and conversions (§14.5.13). In a `checked` context, an overflow produces a compile-time error or causes a `System.OverflowException` to be thrown. In an `unchecked` context, overflows are ignored and any high-order bits that do not fit in the destination type are discarded.

---

byte/sbyte naming oddity

In C#, the 16-bit, 32-bit, and 64-bit signed integral types are named short, int, and long, while the corresponding unsigned integral types are named ushort, uint, and ulong—that is, with a leading u. However, the signed 8-bit integral type is called sbyte, and the unsigned 8-bit integral type is called byte. This appears to be strangely inconsistent. Why are the signed and unsigned 8-bit integral types not named byte and ubyte, respectively? The reason for this inconsistency is that both the common English usage of the word "byte" and the most common and useful usage when writing programs are as an unsigned 8-bit integer. For example, consider the task of reading two bytes from a stream (most significant byte first), and combining them to form an unsigned 16-bit number. If byte is unsigned, the code is straightforward:

```
byte b1 = reader.ReadByte();
byte b2 = reader.ReadByte();
int result = (b1 << 8) + b2;
```

If byte is signed, the code is much more confusing:

```
byte b1 = reader.ReadByte();
byte b2 = reader.ReadByte();
int result = ((b1 & 0xFF) << 8) + (b2 & 0xFF);
```

Experience with programming languages having no unsigned byte type showed that a very common programming error when dealing with bytes was forgetting the "& 0xFF" in situations like the preceding one leading to obscure bugs. Thus, it was felt that using the common word "byte" for an unsigned 8-bit integer would be most familiar to programmers, would be most useful in practice, and would lead to fewer programming errors. Using the common word for uncommon usage would simply be irritating and error prone. The designers felt that these considerations considerably outweighed the argument for consistency. This left the somewhat unfortunate word "sbyte" as the best available name for a signed 8-bit integer.

11.1.6 Floating point types

C# supports two floating-point types: `float` and `double`. The `float` and `double` types are represented using the 32-bit single-precision and 64-bit double-precision IEC 60559 formats, which provide the following sets of values:

- Positive zero and negative zero. In most situations, positive zero and negative zero behave identically as the simple value zero, but certain operations distinguish between the two (§14.7).

> **Two's company, three's a crowd**
>
> There are only two zeros in a floating-point type: positive zero (+0) and negative zero (−0). The "simple value zero" (0) is the same zero as positive zero.

- Positive infinity and negative infinity. Infinities are produced by such operations as dividing a non-zero number by zero. [*Example*: `1.0 / 0.0` yields positive infinity, and `-1.0 / 0.0` yields negative infinity. *end example*]
- The *Not-a-Number* value, often abbreviated NaN. NaNs are produced by invalid floating-point operations, such as dividing zero by zero.
- The finite set of non-zero values of the form $s \times m \times 2^e$, where s is 1 or −1, and m and e are determined by the particular floating-point type: For `float`, $0 < m < 2^{24}$ and $-149 \leq e \leq 104$, and for `double`, $0 < m < 2^{53}$ and $-1075 \leq e \leq 970$. Denormalized floating-point numbers are considered valid non-zero values. C# neither requires nor forbids that a conforming implementation support denormalized floating-point numbers.

The `float` type can represent values ranging from approximately 1.5×10^{-45} to 3.4×10^{38} with a precision of 7 digits.

The `double` type can represent values ranging from approximately 5.0×10^{-324} to 1.7×10^{308} with a precision of 15–16 digits.

> **The other floating point type**
>
> The distinction between the "floating-point" types, `float` and `double`, and the `decimal` type is somewhat arbitrary. Technically, the former are binary floating-point types and the latter is a decimal floating-point type. However, the differences in base, range, and precision do have some consequences; see §11.1.7.

The floating-point operators, including the assignment operators, never produce exceptions. Instead, in exceptional situations, floating-point operations produce zero, infinity, or NaN, as described below:

- The result of a floating-point operation is rounded to the nearest representable value in the destination format. This may cause a non-zero value to be rounded to zero.
- If the magnitude of the result of a floating-point operation is too large for the destination format, the result of the operation becomes positive infinity or negative infinity.
- If a floating-point operation is invalid, the result of the operation becomes NaN.
- If one or both operands of a floating-point operation is NaN, the result of the operation becomes NaN.

Floating-point operations can be performed with higher precision than the result type of the operation. [*Example*: Some hardware architectures support an "extended" or "long double" floating-point type with greater range and precision than the `double` type, and implicitly perform all floating-point operations using this higher precision type. Only at excessive cost in performance can such hardware architectures be made to perform floating-point operations with *less* precision, and rather than require an implementation to forfeit both performance and precision, C# allows a higher precision type to be used for all floating-point operations. Other than delivering more precise results, this rarely has any measurable effects. However, in expressions of the form `x * y / z`, where the multiplication produces a result that is outside the `double` range, but the subsequent division brings the temporary result back into the `double` range, the fact that the expression is evaluated in a higher range format can cause a finite result to be produced instead of an infinity. *end example*]

Rarity is relative

The use of higher precision can cause odd results in some situations. For instance, consider the following class:

```
class Precision
{
  float member;

  float f1 = 2.82323f;
  float f2 = 2.3f;

  float Calc()
  {
    return f1 * f2;
  }

  void FloatTest()
  {
    member = Calc();
    float local = Calc();
    Console.WriteLine(local == member);
    Console.WriteLine(Calc() == member);
    Console.WriteLine((f1 * f2) == member);
  }
}
```

Using the current Microsoft and Mono compilers and runtimes on a Pentium III, the method `FloatTest()` outputs `True`, `True`, and `False`; while the same Microsoft compiler and runtime on a Pentium M machine outputs `False`, `False`, and `False`. The `False` results are due to the compilers using register-based operations for some calculations, which have higher precision than values stored and retrieved from `float` variables. Such higher precision operations are provided by a number of architectures, including the Intel x86 used in these tests. However, different compilers, running on the same or different architectures, may produce different output.

This is one reason to prefer "fuzzy" comparisons (i.e., checking whether a variable's value is within a range, rather than whether it has a particular exact value) when dealing with floating-point data.

11.1.7 The decimal type

The decimal type is a 128-bit data type suitable for financial and monetary calculations. The decimal type can represent values including those in the range 1×10^{-28} through 1×10^{28} with at least 28 significant digits.

The finite set of values of type decimal are of the form $(-1)^s \times c \times 10^{-e}$, where the sign s is 0 or 1, the coefficient c is given by $0 \le c < Cmax$, and the scale e is such that $Emin \le e \le Emax$, where $Cmax$ is at least 1×10^{28}, $Emin \le 0$, and $Emax \ge 28$. The decimal type does not necessarily support signed zeros, infinities, or NaN's.

A decimal is represented as an integer scaled by a power of ten. For decimals with an absolute value less than 1.0m, the value is exact to at least the 28th decimal place. For decimals with an absolute value greater than or equal to 1.0m, the value is exact to at least 28 digits. Contrary to the float and double data types, decimal fractional numbers such as 0.1 can be represented exactly in the decimal representation. In the float and double representations, such numbers often have non-terminating binary expansions, making those representations more prone to round-off errors.

The result of an operation on values of type decimal is that which would result from calculating an exact result (preserving scale, as defined for each operator) and then rounding to fit the representation. Results are rounded to the nearest representable value, and, when a result is equally close to two representable values, to the value that has an even number in the least significant digit position (this is known as "banker's rounding"). That is, results are exact to at least the 28th decimal place. Note that rounding may produce a zero value from a non-zero value.

If a decimal arithmetic operation produces a result whose magnitude is too large for the decimal format, a System.OverflowException is thrown.

The decimal type has greater precision but may have a smaller range than the floating-point types. Thus, conversions from the floating-point types to decimal might produce overflow exceptions, and conversions from decimal to the floating-point types might cause loss of precision or overflow exceptions. For these reasons, no implicit conversions exist between the floating-point types and decimal, and without explicit casts, a compile-time error occurs when floating-point and decimal operands are directly mixed in the same expression.

IEEE decimal

The CLI committee spent some time discussing whether it should adopt the proposed IEEE 754r 128-bit decimal floating point for the decimal type. IEEE Decimal provides 34 decimal digits of precision and an exponent range from 10^{-6143} to 10^{6144}, which is far greater than that specified in C# 1.0 while using the same number of bits. Adopting IEEE Decimal would also make decimal a superset of double (which is already a superset of float). If C# adopted IEEE Decimal, it would provide benefits to conversions (§13.1.2, §13.2.1) and constant expressions (§14.16).

However, it was decided for the benefit of existing implementations and those with stored decimal data that the specification would be changed to *allow* but *not require* the use of IEEE Decimal. The C# committee decided to adopt the same approach.

Using IEEE decimal in C#: supporting legacy data

It has been determined that a C# implementation using IEEE Decimal could store the IEEE format in a way that would allow existing CLI/C# 1.0 decimal data to be detected when reading binary data from files, and hence be autoconverted to the IEEE Decimal format. This is possible because the 1.0 decimal format lays out its decimal data in the 128 bits thus:

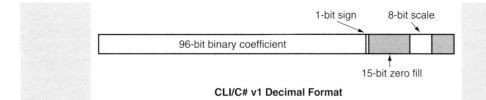

CLI/C# v1 Decimal Format

where there are 15 bits in the fourth word that are always 0. The IEEE decimal encoding uses a compression scheme called *Densely Packed Decimal*, which stores three digits in each group of 10 bits in the significand, and in each of those groups a sequence of all ones never occurs:

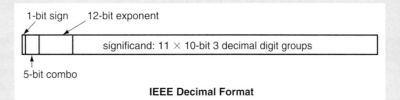

IEEE Decimal Format

One of those groups, fortuitously, falls wholly within the 15-bit all-zeros field on the CLI 1.0 decimal format, so if the IEEE format is stored with all bits inverted (a simple and efficient modification), it can never have all zeros in the relevant 10 bits and can therefore always be distinguished from 1.0 data:

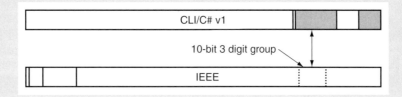

For full details of IEEE Decimal format, see: http://www2.hursley.ibm.com/decimal/.

Mike Cowlishaw

11.1.8 The bool type

The `bool` type represents Boolean logical quantities. The possible values of type `bool` are `true` and `false`.

No standard conversions exist between `bool` and other types. In particular, the `bool` type is distinct and separate from the integral types, and a `bool` value cannot be used in place of an integral value, and vice versa.

[*Note*: In the C and C++ languages, a zero integral or floating-point value, or a null pointer can be converted to the Boolean value `false`, and a non-zero integral or floating-point value, or a non-null pointer can be converted to the Boolean value `true`. In C#, such conversions are accomplished by explicitly comparing an integral or floating-point value to zero, or by explicitly comparing an object reference to `null`. *end note*]

Strong Booleans

As stated earlier there are no implicit conversions between Booleans and other types; this is a Good Thing™ for many reasons; one of them is that mistakes such as writing "=" instead of "==" in `if (x=y) {...}` are caught by the type system when `x` and `y` are not Booleans. C# follows Java in this.

11.1.9 Enumeration types

An enumeration type is a distinct type with named constants. Every enumeration type has an underlying type, which shall be `byte`, `sbyte`, `short`, `ushort`, `int`, `uint`, `long` or `ulong`. Enumeration types are defined through enumeration declarations (§21.1). The direct base type of every enumeration type is the class `System.Enum`. The direct base class of `System.Enum` is `System.ValueType`.

Weak enums: distinct but similar

Enumerations in C# are distinct types but not strong ones; the boundary between an enumeration type and its underlying type is blurry. This is covered in detail in §21, its subclauses, and annotations.

11.2 Reference types

A reference type is a class type, an interface type, an array type, or a delegate type.

reference-type:
  class-type
  interface-type
  array-type
  delegate-type

class-type:
  type-name
  object
  string

interface-type:
  type-name

array-type:
  non-array-type   rank-specifiers

non-array-type:
  value-type
  class-type
  interface-type
  delegate-type
  type-parameter

rank-specifiers:
  rank-specifier
  rank-specifiers   rank-specifier

rank-specifier:
   [*dim-separators$_{opt}$*]

dim-separators:
  ,
  dim-separators ,

delegate-type:
  type-name

A reference type value is a reference to an ***instance*** of the type, the latter known as an ***object***. The special value `null` is compatible with all reference types and indicates the absence of an instance.

Objects vs. values

The C# specification tries to be consistent in naming instances of reference types as *objects* and instances of value types as *values*.

11.2.1 Class types

A class type defines a data structure that contains data members (constants and fields), function members (methods, properties, events, indexers, operators, instance constructors, finalizers, and static constructors), and nested types. Class types support inheritance, a mechanism whereby derived classes can extend and specialize base classes. Instances of class types are created using *object-creation-expression*s (§14.5.10.1).

Class types are described in §17.

11.2.2 The object type

The `object` class type is the ultimate base class of all other types. Every type in C# directly or indirectly derives from the `object` class type.

The keyword `object` is simply an alias for the predefined class `System.Object`.

11.2.3 The string type

The `string` type is a sealed class type that inherits directly from `object`. Instances of the `string` class represent Unicode character strings.

Values of the `string` type can be written as string literals (§9.4.4).

The keyword `string` is simply an alias for the predefined class `System.String`.

Strings are immutable

Though never explicitly highlighted in the Standard, instances of the `string` type are immutable in C#. This comes from the C# Standard library (Annex D) being based on the CLI Standard Library and including the definitions of the latter's types, by reference, from the CLI Standard.

In C# terms this means that string instances are value-like (so a string object once created never changes its value) yet have reference semantics, so strings are copied by reference not by value. String instances should never be compared using *identity* but by using *equality* (§14.9). Indeed, different string references with the same value may refer to the same string object even when this is not immediately obvious (§9.4.4.5), thus making identity testing more or less meaningless.

Insecure strings

For security critical applications it is sometimes recommended that strings not be used to store sensitive information, such as passwords:

- String values may be discoverable in plain text within the application image. For example, if your process is swapped out, the swap file may be accessible and contain the plain text of string values, depending on the host operating system.
- The preceding issue may be compounded by these factors:
  - Strings are reference types. The garbage collector can relocate (unpinned) strings, thus copying the sensitive information to several memory locations.
  - Strings are immutable. You can update a string variable to refer to an empty string, but thanks to garbage collection, the old string value will remain in memory for an arbitrary period of time.

There is no standardized secure string alternative in C# (or the CLI) but your platform may provide one. For example, Microsoft's CLR and Novell's Mono both have a `SecureString` class (in the `System.Security` namespace), but, depending on use, one of its constructors may be insecure.

11.2.4 Interface types

An interface defines a contract. A class or struct that implements an interface shall adhere to its contract. An interface can inherit from multiple base interfaces, and a class or struct can implement multiple interfaces.

Interface types are described in §20.

Interface inheritance is not class inheritance

The word "inheritance" means something different for interfaces than for classes; it means that the interface requires that its "base" interfaces be implemented. This is covered in an annotation on §20.1.2.

11.2.5 Array types

An array is a data structure that contains zero or more variables which are accessed through computed indices. The variables contained in an array, also called the elements of the array, are all of the same type, and this type is called the element type of the array.

Array types are described in §19.

11.2.6 Delegate types

A delegate is a data structure that refers to one or more methods, and for instance methods, it also refers to their corresponding object instances.

[*Note*: The closest equivalent of a delegate in C or C++ is a function pointer, but whereas a function pointer can only reference static functions, a delegate can reference both static and instance methods. In the latter case, the delegate stores not only a reference to the method's entry point, but also a reference to the object instance on which to invoke the method. *end note*]

Delegate types are described in §22.

11.2.7 The null type

The null literal (§9.4.4.6) evaluates to the ***null value***, which is used to denote a reference not pointing at any object or array, or the absence of a value. The ***null type*** has a single value, which is the null value. Hence an expression whose type is the null type can evaluate only to the null value. There is no way to explicitly write the null type and, therefore, no way to use it in a declared type.

Moreover, the null type can never be the type inferred for a type parameter (§25.6.4).

> **Pseudo-type**
>
> The ***null type*** is a pseudo-type introduced in the Standard so that the use of the ***null value*** can be described in an orthogonal way.
>
> For example: conversions (§13) are defined between *types*. When defining implicit reference conversions (§13.1.4) assignment of the null literal is covered by including a case from the ***null type*** to any reference type. All the other cases are similarly defined with respect to types and not values.

11.3 Boxing and unboxing

The concept of boxing and unboxing is central to C#'s type system. It provides a bridge between *value-type*s and *reference-type*s by permitting any value of a *value-type* to be converted to and from type `object`. Boxing and unboxing enables a unified view of the type system wherein a value of any type can ultimately be treated as an object.

> **Can you tell whether a struct instance is boxed?**
>
> The answer to this question is no. You cannot determine, in a simple, platform-neutral, bullet-proof way, whether a struct instance is boxed or not. However, there is a way that gets close on both the Microsoft and Mono runtimes at the time of writing (and will probably continue to work), but it is not bulletproof.
>
> Using unsafe code, you can take the address of the struct instance and compare the address to an address known to be on the stack and to an address known to be on the heap. If the address is nearer to the known stack address than to the known heap address, then it might be assumed to be on the stack; if the address is nearer to the known heap address, then it might assumed to be on the heap. Here is a utility class for performing the address comparisons:
>
> ```
> public unsafe static class Address
> {
>   public static bool IsOnHeap(ref int field)
>   {
>     return HeapDiff(ref field) < StackDiff(ref field);
>   }
>
>   public static bool IsOnStack(ref int field)
>   {
>     return StackDiff(ref field) < HeapDiff(ref field);
>   }
>
>   private static long StackDiff(ref int field)
>   {
>     return System.Math.Abs(Address.Of(ref field) - Address.OnStack());
>   }
> ```

```
    private static long HeapDiff(ref int field)
    {
       return System.Math.Abs(Address.Of(ref field) - Address.OnHeap());
    }

    private static int * Of(ref int field)
    {
       fixed(int * ptr = &field)
       {
          return ptr;
       }
    }

    private static int * OnStack()
    {
       return new S().YourAddress();
    }

    private static int * OnHeap()
    {
       return obj.YourAddress();
    }

    private interface IAddressable
    {
       int * YourAddress();
    }

    private struct S : IAddressable
    {
       public int * YourAddress()
       {
          return Address.Of(ref field);
       }

       private int field;
    }

    private static readonly IAddressable obj = new S();
}
```

And here is an example of it in action:

```
class App
{
   static void Main()
   {
      Eg v = new Eg();
      System.Console.WriteLine(v.IsBoxed()); // false

      Eg copy = v;
      System.Console.WriteLine(copy.IsBoxed()); // false

      IBoxable i = copy;
      System.Console.WriteLine(i.IsBoxed()); // true
```

```
      System.Console.WriteLine(Eg.StaticValue.IsBoxed()); // true
  }
}

struct Eg : IBoxable
{
   public static Eg StaticValue = new Eg();

   public bool IsBoxed()
   {
      return Address.IsOnHeap(ref field);
   }

   private int field;
}

interface IBoxable
{
  bool IsBoxed();
}
```

To re-emphasize: This is *not* guaranteed to always work:

- If memory were getting really tight, then you might get incorrect results since the "top" of the heap could get very close to the "bottom" of the stack.
- A nonboxed struct might not be allocated on the stack; it could be in the heap, in thread-local storage, or even in some other kind of storage (see the annotation on §18).
- In a multithreaded application there are multiple stacks, and these could be with the same region of memory as heap structures.

This code was developed for informal tests, and is intended to be used solely for such. For example, it can be used to indicate that boxing is avoided, as when passing a struct to a generic method whose parameter type is constrained to be a value type realizing a given interface.

We offer a bar of Toblerone® to the first person producing a platform-neutral, bulletproof version.

11.3.1 Boxing conversions

A boxing conversion permits any *non-nullable-value-type* to be implicitly converted to `object` or `System.ValueType` or to any *interface-type* implemented by the *non-nullable-value-type*. Furthermore, there is an implicit boxing conversion from any enumeration type to `System.Enum`. Boxing a value of a *non-nullable-value-type* consists of allocating an object instance and copying the *value-type* value into that instance. A boxing conversion is also permitted on a *nullable-type*. A nullable type `T?` has boxing conversions to the same set of types as `T`. A boxing conversion from a nullable type `T?` is processed as follows:

- If the source value is null (`HasValue` property is false), the result is a null reference of the target type.
- Otherwise, the result is a reference to a boxed `T` produced by unwrapping and boxing the source value.

[*Note*: As a consequence of this, if v is a value of a nullable type and vb is the result of boxing v, then the four expressions `vb==null`, `v==null`, `null==vb`, and `null==v` produce the same result.

The actual process of boxing a value of a *value-type* is best explained by imagining the existence of a **boxing class** for that type. For example, for any *value-type* T, the boxing class behaves as if it were declared as follows:

```
sealed class T_Box
{
  T value;

  public T_Box(T t)
  {
    value = t;
  }
}
```

Boxing of a value v of type T now consists of executing the expression `new T_Box(v)`, and returning the resulting instance as a value of type `object`. Thus, the statements

```
int i = 123;
object box = i;
```

conceptually correspond to

```
int i = 123;
object box = new int_Box(i);
```

Boxing classes like `T_Box` and `int_Box` above don't actually exist and the dynamic type of a boxed value isn't actually a class type. Instead, a boxed value of type T has the dynamic type T, and a dynamic type check using the `is` operator can simply reference type T. For example,

```
int i = 123;
object box = i;
if (box is int)
{
  Console.Write("Box contains an int");
}
```

will output the string "`Box contains an int`" on the console.

White lies and diaphanous types

As explained in an annotation on §11, the C# type system is based on that of the CLI, but the two systems are not identical. The CLI has *anonymous* box types and explicit (un)boxing. C# has implicit (un)boxing, and now this clause introduces diaphanous box types and a few white lies.

To explain (un)boxing, this clause introduces a type `T_Box`, which is a reference type, but then states it does not really exist—even anonymously.

Now a boxed value type is a reference type and derives from `System.ValueType`, yet apparently it is not a class type…. What then is it? Apparently it is a value type, but that cannot be true as it is definitely an object…. Confused?

What this clause is really saying is that every value type in C# also has a reference type form termed a *boxed value type*, but the type testing operator `is` does *not* distinguish between the two forms; in C# they are defined to be of the same type. This is the only case in C# where one type can exist in two different representations.

The context often allows one to determine the current form of a value type. For example:

```
struct V { ...}

V aValue = new V();              // aValue is a value type
System.ValueType aRef = aValue;  // aValue is boxed, aRef contains a
                                 // reference to the box object
                           // dynamic type is a sub-type of ValueType
```

However, there are cases where determining the form is nontrivial. For example:

```
struct V
{
  int x;

  public void InstanceMethod()
  {
    this.x = 42;  // "this" could refer to the value
                  // or reference form of V
  }
}
```

Unfortunately, there is a least one case in C#, the invocation of a method on a boxed value type (§14.4.3.1), where these diaphanous types do impact the semantics of the operation and the result may be surprising.

The design of C# would be more orthogonal if the boxed forms of value types were distinguishable and had proper names (say, System.Boxed<T>), but such a design would be difficult (or impossible) to implement on the CLI—which is a key platform for C#. Just like FORTRAN and C before it, the design of C# has been influenced by its target platform, and not necessarily for the better.

A boxing conversion implies *making a copy* of the value being boxed. This is different from a conversion of a *reference-type* to type object, in which the value continues to reference the same instance and simply is regarded as the less derived type object. For example, given the declaration

```
struct Point
{
  public int x, y;

  public Point(int x, int y)
  {
    this.x = x;
    this.y = y;
  }
}
```

the following statements

```
Point p = new Point(10, 10);
object box = p;
p.x = 20;
Console.Write(((Point)box).x);
```

will output the value 10 on the console because the implicit boxing operation that occurs in the assignment of p to box causes the value of p to be copied. Had Point been declared a class instead, the value 20 would be output because p and box would reference the same instance. *end note*]

11.3.2 Unboxing conversions

An unboxing conversion permits an explicit conversion from object or System.ValueType to any *non-nullable-value-type* or from any *interface-type* to any *non-nullable-value-type* that implements the *interface-type*. Furthermore, there is an explicit unboxing conversion from System.Enum to any enumeration type. An unboxing operation consists of first checking that the object instance is a boxed value of the given *value-type*, and then copying the value out of the instance.

A nullable-type T? has unboxing conversions from the same set of types as T. An unboxing conversion permits an explicit conversion from object or System.ValueType to any *nullable-type* or from any *interface-type* to any *nullable-type* whose underlying type implements the *interface-type*. Furthermore, there is an explicit unboxing conversion from System.Enum to any *nullable-type* whose underlying type is an enumeration type. An unboxing conversion to a nullable-type T? is processed as follows:

- If the source is a null reference, the result is a null value of type T?.
- If the source is a reference to a boxed T, the result is a T? produced by unboxing and wrapping the source.
- Otherwise, a System.InvalidCastException is thrown.

Referring to the imaginary boxing class described in the previous subclause, an unboxing conversion of an object box to a *value-type* T consists of executing the expression ((T_Box)box).value. [*Example*: Thus, the statements

```
object box = 123;
int i = (int)box;
```

conceptually correspond to

```
object box = new int_Box(123);
int i = ((int_Box)box).value;
```

end example]

For an unboxing conversion to a given *value-type* to succeed at run-time, the value of the source operand shall be a reference to an object that was previously created by boxing a value of that *value-type*. If the source operand is null a System.NullReferenceException is thrown. If the source operand is a reference to an incompatible object, a System.InvalidCastException is thrown.

Sometimes your host bites...

This annotation relates to the behavior of certain C# compilers. This behavior breaks the C# type system and is **not** intentional; the compiler teams did not design it in. Rather, the behavior is unfortunately inherited from the host platform, and the compiler teams determined it was too costly to design it out, while other compiler teams could conceivably come to a different conclusion. The Standard committee discussed this matter and decided not to break the C# type system in order to accommodate these platforms.

You are strongly advised not to write code that which relies on this behavior

This behavior is documented only so that when your code fails to throw exceptions when it should, you will know why and be able to track down the problem. Compilers may change, and the platform behavior may change.

Some host platforms, such as the CLI, provide unboxing as a single *instruction*, while others, such as the Pentium, will compile it to a number of instructions. Obviously, if there is an instruction, compiler teams will wish to use it. If the instruction does not exactly meet the C# specification, they have to decide whether to allow their compiler to be nonconforming or to adopt a more complicated, and probably expensive, solution.

Some current C# compilers are known to "accidentally" allow the unboxing of:

- an integral type to an enum type whose underlying type is that integral type;
- an enum type to its underlying type; and
- an enum type to another enum type whose underlying type is the same.

This behavior is known to occur using the Microsoft VS 2005 C# compiler running on Microsoft's CLR v2.0. The Microsoft C# team has stated that they originally accepted this behavior, hoping the CLR would be fixed so that it did not occur. Other permutations of compilers and platforms may or may not behave in this way.

We do not guarantee that these are the only rogue conversions that compilers provide! However, we have provided information on some invalid reference conversions that we are also aware of in §13.2.3.

[*Note*: The behavior described here does not conform to the CLI Standard either.]

11.4 Nullable types

A ***nullable type*** is a structure that combines a value of the underlying type together with a null indicator. More precisely, an instance of a nullable type has two public read-only properties: `HasValue`, of type `bool`, and `Value`, of the nullable type's underlying type. `HasValue` is true for a non-null instance and false for a null instance. When `HasValue` is true, the `Value` property returns the contained value. When `HasValue` is false, an attempt to access the `Value` property results in an exception. A nullable type is classified as a value type (§11.1).

> *nullable-type:*
>   *non-nullable-value-type*   ?

The ***non-nullable-value-type*** specified before the ? modifier in a nullable type is called the ***underlying type*** of the nullable type. The underlying type of a nullable type shall be any non-nullable value type or any type parameter that is constrained (§25.7) to non-nullable value types (that is, any type parameter with a `struct` constraint). The underlying type of a nullable type shall not be a nullable type or a reference type. [*Example*: int?? and string? are invalid types. *end example*]

A nullable type can represent all values of its underlying type plus an additional null value.

T? and System.Nullable<T> denote the same type.

11.4.1 Members
An instance of a nullable type T? has two public read-only properties:

- A HasValue property of type `bool`
- A Value property of type T

An instance for which HasValue is true is said to be non-null. A non-null instance contains a known value and Value returns that value.

An instance for which HasValue is false is said to be null. Attempting to read the Value of a null instance causes a System.InvalidOperationException to be thrown.

In addition to the default constructor, every nullable type T? has a public constructor that takes a single argument of type T. Given a value x of type T, a constructor invocation of the form

```
new T? (x)
```

creates a non-null instance of T? for which the Value property is x.

It is never necessary to explicitly invoke a nullable type's constructor, since equivalent functionality is provided as an implicit conversion from T to T?.

Default value

The default value for a nullable type is an instance for which HasValue is false (§12.2).

To be, or not to be...a value type

A nullable type *T?* in C# is just an alias for System.Nullable<*T*>, which is a *value type*. However, C#, taking a lead from the CLI, treats nullable types as a third category distinct from value types and reference types. However, this third category is not a "first-class citizen" and sometimes nullable types are treated as value types, sometimes not. This nebulous status is particularly noticeable with generic constraints (see annotation on §25.7) and boxing (§11.3).

11.4.2 Implemented interfaces
A type of the form T?, which is an alias for System.Nullable<T>, implements no interfaces (§20). In particular, this means it does not implement any interface that the underlying type T does.

12 Variables

Variables represent storage locations. Every variable has a type that determines what values can be stored in the variable. C# is a type-safe language, and the C# compiler guarantees that values stored in variables are always of the appropriate type. The value of a variable can be changed through assignment or through use of the ++ and – – operators.

> **Aliasing**
>
> Passing a variable as a *reference parameter* (§12.1.5) or an *output parameter* (§12.1.6) creates an *alias* of the variable. The value of a variable can also be changed through assignment to an alias or through use of the ++ and – – operators on an alias.

A variable shall be *definitely assigned* (§12.3) before its value can be obtained.

As described in the following subclauses, variables are either *initially assigned* or *initially unassigned*. An initially assigned variable has a well-defined initial value and is always considered definitely assigned. An initially unassigned variable has no initial value. For an initially unassigned variable to be considered definitely assigned at a certain location, an assignment to the variable shall occur in every possible execution path leading to that location.

12.1 Variable categories

C# defines seven categories of variables: static variables, instance variables, array elements, value parameters, reference parameters, output parameters, and local variables. The subclauses that follow describe each of these categories.

[*Example*: In the following code

```
class A
{
  public static int x;
  int y;

  void F(int[] v, int a, ref int b, out int c)
  {
    int i = 1;
    c = a + b++;
  }
}
```

x is a static variable, y is an instance variable, v[0] is an array element, a is a value parameter, b is a reference parameter, c is an output parameter, and i is a local variable. *end example*]

12.1.1 Static variables
A field declared with the static modifier is called a *static variable*. A static variable comes into existence before execution of the static constructor (§17.11) for its containing type, and ceases to exist when the associated application domain ceases to exist.

The initial value of a static variable is the default value (§12.2) of the variable's type.

For the purposes of definite assignment checking, a static variable is considered initially assigned.

12.1.2 Instance variables
A field declared without the static modifier is called an *instance variable*.

12.1.2.1 Instance variables in classes

An instance variable of a class comes into existence when a new instance of that class is created, and ceases to exist when there are no references to that instance and the instance's finalizer (if any) has executed.

The initial value of an instance variable of a class is the default value (§12.2) of the variable's type.

For the purpose of definite assignment checking, an instance variable is considered initially assigned.

12.1.2.2 Instance variables in structs

An instance variable of a struct has exactly the same lifetime as the struct variable to which it belongs. In other words, when a variable of a struct type comes into existence or ceases to exist, so too do the instance variables of the struct.

The initial assignment state of an instance variable of a struct is the same as that of the containing struct variable. In other words, when a struct variable is considered initially assigned, so too are its instance variables, and when a struct variable is considered initially unassigned, its instance variables are likewise unassigned.

12.1.3 Array elements

The elements of an array come into existence when an array instance is created, and cease to exist when there are no references to that array instance.

The initial value of each of the elements of an array is the default value (§12.2) of the type of the array elements.

For the purpose of definite assignment checking, an array element is considered initially assigned.

12.1.4 Value parameters

A parameter declared without a `ref` or `out` modifier is a ***value parameter***.

A value parameter comes into existence upon invocation of the function member (method, instance constructor, accessor, or operator) to which the parameter belongs, and is initialized with the value of the argument given in the invocation. A value parameter ceases to exist upon return of the function member (except when the value parameter is captured by an anonymous method (§14.5.15.3.1) or the function member body is an iterator block (§26)).

For the purpose of definite assignment checking, a value parameter is considered initially assigned.

12.1.5 Reference parameters

A parameter declared with a `ref` modifier is a ***reference parameter***.

A reference parameter does not create a new storage location. Instead, a reference parameter represents the same storage location as the variable given as the argument in the function member invocation. Thus, the value of a reference parameter is always the same as the underlying variable.

The following definite assignment rules apply to reference parameters. [*Note*: The rules for output parameters are different, and are described in §12.1.6. *end note*]

- A variable shall be definitely assigned (§12.3) before it can be passed as a reference parameter in a function member invocation.
- Within a function member, a reference parameter is considered initially assigned.

Within an instance method or instance accessor of a struct type, the `this` keyword behaves exactly as a reference parameter of the struct type (§14.5.7).

Examples

Reference parameters are also found in, for example, C++ and Pascal, but not in Java. While reference parameters provide significant advantages in certain situations, there are not many examples of their use in the CLI Standard Libraries—out of approximately 3200 methods only 46 use reference parameters. Therefore, we provide a few examples of their use here to illustrate when they are of benefit.

Example: linked data structures

Reference parameters are useful when adding/removing items from linked data structures as they allow the *location* containing a reference to an item, rather than the reference itself, to be passed. Should the reference need to be changed to another item, the location can be updated. An example of this kind of usage can be found in the annotation on §14.5.15.3.1 in the method to insert items into a tree. The code of interest here is:

```
public class Tree<T>
{
  // Nested type for tree nodes
  class Node
  {
    public Node Left;
    public T Item;
    public Node Right;

    public Node(T nodeItem)
    {
      Left = Right = null;
      Item = nodeItem;
    }

    public Node()
    {
      Left = Right = null;
      Item = default(T);
    }

  }

  Comparison<T> cFun;    // ordering function
  Node root;             // root of tree
  long count;            // number of items in tree

  ...

  public void Add(T value)
  {
    Add(value, ref root);
  }

  private void Add(T value, ref Node node)
  {
    if (node == null)
    {
```

```
            node = new Node(value);
            count++;
        }
        else
        {
          int order = cFun(value, node.Item);
          if (order < 0)
            Add(value, ref node.Left);
          else if (order > 0)
            Add(value, ref node.Right);
        }
      }
    }
```

The use of reference parameters allows a straightforward recursive algorithm to be used without the need for (re)assignments; without reference parameters the addition code would need to be:

```
public void Add(T value)
{
  root = Add(value, root);
}

private Node Add(T value, Node node)
{
  if (node == null)
  {
    node = new Node(value);
    count++;
  }
  else
  {
    int order = cFun(value, node.Item);
    if (order < 0)
      node.Left = Add(value, node.Left);
    else if (order > 0)
      node.Right = Add(value, node.Right);
  }
  return node;
}
```

This version redundantly reassigns references all the way down the path to the newly added node.

Example: avoiding repeated index calculations

Reference parameters are particularly useful where multiple accesses to the same array elements are needed and the index calculations are non-trivial. By abstracting out the code that accesses the array elements and passing them in as reference parameters, the index calculations are only performed once.

The Fast Fourier Transform (FFT) algorithm performs a lot of this kind of calculation in a process called a *butterfly*. The following methods are taken from a C# FFT and demonstrate this use of reference parameters:

```
    private void Butterfly(ComplexDouble T,
                           ref ComplexDouble Xi,
                           ref ComplexDouble Xj)

    {
      T *= Xj;
      Xj = Xi - T;
      Xi += T;
    }

    // Perform FFT
    public void Transform(int[] data)
    {
      // Initialise X with permutation of data
      UpdateData(data);

      // step = 2 ^ (level-1)
      // increm = 2 ^ level;
      uint step = 1;
      for (uint level = 1; level <= logPoints; level++)
      {
        uint increm = step * 2;
        for (uint j = 0; j < step; j++)
        {
          // Precalculated exp ( - 2 * pi * j / 2 ^ level )
          ComplexDouble V = W[ level][ j];
          for (uint i = j; i < points; i += increm)
          {
            Butterfly(V, ref X[ i], ref X[ i + step]);
              // Calculate indices once
          }
        }
        step = increm;
      }
    }
```

Note: See the annotation on §25.7 for the reason why this example uses `ComplexDouble`, a class that provides double-precision complex numbers, rather than `Complex<Double>`, a generic complex number class.

Example: avoiding simple reassignment errors

A nice example of a method with a reference parameter is `Array<T>.Resize(ref T[] array, int newSize)` from the CLI Standard Library. Instead of writing the error-prone

```
    Wibble[] array;
    ...
    array = Array<Wibble>.Resize(array, 42);
```

you can write:

```
    Wibble[] array;
    ...
    Array<Wibble>.Resize(ref array, 42);
```

12.1.6 Output parameters

A parameter declared with an `out` modifier is an ***output parameter***.

An output parameter does not create a new storage location. Instead, an output parameter represents the same storage location as the variable given as the argument in the function member invocation. Thus, the value of an output parameter is always the same as the underlying variable.

The following definite assignment rules apply to output parameters. [*Note*: The rules for reference parameters are different, and are described in §12.1.5. *end note*]

- A variable need not be definitely assigned before it can be passed as an output parameter in a function member invocation.
- Following the normal completion of a function member invocation, each variable that was passed as an output parameter is considered assigned in that execution path.
- Within a function member, an output parameter is considered initially unassigned.
- Every output parameter of a function member shall be definitely assigned (§12.3) before the function member returns normally.

Within an instance constructor of a struct type, the `this` keyword behaves exactly as an output or reference parameter of the struct type, depending on whether the constructor declaration includes a constructor initializer (§14.5.7).

Output parameters vs. reference parameters

At runtime, an output parameter behaves exactly as a reference parameter: Assignments to the formal parameter immediately affect the actual parameter, and vice versa.

The difference between an output parameter and a reference parameter lies only in the definite assignment rules, checked at compile time. Whereas a reference parameter is definitely assigned at the beginning of the method body, an output parameter is not; conversely, the output parameter must be definitely assigned before leaving the method body. Correspondingly, a variable used as reference argument must be definitely assigned before a call to the method, whereas one used as output argument need not. Consider the following, very contrived code fragment, which demonstrates the differences:

```
public void RefCaller()
{
  int a;
  a = 0;                 // initialization needed before call
  RefAssign(ref a);   // may alter value of a
}

public void OutCaller()
{
  int a;                 // no initialization needed before call
  OutAssign(out a);   // a will be assigned to during call
}

public void RefAssign(ref int value)
{
  ...                    // no assignment needed before return
}
```

```
public void OutAssign(out int value)
{
  value = 42;          // assignment needed before return
}
```

In addition to indicating that the parameter will be used only to return a value, an output parameter avoids the pointless initialization that a reference parameter would need before the method call.

Using output parameters to return multiple results

Output parameters are useful when a method needs to return multiple results, and those results should not naturally be packaged as a single value.

For example, when searching a dictionary for a key k, the search may succeed and return a corresponding value v, or it may fail and return no value. Failure could be indicated by throwing an exception, but that is slow, the corresponding exception handler code is often ugly, and basically it is wrong to consider "key not found" as an exceptional outcome. Failure cannot in general be indicated by returning null, because that may be a valid result in itself.

An efficient and general solution is to let the search method return a Boolean indicating success or failure, and return the search result via an output parameter. Indeed, this is what is done in the standard generic collection library and in the C5 generic collection library (at http://www.itu.dk/research/c5/). The C5.IDictionary<K,V> lookup method Find(K k, out V v) can be used in convenient idioms such as these:

```
V res;
if (dict.Find(k, out res) && res.Count > 1)
  ...
else
  ...
```

To satisfy the requirement that the output parameter v is definitely assigned, the Find(K k, out V v) method must assign the default value for type V to it when returning false:

```
public virtual bool Find(K key, out V value)
{
  if (...)
  {
    value = p.Value;
    return true;
  }
  else
  {
    value = default(V);
    return false;
  }
}
```

Note that output parameters are quite rare in the CLI Standard Libraries: only 3 of 3191 methods have an output parameter.

12.1.7 Local variables

A *local variable* is declared by a *local-variable-declaration*, *foreach-statement*, or *specific-catch-clause* of a *try-statement*. For a *foreach-statement*, the local variable is an iteration variable

(§15.8.4). For a *specific-catch-clause*, the local variable is an exception variable (§15.10). A local variable declared by a *foreach-statement* or *specific-catch-clause* is considered initially assigned.

A *local-variable-declaration* can occur in a *block*, a *for-statement*, a *switch-block*, or a *using-statement*.

The lifetime of a local variable is the portion of program execution during which storage is guaranteed to be reserved for it. This lifetime extends from entry into the scope with which it is associated, at least until execution of that scope ends in some way. (Entering an enclosed *block*, calling a method, or yielding a value from an iterator block suspends, but does not end, execution of the current scope.) If the local variable is captured by an anonymous method, the lifetime of the variable is extended at least until all referencing delegates are eligible for garbage collection (§14.5.15.3.1). If the parent scope is entered recursively or iteratively, a new instance of the local variable is created each time, and its *local-variable-initializer*, if any, is evaluated each time. [*Note*: A local variable is instantiated each time its scope is entered. This behavior is visible to user code containing anonymous methods. *end note*]

A local variable introduced by a *local-variable-declaration* is not automatically initialized and thus has no default value. Such a local variable is considered initially unassigned. A *local-variable-declaration* can include a *local-variable-initializer*, in which case the variable is considered definitely assigned in its entire scope, except within the expression provided in the *local-variable-initializer*.

Within the scope of a local variable, it is a compile-time error to refer to that local variable in a textual position that precedes its *local-variable-declarator*.

[*Note*: The actual lifetime of a local variable is implementation-dependent. For example, a compiler might statically determine that a local variable in a block is only used for a small portion of that block. Using this analysis, the compiler could generate code that results in the variable's storage having a shorter lifetime than its containing block.

The storage referred to by a local reference variable is reclaimed independently of the lifetime of that local reference variable (§10.9). *end note*]

Extended life or early death

Local variables are often assumed to be "stack allocated": created on entry to a block and destroyed on exit from the block. While true in many programming languages, it is not so in C#.

As stated in the preceding text, if a local variable is captured by an anonymous method (§14.5.15), the lifetime of a local variable may extend long after the scope it was declared in has ceased to exist. This has implications for memory use and garbage collection, which are covered in an annotation on §14.5.15.3.1.

Also as stated in the preceding text, a locally variable may experience early death and not survive until the end of the block in which it is declared. This also has implications for memory use and garbage collection, but in the opposite way: Objects may be reclaimed and finalizers (§17.12) executed earlier than expected. This is covered in annotations on §10.9 and §15.13.

12.2 Default values

The following categories of variables are automatically initialized to their default values:

- Static variables
- Instance variables of class instances
- Array elements

The default value of a variable depends on the type of the variable and is determined as follows:

- For a variable of a *value-type*, the default value is the same as the value computed by the *value-type*'s default constructor (§11.1.2).

> ### Recursive initialization
>
> The default constructor sets all the instance variables of a *value-type* to their default values, so this is a recursive definition. This explains why §12.3.1 states that the instance variables of an initially assigned struct variable are themselves initially assigned.

- For a variable of a *reference-type*, the default value is `null`.

[*Note*: Initialization to default values is typically done by having the memory manager or garbage collector initialize memory to all-bits-zero before it is allocated for use. For this reason, it is convenient to use all-bits-zero to represent the null reference.*end note*]

The default value of a nullable type is an instance for which the `HasValue` property is false. Referencing the `Value` property of a default value of a nullable type results in an exception of type `System.InvalidOperationException`. The default value is also known as the ***null value*** of the nullable type. An implicit conversion exists from the `null` type (§11.2.7) to any nullable type, and this conversion produces the null value of the type.

> ### Pointless instance field initialization
>
> Some developers explicitly initialize instance fields to their default value; for example:
>
> ```
> class NotAdvised
> {
>   int field1 = 0;
>   bool field2 = false;
>   double field3 = 0.0;
>   string field4 = null;
> }
> ```
>
> This is quite common but has no effect whatsoever. To improve performance many compilers will remove such initialization.
>
> One argument in favor of such apparently pointless field initialization is that it prevents misunderstandings about default values; for instance, the default value for a string field is null, not the empty string. Another argument in favor is that the initializations make the intent of the developer clear. On the other hand, if the fields are subsequently assigned different values in all constructors, then the explicit field initialization is misleading and should be considered bad practice.
>
> *Marek Safar*

12.3 Definite assignment

At a given location in the executable code of a function member, a variable is said to be ***definitely assigned*** if the compiler can prove, by a particular static flow analysis (§12.3.3), that the variable has been automatically initialized or has been the target of at least one assignment. [*Note*: Informally stated, the rules of definite assignment are:

- An initially assigned variable (§12.3.1) is always considered definitely assigned.
- An initially unassigned variable (§12.3.2) is considered definitely assigned at a given location if all possible execution paths leading to that location contain at least one of the following:
    - A simple assignment (§14.14.1) in which the variable is the left operand.
    - An invocation expression (§14.5.5) or object creation expression (§14.5.10.1) that passes the variable as an output parameter.
    - For a local variable, a local variable declaration (§15.5) that includes a variable initializer.

The formal specification underlying the above informal rules is described in §12.3.1, §12.3.2, and §12.3.3. *end note*]

The definite assignment states of instance variables of a *struct-type* variable are tracked individually as well as collectively. In additional to the rules above, the following rules apply to *struct-type* variables and their instance variables:

- An instance variable is considered definitely assigned if its containing *struct-type* variable is considered definitely assigned.
- A *struct-type* variable is considered definitely assigned if each of its instance variables is considered definitely assigned.

Definite assignment is a requirement in the following contexts:

- A variable shall be definitely assigned at each location where its value is obtained. [*Note*: This ensures that undefined values never occur. *end note*] The occurrence of a variable in an expression is considered to obtain the value of the variable, except when
    - the variable is the left operand of a simple assignment,
    - the variable is passed as an output parameter, or
    - the variable is a *struct-type* variable and occurs as the left operand of a member access.
- A variable shall be definitely assigned at each location where it is passed as a reference parameter. [*Note*: This ensures that the function member being invoked can consider the reference parameter initially assigned. *end note*]
- All output parameters of a function member shall be definitely assigned at each location where the function member returns (through a `return` statement or through execution reaching the end of the function member body). [*Note*: This ensures that function members do not return undefined values in output parameters, thus enabling the compiler to consider a function member invocation that takes a variable as an output parameter equivalent to an assignment to the variable. *end note*]
- The `this` variable of a *struct-type* instance constructor shall be definitely assigned at each location where that instance constructor returns.

Definitely assigned, maybe…

Taking the address of a variable also causes the variable to be classified as definitely assigned (§27.5.4), even though the operation does not involve assignment. For example:

```
class DefiniteAssignment
{
  static void Main()
  {
    int value;
```

```
         unsafe { int* ptr = &value; }
         System.Console.WriteLine(value);  // OK, as 'value' is classified
                                // as definitely assigned after '&value'
      }
   }
```

This may seem surprising, but §27.5.4 clarifies:

It is the responsibility of the programmer to ensure that correct initialization of the variable actually does take place in this situation.

12.3.1 Initially assigned variables

The following categories of variables are classified as initially assigned:

- Static variables
- Instance variables of class instances
- Instance variables of initially assigned struct variables
- Array elements
- Value parameters
- Reference parameters
- Variables declared by a `catch` clause, a `foreach` statement, or a `using` statement.

12.3.2 Initially unassigned variables

The following categories of variables are classified as initially unassigned:

- Instance variables of initially unassigned struct variables.
- Output parameters, including the `this` variable of struct instance constructors without a constructor initializer.
- Local variables, except those declared in a `catch` clause, a `foreach` statement, or a `using` statement.

12.3.3 Precise rules for determining definite assignment

In order to determine that each used variable is definitely assigned, the compiler shall use a process that is equivalent to the one described in this subclause.

The compiler processes the body of each function member that has one or more initially unassigned variables. For each initially unassigned variable v, the compiler determines a **definite assignment state** for v at each of the following points in the function member:

- At the beginning of each statement
- At the end point (§15.1) of each statement
- On each arc which transfers control to another statement or to the end point of a statement
- At the beginning of each expression
- At the end of each expression

The definite assignment state of v can be either:

- Definitely assigned. This indicates that on all possible control flows to this point, v has been assigned a value.
- Not definitely assigned. For the state of a variable at the end of an expression of type `bool`, the state of a variable that isn't definitely assigned might (but doesn't necessarily) fall into one of the following sub-states:

     ○ Definitely assigned after true expression. This state indicates that v is definitely assigned if the Boolean expression evaluated as true, but is not necessarily assigned if the Boolean expression evaluated as false.

     ○ Definitely assigned after false expression. This state indicates that v is definitely assigned if the Boolean expression evaluated as false, but is not necessarily assigned if the Boolean expression evaluated as true.

The following rules govern how the state of a variable v is determined at each location.

Current compilers, constant expressions, and definite assignment

The Standard does not take into account constant expressions (§14.16) when specifying the rules for definite assignment. However, the Mono and Microsoft compilers current at the time of writing both extend the rules for definite assignment as follows:

- For an `if` statement *stmt* of the form:

  `if ( expr ) then-stmt else else-stmt`

  where *expr* is a constant expression, then:

       ○ If *expr* evaluates to *True*, then the definite assignment of variables is determined as if the statement were replaced by *then-stmt*.

       ○ Otherwise, if *expr* evaluates to *False*, then the definite assignment of variables is determined as if the statement were replaced by *else-stmt*, if such exists, or by an *empty-statement*, if the *else-stmt* is omitted.

  For example, the following code fragment is accepted by both the current Mono and Microsoft compilers:

  ```
  int c, x;

  if (4 > 3)
  {
    c = 6;
  }


  x = c;  // Standard: invalid, c not definitely assigned.
          // Mono & Microsoft: OK
  ```

- For a `while` statement *stmt* of the form:

  `while ( expr ) while-body`

  then:

       ○ If *expr* is a constant expression that evaluates to *True*, then the definite assignment of variables is determined as if the statement were replaced by *while-body* and any contained `continue` or `break` statements replaced by `goto` statements to the start or after the end of the *while-body*, respectively.

  For example, the following code fragment is accepted by both the current Mono and Microsoft compilers:

  ```
  int e, x;

  while (4 > 3)
  {
    e = 8;
    break;
  }
  ```

```
x = e;  // Standard: invalid, e not definitely assigned.
        // Mono & Microsoft: OK, but unreachable code
```

Note: We offer no guarantees that the this list of extensions to the definite assignment rules by these two compilers is exhaustive!

These extensions will seem intuitively correct to many, but, as with any non standard extension, different compilers, or future releases of the same compiler, may behave differently. Care is therefore advised if relying on this behavior.

12.3.3.1 General rules for statements

- v is not definitely assigned at the beginning of a function member body.
- v is definitely assigned at the beginning of any unreachable statement.

> **Arriving from the unreachable**
>
> The second bullet might strike some as odd. If a statement is unreachable, how can the definite assignment status of any variable within it matter?
>
> The answer can be determined from the bullet following this annotation, where the definite assignment status at the start of a statement depends on its status at all control flows into the start of the statement. If one of those inflows comes from a statement whose own start in unreachable, then a naive analysis for a particular variable, v, might proceed as follows:
>
> - if: on each of the reachable inflows, v is definitely assigned
> - but: on any of the unreachable inflows, v is not definitely assigned
> - then: at the start of the statement, v is not definitely assigned
>
> But that is the wrong answer. Defining all variables to be definitely assigned at the start of an unreachable statement is just a device to handle this problem.
>
> The same can be stated from a more logical point of view: If "definitely assigned" is understood as "there is no flow to this point on which the variable could be not yet assigned," then clearly any variable is definitely assigned at the start of an unreachable statement.

- The definite assignment state of v at the beginning of any other statement is determined by checking the definite assignment state of v on all control flow transfers that target the beginning of that statement. If (and only if) v is definitely assigned on all such control flow transfers, then v is definitely assigned at the beginning of the statement. The set of possible control flow transfers is determined in the same way as for checking statement reachability (§15.1).
- The definite assignment state of v at the end point of a block, `checked`, `unchecked`, `if`, `while`, `do`, `for`, `foreach`, `lock`, `using`, or `switch` statement is determined by checking the definite assignment state of v on all control flow transfers that target the end point of that statement. If v is definitely assigned on all such control flow transfers, then v is definitely assigned at the end point of the statement. Otherwise, v is not definitely assigned at the end point of the statement. The set of possible control flow transfers is determined in the same way as for checking statement reachability (§15.1).

12.3.3.2 Block statements, checked, and unchecked statements

The definite assignment state of v on the control transfer to the first statement of the statement list in the block (or to the end point of the block, if the statement list is empty) is the same as the definite assignment statement of v before the block, `checked`, or `unchecked` statement.

12.3.3.3 Expression statements

For an expression statement *stmt* that consists of the expression *expr*:

- v has the same definite assignment state at the beginning of *expr* as at the beginning of *stmt*.
- If v if definitely assigned at the end of *expr*, it is definitely assigned at the end point of *stmt*; otherwise, it is not definitely assigned at the end point of *stmt*.

12.3.3.4 Declaration statements

- If *stmt* is a declaration statement without initializers, then v has the same definite assignment state at the end point of *stmt* as at the beginning of *stmt*.
- If *stmt* is a declaration statement with initializers, then the definite assignment state for v is determined as if *stmt* were a statement list, with one assignment statement for each declaration with an initializer (in the order of declaration).

12.3.3.5 If statements

For an `if` statement *stmt* of the form:

```
if ( expr ) then-stmt else else-stmt
```

- v has the same definite assignment state at the beginning of *expr* as at the beginning of *stmt*.
- If v is definitely assigned at the end of *expr*, then it is definitely assigned on the control flow transfer to *then-stmt* and to either *else-stmt* or to the end-point of *stmt* if there is no else clause.
- If v has the state "definitely assigned after true expression" at the end of *expr*, then it is definitely assigned on the control flow transfer to *then-stmt*, and not definitely assigned on the control flow transfer to either *else-stmt* or to the end-point of *stmt* if there is no else clause.
- If v has the state "definitely assigned after false expression" at the end of *expr*, then it is definitely assigned on the control flow transfer to *else-stmt*, and not definitely assigned on the control flow transfer to *then-stmt*. It is definitely assigned at the end-point of *stmt* if and only if it is definitely assigned at the end-point of *then-stmt*.
- Otherwise, v is considered not definitely assigned on the control flow transfer to either the *then-stmt* or *else-stmt*, or to the end-point of *stmt* if there is no else clause.

Definitely confused?

At first, reading the preceding rules may be a little confusing to some, particularly the lack of symmetry between the third and fourth bullets. Why does the fourth have the last sentence, which is lacking in the third? Well, the rules do make sense, honest, but the following reformulation may help those confused—at least we hope it does not increase confusion! The rules include some statements already covered under the general rules for join points (§12.3.3.1, fourth bullet) (i.e., points reachable by more than one path, such as the end of an if statement.)

- v has the same definite assignment state at the beginning of *expr* as at the beginning of *stmt*.

- If v is definitely assigned at the end of *expr*, then it is definitely assigned on the control flow transfer to *then-stmt*, on the control flow transfer to *else-stmt* (if one exists), and at the end-point of *stmt*.
- If v has the state "definitely assigned after true expression" at the end of *expr*, then it is definitely assigned on the control flow transfer to *then-stmt*, and not definitely assigned on the control flow transfer to *else-stmt* (if one exists). It is definitely assigned at the end-point of *stmt* if and only if it is definitely assigned at the end-point of *else-stmt*.
- If v has the state "definitely assigned after false expression" at the end of *expr*, then it is definitely assigned on the control flow transfer to *else-stmt*, and not definitely assigned on the control flow transfer to *then-stmt*. It is definitely assigned at the end-point of *stmt* if and only if it is definitely assigned at the end-point of *then-stmt*.
- Otherwise, v is considered not definitely assigned on the control flow transfer to the *then-stmt* and not definitely assigned on the control flow transfer to *else-stmt* (if such exists). It is definitely assigned at the end-point of *stmt* if and only if *else-stmt* exists and v is definitely assigned both at the end-point of *then-stmt* and at the end-point of *else-stmt*.

12.3.3.6 Switch statements

In a `switch` statement *stmt* with a controlling expression *expr*:

- The definite assignment state of v at the beginning of *expr* is the same as the state of v at the beginning of *stmt*.
- The definite assignment state of v on the control flow transfer to a reachable switch block statement list is the same as the definite assignment state of v at the end of *expr*.

12.3.3.7 While statements

For a `while` statement *stmt* of the form:

```
while ( expr ) while-body
```

- v has the same definite assignment state at the beginning of *expr* as at the beginning of *stmt*.
- If v is definitely assigned at the end of *expr*, then it is definitely assigned on the control flow transfer to *while-body* and to the end point of *stmt*.
- If v has the state "definitely assigned after true expression" at the end of *expr*, then it is definitely assigned on the control flow transfer to *while-body*, but not definitely assigned at the end-point of *stmt*.
- If v has the state "definitely assigned after false expression" at the end of *expr*, then it is definitely assigned on the control flow transfer to the end point of *stmt*, but not definitely assigned on the control flow transfer to *while-body*.

12.3.3.8 Do statements

For a `do` statement *stmt* of the form:

```
do do-body while ( expr ) ;
```

- v has the same definite assignment state on the control flow transfer from the beginning of *stmt* to *do-body* as at the beginning of *stmt*.
- v has the same definite assignment state at the beginning of *expr* as at the end point of *do-body*.

- If v is definitely assigned at the end of *expr*, then it is definitely assigned on the control flow transfer to the end point of *stmt*.
- If v has the state "definitely assigned after false expression" at the end of *expr*, then it is definitely assigned on the control flow transfer to the end point of *stmt*, but not definitely assigned on the control flow transfer to *do-body*.

12.3.3.9 For statements

Definite assignment checking for a `for` statement of the form:

```
for ( for-initializer ; for-condition ; for-iterator ) embedded-statement
```

is done as if the statement were written:

```
{
  for-initializer ;
  while ( for-condition )
  {
    embedded-statement ;
LLoop:
    for-iterator ;
  }
}
```

with `continue` statements that target the `for` statement being translated to `goto` statements targeting the label `LLoop`. If the *for-condition* is omitted from the `for` statement, then evaluation of definite assignment proceeds as if *for-condition* were replaced with `true` in the above expansion.

12.3.3.10 Break, continue, and goto statements

The definite assignment state of v on the control flow transfer caused by a `break`, `continue`, or `goto` statement is the same as the definite assignment state of v at the beginning of the statement.

12.3.3.11 Throw statements

For a statement *stmt* of the form

```
throw expr ;
```

the definite assignment state of v at the beginning of *expr* is the same as the definite assignment state of v at the beginning of *stmt*.

12.3.3.12 Return statements

For a statement *stmt* of the form

```
return expr ;
```

- The definite assignment state of v at the beginning of *expr* is the same as the definite assignment state of v at the beginning of *stmt*.
- If v is an output parameter, then it shall be definitely assigned either:
    - after *expr*
    - or at the end of the `finally` block of a `try-finally` or `try-catch-finally` that encloses the `return` statement.

For a statement *stmt* of the form:

```
return ;
```

- If v is an output parameter, then it shall be definitely assigned either:
    - before *stmt*
    - or at the end of the `finally` block of a `try-finally` or `try-catch-finally` that encloses the `return` statement.

12.3.3.13 Try-catch statements

For a statement *stmt* of the form:

```
try try-block
catch ( ... ) catch-block-1
...
catch ( ... ) catch-block-n
```

- The definite assignment state of v at the beginning of *try-block* is the same as the definite assignment state of v at the beginning of *stmt*.
- The definite assignment state of v at the beginning of *catch-block-i* (for any *i*) is the same as the definite assignment state of v at the beginning of *stmt*.
- The definite assignment state of v at the end-point of *stmt* is definitely assigned if (and only if) v is definitely assigned at the end-point of *try-block* and every *catch-block-i* (for every *i* from 1 to *n*).

12.3.3.14 Try-finally statements

For a `try` statement *stmt* of the form:

```
try try-block finally finally-block
```

- The definite assignment state of v at the beginning of *try-block* is the same as the definite assignment state of v at the beginning of *stmt*.
- The definite assignment state of v at the beginning of *finally-block* is the same as the definite assignment state of v at the beginning of *stmt*.
- The definite assignment state of v at the end-point of *stmt* is definitely assigned if (and only if) either:
    - v is definitely assigned at the end-point of *try-block*
    - v is definitely assigned at the end-point of *finally-block*

If a control flow transfer (such as a `goto` statement) is made that begins within *try-block*, and ends outside of *try-block*, then v is also considered definitely assigned on that control flow transfer if v is definitely assigned at the end-point of *finally-block*. (This is not an only if—if v is definitely assigned for another reason on this control flow transfer, then it is still considered definitely assigned.)

12.3.3.15 Try-catch-finally statements

Definite assignment analysis for a `try-catch-finally` statement of the form:

```
try try-block
catch ( ... ) catch-block-1
...
catch ( ... ) catch-block-n
finally finally-block
```

is done as if the statement were a `try-finally` statement enclosing a `try-catch` statement:

```
try
{
  try try-block
  catch ( ... ) catch-block-1
  ...
  catch ( ... ) catch-block-n
}
finally finally-block
```

[*Example*: The following example demonstrates how the different blocks of a `try` statement (§15.10) affect definite assignment.

```
class A
{
  static void F()
  {
    int i, j;
    try
    {
      goto LABEL;
      // neither i nor j definitely assigned
      i = 1;
      // i definitely assigned
    }

    catch
    {
      // neither i nor j definitely assigned
      i = 3;
      // i definitely assigned
    }

    finally
    {
      // neither i nor j definitely assigned
      j = 5;
      // j definitely assigned
    }
    // i and j definitely assigned
    LABEL:;
      // j definitely assigned

  }
}
```

end example]

12.3.3.16 Foreach statements

For a `foreach` statement *stmt* of the form:

```
foreach ( type identifier in expr ) embedded-statement
```

- The definite assignment state of *v* at the beginning of *expr* is the same as the state of *v* at the beginning of *stmt*.

- The definite assignment state of v on the control flow transfer to *embedded-statement* or to the end point of *stmt* is the same as the state of v at the end of *expr*.

12.3.3.17 Using statements
For a `using` statement *stmt* of the form:

```
using ( resource-acquisition ) embedded-statement
```

- The definite assignment state of v at the beginning of *resource-acquisition* is the same as the state of v at the beginning of *stmt*.
- The definite assignment state of v on the control flow transfer to *embedded-statement* is the same as the state of v at the end of *resource-acquisition*.

12.3.3.18 Lock statements
For a `lock` statement *stmt* of the form:

```
lock ( expr ) embedded-statement
```

- The definite assignment state of v at the beginning of *expr* is the same as the state of v at the beginning of *stmt*.
- The definite assignment state of v on the control flow transfer to *embedded-statement* is the same as the state of v at the end of *expr*.

12.3.3.19 General rules for simple expressions
The following rule applies to these kinds of expressions: literals (§14.5.1), simple names (§14.5.2), member access expressions (§14.5.4), non-indexed base access expressions (§14.5.8), and `typeof` expressions (§14.5.11).

- The definite assignment state of v at the end of such an expression is the same as the definite assignment state of v at the beginning of the expression.

12.3.3.20 General rules for expressions with embedded expressions
The following rules apply to these kinds of expressions: parenthesized expressions (§14.5.3), element access expressions (§14.5.6), base access expressions with indexing (§14.5.8), increment and decrement expressions (§14.5.9, §14.6.5), cast expressions (§14.6.6), unary +, -, ~, * expressions, binary +, -, *, /, %, <<, >>, <, <=, >, >=, ==, !=, is, as, &, |, ^ expressions (§14.7, §14.8, §14.9, §14.10), compound assignment expressions (§14.14.2), `checked` and `unchecked` expressions (§14.5.13), array and delegate creation expressions (§14.5.10).

Each of these expressions has one or more sub-expressions that are unconditionally evaluated in a fixed order. [*Example*: The binary % operator evaluates the left hand side of the operator, then the right hand side. An indexing operation evaluates the indexed expression, and then evaluates each of the index expressions, in order from left to right. *end example*] For an expression *expr*, which has sub-expressions $expr_1$, $expr_2$, ..., $expr_n$, evaluated in that order:

- The definite assignment state of v at the beginning of $expr_1$ is the same as the definite assignment state at the beginning of *expr*.
- The definite assignment state of v at the beginning of $expr_i$ (i greater than one) is the same as the definite assignment state at the end of $expr_{i-1}$.
- The definite assignment state of v at the end of *expr* is the same as the definite assignment state at the end of $expr_n$.

12.3.3.21 Invocation expressions and object creation expressions

For an invocation expression *expr* of the form:

```
primary-expression ( arg₁, arg₂, …, argₙ )
```

or an object creation expression *expr* of the form:

```
new type ( arg₁, arg₂, …, argₙ )
```

- For an invocation expression, the definite assignment state of v before *primary-expression* is the same as the state of v before *expr*.
- For an invocation expression, the definite assignment state of v before arg_1 is the same as the state of v after *primary-expression*.
- For an object creation expression, the definite assignment state of v before arg_1 is the same as the state of v before *expr*.
- For each argument arg_i, the definite assignment state of v after arg_i is determined by the normal expression rules, ignoring any `ref` or `out` modifiers.
- For each argument arg_i for any i greater than one, the definite assignment state of v before arg_i is the same as the state of v after arg_{i-1}.
- If the variable v is passed as an `out` argument (i.e., an argument of the form "`out v`") in any of the arguments, then the state of v after *expr* is definitely assigned. Otherwise, the state of v after *expr* is the same as the state of v after arg_n.

Trying to peek at an uninitialized variable

It is vital that the fourth bullet specifies that `out` is ignored. This is to prevent code such as this:

```
class HackAttempt
{
  public static void SeeUnitializedY(out int x, int y)
  {
    System.Console.WriteLine(y);
    x = 42;
  }

  public static void Main()
  {
    int y;
    F(out y, y);
  }
}
```

Here the invocation expression `F(out y, y)` is illegal as, ignoring the `out` modifier, y is not definitely assigned.

As of the time of writing, the Mono compiler incorrectly accepts this program.

12.3.3.22 Simple assignment expressions

For an expression *expr* of the form *w=expr-rhs*:

- The definite assignment state of v before *w* is the same as the definite assignment state of v before *expr*.
- The definite assignment state of v before *expr-rhs* is the same as the definite assignment state of v after *w*.

- If *w* is the same variable as *v*, then the definite assignment state of *v* after *expr* is definitely assigned. Otherwise, the definite assignment state of *v* after *expr* is the same as the definite assignment state of *v* after *expr-rhs*.

[*Example*: In the following code

```
class A
{
  static void F(int[] arr)
  {
    int x;

    arr[x = 1] = x;   // ok
  }
}
```

the variable x is considered definitely assigned after arr[x = 1] is evaluated as the left hand side of the second simple assignment. *end example*]

12.3.3.23 && expressions
For an expression *expr* of the form *expr-first* && *expr-second*:

- The definite assignment state of *v* before *expr-first* is the same as the definite assignment state of *v* before *expr*.
- The definite assignment state of *v* before *expr-second* is definitely assigned if the state of *v* after *expr-first* is either definitely assigned or "definitely assigned after true expression". Otherwise, it is not definitely assigned.
- The definite assignment state of *v* after *expr* is determined by:
  - If the state of *v* after *expr-first* is definitely assigned, then the state of *v* after *expr* is definitely assigned.
  - Otherwise, if the state of *v* after *expr-second* is definitely assigned, and the state of *v* after *expr-first* is "definitely assigned after false expression", then the state of *v* after *expr* is definitely assigned.
  - Otherwise, if the state of *v* after *expr-second* is definitely assigned or "definitely assigned after true expression", then the state of *v* after *expr* is "definitely assigned after true expression".
  - Otherwise, if the state of *v* after *expr-first* is "definitely assigned after false expression", and the state of *v* after *expr-second* is "definitely assigned after false expression", then the state of *v* after *expr* is "definitely assigned after false expression".
  - Otherwise, the state of *v* after *expr* is not definitely assigned.

[*Example*: In the following code

```
class A
{
  static void F(int x, int y)
  {
    int i;
    if (x >= 0 && (i = y) >= 0)
    {
      // i definitely assigned
    }
    else
    {
```

```
      // i not definitely assigned
    }
      // i not definitely assigned
  }
}
```

the variable i is considered definitely assigned in one of the embedded statements of an if statement but not in the other. In the if statement in method F, the variable i is definitely assigned in
the first embedded statement because execution of the expression (i = y) always precedes
execution of this embedded statement. In contrast, the variable i is not definitely assigned in
the second embedded statement, since x >= 0 might have tested false, resulting in the variable
i's being unassigned. *end example*]

12.3.3.24 || expressions

For an expression *expr* of the form *expr-first* | | *expr-second*:

- The definite assignment state of *v* before *expr-first* is the same as the definite assignment
  state of *v* before *expr*.
- The definite assignment state of *v* before *expr-second* is definitely assigned if the state of *v*
  after *expr-first* is either definitely assigned or "definitely assigned after false expression".
  Otherwise, it is not definitely assigned.
- The definite assignment statement of *v* after *expr* is determined by:
  - If the state of *v* after *expr-first* is definitely assigned, then the state of *v* after *expr* is
    definitely assigned.
  - Otherwise, if the state of *v* after *expr-second* is definitely assigned, and the state of *v*
    after *expr-first* is "definitely assigned after true expression", then the state of *v* after
    expr is definitely assigned.
  - Otherwise, if the state of *v* after *expr-second* is definitely assigned or "definitely
    assigned after false expression", then the state of *v* after *expr* is "definitely assigned
    after false expression".
  - Otherwise, if the state of *v* after *expr-first* is "definitely assigned after true expres-
    sion", and the state of *v* after *expr-second* is "definitely assigned after true expres-
    sion", then the state of *v* after *expr* is "definitely assigned after true expression".
  - Otherwise, the state of *v* after *expr* is not definitely assigned.

[*Example*: In the following code

```
class A
{
  static void G(int x, int y)
  {
    int i;
    if (x >= 0 || (i = y) >= 0)
    {
      // i not definitely assigned
    }
    else
    {
      // i definitely assigned
    }
      // i not definitely assigned
  }
}
```

the variable `i` is considered definitely assigned in one of the embedded statements of an `if` statement but not in the other. In the `if` statement in method `G`, the variable `i` is definitely assigned in the second embedded statement because execution of the expression `(i = y)` always precedes execution of this embedded statement. In contrast, the variable `i` is not definitely assigned in the first embedded statement, since `x >= 0` might have tested true, resulting in the variable `i`'s being unassigned. *end example*]

12.3.3.25 ! expressions

For an expression *expr* of the form `!`*expr-operand*:

- The definite assignment state of *v* before *expr-operand* is the same as the definite assignment state of *v* before *expr*.
- The definite assignment state of *v* after *expr* is determined by:
  - If the state of *v* after *expr-operand* is definitely assigned, then the state of *v* after *expr* is definitely assigned.
  - If the state of *v* after *expr-operand* is not definitely assigned, then the state of *v* after *expr* is not definitely assigned.
  - If the state of *v* after *expr-operand* is "definitely assigned after false expression", then the state of *v* after *expr* is "definitely assigned after true expression".
  - If the state of *v* after *expr-operand* is "definitely assigned after true expression", then the state of *v* after *expr* is "definitely assigned after false expression".

12.3.3.26 ?: expressions

For an expression *expr* of the form *expr-cond*`?` *expr-true*`:` *expr-false*:

- The definite assignment state of *v* before *expr-cond* is the same as the state of *v* before *expr*.
- The definite assignment state of *v* before *expr-true* is definitely assigned if and only if the state of *v* after *expr-cond* is definitely assigned or "definitely assigned after true expression".
- The definite assignment state of *v* before *expr-false* is definitely assigned if and only if the state of *v* after *expr-cond* is definitely assigned or "definitely assigned after false expression".
- The definite assignment state of *v* after *expr* is determined by:
  - If *expr-cond* is a constant expression (§14.16) with value `true` then the state of *v* after *expr* is the same as the state of *v* after *expr-true*.
  - Otherwise, if *expr-cond* is a constant expression (§14.16) with value `false` then the state of *v* after *expr* is the same as the state of *v* after *expr-false*.
  - Otherwise, if the state of *v* after *expr-true* is definitely assigned and the state of *v* after *expr-false* is definitely assigned, then the state of *v* after *expr* is definitely assigned.
  - Otherwise, the state of *v* after *expr* is not definitely assigned.

12.3.3.27 Anonymous method expressions

The definite assignment state of a parameter of an anonymous method (§14.5.15) is the same as for a parameter of a named method. That is, reference parameters and value parameters are initially definitely assigned and output parameters are initially unassigned. Furthermore, output parameters shall be definitely assigned before the anonymous method returns normally (§12.1.6).

The definite assignment state of an outer variable *v* on the control transfer to the *block* of an *anonymous-method-expression* is the same as the definite assignment state of *v* before the *anonymous-method-expression.* That is, definite assignment of outer variables is inherited from the context of the *anonymous-method-expression.* Within the *block* of an *anonymous-method-expression*, definite assignment evolves as in a normal block (§12.3.3).

The definite assignment state of a variable *v* after an *anonymous-method-expression* is the same as its definite assignment state before the *anonymous-method-expression.*

[*Example*: The example

```
delegate bool Filter(int i);

void F()
{
  int max;

  // Error, max is not definitely assigned
  Filter f = delegate(int n) { return n < max; };

  max = 5;
  DoWork(f);
}
```

generates a compile-time error since max is not definitely assigned where the anonymous method is declared. *end example*] [*Example*: The example

```
delegate void D();

void F()
{
  int n;
  D d = delegate { n = 1; };

  d();

  // Error, n is not definitely assigned
  Console.WriteLine(n);
}
```

also generates a compile-time error since the assignment to n in the anonymous method has no affect on the definite assignment state of n outside the anonymous method. *end example*]

12.3.3.28 Yield statements
For a `yield return` statement *stmt* of the form:

```
yield return expr;
```

- A variable *v* has the same definite assignment state at the beginning of *expr* as at the beginning of *stmt*.
- If a variable *v* is definitely assigned at the end of *expr*, it is definitely assigned at the end point of *stmt*; otherwise, it is not definitely assigned at the end point of *stmt*.

12.3.3.29 ?? expressions
For an expression *expr* of the form

```
expr-first ??
expr-second
```

- The definite assignment state of v before *expr-first* is the same as the definite assignment state of v before *expr*.
- The definite assignment state of v before *expr-second* is the same as the definite assignment state after *expr-first*.
- The definite assignment state of v after *expr* is the same as the definite assignment state after *expr-first*.

Alternative definite assignment rules for the ?? operator

It was discovered at a late stage that the Standard omitted definite assignment rules for the null-coalescing operator (??). Two sets of rules were then proposed by Peter Sestoft: a basic set of rules, which is the one adopted in the standard, and a more liberal set of rules, which are as follows:

First, an extra assignment state (§12.3.3) for variables is needed: *Definitely assigned after null expression.*

Then the liberal rules go like this:

Let *expr* be *expr-first* ?? *expr-second*. Then

- The definite assignment state of v before *expr-first* is the same as the definite assignment state of v before *expr*.
- The definite assignment state of v before *expr-second* is definitely assigned if the state after *expr-first* is either definitely assigned or "definitely assigned after null expression." Otherwise, it is not definitely assigned.
- The definite assignment state of v after *expr* is determined by:
  - If the state of v after *expr-first* is definitely assigned, then the state of v after *expr* is definitely assigned.
  - Otherwise, if the state of v after *expr-second* is definitely assigned, and the state after *expr-first* is "definitely assigned after null expression," then the state of v after *expr* is definitely assigned.
  - Otherwise, if the state of v after *expr-second* is definitely assigned or "definitely assigned after null expression," then the state of v after *expr* is "definitely assigned after null expression."

However, these more liberal rules were not adopted because Peter Hallam discovered they would be unsound. Namely, there is a subtle interaction between implicit conversions and the behavior of the null-coalescing operator (??), as explained in the §14.12 annotation. The liberal rules for definite assignment proposed here would deem variable test definitely assigned after executing the following code fragment, but implicit conversion in combination with the §14.12 rules for (??) would mean that variable test has not actually been assigned and that is bad:

```
class A {}
class B
{
  public static implicit operator B (A a) { return null; }
}

B test;                          // Variable test is unassigned
B b = null;
A a = new A();
B r = a ?? (test = new B());   // Assignment to test *not* executed!
```

Incidentally, it was also discovered that at least one compiler mistakenly accepts this code.

(This annotation was made using the online Wiki via Scandinavian Airlines onboard wireless while cruising at 34,000 feet, crossing the Greenland ice sheet.)

12.4 Variable references

A *variable-reference* is an *expression* that is classified as a variable. A *variable-reference* denotes a storage location that can be accessed both to fetch the current value and to store a new value.

> *variable-reference:*
>   *expression*

[*Note*: In C and C++, a *variable-reference* is known as an *lvalue.end note*]

"classified as a variable"

The following table lists the kinds of expressions classified as variables:

Clause	Production	*variable-reference*
§14.5.2	*simple-name*	A *simple-name* that refers to: • a local variable of the current method; • a method parameter of the current method; • an instance or static non-readonly field in the current class or struct; • a static non-readonly field in any enclosing class or struct.
§14.5.4	*member-access*	A *member-access* of the form E.I and: • E is a class or struct type and I is a non-readonly static field; or • the type of E is a class or struct type and I is a non-readonly instance field.
§14.5.6	*element-access*	An *element-access* of the form E[E_1, ..., E_n], $n \geq 1$, and E is a value of *array-type*.
§14.5.7	*this-access*	A *this-access* used as a *primary-expression* in an instance constructor, instance method or instance accessor of a struct. *Note:* If the *this-access* is within an iterator block of an instance member, the variable referenced is a *copy* of the struct for which the member was invoked (§26.1.4).
§14.5.8	*base-access*	A *base-access* of the form base.I where I is a non-readonly instance field.
§27.5.1	*pointer-indirection-expression*	A *pointer-indirection-expression* within an unsafe context (§27.1).

The reference to C and C++ *lvalues* is misleading as C# is far more restrictive than C/C++. For example, the following is valid in C++:

```
int a, b;
bool p;
...
(p ? a : b) = 6;
```

However, it is invalid in C# as a *conditional-expression* is not classified as a variable.

12.5 Atomicity of variable references

Reads and writes of the following data types shall be atomic: `bool`, `char`, `byte`, `sbyte`, `short`, `ushort`, `uint`, `int`, `float`, and reference types. In addition, reads and writes of enum types with an underlying type in the previous list shall also be atomic. Reads and writes of other types, including `long`, `ulong`, `double`, and `decimal`, as well as user-defined types, need not be atomic. Aside from the library functions designed for that purpose, there is no guarantee of atomic read-modify-write, such as in the case of increment or decrement.

Atomicity vs. volatility

Note that atomicity is a separate issue from volatility. The specification guarantees that if an `int` variable has value 0, and one thread assigns 257 to the variable, then no thread will see any other intermediate value. Without the guarantee, the four bytes of memory holding the `int` variable might be updated nonatomically, and another thread might temporarily see the value 1 or the value 256 in the variable. However, the clause *does not* guarantee that the (atomic) change in value will be immediately observable by other threads. See clauses §17.4.3 and §15.12 for more information on this topic.

Jon Skeet

13 Conversions

A *conversion* enables an expression of one type to be treated as another type. Conversions can be *implicit* or *explicit*, and this determines whether an explicit cast is required. [*Example*: For instance, the conversion from type `int` to type `long` is implicit, so expressions of type `int` can implicitly be treated as type `long`. The opposite conversion, from type `long` to type `int`, is explicit, so an explicit cast is required.

```
int a = 123;
long b = a;      // implicit conversion from int to long
int c = (int) b; // explicit conversion from long to int
```

end example] Some conversions are defined by the language. Programs can also define their own conversions (§13.4).

13.1 Implicit conversions

The following conversions are classified as implicit conversions:

- Identity conversions
- Implicit numeric conversions
- Implicit enumeration conversions
- Implicit reference conversions
- Boxing conversions
- Implicit type parameter conversions
- Implicit constant expression conversions
- User-defined implicit conversions
- Implicit conversions from an anonymous method expression to a compatible delegate type
- Implicit conversion from a method group to a compatible delegate type
- Conversions from the `null` type (§11.2.7) to any nullable type
- Implicit nullable conversions
- Lifted user-defined implicit conversions

Implicit conversions can occur in a variety of situations, including function member invocations (§14.4.3), cast expressions (§14.6.6), and assignments (§14.14).

The pre-defined implicit conversions always succeed and never cause exceptions to be thrown. [*Note*: Properly designed user-defined implicit conversions should exhibit these characteristics as well. *end note*]

13.1.1 Identity conversion

An identity conversion converts from any type to the same type. This conversion exists only such that an entity that already has a required type can be said to be convertible to that type.

13.1.2 Implicit numeric conversions

The implicit numeric conversions are:

- From `sbyte` to `short`, `int`, `long`, `float`, `double`, or `decimal`.
- From `byte` to `short`, `ushort`, `int`, `uint`, `long`, `ulong`, `float`, `double`, or `decimal`.
- From `short` to `int`, `long`, `float`, `double`, or `decimal`.
- From `ushort` to `int`, `uint`, `long`, `ulong`, `float`, `double`, or `decimal`.
- From `int` to `long`, `float`, `double`, or `decimal`.

- From `uint` to `long`, `ulong`, `float`, `double`, or `decimal`.
- From `long` to `float`, `double`, or `decimal`.
- From `ulong` to `float`, `double`, or `decimal`.
- From `char` to `ushort`, `int`, `uint`, `long`, `ulong`, `float`, `double`, or `decimal`.
- From `float` to `double`.

Conversions from `int`, `uint`, `long` or `ulong` to `float` and from `long` or `ulong` to `double` can cause a loss of precision, but will never cause a loss of magnitude. The other implicit numeric conversions never lose any information.

There are no implicit conversions to the `char` type, so values of the other integral types do not automatically convert to the `char` type.

Loss of precision

Precision may be lost in an implicit integral to floating-point conversion as the number of significant digits in the former is greater than in the latter. However, the numeric range of the floating-point types is greater than that of the integral ones, so no loss of magnitude can occur. For example, consider the code fragment:

```
Console.WriteLine(long.MaxValue);
Console.WriteLine((float)long.MaxValue);
```

This outputs:

```
9223372036854775807
9.223372E+18
```

The loss of significant digits can be seen; however, there is no loss of magnitude as the first number is 9.223372036854775807E+18. The loss of precision is 36875854707, which though it looks large is only ~4E-7%.

13.1.3 Implicit enumeration conversions

An implicit enumeration conversion permits the *decimal-integer-literal*0 to be converted to any *enum-type*.

Equal rights for hexadecimals

The Microsoft and Mono C# compilers also allow a *hexadecimal-integer-literal* to be implicitly converted to an enum type. This was assumed to be a simple consequence of the definition of conforming implementation (of a C# compiler) in §2:

> *A conforming implementation of C# is permitted to provide additional types, values, objects, properties, and methods beyond those described in this International Standard, provided they do not alter the behavior of any strictly conforming program. Conforming implementations are required to diagnose programs that use extensions that are ill formed according to this International Standard. Having done so, however; they can compile and execute such programs. (The ability to have extensions implies that a conforming implementation reserves no identifiers other than those explicitly reserved in this International Standard.)*

However, a careful reading shows that this is not one of the permitted extensions. Therefore, strictly speaking, a conforming compiler must issue a diagnostic if it allows a *hexadecimal-integer-literal* to enum type implicit conversion. Neither the Microsoft nor the Mono compilers issue such a warning. Bugs like this make us wish that work on the Annotated Standard had got under way somewhat earlier, in time for this to be fixed in the published Standard.

(See also the "Switching on nullables" annotation in §15.7.2.)

13.1.4 Implicit reference conversions
The implicit reference conversions are:

- From any *reference-type* to `object`.
- From any *class-type* S to any *class-type* T, provided S is derived from T.
- From any *class-type* S to any *interface-type* T, provided S implements T.
- From any *interface-type* S to any *interface-type* T, provided S is derived from T.
- From an *array-type* S with an element type S_E to an *array-type* T with an element type T_E, provided all of the following are true:
    - S and T differ only in element type. In other words, S and T have the same number of dimensions.
    - An implicit reference conversion exists from S_E to T_E.
- From a one-dimensional *array-type* S[] to `System.Collections.Generic.IList<S>` and base interfaces of this interface.
- From a one-dimensional *array-type* S[] to `System.Collections.Generic.IList<T>` and base interfaces of this interface, provided there is an implicit reference conversion from S to T.
- From any *array-type* to `System.Array`.
- From any *delegate-type* to `System.Delegate`.
- From any *array-type* to any interface implemented by `System.Array`.
- From any *delegate-type* to `System.ICloneable`.
- From the null type (§11.2.7) to any *reference-type*.

For a *type-parameter* T that is known to be a reference type (§25.7), the following implicit reference conversions exist:

- From T to its effective base class C, from T to any base class of C, and from T to any interface implemented by C.
- From T to an *interface-type* I in T's effective interface set and from T to any base interface of I.
- From T to a type parameter U provided that T depends on U (§25.7). [*Note*: Since T is known to be a reference type, within the scope of T, the run-time type of U will always be a reference type, even if U is not known to be a reference type at compile-time. *end note*]
- From the null type (§11.2.7) to T.

The implicit reference conversions are those conversions between *reference-type*s that can be proven to always succeed, and therefore require no checks at run-time.

Conversions to implemented interfaces
Since a class inherits all interface implementations provided by its base classes (§20.4 and subclauses), an implicit reference conversion exists from the class to every interface implemented by a base class.

In the example

```
interface I { ...}
class T :  I { ...}
class S :  T { ...}
```

S implements I since I is in T's base class list. Consequently, there exists an implicit reference conversion from S to I.

A specific case of this is when S is an arbitrary delegate type, T is System.Delegate, and I is an arbitrary interface implemented by System.Delegate. (Although C# only specifies the System.ICloneable interface for System.Delegate and this is explicitly mentioned in the preceding text, it is conformant for an implementation to include others. For example, the CLI Standard Library includes System.Runtime.Serialization.ISerializable.) In such a case, there exists an implicit reference conversion from the delegate type to the interface.

Nicu Georgian Fruja

Reference conversions, implicit or explicit, never change the referential identity of the object being converted. [*Note*: In other words, while a reference conversion can change the type of the reference, it never changes the type or value of the object being referred to. *end note*]

13.1.5 Boxing conversions

A boxing conversion permits any *non-nullable-value-type* to be implicitly converted to the type object or System.ValueType or to any *interface-type* implemented by the *non-nullable-value-type*, and any enum type to be implicitly converted to System.Enum as well. Boxing a value of a *non-nullable-value-type* consists of allocating an object instance and copying the value into that instance. An enum can be boxed to the type System.Enum, since that is the direct base class for all enums (§21.4). A struct or enum can be boxed to the type System.ValueType, since that is the direct base class for all structs (§18.3.2) and a base class for all enums.

Leave my box alone...

The specification states that boxing *consists of allocating an object instance*, which disallows the caching of boxed values (e.g., to reuse the same object when repeatedly boxing the same value). This behavior is certainly intentional and referred to elsewhere; for example, see §14.9.6.

The Java specification allows caching of boxed values, and Sun's Java runtime (version 1.5.0) keeps boxed values for the integers –127 to 127 inclusive.

C#'s choice has potential impacts on memory usage and performance, but whether these are positive or negative is application dependent.

Apart from this, the caching or not of boxed values impacts only reference (identity) equality. For a discussion of the subtleties of reference equality, see the annotation on §14.9.

A *nullable-type* has a boxing conversion to the same set of types to which the *nullable-type*'s underlying type has boxing conversions. A boxing conversion applied to a value of a *nullable-type* proceeds as follows:

- If the HasValue property of the nullable value evaluates to false, then the result of the boxing conversion is the null reference of the appropriate type.
- Otherwise, the result is obtained by boxing the result of evaluating the Value property on the nullable value.

For a *type-parameter* T that is *not* known to be a reference type (§25.7), the following conversions involving T are considered to be boxing conversions at compile-time. At run-time, if T is a value type, the conversion is executed as a boxing conversion. At run-time, if T is a reference type, the conversion is executed as an implicit reference conversion or identity conversion.

- From T to its effective base class C, from T to any base class of C, and from T to any interface implemented by C. [*Note*: C will be one of the types System.Object, System.ValueType, or `System.Enum` (otherwise `T` would be known to be a reference type and §13.1.4 would apply instead of this clause). *end note*]

- From `T` to an *interface-type* `I` in `T`'s effective interface set and from `T` to any base interface of `I`.

Boxing conversions are described further in §11.3.1.

13.1.6 Implicit type parameter conversions

This clause details implicit conversions involving type parameters that are not classified as implicit reference conversions or implicit boxing conversions.

For a *type-parameter* `T` that is *not* known to be a reference type, there is an implicit conversion from `T` to a type parameter `U` provided `T` depends on `U`. At run-time, if `T` is a value type and `U` is a reference type, the conversion is executed as a boxing conversion. At run-time, if both `T` and `U` are value types, then `T` and `U` are necessarily the same type and no conversion is performed. At run-time, if `T` is a reference type, then `U` is necessarily also a reference type and the conversion is executed as an implicit reference conversion or identity conversion (§25.7).

13.1.7 Implicit constant expression conversions

An implicit constant expression conversion permits the following conversions:

- A *constant-expression* (§14.16) of type `int` can be converted to type `sbyte`, `byte`, `short`, `ushort`, `uint`, or `ulong`, provided the value of the *constant-expression* is within the range of the destination type.
- A *constant-expression* of type `long` can be converted to type `ulong`, provided the value of the *constant-expression* is not negative.

> **Mind your constants**
>
> That constant expressions may undergo implicit conversions while similar non-constant ones do not can be surprising. For example, consider the code fragment:
>
> ```
> const int i1 = 3;
> byte b1 = i1 + 1;   // OK
>
> int i2 = 3;
> byte b2 = i2 + 1;   // compile-time error
> ```
>
> For a related issue, see the annotation on §14.16.

13.1.8 User-defined implicit conversions

A user-defined implicit conversion consists of an optional standard implicit conversion, followed by execution of a user-defined implicit conversion operator, followed by another optional standard implicit conversion. The exact rules for evaluating user-defined conversions are described in §13.4.3.

13.2 Explicit conversions

The following conversions are classified as explicit conversions:

- All implicit conversions
- Explicit numeric conversions
- Explicit enumeration conversions

- Explicit reference conversions
- Explicit interface conversions
- Unboxing conversions
- Explicit type parameter conversions
- User-defined explicit conversions
- Explicit nullable conversions
- Lifted user-defined explicit conversions

Explicit conversions can occur in cast expressions (§14.6.6).

The set of explicit conversions includes all implicit conversions. [*Note*: This means that redundant cast expressions are allowed. *end note*]

Being explicitly implicit

The terminology here is potentially confusing. For example, consider the following code fragment:

```
int j = 42;
long k = (long)j;
```

A conversion from `int` to `long` is an implicit numeric conversion (§13.1.2). An implicit numeric conversion is an implicit conversion (§13.1), and an implicit conversion is an explicit conversion (§13.2). So in the code fragment, the cast specifies an implicit numeric conversion explicitly, and hence is not required. This is distinct from explicit numeric conversions (§13.2.1) where a cast is required, for example:

```
long r = 42;
int t = (int)r;
```

In summary, an implicit conversion written explicitly is not the same as an explicit conversion.

Jon Skeet

The explicit conversions that are not implicit conversions are conversions that cannot be proven always to succeed, conversions that are known possibly to lose information, and conversions across domains of types sufficiently different to merit explicit notation.

13.2.1 Explicit numeric conversions

The explicit numeric conversions are the conversions from a *numeric-type* to another *numeric-type* for which an implicit numeric conversion (§13.1.2) does not already exist:

- From `sbyte` to `byte`, `ushort`, `uint`, `ulong`, or `char`.
- From `byte` to `sbyte` or `char`.
- From `short` to `sbyte`, `byte`, `ushort`, `uint`, `ulong`, or `char`.
- From `ushort` to `sbyte`, `byte`, `short`, or `char`.
- From `int` to `sbyte`, `byte`, `short`, `ushort`, `uint`, `ulong`, or `char`.
- From `uint` to `sbyte`, `byte`, `short`, `ushort`, `int`, or `char`.
- From `long` to `sbyte`, `byte`, `short`, `ushort`, `int`, `uint`, `ulong`, or `char`.
- From `ulong` to `sbyte`, `byte`, `short`, `ushort`, `int`, `uint`, `long`, or `char`.
- From `char` to `sbyte`, `byte`, or `short`.
- From `float` to `sbyte`, `byte`, `short`, `int`, `uint`, `long`, `ulong`, `char`, or `decimal`.

- From `double` to `sbyte`, `byte`, `short`, `ushort`, `int`, `uint`, `long`, `ulong`, `char`, `float`, or `decimal`.
- From `decimal` to `sbyte`, `byte`, `short`, `ushort`, `int`, `uint`, `long`, `ulong`, `char`, `float`, or `double`.

Because the explicit conversions include all implicit and explicit numeric conversions, it is always possible to convert from any *numeric-type* to any other *numeric-type* using a cast expression (§14.6.6).

The explicit numeric conversions possibly lose information or possibly cause exceptions to be thrown. An explicit numeric conversion is processed as follows:

- For a conversion from an integral type to another integral type, the processing depends on the overflow checking context (§14.5.13) in which the conversion takes place:
    - In a `checked` context, the conversion succeeds if the value of the source operand is within the range of the destination type, but throws a `System.OverflowException` if the value of the source operand is outside the range of the destination type.
    - In an `unchecked` context, the conversion always succeeds, and proceeds as follows.
        - If the source type is larger than the destination type, then the source value is truncated by discarding its "extra" most significant bits. The result is then treated as a value of the destination type.
        - If the source type is smaller than the destination type, then the source value is either sign-extended or zero-extended so that it is the same size as the destination type. Sign-extension is used if the source type is signed; zero-extension is used if the source type is unsigned. The result is then treated as a value of the destination type.
        - If the source type is the same size as the destination type, then the source value is treated as a value of the destination type
- For a conversion from `decimal` to an integral type, the source value is rounded towards zero to the nearest integral value, and this integral value becomes the result of the conversion. If the resulting integral value is outside the range of the destination type, a `System.OverflowException` is thrown.
- For a conversion from `float` or `double` to an integral type, the processing depends on the overflow-checking context (§14.5.13) in which the conversion takes place:
    - In a `checked` context, the conversion proceeds as follows:
        - The value is rounded towards zero to the nearest integral value. If this integral value is within the range of the destination type, then this value is the result of the conversion.
        - Otherwise, a `System.OverflowException` is thrown.
    - In an `unchecked` context, the conversion always succeeds, and proceeds as follows.
        - The value is rounded towards zero to the nearest integral value. If this integral value is within the range of the destination type, then this value is the result of the conversion.
        - Otherwise, the result of the conversion is an unspecified value of the destination type.
- For a conversion from `double` to `float`, the `double` value is rounded to the nearest `float` value. This rounding may cause a non-zero value to be rounded to a zero value

of the same sign. If the magnitude of the `double` value is too large to represent as a `float`, the result becomes positive infinity or negative infinity. If the `double` value is NaN, the result is also NaN.

- For a conversion from `float` or `double` to `decimal`, the source value is converted to `decimal` representation and rounded to the nearest number if required (§11.1.7). This rounding may cause a non-zero value to be rounded to zero. If the source value's magnitude is too large to represent as a `decimal`, or that value is a NaN or infinity, yet the `decimal` representation does not support NaNs or infinities, respectively, a `System.OverflowException` is thrown.

- For a conversion from `decimal` to `float` or `double`, the `decimal` value is rounded to the nearest `double` or `float` value. However, if the value being converted is not within the range of the destination type, a `System.OverflowException` is thrown.

Why no double to decimal implicit conversions?

Programmers are often surprised by this:

```
decimal d = 42.42;  // compile time error?!
```

and wonder why an explicit decimal suffix is required:

```
decimal d = 42.42M;  // ok
```

The type of 42.42 is double, so the first statement will only compile if there is an implicit conversion from double to decimal. But as the standard specifies, this conversion is explicit. This is because making the conversion implicit would create problems with precision. Consider, for example:

```
decimal d = 1.2345678901234567890123;
```

If the literal is interpreted as a double literal, which has only 17 digits of precision, then it must be truncated to 1.234567890123456 and then converted to a decimal. The result would be a decimal with less precision than the programmer presumably expected. Changing the rules so that full precision was maintained was considered, but rejected, as it would have required substantial changes to the language. These dual decimal/double literals would need a new and strange intermediate type, which is of type double, but somehow maintains more precision than a double. Even if this change were made, there would still be potential confusion. For example, it is hard to understand how much precision with which the following constant expression is calculated:

```
decimal d = 1.2345678901234567890123 + 3.2345678901234567890123;
```

As things stand now, every expression has a well-defined type.

Decimal conversion exceptions dependent on format

As mentioned earlier (see annotation on §11.1.7), some time was spent discussing whether C# 2.0 should adopt the proposed IEEE 754r 128-bit decimal floating point for the `decimal` type. Had this been done, then the minimum precision and range of `decimal` would have been a superset of those for `double`. This would have allowed implicit conversions from `double` to `decimal`, and all real literals to be typed `decimal` by default with constant expressions implicitly downcast to the required precision.

Though IEEE Decimal is not required, it is *allowed*. This is the reason why the preceding clause on converting `decimal` to `float` or `double` allows for `System.OverflowException` to be thrown as explained in §11.1.7. However, the compilers from Microsoft and Mono current at the time of writing will never throw this exception as their `decimal` range is within that of both `float` and `double`–only the precision is greater.

Similarly, the preceding clause on converting `float` or `double` to `decimal` allows for `System.OverflowException` to be thrown if NaNs or infinities are involved. However, IEEE Decimal does support NaNs and infinities, so an implementation using this format will never throw an exception in these circumstances. In contrast, the compilers from Microsoft and Mono current at the time of writing do not support NaNs and infinities for `decimal` and will therefore throw an exception in these circumstances.

13.2.2 Explicit enumeration conversions

The explicit enumeration conversions are:

- From `sbyte`, `byte`, `short`, `ushort`, `int`, `uint`, `long`, `ulong`, `char`, `float`, `double`, or `decimal` to any *enum-type*.
- From any *enum-type* to `sbyte`, `byte`, `short`, `ushort`, `int`, `uint`, `long`, `ulong`, `char`, `float`, `double`, or `decimal`.
- From any *enum-type* to any other *enum-type*.

An explicit enumeration conversion between two types is processed by treating any participating *enum-type* as the underlying type of that *enum-type*, and then performing an implicit or explicit numeric conversion between the resulting types. [*Example*: Given an *enum-type* E with and underlying type of `int`, a conversion from E to `byte` is processed as an explicit numeric conversion (§13.2.1) from `int` to `byte`, and a conversion from `byte` to E is processed as an implicit numeric conversion (§13.1.2) from `byte` to `int`. *end example*]

Dubious explicit enum conversions

It might be surprising to some that floating point to enum conversions are provided. For example, why support casting on the CLI from `1032.1032` to an `AttributeTarget` (the result happens to be `Class | Interface`)?

The provision of these conversions stems from the weak nature of C# enumerated types; see annotation on §21.

It is recommended that these conversions are avoided; they obfuscate without benefit.

13.2.3 Explicit reference conversions

The explicit reference conversions are:

- From `object` to any *reference-type*.
- From any *class-type* S to any *class-type* T, provided S is a base class of T.
- From any *class-type* S to any *interface-type* T, provided S is not sealed and provided S does not implement T.
- From any *interface-type* S to any *class-type* T, provided T is not sealed or provided T implements S.
- From any *interface-type* S to any *interface-type* T, provided S is not derived from T.
- From an *array-type* S with an element type S_E to an *array-type* T with an element type T_E, provided all of the following are true:
  - S and T differ only in element type. (In other words, S and T have the same number of dimensions.)
  - An explicit reference conversion exists from S_E to T_E.

- From `System.Array` and the interfaces it implements, to any *array-type*.
- From `System.Delegate` and the interfaces it implements, to any *delegate-type*.
- From a one-dimensional *array-type* `S[ ]` to `System.Collections.Generic.IList<T>` and its base interfaces, provided there is an explicit reference conversion from `S` to `T`.
- From `System.Collections.Generic.IList<T>` and its base interfaces to a one-dimensional *array-type* `S[ ]`, provided there is an implicit or explicit reference conversion from `S[ ]` to `System.Collections.Generic.IList<T>`. This is precisely when either `S` and `T` are the same type or there is an implicit or explicit reference conversion from `S` to `T`.

For a *type-parameter* `T` that is known to be a reference type (§25.7), the following explicit reference conversions exist:

- From the effective base class `C` of `T` to `T` and from any base class of `C` to `T`.
- From any *interface-type* to `T`.
- From `T` to any *interface-type* `I` provided there isn't already an implicit reference conversion from `T` to `I`.
- From a *type-parameter* `U` to `T` provided that `T` depends on `U` (§25.7). [*Note*: Since `T` is known to be a reference type, within the scope of `T`, the run-time type of `U` will always be a reference type, even if `U` is not known to be a reference type at compile-time. *end note*]

The explicit reference conversions are those conversions between *reference-type*s that require run-time checks to ensure they are correct.

For an explicit reference conversion to succeed at run-time, the value of the source operand shall be `null`, or the runtime type of the object referenced by the source operand shall be a type that can be converted to the destination type by an implicit reference conversion (§13.1.4). If an explicit reference conversion fails, a `System.InvalidCastException` is thrown.

Reference conversions, implicit or explicit, never change the referential identity of the object being converted. [*Note*: In other words, while a reference conversion can change the type of the reference, it never changes the type or value of the object being referred to. *end note*]

Never changes, maybe...

The preceding statement refers to *standard* reference conversions. It does not refer to *user-defined* reference conversions. A user-defined conversion may or may not change the referential identity of the object being converted. For example, consider:

```
class SpecialArray<T>
{
  private T[ ] store;

  public SpecialArray(int size)
  {
    store = new T[ size] ;
  }

  public static explicit operator T[ ] (SpecialArray<T> from)
  {
    return from.store;
  }
  . . .
}
```

Here the class `SpecialArray<T>` provides a user-defined explicit conversion to `T[]` that returns a reference to a different object (namely, the array `store`) than the object being converted.

A user-defined conversion, being a method, can in fact perform all sorts of operations and side effects. However it is *most strongly recommended* that it does not!

Conversion from System.Collections.Generic.IList<T>

By definition a standard (i.e., not user-defined) reference conversion not only leaves the converted object unchanged, but also returns a reference to precisely that object, not to another (new or existing) object. These requirements require runtime, as well as compile time, checking.

According to the preceding bullet list, there is an explicit reference conversion from `SCG.IList<T>` to `T[]`, where `SCG` abbreviates `System.Collections.Generic`. It follows that this explicit reference conversion can succeed only if the object of type `SCG.IList<T>` is represented exactly as a one-dimensional C# array. In all other cases, this explicit conversion must throw `InvalidCastException` at runtime.

In particular, consider any user-defined generic class `MyList<T>` that implements `SCG.IList<T>`:

```
using SCG = System.Collections.Generic;

class MyList<T> : SCG.IList<T>
{
  ...
}
```

From the bullets, one might naively expect that a `MyList<T>` object can be converted to a `T[]`. Indeed, because there exists an explicit conversion from `SCG.IList<int>` to `int[]`, the following code will compile OK. However, that is all that "exists" means; at runtime the third line will fail with an `InvalidCastException`:

```
MyList<int> list = new MyList<int>();
SCG.IList<int> ilist = list;       // Compiles and runs OK
int[] arr = (int[])ilist;          // Compiles OK, but fails at runtime
```

One can declare a conversion (explicit or implicit) from `MyList<T>` to `T[]`, but that does not make the last line in the preceding example succeed at runtime, because it will use the standard explicit conversion from `SCG.IList<T>`, which throws `InvalidCastException`. Also, one cannot declare a conversion from `MyList<T>` to an interface such as `SCG.IList<T>` (§17.9.3).

An explicit conversion to `T[]` succeeds at runtime only if the given `SCG.IList<T>` object is actually a one-dimensional array:

```
SCG.IList<int> ilist = new int[4];  // Compiles and runs OK
int[] arr = (int[])ilist;           // Compiles and runs OK
```

An explicit conversion to `T[]` fails at runtime for instances of `SCG.List<T>`, even though `SCG.List<T>` is an array-based list.

Mauled by the host, again...

This annotation relates to the behavior of certain C# compilers. This behavior breaks the C# type system and is **not** intentional; the compiler teams did not design it in. Rather, the behavior is unfortunately inherited from the host platform and the compiler teams determined it was too costly to design it out; other compiler teams might conceivably come to a different conclusion. The Standard committee discussed this matter and decided not to break the C# type system in order to accommodate these platforms.

You are strongly advised not write to code that relies on this behavior

This behavior is documented only so that when your code fails to throw exceptions when it should, you will know why and be able to track down the problem. Compilers may change, and the platform behavior may change.

Some host platforms, such as the CLI, may provide type conversion as an *instruction*, while others, such as the Pentium, compile it into a number of instructions. Obviously, if there is an instruction, compiler teams will wish to use it. If the instruction does not exactly meet the C# specification, they have to decide whether to allow their compiler to be nonconforming or to adopt a more complicated, and probably expensive, solution.

Some C# compilers are known to "accidentally" allow the conversion of a signed integral array to an object and then to an unsigned integral array, where the integral types are the same size, and vice-versa.

This behavior **does not** convert the elements of the array but rather reinterprets the bit-pattern as the other type. The result may not be mathematically correct, and any exceptions that the conversion from signed to unsigned (or vice-versa) should have generated will not be thrown.

This behavior is known to occur using the Microsoft VS 2005 C# compiler running on Microsoft's CLR v2.0. Other permutations of compilers and platforms may or may not behave in this way.

We do not guarantee that these are the only rogue conversions that compilers provide! However, we have provided information on some invalid unboxing conversions that we are also aware of in §11.3.2.

[*Note*: The behavior described here is allowed by the CLI Standard.]

13.2.4 Unboxing conversions

An unboxing conversion permits an explicit conversion from type `object` or `System.Value-Type` to any *non-nullable-value-type*, or from any *interface-type* to any *non-nullable-value-type* that implements the *interface-type*, and from the type `System.Enum` to any enumeration type. An unboxing operation consists of first checking that the object instance is a boxed value of the given *value-type* or enumeration type, and then copying the value out of the instance. An enum can be unboxed from the type `System.Enum`, since that is the direct base class for all enum types (§21.4). A struct or enum can be unboxed from the type `System.ValueType`, since that is the direct base class for all structs (§18.3.2) and a base class for all enums.

An unboxing conversion permits an explicit conversion from `object` or `System.ValueType` to any *nullable-type* or from any *interface-type* to any *nullable-type* whose underlying type implements the *interface-type* and from `System.Enum` to any *nullable-type* whose underlying type is an enumeration type. An unboxing conversion from an expression `e` of type `T` to a nullable type `V?` proceeds as follows:

- If `e` is `null` the result is the null value of type `V?`.
- Otherwise, the result is equivalent to an unboxing from `e` to `V`, followed by a wrapping (§13.7) from `V` to `V?`.

For a *type-parameter* `T` that is *not* known to be a reference type (§25.7), the following conversions involving `T` are considered to be unboxing conversions at compile-time. At run-time, if `T` is a value type, the conversion is executed as an unboxing conversion. At run-time, if `T` is a reference type, the conversion is executed as an explicit reference conversion or identity conversion.

- From the effective base class `C` of `T` to `T` and from any base class of `C` to `T`. [*Note*: `C` will be one of the types `System.Object`, `System.ValueType`, or `System.Enum` (otherwise `T` would be known to be a reference type and §13.2.3 would apply instead of this clause). *end note*]
- From any *interface-type* to `T`.

Unboxing conversions are described further in §11.3.2.

13.2.5 Explicit type parameter conversions

This clause details explicit conversions involving type parameters that are not classified as explicit reference conversions or explicit unboxing conversions.

For a *type-parameter* `T` that is *not* known to be a reference type (§25.7), the following explicit conversions exist:

- From `T` to any *interface-type* `I` provided there is not already an implicit conversion from `T` to `I`. This conversion consists of an implicit boxing conversion (§13.1.5) from `T` to `object` followed by an explicit reference conversion from `object` to `I`. At run-time, if `T` is a value type, the conversion is executed as a boxing conversion followed by an explicit reference conversion. At run-time, if `T` is a reference type, the conversion is executed as an explicit reference conversion.
- From a type parameter `U` to `T` provided that `T` depends on `U` (§25.7). At run-time, if `T` is a value type and `U` is a reference type, the conversion is executed as an unboxing conversion. At run-time, if both `T` and `U` are value types, then `T` and `U` are necessarily the same type and no conversion is performed. At run-time, if `T` is a reference type, then `U` is necessarily also a reference type and the conversion is executed as an explicit reference conversion or identity conversion.

13.2.6 User-defined explicit conversions

A user-defined explicit conversion consists of an optional standard explicit conversion, followed by execution of a user-defined implicit or explicit conversion operator, followed by another optional standard explicit conversion. The exact rules for evaluating user-defined conversions are described in §13.4.4.

13.3 Standard conversions

The standard conversions are those pre-defined conversions that can occur as part of a user-defined conversion.

13.3.1 Standard implicit conversions

The following implicit conversions are classified as standard implicit conversions:

- Identity conversions (§13.1.1)
- Implicit numeric conversions (§13.1.2)
- Implicit reference conversions (§13.1.4)
- Boxing conversions (§13.1.5)
- Implicit type parameter conversions (§13.1.6)
- Implicit constant expression conversions (§13.1.7)
- Implicit nullable conversions (§13.7.2)

The standard implicit conversions specifically exclude user-defined implicit conversions.

13.3.2 Standard explicit conversions

The standard explicit conversions are all standard implicit conversions plus the subset of the explicit conversions for which an opposite standard implicit conversion exists. [*Note*: In other words, if a standard implicit conversion exists from a type A to a type B, then a standard explicit conversion exists from type A to type B and from type B to type A. *end note*]

13.4 User-defined conversions

C# allows the pre-defined implicit and explicit conversions to be augmented by ***user-defined conversions***. User-defined conversions are introduced by declaring conversion operators (§17.9.3) in class and struct types.

13.4.1 Permitted user-defined conversions

C# permits only certain user-defined conversions to be declared. In particular, it is not possible to redefine an already existing implicit or explicit conversion.

The restrictions that apply to user-defined conversions are specified in §17.9.3.

13.4.2 Evaluation of user-defined conversions

A user-defined conversion converts a value from its type, called the ***source type***, to another type, called the ***target type***. Evaluation of a user-defined conversion centers on finding the ***most specific*** user-defined conversion operator for the particular source and target types. This determination is broken into several steps:

- Finding the set of classes and structs from which user-defined conversion operators will be considered. This set consists of the source type and its base classes and the target type and its base classes (with the implicit assumptions that only classes and structs can declare user-defined operators, and that non-class types have no base classes). Trailing ? modifiers, if any, are removed from the source and target types before determining the set of types from which user-defined conversion operators will be considered. For example, when converting from a type S? to a type T?, the set of types from which user-defined conversion operators will be considered consists of S and T.
- From that set of types, determining which user-defined conversion operators are applicable. For a conversion operator to be applicable, it shall be possible to perform a standard conversion (§13.3) from the source type to the operand type of the operator, and it shall be possible to perform a standard conversion from the result type of the operator to the target type. When the source and target types are both nullable, the set of applicable

conversion operators includes not just user-defined conversion operators but also lifted conversion operators (§13.7.3). If the set of applicable user-defined conversion operators is empty then there is no user-defined conversion from the source type to the target type.

- From the set of applicable user-defined operators, determining which operator is unambiguously the most specific. In general terms, the most specific operator is the operator whose operand type is "closest" to the source type and whose result type is "closest" to the target type. The exact rules for establishing the most specific user-defined conversion operator are defined in the following subclauses.

For the purposes of overload resolution, a user-defined conversion from the source type to the target type exists if and only if the set of applicable user-defined conversion operators is non-empty. If the set of applicable operators is non-empty but does not contain a unique most specific operator, the user-defined conversion is deemed to exist even though application of the conversion will always produce a compile-time error.

Once a most specific user-defined conversion operator has been identified, the actual execution of the user-defined conversion involves up to three steps:

- First, if required, performing a standard conversion from the source type to the operand type of the user-defined conversion operator.
- Next, invoking the user-defined conversion operator to perform the conversion.
- Finally, if required, performing a standard conversion from the result type of the user-defined conversion operator to the target type.

Evaluation of a user-defined conversion never involves more than one user-defined conversion operator. In other words, a conversion from type S to type T will never first execute a user-defined conversion from S to X and then execute a user-defined conversion from X to T.

Exact definitions of evaluation of user-defined implicit or explicit conversions are given in the following subclauses. The definitions make use of the following terms:

- If a standard implicit conversion (§13.3.1) exists from a type A to a type B, and if neither A nor B are *interface-type*s, then A is said to be **encompassed by** B, and B is said to **encompass** A.
- The **most encompassing type** in a set of types is the one type that encompasses all other types in the set. If no single type encompasses all other types, then the set has no most encompassing type. In more intuitive terms, the most encompassing type is the "largest" type in the set—the one type to which each of the other types can be implicitly converted.
- The **most encompassed type** in a set of types is the one type that is encompassed by all other types in the set. If no single type is encompassed by all other types, then the set has no most encompassed type. In more intuitive terms, the most encompassed type is the "smallest" type in the set—the one type that can be implicitly converted to each of the other types.

13.4.3 User-defined implicit conversions

A user-defined implicit conversion from type S to type T is processed as follows:

- Determine the types S0 and T0 that result from removing the trailing ? modifiers, if any, from S and T.
- Find the set of types, D, from which user-defined conversion operators will be considered. This set consists of S0 (if S0 is a class or struct), the base classes of S0 (if S0 is a class), the

effective base class of S0 and its base classes (if S0 is a type parameter), and T0 (if T0 is a class or struct).

- Find the set of applicable conversion operators, U. This set consists of the user-defined and, if S and T are both nullable, lifted implicit conversion operators (§13.7.3) declared by the classes or structs in D that convert from a type encompassing S to a type encompassed by T. If U is empty, there is no conversion, and a compile-time error occurs.
- Find the most specific source type, SX, of the operators in U:
  - If any of the operators in U convert from S, then SX is S.
  - Otherwise, SX is the most encompassed type in the combined set of source types of the operators in U. If exactly one most encompassed type cannot be found, then the conversion is ambiguous and a compile-time error occurs.
- Find the most specific target type, TX, of the operators in U:
  - If any of the operators in U convert to T, then TX is T.
  - Otherwise, TX is the most encompassing type in the combined set of target types of the operators in U. If exactly one most encompassing type cannot be found, then the conversion is ambiguous and a compile-time error occurs.
- Find the most specific conversion operator:
  - If U contains exactly one user-defined conversion operator that converts from SX to TX, then this is the most specific conversion operator.
  - Otherwise, if U contains exactly one lifted conversion operator that converts from SX to TX, then this is the most specific conversion operator.
  - Otherwise, the conversion is ambiguous and a compile-time error occurs.
- Finally, apply the conversion:
  - If S is not SX, then a standard implicit conversion from S to SX is performed.
  - The most specific conversion operator is invoked to convert from SX to TX.
  - If TX is not T, then a standard implicit conversion from TX to T is performed.

13.4.4 User-defined explicit conversions

A user-defined explicit conversion from type S to type T is processed as follows:

- Determine the types S0 and T0 that result from removing the trailing ? modifiers, if any, from S and T.
- Find the set of types, D, from which user-defined conversion operators will be considered. This set consists of S0 (if S0 is a class or struct), the base classes of S0 (if S0 is a class), the effective base class of S0 and its base classes (if S0 is a type parameter),T0 (if T0 is a class or struct), the base classes of T0 (if T0 is a class), and the effective base class of T0 and its base classes (if T0 is a type parameter).
- Find the set of applicable conversion operators, U. This set consists of the user-defined and, if S and T are both nullable, lifted implicit or explicit conversion operators (§13.7.3) declared by the classes or structs in D that convert from a type encompassing or encompassed by S to a type encompassing or encompassed by T. If U is empty, there is no conversion, and a compile-time error occurs.
- Find the most specific source type, SX, of the operators in U:
  - If any of the operators in U convert from S, then SX is S.
  - Otherwise, if any of the operators in U convert from types that encompass S, then SX is the most encompassed type in the combined set of source types of those operators. If exactly one most encompassed type cannot be found, then the conversion is ambiguous and a compile-time error occurs.

- Otherwise, SX is the most encompassing type in the combined set of source types of the operators in U. If exactly one most encompassing type cannot be found, then the conversion is ambiguous and a compile-time error occurs.
- Find the most specific target type, TX, of the operators in U:
  - If any of the operators in U convert to T, then TX is T.
  - Otherwise, if any of the operators in U convert to types that are encompassed by T, then TX is the most encompassing type in the combined set of target types of those operators. If exactly one most encompassing type cannot be found, then the conversion is ambiguous and a compile-time error occurs.
  - Otherwise, TX is the most encompassed type in the combined set of target types of the operators in U. If exactly one most encompassed type cannot be found, then the conversion is ambiguous and a compile-time error occurs.
- Find the most specific conversion operator:
  - If U contains exactly one user-defined conversion operator that converts from SX to TX, then this is the most specific conversion operator.
  - Otherwise, if U contains exactly one lifted conversion operator that converts from SX to TX, then this is the most specific conversion operator.
  - Otherwise, the conversion is ambiguous and a compile-time error occurs.
- Finally, apply the conversion:
  - If S is not SX, then a standard explicit conversion from S to SX is performed.
  - The most specific conversion operator is invoked to convert from SX to TX.
  - If TX is not T, then a standard explicit conversion from TX to T is performed.

13.5 Anonymous method conversions

An implicit conversion (§13.1) exists from an *anonymous-method-expression* (§14.5.15) to any **compatible** delegate type. If D is a delegate type, and A is an *anonymous-method-expression*, then D is compatible with A if and only if the following two conditions are met.

Anecdote: Mono widget design improves C#

This might have been the only contribution to the specification from the Mono team that made it through Anders's filter. Although Michael Meeks suggested this idea to the Mono team, it seems that the same issues might have been raised by others and that Microsoft would have implemented this anyway.

The GUI libraries that we use in Unix are based on a set of object-oriented patterns built on top of C. To make development more pleasant with C, the GUI classes are developed with an event system. Most developers will not extend a C-class when they want to alter the behavior of a widget, but instead will do this by connecting to the various events that the widgets trigger.

When we bound this GUI library for use by Mono developers, we exposed this familiar technique to them. At the time, developers had to write code like this:

```
Gtk.Entry password = new Gtk.Entry();
password.TextInserted += new Gtk.TextDeletedHandler(check_password);

Gtk.Button ok = new Gtk.Button("Ok");
ok.Clicked += new EventHandler(ProcessForm);
```

Developers claimed, with just reason, that although C# was a very nice upgrade to use C to develop applications, they could not understand why the compiler could not do some of the work as the information was already available for it to use. They wished to write:

```
Gtk.Entry password = new Gtk.Entry();
password.TextInserted += check_password;

Gtk.Button ok = new Gtk.Button("Ok");
ok.Clicked += ProcessForm;
```

This is just what we have now.

Miguel de Icaza

- First, the parameter types of D shall be compatible with A:
  - If A does not contain an *anonymous-method-signature*, then D can have zero or more parameters of any type, as long as no parameter of D has the out parameter modifier.
  - If A has an *anonymous-method-signature*, then D shall have the same number of parameters and each parameter of A shall be compatible with the corresponding parameter of D. A parameter of A is considered compatible with a parameter of D if they are both of the same type and the presence or absence of the ref or out modifier on the parameter of A matches the corresponding parameter of D. Whether the final parameter of D is a *parameter-array* is not considered when determining the compatibility of A and D. A parameter which has the *parameter-array* modifier is compatible with a parameter without the *parameter-array* modifier if they are both of the same type.
- Second, the return type of D shall be compatible with A. For these rules, A is not considered to contain the *block* of any other anonymous methods:
  - If D is declared with a void return type, then any return statement contained in A shall not specify an expression.
  - If D is declared with a return type of R, then any return statement contained in A shall specify an expression which is implicitly convertible (§13.1) to R. Furthermore, the end-point of the *block* of A shall not be reachable. [*Note*: The *block* of an *anonymous-method-expression* is always considered reachable, even if it is contained in a statement that is unreachable. See §15.1. *end note*]

Besides the implicit conversions to compatible delegate types, no other conversions exist from an *anonymous-method-expression*, not even to the type object.

[*Example*: The following examples illustrate these rules:

```
delegate void D(int x);

D d1 = delegate {};                     // Ok
D d2 = delegate() {};                   // Error, signature mismatch
D d3 = delegate(long x) {};             // Error, signature mismatch
D d4 = delegate(int x) {};              // Ok
D d5 = delegate(int x) { return; };     // Ok
D d6 = delegate(int x) { return x; };   // Error, return type mismatch

delegate void E(out int x);

E e1 = delegate {};                     // Error, E has an out parameter
E e2 = delegate(out int x) { x = 1; };  // Ok
E e3 = delegate(ref int x) { x = 1; };  // Error, signature mismatch
```

```
delegate int P(params int[] a);

P p1 = delegate { };                    // Error, end of block reachable
P p2 = delegate { return; };            // Error, return type mismatch
P p3 = delegate { return 1; };          // Ok
P p4 = delegate { return "Hello"; };    // Error, return type mismatch
P p5 = delegate(int[] a)                // Ok
   {
      return a[0];
   };
P p6 = delegate(params int[] a)         // Error, params modifier
   {
      return a[0];
   };
P p7 = delegate(int[] a)                // Error, return type mismatch
   {
      if (a.Length > 0) return a[0];
      return "Hello";
   };

delegate object Q(params int[] a);

Q q1 = delegate(int[] a)                // Ok
   {
      if (a.Length > 0) return a[0];
      return "Hello";
   };
```
end example]

A *delegate-creation-expression* (§14.5.10.3) can be used as an alternate syntax for converting an anonymous method to a delegate type.

13.6 Method group conversions

Similar to the implicit anonymous method conversions described in §13.5, an implicit conversion exists from a method group (§14.1) to a compatible delegate type. If D is a delegate type, and E is an expression that is classified as a method group, then D is compatible with E if and only if E contains at least one method that is applicable in its normal form (§14.4.2.1) to any argument list (§14.4.1) having types and modifiers matching the parameter types and modifiers of D.

The compile-time application of the conversion from E to D is the same as the compile-time processing of the delegate creation expression new D(E) (§14.5.10.3). Note that the existence of an implicit conversion from E to D just indicates that the set of applicable methods is not empty, but does not guarantee that the compile-time application of the conversion will succeed without error.

Non-orthogonality

While an implicit conversion is defined to be equivalent to the expression new D(E), there is a non-orthogonality in that if E is itself a delegate then an implicit conversion does not exist. This may be surprising and is covered in an annotation on §14.5.10.3.

[*Example*: In the following code

```
using System;
using System.Windows.Forms;

class AlertDialog
{
  Label message = new Label();
  Button okButton = new Button();
  Button cancelButton = new Button();

  public AlertDialog()
  {
    okButton.Click += new EventHandler(OkClick);
    cancelButton.Click += new EventHandler(CancelClick);
    ...
  }

  void OkClick(object sender, EventArgs e)
  {
    ...
  }

  void CancelClick(object sender, EventArgs e)
  {
    ...
  }
}
```

the constructor creates two delegate instances using the `new` operator. Implicit method group conversions permit this to be shortened to

```
public AlertDialog()
{
  okButton.Click += OkClick;
  cancelButton.Click += CancelClick;
  ...
}
```

end example]

As with all other implicit and explicit conversions, the cast operator can be used to explicitly perform a particular conversion. [*Example*: Thus, the example

```
object obj = new EventHandler(myDialog.OkClick);
```

could instead be written

```
object obj = (EventHandler)myDialog.OkClick;
```

end example]

Although method groups and anonymous method expressions can influence overload resolution, they do not participate in type inferencing (§25.6.4).

Through a glass darkly...

The rules for implicit conversions from method groups may produce results that surprise some people.

As the reference to §14.4.2.1 earlier indicates, the rules for overload resolution are involved in the conversion process. Overload resolution in C# (§14.4.2) may insert code to perform implicit conversions (§13.1) *before* a method is called. For example, consider the code fragment:

```
void M(long l) { ...}
...
int x;
...
M(x);
```

The method M takes an argument of type long. A value of type int cannot be passed, as the runtime representations of long and int are different. However, C# provides an implicit conversion from int to long (§13.1.2) and thus converts the call to:

```
M((long)x);
```

This is correct as the cast (§14.6.6) is compiled to produce the code to convert the int value to a long before the method call is made.

Delegate (§22) invocation behaves the same as any other method invocation (§14.5.5) and so overload resolution (§14.4.2) may be involved and implicit conversions (§13.1) may be inserted.

However, a delegate is just a reference to a method, and a call to a delegate is just redirected to a method *without any representation changes* to the supplied arguments. Therefore, when a delegate is created (§14.5.10.3) from a method name, the usual lookup process is applied to discover to which method the name refers. This involves the usual overload resolution search (§14.4.2), and then the method is checked for *consistency* (§22.1) with the delegate. This check disallows implicit conversions, which involve representation changes, and so makes the call redirection possible. For example:

```
delegate void Dint(int x);
delegate void Dlong(long y);

void M(long z) { ...}
...
Dint d1 = new Dint(M);    // invalid as M requires a long and a conversion
                          // from int to long is a representation change
Dlong d2 = new Dlong(M); // valid
```

The source of potential confusion arises from the split between:

- locating candidate methods, which involves overload resolution (§14.4.2);
- the separate application of the consistency check (§22.1); and
- the decision that during overload resolution an implicit conversion shall be deemed to exist if overload resolution locates a candidate (first paragraph of this clause) **but** before the consistency check has been applied (second paragraph of this clause).

This produces the potentially surprising result:

```
delegate void Dint(int x);
delegate void Dlong(long y);

void M(long z) { ...}

void F(Dint di) { ...}
void F(Dlong dl) { ...}
...
Dint d1 = new Dint(M); // invalid as M requires a long and a conversion
```

```
                          // from int to long is a representation change
    Dlong d2 = new Dlong(M); // valid

    F(M);                     // error, ambiguous although d1 = new Dint(M) is invalid
```

This result stems directly from the preceding split; the overload resolution produces an ambiguous error as an implicit conversion from M to D1 is deemed to exist despite the fact that the next stage of compilation will reject it as M is not consistent D1.

At the time of writing the current Microsoft compiler follows the above definition and reports an error. However the current Mono compiler defines the implicit conversion to exist *if and only if* the method is consistent with the delegate, and thus resolves the call to refer to the method void F(Dlong d1).

It is hard to fault Mono's choice...

13.7 Conversions involving nullable types

The following terms are used in the subsequent sections:

- The term *wrapping* denotes the process of packaging a value, of type T, in an instance of type T?. A value x of type T is wrapped to type T? by evaluating the expression new T?(x).
- The term *unwrapping* denotes the process of obtaining the value, of type T, contained in an instance of type T?. A value x of type T? is unwrapped to type T by evaluating the expression x.Value. Attempting to unwrap a null instance causes a System.InvalidOperationException to be thrown.

Wrapping conversions

Wrapping and unwrapping can also be done by conversions; see §13.7.2 (and also §11.4.1).

13.7.1 Null type conversions

An implicit conversion exists from the null type (§11.2.7) to any nullable type. This conversion produces the null value (§12.2) of the given nullable type.

13.7.2 Nullable conversions

Nullable conversions permit predefined conversions that operate on non-nullable value types to also be used with nullable forms of those types. For each of the predefined implicit or explicit conversions that convert from a non-nullable value type S to a non-nullable value type T (§13.1.1, §13.1.2, §13.1.3, §13.1.7, §13.2.1, and §13.2.2), the following nullable conversions exist:

- An implicit or explicit conversion from S? to T?.
- An implicit or explicit conversion from S to T?.
- An explicit conversion from S? to T.

A nullable conversion is itself classified as an implicit or explicit conversion.

Nullable "identity" conversions

Note that the identity conversion (§13.1.1) is included, so the following conversions exist:

- An implicit conversion from S to S? (see also §11.4.1).
- An explicit conversion from S? to S.

Certain nullable conversions are classified as standard conversions and can occur as part of a user-defined conversion. Specifically, all implicit nullable conversions are classified as standard implicit conversions (§13.3.1), and those explicit nullable conversions that satisfy the requirements of §13.3.2 are classified as standard explicit conversions.

Evaluation of a nullable conversion based on an underlying conversion from S to T proceeds as follows:

- If the nullable conversion is from S? to T?:
  - If the source value is null (HasValue property is false), the result is the null value of type T?.
  - Otherwise, the conversion is evaluated as an unwrapping from S? to S, followed by the underlying conversion from S to T, followed by a wrapping from T to T?.
- If the nullable conversion is from S to T?, the conversion is evaluated as the underlying conversion from S to T followed by a wrapping from T to T?.
- If the nullable conversion is from S? to T, the conversion is evaluated as an unwrapping from S? to S followed by the underlying conversion from S to T.

13.7.3 Lifted conversions

Given a user-defined conversion operator that converts from a non-nullable value type S to a non-nullable value type T, a ***lifted conversion operator*** exists that converts from S? to T?. This lifted conversion operator performs an unwrapping from S? to S followed by the user-defined conversion from S to T followed by a wrapping from T to T?, except that a null valued S? converts directly to a null valued T?.

A lifted conversion operator has the same implicit or explicit classification as its underlying user-defined conversion operator.

The same, but different

By §13.7.3 a standard implicit conversion from S to S? and a standard explicit conversion from S? to S exist. By §13.4.2 a user-defined conversion is evaluated as an optional standard conversion, followed by the user-defined conversion, followed finally by another optional standard conversion. Therefore, the following conversions exist given a user-defined conversion operator that converts from a non-nullable value type S to a non-nullable value type T:

- an implicit or explicit conversion from S? to T? (lifted conversion)
- an implicit or explicit conversion from S to T? (user-defined conversion S to T, standard implicit conversion T to T?)
- an explicit conversion from S? to T (standard explicit conversion S? to S, user-defined conversion S to T)

This list is just the same as the one for nullable conversions (§13.7.3) but applied to user-defined rather than predefined conversions.

14 Expressions

An expression is a sequence of operators and operands. This clause defines the syntax, order of evaluation of operands and operators, and meaning of expressions.

14.1 Expression classifications

An expression is classified as one of the following:

- A value. Every value has an associated type.
- A variable. Every variable has an associated type, namely the declared type of the variable.

> See the annotation on §12.4 for a table of those expressions classified as a variable.

- A namespace. An expression with this classification can only appear as the left-hand side of a *member-access* (§14.5.4). In any other context, an expression classified as a namespace causes a compile-time error.
- A type. An expression with this classification can only appear as the left-hand side of a *member-access* (§14.5.4). In any other context, an expression classified as a type causes a compile-time error.
- A method group, which is a set of overloaded methods resulting from a member lookup (§14.3). A method group can have an associated instance expression. When an instance method is invoked, the result of evaluating the instance expression becomes the instance represented by this (§14.5.7). A method group can be used in an *invocation-expression* (§14.5.5), used in a *delegate-creation-expression* (§14.5.10.3), or implicitly converted to a compatible delegate type. In any other context, an expression classified as a method group causes a compile-time error.
- An anonymous method. An expression with this classification can be used in a *delegate-creation-expression* (§14.5.10.3) or implicitly converted to a compatible delegate type. In any other context, an expression classified as an anonymous method causes a compile-time error.
- A property access. Every property access has an associated type, namely the type of the property. Furthermore, a property access can have an associated instance expression. When an accessor (the get or set block) of an instance property access is invoked, the result of evaluating the instance expression becomes the instance represented by this (§14.5.7).
- An event access. Every event access has an associated type, namely the type of the event. Furthermore, an event access can have an associated instance expression. An event access can appear as the left-hand operand of the += and -= operators (§14.14.3). In any other context, an expression classified as an event access causes a compile-time error.
- An indexer access. Every indexer access has an associated type, namely the element type of the indexer. Furthermore, an indexer access has an associated instance expression and an associated argument list. When an accessor (the get or set block) of an indexer access is invoked, the result of evaluating the instance expression becomes the instance represented by this (§14.5.7), and the result of evaluating the argument list becomes the parameter list of the invocation.

- Nothing. This occurs when the expression is an invocation of a method with a return type of `void`. An expression classified as nothing is only valid in the context of a *statement-expression* (§15.6).

The final result of an expression is never a namespace, type, method group, anonymous method, or event access. Rather, as noted above, these categories of expressions are intermediate constructs that are only permitted in certain contexts.

A property access or indexer access is always reclassified as a value by performing an invocation of the *get-accessor* or the *set-accessor*. The particular accessor is determined by the context of the property or indexer access: If the access is the target of an assignment, the *set-accessor* is invoked to assign a new value (§14.14.1). Otherwise, the *get-accessor* is invoked to obtain the current value (§14.1.1).

14.1.1 Values of expressions

Most of the constructs that involve an expression ultimately require the expression to denote a *value*. In such cases, if the actual expression denotes a namespace, a type, or nothing, a compile-time error occurs. However, if the expression denotes a property access, an indexer access, or a variable, the value of the property, indexer, or variable is implicitly substituted:

- The value of a variable is simply the value currently stored in the storage location identified by the variable. A variable shall be considered definitely assigned (§12.3) before its value can be obtained, or otherwise a compile-time error occurs.
- The value of a property access expression is obtained by invoking the *get-accessor* of the property. If the property has no *get-accessor*, a compile-time error occurs. Otherwise, a function member invocation (§14.4.3) is performed, and the result of the invocation becomes the value of the property access expression.
- The value of an indexer access expression is obtained by invoking the *get-accessor* of the indexer. If the indexer has no *get-accessor*, a compile-time error occurs. Otherwise, a function member invocation (§14.4.3) is performed with the argument list associated with the indexer access expression, and the result of the invocation becomes the value of the indexer access expression.

14.2 Operators

Expressions are constructed from **operands** and **operators**. The operators of an expression indicate which operations to apply to the operands. [*Example*: Examples of operators include +, -, *, /, and `new`. Examples of operands include literals, fields, local variables, and expressions. *end example*]

There are three kinds of operators:

- Unary operators. The unary operators take one operand and use either prefix notation (such as `-x`) or postfix notation (such as `x++`).
- Binary operators. The binary operators take two operands and all use infix notation (such as `x + y`).
- Ternary operator. Only one ternary operator, `? :`, exists; it takes three operands and uses infix notation (`c ? x : y`).

The order of evaluation of operators in an expression is determined by the **precedence** and **associativity** of the operators (§14.2.1).

The order in which operands in an expression are evaluated, is left to right. [*Example*: In `F(i) + G(i++) * H(i)`, method `F` is called using the old value of `i`, then method `G` is called with the old value of `i`, and, finally, method `H` is called with the new value of `i`. This is separate from and unrelated to operator precedence. *end example*]

Certain operators can be **overloaded**. Operator overloading (§14.2.2) permits user-defined operator implementations to be specified for operations where one or both of the operands are of a user-defined class or struct type.

Operand order of evaluation

C/C++ programmers in particular should note that operand evaluation in a C# expression proceeds from left to right.

```
int value = v++ * v;       // computes v * (v+1) in C#,
                           // but is unspecified in C/C++
```

This left to right evaluation is fundamental and can be relied on:

```
int x;
int value = Method(out x) + x; // compiles ok
```

It is **most strongly advised** that code such as this **not** be written, even in C#, but it is nevertheless well defined.

14.2.1 Operator precedence and associativity

When an expression contains multiple operators, the **precedence** of the operators controls the order in which the individual operators are evaluated. [*Note*: For example, the expression `x + y * z` is evaluated as `x + (y * z)` because the `*` operator has higher precedence than the binary `+` operator. *end note*] The precedence of an operator is established by the definition of its associated grammar production. [*Note*: For example, an *additive-expression* consists of a sequence of *multiplicative-expression*s separated by `+` or `-` operators, thus giving the `+` and `-` operators lower precedence than the `*`, `/`, and `%` operators. *end note*]

[*Note*: The following table summarizes the operators in order of precedence from highest to lowest:

Subclause	Category	Operators
§14.5	Primary	`x.y  f(x)  a[x]  x++  x--  new` `typeof  checked  unchecked`
§14.6	Unary	`+  -  !  ~  ++x  --x  (T)x`
§14.7	Multiplicative	`*  /  %`
§14.7	Additive	`+  -`
§14.8	Shift	`<<  >>`
§14.9	Relational and type-testing	`<  >  <=  >=  is  as`
§14.9	Equality	`==  !=`
§14.10	Logical AND	`&`
§14.10	Logical XOR	`^`
§14.10	Logical OR	`|`
§14.11	Conditional AND	`&&`
§14.11	Conditional OR	`||`

§14.12	Null Coalescing	??
§14.13	Conditional	? :
§14.14	Assignment	= *= /= %= += -= <<= >>= &= ^= |=

Erratum and clarification

Erratum: The first row of the preceding table is incorrect, as a few operators have been accidentally omitted.

Clarification: Though "precedence" is usually used in relation to operators only, the grammar rules define how an expression is parsed, and these cover nonoperator subexpressions as well.

Making these changes, the first row of the table would become:

| §14.5 | Primary | *literal simple-name member-access parenthesized-expression anonymous-method-expression* f(x) a[x] x++ x-- this.x this[x] base.x base[x] new typeof checked unchecked sizeof default |

end note]

When an operand occurs between two operators with the same precedence, the ***associativity*** of the operators controls the order in which the operations are performed:

- Except for the assignment operators and the null coalescing operator, all binary operators are ***left-associative***, meaning that operations are performed from left to right.
  [*Example*: x + y + z is evaluated as (x + y) + z. *end example*]
- The assignment operators, null coalescing operator and the conditional operator (? :) are ***right-associative***, meaning that operations are performed from right to left.
  [*Example*: x = y = z is evaluated as x = (y = z). *end example*]

Precedence and associativity can be controlled using parentheses. [*Example*: x + y * z first multiplies y by z and then adds the result to x, but (x + y) * z first adds x and y and then multiplies the result by z. *end example*]

14.2.2 Operator overloading

All unary and binary operators have predefined implementations that are automatically available in any expression. In addition to the predefined implementations, user-defined implementations can be introduced by including operator declarations (§17.9) in classes and structs. User-defined operator implementations always take precedence over predefined operator implementations: Only when no applicable user-defined operators implementations exist are the predefined operator implementations considered, as described in §14.2.3 and §14.2.4.

The ***overloadable unary operators*** are:

    + - ! ~ ++ -- true false

[*Note*: Although true and false are not used explicitly in expressions (and therefore are not included in the precedence table in §14.2.1), they are considered operators because they are invoked in several expression contexts: Boolean expressions (§14.17) and expressions involving the conditional operator (§14.13) and conditional logical operators (§14.11). *end note*]

The ***overloadable binary operators*** are:

```
+ - * / % & | ^ << >> == != > < >= <=
```

Only the operators listed above can be overloaded. In particular, it is not possible to overload member access, method invocation, or the `=`, `&&`, `||`, `??`, `? :`, `checked`, `unchecked`, `new`, `typeof`, `as`, and `is` operators.

When a binary operator is overloaded, the corresponding assignment operator, if any, is also implicitly overloaded. [*Example*: An overload of operator `*` is also an overload of operator `*=`. This is described further in §14.14. *end example*] The assignment operator itself (`=`) cannot be overloaded. An assignment always performs a simple bit-wise copy of a value into a variable.

Cast operations, such as `(T)x`, are overloaded by providing user-defined conversion operators (§13.4).

Element access, such as `a[x]`, is not considered an overloadable operator. Instead, user-defined indexing is supported through indexers (§17.8).

In expressions, operators are referenced using operator notation, and in declarations, operators are referenced using functional notation. The following table shows the relationship between operator and functional notations for unary and binary operators. In the first entry, *op* denotes any overloadable unary prefix operator. In the second entry, *op* denotes the unary postfix `++` and `--` operators. In the third entry, *op* denotes any overloadable binary operator. [*Note*: For an example of overloading the `++` and `--` operators see §17.9.1. *end note*]

Operator notation	Functional notation
op x	operator *op*(x)
x *op*	operator *op*(x)
x *op* y	operator *op*(x, y)

User-defined operator declarations always require at least one of the parameters to be of the class or struct type that contains the operator declaration. [*Note*: Thus, it is not possible for a user-defined operator to have the same signature as a predefined operator. *end note*]

User-defined operator declarations cannot modify the syntax, precedence, or associativity of an operator. [*Example*: The `/` operator is always a binary operator, always has the precedence level specified in §14.2.1, and is always left-associative. *end example*]

[*Note*: While it is possible for a user-defined operator to perform any computation it pleases, implementations that produce results other than those that are intuitively expected are strongly discouraged. For example, an implementation of `operator ==` should compare the two operands for equality and return an appropriate `bool` result. *end note*]

The descriptions of individual operators in §14.5 through §14.14 specify the predefined implementations of the operators and any additional rules that apply to each operator. The descriptions make use of the terms ***unary operator overload resolution***, ***binary operator overload resolution***, ***numeric promotion***, and ***lifted operators*** definitions of which are found in the following subclauses.

14.2.3 Unary operator overload resolution

An operation of the form *op* x or x *op*, where *op* is an overloadable unary operator, and x is an expression of type X, is processed as follows:

- The set of candidate user-defined operators provided by X for the operation `operator` *op* `(x)` is determined using the rules of §14.2.5.

- If the set of candidate user-defined operators is not empty, then this becomes the set of candidate operators for the operation. Otherwise, the predefined unary `operator` *op* implementations become the set of candidate operators for the operation. If type X is not an enum type, then any predefined unary operator with a parameter type that is an enum type is removed from consideration. The predefined implementations of a given operator are specified in the description of the operator (§14.5 and §14.6).
- The overload resolution rules of §14.4.2 are applied to the set of candidate operators to select the best operator with respect to the argument list `(x)`, and this operator becomes the result of the overload resolution process. If overload resolution fails to select a single best operator, a compile-time error occurs.

14.2.4 Binary operator overload resolution

An operation of the form x *op* y, where *op* is an overloadable binary operator, x is an expression of type X, and y is an expression of type Y, is processed as follows:

- The set of candidate user-defined operators provided by X and Y for the operation `operator` *op*`(x, y)` is determined. The set consists of the union of the candidate operators provided by X and the candidate operators provided by Y, each determined using the rules of §14.2.5. If X and Y are the same type, or if X and Y are derived from a common base type, then shared candidate operators only occur in the combined set once.
- If the set of candidate user-defined operators is not empty, then this becomes the set of candidate operators for the operation. Otherwise, the predefined binary `operator` *op* implementations become the set of candidate operators for the operation. If neither X nor Y is an enum type, then any predefined binary operator with a parameter type that is an enum type is removed from consideration. Similarly, if neither X nor Y is a delegate type, then any predefined binary operator with a parameter type that is a delegate type is removed from consideration. The predefined implementations of a given operator are specified in the description of the operator (§14.7 through §14.14).
- The overload resolution rules of §14.4.2 are applied to the set of candidate operators to select the best operator with respect to the argument list `(x, y)`, and this operator becomes the result of the overload resolution process. If overload resolution fails to select a single best operator, a compile-time error occurs.

14.2.5 Candidate user-defined operators

Given a type T and an operation `operator` *op*`(A)`, where *op* is an overloadable operator and A is an argument list, the set of candidate user-defined operators provided by T for `operator` *op*`(A)` is determined as follows:

- Determine the type T0 that results from removing the trailing `?` modifiers, if any, from T.
- For all `operator` *op* declarations in T0, if at least one operator is applicable (§14.4.2.1) with respect to the argument list A, then the set of candidate operators consists of all applicable `operator` *op* declarations in T0. The lifted forms of the operators (§14.2.7) declared in T0 are considered to also be declared by T0.
- Otherwise, if T0 is `object`, the set of candidate operators is empty.
- Otherwise, the set of candidate operators provided by T0 is the set of candidate operators provided by the direct base class of T0, or the effective base class of T0 if T0 is a type parameter.

14.2.6 Numeric promotions

This subclause is informative.

Numeric promotion consists of automatically performing certain implicit conversions of the operands of the predefined unary and binary numeric operators. Numeric promotion is not a distinct mechanism, but rather an effect of applying overload resolution to the predefined operators. Numeric promotion specifically does not affect evaluation of user-defined operators, although user-defined operators can be implemented to exhibit similar effects.

As an example of numeric promotion, consider the predefined implementations of the binary *operator:

```
int operator * (int x, int y);
uint operator * (uint x, uint y);
long operator * (long x, long y);
ulong operator * (ulong x, ulong y);
void operator * (long x, ulong y);
void operator * (ulong x, long y);
float operator * (float x, float y);
double operator * (double x, double y);
decimal operator * (decimal x, decimal y);
```

When overload resolution rules (§14.4.2) are applied to this set of operators, the effect is to select the first of the operators for which implicit conversions exist from the operand types. [*Example*: For the operation b * s, where b is a byte and s is a short, overload resolution selects opera-tor * (int, int) as the best operator. Thus, the effect is that b and s are converted to int, and the type of the result is int. Likewise, for the operation i * d, where i is an int and d is a dou-ble, overload resolution selects operator * (double, double) as the best operator. *end example*]

End of informative text.

Land of surprises

Though this clause and its two children are informative, they are a summary of the combined effect of:

- the rules for implicit numeric conversions (§13.1.2);
- the rules for better conversion (§14.4.2.3); and
- the available arithmetic (§14.7), relational (§14.9), and integral logical (§14.10.1) operators.

The following diagram shows which operator will be selected as a result of these rules and definitions based on the types of the operands. The bold boxes indicate the provided operators, all of which have signatures of the form: *T* operator(*T* left, *T* right). To locate which operator will be used, start at the two boxes representing the types of the operands and follow the arrows to the closest bold box:

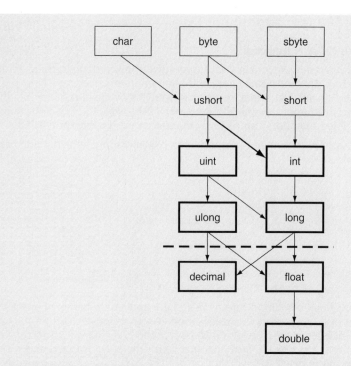

There are two particular cases to note:

- For all combinations of two operands of types `char`, `byte`, or `ushort` there are two closest operators: `int` and `uint`. This is where the better conversion rules (§14.4.2.3) come into play and `int` is chosen (indicated in the diagram by the bold arrow).
- For the combinations `long,ulong`, and `ulong,long` there are also two choices: `float` and `decimal`. There are no rules to resolve this, so the combinations are ambiguous and explicit casting must be used to resolve the situation.

Other choices could have been made for resolving combinations of numeric operands, but there is no single 'right' solution. C# chooses that in the absence of explicit casts, combinations of integral operands should always produce an integral result, and that increasing the size of integral results was better than having more cases where overflow is possible.

Other languages have made different choices. Java does not have unsigned integral types and this choice simplified its options. C/C++ do have both signed and unsigned integral types; these choose to use mathematically incorrect conversions between signed and unsigned values rather than promote the size of the result—this choice is arguably wrong! Finally Ada, which has a much wider range of numeric types than C#, always requires explicit casting to avoid any possible confusion.

C#'s choices do produce a number of surprises, covered by annotations in §14.4.2.3 and §14.10.1.

To avoid surprises in mixed-type arithmetic expressions, liberal use of explicit casts is recommended.

Into the void

As mentioned in the previous annotation, the operand combinations `long`,`ulong` and `ulong`, `long` are ambiguous and a compile time error will be produced should an attempt be made to use them.

The Standard contains additional operator definitions for the arithmetic (§14.7), relational (§14.9), and integral logical (§14.10.1) operators of the forms:

```
void op(long x, ulong y);
void op(ulong x, long y);
```

These operators are uncallable as they have a return type of `void`, and hence are rather peculiar entities. They do not alter the fact that the `long`,`ulong` and `ulong`,`long` operand combinations are invalid.

The existence of these uncallable operators is an artifact of a particular implementation strategy that crept into the Standard. It is safe to ignore them completely and rely on the implicit conversions rules.

Note: These imaginary operators are very peculiar as their signatures are invalid; it is not possible to declare an operator (§17.9) that returns `void`. Unfortunately, however, as the Standard includes them, an implementation may choose to allow the import of similar operators from libraries (which could, of course, not be written in C#). Indeed, the CLI does allow the definition of such unusable operators, and at least one of the current C# compilers allows "access" to them—producing compile time error messages if such an attempt is made, as `void` is an invalid type for a value!

Loosely literal

An integral literal without a suffix is given the first type of: `int`, `uint`, `long`, and `ulong` in which the value can be represented (§9.4.4.2). This gives rise to the behavior that adding, say, zero can change the type of a value. Consider:

```
uint u;
int i = 0;

... (u + i) ... // the type of the addition is long
... (u + 0) ... // also long
```

The result of the second expression in particular might be surprising to some.

However, both the Microsoft and Mono compilers current at the time of writing "bend" the definition of literals in §9.4.4.2. In these compilers, if an integral literal without a suffix is combined with a non-literal integral expression of type *T*, then if the literal is a valid value of type *T* it is typed as such and not according to the rules in §9.4.4.2. In the preceding example, this means that the *second* expression will have type `uint`, as `0` is a valid `uint` value. The *first* will still have the type `long`.

When using these compilers, some readers may find it surprising that the two expressions have different types.

The same recommendation as in the previous annotation is made: When combining expressions of different numeric types, explicit casting reduces the opportunities for confusion.

Reasons for numeric promotion

The question of why an expression such as `short + short` results in an `int` often comes up. It is usually met with an answer involving overflows, suggesting that the C# specification is trying to avoid problems when both operands are more than half the maximum `short` value. However, this line of reasoning falls apart when one considers operators with `int` operands—the result would have to be a `uint` or `long` for consistency.

A more practical reason is efficiency; most modern processors tend to be optimized to work with operands of at least 32 bits. On some architectures, compilers may need to use 32 bit operations and generate additional code to reduce the result of the operation to fewer bits. Though these details need be of no direct concern to the programmer, in hiding the details the costs imposed would also be hidden and these costs could be significant. By adopting numeric promotion, the use of higher precision operations is more obvious, and any reduction of the result must be explicitly requested by casting. However, numeric promotions can make code significantly harder to read where several calculations are performed on sub-int values.

C# is, of, course, not alone in taking this route; for example, both Java and C do likewise, and there are also languages that provide operators for all numeric sizes and do not do promotion (i.e., Ada). In 2020, will people wonder why `int + int` does not result in a `long`?

Jon Skeet

14.2.6.1 Unary numeric promotions

This subclause is informative.

Unary numeric promotion occurs for the operands of the predefined +, −, and ~ unary operators. Unary numeric promotion simply consists of converting operands of type `sbyte`, `byte`, `short`, `ushort`, or `char` to type `int`. Additionally, for the unary − operator, unary numeric promotion converts operands of type `uint` to type `long`.

End of informative text.

14.2.6.2 Binary numeric promotions

This subclause is informative.

Binary numeric promotion occurs for the operands of the predefined +, −, *, /, %, &, |, ^, ==, !=, >, <, >=, and <= binary operators. Binary numeric promotion implicitly converts both operands to a common type which, in case of the non-relational operators, also becomes the result type of the operation. Binary numeric promotion consists of applying the following rules, in the order they appear here:

- If either operand is of type `decimal`, the other operand is converted to type `decimal`, or a compile-time error occurs if the other operand is of type `float` or `double`.
- Otherwise, if either operand is of type `double`, the other operand is converted to type `double`.
- Otherwise, if either operand is of type `float`, the other operand is converted to type `float`.
- Otherwise, if either operand is of type `ulong`, the other operand is converted to type `ulong`, or a compile-time error occurs if the other operand is of type `sbyte`, `short`, `int`, or `long`.
- Otherwise, if either operand is of type `long`, the other operand is converted to type `long`.
- Otherwise, if either operand is of type `uint` and the other operand is of type `sbyte`, `short`, or `int`, both operands are converted to type `long`.
- Otherwise, if either operand is of type `uint`, the other operand is converted to type `uint`.
- Otherwise, both operands are converted to type `int`.

[*Note*: The first rule disallows any operations that mix the `decimal` type with the `double` and `float` types. The rule follows from the fact that there are no implicit conversions between the `decimal` type and the `double` and `float` types. *end note*]

[*Note*: Also note that it is not possible for an operand to be of type `ulong` when the other operand is of a signed integral type. The reason is that no integral type exists that can represent the full range of `ulong` as well as the signed integral types. *end note*]

In both of the above cases, a cast expression can be used to explicitly convert one operand to a type that is compatible with the other operand.

[*Example*: In the following code

```
decimal AddPercent(decimal x, double percent)
{
    return x * (decimal) (1.0 + percent / 100.0);
}
```

a compile-time error occurs because a `decimal` cannot be multiplied by a `double`. The error is resolved by explicitly converting the second operand to `decimal, as follows`:

```
decimal AddPercent(decimal x, double percent)
{
    return x * (decimal)(1.0 + percent / 100.0);
}
```

end example]

End of informative text.

14.2.7 Lifted operators

Lifted operators permit predefined and user-defined operators that operate on non-nullable value types to also be used with nullable forms of those types. Lifted operators are constructed from predefined and user-defined operators that meet certain requirements, as described in the following:

- For the unary operators

+   ++   -   --   !   ~

a lifted form of an operator exists if the operand and result types are both non-nullable value types. The lifted form is constructed by adding a single ? modifier to the operand and result types. The lifted operator produces a null value if the operand is null. Otherwise, the lifted operator unwraps the operand, applies the underlying operator, and wraps the result.

- For the binary operators

+   -   *   /   %   & | ^   <<   >>

a lifted form of an operator exists if the operand and result types are all non-nullable value types. The lifted form is constructed by adding a single ? modifier to each operand and result type. The lifted operator produces a null value if one or both operands are null (an exception being the & and | operators of the `bool?` type, as described in §14.10.4). Otherwise, the lifted operator unwraps the operands, applies the underlying operator, and wraps the result.

- For the equality operators

==   !=

a lifted form of an operator exists if the operand types are both non-nullable value types and if the result type is `bool`. The lifted form is constructed by adding a single ? modifier to each operand type. The lifted operator considers two null values equal, and a null value unequal to any non-null value. If both operands are non-null, the lifted operator unwraps the operands and applies the underlying operator to produce the `bool` result.

- For the relational operators

  ```
  <  >  <=  >=
  ```

a lifted form of an operator exists if the operand types are both non-nullable value types and if the result type is `bool`. The lifted form is constructed by adding a single `?` modifier to each operand type. The lifted operator produces the value `false` if one or both operands are null. Otherwise, the lifted operator unwraps the operands and applies the underlying operator to produce the `bool` result.

The lifted forms of the predefined operators are themselves considered predefined operators.

Null values in C# and in SQL

This clause is interesting as it sometimes varies from what might be expected by a C# programmer, and it sometimes varies from what might be expected by an SQL developer. Furthermore, C# has made different choices for nullable types and null than for the analogous case of floating-point types and NaNs (§14.9.2).

As shown by the following table, C# and SQL arithmetic and logical operators agree, but the comparison, equality, and inequality operators do not.

	C#		SQL	
Arithmetics	1 + null	null	1 + NULL	NULL
Equality	null == null	true	NULL = NULL	NULL
Inequality	null != null	false	NULL <> NULL	NULL
Comparison	1 < null	false	1 < NULL	NULL
Comparison	1 == null	false	1 = NULL	NULL
Comparison	1 > null	false	1 > NULL	NULL
Logical and	null & false	false	NULL AND FALSE	FALSE
Logical and	false & null	false	FALSE AND NULL	FALSE
Logical and	true & null	null	TRUE AND NULL	NULL
Logical and	null & true	null	NULL AND TRUE	NULL
Logical and	null & null	null	NULL AND NULL	NULL
Logical or	null | false	null	NULL OR FALSE	NULL
Logical or	false | null	null	FALSE OR NULL	NULL
Logical or	true | null	true	TRUE OR NULL	TRUE
Logical or	null | true	true	NULL OR TRUE	TRUE
Logical or	null | null	null	NULL OR NULL	NULL

In neither language does it hold true that for two values x and y, exactly one of x < y, x > y, or x == y is true. When one of the operands is null, all three expressions are false in C# and all three are null in SQL.

Moreover, when both x and y are `null` the expression `null == null` produces true in C#, as would be expected by a developer used to reference comparison, but in SQL the result is null.

In the analogous situation with floating-point numbers and NaNs, C# adheres to IEC 60559 arithmetics:

	C#	
Arithmetics	1.0 + NaN	NaN
Equality	NaN == NaN	false
Inequality	NaN != NaN	true
Comparison	1.0 < NaN	false
Comparison	1.0 == NaN	false
Comparison	1.0 > NaN	false

As can be seen, `NaN == z` is false, even if z is NaN. So, on similar values, C# floating-point, C# `int?` (that is, nullable `int`), and SQL all differ from each other.

Note: The method `Equals` applied to two NaNs returns true; see annotation on §14.9.2. For nullables, the method `Equals` follows the "==" operator.

The balance that has been struck between similarity to SQL and C#-like equality is a reasonable one. However, it may take a while before developers can reliably predict results without recourse to the specification. The different treatment of nulls and NaNs does not help in this respect.

Jon Skeet

14.3 Member lookup

A member lookup is the process whereby the meaning of a name in the context of a type is determined. A member lookup can occur as part of evaluating a *simple-name* (§14.5.2) or a *member-access* (§14.5.4) in an expression.

Member lookup considers not only the name of a member but also the number of type parameters the member has and whether the member is accessible. For the purposes of member lookup, generic methods and nested generic types have the number of type parameters indicated in their respective declarations and all other members have zero type parameters.

A member lookup of a name N with K type parameters in a type T is processed as follows:

- First, a set of accessible members named N is determined:
  - If T is a type parameter, then the set is the union of the sets of accessible members named N in each of the types specified as a primary constraint or secondary constraint (§25.7) for T, along with the set of accessible members named N in `object`.
  - Otherwise, the set consists of all accessible (§10.5) members named N in T, including inherited members and the accessible members named N in `object`. If T is a constructed type, the set of members is obtained by substituting type arguments as described in §25.5.4. Members that include an `override` modifier are excluded from the set.
- Next, if the set of accessible members is empty, the member lookup does not produce a match and no further steps are taken.
- Next, if K is zero, remove all nested types whose declaration included type parameters. If K is not zero, remove all members with a different number of type parameters. Note that when K is zero, we do not remove all methods having type parameters, since the type inference process (§25.6.4) might be able to infer the type arguments.

- Next, members that are hidden by other members are removed from the set. Members that are removed during this step may still cause other members to be removed. For every member S.M in the set, where S is the type in which the member M is declared, the following rules are applied:
    - If M is a constant, field, property, event, enumeration member, or type declaration then all members declared in a base type of S are removed from the set.
    - If M is a method, then all non-method members declared in a base type of S are removed from the set.
- Next, interface members that are hidden by class members are removed from the set. This step only has an effect if T is a type parameter and T has both an effective base class other than object and a non-empty effective interface set (§25.7). For every member S.M in the set, where S is the type in which the member M is declared, the following rules are applied if S is a class declaration other than object:
    - If M is a constant, field, property, event, enumeration member, or type declaration, then all members declared in an interface declaration are removed from the set.
    - If M is a method, then all non-method members declared in an interface declaration are removed from the set.
- Finally, having removed hidden members, the result of the lookup is determined:
    - If the set consists of a single member that is not a method, then this member is the result of the lookup.
    - Otherwise, if the set contains only methods, then this group of methods is the result of the lookup.
    - Otherwise, the lookup is ambiguous, and a compile-time error occurs.

For member lookups in types other than type parameters and interfaces, and member lookups in interfaces that are strictly single-inheritance (each interface in the inheritance chain has exactly zero or one direct base interface), the effect of the lookup rules is simply that derived members hide base members with the same name. Such single-inheritance lookups are never ambiguous. The ambiguities that can possibly arise from member lookups in multiple-inheritance interfaces are described in §20.2.5.

14.3.1 Base types

For purposes of member lookup, a type T is considered to have the following base types:

- If T is object, then T has no base type.
- If T is an *enum-type*, the base types of T are the class types System.Enum, System. ValueType, and object.
- If T is a *struct-type*, the base types of T are the class types System.ValueType and object.
- If T is a *class-type*, the base types of T are the base classes of T, including the class type object.
- If T is an *interface-type*, the base types of T are the base interfaces of T and the class type object.
- If T is an *array-type*, the base types of T are the class types System.Array and object.
- If T is a *delegate-type*, the base types of T are the class types System.Delegate and object.
- If T is a *nullable-type*, the base types of T are the class types System.ValueType and object.

14.4 Function members

Function members are members that contain executable statements. Function members are always members of types and cannot be members of namespaces. C# defines the following categories of function members:

- Methods
- Properties
- Events
- Indexers
- User-defined operators
- Instance constructors
- Static constructors
- Finalizers

Except for static constructors and finalizers (which cannot be invoked explicitly), the statements contained in function members are executed through function member invocations. The actual syntax for writing a function member invocation depends on the particular function member category.

The argument list (§14.4.1) of a function member invocation provides actual values or variable references for the parameters of the function member.

Invocations of methods, indexers, operators, and instance constructors employ overload resolution to determine which of a candidate set of function members to invoke. This process is described in §14.4.2.

Once a particular function member has been identified at compile-time, possibly through overload resolution, the actual run-time process of invoking the function member is described in §14.4.3.

[*Note*: The following table summarizes the processing that takes place in constructs involving the six categories of function members that can be explicitly invoked. In the table, e, x, y, and `value` indicate expressions classified as variables or values, T indicates an expression classified as a type, F is the simple name of a method, and P is the simple name of a property.

Construct	Example	Description
Method invocation	`F(x,y)`	Overload resolution is applied to select the best method F in the containing class or struct. The method is invoked with the argument list `(x, y)`. If the method is not `static`, the instance expression is `this`.
	`T.F(x,y)`	Overload resolution is applied to select the best method F in the class or struct T. A compile-time error occurs if the method is not `static`. The method is invoked with the argument list `(x, y)`.
	`e.F(x, y)`	Overload resolution is applied to select the best method F in the class, struct, or interface given by the type of e. A compile-time error occurs if the method is `static`. The method is invoked with the instance expression e and the argument list `(x, y)`.
Property access	`P`	The `get` accessor of the property P in the containing class or struct is invoked. A compile-time error occurs if P is write-only. If P is not `static`, the instance expression is `this`.
	`P = value`	The `set` accessor of the property P in the

		containing class or struct is invoked with the argument list `(value)`. A compile-time error occurs if P is read-only. If P is not `static`, the instance expression is `this`.
	`T.P`	The `get` accessor of the property P in the class or struct T is invoked. A compile-time error occurs if P is not `static` or if P is write-only.
	`T.P = value`	The `set` accessor of the property P in the class or struct T is invoked with the argument list `(value)`. A compile-time error occurs if P is not `static` or if P is read-only.
	`e.P`	The `get` accessor of the property P in the class, struct, or interface given by the type of e is invoked with the instance expression e. A compile-time error occurs if P is `static` or if P is write-only.
	`e.P = value`	The `set` accessor of the property P in the class, struct, or interface given by the type of e is invoked with the instance expression e and the argument list `(value)`. A compile-time error occurs if P is `static` or if P is read-only.
Event access	`E += value`	The `add` accessor of the event E in the containing class or struct is invoked. If E is not `static`, the instance expression is `this`.
	`E -= value`	The `remove` accessor of the event E in the containing class or struct is invoked. If E is not `static`, the instance expression is `this`.
	`T.E += value`	The `add` accessor of the event E in the class or struct T is invoked. A compile-time error occurs if E is not `static`.
	`T.E -= value`	The `remove` accessor of the event E in the class or struct T is invoked. A compile-time error occurs if E is not `static`.
	`e.E += value`	The `add` accessor of the event E in the class, struct, or interface given by the type of e is invoked with the instance expression e. A compile-time error occurs if E is `static`.
	`e.E -= value`	The `remove` accessor of the event E in the class, struct, or interface given by the type of e is invoked with the instance expression e. A compile-time error occurs if E is `static`.
Indexer access	`e[x, y]`	Overload resolution is applied to select the best indexer in the class, struct, or interface given by the type of e. The `get` accessor of the indexer is invoked with the instance expression e and the argument list `(x, y)`. A compile-time error occurs if the indexer is write-only.
	`e[x, y] = value`	Overload resolution is applied to select the best indexer in the class, struct, or interface given by the type of e. The `set` accessor of the indexer is invoked with the instance expression e and the argument list `(x, y, value)`. A compile-time error occurs if the indexer is read-only.
Operator invocation	`-x`	Overload resolution is applied to select the best unary operator in the class or struct given by the type of x. The selected operator is invoked with the argument list `(x)`.

	x + y	Overload resolution is applied to select the best binary operator in the classes or structs given by the types of x and y. The selected operator is invoked with the argument list (x, y).
Instance constructor invocation	new T(x, y)	Overload resolution is applied to select the best instance constructor in the class or struct T. The instance constructor is invoked with the argument list (x, y).

end note]

14.4.1 Argument lists

Every function member invocation includes an argument list, which provides actual values or variable references for the parameters of the function member. The syntax for specifying the argument list of a function member invocation depends on the function member category:

- For instance constructors, methods, and delegates, the arguments are specified as an *argument-list*, as described below.
- For properties, the argument list is empty when invoking the get accessor, and consists of the expression specified as the right operand of the assignment operator when invoking the set accessor.
- For events, the argument list consists of the expression specified as the right operand of the += or -= operator.
- For indexers, the argument list consists of the expressions specified between the square brackets in the indexer access. When invoking the set accessor, the argument list additionally includes the expression specified as the right operand of the assignment operator. [*Note*: The additional argument is not used for overload resolution, just during invocation of the set accessor. *end note*]
- For user-defined operators, the argument list consists of the single operand of the unary operator or the two operands of the binary operator.

The arguments of properties (§17.6), events (§17.7), and user-defined operators (§17.9) are always passed as value parameters (§17.5.1.1). The arguments of indexers (§17.8) are always passed as value parameters (§17.5.1.1) or parameter arrays (§17.5.1.4). Reference and output parameters are not supported for these categories of function members.

The arguments of an instance constructor, method, or delegate invocation are specified as an *argument-list*:

> *argument-list:*
>   *argument*
>   *argument-list* , *argument*
>
> *argument:*
>   *expression*
>   ref *variable-reference*
>   out *variable-reference*

An *argument-list* consists of one or more *argument*s, separated by commas. Each argument can take one of the following forms:

- An *expression*, indicating that the argument is passed as a value parameter (§17.5.1.1).
- The keyword `ref` followed by a *variable-reference* (§12.3.3.29), indicating that the argument is passed as a reference parameter (§17.5.1.2). A variable shall be definitely assigned (§12.3) before it can be passed as a reference parameter.
- The keyword `out` followed by a *variable-reference* (§12.3.3.29), indicating that the argument is passed as an output parameter (§17.5.1.3). A variable is considered definitely assigned (§12.3) following a function member invocation in which the variable is passed as an output parameter.

Passing a volatile field (§17.4.3) as a reference parameter or output parameter causes a warning, since the field may not be treated as volatile by the invoked method.

> ### Unrealistic optimism
>
> In practice the phrase "may not" is unrealistically optimistic. It is extremely unlikely that a volatile field passed as a reference or output parameter will be treated as volatile in the callee. To our knowledge none of the implementations current at the time of writing do so, and it would probably take computer hardware architectural changes before compiler writers even consider supporting such semantics.
>
> For an example discussing this, see the annotation "Unrealistic optimism redux" on §17.4.3.

During the run-time processing of a function member invocation (§14.4.3), the expressions or variable references of an argument list are evaluated in order, from left to right, as follows:

- For a value parameter, the argument expression is evaluated and an implicit conversion (§13.1) to the corresponding parameter type is performed. The resulting value becomes the initial value of the value parameter in the function member invocation.
- For a reference or output parameter, the variable reference is evaluated and the resulting storage location becomes the storage location represented by the parameter in the function member invocation. If the variable reference given as a reference or output parameter is an array element of a *reference-type*, a run-time check is performed to ensure that the element type of the array is identical to the type of the parameter. If this check fails, a `System.ArrayTypeMismatchException` is thrown.

Methods, indexers, and instance constructors can declare their right-most parameter to be a parameter array (§17.5.1.4). Such function members are invoked either in their normal form or in their expanded form depending on which is applicable (§14.4.2.1):

- When a function member with a parameter array is invoked in its normal form, the argument given for the parameter array shall be a single expression of a type that is implicitly convertible (§13.1) to the parameter array type. In this case, the parameter array acts precisely like a value parameter.
- When a function member with a parameter array is invoked in its expanded form, the invocation shall specify zero or more arguments for the parameter array, where each argument is an expression of a type that is implicitly convertible (§13.1) to the element type of the parameter array. In this case, the invocation creates an instance of the parameter array type with a length corresponding to the number of arguments, initializes the elements of the array instance with the given argument values, and uses the newly created array instance as the actual argument.

Hidden (small) costs of parameter arrays

When calling a method that uses a parameter array, it is not always entirely obvious to the reader that an array will be invisibly created. For instance, consider the code fragment that calls the CLI method `string.Split`:

```
string[] bits = someString.Split(',');
```

It looks like the parameter to the `Split` method is a constant character, but in fact the argument is a parameter array, and each time the line is executed a new char array may be created. While this is rarely likely to be an issue, in some tight loops it may make a significant difference compared with creating the character array once and reusing it, for example:

```
static readonly char[] CommaForSplitting = { ',' };
...
string[] bits = someString.Split(CommaForSplitting);
```

Of course, this approach does not work if the method being called might modify the contents of the array.

Though a compiler can also sometimes determine that expressions inside a loop are invariant and make similar optimizations, it is unlikely a compiler will determine that a parameter array is not modified by the callee and hence invariant.

Jon Skeet

The expressions of an argument list are always evaluated in the order they are written. [*Example*: Thus, the example

```
class Test
{
  static void F(int x, int y, int z)
  {
    System.Console.WriteLine("x = {0}, y = {1}, z = {2}", x, y, z);
  }

  static void Main()
  {
    int i = 0;
    F(i++, i++, i++);
  }
}
```

produces the output

```
x = 0, y = 1, z = 2
```

end example]

String formatting not part of the Standard

The string formatting `System.Console.WriteLine(...)` used in the preceding example is from the CLI Standard and not part of the C# Standard. The behavior of method `WriteLine (String, params Object)` is prescribed by the CLI Standard's `System.IO.TextWriter` class, and the interpretation of format strings is prescribed by the CLI Standard's `System. String.Format` method.

The array covariance rules (§19.5) permit a value of an array type A[ ] to be a reference to an instance of an array type B[ ], provided an implicit reference conversion exists from B to A. Because of these rules, when an array element of a *reference-type* is passed as a reference or output parameter, a run-time check is required to ensure that the actual element type of the array is *identical* to that of the parameter. [*Example*: In the following code

```
class Test
{
  static void F(ref object x) {...}

  static void Main()
  {
    object[] a = new object[10];
    object[] b = new string[10];
    F(ref a[0]);      // Ok
    F(ref b[1]);      // ArrayTypeMismatchException
  }
}
```

the second invocation of F causes a System.ArrayTypeMismatchException to be thrown because the actual element type of b is string and not object. *end example*]

When a function member with a parameter array is invoked in its expanded form, the invocation is processed exactly as if an array creation expression with an array initializer (§14.5.10.2) was inserted around the expanded parameters. [*Example*: Given the declaration

```
void F(int x, int y, params object[] args);
```

the following invocations of the expanded form of the method

```
F(10, 20);
F(10, 20, 30, 40);
F(10, 20, 1, "hello", 3.0);
```

correspond exactly to

```
F(10, 20, new object[] {});
F(10, 20, new object[] {30, 40});
F(10, 20, new object[] {1, "hello", 3.0});
```

In particular, note that an empty array is created when there are zero arguments given for the parameter array. *end example*]

14.4.2 Overload resolution

Overload resolution is a compile-time mechanism for selecting the best function member to invoke given an argument list and a set of candidate function members. Overload resolution selects the function member to invoke in the following distinct contexts within C#:

- Invocation of a method named in an *invocation-expression* (§14.5.5).
- Invocation of an instance constructor named in an *object-creation-expression* (§14.5.10.1).
- Invocation of an indexer accessor through an *element-access* (§14.5.6).
- Invocation of a predefined or user-defined operator referenced in an expression (§14.2.3 and §14.2.4).

Each of these contexts defines the set of candidate function members and the list of arguments in its own unique way. However, once the candidate function members and the argument list have been identified, the selection of the best function member is the same in all cases:

- First, the set of candidate function members is reduced to those function members that are applicable with respect to the given argument list (§14.4.2.1). If this reduced set is empty, a compile-time error occurs.
- Then, given the set of applicable candidate function members, the best function member in that set is located. If the set contains only one function member, then that function member is the best function member. Otherwise, the best function member is the one function member that is better than all other function members with respect to the given argument list, provided that each function member is compared to all other function members using the rules in §14.4.2.2. If there is not exactly one function member that is better than all other function members, then the function member invocation is ambiguous and a compile-time error occurs.

The following subclauses define the exact meanings of the terms ***applicable function member*** and ***better function member***.

> ### Overload resolution: C# vs. CIL
>
> Overloading is resolved at compile time, and the chosen method is identified by its unique fully qualified name. This is the usual way languages handle overloading.
>
> Most platforms, including the CLI, allow overloading but do not support any overloading resolution; for example, the CLI has no CIL method call instruction that performs overload resolution.
>
> By not having overload resolution, a platform need not constrain the types that may be overloaded. For example, the CLI permits overloads that, in some languages—even languages targeting the CLI—might be ambiguous.
>
> Therefore, if using overloading in C# code intended for use from other languages, careful consideration should be given to the overload resolution algorithm of those languages.

14.4.2.1 Applicable function member

A function member is said to be an ***applicable function member*** with respect to an argument list A when all of the following are true:

- The number of arguments in A is identical to the number of parameters in the function member declaration.
- For each argument in A, the parameter passing mode of the argument (i.e., value, `ref`, or `out`) is identical to the parameter passing mode of the corresponding parameter, and
    - for a value parameter or a parameter array, an implicit conversion (§13.1) exists from the type of the argument to the type of the corresponding parameter, or
    - for a `ref` or `out` parameter, the type of the argument is identical to the type of the corresponding parameter. [*Note*: After all, a `ref` or `out` parameter is an alias for the argument passed. *end note*]

For a function member that includes a parameter array, if the function member is applicable by the above rules, it is said to be applicable in its ***normal form***. If a function member that includes a parameter array is not applicable in its normal form, the function member might instead be applicable in its ***expanded form***:

- The expanded form is constructed by replacing the parameter array in the function member declaration with zero or more value parameters of the element type of the parameter array such that the number of arguments in the argument list A matches the total number of parameters. If A has fewer arguments than the number of fixed parameters in the function member declaration, the expanded form of the function member cannot be constructed and is thus not applicable.

- Otherwise, the expanded form is applicable if for each argument in A the parameter passing mode of the argument is identical to the parameter passing mode of the corresponding parameter, and

    o for a fixed value parameter or a value parameter created by the expansion, an implicit conversion (§13.1) exists from the type of the argument to the type of the corresponding parameter, or

    o for a ref or out parameter, the type of the argument is identical to the type of the corresponding parameter.

14.4.2.2 Better function member

Given an argument list A with a sequence of argument types $\{A_1, A_2, ..., A_N\}$ and two applicable function members M_P and M_Q with parameter types $\{P_1, P_2, ..., P_N\}$ and $\{Q_1, Q_2, ..., Q_N, M_P\}$, after expansion and type argument substitution,is defined to be a ***better function member*** than M_Q if

- for each argument, the implicit conversion from A_X to P_X is not worse than the implicit conversion from A_X to Q_X, and
- for at least one argument, the conversion from A_X to P_X is better than the conversion from A_X to Q_X.

When performing this evaluation, if M_P or M_Q is applicable only in its expanded form, then P_X or Q_X refers to a parameter in the expanded form of the parameter list.

In case the expanded parameter types $\{P_1, P_2, ..., P_N\}$ and $\{Q_1, Q_2, ..., Q_N\}$, are identical, the following tie-breaking rules are applied to determine the better function member by comparing the given uninstantiated and unexpanded parameter types $\{R_1, R_2, ..., R_K\}$ and $\{S_1, S_2, ..., S_L\}$ of the function members M_P and M_Q respectively. In this case, the better function member is determined by the following rules:

- If one of M_P and M_Q is non-generic, but the other is generic, then the non-generic is better.
- Otherwise, if one of M_P and M_Q is applicable in its non-expanded form (or has no params array) and the other is applicable only in its expanded form (and has a params array), then the non-expanded method is better.
- Otherwise, if the numbers of parameters K in M_P and L in M_Q are different, then the method with more parameters is better. Note that this can only occur if both methods have params arrays and are only applicable in their expanded forms.
- Otherwise, the number of parameters K in M_P and L in M_Q are the same, and if one method has ***more specific*** parameter types, then that method is better. The given parameter types $\{R_1, R_2, ..., R_K\}$ are defined to be more specific than the given parameter types $\{S_1, S_2, ..., S_L\}$ if each given parameter R_X is not less specific than S_X, and at least one given parameter, R_X is more specific than S_X. A type parameter is less specific than a non-type parameter. Recursively, a constructed type is more specific than another constructed type (with the same number of type arguments) if at least one type argument is more specific and no type argument is less specific than the corresponding type argument in the other. An array type is more specific than another array type (with the same number of dimensions) if the element type of the first is more specific than the element type of the second.

- Otherwise, if one member is a lifted operator and the other member is an unlifted operator, then the unlifted operator is better.
- Otherwise, neither method is better.

14.4.2.3 Better conversion

Given an implicit conversion C_1 that converts from a type S to a type T_1, and an implicit conversion C_2 that converts from a type S to a type T_2, the ***better conversion*** of the two conversions is determined as follows:

- If T_1 and T_2 are the same type, neither conversion is better.
- If S is T_1, C_1 is the better conversion.
- If S is T_2, C_2 is the better conversion.
- If an implicit conversion from T_1 to T_2 exists, and no implicit conversion from T_2 to T_1 exists, C_1 is the better conversion.
- If an implicit conversion from T_2 to T_1 exists, and no implicit conversion from T_1 to T_2 exists, C_2 is the better conversion.
- If T_1 is sbyte and T_2 is byte, ushort, uint, or ulong, C_1 is the better conversion.
- If T_2 is sbyte and T_1 is byte, ushort, uint, or ulong, C_2 is the better conversion.
- If T_1 is short and T_2 is ushort, uint, or ulong, C_1 is the better conversion.
- If T_2 is short and T_1 is ushort, uint, or ulong, C_2 is the better conversion.
- If T_1 is int and T_2 is uint, or ulong, C_1 is the better conversion.
- If T_2 is int and T_1 is uint, or ulong, C_2 is the better conversion.
- If T_1 is long and T_2 is ulong, C_1 is the better conversion.
- If T_2 is long and T_1 is ulong, C_2 is the better conversion.
- Otherwise, neither conversion is better.

If an implicit conversion C_1 is defined by these rules to be a better conversion than an implicit conversion C_2, then it is also the case that C_2 is a ***worse conversion*** than C_1.

Lost digits

As discussed in the annotation on §14.2.6, it is problematic to marry subclass type conversions with numerical type conversions, as C# and many other languages attempt to do for the convenience of the programmer. The various numeric types in most languages, including C#, cannot be uniquely organized in a subtype hierarchy: Range and precision provide two different and conflicting dimensions along which the hierarchy could be organized.

There are implicit conversions from long to float, from long to double, and from float to double. By the rules here for *better conversion* this means that the conversion from long to float is better than the one from long to double. But the former is numerically worse because the precision loss is greater. So seen from a numerical point of view, the conversion to double would be better.

Better conversion pitfall

The preceding fourth and fifth rules ("If an implicit conversion from ...") might cause confusing behavior. Consider the following:

```
public class A
{
  public static implicit operator B(A a)
  {
    return new B();
  }
}

public class B { ...}

class Example
{
  static void Method(A a, B b) { ...} // definition 1
  static void Method(B b, A a) { ...} // definition 2

  static void Main()
  {
    A a = new A();
    Method(a, null);
  }
}
```

The call `Method(a, null)` is ambiguous. This may seem odd; definition 1 appears preferable given the first parameter, until we consider the fourth and fifth rules and the second parameter. The null type is convertible to both `A` and `B`, but because there is also a conversion from `A` to `B`, definition 2 is preferable for that parameter. Therefore, neither definition is best, and an error is reported.

The rules are designed to select the most derived ("deepest") type in a subtype hierarchy. It is when the types are not directly related and cross-hierarchy conversions are defined, as shown in the previous example, that confusion is most likely to occur.

Jon Skeet

14.4.3 Function member invocation

This subclause describes the process that takes place at run-time to invoke a particular function member. It is assumed that a compile-time process has already determined the particular member to invoke, possibly by applying overload resolution to a set of candidate function members.

For purposes of describing the invocation process, function members are divided into two categories:

- Static function members. These are static methods, static property accessors, and user-defined operators. Static function members are always non-virtual.
- Instance function members. These are instance methods, instance constructors, instance property accessors, and indexer accessors. Instance function members are either non-virtual or virtual, and are always invoked on a particular instance. The instance is computed by an instance expression, and it becomes accessible within the function member as `this` (§14.5.7). For an instance constructor, the instance expression is taken to be the newly allocated object.

The run-time processing of a function member invocation consists of the following steps, where M is the function member and, if M is an instance member, E is the instance expression:

- If M is a static function member:
    - The argument list is evaluated as described in §14.4.1.
    - M is invoked.
- If M is an instance function member declared in a *value-type*:
    - E is evaluated. If this evaluation causes an exception, then no further steps are executed. For an instance constructor, this evaluation consists of allocating the storage (typically from an execution stack) for the new object. In this case E is classified as a variable.
    - If E is not classified as a variable, then a temporary local variable of E's type is created and the value of E is assigned to that variable. E is then reclassified as a reference to that temporary local variable. The temporary variable is accessible as this within M, but not in any other way. Thus, only when E is a true variable is it possible for the caller to observe the changes that M makes to this.
    - The argument list is evaluated as described in §14.4.1.
    - M is invoked. The variable referenced by E becomes the variable referenced by this.
- If M is an instance function member declared in a *reference-type*:
    - E is evaluated. If this evaluation causes an exception, then no further steps are executed. For an instance constructor, this evaluation consists of allocating (typically from a garbage-collected heap) the storage for the new object.
    - The argument list is evaluated as described in §14.4.1.
    - The value of E is checked to be valid: if the type of E is a *reference-type*, and the value of E is null, a System.NullReferenceException is thrown and no further steps are executed.
    - The function member implementation to invoke is determined:
        - If the compile-time type of E is an interface, the function member to invoke is the implementation of M provided by the run-time type of the instance referenced by E. This function member is determined by applying the interface mapping rules (§20.4.2).
        - Otherwise, if M is a virtual function member, the function member to invoke is the implementation of M provided by the run-time type of the instance referenced by E. This function member is determined by applying the rules for determining the most derived implementation (§17.5.3) of M with respect to the run-time type of the instance referenced by E.
        - Otherwise, M is a non-virtual function member, and the function member to invoke is M itself.
    - The function member implementation determined in the step above is invoked. If the type of E is a *value-type*, then the variable referenced by E becomes the variable referenced by this; otherwise, the type of E is a *reference-type* and the object referenced by E becomes the object referenced by this.

[*Note*: If the type of E is a *value-type*, no boxing occurs even if M is an instance member function declared in a *reference-type*. *end note*]

No boxing

If a `struct` called `S` declares an override of `object.ToString` or `object.GetHashCode` or `object.Equals`, then calling these methods on an expression of type `S` does *not* box. Likewise, if `S` declares an *implicit* member implementation of an interface member `M`, then calling `M` on an expression of type `S` does *not* box. For example:

```
interface I
{
  void M();
}

struct S : I
{
  ...
  public override string ToString() { ...}
  public override int GetHashCode() { ...}
  public override bool Equals(object other) { ...}
  public void M() { ...}
}

class NoBoxing
{
  static void Main()
  {
    S value = new S();
    string s = value.ToString();    // no boxing
    int hc = value.GetHashCode();  // no boxing
    bool eq = value.Equals(null);  // no boxing
    value.M();                      // no boxing
  }
}
```

See also the annotation in §25.7.3.

14.4.3.1 Invocations on boxed instances

A function member implemented in a *value-type* can be invoked through a boxed instance of that *value-type* in the following situations:

- When the function member is an `override` of a method inherited from type `object` and is invoked through an instance expression of type `object`.
- When the function member is an implementation of an interface function member and is invoked through an instance expression of an *interface-type*.
- When the function member is invoked through a delegate.

In these situations, the boxed instance is considered to contain a variable of the *value-type*, and this variable becomes the variable referenced by `this` within the function member invocation. [*Note*: In particular, this means that when a function member is invoked on a boxed instance, it is possible for the function member to modify the value contained in the boxed instance. *end note*]

From diaphanous to concrete

As covered in the annotation on §11.3.1, C# goes to some lengths to make the representation change between value types and boxed value types as diaphanous as possible so as to present a unified view of the type system (§11). The preceding note highlights a very important situation where existence of the representation change becomes far more concrete, and the possibly surprising results of this. This issue is covered in detail in an annotation on §22.2.

But wait, there is more...

This clause refers to function members implemented *in* a *value-type*. A boxed enumeration type (§11.1.9) is a subtype of `System.Enum`, which in turn is a subtype of `System.Value-Type`. All other boxed value types are subtypes of `System.ValueType`. Though C# does not mandate any methods for these two classes (Annex D), a particular implementation may provide them. In such a case those methods may be invoked on boxed instances using the normal rules of C#.

For example, the CLI Standard Library provides a `CompareTo()` method in `System.Enum`. The following code fragment shows how this may be invoked from C# hosted on the CLI:

```
enum Colour { Red, Green, Blue };

public static void CLIBoxedCompareExample()
{
   Enum obj_1 = Colour.Green;
   Enum obj_2 = Colour.Blue;

   int comp_1 = obj_1.CompareTo(Colour.Red);
   int comp_2 = obj_1.CompareTo(obj_2);

   Console.WriteLine("comp_1 = { 0}, comp_2 = { 1} ", comp_1, comp_2);
}
```

When `CLIBoxedCompareExample()` is invoked, the output is:

```
comp_1 = 1, comp_2 = -1
```

14.5 Primary expressions

Primary expressions include the simplest forms of expressions.

primary-expression:
  array-creation-expression
  primary-no-array-creation-expression

primary-no-array-creation-expression:
  literal
  simple-name
  parenthesized-expression
  member-access
  invocation-expression
  element-access
  this-access
  base-access
  post-increment-expression

> post-decrement-expression
> object-creation-expression
> delegate-creation-expression
> typeof-expression
> checked-expression
> unchecked-expression
> default-value-expression
> anonymous-method-expression

Primary expressions are divided between *array-creation-expression*s and *primary-no-array-creation-expression*s. Treating *array-creation-expression* in this way, rather than listing it along with the other simple expression forms, enables the grammar to disallow potentially confusing code such as

```
object o = new int[3][1] ;
```

which would otherwise be interpreted as

```
object o = (new int[3] )[1] ;
```

A *primary-expression* is permitted to reference a static class (§17.1.1.3) if the *primary-expression* is the E in a *member-access* (§14.5.4) of the form E.I.

14.5.1 Literals

A *primary-expression* that consists of a *literal* (§9.4.4) is classified as a value.

> *literal::*
>   *boolean-literal*
>   *integer-literal*
>   *real-literal*
>   *character-literal*
>   *string-literal*
>   *null-literal*

14.5.2 Simple names

A *simple-name* consists of an identifier, optionally followed by a type argument list:

> *simple-name:*
>   *identifier   type-argument-list$_{opt}$*

A *simple-name* is either of the form I or of the form I<A$_1$, ..., A$_K$>, where I is a single identifier and <A$_1$, ..., A$_K$> is an optional *type-argument-list*. When no *type-argument-list* is specified, consider K to be zero. The *simple-name* is evaluated and classified as follows:

- If K is zero and the *simple-name* appears within a *block* and if the *block*'s (or an enclosing *block*'s) local variable declaration space (§10.3) contains a local variable, parameter or constant with name I, then the *simple-name* refers to that local variable, parameter or constant and is classified as a variable or value.
- If K is zero and the *simple-name* appears within the body of a generic method declaration and if that declaration includes a type parameter with name I, then the *simple-name* refers to that type parameter.

- Otherwise, for each instance type T (§25.1.2), starting with the instance type of the immediately enclosing type declaration and continuing with the instance type of each enclosing class or struct declaration (if any):
  - If K is zero and the declaration of T includes a type parameter with name I, then the *simple-name* refers to that type parameter.
  - Otherwise, if a member lookup (§14.3) of I in T with K type arguments produces a match:
    - If T is the instance type of the immediately enclosing class or struct type and the lookup identifies one or more methods, the result is a method group with an associated instance expression of this. If a type argument list was specified, it is used in calling a generic method (§25.6.3).
    - Otherwise, if T is the instance type of the immediately enclosing class or struct type, if the lookup identifies an instance member, and if the reference occurs within the *block* of an instance constructor, an instance method, or an instance accessor, the result is the same as a member access (§14.5.4) of the form this.I. This can only happen when K is zero.
    - Otherwise, the result is the same as a member access (§14.5.4) of the form T.I or T.I<A_1, ..., A_K>. In this case, it is a compile-time error for the *simple-name* to refer to an instance member.
- Otherwise, for each namespace N, starting with the namespace in which the *simple-name* occurs, continuing with each enclosing namespace (if any), and ending with the global namespace, the following steps are evaluated until an entity is located:
  - If K is zero and I is the name of a namespace in N, then:
    - If the location where the *simple-name* occurs is enclosed by a namespace declaration for N and the namespace declaration contains an *extern-alias-directive* or *using-alias-directive* that associates the name I with a namespace or type, then the *simple-name* is ambiguous and a compile-time error occurs.
    - Otherwise, the *simple-name* refers to the namespace named I in N.
  - Otherwise, if N contains an accessible type having name I and K type parameters, then:
    - If K is zero and the location where the *simple-name* occurs is enclosed by a namespace declaration for N and the namespace declaration contains an *extern-alias-directive* or *using-alias-directive* that associates the name I with a namespace or type, then the *simple-name* is ambiguous and a compile-time error occurs.
    - Otherwise, the *simple-name* refers to the type constructed with the given type arguments.
  - Otherwise, if the location where the *simple-name* occurs is enclosed by a namespace declaration for N:
    - If K is zero and the namespace declaration contains an *extern-alias-directive* or *using-alias-directive* that associates the name I with an imported namespace or type, then the *simple-name* refers to that namespace or type.
    - Otherwise, if the namespaces imported by the *using-namespace-directive*s of the namespace declaration contain exactly one type having name I and K type parameters, then the *simple-name* refers to that type constructed with the given type arguments.

- Otherwise, if the namespaces imported by the *using-namespace-directive*s of the namespace declaration contain more than one type having name I and K type parameters, then the *simple-name* is ambiguous and an error occurs.

[*Note*: This entire step is exactly parallel to the corresponding step in the processing of a *namespace-or-type-name* (§10.8). *end note*]

- Otherwise, the *simple-name* is undefined and a compile-time error occurs.

14.5.2.1 Invariant meaning in blocks

For each occurrence of a given identifier as a *simple-name* in an expression or declarator, every other occurrence of the same identifier as a *simple-name* in an expression or declarator within the immediately enclosing *block* (§15.2) or *switch-block* (§15.7.2) shall refer to the same entity. [*Note*: This rule ensures that the meaning of a name is always the same within a block. *end note*]

[*Example*: The example

```
class Test
{
  double x;

  void F(bool b)
  {
    x = 1.0;
    if (b)
    {
      int x = 1;
    }
  }
}
```

results in a compile-time error because x refers to different entities within the outer block (the extent of which includes the nested block in the if statement). In contrast, the example

```
class Test
{
  double x;

  void F(bool b)
  {
    if (b)
    {
      x = 1.0;
    }
    else
    {
      int x = 1;
    }
  }
}
```

is permitted because the name x is never used in the outer block. *end example*]

Simpler confusion

The "invariant meaning" rule was intended to be less confusing than the "local declarations may not hide each other" rule of Java and other languages. After all, by requiring wherever a simple name is placed within a block, including within any nested blocks, that it must be in the scope of the *same* declaration, the potential for confusion must surely be reduced?

However, it is clear that some find the rule more confusing. The first program fragment in this clause provides an example, as it can be argued that the assignment is clearly to the class field, which is hidden by no local declaration.

Furthermore, a valid existing program with a local declaration in a nested block may be invalidated by the introduction of an assignment in an outer block to a field of the type.

Neither of these situations causes a problem with Java's "local declarations may not hide each other" rule.

Recommendation: Avoid using a name for a local variable in a nested block that is also used as a name for a field in the enclosing type. Check carefully when versioning a type to maintain this guideline, changing local names if required.

The committee also considered a third alternative: using the `new` keyword to allow a local variable declaration to hide another declaration, in a manner similar to using `new` as a member declaration modifier. However, renaming local variables, as required by "invariant meaning" or "local declarations may not hide each other" rules, was felt to be far clearer than allowing hiding, so this alternative was discarded.

Note that the invariant meaning rule considers scope and not whether the simple name can be referenced; see §10.7 and associated annotation for an explanation of the difference.

[*Note*: The rule of invariant meaning applies only to simple names. It is perfectly valid for the same identifier to have one meaning as a simple name and another meaning as right operand of a member access (§14.5.4). *end note*] [*Example*:

```
struct Point
{
  int x, y;

  public Point(int x, int y)
  {
    this.x = x;
    this.y = y;
  }
}
```

The example above illustrates a common pattern of using the names of fields as parameter names in an instance constructor. In the example, the simple names `x` and `y` refer to the parameters, but that does not prevent the member access expressions `this.x` and `this.y` from accessing the fields. *end example*]

14.5.3 Parenthesized expressions

A *parenthesized-expression* consists of an *expression* enclosed in parentheses.

> *parenthesized-expression:*
> (*expression*)

A *parenthesized-expression* is evaluated by evaluating the *expression* within the parentheses. If the *expression* within the parentheses denotes a namespace or type, a compile-time error occurs.

Otherwise, the result of the *parenthesized-expression* is the result of the evaluation of the contained *expression*.

14.5.4 Member access

A *member-access* consists of a *primary-expression*, a *predefined-type*, or a *qualified-alias-member*, followed by a "." token, followed by an *identifier*, optionally followed by a *type-argument-list*.

> *member-access:*
>   *primary-expression* . *identifier* *type-argument-list*_{opt}
>   *predefined-type* . *identifier* *type-argument-list*_{opt}
>   *qualified-alias-member* . *identifier* *type-argument-list*_{opt}
>
> *predefined-type:* one of
>   ```
>   bool    byte    char    decimal  double  float   int      long
>   object  sbyte   short   string   uint    ulong   ushort
>   ```

qualified-alias-member is defined in §16.7.

A *member-access* is either of the form $E.I$ or of the form $E.I<A_1, \ldots, A_K>$, where E is a *primary-expression, predefined-type* or *qualified-alias-member*, I is a single identifier and $<A_1, \ldots, A_K>$ is an optional *type-argument-list*. When no *type-argument-list* is specified, consider K to be zero. The *member-access* is evaluated and classified as follows:

- If K is zero and E is a namespace and E contains a nested namespace with name I, then the result is that namespace.
- Otherwise, if E is a namespace and E contains an accessible type having name I and K type parameters, then the result is that type constructed with the given type arguments.
- If E is a classified as a type, if E is not a type parameter, and if a member lookup (§14.3) of I in E with K type parameters produces a match, then $E.I$ is evaluated and classified as follows: [*Note*: When the result of such a member lookup is a method group and K is zero, the method group can contain methods having type parameters. This allows such methods to be considered for type argument inferencing. *end note*]
  - If I identifies a type, then the result is that type constructed with the given type and any inferred arguments.
  - If I identifies one or more methods, then the result is a method group with no associated instance expression.
  - If I identifies a `static` property, then the result is a property access with no associated instance expression.
  - If I identifies a `static` field:
    - If the field is `readonly` and the reference occurs outside the static constructor of the class or struct in which the field is declared, then the result is a value, namely the value of the static field I in E.
    - Otherwise, the result is a variable, namely the static field I in E.
  - If I identifies a `static` event:
    - If the reference occurs within the class or struct in which the event is declared, and the event was declared without *event-accessor-declarations* (§17.7), then $E.I$ is processed exactly as if I were a static field.
    - Otherwise, the result is an event access with no associated instance expression.
  - If I identifies a constant, then the result is a value, namely the value of that constant.

- o If I identifies an enumeration member, then the result is a value, namely the value of that enumeration member.
  - o Otherwise, E.I is an invalid member reference, and a compile-time error occurs.
- If E is a property access, indexer access, variable, or value, the type of which is T, and a member lookup (§14.3) of I in T with K type arguments produces a match, then E.I is evaluated and classified as follows:
  - o First, if E is a property or indexer access, then the value of the property or indexer access is obtained (§14.1.1) and E is reclassified as a value.
  - o If I identifies one or more methods, then the result is a method group with an associated instance expression of E. If a type argument list was specified, the method group consists only of generic methods having K type parameters and the type argument list is implicitly applied to each method in the method group (§25.6.3). If no type argument list was specified, the method group may contain both generic and non-generic methods.
  - o If I identifies an instance property, then the result is a property access with an associated instance expression of E.
  - o If T is a *class-type* and I identifies an instance field of that *class-type*:
    - If the value of E is null, then a System.NullReferenceException is thrown.
    - Otherwise, if the field is readonly and the reference occurs outside an instance constructor of the class in which the field is declared, then the result is a value, namely the value of the field I in the object referenced by E.
    - Otherwise, the result is a variable, namely the field I in the object referenced by E.
  - o If T is a *struct-type* and I identifies an instance field of that *struct-type*:
    - If E is a value, or if the field is readonly and the reference occurs outside an instance constructor of the struct in which the field is declared, then the result is a value, namely the value of the field I in the struct instance given by E.
    - Otherwise, the result is a variable, namely the field I in the struct instance given by E.
  - o If I identifies an instance event:
    - If the reference occurs within the class or struct in which the event is declared, and the event was declared without *event-accessor-declarations* (§17.7), then E.I is processed exactly as if I was an instance field.
    - Otherwise, the result is an event access with an associated instance expression of E.
- Otherwise, E.I is an invalid member reference, and a compile-time error occurs.

14.5.4.1 Identical simple names and type names

In a member access of the form E.I, if E is a single identifier, and if the meaning of E as a *simple-name* (§14.5.2) is a constant, field, property, local variable, or parameter with the same type as the meaning of E as a *type-name* (§10.8), then both possible meanings of E are permitted. The two possible meanings of E.I are never ambiguous, since I shall necessarily be a member of the type E in both cases. In other words, the rule simply permits access to the static members and nested types of E where a compile-time error would otherwise have occurred. [*Example*:

```
struct Color
{
  public static readonly Color White = new Color(...);
  public static readonly Color Black = new Color(...);

  public Color Complement() {...}
}

class A
{
  public Color Color;            // Field A.Color of type Color

  void F()
  {
    Color = Color.Black;         // References Color.Black
    Color = Color.Complement();  // Invokes Complement() on A.Color
  }

  static void G()
  {
    Color c = Color.White;       // References Color.White
  }
}
```

Within the A class, those occurrences of the Color identifier that reference the Color type are underlined, and those that reference the Color field are not underlined. *end example*]

14.5.5 Invocation expressions

An *invocation-expression* is used to invoke a method.

> *invocation-expression:*
>   *primary-expression*   (*argument-list*$_{opt}$)

The *primary-expression* of an *invocation-expression* shall be a method group or a value of a *delegate-type*. If the *primary-expression* is a method group, the *invocation-expression* is a method invocation (§14.5.5.1). If the *primary-expression* is a value of a *delegate-type*, the *invocation-expression* is a delegate invocation (§14.5.5.2). If the *primary-expression* is neither a method group nor a value of a *delegate-type*, a compile-time error occurs.

The optional *argument-list* (§14.4.1) provides values or variable references for the parameters of the method.

The result of evaluating an *invocation-expression* is classified as follows:

- If the *invocation-expression* invokes a method or delegate that returns void, the result is nothing. An expression that is classified as nothing cannot be an operand of any operator, and is permitted only in the context of a *statement-expression* (§15.6).
- Otherwise, the result is a value of the type returned by the method or delegate.

14.5.5.1 Method invocations

For a method invocation, the *primary-expression* of the *invocation-expression* shall be a method group. The method group identifies the one method to invoke or the set of overloaded methods from which to choose a specific method to invoke. In the latter case, determination of the specific method to invoke is based on the context provided by the types of the arguments in the *argument-list*.

What is not considered during overload resolution?

Explicit implementations of interface methods (§20.4.1) take no part in overload resolution as they are only callable via an interface reference. Note that interfaces cannot derive from other interfaces in C#; they can only require other interfaces to also be implemented (§20.1.2).

Method overrides also take no part in overload resolution, but if overloading resolves to a virtual method, then usual invocation rules apply and an override may be invoked. Method overrides are excluded as overload resolution uses a method group (§14.1), which is a set of overloaded methods resulting from a member lookup (§14.3), and method lookup excludes override methods.

The compile-time processing of a method invocation of the form M(A), where M is a method group (possibly including a *type-argument-list*), and A is an optional *argument-list*, consists of the following steps:

- The set of candidate methods for the method invocation is constructed. For each method F associated with the method group M:
    - If F is non-generic, F is a candidate when:
        - M has no type argument list, and
        - F is applicable with respect to A (§14.4.2.1).
    - If F is generic and M has no type argument list, F is a candidate when:
        - Type inference (§25.6.4) succeeds, inferring a list of type arguments for the call, and
        - Once the inferred type arguments are substituted for the corresponding method type parameters, all constructed types in the parameter list of F satisfy their constraints (§25.7.1), and the parameter list of F is applicable with respect to A (§14.4.2.1), and
    - If F is generic and M includes a type argument list, F is a candidate when:
        - F has the same number of method type parameters as were supplied in the type argument list, and
        - Once the type arguments are substituted for the corresponding method type parameters, all constructed types in the parameter list of F satisfy their constraints (§25.7.1), and the parameter list of F is applicable with respect to A (§14.4.2.1).
- The set of candidate methods is reduced to contain only methods from the most derived types: For each method C.F in the set, where C is the type in which the method F is declared, all methods declared in a base type of C are removed from the set. Furthermore, if C is a class type other than object, all methods declared in an interface type are removed from the set. [*Note*: This latter rule only has affect when the method group was the result of a member lookup on a type parameter having an effective base class other than object and a non-empty effective interface set (§25.7). *end note*]
- If the resulting set of candidate methods is empty, then no applicable methods exist, and a compile-time error occurs.
- The best method of the set of candidate methods is identified using the overload resolution rules of §14.4.2. If a single best method cannot be identified, the method invocation is ambiguous, and a compile-time error occurs. When performing overload resolution, the parameters of a generic method are considered after substituting the type arguments (supplied or inferred) for the corresponding method type parameters.
- Final validation of the chosen best method is performed:

   ○ The method is validated in the context of the method group: If the best method is a static method, the method group shall have resulted from a *simple-name* or a *member-access* through a type. If the best method is an instance method, the method group shall have resulted from a *simple-name*, a *member-access* through a variable or value, or a *base-access*. If neither of these requirements is true, a compile-time error occurs.
   ○ If the best method is a generic method, the type arguments (supplied or inferred) are checked against the constraints (§25.7.1) declared on the generic method. If any type argument does not satisfy the corresponding constraint(s) on the type parameter, a compile-time error occurs.

Once a method has been selected and validated at compile-time by the above steps, the actual run-time invocation is processed according to the rules of function member invocation described in §14.4.3.

[*Note*: The intuitive effect of the resolution rules described above is as follows: To locate the particular method invoked by a method invocation, start with the type indicated by the method invocation and proceed up the inheritance chain until at least one applicable, accessible, non-override method declaration is found. Then perform overload resolution on the set of applicable, accessible, non-override methods declared in that type and invoke the method thus selected. *end note*]

Sometimes there is no right answer...

Overloading is a controversial subject in programming languages; on the one hand it is often very convenient, while on the other it can produce confusion and be difficult to define precise intuitive rules. In object-oriented languages, inheritance and virtual methods add to the complexity. There is good reason why overloading is sometimes referred to as "ad hoc polymorphism."

The preceding rules precisely define how overloading works in C#; they cannot be said to be trivially intuitive, but that is the nature of the subject matter, not a criticism of C#. Here we will present some of the cases to help you know which method will be called in a given situation.

Consider the code fragment:

```
public class BasicMath
{
  // compute gamma for natural numbers (gamma(n) = factorial(n-1))
  public ulong Gamma(ulong val) { ...}
}

public class AdvancedMath : BasicMath { ...}

public class Client
{
  static public void Test()
  {
    AdvancedMath sm = new AdvancedMath();
    ulong ans = (ulong)sm.Gamma(11UL);
  }
}
```

This does not (yet) involve overloading and the call `sm.Gamma(11UL)` trivially invokes method `BasicMath.Gamma(ulong)`.

Now add the following method to the `AdvancedMath` class:

```
// compute general gamma function
public double Gamma(double val) { ...}
```

There are now two versions of `Gamma`, one in each class. The call `sm.Gamma(11UL)` now invokes the method `AdvancedMath.Gamma(double)`.

This may be counter-intuitive to some. In this example, the intention would appear to be that if the gamma of a natural number is required the (fast and precise) method from `BasicMath` is used, while for the gamma of a floating-point value the (probably slower and inexact) method from `AdvancedMath` is invoked. How did the addition of the gamma for floating-point stop the call resolving to the gamma for natural numbers?

In C#, the rules in this clause state that if an *applicable function member* (§14.4.2.1) is found in a particular class, then methods from base classes of that class are discounted.

Therefore, when resolving the call `sm.Gamma(11UL)`, the method `AdvancedMath.Gamma (double)` is selected, even though it requires an implicit conversion to convert the literal `11UL` to `double`.

However, if `Gamma(double)` is removed from the `AdvancedMath` class and placed into the `BasicMath` class, so that now both versions are in the same class, the call `sm.Gamma (11UL)` invokes the method `BasicMath.Gamma(ulong)`.

This result is produced as `Gamma(ulong)` is a *better function member* (§14.4.2.2) than `Gamma (double)` for the call `sm.Gamma(11UL)`.

Rule 1: In C#, methods in derived classes are always preferred over those in their base classes, even if implicit conversions are required before invoking the former and are not required to invoke the latter. (Remember this is a design choice; it is neither right nor wrong.)

Next consider the following example, contributed by Jon Skeet, which adds overriding to the mix:

```
public class Basic
{
  public virtual void Compute(int val) { ...}
}

public class Advanced : Basic
{
  public override void Compute(int val) { ...}
  public virtual void Compute(double val) { ...}
}

public class Client
{
  public static void Test()
  {
    Advanced a = new Advanced();
    a.Compute(5);
  }
}
```

Intuition might suggest that for the call `a.Compute(5)` the methods in class `Advanced` take precedence over those in class `Basic`, and that the *better function member* from class `Advanced` is `Compute(int)`. However, the method actually invoked is `Advanced.Compute(double)`.

This choice is determined as follows:

- As explained in the preceding annotation, override methods are excluded from consideration, ruling out method `Advanced.Compute(int)`;
- Method `Advanced.Compute(double)` is applicable, so any method in class `Basic` is discounted;
- This leaves `Advanced.Compute(double)` as the only available choice.

Rule 2: Method overrides are not considered when resolving overloading. However, if overloading resolves to a virtual method that is overridden, then, as usual, the override is the actual method called. (Again, remember this is a design choice; it is neither right nor wrong.)

As has been shown, overloading can make it difficult to determine which method will be invoked. The preceding simplified rules should help. We also offer the following guidelines (neither original):

- Keep all overloads of a particular method in the same class, do not disperse them among classes in an inheritance hierarchy. This avoids the issue where an intuitively less-applicable method in a derived class is selected over a more applicable method in a base class. (Peter Hallam from Microsoft's C# team advocates this guideline.)
- Do not override and overload the same method in the same class. This avoids the issue of when an intuitively less applicable method in a class is selected over a more applicable override method in the same class.

14.5.5.2 Delegate invocations

For a delegate invocation, the *primary-expression* of the *invocation-expression* shall be a value of a *delegate-type*. Furthermore, considering the *delegate-type* to be a function member with the same parameter list as the *delegate-type*, the *delegate-type* shall be applicable (§14.4.2.1) with respect to the *argument-list* of the *invocation-expression*.

The run-time processing of a delegate invocation of the form `D(A)`, where `D` is a *primary-expression* of a *delegate-type* and `A` is an optional *argument-list*, consists of the following steps:

- `D` is evaluated. If this evaluation causes an exception, no further steps are executed.
- The argument list `A` is evaluated. If this evaluation causes an exception, no further steps are executed.
- The value of `D` is checked to be valid. If the value of `D` is `null`, a `System.NullReferenceException` is thrown and no further steps are executed.
- Otherwise, `D` is a reference to a delegate instance. A function member invocation (§14.4.3) is performed on each callable entity referenced by the delegate. If invocation of a callable entity causes an exception, the remaining callable entities are not invoked. Otherwise, the return result of the invocation is the result returned from the last callable entity.

Raising events and thread safety

A common piece of advice is to check that a delegate is not null before invoking it, like this:

```
delegate void FrobEventHandler(object sender, FrobEventArgs args);

class DontDoThis
{
  public event FrobEventHandler FrobEvent;
```

```
    protected virtual void OnFrob(FrobEventArgs args)
    {
      if (FrobEvent != null)
      {
        FrobEvent(this, args);
      }
    }
  }
```

Unfortunately, this is not thread safe. Consequently, you might see advice recommending this:

```
class DoThis
{
  public event FrobEventHandler FrobEvent;

  protected virtual void OnFrob(FrobEventArgs args)
  {
    FrobEventHandler toRaise = FrobEvent;
    if (toRaise != null)
    {
      toRaise(this, args);
    }
  }
}
```

This is thread safe. However, you might occasionally read advice telling you that using a local temporary variable (such as `toRaise`) does *not* make the code thread safe because a compiler could optimize it away. The C# committee discussed this and unanimously agreed that a conforming C# compiler cannot do this as it is not a thread-safe optimization. In fact, Microsoft has removed optimizations from its 64-bit JIT compiler precisely for this reason.

Note that this design, in avoiding getting caught by an update that makes the event null, can also miss an update that adds a delegate to the event after the `toRaise` local copy is made. Attempting to avoid this would require locking the event over the call invoking it, and this raises potential deadlock issues and so is not advised! Missing such an update is just normal behavior when concurrency is involved.

14.5.6 Element access

An *element-access* consists of a *primary-no-array-creation-expression*, followed by a "[" token, followed by an *expression-list*, followed by a "] " token. The *expression-list* consists of one or more *expression*s, separated by commas.

> *element-access:*
>   *primary-no-array-creation-expression* [*expression-list*   ]
>
> *expression-list:*
>   *expression*
>   *expression-list*   ,   *expression*

If the *primary-no-array-creation-expression* of an *element-access* is a value of an *array-type*, the *element-access* is an array access (§14.5.6.1). Otherwise, the *primary-no-array-creation-expression* shall be a variable or value of a class, struct, or interface type that has one or more indexer members, in which case the *element-access* is an indexer access (§14.5.6.2).

14.5.6.1 Array access

For an array access, the *primary-no-array-creation-expression* of the *element-access* shall be a value of an *array-type*. The number of expressions in the *expression-list* shall be the same as the rank of the *array-type*, and each expression shall be of type int, uint, long, ulong, or of a type that can be implicitly converted to one or more of these types.

The result of evaluating an array access is a variable of the element type of the array, namely the array element selected by the value(s) of the expression(s) in the *expression-list*.

The run-time processing of an array access of the form P[A] , where P is a *primary-no-array-creation-expression* of an *array-type* and A is an *expression-list*, consists of the following steps:

- P is evaluated. If this evaluation causes an exception, no further steps are executed.
- The index expressions of the *expression-list* are evaluated in order, from left to right. Following evaluation of each index expression, an implicit conversion (§13.1) to one of the following types is performed: int, uint, long, ulong. The first type in this list for which an implicit conversion exists is chosen. For instance, if the index expression is of type short then an implicit conversion to int is performed, since implicit conversions from short to int and from short to long are possible. If evaluation of an index expression or the subsequent implicit conversion causes an exception, then no further index expressions are evaluated and no further steps are executed.

> **Array indexing corner case**
>
> Nicu Fruja proposed the following program, which uses index expressions of mixed types, ulong and long, to index into a two-dimensional array:
>
> ```
> class App
> {
>   static void Main()
>   {
>     int[ ,] a = new int[ 2,2] ;
>     ulong i = 1;
>     long j = 1;
>     int value = a[ i,j] ;
>   }
> }
> ```
>
> The current Mono compiler accepts this, but the Microsoft one fails to compile this program, issuing the following diagnostics:
>
> ```
> error: Cannot implicitly convert 'ulong' to 'int'.
> error: Cannot implicitly convert 'long' to 'int'.
> ```
>
> It seems implausible that this is in accordance with the intentions of the Standard, but the preceding phrase, "each expression shall be of type," *could* be interpreted as saying that all expressions must be of the same type. Also, the description of the runtime processing of the index value, "The first type in this list for which an implicit conversion exists is chosen," may lead the implementer to think that all index expressions must be convertible to the same type. On the contrary, the phrases "each index expression," "if the index expression," and "no further index expressions" suggest each index is processed and typed independently.

- The value of P is checked to be valid. If the value of P is null, a System.NullReferenceException is thrown and no further steps are executed.
- The value of each expression in the *expression-list* is checked against the actual bounds of each dimension of the array instance referenced by P. If one or more values are out of range, a System.IndexOutOfRangeException is thrown and no further steps are executed.
- The location of the array element given by the index expression(s) is computed, and this location becomes the result of the array access.

Red Katipo

At the time of writing, both the Mono and Microsoft implementations deviate from the Standard by not throwing System.IndexOutOfRangeException if the index type is an out-of-range long. Instead, they both throw System.OverflowException. For example, consider:

```
int[] vals = new int[42];

long ix = long.MaxValue;

vals[ix] = 56;        // Mono and MS: OverflowException,
                      // should be IndexOutOfBoundsException
```

Both these compilers execute on CLI implementations and provide a (non-Standard) Array.SetValue method, which takes a long index. This gets a little closer to the C# specification (even though it need not):

```
vals.SetValue(56, ix);  // Mono and MS: ArgumentOutOfRangeException
```

When using int indexes (including when using the CLI Standard Array.SetValue, which takes an int index), both compilers throw System.IndexOutOfRangeException.

The same issue occurs for reads using array indexing and the matching CLI Standard Array.GetValue methods.

Like the Red Katipo, a rare New Zealand spider that can bite, indexing arrays with longs is rare, so this bug should rarely bite.

14.5.6.2 Indexer access

For an indexer access, the *primary-no-array-creation-expression* of the *element-access* shall be a variable or value of a class, struct, or interface type, and this type shall implement one or more indexers that are applicable with respect to the *expression-list* of the *element-access*.

The compile-time processing of an indexer access of the form P[A], where P is a *primary-no-array-creation-expression* of a class, struct, or interface type T, and A is an *expression-list*, consists of the following steps:

- The set of indexers provided by T is constructed. The set consists of all indexers declared in T or a base type of T that are not override declarations and are accessible in the current context (§10.5).
- The set is reduced to those indexers that are applicable and not hidden by other indexers. The following rules are applied to each indexer S.I in the set, where S is the type in which the indexer I is declared:
  - o If I is not applicable with respect to A (§14.4.2.1), then I is removed from the set.

- o If I is applicable with respect to A (§14.4.2.1), then all indexers declared in a base type of S are removed from the set.
- If the resulting set of candidate indexers is empty, then no applicable indexers exist, and a compile-time error occurs.
- The best indexer of the set of candidate indexers is identified using the overload resolution rules of §14.4.2. If a single best indexer cannot be identified, the indexer access is ambiguous, and a compile-time error occurs.
- The index expressions of the *expression-list* are evaluated in order, from left to right. The result of processing the indexer access is an expression classified as an indexer access. The indexer access expression references the indexer determined in the step above, and has an associated instance expression of P and an associated argument list of A.

Depending on the context in which it is used, an indexer access causes invocation of either the *get-accessor* or the *set-accessor* of the indexer. If the indexer access is the target of an assignment, the *set-accessor* is invoked to assign a new value (§14.14.1). In all other cases, the *get-accessor* is invoked to obtain the current value (§14.1.1).

14.5.7 This access

A *this-access* consists of the reserved word this.

> *this-access:*
>   this

A *this-access* is permitted only in the *block* of an instance constructor, an instance method, or an instance accessor. It has one of the following meanings:

- When this is used in a *primary-expression* within an instance constructor of a class, it is classified as a value. The type of the value is the class within which the usage occurs, and the value is a reference to the object being constructed.
- When this is used in a *primary-expression* within an instance method or instance accessor of a class, it is classified as a value. The type of the value is the class within which the usage occurs, and the value is a reference to the object for which the method or accessor was invoked.
- When this is used in a *primary-expression* within an instance constructor of a struct, it is classified as a variable. The type of the variable is the struct within which the usage occurs, and the variable represents the struct being constructed. The this variable of an instance constructor of a struct behaves exactly the same as:
  - o an out parameter of the struct type if the constructor declaration has no constructor initializer. In particular, this means that the variable shall be definitely assigned in every execution path of the instance constructor.
  - o a ref parameter of the struct type if the constructor declaration has a constructor initializer. In particular, this means that the variable is considered initially assigned.
- When this is used in a *primary-expression* within an instance method or instance accessor of a struct, it is classified as a variable. The type of the variable is the struct within which the usage occurs, and the variable represents the struct for which the method or accessor was invoked. The this variable of an instance method of a struct behaves exactly the same as a ref parameter of the struct type.

Use of `this` in a *primary-expression* in a context other than the ones listed above is a compile-time error. In particular, it is not possible to refer to `this` in a static method, a static property accessor, or in a *variable-initializer* of a field declaration.

> **this = that?**
>
> The idea of `this` being a variable in struct types may come as a surprise to some readers (as it did to me). In particular, assigning to `this` may appear downright odd, but it does have plausible uses; for an example, see annotation on §18.3.8.
>
> *Jon Skeet*

14.5.8 Base access

A *base-access* consists of the reserved word `base` followed by either a "." token and an identifier and optional *type-argument-list* or an *expression-list* enclosed in square brackets:

> *base-access:*
>   `base`   .   *identifier*   *type-argument-list*_{opt}
>   `base`   [*expression-list*   ]

A *base-access* is used to access base class members that are hidden by similarly named members in the current class or struct. A *base-access* is permitted only in the *block* of an instance constructor, an instance method, or an instance accessor. When `base.I` occurs in a class or struct, `I` shall denote a member of the base class of that class or struct. Likewise, when `base[E]` occurs in a class, an applicable indexer shall exist in the base class.

At compile-time, *base-access* expressions of the form `base.I` and `base[E]` are evaluated exactly as if they were written `((B)this).I` and `((B)this)[E]`, where `B` is the base class of the class or struct in which the construct occurs. Thus, `base.I` and `base[E]` correspond to `this.I` and `this[E]`, except `this` is viewed as an instance of the base class.

When a *base-access* references a virtual function member (a method, event, property, or indexer), the determination of which function member to invoke at run-time (§14.4.3) is changed. The function member that is invoked is determined by finding the most derived implementation (§17.5.3) of the function member with respect to `B` (instead of with respect to the run-time type of `this`, as would be usual in a non-base access). Thus, within an `override` of a `virtual` function member, a *base-access* can be used to invoke the inherited implementation of the function member. If the function member referenced by a *base-access* is abstract, a compile-time error occurs.

> **Base access is nonvirtual**
>
> Given the following classes
>
> ```
> class A
> {
>     public virtual void M() {}
> }
>
> class B : A
> {
>     public override void M() {}
> }
>
> class C : B {}
> ```

it is important to realize the difference between this:

```
class D1 : C
{
  public override void M()
  {
    (this as C).M(); // ooops...
  }
}
```

and this:

```
class D2 : C
{
  public override void M()
  {
    base.M();
  }
}
```

- In D1 the call `(this as C).M()`, or equivalently `((C)this).M()`, causes infinite recursion. This is because it calls (virtually) the most derived implementation of M in `this`, which is of course itself.
- In D2 the call `base.M()` does *not* cause infinite recursion. This is because it calls (non-virtually) the most derived implementation of M with respect to C, which in this case is the implementation of M that C inherits from B.

See also §17.5.3 and associated annotations.

[*Note*: Being non-virtual, a `base.M()` call is most likely somewhat faster than a virtual call `M()` to a (virtual) method declared in the base class. However, it is **strongly discouraged** to speculate on this sort of optimization.]

No override bypass

The *base-access* does not allow an inherited override method to be bypassed by calling, on the current instance, the method that the inherited override itself overrode. Put another way, you cannot perform a `base.base...` access. For example, consider the code fragment:

```
class A
{
  public virtual void M() {...}
}

class B : A
{
  public override void M() {...}
}

class C : B
{
```

```
   public override void M()
   {
     base.M(); // call B.M on this
     // no way to call A.M on this
     ...
   }
 }
```

C# provides no way within class C to invoke the method A.M on an instance of C, such as this. This prevents the override in class B from being bypassed.

Note: The CLI does support bypassing an override in this way. This means that if a C# class is to be consumed by another language running on the CLI, it is not guaranteed that any overrides will not be bypassed.

14.5.9 Postfix increment and decrement operators

post-increment-expression:
   primary-expression ++

post-decrement-expression:
   primary-expression --

The operand of a postfix increment or decrement operation shall be an expression classified as a variable, a property access, or an indexer access. The result of the operation is a value of the same type as the operand.

If the operand of a postfix increment or decrement operation is a property or indexer access, the property or indexer shall have both a get and a set accessor. If this is not the case, a compile-time error occurs.

Unary operator overload resolution (§14.2.3) is applied to select a specific operator implementation. Predefined ++ and -- operators exist for the following operand types: sbyte, byte, short, ushort, int, uint, long, ulong, char, float, double, decimal, and any enum type. The result type of each of these predefined operators is the same as the operand type. The predefined ++ operators return the value produced by adding 1 to the operand, and the predefined -- operators return the value produced by subtracting 1 from the operand. In a checked context, if the result of this addition or subtraction is outside the range of the result type and the result type is an integral type or enum type, a System.OverflowException is thrown.

Overflow eventually...

While overflow is possible when operating on enum types, it must be remembered that enums have many "invisible" values that must be traversed before an overflow condition exists. Consider the code fragment:

```
enum Shop { Asda, Foodtown, Bilka };
...
Shop s = Bilka;
s++; // will NOT overflow
```

The type Shop has 2^{32} values, not 3 as it might appear, and the postfix increment operator would need to be applied $2^{31} - 2$ times to the value Bilka before overflow occurs. This contrasts with languages with strong enums, such as Pascal and Ada, where applying the successor function just once to Bilka would produce an error.

There shall be an implicit conversion from the return type of the selected unary operator to the type of the *primary-expression*, otherwise a compile-time error occurs.

The run-time processing of a postfix increment or decrement operation of the form `x++` or `x--` consists of the following steps:

- If `x` is classified as a variable:
  - `x` is evaluated to produce the variable.
  - The value of `x` is saved.
  - The saved value of `x` is converted to the operand type of the selected operator and the operator is invoked with this value as its argument.
  - The value returned by the operator is converted to the type of `x` and stored in the location given by the evaluation of `x`.
  - The saved value of `x` becomes the result of the operation.
- If `x` is classified as a property or indexer access:
  - The instance expression (if `x` is not `static`) and the argument list (if `x` is an indexer access) associated with `x` are evaluated, and the results are used in the subsequent `get` and `set` accessor invocations.
  - The `get` accessor of `x` is invoked and the returned value is saved.
  - The saved value of x is converted to the operand type of the selected operator and the operator is invoked with this value as its argument.
  - The value returned by the operator is converted to the type of x and the `set` accessor of x is invoked with this value as its `value` argument.
  - The saved value of `x` becomes the result of the operation.

The `++` and `--` operators also support prefix notation (§14.6.5). The result of `x++` or `x--` is the value of `x` *before* the operation, whereas the result of `++x` or `--x` is the value of `x` *after* the operation. In either case, `x` itself has the same value after the operation.

An `operator ++` or `operator --` implementation can be invoked using either postfix or prefix notation. It is not possible to have separate operator implementations for the two notations.

Lifted (§14.2.7) forms of the unlifted predefined postfix increment and decrement operators defined above are also predefined.

14.5.10 The new operator

The `new` operator is used to create new instances of types.

There are three forms of `new` expressions:

- Object creation expressions are used to create new instances of class types and value types.
- Array creation expressions are used to create new instances of array types.
- Delegate creation expressions are used to create new instances of delegate types.

The `new` operator implies creation of an instance of a type, but does not necessarily imply dynamic allocation of memory. In particular, instances of value types require no additional memory beyond the variables in which they reside, and no dynamic allocations occur when `new` is used to create instances of value types.

New for old?

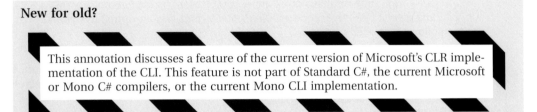

This annotation discusses a feature of the current version of Microsoft's CLR implementation of the CLI. This feature is not part of Standard C#, the current Microsoft or Mono C# compilers, or the current Mono CLI implementation.

When targeting the CLI, a C# compiler uses the CLI's `newobj` instruction to implement the `new` operator. Like the C# operator, the CLI instruction creates a new instance of a type. However, when executing on the current Microsoft CLR implementation, there is at least one case where using the `newobj` instruction on a reference type does not create a new instance of a type. Consider:

```
void NewOldObjects()
{
  string a = string.Empty;
  string b = new string(new char[ 0] );
  string c = new string(new char[ 0] );

  System.Console.WriteLine((object)a == (object)b);
  System.Console.WriteLine((object)b == (object)c);
  System.Console.WriteLine((object)a == (object)c);
}
```

On the current version of Microsoft's CLR, this example prints `True True True`, indicating that the three variables all refer to the same object. Presumably this is an optimization, but probably not one for which it is worth violating the CLI specification. Note that executing the same compiled assembly on Mono's runtime correctly prints `False False False`.

However, the impact of this behavior by Microsoft's CLR should be minuscule on most, if not all, C# programs. Strings are immutable and behave like values but have reference semantics (§11.2.3), and comparisons between strings should not be based on *identity* but on *equality* (§14.9).

The result on Microsoft's CLR is *not* a lack of conformance by either the Microsoft or Mono C# compilers.

Jon Skeet

14.5.10.1 Object creation expressions
An *object-creation-expression* is used to create a new instance of a *class-type* or a *value-type*.

> *object-creation-expression:*
>   new *type* (*argument-list*_{opt})

The *type* of an *object-creation-expression* shall be a *class-type*, a *value-type*, or a *type-parameter* having the *constructor-constraint* or the value type constraint (§25.7). The *type* cannot be an `abstract` *class-type*.

The optional *argument-list* (§14.4.1) is permitted only if the *type* is a *class-type* or a *struct-type*, and not a *type-parameter*.

The compile-time processing of an *object-creation-expression* of the form new T(A), where T is a *class-type*, a *value-type*, or a *type-parameter*, and A is an optional *argument-list*, consists of the following steps:

- If T is a *value-type* and A is not present:
    - ○ The *object-creation-expression* is a default constructor invocation. The result of the *object-creation-expression* is a value of type T, namely the default value for T as defined in §11.1.2.
- Otherwise, if T is a *class-type* or a *struct-type*:
    - ○ If T is an abstract*class-type*, a compile-time error occurs.
    - ○ The instance constructor to invoke is determined using the overload resolution rules of §14.4.2. The set of candidate instance constructors consists of all accessible instance constructors declared in T. If the set of candidate instance constructors is empty, or if a single best instance constructor cannot be identified, a compile-time error occurs.
    - ○ The result of the *object-creation-expression* is a value of type T, namely the value produced by invoking the instance constructor determined in the step above.
- Otherwise, if T is a *type-parameter*:
    - ○ If A is present, a compile-time error occurs.
    - ○ Otherwise, if T has the *constructor-constraint* or the value type constraint, the result of the object-creation-expression is a value of type T.
    - ○ Otherwise, the *object-creation-expression* is invalid, and a compile-time error occurs.
- Otherwise, the *object-creation-expression* is invalid, and a compile-time error occurs.

The run-time processing of an *object-creation-expression* of the form new T(A), where T is *class-type*, a *struct-type*, or a *type-parameter*, and A is an optional *argument-list*, consists of the following steps:

- If T is a *class-type*:
    - ○ A new instance of class T is allocated. If there is not enough memory available to allocate the new instance, a System.OutOfMemoryException is thrown and no further steps are executed.
    - ○ All fields of the new instance are initialized to their default values (§12.2).
    - ○ The instance constructor is invoked according to the rules of function member invocation (§14.4.3). A reference to the newly allocated instance is automatically passed to the instance constructor and the instance can be accessed from within that constructor as this.
- If T is a *struct-type*:
    - ○ An instance of type T is created by allocating a temporary local variable. Since an instance constructor of a *struct-type* is required to definitely assign a value to each field of the instance being created, no initialization of the temporary variable is necessary.
    - ○ The instance constructor is invoked according to the rules of function member invocation (§14.4.3). A reference to the newly allocated instance is automatically passed to the instance constructor and the instance can be accessed from within that constructor as this.
- If T is a *type-parameter*:
    - ○ If T evaluates at run-time to a value type, the result is the default value of this type (§11.1.2). This is always the case if T has the value type constraint.

 o Otherwise, T shall evaluate at run-time to a non-abstract class type having a public constructor taking no parameters. The result is a new instance of this class type:

- A new instance of the class is allocated. If there is not enough memory available to allocate the new instance, a System.OutOfMemoryException is thrown and no further steps are executed.
- All fields of the new instance are initialized to their default values (§12.2).
- The instance constructor is invoked according to the rules of function member invocation (§14.4.3). A reference to the newly allocated instance is automatically passed to the instance constructor and the instance can be accessed from within that constructor as this.

[*Note*: The run-time type need not be accessible to the code containing the *object-creation-expression*. Nevertheless, the run-time environment shall support invoking the constructor. *end note*]

14.5.10.2 Array creation expressions

An *array-creation-expression* is used to create a new instance of an *array-type*.

> *array-creation-expression:*
> new *non-array-type* [*expression-list*] *rank-specifiers$_{opt}$* *array-initializer$_{opt}$*
> new *array-type* *array-initializer*

An array creation expression of the first form allocates an array instance of the type that results from deleting each of the individual expressions from the expression list. [*Example*: The array creation expression new int[10,20] produces an array instance of type int[,], and the array creation expression new int[10][,] produces an array of type int[ ][,]. *end example*] Each expression in the expression list shall be of type int, uint, long, or ulong, or of a type that can be implicitly converted to one or more of these types. The value of each expression determines the length of the corresponding dimension in the newly allocated array instance. Since the length of an array dimension shall be nonnegative, it is a compile-time error to have a constant expression with a negative value, in the expression list.

Except in an unsafe context (§27.1), the layout of arrays is unspecified.

If an array creation expression of the first form includes an array initializer, each expression in the expression list shall be a constant expression (§14.16) and the rank and dimension lengths specified by the expression list shall match those of the array initializer.

In an array creation expression of the second form, the rank of the specified array type shall match that of the array initializer. The individual dimension lengths are inferred from the number of elements in each of the corresponding nesting levels of the array initializer. Thus, the expression

```
new int[,] {{0, 1} , {2, 3} , {4, 5}}
```

exactly corresponds to

```
new int[3, 2] {{0, 1} , {2, 3} , {4, 5}}
```

Array initializers are described further in §19.7.

The result of evaluating an array creation expression is classified as a value, namely a reference to the newly allocated array instance. The run-time processing of an array creation expression consists of the following steps:

- The dimension length expressions of the *expression-list* are evaluated in order, from left to right. Following evaluation of each expression, an implicit conversion (§13.1) to one of the following types is performed: int, uint, long, ulong. The first type in this list for which an implicit conversion exists is chosen. If evaluation of an expression or the subsequent implicit conversion causes an exception, then no further expressions are evaluated and no further steps are executed.
- The computed values for the dimension lengths are validated, as follows: If one or more of the values are less than zero, a System.OverflowException is thrown and no further steps are executed.
- An array instance with the given dimension lengths is allocated. If there is not enough memory available to allocate the new instance, a System.OutOfMemoryException is thrown and no further steps are executed.
- All elements of the new array instance are initialized to their default values (§12.2).
- If the array creation expression contains an array initializer, then each expression in the array initializer is evaluated and assigned to its corresponding array element. The evaluations and assignments are performed in the order the expressions are written in the array initializer—in other words, elements are initialized in increasing index order, with the rightmost dimension increasing first. If evaluation of a given expression or the subsequent assignment to the corresponding array element causes an exception, then no further elements are initialized (and the remaining elements will thus have their default values).

An array creation expression permits instantiation of an array with elements of an array type, but the elements of such an array shall be manually initialized. [*Example*: The statement

```
int[][] a = new int[100][];
```

creates a single-dimensional array with 100 elements of type int[]. The initial value of each element is null. It is not possible for the same array creation expression to also instantiate the sub-arrays (without an array initializer), and the statement

```
int[][] a = new int[100][5];    // Error
```

results in a compile-time error. Instantiation of the sub-arrays can instead be performed manually or using an array initializer, as in

```
int[][] a = new int[100][];
for (int i = 0; i < 100; i++) a[i] = new int[5];

int[][] b = new int[3][] {new int[1], new int[2], new int[3]};
```

end example]

Java difference

Note that, unlike in C#, in Java the declaration:

```
int[][] a = new int[100][5];    // Java code
```

is legal and performs nested allocations. The Java declaration is directly equivalent to the C# code given before, that is:

```
int[][] a = new int[100][];
for (int i = 0; i < 100; i++)
  a[i] = new int[5];
```

[*Note*: When an array of arrays has a "rectangular" shape, that is when the sub-arrays are all of the same length, it is more efficient to use a multi-dimensional array. In the example above, instantiation of the array of arrays creates 101 objects—one outer array and 100 sub-arrays. In contrast,

```
int[,] = new int[100, 5];
```

creates only a single object, a two-dimensional array, and accomplishes the allocation in a single statement. *end note*]

14.5.10.3 Delegate creation expressions

A *delegate-creation-expression* is used to create a new instance of a *delegate-type*.

> *delegate-creation-expression*:
>   new   *delegate-type*   (*expression*   )

The argument of a delegate creation expression shall be a method group (§14.1), an *anonymous-method-expression* (§14.5.15), or a value of a *delegate-type*. If the argument is a method group, it identifies the method, type arguments (for a generic method) and, for an instance method, the object for which to create a delegate. If the argument is a value of a *delegate-type*, it identifies a delegate instance of which to create a copy.

If the *expression* is an *anonymous-method-expression* (§14.5.15), then the anonymous method is converted to the given delegate type using the implicit conversion rules defined in §13.5. [*Example*: If D is a delegate type, then the expression

```
new D(delegate { Console.WriteLine("hello"); } )
```

is equivalent to the expression

```
(D) delegate { Console.WriteLine("hello"); }
```

end example]

The compile-time processing of a *delegate-creation-expression* of the form new D(E), where D is a *delegate-type* and E is an *expression*, consists of the following steps:

- If E is a method group:
  - A single method is selected corresponding to a method invocation (§14.5.5.1) of the form E(A), with the following modifications:
    - The parameter types and modifiers (ref or out) of D are used as the argument types and modifiers of the argument list A.
    - The candidate methods considered are only those methods that are applicable in their normal form (§14.4.2.1), not those applicable only in their expanded form.
    - If the algorithm of §14.5.5.1 produces an error, then a compile-time error occurs. Otherwise the algorithm produces a single best method M, together with its type arguments (if the method is generic), having the same number of parameters as D.
  - If the selected M is not consistent (§22.1) with the delegate type D, a compiler-time error occurs.
  - If the method M is an instance method, the instance expression associated with E determines the target object of the delegate.
  - The result is a value of type D, namely a newly created delegate that refers to the method M and target object.

- Otherwise, if E is a value of a *delegate-type*:
  - ○ If D and E have different numbers of parameters, a compile-time error occurs.
  - ○ If there is not an identity conversion or implicit reference conversion from the return type of E to the return type of D, a compile-time error occurs.
  - ○ If for some parameter of D there is not an identity conversion or implicit reference conversion from the parameter type to the corresponding parameter type of E, a compile-time error occurs.
  - ○ If any parameter of D or E has a parameter modifier (ref or out), then the other corresponding parameter must have the same modifier and the same type.
  - ○ The result is a value of type D, namely a newly created delegate that refers to the same invocation list as E.
- Otherwise, the delegate creation expression is invalid, and a compile-time error occurs.

The run-time processing of a *delegate-creation-expression* of the form new D(E), where D is a *delegate-type* and E is an *expression*, consists of the following steps:

- If E is a method group:
  - ○ If the method selected at compile-time is a static method, the target object of the delegate is null. Otherwise, the selected method is an instance method, and the target object of the delegate is determined from the instance expression associated with E:
    - The instance expression is evaluated. If this evaluation causes an exception, no further steps are executed.
    - If the instance expression is of a *reference-type*, the value computed by the instance expression becomes the target object. If the target object is null, a System.NullReferenceException is thrown and no further steps are executed.
    - If the instance expression is of a *value-type*, a boxing operation (§11.3.1) is performed to convert the value to an object, and this object becomes the target object.
  - ○ A new instance of the delegate type D is allocated. If there is not enough memory available to allocate the new instance, a System.OutOfMemoryException is thrown and no further steps are executed.
  - ○ The new delegate instance is initialized with a reference to the method that was determined at compile-time and a reference to the target object computed above.
- If E is a value of a *delegate-type*:
  - ○ E is evaluated. If this evaluation causes an exception, no further steps are executed.
  - ○ If the value of E is null, a System.NullReferenceException is thrown and no further steps are executed.
  - ○ A new instance of the delegate type D is allocated. If there is not enough memory available to allocate the new instance, a System.OutOfMemoryException is thrown and no further steps are executed.
  - ○ The new delegate instance is initialized with references to the same invocation list as the delegate instance given by E.

Name equivalence and conversions

Delegate types, like other types in C#, use *name equivalence*: Two delegate types are compatible with each other *if and only if* they are instances of exactly the same delegate type. This is where conversions come in, but the behavior may be a little surprising. For example, given the declarations:

```
delegate void D1(int x);
delegate void D2(int y);

static void M(int z) {}
```

then, by §13.6, the method M can be converted to both D1 and D2 using implicit conversions:

```
D1 di1 = M;
D2 di2 = M;
```

If an implicit conversion exists, then an explicit (§13.3.2) one exists also:

```
di1 = (D1)M;
di2 = (D2)M;
```

These assignments are defined (§13.6) to be respectively, equivalent to the delegate creation expressions (§14.5.10.3):

```
di1 = new D1(M);
di2 = new D2(M);
```

However, when converting from one delegate to another, name equivalence is used, so, with no implicit or explicit conversions defined, the following are invalid:

```
di2 = di1;       // Invalid
di2 = (D2)di1;   // Invalid
```

Despite this, one can create one type of delegate from the other simply by using a new expression (§14.5.10.3):

```
di2 = new D2(di1);
```

The lack of orthogonality here may be surprising.

The method and object to which a delegate refers are determined when the delegate is instantiated and then remain constant for the entire lifetime of the delegate. In other words, it is not possible to change the target method or object of a delegate once it has been created. [*Note*: Remember, when two delegates are combined or one is removed from another, a new delegate results; no existing delegate has its content changed. *end note*]

It is not possible to create a delegate that refers to a property, indexer, user-defined operator, instance constructor, finalizer, or static constructor.

[*Example*: As described above, when a delegate is created from a method group, the formal parameter list and return type of the delegate determine which of the overloaded methods to select. In the example

```
delegate double DoubleFunc(double x);

class A
{
  DoubleFunc f = new DoubleFunc(Square);

  static float Square(float x)
  {
    return x * x;
  }
}
```

```
static double Square(double x)
{
  return x * x;
}
}
```

the A.f field is initialized with a delegate that refers to the second Square method because overload resolution with an argument list consisting of a lone double value would choose that method. Had the second Square method not been present, a compile-time error would have occurred.

The definition of a method being consistent with a delegate type (§22.1) permits covariance in the return type and contra-variance in the parameter types. That is, the method return type may be more specific than the delegate return type and the method parameter types may be less specific than the delegate parameter types. In the example

```
delegate object StrToObj(string s);

class A
{
  StrToObj f = new StrToObj(ObjToStr);

  static string ObjToStr(object x)
  {
    return x.ToString();
  }

}
```

the method ObjToStr is used to create a delegate of type StrToObj. The method is consistent with the delegate type since there is an implicit reference conversion from the parameter type of the delegate to the parameter type of the method and an implicit reference conversion from the return type of the method to the return type of the delegate.

Here's another variance-related example:

```
delegate void D1(int i);
delegate void D2(long l);

class Program
{
  static void M(long l) {}
  static void F(D1 d) {}
  static void F(D2 d) {}

  static void Main()
  {
    D1 d1 = new D1(M);
          // Error: M is compatible with D1,
          // but inconsistent, because the conversion from
          // int to long is not an implicit reference
          // conversion.
```

```
        F(M); // Error: ambiguity between F(D1) and F(D2). M is
              // compatible with both D1 and D2. However M is
              // consistent with D2, while inconsistent with D1.
    }
}
```

end example]

Creating a delegate from a delegate

As noted in the preceding annotation, two delegate types such as `FromInt` and `ToFloat` are distinct types even though they have the same return types and the same formal parameter lists:

```
public delegate float FromInt(int x);
public delegate float ToFloat(int x);
```

Thus, if a method `Producer` returns a `FromInt` and we want to pass that delegate to a method `Consumer` that expects a `ToFloat` argument, we need a delegate creation expression to create a `ToFloat` delegate from a `FromInt` delegate:

```
Consumer(new ToFloat(Producer()))
```

This scenario is particularly likely when the `Producer` and `Consumer` methods are from different libraries, independently developed. Otherwise, a single delegate type would suffice.

In C# 1.0, that was the only real use of delegate creation expressions where the argument was a value of a delegate type, because the delegate types had to be structurally identical for the delegate creation expression to be applicable. In C# 2.0, parameter contravariance and return type covariance mean that the delegate types no longer have to be structurally identical, so delegate creation expressions are more useful.

Here is a C# 2.0 example with both contravariance and covariance:

```
delegate string First(object o);
delegate object Second(string x);

class Test
{
    static void Main()
    {
        First f = new First(Foo);
        Second s = new Second(f);
    }

    static string Foo(object o)
    {
        return "";
    }
}
```

[Note: For one way to avoid non-matching delegate types, see §25.4.]

Jon Skeet

Breaking change

The introduction of covariance and contravariance in delegate creation causes one of the few breaking changes in the transition to C# 2.0: The method selected in a delegate creation expression may be different in C# 2.0 than in C# 1.0. Consider the following:

```
using System;

class B
{
  public void Foo(string x)
  {
    Console.WriteLine("B.Foo(string)");
  }
}

class D : B
{
  public void Foo(object o)
  {
    Console.WriteLine("D.Foo(object)");
  }
}

class Test
{
  delegate void StringDelegate(string x);

  static void Main()
  {
    D d = new D();
    StringDelegate sd = new StringDelegate(d.Foo);
    sd("Hello");
  }
}
```

In C# 1.0 there would be only one candidate for `Foo` in the `new StringDelegate(d.Foo)` expression; namely, `B.Foo`, but in C# 2.0 there two candidates due to contravariance.

The current Microsoft C# compiler produces a warning to indicate that the behavior has changed due to new language rules. However, neither the current Microsoft compiler nor current Mono produces a warning about the following, where there is an extra candidate thanks to covariance:

```
using System;

class B
{
  public object Foo()
  {
    Console.WriteLine("B.Foo");
    return null;
  }
}
```

```
class D : B
{
  new public string Foo()
  {
    Console.WriteLine("D.Foo");
    return null;
  }
}

class Test
{
  delegate object StringDelegate();

  static void Main()
  {
    D d = new D();
    StringDelegate sd = new StringDelegate(d.Foo);
    sd();
  }
}
```

In both examples, method B.Foo is called in C# 1.0 whereas method D.Foo is called in C# 2.0.

Jon Skeet

14.5.11 The typeof operator

The typeof operator is used to obtain the System.Type object for a type.

typeof-expression:
  typeof (*type*)
  typeof (*unbound-type-name*)
  typeof (void)

unbound-type-name:
  identifier generic-dimension-specifier$_{opt}$
  *identifier *::* identifier generic-dimension-specifier$_{opt}$*
  unbound-type-name . identifier generic-dimension-specifier$_{opt}$

generic-dimension-specifier:
  < commas$_{opt}$ >

commas:
  ,
  commas ,

The first form of *typeof-expression* consists of a typeof keyword followed by a parenthesized *type*. The result of an expression of this form is the System.Type object for the indicated type. There is only one System.Type object for any given type. [*Note*: This means that for type T, typeof(T) == typeof(T) is always true. *end note*]

The second form of *typeof-expression* consists of a typeof keyword followed by a parenthesized *unbound-type-name*. [*Note*: An *unbound-type-name* is very similar to a *type-name* (§10.8) except that an *unbound-type-name* contains *generic-dimension-specifiers* where a *type-name* contains *type-argument-list*s. *end note*] When the operand of a *typeof-expression* is a sequence of tokens that satisfies the grammars of both *unbound-type-name* and *type-name*, namely when it contains neither a *generic-dimension-specifier* nor a *type-argument-list*, the sequence of tokens is considered to be a *type-name*. The meaning of an *unbound-type-name* is determined as follows:

- Convert the sequence of tokens to a *type-name* by replacing each *generic-dimension-specifier* with a *type-argument-list* having the same number of commas and the keyword `object` as each *type-argument*.
- Evaluate the resulting *type-name*, while ignoring all type parameter constraints.
- The *unbound-type-name* resolves to the **unbound generic type** associated with the resulting constructed type (§25.5).

The result of the *typeof-expression* is the `System.Type` object for the resulting unbound generic type.

The third form of *typeof-expression* consists of a `typeof` keyword followed by a parenthesized `void` keyword. The result of an expression of this form is the `System.Type` object that represents the absence of a type. The type object returned by `typeof(void)` is distinct from the type object returned for any type. [*Note*: This special type object is useful in class libraries that allow reflection onto methods in the language, where those methods wish to have a way to represent the return type of any method, including void methods, with an instance of `System.Type`. *end note*]

[*Example*: The example

```
using System;

class Test
{
  static void Main()
  {
    Type[] t =
    {
      typeof(int),
      typeof(System.Int32),
      typeof(string),
      typeof(double[]),
      typeof(void)    };
    for (int i = 0; i < t.Length; i++)
    {
      Console.WriteLine(t[i].FullName);
    }
  }
}
```

produces the following output:

```
System.Int32
System.Int32
System.String
System.Double[]
System.Void
```

Note that `int` and `System.Int32` are the same type. *end example*]

The `typeof` operator can be used on a *type-parameter* (§25.1.1). The result is the `System.Type` object for the run-time type that was bound to the type-parameter. The `typeof` operator can also be used on a constructed type (§25.5) or an unbound generic type. The `System.Type` object for an unbound generic type is not the same as the `System.Type` object of the instance type. The instance type is always a closed constructed type at run-time so its `System.Type` object depends on the run-time type arguments in use, while the unbound generic type has no type arguments. [*Example*:

```
class X<T>
{
  public static void PrintTypes()
  {
    Console.WriteLine(typeof(T).FullName);
    Console.WriteLine(typeof(X<T>).FullName);
    Console.WriteLine(typeof(X<X<T>>).FullName);
    Console.WriteLine(typeof(X<>).FullName);
  }
}

class M
{
  static void Main()
  {
    X<int>.PrintTypes();
    X<string>.PrintTypes();
  }
}
```

The above program might print:

```
System.Int32

X`1[[System.Int32, mscorlib, Version=2.0.3600.0, Culture=neutral,
                  PublicKeyToken=b77a5c561934e089]]

X`1[[X`1[[System.Int32, mscorlib, Version=2.0.3600.0, Culture=
      neutral, PublicKeyToken=b77a5c561934e089]], CSharpEcmaExample,
      Version=1.0.1717.35787, Culture=neutral, PublicKeyToken=null]]

X`1

System.String

X`1[[System.String, mscorlib, Version=2.0.3600.0, Culture=
                  neutral, PublicKeyToken=b77a5c561934e089]]

X`1[[X`1[[System.String, mscorlib, Version=2.0.3600.0, Culture=
      neutral, PublicKeyToken=b77a5c561934e089]], CSharpEcmaExample,
      Version=1.0.1717.35787, Culture=neutral, PublicKeyToken=null]]
X`1
```

Note that the result of `typeof(X<>)` does not depend on the type argument but the result of `typeof(X<T>)` does depend on the type argument. *end example*]

typeof(Generic<,>)

None of the previous examples show `typeof` being used on a multi-argument *unbound-type-name* such as `Generic<,>`, but this is also allowed. Here is an example that also shows how the resulting `Type` can be bound using reflection:

```
public class Generic<A,B> { ...}

public class Example
{
  public static void Main(string[] args)
  {
    Type unbound = typeof(Generic<,>);

    // bind using CLI reflection
    Type[] types = { Type.GetType(args[0]), Type.GetType(args[1]) };
    Type bound = unbound.MakeGenericType(types);
    object o = Activator.CreateInstance(bound);
    Generic<string,int> ok = (Generic<string,int>)o;
    ...
  }
}
```

Note: Remember reflection is not part of C#, but is included in Standard CLI.

14.5.12 The sizeof operator

The sizeof operator returns the number of 8-bit bytes occupied by a variable of a given type. The type specified as an operand to sizeof shall be an unmanaged-type (§27.2).

> *sizeof-expression:*
>   sizeof (*unmanaged-type*)

For certain predefined types the sizeof operator yields a constant int value as shown in the table below:

Expression	Result
sizeof(sbyte)	1
sizeof(byte)	1
sizeof(short)	2
sizeof(ushort)	2
sizeof(int)	4
sizeof(uint)	4
sizeof(long)	8
sizeof(ulong)	8
sizeof(char)	2
sizeof(float)	4
sizeof(double)	8
sizeof(bool)	1
sizeof(decimal)	16

For all other operand types, the sizeof operator is specified in §27.5.8.

Marshal.SizeOf != sizeof

This annotation applies to Microsoft's CLR only and not to Standard C# or CLI.

The Microsoft CLR supports interoperation with Microsoft COM code, where the former is referred to as *managed code* and the latter as *unmanaged code*. Similarly, CLR types are referred to as *managed types* and COM types as *unmanaged types*. The (unmanaged) COM types are different from the CLR's *unmanaged-type* covered in this clause and §27.2.

The Microsoft CLR contains a class called `Marshal` (in the `System.Runtime.InteropServices` namespace) containing a static method called `SizeOf` that accepts a parameter of type `System.Type`. This method returns the size of a CLR *unmanaged-type* when converted to a COM unmanaged type. The method is *not* an alternative to `sizeof` and the two may return different results for the same *unmanaged-type*. For example, the following code fragment produces the output shown in the comments:

```
Console.WriteLine(Marshal.SizeOf(typeof(char)); // 1
Console.WriteLine(sizeof(char));                 // 2
```

14.5.13 The checked and unchecked operators

The `checked` and `unchecked` operators are used to control the ***overflow-checking context*** for integral-type arithmetic operations and conversions.

checked-expression:
  checked (*expression*)

unchecked-expression:
  unchecked (*expression*)

The `checked` operator evaluates the contained expression in a checked context, and the `unchecked` operator evaluates the contained expression in an unchecked context. A *checked-expression* or *unchecked-expression* corresponds exactly to a *parenthesized-expression* (§14.5.3), except that the contained expression is evaluated in the given overflow checking context.

The overflow checking context can also be controlled through the `checked` and `unchecked` statements (§15.11).

The following operations are affected by the overflow checking context established by the `checked` and `unchecked` operators and statements:

- The predefined ++ and -- unary operators (§14.5.9 and §14.6.5), when the operand type is an integral or enum type.
- The predefined - unary operator (§14.6.2), when the operand type is an integral type.
- The predefined +, -, *, and / binary operators (§14.7), when the operand types are integral or enum types.
- Explicit numeric conversions (§13.2.1) from one integral or enum type to another integral or enum type, or from `float` or `double` to an integral or enum type.

When one of the above operations produces a result that is too large to represent in the destination type, the context in which the operation is performed controls the resulting behavior:

- In a `checked` context, if the operation is a constant expression (§14.16), a compile-time error occurs. Otherwise, when the operation is performed at run-time, a `System.OverflowException` is thrown.
- In an `unchecked` context, the result is truncated by discarding any high-order bits that do not fit in the destination type.

Checked expression pitfall

The following is valid:

```
v += 100;
```

but the following is not:

```
checked(v += 100);
```

This is because *checked-expression* (and likewise *unchecked-expression*) is not an instance of *statement-expression* (§15.6), and hence not a valid statement.

To check (not check) a *statement-expression*, it should be written so that the *checked-expression* (*unchecked-expression*) is a subexpression, as in:

```
v = checked(v + 100);
```

or the *checked-statement* (*unchecked-statement*) should be used, as in:

```
checked
{
   v += 100;
}
```

For non-constant expressions (§14.16) that are not enclosed by any `checked` or `unchecked` operators or statements, the default overflow checking context is `unchecked`, unless external factors (such as compiler switches and execution environment configuration) call for `checked` evaluation.

For constant expressions (§14.16), the default overflow checking context is always `checked`. Unless a constant expression is explicitly placed in an `unchecked` context, overflows that occur during the compile-time evaluation of the expression always cause compile-time errors.

(Un)checked constants

As stated in the preceding paragraph, the default overflow checking context is checked for constant expressions (§14.16), and overflows that occur during their evaluation cause compile time errors. This can be changed as for other expressions by using the `checked` and `unchecked` operators.

However, the compilers current at the time of writing have been observed behaving most bizarrely when dealing with constant expressions and overflow; indeed, the behavior can be so odd that we hesitate to detail it in case the compilers are fixed (which we must hope) by the time you read this and then you fail to believe us! There is one example, though, that we shall give; it deserves recording for posterity!

```
byte b;
b = checked((byte)2048F);  // compile-time error
b = checked((byte)2047F);  // OK!!!!!
```

Apparently, when converting from a `float` constant to a `byte` this particular compiler uses the new "Big Bytes™" range ☺, and you will have to guess what value is assigned to b!

Having warned you about this, it should be noted that generating overflows in constant expressions should not be usual practice, except possibly in the case of hexadecimal constants covered later in the clause, so if you are bitten by this bizarre behavior, you should first consider carefully whether your code might best be written another way.

[*Note*: Developers might benefit if they exercise their code using checked mode (as well as unchecked mode). It also seems reasonable that, unless otherwise requested, the default overflow checking context is set to checked when debugging is enabled. *end note*]

[*Example*: In the following code

```
class Test
{
   static readonly int x = 1000000;
   static readonly int y = 1000000;

   static int F()
   {
      return checked(x * y);    // Throws OverflowException
   }

   static int G()
   {
      return unchecked(x * y);  // Returns -727379968
   }

   static int H()
   {
      return x * y;             // Depends on default
   }
}
```

no compile-time errors are reported since neither of the expressions can be evaluated at compile-time. At run-time, the F method throws a System.OverflowException, and the G method returns –727379968 (the lower 32 bits of the out-of-range result). The behavior of the H method depends on the default overflow-checking context for the compilation, but it is either the same as F or the same as G. *end example*]

[*Example*: In the following code

```
class Test
{
   const int x = 1000000;
   const int y = 1000000;

   static int F()
   {
      return checked(x * y);    // Compile error, overflow
   }

   static int G()
   {
      return unchecked(x * y);  // Returns -727379968
   }
```

```
static int H()
{
  return x * y;                    // Compile error, overflow
}
}
```

the overflows that occur when evaluating the constant expressions in F and H cause compile-time errors to be reported because the expressions are evaluated in a checked context. An overflow also occurs when evaluating the constant expression in G, but since the evaluation takes place in an unchecked context, the overflow is not reported. *end example*]

The checked and unchecked operators only affect the overflow checking context for those operations that are textually contained within the "(" and ")" tokens. The operators have no effect on function members that are invoked as a result of evaluating the contained expression. [*Example*: In the following code

```
class Test
{
  static int Multiply(int x, int y)
  {
    return x * y;
  }

  static int F()
  {
    return checked(Multiply(1000000, 1000000));
  }
}
```

the use of checked in F does not affect the evaluation of x * y in Multiply, so x * y is evaluated in the default overflow checking context. *end example*]

The unchecked operator is convenient when writing constants of the signed integral types in hexadecimal notation. [*Example*:

```
class Test
{
  public const int AllBits = unchecked((int)0xFFFFFFFF);

  public const int HighBit = unchecked((int)0x80000000);
}
```

Both of the hexadecimal constants above are of type uint. Because the constants are outside the int range, without the unchecked operator, the casts to int would produce compile-time errors. *end example*]

[*Note*: The checked and unchecked operators and statements allow programmers to control certain aspects of some numeric calculations. However, the behavior of some numeric operators depends on their operands' data types. For example, multiplying two decimals always results in an exception on overflow *even* within an explicitly unchecked construct. Similarly, multiplying two floats never results in an exception on overflow *even* within an explicitly checked construct. In addition, other operators are *never* affected by the mode of checking, whether default or explicit. As a service to programmers, it is recommended that the compiler issue a warning when there is an arithmetic expression within an explicitly checked or unchecked context (by operator or statement) that cannot possibly be affected by the specified mode of checking. Since such a warning is not required, the compiler has flexibility in determining the circumstances that merit the issuance of such warnings. *end note*]

The meaning of (un)checked

Some confusion surrounds the `checked` and `unchecked` operators and statements (§15.11); some of it stems from the use of the term ***overflow-checking context***. These operators *do not* control all overflow exceptions that might occur in the expressions they enclose, or stop such exceptions being handled by `try` statements (§15.10) or thrown by `throw` statements (§15.9.5).

Some integral and enum operators (++, --, + (unary and binary), – (unary and binary), *, and /) and some explicit conversions (from one integral or enum type to another, and from `float`/`double` to an integral or enum) exist in two forms: One checks overflow and one does not. For example, the * operator on `int` is actually one of two operators:

```
int operator *checked(int x, int y);
int operator *unchecked(int x, int y);
```

[Note: The divide operator is a little different from the others in how the two versions handle overflow; see §14.7.2. However, the two versions of divide do not differ in how they handle divide-by-zero.]

The overflow checking context controls which operator version, of those that have two versions, is used. For example, consider the method:

```
int Mixed(int a, int b, int c, int d)
{
    return checked( (a * unchecked(b * c)) << d );
}
```

This is translated to:

```
int Mixed(int a, int b, int c, int d)
{
    return (a *checked (b *unchecked c)) << d;
}
```

Note that the << operator is unaffected as it does not come in two versions.

14.5.14 Default value expression

A default value expression is used to obtain the default value (§12.2) of a type. Typically a default value expression is used for type parameters (§25.1.1), since it might not be known if the type parameter is a value type or a reference type. (No conversion exists from the `null` type (§11.2.7) to a type parameter unless the type parameter is known to be a reference type (§25.7).)

> *default-value-expression:*
>   `default` (*type*)

If the *type* in a *default-value-expression* evaluates at run-time to a reference type, the result is `null` converted to that type. If the *type* in a *default-value-expression* evaluates at run-time to a value type, the result is the *value-type*'s default value (§11.1.2).

Historical aside

An early proposal to the Standard committee used the grammar *type*.`default` for *default-value-expression* (e.g., `int.default`). This was even implemented in an early development release of one C# compiler, but was changed to the preceding syntax (e.g., `default(int)`) to match that used for `typeof` (§14.5.11) and `sizeof` expressions (§14.5.12).

14.5.15 Anonymous methods

Breaking the ties that bind...

Anonymous methods and iterators (§26) are new features introduced in C# 2.0 that fundamentally change the nature of the language.

Previously, C#, in a similar way to C and pre-1.5 Java, had a very clear correspondence with the underlying (virtual) machine—read a C# fragment and the corresponding machine language could be easily determined, and vice versa.

In C# 2.0 this correspondence may be less clear, as for many high-level languages. Anonymous methods bring expressive power while also introducing subtleties: Small changes in the program text can produce much larger changes in produced code and program behavior or performance. The annotations in this section expand on these issues.

Anonymous methods used in conjunction with visitor style enumeration provide an alternative to the use of handwritten enumerators or `yield`-based iterators (§26). Annotations in this section (§14.5.15.3.1) and later (§26.1.4) compare the relative merits of the approaches.

An *anonymous-method-expression* defines an **anonymous method** and evaluates to a value referencing the method:

> *anonymous-method-expression:*
>   `delegate` *anonymous-method-signature$_{opt}$*   *block*
>
> *anonymous-method-signature:*
>   (*anonymous-method-parameter-list$_{opt}$*   )
>
> *anonymous-method-parameter-list:*
>   *anonymous-method-parameter*
>   *anonymous-method-parameter-list* , *anonymous-method-parameter*
>
> *anonymous-method-parameter:*
>   *parameter-modifier$_{opt}$* *type* *identifier*

The type of an *anonymous-method-expression* is a delegate type, which is inferred from the context of that expression. (The inference rules are described in §13.5.)

An *anonymous-method-expression* can be used in a *delegate-creation-expression* (§14.5.10.3). All other valid uses of an *anonymous-method-expression* depend on the implicit conversions defined in §13.5.

An *anonymous-method-expression* defines a new declaration space for parameters, locals and constants and a new declaration space for labels (§10.3).

Anonymous sharing

The grammar for *anonymous-method-expression* does *not* use the `new` keyword. This is deliberate, and is intended to allow the possibility of optimization where delegates may be preallocated and shared.

For example, if an *anonymous-method-expression* appears within a loop but captures no variables declared inside the loop, then it is a significant optimization to allocate a single delegate instead of allocating one for each iteration. Note that the definition of the `foreach` statement (§15.8.4) was changed subtly in this version of the Standard, and that change increases the chances a compiler can optimize anonymous methods within the loop.

The choice here is an interesting contrast to boxing, where sharing is explicitly disallowed; see the annotation on §13.1.5.

14.5.15.1 Anonymous method signatures

The optional *anonymous-method-signature* defines the names and types of the formal parameters for the anonymous method. The scope of the parameters of the anonymous method is the *block*. It is a compile-time error for the name of a parameter of the anonymous method to match the name of a local variable, local constant or parameter whose scope includes the *anonymous-method-expression*.

If an *anonymous-method-expression* has an *anonymous-method-signature*, then the set of compatible delegate types is restricted to those that have the same parameter types and modifiers, in the same order (§13.5). In contrast to method groups, contra-variance of anonymous method parameter types is not supported (§14.5.10.3). If an *anonymous-method-expression* doesn't have an *anonymous-method-signature*, then the set of compatible delegate types is restricted to those that have no `out` parameters.

Note that an *anonymous-method-signature* cannot include attributes or a *parameter-array*. Nevertheless, an *anonymous-method-signature* may be compatible with a delegate type whose *formal-parameter-list* contains a *parameter-array*.

14.5.15.2 Anonymous method blocks

The *block* of an *anonymous-method-expression* is subject to the following rules:

- If the anonymous method includes a signature, the parameters specified in the signature are available in the *block*. If the anonymous method has no signature, it can be converted to a delegate type having parameters (§13.5), but the parameters cannot be accessed in the *block*.
- Except for `ref` or `out` parameters specified in the signature (if any) of the nearest enclosing anonymous method, it is a compile-time error for the *block* to access a `ref` or `out` parameter.
- When the type of `this` is a struct type, it is a compile-time error for the *block* to access `this`. This is true whether the access is explicit (as in `this.x`) or implicit (as in `x`, where `x` is an instance member of the struct). This rule simply prohibits such access and does not affect whether member lookup results in a member of the struct.
- The *block* has access to the outer variables (§14.5.15.3) of the anonymous method. Access of an outer variable will reference the instance of the variable that is active at the time the *anonymous-method-expression* is evaluated (§14.5.15.4).
- It is a compile-time error for the *block* to contain a `goto` statement, `break` statement, or `continue` statement whose target is outside the *block* or within the *block* of a contained anonymous method.
- A `return` statement in the *block* returns control from an invocation of the nearest enclosing anonymous method, not from the enclosing function member. An expression specified in a `return` statement shall be compatible with the delegate type to which the nearest enclosing *anonymous-method-expression* is converted (§14.5.15.4).

It is explicitly unspecified whether there is any way to execute the *block* of an anonymous method other than through evaluation and invocation of the *anonymous-method-expression*. In particular, a compiler might choose to implement an anonymous method by synthesizing one or more named methods or types. The names of any such synthesized elements shall be in the space reserved for implementations (that is, the names shall contain two consecutive underscore characters).

14.5.15.3 Outer variables

Any local variable, value parameter, or parameter array whose scope includes an *anonymous-method-expression* is called an **outer variable** of that *anonymous-method-expression*. In an instance function member of a class, the `this` value is considered a value parameter and is an outer variable of any *anonymous-method-expression* contained within that function member.

14.5.15.3.1 Captured outer variables

When an oter variable is referenced by an anonymous method, the outer variable is said to have been **captured** by the anonymous method. Ordinarily, the lifetime of a local variable is limited to execution of the block or statement with which it is associated (§12.1.7). However, the lifetime of a captured outer variable is extended at least until the delegate referring to the anonymous method becomes eligible for garbage collection.

[*Example*: In the following code

```
using System;

delegate int D();

class Test
{
  static D F()
  {
    int x = 0;
    D result = delegate { return ++x; };
    return result;
  }

  static void Main()
  {
    D d = F();
    Console.WriteLine(d());
    Console.WriteLine(d());
    Console.WriteLine(d());
  }
}
```

the local variable x is captured by the anonymous method, and the lifetime of x is extended at least until the delegate returned from F becomes eligible for garbage collection. Since each invocation of the anonymous method operates on the same instance of x, the output of the example is:

```
1
2
3
```

end example]

Captured local variables: modification and lifetime

As the preceding example shows, a captured local variable can be modified by an anonymous method. This is very different, for example, from the way anonymous classes in Java behave—where only read-only local variables may be captured.

To allow modification, the lifetime of the local variable is changed and becomes dynamic. As explained later (§14.5.15.5), an implementation may achieve this by allocating objects and transforming every access to a captured local variable, including those in the declaring block, to be an access to a field in an object.

In addition to (drastically) changing the lifetime of the variable, it will typically slow down accesses somewhat.

Captured variable pitfall

A pitfall when creating anonymous methods within a loop is to assume that the control variable of a loop is captured with the value it has at creation. However, as it is the variable (lvalue), and not its value (rvalue), that is captured, the value at the time the anonymous method is *called* will be seen. This is often the value at loop termination. For example, consider:

```
delegate void D();

class Test
{
  static void DoIt(int v)
  {
    System.Console.WriteLine(v);
  }

  static void Main()
  {
    D[] arr = new D[5];

    for (int i = 0; i < 5; ++i)
    {
      arr[i] = delegate { DoIt(i); };
    }

    for (int i = 0; i < 5; ++i)
    {
      arr[i]();
    }
  }
}
```

This program will output 5 five times.

To capture the current value of a loop variable, a new variable can be declared within the loop into which the current value of the loop variable is copied. The anonymous method expression can now reference this introduced variable. As the declaration is within the loop, a new variable will be created for each iteration, and every anonymous method created will capture a *different* variable. For example, consider:

```
delegate void D();

class Test
{
  static void DoIt(int v)
  {
    System.Console.WriteLine(v);
  }

  static void Main()
  {
    D[] arr = new D[5];

    for (int i = 0; i < 5; ++i)
    {
      int v = i;
      arr[i] = delegate { DoIt(v); };
    }

    for (int i = 0; i < 5; ++i)
    {
      arr[i]();
    }
  }
}
```

This program will output the numbers 0 to 4.

Paolo Molaro

Caution: space leaks

When a local variable is captured its lifetime is changed and may extend well beyond its immediately apparent scope. Consequently, care needs to be exercised to avoid introducing "space leaks"—that is, accidentally holding onto references to large allocated structures past the point when they are needed, and thus preventing them from being garbage collected. While this problem is present in any language with dynamic allocation, and in particular in Java's anonymous classes, the ability to modify captured variables in C# may, depending on the implementation, introduce new hard-to-spot ways of creating space leaks compared to Java.

Unfortunately, the problem can be implementation dependent; see the annotation on §14.5.15.3.2.

Visitor-style enumeration

The use of anonymous methods, captured outer variables, and "visitor" style methods defined on data structures can be a good alternative to the use of "iterator" style methods, and may also provide worthwhile performance improvements.

We will use the following simple non-linear data structure in this and related annotations:

```
public class Tree<T>
{
  // Nested type for tree nodes
  private class Node
```

```
{
  public Node Left;
  public T Item;
  public Node Right;

  public Node(T nodeItem)
  {
    Left = Right = null;
    Item = nodeItem;
  }

  public Node() : this( default(T) ) {}
}

private Comparison<T> cFun;   // ordering function
private Node root;           // root of tree
private long count;          // number of items in tree

public Tree(Comparison<T> comp)
{
  cFun = comp;
  root = null;
  count = 0;
}

public Tree() : this( Comparer<T>.Default.Compare ) {}

public long Count
{
  get { return count; }
}

public void Add(T value)
{
  Add(value, ref root);
}

private void Add(T value, ref Node current)
{
  if (current == null)
  {
    current = new Node(value);
    count++;
  }
  else
  {
    int order = cFun(value, current.Item);
    if (order < 0)
      Add(value, ref current.Left);
    else if (order > 0)
      Add(value, ref current.Right);
  }
}
}
```

A visitor-style inorder enumerator for this data structure may be defined like this:

```
// Delegate visitor ("Internal enumerator")
private void ForEach(Action<T> act, Node current)
{
    if (current.Left != null)
        ForEach(act, current.Left);

    act(current.Item);

    if (current.Right != null)
        ForEach(act, current.Right);
}

public void ForEach(Action<T> act)
{
    if (root != null)
        ForEach(act, root);
}
```

A simple use of `ForEach` to count the items in a `Tree<T>` may be coded as follows:

```
int TreeCount<T>(Tree<T> aTree)
{
    int count = 0;

    aTree.ForEach(delegate (T ignore) { count++; });

    return count;
}
```

Obviously, using the `Count` property would be better in this particular case. However, the (maybe surprising), observation is that anonymous method/visitor-based enumeration can be an order of magnitude faster than iterator-based enumeration. See the annotation on clause §26.1.4 for a performance comparison.

Note the explicit (`T ignore`) is the preceding delegate expression. Though C# does not require this, and will infer it if omitted, including it makes it clear it is passed and ignored rather than not passed at all.

Note: The use of reference parameters in the `Add` method is to simplify the algorithm. This is discussed in the annotation on §12.1.5.

14.5.15.3.2 Instantiation of local variables

A local variable is considered to be ***instantiated*** when execution enters the scope of the variable. [*Example*: When the following method is invoked, the local variable `x` is instantiated and initialized three times—once each iteration of the loop.

```
static void F()
{
    for (int i = 0; i < 3; i++)
    {
        int x = i * 2 + 1;
        ...
    }
}
```

However, moving the declaration of x outside the loop results in a single instantiation of x:

```
static void F()
{
  int x;
  for (int i = 0; i < 3; i++)
  {
    x = i * 2 + 1;
    ...
  }
}
```

end example]

Ordinarily, there is no way to observe exactly how often a local variable is instantiated—because the lifetimes of the instantiations are disjoint, it is possible for each instantiation to simply use the same storage location. However, when an anonymous method captures a local variable, the effects of instantiation become apparent. [*Example*: The example

```
using System;

delegate void D();

class Test
{
  static D[] F()
  {
    D[] result = new D[3];
    for (int i = 0; i < 3; i++)
    {
      int x = i * 2 + 1;
      result[i] = delegate { Console.WriteLine(x); };
    }
    return result;
  }

  static void Main()
  {
    foreach (D d in F()) d();
  }
}
```

produces the output:

```
1
3
5
```

However, when the declaration of x is moved outside the loop:

```
static D[] F()
{
  D[] result = new D[3];
  int x;
  for (int i = 0; i < 3; i++)
  {
    x = i * 2 + 1;
```

```
      result[i] = delegate { Console.WriteLine(x); };
   }
   return result;
}
```

the output is:

```
5
5
5
```

Note that the three delegates created in the version of F directly above will be equal according to the equality operator (§14.9.8). Furthermore, note that the compiler is permitted (but not required) to optimize the three instantiations into a single delegate instance (§14.5.15.4). *end example*]

It is possible for anonymous method delegates to share some captured variables yet have separate instances of others. [*Example*: If F is changed to

```
static D[] F()
{
   D[] result = new D[3];
   int x = 0;
   for (int i = 0; i < 3; i++)
   {
      int y = 0;
      result[i] = delegate { Console.WriteLine("{0} {1} ", ++x, ++y); };
   }
   return result;
}
```

the three delegates capture the same instance of x but separate instances of y, and the output is:

```
1 1
2 1
3 1
```

end example]

Separate anonymous methods can capture the same instance of an outer variable. [*Example*: In the following code:

```
using System;

delegate void Setter(int value);

delegate int Getter();

class Test
{
   static void Main()
   {
      int x = 0;
      Setter s = delegate(int value) { x = value; };
      Getter g = delegate { return x; };
      s(5);
      Console.WriteLine(g());
```

```
      s(10);
      Console.WriteLine(g());
   }
}
```

the two anonymous methods capture the same instance of the local variable x, and they can thus "communicate" through that variable. The output of the example is:

```
5
10
```

end example]

Caution: local variables shared between threads

One consequence of the specification of captured outer variables is that a local variable can now be accessed from multiple concurrent threads. This was not possible in C# prior to the adoption of anonymous delegates.

Here is a contrived example of two threads sharing a local variable i:

```
public static void Main()
{
   int i = 0;
   ThreadStart t1 = delegate
           { for (;;)
               {
                  Thread.Sleep(102);
                  i++;
               }
           };

   ThreadStart t2 = delegate
           { for (;;)
               {
                  Thread.Sleep(500);
                  Console.WriteLine(i);
               }
           };

   new Thread(t1).Start();
   new Thread(t2).Start();
}
```

Caution: implementation-dependent space leaks

When a local variable is captured, its lifetime is changed and may extend well beyond its immediately apparent scope. Consequently, care needs to be exercised to avoid introducing "space leaks"—as explained in the annotation on 14.5.15.3.1.

The following, rather contrived example illustrates the possible pitfalls. First, a class provides a delegate to compute a math function:

```
// for simplicity this example is not thread safe
class MathUtil
{
   public delegate int Compute(int x);
```

```
private delegate void Procedure();

// Return a method to sum the squares n to max
// Internally uses separate computation delegate
// so only ever computes the sum of squares from
// 1 to max once however many times it is called.
public static Compute SumSquaresTo(int max)
{
  int totalRangeSum = 0;
  int[] squares = new int[max+1];   // working array

  // delay computation of sum of squares 1 to max
  // by wrapping in a delegate
  Procedure calculate =
    delegate
    {
      // compute max * (max + 1) * (2 * max + 1) / 6 the hard way...

      // initialise array
      squares[0] = 0; // unused element
      for (int i = 1; i <= max; i++)
        squares[i] = i * i;

      totalRangeSum = 0;
      foreach (int x in squares)
        totalRangeSum += x;
    };

  return
    delegate (int start)
    {
      // do the computation if needed
      if (calculate != null)
      {
        calculate();
        calculate = null;
        // calculate now eligible for garbage collection
        // squares no longer needed or visibly referenced
      }

      // need to subtract sum of squares 1 to (start - 1) from
      // sum squares 1 to max, found in totalRangeSum

      return totalRangeSum - (start * (start - 1) * (2 * start - 1))/6;
    };
  }
}
```

In this example, the local variables, totalRangeSum and squares, from the same declaration space are both captured by anonymous methods whose lifetime extends beyond that of declaration space itself. Only the calculate anonymous method references the array squares, and this method is made eligible for garbage collection the first time the second anonymous method is called, so there is no longer any *visible* reference to squares after this.

The following method uses the MathUtil class:

```
static void Main()
{
    const int MAX = 1000;

    MathUtil.Compute doSumFrom = MathUtil.SumSquaresTo(MAX);

    Console.WriteLine("Sum of squares 1 to {0} = {1}",
                            MAX, doSumFrom(1));
    // the array "squares" may still be referenced...
    Console.WriteLine("Sum of squares 500 to {0} = {1}",
                            MAX, doSumFrom(500));
    Console.WriteLine("Sum of squares 1000 to {0} = {1}",
                            MAX, doSumFrom(1000));
}
```

This all looks OK and executes as expected. The catch, unfortunately, is that the two main C# compilers current at the time of writing follow the implementation strategy outlined in §14.5.15.5 and place both totalRangeSum and squares into the same object. This means there exists a hidden reference to the array squares as long as there is one to doSumFrom, despite the programmer explicitly making the delegate previously bound to calculate available for garbage collection. So there is an *implementation-dependent* space leak.

14.5.15.4 Anonymous method evaluation

The run-time evaluation of an *anonymous-method-expression* produces a delegate instance which references the anonymous method and the (possibly empty) set of captured outer variablesthat are active at the time of the evaluation. When a delegate resulting from an *anonymous-method-expression* is invoked, the body of the anonymous method is executed. The code in the body is executed using the set of captured outer variables referenced by the delegate.

The invocation list of a delegate produced from an *anonymous-method-expression* contains a single entry. The exact target object and target method of the delegate are unspecified. In particular, it is unspecified whether the target object of the delegate is null, the this value of the enclosing function member, or some other object.

Evaluation of semantically identical *anonymous-method-expression*s with the same (possibly empty) set of captured outer variable instances is permitted (but not required) to return the same delegate instance. The term "semantically identical" is used here to mean that execution of the anonymous methods will produce, in all cases, the same effects given the same arguments. [*Example*: This rule permits code such as the following to be optimized.

```
delegate double Function(double x);

class Test
{
    static double[] Apply(double[] vector, Function func)
    {
        double[] result = new double[vector.Length];
        for (int i = 0; i < vector.Length; i++)
        {
            result[i] = func(vector[i]);
```

```
    }
    return result;
  }

  static void F(double[] vx, double[] vy)
  {
    double[] rx = Apply(vx, delegate(double x)
    {
      return Math.Sin(x);
    });
    double[] ry = Apply(vy, delegate(double y)
    {
      return Math.Sin(y);
    });
    ...
  }
}
```

Since the two anonymous method delegates have the same (empty) set of captured outer variables, and since the anonymous methods are semantically identical, the compiler is permitted to have the delegates refer to the same target method. Indeed, the compiler is permitted to return the very same delegate instance from both anonymous method expressions.

end example]

Interlude: call-by-name

In "Visitor-style enumeration" (§14.5.15.3.1) we demonstrated a very practical use of anonymous methods, while some of the other annotations have warned of the pitfalls to avoid. Delegates, in general, and anonymous methods, in particular, open up interesting algorithmic possibilities. This interlude covers a little history and realizes some of the examples in C#; hopefully this is at least fun and maybe will spark some practical ideas.

C# by default uses *call-by-value* for parameter passing. That is, the value of the argument expression is used to initialize the local parameter variable (§17.5.1.1). C# also provides *call-by-reference* where the local parameter is an alias for the variable passed as the argument (§17.5.1.2, §17.5.1.3). Algol 60, one of the earliest programming languages, introduced *call-by-name* for parameter passing. This is defined in the *Revised Report on the Algorithmic Language Algol 60* as:

> **4.7.3.2. Name replacement (call by name).** Any formal parameter not quoted in the value list *[that is not specified as call-by-value]* is replaced, throughout the procedure body, by the corresponding actual parameter, after enclosing this latter in parentheses wherever syntactically possible. Possible conflicts between identifiers inserted through this process and other identifiers already present within the procedure body will be avoided by suitable systematic changes of the formal or local identifiers involved.

What this is describing is "string replacement"—Every occurrence of the parameter name is replaced by the actual argument text, with any local variable in the procedure renamed if it conflicts with a variable referenced in the argument text. The latter, given Algol 60's scope rules, means that the variable references in the substituted arguments will reference the variables in scope at the point of call. Recasting this in pseudo-C#, consider the method:

```
int Strange(name int x, name int f)
{
  int sum;
  x = 1;
```

```
    sum = f;
    x = 2;
    sum += f;
    return sum;
}
```

where `name` is used to indicate call-by-name. Then, by the preceding definition, the code fragment:

```
int M(int k) { ...}
...
int sum, k;
...
sum = Strange(k, M(k));
```

results in the following expansion of the body of `Strange`:

```
{
    int sum1;
    k = 1;
    sum1 = M(k);
    k = 2;
    sum1 += M(k);
    return sum1;
}
```

It should not come as a surprise that call-by-name was not actually implemented this way, as it would have required string substitution, variable renaming, and the compilation of the resulting body at every call site. Rather, a call-by-name parameter x was in general passed as two procedures, sometimes called *thunks*: one to get the value of x and one to set the value of x. Each use of x would then be replaced by a call to the first thunk, and each assignment to x would be replaced by a call to the second thunk. Correspondingly, the argument expression would be compiled into two thunks. The first one, when called, would evaluate the argument expression and return its value. The second thunk would be called to set the value of the argument expression—which makes sense only if the argument expression has an lvalue; for instance, if it is a variable occurrence y or an array indexing expression a[y] .

For a parameter not assigned to within the procedure, only the first thunk would be needed. Let us next consider how this special case could be implemented in C#.

Call-by-name in C#

In C# we can represent the type "expression returning T" using the delegate:

```
delegate T Expr<T>()
```

and using this we can re-implement our example in real C# (since `f` is not assigned to):

```
int Strange(ref int x, Expr<int> f)
{
    int sum;
    x = 1;
    sum = f();
    x = 2;
    sum += f();
    return sum;
}
```

The call becomes a little more verbose:

```
sum = Strange(ref k, delegate { return M(k); } );
```

This has exactly the same semantics as the Algol 60 version due to the variable capture semantics of anonymous methods.

Jensen's device

In the early 60s, Danish computer scientist Jørn Jensen wrote a procedure to demonstrate the power of call-by-name; this became known as *Jensen's device*. The procedure is deceptively simple; here it is cast into C#:

```
double Jensen(ref int ix, int start, int end, Expr<double> item)
{
  double total = 0;
  for (ix = start; ix <= end; ix++)
    total += item();
  return total;
}
```

Jensen used this to compute harmonic numbers, but to show its capabilities we will sum part of an array:

```
double[] test1 ={ 2, 3, 4, 5, 6, 7, 8 };
int ix = 0;
double sum;

sum = Jensen(ref ix, 3, 5, delegate { return test1[ ix] ; } );
```

The variable sum will be set to 18. Does this not seem powerful? Well, consider that calls to Jensen can be easily nested:

```
double[ ,] test2 ={ { 1, 2, 3 }, { 4, 5, 6 }, { 7, 8, 9 } };
int ix = 0, iy = 0;
double sum;

// sum should be 24
sum = Jensen
    (ref ix, 1, 2,
    delegate
    {
      return Jensen(ref iy, 0, 1,
            delegate { return test2[ ix, iy] ; }
            );
    }
    );
```

This sums a rectangular section of a two-dimensional array. By further nesting, any contiguous part of an *n*-dimensional array can be summed.

Man or boy?

Later, in the *Algol Bulletin* 17 (July 1964) and 19 (Jan 1965), Donald Knuth presented a test to determine whether Algol 60 compilers implemented call-by-name properly (the "men") or not (the "boys"). Here it is recast in C#:

```
// Man or boy by Knuth
int A(int k, Expr<int> x1, Expr<int> x2, Expr<int> x3, Expr<int> x4,
                                                       Expr<int> x5)

{
  Expr<int> B = null;

  B = delegate { k--; return A(k, B, x1, x2, x3, x4); };

  return k <= 0 ? x4() + x5() : B();
}

// C# convenience method
Expr<int> Const(int v)
{
  return delegate { return v; };
}

// The test, res should be -67...
int res = A(10, Const(1), Const(-1), Const(-1), Const(1), Const(0));
```

Try this out on your favorite C# implementation. If the result is −67, then anonymous methods are implemented correctly! (For the terminally curious, this example generates 722 unique instances of B, 306 of which are never called, 352 are called once, and the remaining ones, between 2 and 63 times each.)

With great power...

...comes great responsibility. Anonymous methods and local variable capture, if misused, will see variables magically changing value, space leaks, and totally incomprehensible code. Call-by-name was also available in Simula 67 but then did not appear again in programming languages until it was re-introduced in a more limited, safer, and probably more useful form as *call-by-need* in non-strict functional languages, such as Haskell. Call-by-need gives (most of) the power without the pain of call-by-name, but that is an interlude for another time...

14.5.15.5 Implementation example

[*Note*: This subclause describes a possible implementation of anonymous methods in terms of standard C# constructs. The implementation described here is by no means a mandated implementation, nor is it the only one possible.

The remainder of this subclause gives several examples of code that contains anonymous methods with different characteristics. For each example, a corresponding translation to code that uses only standard C# constructs is provided. In the examples, the identifier D is assumed to represent the following delegate type:

```
public delegate void D();
```

The simplest form of an anonymous method is one that captures no outer variables:

```
class Test
{
  static void F()
  {
    D d = delegate { Console.WriteLine("test"); };
  }
}
```

This can be translated to a delegate instantiation that references a compiler-generated static method in which the code of the anonymous method is placed:

```
class Test
{
  static void F()
  {
    D d = new D(__Method1);
  }

  static void __Method1()
  {
    Console.WriteLine("test");
  }
}
```

In the following example, the anonymous method references instance members of `this`:

```
class Test
{
  int x;

  void F()
  {
    D d = delegate { Console.WriteLine(x); };
  }
}
```

This can be translated to a compiler-generated instance method containing the code of the anonymous method:

```
class Test
{
  int x;

  void F()
  {
    D d = new D(__Method1);
  }

  void __Method1()
  {
    Console.WriteLine(x);
  }
}
```

In this example, the anonymous method captures a local variable:

```
class Test
{
  void F()
  {
    int y = 123;
    D d = delegate { Console.WriteLine(y); };
  }
}
```

The lifetime of the local variable shall now be extended to at least the lifetime of the anonymous method delegate. This can be achieved by "lifting" the local variable into a field of a compiler-generated class. Instantiation of the local variable (§14.5.15.3.2) then corresponds to creating an instance of the compiler-generated class, and accessing the local variable corresponds to accessing a field in the instance of the compiler-generated class. Furthermore, the anonymous method becomes an instance method of the compiler-generated class:

```
class Test
{
  void F()
  {
    __Locals1 __locals1 = new __Locals1();
    __locals1.y = 123;
    D d = new D(__locals1.__Method1);
  }

  class __Locals1
  {
    public int y;

    public void __Method1()
    {
      Console.WriteLine(y);
    }
  }
}
```

Finally, the following anonymous method captures this as well as two local variables with different lifetimes:

```
class Test
{
  int x;

  void F()
  {
    int y = 123;
    for (int i = 0; i < 10; i++)
    {
      int z = i * 2;
      D d = delegate { Console.WriteLine(x + y + z); };
    }
  }
}
```

Here, a compiler-generated class is created for each statement block in which locals are captured such that the locals in the different blocks can have independent lifetimes. An instance of __Locals2, the compiler-generated class for the inner statement block, contains the local variable z and a field that references an instance of __Locals1. An instance of __Locals1, the compiler-generated class for the outer statement block, contains the local variable y and a field that references this of the enclosing function member. With these data structures it is possible to reach all captured outer variables through an instance of __Locals2, and the code of the anonymous method can thus be implemented as an instance method of that class.

```
class Test
{
  void F()
  {
    __Locals1 __locals1 = new __Locals1();
    __locals1.__this = this;
    __locals1.y = 123;
    for (int i = 0; i < 10; i++)
    {
      __Locals2 __locals2 = new __Locals2();
      __locals2.__locals1 = __locals1;
      __locals2.z = i * 2;
      D d = new D(__locals2.__Method1);
    }
  }

  class __Locals1
  {
    public Test __this;
    public int y;
  }

  class __Locals2
  {
    public __Locals1 __locals1;
    public int z;

    public void __Method1()
    {
      Console.WriteLine(__locals1.__this.x + __locals1.y + z);
    }
  }
}
```

end note]

Anonymous methods, generic parameters, and a bug

The preceding implementation sketch helps explain why a prerelease compiler did not implement the following example correctly. But first let us explain what the example tries to achieve. The generic delegate types called Function are defined in (§25.4). The function *Curry* is well known from functional programming. It takes a two-argument function, $f : A \times B \to C$, and returns a one-argument function that, when applied to an *A*, returns a one-argument function that, when applied to a *B*, returns a *C*, that is *Curry* : $(A \times B \to C) \to (A \to (B \to C))$.

In C# terms, Curry takes as argument a two-argument delegate f of type Function<A,B,C> and returns a one-argument delegate that, when applied to an A, returns one-argument delegate:

```
public static Function<A,Function<B,C>>
    Curry<A,B,C> (Function<A, B,C> f)
{
  return delegate(A x)
  {
    return delegate(B y)
```

```
        {
            return f(x, y);
        };
    };
}
```

When we tried this back in 2003 on a pre-release version of Microsoft's compiler, it generated ill-formed bytecode, which subsequently caused a Fatal Execution Engine Error at runtime. Obviously, the delegate classes created for the two anonymous methods should be generic, and they were. However, in the bytecode, the type parameter occurrences in those classes were compiled as references to type parameters of a generic method rather than as type parameters of a generic class. The CIL bytecode (but not C#) makes this distinction, and apparently the implementer had overlooked it.

14.6 Unary expressions

unary-expression:
   primary-expression
   + *unary-expression*
   – *unary-expression*
   ! *unary-expression*
   ~ *unary-expression*
   pre-increment-expression
   pre-decrement-expression
   cast-expression

14.6.1 Unary plus operator

For an operation of the form +x, unary operator overload resolution (§14.2.3) is applied to select a specific operator implementation. The operand is converted to the parameter type of the selected operator, and the type of the result is the return type of the operator. The predefined unary plus operators are:

```
int operator +(int x);
uint operator +(uint x);
long operator +(long x);
ulong operator +(ulong x);
float operator +(float x);
double operator +(double x);
decimal operator +(decimal x);
```

For each of these operators, the result is simply the value of the operand.

Lifted (§14.2.7) forms of the unlifted predefined unary plus operators defined above are also predefined.

14.6.2 Unary minus operator

For an operation of the form –x, unary operator overload resolution (§14.2.3) is applied to select a specific operator implementation. The operand is converted to the parameter type of the selected operator, and the type of the result is the return type of the operator. The predefined negation operators are:

- Integer negation:

    ```
    int operator -(int x);
    long operator -(long x);
    ```

    The result is computed by subtracting x from zero. In a `checked` context, if the value of x is the smallest `int` or `long` (-2^{31} or -2^{63}, respectively), a `System.OverflowException` is thrown. In an `unchecked` context, if the value of x is the smallest `int` or `long`, the result is that same value and the overflow is not reported.

    If the operand of the negation operator is of type `uint`, it is converted to type `long`, and the type of the result is `long`. An exception is the rule that permits the `int` value –2147483648 (-2^{31}) to be written as a decimal integer literal (§9.4.4.2).

- Negation of `ulong` is an error:

    ```
    void operator -(ulong x);
    ```

    Selection of this operator by unary operator overload resolution (§14.2.3) always results in a compile-time error. Consequently, if the operand of the negation operator is of type `ulong`, a compile-time error occurs. An exception is the rule that permits the `long` value –9223372036854775808 (-2^{63}) to be written as a decimal integer literal (§9.4.4.2).

- Floating-point negation:

    ```
    float operator -(float x);
    double operator -(double x);
    ```

    The result is the value of x with its sign inverted. If x is NaN, the result is also NaN.

- Decimal negation:

    ```
    decimal operator -(decimal x);
    ```

    The result is computed by subtracting x from zero.

    Decimal negation is equivalent to using the unary minus operator of type `System.Decimal`.

Lifted (§14.2.7) forms of the unlifted predefined unary minus operators defined above are also predefined.

14.6.3 Logical negation operator

For an operation of the form `!x`, unary operator overload resolution (§14.2.3) is applied to select a specific operator implementation. The operand is converted to the parameter type of the selected operator, and the type of the result is the return type of the operator. Only one predefined logical negation operator exists:

```
bool operator !(bool x);
```

This operator computes the logical negation of the operand: If the operand is `true`, the result is `false`. If the operand is `false`, the result is `true`.

Lifted (§14.2.7) forms of the unlifted predefined logical negation operator defined above are also predefined.

14.6.4 Bitwise complement operator

For an operation of the form ~x, unary operator overload resolution (§14.2.3) is applied to select a specific operator implementation. The operand is converted to the parameter type of the selected operator, and the type of the result is the return type of the operator. The predefined bitwise complement operators are:

```
int operator ~ (int x);
uint operator ~ (uint x);
long operator ~ (long x);
ulong operator ~ (ulong x);
```

For each of these operators, the result of the operation is the bitwise complement of x.

Every enumeration type E implicitly provides the following bitwise complement operator:

```
E operator ~ (E x);
```

The result of evaluating ~x, where x is an expression of an enumeration type E with an underlying type U, is exactly the same as evaluating unchecked((E)(~(U)x)). This operator is only considered by unary operator overload resolution when the operand type is the enum type E (§14.2.3).

Lifted (§14.2.7) forms of the unlifted predefined bitwise complement operators defined above are also predefined.

14.6.5 Prefix increment and decrement operators

pre-increment-expression:
    ++   *unary-expression*

pre-decrement-expression:
    --   *unary-expression*

The operand of a prefix increment or decrement operation shall be an expression classified as a variable, a property access, or an indexer access. The result of the operation is a value of the same type as the operand.

> **Obscure C++ difference**
>
> Note that the result of the ++ and -- operators is a value and not a variable.
>
> ```
> int m = 42;
> m++++; // compile-time error in C# and C++
> ++++m; // compile-time error in C#, legal in C++!
> ```

If the operand of a prefix increment or decrement operation is a property or indexer access, the property or indexer shall have both a get and a set accessor. If this is not the case, a compile-time error occurs.

Unary operator overload resolution (§14.2.3) is applied to select a specific operator implementation. Predefined ++ and -- operators exist for the following operand types: sbyte, byte, short, ushort, int, uint, long, ulong, char, float, double, decimal, and any enum type. The result type of each of these predefined operators is the same as the operand type. The predefined ++ operators return the value produced by adding 1 to the operand, and the predefined -- operators return the value produced by subtracting 1 from the operand. In a checked context, if the result of this addition or subtraction is outside the range of the result type and the result type is an integral type or enum type, a System.OverflowException is thrown.

There shall be an implicit conversion from the return type of the selected unary operator to the type of the *primary-expression*, otherwise a compile-time error occurs.

The run-time processing of a prefix increment or decrement operation of the form ++x or --x consists of the following steps:

- If x is classified as a variable:
  - x is evaluated to produce the variable.
  - The value of x is converted to the operand type of the selected operator and the operator is invoked with this value as its argument.
  - The value returned by the operator is converted to the type of x. The resulting value is stored in the location given by the evaluation of x and becomes the result of the operation.
- If x is classified as a property or indexer access:
  - The instance expression (if x is not static) and the argument list (if x is an indexer access) associated with x are evaluated, and the results are used in the subsequent get and set accessor invocations.
  - The get accessor of x is invoked.
  - The value returned by the get accessor is converted to the operand type of the selected operator and operator is invoked with this value as its argument.
  - The value returned by the operator is converted to the type of x. The set accessor of x is invoked with this value as its value argument. This value also becomes the result of the operation.

The ++ and -- operators also support postfix notation (§14.5.9). The result of x++ or x-- is the value of x *before* the operation, whereas the result of ++x or --x is the value of x *after* the operation. In either case, x itself has the same value after the operation.

An operator ++ or operator -- implementation can be invoked using either postfix or prefix notation. It is not possible to have separate operator implementations for the two notations.

Lifted (§14.2.7) forms of the unlifted predefined prefix increment and decrement operators defined above are also predefined.

14.6.6 Cast expressions

A *cast-expression* is used to convert explicitly an expression to a given type.

> *cast-expression:*
>   (*type*) *unary-expression*

A *cast-expression* of the form (T)E, where T is a *type* and E is a *unary-expression*, performs an explicit conversion (§13.2) of the value of E to type T. If no explicit conversion exists from the type of E to T, a compile-time error occurs. Otherwise, the result is the value produced by the explicit conversion. The result is always classified as a value, even if E denotes a variable.

The grammar for a *cast-expression* leads to certain syntactic ambiguities. [*Example*: The expression (x) -y could either be interpreted as a *cast-expression* (a cast of -y to type x) or as an *additive-expression* combined with a *parenthesized-expression* (which computes the value x - y). *end example*]

To resolve *cast-expression* ambiguities, the following rule exists: A sequence of one or more *tokens* (§9.4) enclosed in parentheses is considered the start of a *cast-expression* only if at least one of the following are true:

- The sequence of tokens is correct grammar for a *type*, but not for an *expression*.

- The sequence of tokens is correct grammar for a *type*, and the token immediately following the closing parentheses is the token "~", the token "!", the token "(", an *identifier* (§9.4.1), a *literal* (§9.4.4), or any *keyword* (§9.4.3) except `as` and `is`.

The term "correct grammar" above means only that the sequence of tokens shall conform to the particular grammatical production. It specifically does not consider the actual meaning of any constituent identifiers. [*Example*: If `x` and `y` are identifiers, then `x.y` is correct grammar for a type, even if `x.y` doesn't actually denote a type. *end example*]

[*Note*: From the disambiguation rule, it follows that, if `x` and `y` are identifiers, `(x)y`, `(x)(y)`, and `(x)(-y)` are *cast-expression*s, but `(x)-y` is not, even if `x` identifies a type. However, if `x` is a keyword that identifies a predefined type (such as `int`), then all four forms are *cast-expression*s (because such a keyword could not possibly be an expression by itself). *end note*]

14.7 Arithmetic operators

The `*`, `/`, `%`, `+`, and `–` operators are called the arithmetic operators.

> *multiplicative-expression:*
>   *unary-expression*
>   *multiplicative-expression* `*` *unary-expression*
>   *multiplicative-expression* `/` *unary-expression*
>   *multiplicative-expression* `%` *unary-expression*

> *additive-expression:*
>   *multiplicative-expression*
>   *additive-expression* `+` *multiplicative-expression*
>   *additive-expression* `–` *multiplicative-expression*

Void arithmetic

Each of the arithmetic operators provides two versions, which do not return a value (they are marked `void`). These are uncallable operators, which may be ignored. For more details, see the annotations on §14.2.6.

Operator to instruction/method mapping not defined

In the Standard, operator descriptions include a C# signature. However, there is no requirement for these operators to actually exist as members of one of the types of their operand (s). This is usual in languages; one does not expect, for example, that integer addition is implemented by a method but by a machine instruction. This freedom is possible, and implicit in the Standard, because the language to platform mapping is not specified.

For example, the operator:

```
public static string operator+(string, string);
```

is implemented by both Microsoft and Mono compilers running on the CLI using the CLI's `string.Concat(string, string)` method. By contrast, the similar:

```
public static int operator+(int, int);
```

is compiled to a CLI instruction by the same compilers.

(See also the annotation on §14.7.4.)

14.7.1 Multiplication operator

For an operation of the form x * y, binary operator overload resolution (§14.2.4) is applied to select a specific operator implementation. The operands are converted to the parameter types of the selected operator, and the type of the result is the return type of the operator.

The predefined multiplication operators are listed below. The operators all compute the product of x and y.

- Integer multiplication:

```
int operator * (int x, int y);
uint operator * (uint x, uint y);
long operator * (long x, long y);
ulong operator * (ulong x, ulong y);
void operator * (long x, ulong y);
void operator * (ulong x, long y);
```

The operators with void return type always produce a compile-time error. Consequently, it is an error for one operand to be of type long and the other to be of type ulong.

In a checked context, if the product is outside the range of the result type, a System.OverflowException is thrown. In an unchecked context, overflows are not reported and any significant high-order bits outside the range of the result type are discarded.

- Floating-point multiplication:

```
float operator * (float x, float y);
double operator * (double x, double y);
```

The product is computed according to the rules of IEC 60559 arithmetic. The following table lists the results of all possible combinations of nonzero finite values, zeros, infinities, and NaN's. In the table, x and y are positive finite values. z is the result of x * y, rounded to the nearest representable value. If the magnitude of the result is too large for the destination type, z is infinity. Because of rounding, z may be zero even though neither x nor y is zero.

	+y	-y	+0	-0	+∞	-∞	NaN
+x	+z	-z	+0	-0	+∞	-∞	NaN
-x	-z	+z	-0	+0	-∞	+∞	NaN
+0	+0	-0	+0	-0	NaN	NaN	NaN
-0	-0	+0	-0	+0	NaN	NaN	NaN
+∞	+∞	-∞	NaN	NaN	+∞	-∞	NaN
-∞	-∞	+∞	NaN	NaN	-∞	+∞	NaN
NaN	NaN	NaN	NaN	NaN	NaN	NaN	NaN

- Decimal multiplication:

```
decimal operator * (decimal x, decimal y);
```

If the magnitude of the resulting value is too large to represent in the decimal format, a System.OverflowException is thrown. Because of rounding, the result may be zero even though neither operand is zero. The scale of the result, before any rounding, is the sum of the scales of the two operands.

Decimal multiplication is equivalent to using the multiplication operator of type `System.Decimal`.

Lifted (§14.2.7) forms of the unlifted predefined multiplication operators defined above are also predefined.

14.7.2 Division operator

For an operation of the form x / y, binary operator overload resolution (§14.2.4) is applied to select a specific operator implementation. The operands are converted to the parameter types of the selected operator, and the type of the result is the return type of the operator.

The predefined division operators are listed below. The operators all compute the quotient of x and y.

- Integer division:

```
int operator /(int x, int y);
uint operator /(uint x, uint y);
long operator /(long x, long y);
ulong operator /(ulong x, ulong y);
void operator /(long x, ulong y);
void operator /(ulong x, long y);
```

The operators with `void` return type always produce a compile-time error. Consequently, it is an error for one operand to be of type `long` and the other to be of type `ulong`.

If the value of the right operand is zero, a `System.DivideByZeroException` is thrown.

The division rounds the result towards zero, and the absolute value of the result is the largest possible integer that is less than the absolute value of the quotient of the two operands. The result is zero or positive when the two operands have the same sign and zero or negative when the two operands have opposite signs.

> ### Divided we stand
>
> As a consequence of truncating the quotient towards zero, the plausible equivalence `n/d+1 == (n+d)/d` does hold not for integers n and d of opposite signs (i.e., $n < 0 < d$ or $d < 0 < n$). For example, with n = -2 and d = 3, we have that `n/d+1` equates to `((-2)/3)+1`, which evaluates to `0+1`; that is, `1`; whereas `(n+d)/d` equates to `1/3`, which evaluates to `0`.
>
> However, note that the equivalence `(-n)/d == -(n/d) == n/(-d)` does hold. For example, `(-4)/3`, `-(4/3)`, and `4/(-3)` all evaluate to `-1`.
>
> The other option for integer division is to truncate towards $-\infty$, that is, minus infinity, which is the usual mathematical definition sometimes referred to as *quotient*. In this case the first equivalence holds and the second does not.
>
> Truncation towards zero is implemented by most hardware and by most programming languages, and presumably that is why C# adopts it too. The debate between the two choices has gone on almost since the first programming languages; those that provide truncation towards $-\infty$ include APL, Forth, Haskell, Standard ML, Mathematica, and Python. On the other hand, FORTRAN, Java, later versions of C/C++ (earlier versions did not specify), and Ada are among the majority that opt for truncation towards zero.
>
> Similar issues also apply to remainder/modulo operators.

The following table compares truncation towards zero, as provided by C#'s division and remainder operators, and truncation towards –∞, referred to as `quo()` and `mod()`:

x	y	x / y	x % y	quo(x, y)	mod(x, y)
-3	3	-1	0	-1	0
-2	3	0	-2	-1	1
-1	3	0	-1	-1	2
0	3	0	0	0	0
1	3	0	1	0	1
2	3	0	2	0	2
3	3	1	0	1	0
4	3	1	1	1	1
5	3	1	2	1	2
-5	-3	-1	-2	1	-2
-4	-3	-1	-1	1	-1
-3	-3	-1	0	1	0
-2	-3	0	-2	0	-2
-1	-3	0	-1	0	-1
0	-3	0	0	0	0
1	-3	0	1	-1	-2
2	-3	0	2	-1	-1
3	-3	1	0	-1	0

Given one form the other can be easily written. Using integer arithmetic, `int` quotient and modulus can be defined as:

```
static int QuoMod(int dividend, int divisor, out int mod)
{
  int quo;
  bool negDividend = dividend < 0;
  if (negDividend ^ (divisor < 0))
    quo = (dividend - divisor + (negDividend ? 1 : -1))
            /divisor;
  else
    quo = dividend / divisor;
  mod = dividend - quo * divisor;
  return quo;
}
```

Using floating point arithmetic and a CLI Standard library function it can be also defined as:

```
static int QuoMod(int dividend, int divisor, out int mod)
{
  int quo = (int)Math.Floor(((double)dividend)
                       / ((double)divisor));
  mod = dividend - quo * divisor;
  return quo;
}
```

If the left operand is the smallest `int` or `long` value (-2^{31} or -2^{63}, respectively) and the right operand is -1, an overflow occurs. In a `checked` context, this causes a `System.ArithmeticException` (or a subclass thereof) to be thrown. In an `unchecked` context, it is implementation-defined as to whether a `System.ArithmeticException` (or a subclass thereof) is thrown or the overflow goes unreported with the resulting value being that of the left operand.

A touch of Pentium

When the other operators are precise about overflows, why does the division operator have implementation-defined behavior? A possible answer may be found by looking at the CLI's instruction set. There you will find instruction pairs `add`/`add.ovf`, `sub`/`sub.ovf` and `mul`/`mul.ovf`, where the latter member of each pair checks for overflow. However, in CLI there is just `div`, no `div.ovf`. On the Pentium the `div` instruction always checks for overflow; on some other architectures it does not. It seems this little Pentium'ism crept into the CLI so there is only one div instruction, the overflow checking one.

By allowing the implementation defined behavior for division, C# attempts to accommodate these platform variations.

- Floating-point division:

```
float operator / (float x, float y);
double operator / (double x, double y);
```

The quotient is computed according to the rules of IEC 60559 arithmetic. The following table lists the results of all possible combinations of nonzero finite values, zeros, infinities, and NaN's. In the table, x and y are positive finite values. z is the result of x / y, rounded to the nearest representable value. If the magnitude of the result is too large for the destination type, z is infinity. Because of rounding, z may still be zero even though x is not zero and y is not infinite.

	$+y$	$-y$	$+0$	-0	$+\infty$	$-\infty$	NaN
$+x$	$+z$	$-z$	$+\infty$	$-\infty$	$+0$	-0	NaN
$-x$	$-z$	$+z$	$-\infty$	$+\infty$	-0	$+0$	NaN
$+0$	$+0$	-0	NaN	NaN	$+0$	-0	NaN
-0	-0	$+0$	NaN	NaN	-0	$+0$	NaN
$+\infty$	$+\infty$	$-\infty$	$+\infty$	$-\infty$	NaN	NaN	NaN
$-\infty$	$-\infty$	$+\infty$	$-\infty$	$+\infty$	NaN	NaN	NaN
NaN	NaN	NaN	NaN	NaN	NaN	NaN	NaN

- Decimal division:

```
decimal operator / (decimal x, decimal y);
```

If the value of the right operand is zero, a `System.DivideByZeroException` is thrown. If the magnitude of the resulting value is too large to represent in the `decimal` format, a `System.OverflowException` is thrown. Because of rounding, the result may be zero even though the first operand is not zero. The scale of the result, before any rounding, is the closest scale to the preferred scale which will preserve a result equal to the exact result. The preferred scale is the scale of x less the scale of y.

Decimal division is equivalent to using the division operator of type `System.Decimal`.

Lifted (§14.2.7) forms of the unlifted predefined division operators defined above are also predefined.

14.7.3 Remainder operator

For an operation of the form x % y, binary operator overload resolution (§14.2.4) is applied to select a specific operator implementation. The operands are converted to the parameter types of the selected operator, and the type of the result is the return type of the operator.

The predefined remainder operators are listed below. The operators all compute the remainder of the division between x and y.

- Integer remainder:

```
int operator %(int x, int y);
uint operator %(uint x, uint y);
long operator %(long x, long y);
ulong operator %(ulong x, ulong y);
void operator %(long x, ulong y);
void operator %(ulong x, long y);
```

The operators with `void` return type always produce a compile-time error. Consequently, it is an error for one operand to be of type `long` and the other to be of type `ulong`.

The result of x % y is the value produced by x - (x / y) * y. If y is zero, a `System.DivideByZeroException` is thrown.

If the left operand is the smallest `int` or `long` value (-2^{31} or -2^{63}, respectively) and the right operand is -1, it is implementation-defined as to whether a `System.ArithmeticException` (or a subclass thereof) is thrown. A conforming implementation shall not throw an exception for x % y in any case where x / y does not throw an exception.

> **Remainder latitude**
>
> The remainder operator is certainly *allowed*, but *not required*, to throw `ArithmeticException` when computing the remainder of the minimum integer value and -1.
>
> The mathematically correct result for remainder when the divisor is 1 or -1 is of course 0. However, common algorithms for remainder use division, and dividing the minimum integer by -1 produces an overflow in two's complement arithmetic. To allow these algorithms to be used, it is implementation defined whether an exception is thrown. At the time of writing both the Microsoft and Mono implementations will throw an exception in this situation.

- Floating-point remainder:

```
float operator %(float x, float y);
double operator %(double x, double y);
```

The following table lists the results of all possible combinations of nonzero finite values, zeros, infinities, and NaN's. In the table, x and y are positive finite values. z is the result of x % y and is computed as $x - n * y$, rounded to the nearest representable value, where n is the largest integer that is less than or equal to x / y. This method of computing the remainder is analogous to that used for integer operands, but differs from the IEC 60559 definition (in which n is the integer closest to x / y).

	+y	−y	+0	−0	+∞	−∞	NaN
+x	+z	+z	NaN	NaN	+x	+x	NaN
−x	−z	−z	NaN	NaN	−x	−x	NaN
+0	+0	+0	NaN	NaN	+0	+0	NaN
−0	−0	−0	NaN	NaN	−0	−0	NaN
+∞	NaN	NaN	NaN	NaN	NaN	NaN	NaN
−∞	NaN	NaN	NaN	NaN	NaN	NaN	NaN
NaN	NaN	NaN	NaN	NaN	NaN	NaN	NaN

IEC remainder

The CLI provides a method `Math.IEEERemainder` which calculates the IEC 60559 remainder. Unlike for integer quotient, there is no simple algorithm to compute IEC 60559 remainder using only the operations defined by the C# Standard.

- Decimal remainder:

  ```
  decimal operator % (decimal x, decimal y);
  ```

  If the value of the right operand is zero, a `System.DivideByZeroException` is thrown. It is implementation-defined when a `System.ArithmeticException` (or a subclass thereof) is thrown. A conforming implementation shall not throw an exception for x % y in any case where x / y does not throw an exception. The scale of the result, before any rounding, is the larger of the scales of the two operands, and the sign of the result, if non-zero, is the same as that of x.

Further latitude

The situation here is similar to that of integer remainder (see the "Remainder latitude" annotation). The most straightforward way to compute remainder in `decimal` is to use division, and that division may overflow within `decimal` even in cases where the (mathematically correct) remainder would have been representable in the `decimal` type. The wording simply allows implementers to do better if they can.

Decimal remainder is equivalent to using the remainder operator of type `System.Decimal`.

Lifted (§14.2.7) forms of the unlifted predefined remainder operators defined above are also predefined.

14.7.4 Addition operator

For an operation of the form x + y, binary operator overload resolution (§14.2.4) is applied to select a specific operator implementation. The operands are converted to the parameter types of the selected operator, and the type of the result is the return type of the operator.

The predefined addition operators are listed below. For numeric and enumeration types, the predefined addition operators compute the sum of the two operands. When one or both operands are of type string, the predefined addition operators concatenate the string representation of the operands.

- Integer addition:

```
int operator +(int x, int y);
uint operator +(uint x, uint y);
long operator +(long x, long y);
ulong operator +(ulong x, ulong y);
void operator +(long x, ulong y);
void operator +(ulong x, long y);
```

The operators with void return type always produce a compile-time error. Consequently, it is an error for one operand to be of type long and the other to be of type ulong.

In a checked context, if the sum is outside the range of the result type, a System.OverflowException is thrown. In an unchecked context, overflows are not reported and any significant high-order bits outside the range of the result type are discarded.

- Floating-point addition:

```
float operator +(float x, float y);
double operator +(double x, double y);
```

The sum is computed according to the rules of IEC 60559 arithmetic. The following table lists the results of all possible combinations of nonzero finite values, zeros, infinities, and NaN's. In the table, x and y are nonzero finite values, and z is the result of x + y, rounded to the nearest representable value. If x and y have the same magnitude but opposite signs, z is positive zero. If the magnitude of x + y is too large to represent in the destination type, z is an infinity with the same sign as x + y.

	y	+0	−0	+∞	−∞	NaN
x	z	x	x	+∞	−∞	NaN
+0	y	+0	+0	+∞	−∞	NaN
−0	y	+0	−0	+∞	−∞	NaN
+∞	+∞	+∞	+∞	+∞	NaN	NaN
−∞	−∞	−∞	−∞	NaN	−∞	NaN
NaN	NaN	NaN	NaN	NaN	NaN	NaN

- Decimal addition:

```
decimal operator +(decimal x, decimal y);
```

If the magnitude of the resulting value is too large to represent in the `decimal` format, a `System.OverflowException` is thrown. The scale of the result, before any rounding, is the larger of the scales of the two operands.

Decimal addition is equivalent to using the addition operator of type `System.Decimal`.

- Enumeration addition. Every enumeration type implicitly provides the following predefined operators, where `E` is the enum type, and `U` is the underlying type of `E`:

```
E operator +(E x, U y);
E operator +(U x, E y);
```

The operators are evaluated exactly as `(E) ((U) x + (U) y)`. These operators are only considered by overload resolution (§14.2.4) when one of the actual operands is of type `E`.

- String concatenation:

```
string operator +(string x, string y);
string operator +(string x, object y);
string operator +(object x, string y);
```

The binary + operator performs string concatenation when one or both operands are of type `string`. If an operand of string concatenation is `null`, an empty string is substituted. Otherwise, any non-string operand is converted to its string representation by invoking the virtual `ToString` method inherited from type `object`. If `ToString` returns `null`, an empty string is substituted. [*Example*:

```
using System;

class Test
{
  static void Main()
  {
    string s = null;
    Console.WriteLine("s =>" + s + "<"); // displays s = ><
    int i = 1;
    Console.WriteLine("i = " + i);  // displays i = 1
    float f = 1.2300E+15F;
    Console.WriteLine("f = " + f);  // displays f = 1.23E+15
    decimal d = 2.900m;
    Console.WriteLine("d = " + d);  // displays d = 2.900
  }
}
```

end example]

Hidden boxing

In the preceding examples, hidden boxing occurs on the `i`, `f`, and `d` operands. As overload resolution (§14.4.2) specifies, and this clause bullet reiterates, the expression `"i = " + i` resolves to the `operator+(string, object)` thus boxing `i`. To avoid the boxing you can manually call `ToString()`:

```
int i = 1;
Console.WriteLine("i = " + i.ToString());
float f = 1.2300E+15F;
```

```
Console.WriteLine("f = " + f.ToString());
decimal d = 2.900m;
Console.WriteLine("d = " + d.ToString());
```

This is because calling a virtual method on a value type *does not* box (see §14.4.3).

In practice, the run-time overhead incurred by the boxing is low; typically one tenth of the cost of converting to string. However, in this example the conversion to string needs to be done, so some saving will accrue.

Implicitly avoiding the boxing

It is possible when defining a type to include an implicit conversion (§13.4, §17.9.3) to string so that boxing in situations such as the preceding is automatically avoided. For example, consider the program fragment:

```
public struct Complex
{
    double re;
    double im;

    public Complex(double real, double imag) {...}

    public static Complex
    operator +(Complex left, Complex right) {...}

    public static implicit operator string(Complex c)
    {
        return string.Format("({0} + {1} i)",
        c.re.ToString(), c.im.ToString());
    }
    ...
}

class Test
{

    static void Run()
    {
        Complex a = new Complex(1, 2);
        Complex b = new Complex(2, -1);

        Complex c = a + b;

        Console.WriteLine("a = " + a);
        Console.WriteLine("b = " + b);
        Console.WriteLine("c = " + c);
    }
}
```

[Note: string.Format *and the formatting version of* Console.WriteLine *used next are CLI Standard Library methods, not part of Standard C#.]*

By the rules of overloading and better conversion (§14.4.2.3) in the calls to Console.WriteLine the operator used will be string operator +(string x, string y) and no boxing will occur. Note, however, that the call:

```
        Console.WriteLine("a = {0} ", a);
```

would still box a, but that:

```
        Console.WriteLine("a = {0} ", (string)a);
```

would not. (However, in the last case WriteLine probably ends up invoking ToString
() on a string, cheap but pointless!)

Whether this technique is useful is application dependent. It has also been asked, given
that every type inherits ToString(), whether an implicit conversion to string could
have been included in C#. Though this would have been possible, consideration would
need to have been given to fitting it into the overall conversion hierarchy (§13), and in
particular the interplay with numeric promotions (§14.2.6) and the overloading of the
addition operator with both numeric and string types. Given this was not done, such a
conversion is unlikely to be added in future. However, for user-defined types the
approach is certainly applicable.

The result of the string concatenation operator is a string that consists of the
characters of the left operand followed by the characters of the right operand.
The string concatenation operator never returns a null value. A System.
OutOfMemoryException can be thrown if there is not enough memory available
to allocate the resulting string.

- Delegate combination. Every delegate type implicitly provides the following predefined
  operator, where D is the delegate type:

  ```
  D operator +(D x, D y);
  ```

  The binary + operator performs delegate combination when both operands are
  convertible to some delegate type D. (If the operands have different delegate
  types, overload resolution finds no applicable operator and a compile-time error
  occurs.) This operator is only considered by overload resolution (§14.2.4) when
  one of the actual operands is of type D. If the first operand is null, the result of
  the operation is the value of the second operand (even if that is also null).
  Otherwise, if the second operand is null, then the result of the operation is the
  value of the first operand. Otherwise, the result of the operation is a new delegate
  instance whose invocation list consists of the elements in the invocation list of
  the first operand, followed by the elements in the invocation list of the second
  operand. That is, the invocation list of the resulting delegate is the concatenation
  of the invocation lists of the two operands. [*Note*: For examples of delegate
  combination, see §14.7.5 and §22.3. Since System.Delegate is not a delegate
  type, operator + is not defined for it. *end note*]

Lifted (§14.2.7) forms of the unlifted predefined addition operators defined above are also
predefined.

String concatenation efficiency

That only binary string concatenation operators are defined suggests less efficiency than is
usually actually implemented. For instance, consider the following program:

```
using System;

class Test
{
   static void Main()
   {
      string x = "x";
      string y = "y";
      string z = "z";
      string total = x + y + z;
   }
}
```

Normally, one might expect the last statement to be evaluated as (x+y)+z, involving the concatenation initially of "x" and "y" and then of "xy" and "z." This is clearly somewhat inefficient; in fact, the execution time would be quadratic in the number of nonempty strings. However, compilers are free to optimize. For example, the current Microsoft and Mono compilers implement the preceding concatenation by a call to the CLI's `string.Concat` (one of several overloads, depending on the precise situation). This allows a single string to be created, avoiding the $n-2$ intermediate strings that would seem needed for concatenating n strings.

Aside: This optimization is unfortunately overlooked by some people who, having heard "use the CLI's `StringBuilder` to build up strings" insist on doing so, even when using `StringBuilder` would actually be less efficient than the compiler-generated call to `string.Concat`. Such is the peril of learning a rule without fully understanding the reasons behind it.

(See also the annotation on §14.7.)

Jon Skeet

14.7.5 Subtraction operator

For an operation of the form x – y, binary operator overload resolution (§14.2.4) is applied to select a specific operator implementation. The operands are converted to the parameter types of the selected operator, and the type of the result is the return type of the operator.

The predefined subtraction operators are listed below. The operators all subtract y from x.

- Integer subtraction:

```
int operator –(int x, int y);
uint operator –(uint x, uint y);
long operator –(long x, long y);
ulong operator –(ulong x, ulong y);
void operator –(long x, ulong y);
void operator –(ulong x, long y);
```

The operators with `void` return type always produce a compile-time error. Consequently, it is an error for one operand to be of type `long` and the other to be of type `ulong`.

In a `checked` context, if the difference is outside the range of the result type, a `System.OverflowException` is thrown. In an `unchecked` context, overflows are not reported and any significant high-order bits outside the range of the result type are discarded.

- Floating-point subtraction:

```
float operator -(float x, float y);
double operator -(double x, double y);
```

The difference is computed according to the rules of IEC 60559 arithmetic. The following table lists the results of all possible combinations of nonzero finite values, zeros, infinities, and NaNs. In the table, x and y are nonzero finite values, and z is the result of x − y, rounded to the nearest representable value. If x and y are equal, z is positive zero. If the magnitude of x − y is too large to represent in the destination type, z is an infinity with the same sign as x − y.

y	+0	−0	+∞	−∞	NaN
x	z	x	x	−∞	+∞	NaN
+0	−y	+0	+0	−∞	+∞	NaN
−0	−y	−0	+0	−∞	+∞	NaN
+∞	+∞	+∞	+∞	NaN	+∞	NaN
−∞	−∞	−∞	−∞	−∞	NaN	NaN
NaN	NaN	NaN	NaN	NaN	NaN	NaN

Negation, not negative

In the preceding table the −y entries denote the *negation* of y, not that the value is negative. This differs from the other uses of "−" in this table, and the uses in the floating point tables in §14.7.1-4, where it means the value is negative.

[Note: In all the floating point tables in §14.7.1-5, the use of "+" means the value is positive; the lack of any sign means the value may be positive or negative (as in z before) or has no sign (NaN).]

- Decimal subtraction:

```
decimal operator -(decimal x, decimal y);
```

If the magnitude of the resulting value is too large to represent in the decimal format, a System.OverflowException is thrown. The scale of the result, before any rounding, is the larger of the scales of the two operands.

Decimal subtraction is equivalent to using the subtraction operator of type System.Decimal.

- Enumeration subtraction. Every enumeration type implicitly provides the following predefined operator, where E is the enum type, and U is the underlying type of E:

```
U operator -(E x, E y);
```

This operator is evaluated exactly as (U)((U)x - (U)y). In other words, the operator computes the difference between the ordinal values of x and y, and the type of the result is the underlying type of the enumeration.

```
E operator -(E x, U y);
```

This operator is evaluated exactly as (E)((U)x - y). In other words, the operator subtracts a value from the underlying type of the enumeration, yielding a value of the enumeration.

These operators are only considered by overload resolution (§14.2.4) when one of the actual operands is of type E.

- Delegate removal. Every delegate type implicitly provides the following predefined operator, where D is the delegate type:

```
D operator - (D x, D y);
```

The binary – operator performs delegate removal when both operands are convertible to some delegate type D. (If the operands have different delegate types, overload resolution finds no applicable operator and a compile-time error occurs.) This operator is only considered by overload resolution (§14.2.4) when one of the actual operands is of type D. If the first operand is null, the result of the operation is null. Otherwise, if the second operand is null, then the result of the operation is the value of the first operand. Otherwise, both operands represent invocation lists (§22.1) having one or more entries, and the result is a new invocation list consisting of the first operand's list with the second operand's entries removed from it, provided the second operand's list is a proper contiguous sublist of the first's. (For determining sublist equality, corresponding entries are compared as for the delegate equality operator (§14.9.8).) Otherwise, the result is the value of the left operand. Neither of the operands' lists is changed in the process. If the second operand's list matches multiple sublists of contiguous entries in the first operand's list, the right-most matching sublist of contiguous entries is removed. If removal results in an empty list, the result is null. [*Example*:

```
using System;

delegate void D(int x);
class Test
{
  public static void M1(int i) { /* ... */ }
  public static void M2(int i) { /* ... */ }
}

class Demo
{
  static void Main()
  { D cd1 = new D(Test.M1);
    D cd2 = new D(Test.M2);

    D cd3 = cd1 + cd2 + cd2 + cd1;   // M1 + M2 + M2 + M1
    cd3 -= cd1;                       // => M1 + M2 + M2

    cd3 = cd1 + cd2 + cd2 + cd1;     // M1 + M2 + M2 + M1
    cd3 -= cd1 + cd2;                 // => M2 + M1

    cd3 = cd1 + cd2 + cd2 + cd1;     // M1 + M2 + M2 + M1
    cd3 -= cd2 + cd2;                 // => M1 + M1

    cd3 = cd1 + cd2 + cd2 + cd1;     // M1 + M2 + M2 + M1
    cd3 -= cd2 + cd1;                 // => M1 + M2
```

```
        cd3 = cd1 + cd2 + cd2 + cd1;   // M1 + M2 + M2 + M1
        cd3 -= cd1 + cd1;              // => M1 + M2 + M2 + M1
    }
}
```

end example]

Lifted (§14.2.7) forms of the unlifted predefined subtraction operators defined above are also predefined.

Legacy coding style

The preceding code example uses `new` when assigning values to `cd1` and `cd2`. Also, in §8.7.5 one finds this example:

```
public void Disconnect()
{
    Button1.Click -= new EventHandler(Button1_Click);
}
```

This uses `new` for the sole purpose of removing something, which may appear rather unintuitive.

Both examples are legacies from the first version of the C# Standard. In the present version, as a result of the introduction of method group conversions (§13.6), the `new` is no longer required. For example, the preceding can now be written:

```
public void Disconnect()
{
    Button1.Click -= Button1_Click;
}
```

This certainly reads better.

[This annotation was inspired by a comment made by Matthew Strawbridge, one of the book's reviewers.]

14.8 Shift operators

The `<<` and `>>` operators are used to perform bit shifting operations.

shift-expression:
  additive-expression
  shift-expression `<<` *additive-expression*
  shift-expression *right-shift* *additive-expression*

For an operation of the form `x << count` or `x >> count`, binary operator overload resolution (§14.2.4) is applied to select a specific operator implementation. The operands are converted to the parameter types of the selected operator, and the type of the result is the return type of the operator.

When declaring an overloaded shift operator, the type of the first operand shall always be the class or struct containing the operator declaration, and the type of the second operand shall always be `int`.

The predefined shift operators are listed below.

- Shift left:

```
int operator << (int x, int count);
uint operator << (uint x, int count);
long operator << (long x, int count);
ulong operator << (ulong x, int count);
```

The << operator shifts x left by a number of bits computed as described below.

The high-order bits outside the range of the result type of x are discarded, the remaining bits are shifted left, and the low-order empty bit positions are set to zero.

- Shift right:

```
int operator >> (int x, int count);
uint operator >> (uint x, int count);
long operator >> (long x, int count);
ulong operator >> (ulong x, int count);
```

The >> operator shifts x right by a number of bits computed as described below.

When x is of type int or long, the low-order bits of x are discarded, the remaining bits are shifted right, and the high-order empty bit positions are set to zero if x is non-negative and set to one if x is negative.

When x is of type uint or ulong, the low-order bits of x are discarded, the remaining bits are shifted right, and the high-order empty bit positions are set to zero.

For the predefined operators, the number of bits to shift is computed as follows:

- When the type of x is int or uint, the shift count is given by the low-order five bits of count. In other words, the shift count is computed from count & 0x1F.
- When the type of x is long or ulong, the shift count is given by the low-order six bits of count. In other words, the shift count is computed from count & 0x3F.

If the resulting shift count is zero, the shift operators simply return the value of x.

Shift operations never cause overflows and produce the same results in checked and unchecked contexts.

When the left operand of the >> operator is of a signed integral type, the operator performs an *arithmetic* shift right wherein the value of the most significant bit (the sign bit) of the operand is propagated to the high-order empty bit positions. When the left operand of the >> operator is of an unsigned integral type, the operator performs a *logical* shift right wherein high-order empty bit positions are always set to zero. To perform the opposite operation of that inferred from the operand type, explicit casts can be used. [*Example*: If x is a variable of type int, the operation unchecked((int)((uint)x >> y)) performs a logical shift right of x. *end example*]

Lifted (§14.2.7) forms of the unlifted predefined shift operators defined above are also predefined.

Negative shifts

The shift count is of type int, which allows for a *negative* value. However, as the value is always masked to 5 or 6 bits the shift count is always *positive*. C# uses 2's-complement binary arithmetic (§11.1.5) so when shifting an int or uint value by x, $-32 \leq x < 0$, the shift count is $32 - x$. Likewise, when shifting a long or ulong value by x, $-64 \leq x < 0$, the shift count is $64 - x$.

For right hand operand values outside the range ±32 (int or uint) or ±64 (long or ulong) the resultant shift count is a little less obvious, as shown in the following table:

	Shift count	
Right hand operand	int **or** uint	long **or** ulong
$x \geq 0$	x mod 32	x mod 64
$x < 0$	$32 - (|x| \bmod 32)$	$64 - (|x| \bmod 64)$

Some examples:

```
int iv, ir;
long lv, lr;
...
ir = iv << -5;    // shift left 27 bits
lr = lv << -5;    // shift left 59 bits

ir = iv >> -345;  // shift right 25 bits
lr = lv >> -345;  // shift right 25 bits
```

Confused? It is strongly recommended that right hand operand values are kept to the range $0 \leq x \leq 32$ (int or uint) or $0 \leq x \leq 64$ (long or ulong).

Out of bounds shift count behavior?

C# deliberately keeps implementation-defined behaviors to a minimum. They are accepted only when the performance impact of forcing uniform behavior would be excessive (such as for some floating-point precision issues). Hence, the size of each integral type is precisely specified, and the character set is fixed to Unicode.

For shift operations, too, uniform behavior is specified. It can be achieved using a single extra instruction (& 0x1F or & 0x3F) that incurs only a tiny cost on modern processors, especially since it does not reference memory. Unlike for floating-point operations, the difference in shift behavior would be dramatic if left to the whim of the processors; rather than a small difference in precision, completely different integral results would be produced.

In making this decision the committee studied reference materials for a number of different processor architectures. There is little consistency in the behavior for shift counts outside the range −32..+32 for 32-bit operands, and respectively −64..+64 for 64-bit operands:

- x86 (IA-32): mod 32
- PA-RISC: mod 32 (32-bit operand), mod 64 (64-bit operand)
- IA-64: no mod (shift count is unsigned)
- Motorola ColdFire: mod 64
- ARM: mod 256
- Alpha: mod 64
- SPARC: mod 32

Interestingly, the CLI shift instructions do not specify the behavior for out-of-range shift counts, so to obtain C# shift behavior, CLI bitwise-and instructions must be generated by the C# compiler.

In specifying the sizes of integral types, uniform behavior for shifts, etc., C# follows Java.

Zero-extension signed shift

C# provides both signed and unsigned integers; the shift operator >> performs an arithmetic (sign extending) right shift for signed integers and a logical (zero fill) right shift for unsigned integers.

In contrast, Java does not provide unsigned integers and has a special right shift operator, >>>, which performs a logical shift on signed values.

If you need to do a logical right shift on a signed integer in C#, the following method will perform correctly regardless of the current overflow checking state:

```
static int Lsr(int v, int by)
{
   return unchecked((int)((uint)v >> by));
}
```

This, of course, will also work as an inline expression and for long values.

Jon Skeet

14.9 Relational and type-testing operators

The ==, !=, <, >, <=, >=, is and as operators are called the relational and type-testing operators.

> *relational-expression:*
>   *shift-expression*
>   *relational-expression*   <   *shift-expression*
>   *relational-expression*   >   *shift-expression*
>   *relational-expression*   <=   *shift-expression*
>   *relational-expression*   >=   *shift-expression*
>   *relational-expression*   is   *type*
>   *relational-expression*   as   *type*
>
> *equality-expression:*
>   *relational-expression*
>   *equality-expression*   ==   *relational-expression*
>   *equality-expression*   !=   *relational-expression*

The is operator is described in §14.9.10 and the as operator is described in §14.9.11.

The ==, !=, <, >, <= and >= operators are **comparison operators**. For an operation of the form x *op* y, where *op* is a comparison operator, overload resolution (§14.2.4) is applied to select a specific operator implementation. The operands are converted to the parameter types of the selected operator, and the type of the result is the return type of the operator. If both operands of an *equality-expression* have the null type (§11.2.7) (and hence the null value as well), then overload resolution is not performed and the expression evaluates to a constant value of true or false according to whether the operator is == or !=.

Incomparable

Each of the comparison operators provides two versions, which do not return a value (they are marked void). These are uncallable operators, which may be ignored. For more details see the annotations on §14.2.6.

The predefined comparison operators are described in the following subclauses. All predefined comparison operators return a result of type `bool`, as described in the following table.

Operation	Result
x == y	`true` if x is equal to y, `false` otherwise
x != y	`true` if x is not equal to y, `false` otherwise
x < y	`true` if x is less than y, `false` otherwise
x > y	`true` if x is greater than y, `false` otherwise
x <= y	`true` if x is less than or equal to y, `false` otherwise
x >= y	`true` if x is greater than or equal to y, `false` otherwise

All references are equal, but some are more equal than others

Consider the following code fragment:

```
public struct Weird
{
    public int iField;
    public object sField;

    public Weird(int i, string s)
    {
        iField = i;
        sField = s;
    }

    public static bool operator==(Weird a, Weird b)
    {
        return (a.iField == b.iField) && (a.sField == b.sField);
    }

    public public bool operator!=(Weird a, Weird b)
    {
        return !a.iField.Equals(b.iField) || !a.sField.Equals (b.sField);
    }
}

static void Test()
{
    Weird wOne = new Weird(2, "");
    Weird wTwo = new Weird(2, string.Empty);

    Console.WriteLine(wOne == wTwo);
    Console.WriteLine(wOne != wTwo);
    Console.WriteLine(wOne.Equals(wTwo));
}
```

[Note: The operators `==` and `!=` would not normally be written differently as shown here; this code is simply to demonstrate the different results.]

What should the output from a call to `Test()` be? The current Microsoft compiler outputs: `false`, `false`, and `true`, which might strike some as surprising. The current Mono compiler outputs: `true`, `false`, and `true`; this is probably less surprising. However, what is probably most surprising is that *both* are valid according to the Standard.

Two Equivalences

Programming languages often deal with two *equivalence relations*:

1. (Value) Equality: This is the usual "equals" relation on numbers, characters, etc. that determines whether two values are the same. Equality is also provided, or can be provided by the programmer, for other struct and class types and has the same meaning: Do two struct or class instances represent the same value?

2. Reference Identity/Equality: This is only applicable to reference types and determines whether two references refer to the *same* object instance. If two reference values are equivalent according to reference identity then what they refer to must also be equivalent according to value equality; however, of course, the reverse is not true; two object instances may represent the same value but be different objects.

C# provides both of these, but which you get in a given circumstance is not always immediately apparent, which can lead to confusion.

Equivalence on the CLI

The C# Standard Library (Annex D) is defined in terms of the CLI Standard Library. Also, though not reliant on the CLI, the design of C# has been influenced by it and the current C# systems run on CLI implementations. Therefore, to understand C#'s handling of equivalence it helps to look at the CLI first. The CLI is intended to support the various equivalence relations provided by different languages, and to do this the CLI supports four equivalence operations:

1. **Method:** `ReferenceEquals`. The identity relation on references is provided by the static method (*CLI Standard, Partition I, 8.2.5.1*):

   ```
   public static bool object.ReferenceEquals(object objA, object objB);
   ```

   This method is *not* required by the C# Standard (but of course implementations running on the CLI may use it). Also, the result of this method is not particularly meaningful if applied to two boxed value types (see §13.1.5) or two strings (see §9.4.4.5).

2. **Method:** `Equals`. Value equality is provided by the instance method (*CLI Standard, Partition I, 8.2.5.2*):

   ```
   public virtual bool object.Equals(object obj);
   ```

   This method is required by the C# Standard (Annex D).The CLI defines Equals for many of its standard types, including boxed types, but these definitions are not required by the C# Standard.

   Though this method is intended to implement the value equality relation the default implementation of `object.Equals` determines the reference identity relation, so it only provides *partial* value equality unless overridden—if `a.Equals(b)` is `true` then a and b represent the same value, but if it is `false` we only know they *may* not do so. The default implementation of `Value-Type.Equals` performs the pairwise equality of the type's fields.

3. **CIL instruction:** `ceq`. The CIL instruction `ceq` (*CLI Standard, Partition III, 3.21*; also the instructions `beq` *3.21* and `bne` *3.14*) computes the value equality relation for built-in value types (integers, floating-point, characters and Booleans) and user-defined enumeration types. However, it also computes the reference identity relation for object

references. This is the typical behavior of a "machine level" equivalence operation that treats references as an integral pointer/address type.

4. **Operator:** `op_Equality`. The CLI does not really provide "operators" — an operator is just a static method with a particular naming pattern that programming languages running on the CLI may choose to provide operator syntax for. The naming pattern for the equality operator is (*CLI Standard, Partition I, 10.3.2*):

    ```
    public static bool T.op_Equality(T left, T right);
    ```

    The current C# compilers from Microsoft and Mono that run on the CLI use this pattern when compiling C#'s:

    ```
    public static bool T.operator==(T left, T right);
    ```

    There is a corresponding `op_Inequality` used by C# CLI compilers for `operator!=`.

Equivalence in C#

C# provides two standard equivalence operations: the operator `==` (and its inverse `!=`) and the virtual method `Equals`. We describe the two by how they may be realized on the CLI:

a. **Method** `object.Equals`**: partial value equality.**

    The `object.Equals` method is intended for value equality and C# takes its definition from the CLI (Annex D). C# does not specify `Equals` on types other than `object`. This method is covered further in the annotations "The invisible contract," "Equality for all," and "Exploiting the built-in equality on value types" later.

b. **Operator** `==`**: type dependent equivalence.**

    C# predefines this operator over various, but not all, types (see subclauses of §14.9). It can also be user defined for other types (§17.9.2). The following table describes how the current Microsoft and Mono compilers meet the C# requirements for '`==`' on the CLI:

Type	Compiled to	Relation
Predefined integer, floating-point, character and Boolean; any enum	ceq instruction	value equality
decimal	System.Decimal.op_Equality	value equality
string	System.String.Equals	value equality
Any delegate type	System.Delegate.op_Equality	value equality
Any other value type, T	if provided, T.op_Equality, otherwise not supported	value equality *or* not supported
object	ceq	reference identity
Any other class type	if provided, T.op_Equality, otherwise ceq	value equality *or* reference identity

As the table shows, the equivalence relation computed by `==` depends on the types of its arguments. In doing this C# follows Java and also behaves like C, a language without references.

Important: In C# operators are static and operator selection is determined at compile time based on the compile-time type. The consequence of this is that if a particular type's default equivalence relation used for `==` is value equality, whether built in or user defined, then casting to `object` (or any other supertype which does not implement `==`) and then comparing *will change the equivalence relation used* to reference identity. This might seem surprising to some in an OO environment.

The Example Explained

We can now explain why this example produces the results it does, and why both Microsoft and Mono implementations are correct even though they produce different answers. We look at each comparison in turn:

i. `wOne == wTwo`

The example defines `==` by pairwise application of `==` to the two fields `iField` and `sField`. The former is an `int` and so value equality is computed; however, the latter is an `object` and so reference identity is computed. Using the current Microsoft compiler, the string values `""` and `string.Empty` are different objects and so `false` is returned. However, by §9.4.4.5 strings with the same value may be represented by the same object; this is possible as strings are immutable. The current Mono compiler uses the same *object* for both `""` and `string.Empty` and so returns `true`. Both implementations are valid; however, Microsoft produces a semantically incorrect result while Mono gets the semantically correct result by luck.

ii. `wOne != wTwo`

The example defines `!=` by pairwise application of `Equals`. Both `int` and `string` correctly define this to be value equality, and as it is a virtual method, storing the `string` values in `object` fields does not stop the `string.Equals` method being invoked. This version therefore gives the semantically correct result.

iii. `wOne.Equals(wTwo)`

The `Weird` type does not define `Equals` so it inherits the CLI's one from `System.ValueType`, which in turn does a pairwise application of `Equals` to the fields. Therefore, as for `!=` this produces the semantically correct result. However, this version will involve boxing. Also, on a non-CLI hosted implementation this result might be different.

C# has followed Java in making equality type dependent and differs from those languages, such as Eiffel and Algol 68, which provide separate value equality and reference identity relations.

It is unfortunate that confusing, and apparently contradictory, results can easily be obtained when comparing items in C#. Other annotations suggest design approaches that reduce the chances for unexpected results.

The invisible contract

C# has a required method `object.Equals(object)` (Annex D) copied from the CLI Standard library. The semantics of this method, as with all items listed in Annex D, is "included by reference in this International Standard" from the CLI Standard library. This semantics includes the following contract that all implementations must adhere to:

For x, y, and z representing non-null object references or value type instances:

- `x.Equals(x)` returns `true`.
- `x.Equals(y)` returns the same value as `y.Equals(x)`.
- If `x.Equals(y) && y.Equals(z)` returns `true`, then `x.Equals(z)` returns `true`.

- Successive invocations of `x.Equals(y)` return the same value as long as the objects referenced by, or the values of, `x` and `y` are not modified.
- `x.Equals(null)` returns `false`.

Recommendation: The Standard has an *informative* recommendation that an implementation of `Equals` should not throw exceptions. We strongly support this recommendation, and it probably ought to be normative. For example, collection classes would be inefficient if they had to guard against `Equals` throwing exceptions and ensure that internal data structures remained consistent after such an exception.

Furthermore, when overriding `Equals` it is usually required to override `GetHashCode` as it must obey the following contract:

For `x` and `y` representing non-null object references or value type instances:

- If `x.Equals(y)` returns `true`, then `x.GetHashCode() == y.GetHashCode()`.

Recommendation: When overriding `Equals` it is recommended to provide a type-specific version to avoid unnecessary casting or boxing:

```
public bool T.Equals(T other);
```

Recommendation: Though not required by the Standard it is strongly recommended that an implementation of `operator==` adheres to the same contract as `Equals`, and that the corresponding `operator!=` returns the Boolean negation of `operator==`. Indeed, `operator==` and `Equals` should compute *exactly the same* equality relation.

Having said that, there are two standard types, `float` and `double`, for which `operator==` does not adhere to this contract; see the annotation on §14.9.2.

Equality for all

As explained in the second-to-last annotation, the C# operator `operator==` is an equivalence relation, but on some types it computes equality while on others it computes identity. This can lead to potentially confusing results, especially as casting one operand to a base type can change the operation.

To enable equality testing for all types, and identity testing for reference types, one may adopt the following rules:

- Do not define `operator==` or `operator!=` on class types.
- For class types for which you want an equality relation, override `Equals`.
- For value types for which you want an equality relation, define `operator==` and `operator!=`, and override `Equals`.

If these rules are followed then for two expressions `a` and `b`:

- If `a` and `b` are class types: "`a == b`" and "`a != b`" will compute the identity and nonidentity relations. (The result is meaningless if the class types are boxed value types.)
- If `a` and `b` are value types: "`a == b`" and "`a != b`" will compute the equality and nonequality relations. These expressions are likely to be inlined and hence efficient for at least built-in types and user-defined enum types.
- If `a` and `b` are any type, including object, `a.Equals(b)` will compute the equality relation.

A variation on these rules is to define `operator==` and `operator!=` for immutable ("value-like") reference types as well, just as C# does for `string`.

Exploiting the built-in equality on value types

C# requires a 'public virtual bool object.Equals(object obj)' (Annex D) method, and the type System.ValueType (§11.1.1) from which all value types derive. It follows therefore that there is an Equals method on every value type and, by inherited semantics from the Standard CLI library (see Annex D), it computes the equality relation.

However, the C# operator "==" does not operate on a user-defined value type unless that type defines operator==. To define operator== in terms of Equals, you can use the following pattern:

```
public struct S
{
  ...
  public static bool operator==(S left, S right)
  {
    return left.Equals(right);
  }

  public static bool operator!=(S left, S right)
  {
    return !left.Equals(right);
  }
}
```

Your compiler may issue a warning about not overriding Equals. *This warning is there to remind you to keep* operator==, operator!= *and* Equals *in sync with each other, and this code* **is** *doing that but the compiler cannot figure that out.*

Note that as this pattern invokes method Equals on ValueType, this *will* cause boxing to occur as ValueType is a class.

If your type has values that are semantically equal but are represented differently, such as a type for fractions that allows both 1/3 and 4/12 to represent the same number, then you will need to define your own equality by overriding Equals and defining corresponding operator== and operator!= operators.

In all other cases, though the preceding code will always work, it will probably be more expensive than a hand-written method that compares the two struct values field by field. In particular, some compilers use reflection in their default implementation of Equals on value types, which is usually slow. However, if you do not call Equals very much, the savings in development time not defining Equals could easily outweigh any performance penalty—and you should never prematurely optimize...

14.9.1 Integer comparison operators

The predefined integer comparison operators are:

```
bool operator ==(int x, int y);
bool operator ==(uint x, uint y);
bool operator ==(long x, long y);
bool operator ==(ulong x, ulong y);
void operator ==(long x, ulong y);
void operator ==(ulong x, long y);

bool operator !=(int x, int y);
bool operator !=(uint x, uint y);
bool operator !=(long x, long y);
```

```
bool operator !=(ulong x, ulong y);
void operator !=(long x, ulong y);
void operator !=(ulong x, long y);

bool operator <(int x, int y);
bool operator <(uint x, uint y);
bool operator <(long x, long y);
bool operator <(ulong x, ulong y);
void operator <(long x, ulong y);
void operator >(ulong x, long y);

bool operator >(int x, int y);
bool operator >(uint x, uint y);
bool operator >(long x, long y);
bool operator >(ulong x, ulong y);
void operator >(long x, ulong y);
void operator >(ulong x, long y);

bool operator <=(int x, int y);
bool operator <=(uint x, uint y);
bool operator <=(long x, long y);
bool operator <=(ulong x, ulong y);
void operator <=(long x, ulong y);
void operator <=(ulong x, long y);

bool operator >=(int x, int y);
bool operator >=(uint x, uint y);
bool operator >=(long x, long y);
bool operator >=(ulong x, ulong y);
void operator >=(long x, ulong y);
void operator >=(ulong x, long y);
```

Each of these operators compares the numeric values of the two integer operands and returns a `bool` value that indicates whether the particular relation is `true` or `false`. The operators with `void` return type always produce a compile-time error. Consequently, it is an error for one operand to be of type `long` and the other to be of type `ulong`.

Lifted (§14.2.7) forms of the unlifted predefined integer comparison operators defined above are also predefined.

14.9.2 Floating-point comparison operators

The predefined floating-point comparison operators are:

```
bool operator ==(float x, float y);
bool operator ==(double x, double y);

bool operator !=(float x, float y);
bool operator !=(double x, double y);

bool operator <(float x, float y);
bool operator <(double x, double y);

bool operator >(float x, float y);
bool operator >(double x, double y);
```

```
bool operator <=(float x, float y);
bool operator <=(double x, double y);

bool operator >=(float x, float y);
bool operator >=(double x, double y);
```

The operators compare the operands according to the rules of the IEC 60559 standard:

If either operand is NaN, the result is `false` for all operators except `!=`, for which the result is `true`. For any two operands, `x != y` always produces the same result as `!(x == y)`. However, when one or both operands are NaN, the `<`, `>`, `<=`, and `>=` operators do *not* produce the same results as the logical negation of the opposite operator. [*Example*: If either of `x` and `y` is NaN, then `x < y` is `false`, but `!(x >= y)` is `true`. *end example*]

- When neither operand is NaN, the operators compare the values of the two floating-point operands with respect to the ordering

  $$-\infty < -max < \ldots < -min < -0.0 == +0.0 < +min < \ldots < +max < +\infty$$

  where `min` and `max` are the smallest and largest positive finite values that can be represented in the given floating-point format. Notable effects of this ordering are:
    - Negative and positive zeros are considered equal.
    - A negative infinity is considered less than all other values, but equal to another negative infinity.
    - A positive infinity is considered greater than all other values, but equal to another positive infinity.

Lifted (§14.2.7) forms of the unlifted predefined floating-point comparison operators defined above are also predefined.

NaNs may be equal

To conform to IEC 60559 arithmetics, the "`==`" operator returns `false` when applied to two NaNs. However, to conform to its equivalence contract (see annotation on §14.9) the `Equals` method returns `true`. For example, consider:

```
double zero = 0.0;
double nan = zero / zero;

bool b1 = nan == nan;        // evaluates to false
bool b2 = nan.Equals(nan);   // evaluates to true
```

That something is not equal even unto itself might be surprising, but such is IEC 60559 arithmetic. This is one of the exceedingly rare cases where the operator "`==`" and the `Equals` method should return different values.

Note: The IEC 60559 standard is probably better known as IEEE 754.

14.9.3 Decimal comparison operators

The predefined decimal comparison operators are:

```
bool operator ==(decimal x, decimal y);
bool operator !=(decimal x, decimal y);
```

```
bool operator < (decimal x, decimal y);
bool operator > (decimal x, decimal y);
bool operator <= (decimal x, decimal y);
bool operator >= (decimal x, decimal y);
```

Each of these operators compares the numeric values of the two decimal operands and returns a `bool` value that indicates whether the particular relation is `true` or `false`. Each decimal comparison is equivalent to using the corresponding relational or equality operator of type `System.Decimal`.

Lifted (§14.2.7) forms of the unlifted predefined decimal comparison operators defined above are also predefined.

14.9.4 Boolean equality operators

The predefined Boolean equality operators are:

```
bool operator == (bool x, bool y);
bool operator != (bool x, bool y);
```

The result of `==` is `true` if both `x` and `y` are `true` or if both `x` and `y` are `false`. Otherwise, the result is `false`.

The result of `!=` is `false` if both `x` and `y` are `true` or if both `x` and `y` are `false`. Otherwise, the result is `true`. When the operands are of type `bool`, the `!=` operator produces the same result as the `^` operator.

Lifted (§14.2.7) forms of the unlifted predefined Boolean equality operators defined above are also predefined.

14.9.5 Enumeration comparison operators

Every enumeration type implicitly provides the following predefined comparison operators:

```
bool operator == (E x, E y);
bool operator != (E x, E y);

bool operator < (E x, E y);
bool operator > (E x, E y);
bool operator <= (E x, E y);
bool operator >= (E x, E y);
```

The result of evaluating `x` *op* `y`, where `x` and `y` are expressions of an enumeration type `E` with an underlying type `U`, and *op* is one of the comparison operators, is exactly the same as evaluating `((U)x)` *op* `((U)y)`. In other words, the enumeration type comparison operators simply compare the underlying integral values of the two operands. These operators are only considered by overload resolution (§14.2.4) when one of the actual operands is of type `E`.

Lifted (§14.2.7) forms of the unlifted predefined enumeration comparison operators defined above are also predefined.

14.9.6 Reference type equality operators

Every class type `C` implicitly provides the following predefined reference type equality operators:

```
bool operator == (C x, C y);
bool operator != (C x, C y);
```

unless predefined equality operators otherwise exists for `C` (for example, when `C` is `string` or `System.Delegate`).

The operators return the result of comparing the two references for equality or non-equality.

There are special rules for determining when a reference type equality operator is applicable. For an *equality-expression* with operands of type A and B, define A_0 as follows:

- If A is a type parameter *known to be a reference type* (§25.7), let A_0 be the effective base class of A.
- Otherwise, if A is an interface type, a delegate type, an array type, a class type, or the `null` type (§11.2.7), let A_0 be the same as A.
- Otherwise, no reference type equality operator is applicable.

Specification mistake

The statement "Otherwise, no reference type equality operator is applicable" is wrong. Namely, A may be an unconstrained type parameter, and hence not known to be a reference type, yet the comparison `x==null` is legal as defined in the following bullet list (bullets two and three in the second bullet list).

The reason for this specification mistake is that it was decided very late in the Standard process to allow comparison between `null` and an expression whose type is an unconstrained type parameter. The bullets allowing this were added, but the corresponding change was not made here.

Now define A_1 as follows:

- If A_0 is an interface type, a delegate type, `System.Delegate`, or `string`, let A_1 be `object`.
- Otherwise, if A_0 is an array type, let A_1 be `System.Array`.
- Otherwise, A_0 is the `null` type or a class type and let A_1 be the same as A_0.

Define B_0 and B_1 in the same manner. Now determine if any reference type equality operators are applicable as follows:

- If both of the types A and B are the `null` type, then overload resolution is not performed and the result is a constant `true` or `false`, as specified in §14.9.
- Otherwise, if A is the null type, then the reference type equality operator for B_1 is applicable. If B is a type parameter and at runtime the type parameter is a non-nullable value type, the result of the operation is `false`. If B is a type parameter and at runtime the type parameter is a nullable type or reference type, the result is as if the operand of type B is boxed and then compared to `null`.
- Otherwise, if B is the null type, then the reference type equality operator for A_1 is applicable. If A is a type parameter and at runtime the type parameter is a non-nullable value type, the result of the operation is `false`. If A is a type parameter and at runtime the type parameter is a nullable type or reference type, the result is as if the operand of type A is boxed and then compared to `null`.

Boxing not required

In this and the previous bullet, the phrase "as if the operand … is boxed" does not require an implementation to actually box. If at runtime the type parameter is a nullable type, the value of its `HasValue` may be used to determine the result of the comparison. If at runtime the type parameter is a reference type, it may be compared directly with `null`.

- Otherwise, if either A or B is a type parameter that is not known to be a reference type (§25.7), then no reference type equality operator is applicable.
- Otherwise, if there is no identity or reference conversion (implicit or explicit) from A_0 to B_0 or no identity or reference conversion (implicit or explicit) from B_0 to A_0, then no reference type equality operator is applicable.
- Otherwise, if there is an identity or implicit reference conversion from A_1 to B_1, then the reference type equality operator for B_1 is applicable.
- Otherwise, if there is an implicit reference conversion from B_1 to A_1, then the reference type equality operator for A_1 is applicable.
- Otherwise, no reference type equality operator is applicable.

[*Note*: Notable implications of these rules are:

- The predefined reference type equality operators cannot be used to compare two references that are known to be different at compile-time. [*Example*: If the compile-time types of the operands are two class types A and B, and if neither A nor B derives from the other, then it would be impossible for the two operands to reference the same object and no reference type equality operator is applicable. Similarly, if A is a sealed class and B is an interface that A does not implement, then no reference type equality operator is applicable. *end example*]
- The predefined reference type equality operators do not permit value type operands to be compared.
- The predefined reference type equality operators never cause boxing operations to occur for their operands. It would be meaningless to perform such boxing operations, since references to the newly allocated boxed instances would necessarily differ from all other references.

end note]

When the operator overload resolution (§14.2.4) rules would pick an equality operator other than a reference type equality operator, selection of a reference type equality operator can be forced by explicitly casting one or both operands to type object. [*Example*: The example

```
using System;

class Test
{
  static void Main()
  {
    string s = "Test";
    string t = string.Copy(s);
    Console.WriteLine(s == t);
    Console.WriteLine((object)s == t);
    Console.WriteLine(s == (object)t);
    Console.WriteLine((object)s == (object)t);
  }
}
```

produces the output

```
True
False
False
False
```

The s and t variables refer to two distinct string instances containing the same characters. The first comparison outputs True because the predefined string equality operator (§14.9.7) is selected when both operands are of type string. The remaining comparisons all output False because a predefined reference type equality operator is selected when one or both of the operands are of type object.

Note that the above technique is not meaningful for value types. The example

```
class Test
{
  static void Main()
  {
    int i = 123;
    int j = 123;
    System.Console.WriteLine((object)i == (object)j);
  }
}
```

outputs False because the casts create references to two separate instances of boxed int values. *end example*]

14.9.7 String equality operators

The predefined string equality operators are:

```
bool operator ==(string x, string y);
bool operator !=(string x, string y);
```

Two string values are considered equal when one of the following is true:

- Both values are null.
- Both values are non-null references to string instances that have identical lengths and identical characters in each character position.

The string equality operators compare string values rather than string references. When two separate string instances contain the exact same sequence of characters, the values of the strings are equal, but the references are different. [*Note*: As described in §14.9.6, the reference type equality operators can be used to compare string references instead of string values. *end note*]

14.9.8 Delegate equality operators

Every delegate type implicitly provides the following predefined comparison operators, where D is the delegate type:

```
bool operator ==(D x, D y);
bool operator !=(D x, D y);
```

These operators are only considered by overload resolution (§14.2.4) when one of the actual operands is of type D.

The following predefined operators are available for comparing delegates when the delegate type is not known at compile time:

```
bool operator ==(System.Delegate x, System.Delegate y);
bool operator !=(System.Delegate x, System.Delegate y);
```

These latter operators are not considered applicable if the types of the operands are distinct delegate types. [*Example*:

```
delegate void D();
delegate void E();

static bool Compare1(D d, E e)
{
  return d == e;   // Error
}

static bool Compare2(System.Delegate d, E e)
{
  return d == e;   // Ok
}
```

The comparison in `Compare1` produces an error since the types of the operands are distinct delegate types. In this case, none of the delegate equality operators or reference equality operators is applicable since a non-null instance of `D` could never be equal to an instance of `E`. *end example*]

Two delegate instances are considered equal as follows:

- If either of the delegate instances is `null`, they are equal if and only if both are `null`.
- If the delegate instances have different runtime types, they are not equal.
- If both of the delegate instances have an invocation list (§22.1), those instances are equal if and only if their invocation lists are the same length, and each entry in one's invocation list is equal (as defined below) to the corresponding entry, in order, in the other's invocation list.

The following rules govern the equality of invocation list entries:

- If two invocation list entries both refer to the same static method then the entries are equal.
- If two invocation list entries both refer to the same non-static method on the same target object (as defined by the reference equality operators) then the entries are equal.
- Invocation list entries produced from evaluation of semantically identical *anonymous-method-expression*s with the same (possibly empty) set of captured outer variable instances are permitted (but not required) to be equal.
- Invocation list entries produced from evaluation of semantically different *anonymous-method-expression*s or having different sets of captured outer variable instances are never equal.
- An invocation list entry produced from evaluation of an *anonymous-method-expression* is never equal to an invocation list entry produced from a *delegate-creation-expression* on a method group.

Creating unique invocation list items

According to the preceding rules, one can create unique invocation list entries from a single *anonymous-method-expression*, provided each captures a distinct outer variable instance. Method `MakeUniqueVoidDelegate` is a factory of such unique (and effect-less) invocation list entries, as each call to `MakeUniqueVoidDelegate` will create a new instance of variable `captured`, which is then captured by the anonymous method expression:

```
static EventHandler MakeUniqueVoidDelegate()
{
    int captured = 42;
    return delegate { int dummy = captured; } ;
}
```

A plausible use of a unique invocation list entry is to keep an invocation list from ever becoming null after initialization (see annotation in §17.7.1). The idea is to initialize the invocation list with a unique entry and not hold any other reference to the unique entry, so that there is no way to remove it from the invocation list outside the class declaring the event field. Preferably, one should be able to perform the initialization at declaration, in a straightforward manner like this:

```
class Button
{
    public event EventHandler Click = new UniqueVoidDelegate();
    ...
}
```

Jon Jagger invented a very elegant way to do this. Define a public struct type UniqueVoidDelegate that has an implicit conversion from the struct type to a delegate of type EventHandler. Then the new expression will create a struct instance, and the assignment will call the implicit conversion method, which will create a unique invocation list item because the anonymous method expression captures the conversion's parameter:

```
public struct UniqueVoidDelegate
{
    public static implicit
        operator EventHandler(UniqueVoidDelegate captured)
    {
        return delegate { UniqueVoidDelegate dummy = captured; } ;
    }
}
```

Note how the simplicity of use is achieved by a combination of C# features (implicit conversion, anonymous delegates, outer variable instance capture, the rules for invocation list item equality).

14.9.9 Equality operators and nullable types

The == and != operators permit one operand to be a value of a nullable type and the other to have the null type (§11.2.7), even if no predefined or user-defined operator (in unlifted or lifted form) exists for the operation.

For an operation of one of the forms

```
x == null   null == x   x != null   null != x
```

where x is an expression of a nullable type, if operator overload resolution (§14.2.4) fails to find an applicable operator, the result is instead computed from the HasValue property of x. Specifically, the first two forms are translated into !x.HasValue, and last two forms are translated into x.HasValue.

14.9.10 is operator

The is operator is used to dynamically check if the run-time type of an object is compatible with a given type. The result of the operation e is T, where e is an expression and T is a type, is a

Boolean value indicating whether `e` can successfully be converted to type `T` by a reference conversion, a boxing conversion, an unboxing conversion, a wrapping conversion, or an unwrapping conversion. The operation is evaluated as follows:

- If the compile-time type of `e` is the same as `T`, or if an implicit reference conversion (§13.1.4), boxing conversion (§13.1.5), or wrapping conversion (§13.7) exists from the compile-time type of `e` to `T`:
    - If `e` is of a reference type, the result of the operation is equivalent to evaluating `e != null`.
    - If `e` is of a nullable type, the result of the operation is equivalent to evaluating `e != null`.
    - If `e` is of a value type, the result of the operation is `true`.
- Otherwise, if an unwrapping conversion (§13.7) exists from the compile-time type of `e` to `T`, the result of the operation is equivalent to evaluating `e != null`.
- Otherwise, if an explicit reference conversion (§13.2.3) or unboxing conversion (§13.2.4) exists from the compile-time type of `e` to `T`, a dynamic type check is performed:
    - If the value of `e` is `null`, the result is `false`.
    - Otherwise, if `T` is a nullable type, if the runtime type of `e` is the underlying type of `T`, the result is `true`.
    - Otherwise, let `R` be the run-time type of the instance referenced by `e`. If `R` and `T` are the same type, if `R` is a reference type and an implicit reference conversion from `R` to `T` exists, or if `R` is a value type and `T` is an interface type that is implemented by `R`, the result is `true`.
    - Otherwise, the result is `false`.
- Otherwise, if the compile-time type of `e` or `T` is an open type (§25.5.2), a dynamic type check is performed.
- Otherwise, no reference, boxing, wrapping, or unwrapping conversion of `e` to type `T` is possible, and the result of the operation is `false`.

The `is` operator only considers reference conversions, boxing conversions, and unboxing conversions. Other conversions, such as user defined conversions, are not considered by the `is` operator.

14.9.11 as operator

The `as` operator is used to explicitly convert a value to a given reference type or nullable type. When converting to a reference type, the `as` operator uses a reference conversion or a boxing conversion. When converting to a nullable type, the `as` operator uses a wrapping conversion, an unboxing conversion, or a null type conversion (§13.7.1). Unlike a cast expression (§14.6.6), the `as` operator never throws an exception. Instead, if the indicated conversion is not possible, the resulting value is `null`.

In an operation of the form `e as T`, `e` shall be an expression and `T` shall be a reference type, a type parameter that is known to be a reference type (§25.7), or a nullable type. The type of the result is `T`, and the result is always classified as a value. The operation is evaluated as follows:

- If the compile-time type of `e` is the same as `T`, the result is simply the value of `e`.
- Otherwise, if an implicit reference conversion (§13.1.4), boxing conversion (§13.1.5), wrapping conversion (§13.7), or null type conversion (§13.7.1) exists from the compile-time type of `e` to `T`, this conversion is performed and becomes the result of the operation.
- Otherwise, if an explicit reference conversion (§13.2.3) or unboxing conversion (§13.2.4) exists from the compile-time type of `e` to `T`, a dynamic type check is performed:

- o If the value of e is `null`, the result is the value `null` with the compile-time type T.
- o Otherwise, if T is a nullable type, let R be the run-time type of the instance referenced by e. If R is the underlying type of T, then the result is equivalent to unboxing the value given by e to the type T.
- o Otherwise, let R be the run-time type of the instance referenced by e. If R and T are the same type, if R is a reference type and an implicit reference conversion from R to T exists, or if R is a value type and T is an interface type that is implemented by R, the result is the reference given by e with the compile-time type T.
- o Otherwise, the result is the value `null` with the compile-time type T.
- • Otherwise, if the compile-time type of e or T is an open type (§25.5.2), a dynamic type check is performed.
- • Otherwise, the indicated conversion is never possible, and a compile-time error occurs.

The `as` operator only performs reference conversions, boxing conversions, unboxing conversions, and unwrapping conversions. Other conversions, such as user defined conversions, are not possible with the `as` operator and should instead be performed using cast expressions.

The `as` operator can be used with a type parameter T (§25.1.1) as the right-hand side only if T is known to be a reference type (§25.7). This restriction is required because the value `null` might be returned as a result of the operator. [*Example*:

```
class X
{
  public T F<T>(object o) where T: Attribute
  {
    return o as T;        // Ok, T has a class type constraint
  }

  public T G<T>(object o)
  {
    return o as T;        // Error, unconstrained T
  }
}
```

end example]

[*Note*: When constraints are factored in, there are situations where the compiler can conclude that the operation e as T will never succeed, for example, when e is a struct or sealed class that doesn't implement a particular interface, and T is constrained to require that interface. However, a complete specification of those situations is complicated, and the rules given above seem to be the best compromise. *end note*]

is and as ignore user-defined conversions

Note that the `is` (§14.9.10) operator and the `as` operator do *not* consider user-defined conversions (§13.4), not even those that convert between reference types. For example:

```
class One {}

class Two {}

class Three : Two
{
  public static explicit operator One(Three value)
```

```
    {
      return new One();
    }
  }

  class IsAndAs
  {
    static void Main()
    {
      Three third = new Three();

      bool isOne = third is One;      // false, user-defined conversion
                                      // not considered
      bool isTwo = third is Two;      // true

      //One first = third as One;     // compile-time error, user-defined
                                      // conversion not considered
      Two second = third as Two;      // ok

      One anotherOne = (One)third;    // ok, via user-defined conversion
    }
  }
```

See also the annotation in §17.9.3.

Jon Skeet

14.10 Logical operators

The &, ^, and | operators are called the logical operators.

> *and-expression:*
>   *equality-expression*
>   *and-expression*   &   *equality-expression*

> *exclusive-or-expression:*
>   *and-expression*
>   *exclusive-or-expression*   ^   *and-expression*

> *inclusive-or-expression:*
>   *exclusive-or-expression*
>   *inclusive-or-expression* | *exclusive-or-expression*

For an operation of the form x *op* y, where *op* is one of the logical operators, overload resolution (§14.2.4) is applied to select a specific operator implementation. The operands are converted to the parameter types of the selected operator, and the type of the result is the return type of the operator.

The predefined logical operators are described in the following subclauses.

14.10.1 Integer logical operators

The predefined integer logical operators are:

```
int operator &(int x, int y);
uint operator &(uint x, uint y);
long operator &(long x, long y);
ulong operator &(ulong x, ulong y);
void operator &(long x, ulong y);
void operator &(ulong x, long y);

int operator |(int x, int y);
uint operator |(uint x, uint y);
long operator |(long x, long y);
ulong operator |(ulong x, ulong y);
void operator |(long x, ulong y);
void operator |(ulong x, long y);

int operator ^(int x, int y);
uint operator ^(uint x, uint y);
long operator ^(long x, long y);
ulong operator ^(ulong x, ulong y);
void operator ^(long x, ulong y);
void operator ^(ulong x, long y);
```

The `&` operator computes the bitwise logical AND of the two operands, the `|` operator computes the bitwise logical OR of the two operands, and the `^` operator computes the bitwise logical exclusive OR of the two operands. No overflows are possible from these operations. The operators with `void` return type always produce a compile-time error. Consequently, it is an error for one operand to be of type `long` and the other to be of type `ulong`.

Lifted (§14.2.7) forms of the unlifted predefined integer logical operators defined above are also predefined.

Extra bits

Note that due to the behavior of implicit numeric conversions (§13.1.2) as explained under numeric promotions (§14.2.6), the logical operators may produce a result whose bit size is larger than either of the operands. For example, consider:

```
uint flagWord, updatedFlags;
int mask;
...
updatedFlags = flagWord & mask; // error, result is long not uint
```

The result of the bitwise-and of the two 32-bit operands (`int` and `uint`) is 64 bits (`long`). This might be surprising.

See also the annotation on §14.2.6 regarding the treatment of literals.

Bit buckets

Each of the integer logical operators provides two versions that do not return a value: namely those marked `void` in the preceding text. These uncallable operators should be ignored. For more details see the annotations on §14.2.6.

14.10.2 Enumeration logical operators

Every enumeration type `E` implicitly provides the following predefined logical operators:

```
E operator &(E x, E y);
E operator |(E x, E y);
E operator ^(E x, E y);
```

The result of evaluating x *op* y, where x and y are expressions of an enumeration type E with an underlying type U, and *op* is one of the logical operators, is exactly the same as evaluating (E) ((U)x *op* (U)y). In other words, the enumeration type logical operators simply perform the logical operation on the underlying type of the two operands. These operators are only considered by overload resolution (§14.2.4) when one of the actual operands is of type E.

Lifted (§14.2.7) forms of the unlifted predefined enumeration logical operators defined above are also predefined.

14.10.3 Boolean logical operators
The predefined Boolean logical operators are:

```
bool operator &(bool x, bool y);
bool operator |(bool x, bool y);
bool operator ^(bool x, bool y);
```

The result of x & y is true if both x and y are true. Otherwise, the result is false.

The result of x | y is true if either x or y is true. Otherwise, the result is false.

The result of x ^ y is true if x is true and y is false, or x is false and y is true. Otherwise, the result is false. When the operands are of type bool, the ^ operator computes the same result as the != operator.

Forgotten "long-circuiting" operators

Many C# programmers seem to be unaware of these & and | non-short-circuiting, or strict, versions of the && and || (§14.11) operators on bool operands. The & and | operators are best known as bitwise operators on integral operands.

When the short-circuit semantics of && (||) is *not* required, should one use & (|) instead? It is unlikely that the choice of one over the other has any impact on application performance. However, considering semantics, the recommendation is easy: In general, only use the short-circuiting versions if their semantics is *required* for correct operation.

Some find it ironic that the && operator (which has *two* characters) guarantees to evaluate only *one* operand whereas the & operator (which has *one* character) guarantees to evaluate *two* operands.

14.10.4 The bool? logical operators
The nullable Boolean type bool? can represent three values, true, false, and null, and is conceptually similar to the three-valued type used for Boolean expressions in SQL. To ensure that the results produced by the & and | operators for bool? operands are consistent with SQL's three-valued logic, the following predefined operators are provided:

```
bool? operator &(bool? x, bool? y);
bool? operator |(bool? x, bool? y);
```

The following table lists the results produced by these operators for all combinations of the values true, false, and null:

x	y	x & y	x | y
true	true	true	true
true	false	false	true
true	null	null	true
false	true	false	true
false	false	false	false
false	null	false	null
null	true	null	true
null	false	false	null
null	null	null	null

14.11 Conditional logical operators

The `&&` and `||` operators are called the conditional logical operators. They are also called the "short-circuiting" logical operators.

> *conditional-and-expression:*
>   *inclusive-or-expression*
>   *conditional-and-expression* `&&` *inclusive-or-expression*
>
> *conditional-or-expression:*
>   *conditional-and-expression*
>   *conditional-or-expression* `||` *conditional-and-expression*

The `&&` and `||` operators are conditional versions of the `&` and `|` operators:

- The operation x `&&` y corresponds to the operation x `&` y, except that y is evaluated only if x is `true`.
- The operation x `||` y corresponds to the operation x `|` y, except that y is evaluated only if x is `false`.

An operation of the form x `&&` y or x `||` y is processed by applying overload resolution (§14.2.4) as if the operation was written x `&` y or x `|` y. Then,

- If overload resolution fails to find a single best operator, or if overload resolution selects one of the predefined integer logical operators, a compile-time error occurs.
- Otherwise, if the selected operator is one of the predefined Boolean logical operators (§14.10.2), the operation is processed as described in §14.11.1.
- Otherwise, the selected operator is a user-defined operator, and the operation is processed as described in §14.11.2.

It is not possible to directly overload the conditional logical operators. However, because the conditional logical operators are evaluated in terms of the regular logical operators, overloads of the regular logical operators are, with certain restrictions, also considered overloads of the conditional logical operators. This is described further in §14.11.2.

14.11.1 Boolean conditional logical operators

When overload resolution (§14.2.4) for x `&` y or x `|` y selects the predefined Boolean `&` or `|` operator, then x `&&` y or x `||` y is processed as follows:

- The operation x && y is evaluated as `(bool)x ? (bool)y : false`. In other words, x is first evaluated and converted to type `bool`. Then, if x is `true`, y is evaluated and converted to type `bool`, and this becomes the result of the operation. Otherwise, the result of the operation is `false`.
- The operation x || y is evaluated as `(bool)x ? true : (bool)y` In other words, x is first evaluated and converted to type `bool`. Then, if x is `true`, the result of the operation is `true`. Otherwise, y is evaluated and converted to type `bool`, and this becomes the result of the operation.

14.11.2 User-defined conditional logical operators

When overload resolution (§14.2.4) for x & y or x | y selects a user defined & or | operator, then processing x && y or x || y requires that both of the following shall be true, where T is the type in which the selected operator is declared:

- The return type and the type of each parameter of the selected operator shall be T. In other words, the operator shall compute the logical AND or the logical OR of two operands of type T, and shall return a result of type T.
- T shall contain declarations of `operator true` and `operator false`.

A compile-time error occurs if either of these requirements is not satisfied. Otherwise, the && or || operation is evaluated by combining the user-defined `operator true` or `operator false` with the selected user-defined operator:

- The operation x && y is evaluated as `T.false((T)x) ? (T)x : T.&((T)x, y)` where `T.false((T)x)` is an invocation of the `operator false` declared in T, and `T.&((T)x, y)` is an invocation of the selected `operator &` In addition, the value `(T)x` shall only be evaluated once. In other words, x is first evaluated and converted to type T and `operator false` is invoked on the result to determine if x is definitely false. Then, if x is definitely false, the result of the operation is the value previously computed for x converted to type T. Otherwise, y is evaluated, and the selected `operator &` is invoked on the value previously computed for x converted to type T and the value computed for y to produce the result of the operation.
- The operation x || y is evaluated as `T.true((T)x) ? (T)x : T.|((T)x, y)`, where `T.true((T)x)` is an invocation of the `operator true` declared in T, and `T.|((T)x, y)` is an invocation of the selected `operator |`. In addition, the value `(T)x` shall only be evaluated once. In other words, x is first evaluated and converted to type T and `operator true` is invoked on the result to determine if x is definitely true. Then, if x is definitely true, the result of the operation is the value previously computed for x converted to type T. Otherwise, y is evaluated, and the selected `operator |` is invoked on the value previously computed for x converted to type T and the value computed for y to produce the result of the operation.

In either of these operations, the expression given by x is only evaluated once, and the expression given by y is either not evaluated or evaluated exactly once.

---

true/false overloading

I would suggest that the proportion of C# developers who are both aware of true/false operator overloading and also know when they are invoked is vanishingly small—to the extent that from a maintenance point of view, even those who do know about this area should not overload the operators due to the risk of confusing colleagues.

Jon Skeet

14.12 The null coalescing operator

The ?? operator is called the null coalescing operator.

> *null-coalescing-expression:*
>   *conditional-or-expression*
>   *conditional-or-expression* ??   *null-coalescing-expression*

A null coalescing expression of the form a ?? b requires a to be of a nullable type or reference type. If a is non-null, the result of a ?? b is a; otherwise, the result is b. The operation evaluates b only if a is null.

The null coalescing operator is right-associative, meaning that operations are grouped from right to left. *[Example*: An expression of the form a ?? b ?? c is evaluated as a ?? (b ?? c). In general terms, an expression of the form E_1 ?? E_2 ?? ... ?? E_N returns the first of the operands that is non-null, or null if all operands are null. *end example]*

The type of the expression a ?? b depends on which implicit conversions are available between the types of the operands. In order of preference, the type of a ?? b is A0, A, or B, where A is the type of a, B is the type of b, and A0 is the type that results from removing the trailing ? modifier, if any, from A. Specifically, a ?? b is processed as follows:

- If A is not a nullable type or a reference type, a compile-time error occurs.
- If A is a nullable type and an implicit conversion exists from b to A0, the result type is A0. At run-time, a is first evaluated. If a is not null, a is unwrapped to type A0, and this becomes the result. Otherwise, b is evaluated and converted to type A0, and this becomes the result.
- Otherwise, if an implicit conversion exists from b to A, the result type is A. At run-time, a is first evaluated. If a is not null, a becomes the result. Otherwise, b is evaluated and converted to type A, and this becomes the result.
- Otherwise, if an implicit conversion exists from A0 to B, the result type is B. At run-time, a is first evaluated. If a is not null, a is unwrapped to type A0 (unless A and A0 are the same type) and converted to type B, and this becomes the result. Otherwise, b is evaluated and becomes the result.

Otherwise, a and b are incompatible, and a compile-time error occurs.

Subtle interaction with implicit conversions

Peter Hallam discovered a subtle interaction between implicit conversions and the rule expressed by the fourth bullet in the preceding list. The problem is that an implicit conversion may turn a non-null A value into a null B, as in these declarations:

```
class A{}
class B
{
    public static implicit operator B(A a) { return null; }
}
```

Now consider this:

```
B b = null;
A a = new A();
B r = a ?? new B();    // r is null because of conversion!
```

Clearly, `a` is non-null, so the right-hand side of the (`??`) operator is not evaluated, but the non-null A value is converted into a null B value. Hence, somewhat surprisingly, the expression `e1 ?? e2` may evaluate to null without evaluating `e2`. This means that the so-called liberal rules for definite assignment in §12.3 are not sound.

Given the surprise, the committee looked into reformulating the fourth bullet to perform the implicit conversion from A to B *before* the null check. This would seem to cover the case where the implicit conversion results in a null.

However, Anders Hejlsberg produced the following counter-example to this approach:

```
int? iq = ...;
long longValue = 7L;
long result = iq ?? longValue;
```

Given the original fourth bullet, this compiles and the last line is equivalent to this one:

```
long result = iq.HasValue ? (long) iq.Value : longValue;
```

If the fourth bullet were revised to perform the conversion before the null check, for example,

- Otherwise, if an implicit conversion exists from A0 to B, the result type is B. At run-time, a is first evaluated, unwrapped to type A0 (unless A and A0 are the same type) and converted to type B, and if the resulting value is not null it becomes the result. Otherwise, b is evaluated and becomes the result.

Then the last line would be equivalent to this:

```
long result = (long) iq.Value ? (long) iq.Value : longValue;
```

Unfortunately, if `iq` is null, then `iq.Value` will throw an exception. So in attempting to fix one problem another has been introduced

The committee then went on to consider a final formulation, which performs the null test both before *and* after the implicit conversion if required:

- Otherwise, if an implicit conversion exists from A0 to B, the result type is B. At run-time, a is first evaluated. If a is not null, a is unwrapped to type A0 (unless A and A0 are the same type) and converted to type B, then:
  - o If B is a nullable type or a reference type and the resulting value is not null it becomes the result.
  - o Otherwise, if B is not a nullable type or a reference type the resulting value becomes the result.

  Otherwise, b is evaluated and becomes the result.

Using this formulation, our first code example would be equivalent to :

```
B b = null;
A a = new A();
B r = (a != null) && (((B)a) != null) ? (B)a : new B();
```

and the second to:

```
long result = iq.HasValue ? (long) iq.Value : longValue;
```

This final formulation appears to produce the intuitively correct result avoiding the, hopefully rare, surprising case, but at the cost of added complexity in the definition.

Due to the lateness the subtle issue was discovered, and the added complexity of the solution with little time available to check for other interactions it might introduce, the committee resolved to keep the original formulation of the fourth bullet.

14.13 Conditional operator

The ? : operator is called the conditional operator. It is at times also called the ternary operator.

> *conditional-expression:*
>   *null-coalescing-expression*
>   *null-coalescing-expression* ? *expression* : *expression*

A conditional expression of the form b ? x : y first evaluates the condition b. Then, if b is true, x is evaluated and becomes the result of the operation. Otherwise, y is evaluated and becomes the result of the operation. A conditional expression never evaluates both x and y.

The conditional operator is right-associative, meaning that operations are grouped from right to left. [*Example*: An expression of the form a ? b : c ? d : e is evaluated as a ? b : (c ? d : e). *end example*]

The first operand of the ? : operator shall be an expression of a type that can be implicitly converted to bool, or an expression of a type that implements operator true. If neither of these requirements is satisfied, a compile-time error occurs.

The second and third operands of the ? : operator control the type of the conditional expression. Let X and Y be the types of the second and third operands. Then,

- If X and Y are the same type, then this is the type of the conditional expression.
- Otherwise, if an implicit conversion (§13.1) exists from X to Y, but not from Y to X, then Y is the type of the conditional expression.
- Otherwise, if an implicit conversion (§13.1) exists from Y to X, but not from X to Y, then X is the type of the conditional expression.
- Otherwise, no expression type can be determined, and a compile-time error occurs.

The run-time processing of a conditional expression of the form b ? x : y consists of the following steps:

- First, b is evaluated, and the bool value of b is determined:
  - If an implicit conversion from the type of b to bool exists, then this implicit conversion is performed to produce a bool value.
  - Otherwise, the operator true defined by the type of b is invoked to produce a bool value.
- If the bool value produced by the step above is true, then x is evaluated and converted to the type of the conditional expression, and this becomes the result of the conditional expression.
- Otherwise, y is evaluated and converted to the type of the conditional expression, and this becomes the result of the conditional expression.

14.14 Assignment operators

The assignment operators assign a new value to a variable, a property, event, or an indexer element.

> *assignment:*
>   *unary-expression assignment-operator expression*
>
> *assignment-operator:* one of
>   =   +=   -=   *=   /=   %=   &= |=   ^=   <<=   *right-shift-assignment*

The left operand of an assignment shall be an expression classified as a variable, a property access, an indexer access, or an event access.

The = operator is called the ***simple assignment operator***. It assigns the value of the right operand to the variable, property, or indexer element given by the left operand. The left operand of the simple assignment operator shall not be an event access (except as described in §17.7.1). The simple assignment operator is described in §14.14.1.

The operators formed by prefixing an = character with a binary operator are called the ***compound assignment operators***. These operators perform the indicated operation on the two operands, and then assign the resulting value to the variable, property, or indexer element given by the left operand. The compound assignment operators are described in §14.14.2.

The += and -= operators with an event access expression as the left operand are called the ***event assignment operators***. No other assignment operator is valid with an event access as the left operand. The event assignment operators are described in 14.13.3.

The assignment operators are right-associative, meaning that operations are grouped from right to left. [*Example*: An expression of the form a = b = c is evaluated as a = (b = c). *end example*]

14.14.1 Simple assignment

The = operator is called the simple assignment operator. In a simple assignment, the right operand shall be an expression of a type that is implicitly convertible to the type of the left operand. The operation assigns the value of the right operand to the variable, property, or indexer element given by the left operand.

The result of a simple assignment expression is the value assigned to the left operand. The result has the same type as the left operand, and is always classified as a value.

If the left operand is a property or indexer access, the property or indexer shall have a set accessor. If this is not the case, a compile-time error occurs.

The run-time processing of a simple assignment of the form x = y consists of the following steps:

- If x is classified as a variable:
  - x is evaluated to produce the variable.
  - y is evaluated and, if required, converted to the type of x through an implicit conversion (§13.1).
  - If the variable given by x is an array element of a *reference-type*, a run-time check is performed to ensure that the value computed for y is compatible with the array instance of which x is an element. The check succeeds if y is null, or if an implicit reference conversion (§13.1.4) exists from the runtime type of the instance referenced by y to the actual element type of the array instance containing x. Otherwise, a System.ArrayTypeMismatchException is thrown.
  - The value resulting from the evaluation and conversion of y is stored into the location given by the evaluation of x.
- If x is classified as a property or indexer access:
  - The instance expression (if x is not static) and the argument list (if x is an indexer access) associated with x are evaluated, and the results are used in the subsequent set accessor invocation.
  - y is evaluated and, if required, converted to the type of x through an implicit conversion (§13.1).
  - The set accessor of x is invoked with the value computed for y as its value argument.

[*Note*: The array covariance rules (§19.5) permit a value of an array type A[ ] to be a reference to an instance of an array type B[ ] , provided an implicit reference conversion exists from B to A. Because of these rules, assignment to an array element of a *reference-type* requires a run-time check to ensure that the value being assigned is compatible with the array instance. In the example

```
string[] sa = new string[10];
object[] oa = sa;

oa[0] = null;              // Ok
oa[1] = "Hello";           // Ok
oa[2] = new ArrayList();   // ArrayTypeMismatchException
```

the last assignment causes a System.ArrayTypeMismatchException to be thrown because an instance of ArrayList cannot be stored in an element of a string[] . *end note*]

When a property or indexer declared in a *struct-type* is the target of an assignment, the instance expression associated with the property or indexer access shall be classified as a variable. If the instance expression is classified as a value, a compile-time error occurs. [*Note*: Because of §14.5.4, the same rule also applies to fields. *end note*]

[*Example*: Given the declarations:

```
struct Point
{
  int x, y;

  public Point(int x, int y)
  {
    this.x = x;
    this.y = y;
  }

  public int X
  {
    get { return x; }
    set { x = value; }
  }

  public int Y
  {
    get { return y; }
    set { y = value; }
  }
}

struct Rectangle
{
  Point a, b;

  public Rectangle(Point a, Point b)
  {
    this.a = a;
    this.b = b;
  }
```

```
public Point A
{
  get { return a; }
  set { a = value; }
}

public Point B
{
  get { return b; }
  set { b = value; }
}
}
```

in the example

```
Point p = new Point();
p.X = 100;
p.Y = 100;
Rectangle r = new Rectangle();
r.A = new Point(10, 10);
r.B = p;
```

the assignments to p.X, p.Y, r.A, and r.B are permitted because p and r are variables. However, in the example

```
Rectangle r = new Rectangle();
r.A.X = 10;
r.A.Y = 10;
r.B.X = 100;
r.B.Y = 100;
```

the assignments are all invalid, since r.A and r.B are not variables. *end example*]

14.14.2 Compound assignment

An operation of the form x *op*= y is processed by applying binary operator overload resolution (§14.2.4) as if the operation was written x *op* y. Then,

- If the return type of the selected operator is implicitly convertible to the type of x, the operation is evaluated as x = x *op* y, except that x is evaluated only once.
- Otherwise, if the selected operator is a predefined operator, if the return type of the selected operator is explicitly convertible to the type of x, and if y is implicitly convertible to the type of x *or the operator is a shift operator*, then the operation is evaluated as x = (T)(x *op* y), where T is the type of x, except that x is evaluated only once.
- Otherwise, the compound assignment is invalid, and a compile-time error occurs.

The term "evaluated only once" means that in the evaluation of x *op* y, the results of any constituent expressions of x are temporarily saved and then reused when performing the assignment to x. [*Example*: In the assignment A()[B()] += C(), where A is a method returning int[], and B and C are methods returning int, the methods are invoked only once, in the order A, B, C. *end example*]

When the left operand of a compound assignment is a property access or indexer access, the property or indexer shall have both a get accessor and a set accessor. If this is not the case, a compile-time error occurs.

The second rule above permits x *op*= y to be evaluated as x = (T) (x *op* y) in certain contexts. The rule exists such that the predefined operators can be used as compound operators when the left operand is of type `sbyte`, `byte`, `short`, `ushort`, or `char`. Even when both arguments are of one of those types, the predefined operators produce a result of type `int`, as described in §14.2.6.2. Thus, without a cast it would not be possible to assign the result to the left operand.

The intuitive effect of the rule for predefined operators is simply that x *op*= y is permitted if both of x *op* y and x = y are permitted. [*Example*: In the following code

```
byte b = 0;
char ch = '\0';
int i = 0;

b += 1;           // Ok
b += 1000;        // Error, b = 1000 not permitted
b += i;           // Error, b = i not permitted
b += (byte)i;     // Ok

ch += 1;          // Error, ch = 1 not permitted
ch += (char)1;    // Ok
```

the intuitive reason for each error is that a corresponding simple assignment would also have been an error. *end example*]

[*Note*: Compound assignment operations support lifted operators. Since a compound assignment x *op*= y is evaluated as either x = x *op* y or x = (T) (x *op* y), the rules of evaluation implicitly cover lifted operators. *end note*]

14.14.3 Event assignment

If the left operand of a += or -= operator is an event, the expression is classified as an event access, and is evaluated as follows:

- The instance expression, if any, of the event access is evaluated.
- The right operand of the += or -= operator is evaluated, and, if required, converted to the type of the left operand through an implicit conversion (13.1).
- An event accessor of the event is invoked, with argument list consisting of the value computed in the previous step. If the operator was +=, the `add` accessor is invoked; if the operator was -=, the `remove` accessor is invoked.

An event assignment expression does not yield a value. Thus, an event assignment expression is valid only in the context of a *statement-expression* (15.6).

14.15 Expression

An *expression* is either a *conditional-expression* or an *assignment*.

   expression:
     conditional-expression
     assignment

14.16 Constant expressions

A constant expression is an expression that shall be fully evaluated at compile-time. Where an expression is required to be constant this is indicated in the grammar by using *constant-expression*.

constant-expression:
  expression

> ### Expressions can be constant
> It is important to note that the grammar production *constant-expression* does not exclusively define where a "constant expression" may occur. Any occurrence of *expression* in the grammar may be a constant expression if the context allows a value.

The type of a constant expression can be one of the following: sbyte, byte, short, ushort, int, uint, long, ulong, char, float, double, decimal, bool, string, any enumeration type, or the null type (§11.2.7). The following constructs are permitted in constant expressions:

- Literals (including the null literal)
- References to const members of class and struct types.
- References to members of enumeration types.
- Parenthesized sub-expressions, which are themselves constant expressions.
- Cast expressions, provided the target type is one of the types listed above.
- The predefined checked and unchecked, +, −, !, and ~ unary operators.
- The predefined +, −, *, /, %, <<, >>, &, |, ^, &&, ||, ==, !=, <, >, <=, and >= binary operators, provided each operand is of a type listed above.
- The ? : conditional operator.
- sizeof expressions, provided the unmanaged-type is one of the types specified in §14.5.12.
- default value expressions, provided the type is one of the types listed above, or the type is a reference type or a type parameter that is known to be a reference type (§25.7).

The following conversions are permitted in constant expressions:

- Identity conversions
- Numeric conversions
- Enumeration conversions
- Constant expression conversions
- Implicit and explicit reference conversions, provided the source of the conversions is a constant expression that evaluates to the null value.

[*Note*: Other conversions including boxing, unboxing, and implicit reference conversions of non-null values are not permitted in constant expressions. *end note*]

[*Example*: In the following code

```
class C
{
  const object ival = 5;     // error: boxing conversion not permitted
  const object str = "hello"; // error: implicit reference conversion
}
```

the initialization of ival is an error because a boxing conversion is required. The initialization of str is an error because an implicit reference conversion from a non-null value is required. *end example*]

Whenever an *expression* is of one of the types listed above and contains only the constructs listed above, it is a constant expression and shall be evaluated at compile-time. This is true even if the expression is a sub-expression of a larger expression that contains non-constant constructs.

The compile-time evaluation of constant expressions uses the same rules as run-time evaluation of non-constant expressions, except that where run-time evaluation would have thrown an exception, compile-time evaluation causes a compile-time error to occur.

Compile time constant evaluation

The last two paragraphs mandate that constant expressions, whether they are instances of the productions *constant-expression* or *expression*, and including those which are part of larger expressions, **must be** evaluated at compile time. Also, any exceptions that result must be reported as compile-time errors. In some circumstances the result of this might be surprising. For example, consider the code fragment:

```
const int factor = 0;
int count;
...
if (factor != 0)
{
    ...
    count *= 5 / factor;
    ...
}
```

Both the expressions `factor != 0` and `5 / factor` must be evaluated at compile time. Therefore, compilation of this **must** produce a compile-time divide-by-zero error even though it can never occur at run-time.

This error might be even more surprising to some as their expectation might be that the body of the conditional would not be included in the compiled program once the comparison was determined at compile-time to be false. Indeed, both the current Microsoft and Mono compilers do remove the body in such circumstances. However, before deciding whether to remove the body, both compilers correctly check for and report the compile-time error.

If `factor` were not a `const`, this fragment would compile and run without a divide-by-zero error.

For a related issue, see the annotation on §13.1.7.

Unless a constant expression is explicitly placed in an `unchecked` context, overflows that occur in integral-type arithmetic operations and conversions during the compile-time evaluation of the expression always cause compile-time errors (§14.5.13).

Divide by zero always throws

The previous clause mentions overflow but *not* division by zero. This is because divide by zero is *always* checked, even if explicitly placed in a unchecked context (§14.5.13). For example:

```
const int a = 1;
const int b = 0;
int c = unchecked(a / b); // compile-time error

int a = 1;
int b = 0;
int c = unchecked(a / b); // runtime DivideByZeroException
```

Constant expressions are required in the contexts listed below and this is indicated in the grammar by using *constant-expression*. In these contexts, a compile-time error occurs if an expression cannot be fully evaluated at compile-time.

- Constant declarations (§17.3)
- Enumeration member declarations (§21.3)
- `case` labels of a `switch` statement (§15.7.2).
- `goto case` statements (§15.9.3)
- Dimension lengths in an array creation expression (§14.5.10.2) that includes an initializer.
- Attributes (§24)

An implicit constant expression conversion (§13.1.7) permits a constant expression of type `int` to be converted to `sbyte`, `byte`, `short`, `ushort`, `uint`, or `ulong`, provided the value of the constant expression is within the range of the destination type.

14.17 Boolean expressions

A *boolean-expression* is an expression that yields a result of type `bool`.

> *boolean-expression:*
> *expression*

The controlling conditional expression of an *if-statement* (§15.7.1), *while-statement* (§15.8.1), *do-statement* (§15.8.2), or *for-statement* (§15.8.3) is a *boolean-expression*. The controlling conditional expression of the `?` : operator (§14.13) follows the same rules as a *boolean-expression*, but for reasons of operator precedence is classified as a *null-coalescing-expression*.

A *boolean-expression* is required to be of a type that can be implicitly converted to `bool` or of a type that implements `operator true`. [*Note*: As required by §17.9.1, any type that implements `operator true` shall also implement `operator false`. *end note*] If neither requirement is satisfied, a compile-time error occurs.

When a Boolean expression is of a type that cannot be implicitly converted to `bool` but does implement `operator true`, then following evaluation of the expression, the `operator true` implementation provided by that type is invoked to produce a `bool` value.

15 Statements

C# provides a variety of statements. [*Note*: Most of these statements will be familiar to developers who have programmed in C and C++. *end note*]

> *statement:*
>   *labeled-statement*
>   *declaration-statement*
>   *embedded-statement*
>
> *embedded-statement:*
>   *block*
>   *empty-statement*
>   *expression-statement*
>   *selection-statement*
>   *iteration-statement*
>   *jump-statement*
>   *try-statement*
>   *checked-statement*
>   *unchecked-statement*
>   *lock-statement*
>   *using-statement*
>   *yield-statement*

The *embedded-statement* non-terminal is used for statements that appear within other statements. The use of *embedded-statement* rather than *statement* excludes the use of declaration statements and labeled statements in these contexts. [*Example*: The code

```
void F(bool b)
{
  if (b)
    int i = 44;
}
```

results in a compile-time error because an `if` statement requires an *embedded-statement* rather than a *statement* for its if branch. If this code were permitted, then the variable `i` would be declared, but it could never be used. (Note, however, that by placing `i`'s declaration in a block, the example is valid.) *end example*]

15.1 End points and reachability

Every statement has an ***end point***. In intuitive terms, the end point of a statement is the location that immediately follows the statement. The execution rules for composite statements (statements that contain embedded statements) specify the action that is taken when control reaches the end point of an embedded statement. [*Example*: When control reaches the end point of a statement in a block, control is transferred to the next statement in the block. *end example*]

If a statement can possibly be reached by execution, the statement is said to be ***reachable***. Conversely, if there is no possibility that a statement will be executed, the statement is said to be ***unreachable***.

[*Example*: In the following code

```
void F()
{
  Console.WriteLine("reachable");
  goto Label;
  Console.WriteLine("unreachable");
  Label:
  Console.WriteLine("reachable");
}
```

the second invocation of `Console.WriteLine` is unreachable because there is no possibility that the statement will be executed. *end example*]

A warning is reported if the compiler determines that a statement is unreachable. It is specifically not an error for a statement to be unreachable.

[*Note*: To determine whether a particular statement or end point is reachable, the compiler performs flow analysis according to the reachability rules defined for each statement. The flow analysis takes into account the values of constant expressions (§14.16) that control the behavior of statements, but the possible values of non-constant expressions are not considered. In other words, for purposes of control flow analysis, a non-constant expression of a given type is considered to have any possible value of that type.

Flow-analysis vs. unsigned types

Even though the value of a relational expression involving variables of unsigned types may be decidable at compile time, such an expression is not defined as a constant expression (§14.16), so flow analysis does not consider its value.

For example, given a variable x of any unsigned type, the expression x >= 0 always evaluates to `true`, and the expression x < 0 to `false`. However, flow-analysis does not take account of this as neither is a constant expression.

In the example

```
void F()
{
  const int i = 1;
  if (i == 2) Console.WriteLine("unreachable");
}
```

the Boolean expression of the `if` statement is a constant expression because both operands of the `==` operator are constants. As the constant expression is evaluated at compile-time, producing the value `false`, the `Console.WriteLine` invocation is considered unreachable. However, if i is changed to be a local variable

```
void F()
{
  int i = 1;
  if (i == 2) Console.WriteLine("reachable");
}
```

the `Console.WriteLine` invocation is considered reachable, even though, in reality, it will never be executed. *end note*]

The *block* of a function member is always considered reachable. The *block* of an *anonymous-method-expression* is always considered reachable. By successively evaluating the reachability rules of each statement in a block, the reachability of any given statement can be determined.

[*Example*: In the following code

```
void F(int x)
{
  Console.WriteLine("start");
  if (x < 0) Console.WriteLine("negative");
}
```

the reachability of the second `Console.WriteLine` is determined as follows:

- The first `Console.WriteLine` expression statement is reachable because the block of the F method is reachable (§15.2).
- The end point of the first `Console.WriteLine` expression statement is reachable because that statement is reachable (§15.6 and §15.2).
- The `if` statement is reachable because the end point of the first `Console.WriteLine` expression statement is reachable (§15.6 and §15.2).
- The second `Console.WriteLine` expression statement is reachable because the Boolean expression of the `if` statement does not have the constant value `false`.

end example]

There are two situations in which it is a compile-time error for the end point of a statement to be reachable:

- Because the `switch` statement does not permit a switch section to "fall through" to the next switch section, it is a compile-time error for the end point of the statement list of a switch section to be reachable. If this error occurs, it is typically an indication that a `break` statement is missing.
- It is a compile-time error for the end point of the block of a function member that computes a value to be reachable. If this error occurs, it typically is an indication that a `return` statement is missing.

15.2 Blocks

A *block* permits multiple statements to be written in contexts where a single statement is allowed.

> *block:*
> { *statement-list*_{opt} }

A *block* consists of an optional *statement-list* (§15.2.1), enclosed in braces. If the statement list is omitted, the block is said to be empty.

A block can contain declaration statements (§15.5). The scope of a local variable or constant declared in a block is the block.

Within a block, the meaning of a name used in an expression or declarator context shall always be the same (§14.5.2.1).

A block is executed as follows:

- If the block is empty, control is transferred to the end point of the block.
- If the block is not empty, control is transferred to the statement list. When and if control reaches the end point of the statement list, control is transferred to the end point of the block.

The statement list of a block is reachable if the block itself is reachable.

The end point of a block is reachable if the block is empty or if the end point of the statement list is reachable.

15.2.1 Statement lists

A ***statement list*** consists of one or more statements written in sequence. Statement lists occur in *blocks* (§15.2) and in *switch-blocks* (§15.7.2).

> *statement-list:*
>   *statement*
>   *statement-list   statement*

A statement list is executed by transferring control to the first statement. When and if control reaches the end point of a statement, control is transferred to the next statement. When and if control reaches the end point of the last statement, control is transferred to the end point of the statement list.

A statement in a statement list is reachable if at least one of the following is true:

- The statement is the first statement and the statement list itself is reachable.
- The end point of the preceding statement is reachable.
- The statement is a labeled statement and the label is referenced by a reachable `goto` statement.

The end point of a statement list is reachable if the end point of the last statement in the list is reachable.

15.3 The empty statement

An *empty-statement* does nothing.

> *empty-statement:*
>   *;*

An empty statement is used when there are no operations to perform in a context where a statement is required.

Execution of an empty statement simply transfers control to the end point of the statement. Thus, the end point of an empty statement is reachable if the empty statement is reachable.

[*Example*: An empty statement can be used when writing a `while` statement with a null body:

```
bool ProcessMessage() {...}

void ProcessMessages()
{
  while (ProcessMessage())
    ;
}
```

Also, an empty statement can be used to declare a label just before the closing "`}`" of a block:

```
void F()
{
  ...
  if (done) goto exit;
  ...
  exit: ;
}
```

end example]

15.4 Labeled statements

A *labeled-statement* permits a statement to be prefixed by a label. Labeled statements are permitted in blocks, but are not permitted as embedded statements.

> *labeled-statement:*
>   *identifier* : *statement*

A labeled statement declares a label with the name given by the *identifier*. The scope of a label is the whole block in which the label is declared, including any nested blocks. It is a compile-time error for two labels with the same name to have overlapping scopes.

A label can be referenced from `goto` statements (§15.9.3) within the scope of the label. [*Note*: This means that `goto` statements can transfer control within blocks and out of blocks, but never into blocks. *end note*]

Labels have their own declaration space and do not interfere with other identifiers. [*Example*: The example

```
int F(int x)
{
  if (x >= 0) goto x;
  x = -x;
  x: return x;
}
```

is valid and uses the name x as both a parameter and a label. *end example*]

Execution of a labeled statement corresponds exactly to execution of the statement following the label.

In addition to the reachability provided by normal flow of control, a labeled statement is reachable if the label is referenced by a reachable `goto` statement, unless the `goto` statement is inside a `try` that includes a `finally` block whose end point is unreachable, and the labeled statement is outside the `try`.

15.5 Declaration statements

A *declaration-statement* declares a local variable or constant. Declaration statements are permitted in blocks, but are not permitted as embedded statements.

> *declaration-statement:*
>   *local-variable-declaration* ;
>   *local-constant-declaration* ;

15.5.1 Local variable declarations

A *local-variable-declaration* declares one or more local variables.

> *local-variable-declaration:*
>   *type*   *local-variable-declarators*

> *local-variable-declarators:*
>   *local-variable-declarator*
>   *local-variable-declarators*   ,   *local-variable-declarator*

> *local-variable-declarator:*
>   *identifier*
>   *identifier*   =   *local-variable-initializer*

> *local-variable-initializer:*
>   *expression*
>   *array-initializer*

The *type* of a *local-variable-declaration* specifies the type of the variables introduced by the declaration. The type is followed by a list of *local-variable-declarator*s, each of which introduces a new variable. A *local-variable-declarator* consists of an *identifier* that names the variable, optionally followed by an "=" token and a *local-variable-initializer* that gives the initial value of the variable.

The value of a local variable is obtained in an expression using a *simple-name* (§14.5.2), and the value of a local variable is modified using an *assignment* (§14.14). A local variable shall be definitely assigned (§12.3) at each location where its value is obtained.

The scope of a local variable declared in a *local-variable-declaration* is the block in which the declaration occurs. It is an error to refer to a local variable in a textual position that precedes the *local-variable-declarator* of the local variable. Within the scope of a local variable, it is a compile-time error to declare another local variable or constant with the same name.

A local variable declaration that declares multiple variables is equivalent to multiple declarations of single variables with the same type. Furthermore, a variable initializer in a local variable declaration corresponds exactly to an assignment statement that is inserted immediately after the declaration.

[*Example*: The example

```
void F()
{
   int x = 1, y, z = x * 2;
}
```

corresponds exactly to

```
void F()
{
   int x; x = 1;
   int y;
   int z; z = x * 2;
}
```

end example]

15.5.2 Local constant declarations

A *local-constant-declaration* declares one or more local constants.

local-constant-declaration:
   `const` *type* *constant-declarators*

constant-declarators:
   constant-declarator
   constant-declarators , *constant-declarator*

constant-declarator:
   identifier = *constant-expression*

The *type* of a *local-constant-declaration* specifies the type of the constants introduced by the declaration. The type is followed by a list of *constant-declarator*s, each of which introduces a new constant. A *constant-declarator* consists of an *identifier* that names the constant, followed by an "=" token, followed by a *constant-expression* (§14.16) that gives the value of the constant.

The *type* and *constant-expression* of a local constant declaration shall follow the same rules as those of a constant member declaration (§17.3).

The value of a local constant is obtained in an expression using a *simple-name* (§14.5.2).

The scope of a local constant is the block in which the declaration occurs. It is an error to refer to a local constant in a textual position that precedes its *constant-declarator*. Within the scope of a local constant, it is a compile-time error to declare another local variable or constant with the same name.

A local constant declaration that declares multiple constants is equivalent to multiple declarations of single constants with the same type.

15.6 Expression statements

An *expression-statement* evaluates a given expression. The value computed by the expression, if any, is discarded.

expression-statement:
   statement-expression ;

statement-expression:
   invocation-expression
   object-creation-expression
   assignment
   post-increment-expression
   post-decrement-expression
   pre-increment-expression
   pre-decrement-expression

Not all expressions are permitted as statements. [*Note*: In particular, expressions such as x + y and x == 1, that merely compute a value (which will be discarded), are not permitted as statements. *end note*]

Execution of an expression statement evaluates the contained expression and then transfers control to the end point of the expression statement. The end point of an *expression-statement* is reachable if that *expression-statement* is reachable.

15.7 Selection statements

Selection statements select one of a number of possible statements for execution based on the value of some expression.

> *selection-statement:*
>   *if-statement*
>   *switch-statement*

15.7.1 The if statement

The `if` statement selects a statement for execution based on the value of a Boolean expression.

> *if-statement:*
>   if (*boolean-expression*) *embedded-statement*
>   if (*boolean-expression*) *embedded-statement* else *embedded-statement*

An `else` part is associated with the lexically nearest preceding `if` that is allowed by the syntax. [*Example*: Thus, an `if` statement of the form

```
if (x) if (y) F(); else G();
```

is equivalent to

```
if (x)
{
  if (y)
  {
    F();
  }
  else
  {
    G();
  }
}
```

end example]

An `if` statement is executed as follows:

- The *boolean-expression* (§14.17) is evaluated.
- If the Boolean expression yields `true`, control is transferred to the first embedded statement. When and if control reaches the end point of that statement, control is transferred to the end point of the `if` statement.
- If the Boolean expression yields `false` and if an `else` part is present, control is transferred to the second embedded statement. When and if control reaches the end point of that statement, control is transferred to the end point of the `if` statement.
- If the Boolean expression yields `false` and if an `else` part is not present, control is transferred to the end point of the `if` statement.

The first embedded statement of an `if` statement is reachable if the `if` statement is reachable and the Boolean expression does not have the constant value `false`.

The second embedded statement of an `if` statement, if present, is reachable if the `if` statement is reachable and the Boolean expression does not have the constant value `true`.

The end point of an `if` statement is reachable if the end point of at least one of its embedded statements is reachable. In addition, the end point of an `if` statement with no `else` part is reachable if the `if` statement is reachable and the Boolean expression does not have the constant value `true`.

15.7.2 The switch statement

The `switch` statement selects for execution a statement list having an associated switch label that corresponds to the value of the switch expression.

> *switch-statement:*
>   `switch` (*expression*) *switch-block*
>
> *switch-block:*
>   { *switch-sections$_{opt}$* }
>
> *switch-sections:*
>   *switch-section*
>   *switch-sections* *switch-section*
>
> *switch-section:*
>   *switch-labels* *statement-list*
>
> *switch-labels:*
>   *switch-label*
>   *switch-labels* *switch-label*
>
> *switch-label:*
>   `case` *constant-expression* :
>   `default` :

A *switch-statement* consists of the keyword `switch`, followed by a parenthesized expression (called the switch expression), followed by a *switch-block*. The *switch-block* consists of zero or more *switch-section*s, enclosed in braces. Each *switch-section* consists of one or more *switch-labels* followed by a *statement-list* (§15.2.1).

The ***governing type*** of a `switch` statement is established by the switch expression. If the type of the switch expression is `sbyte`, `byte`, `short`, `ushort`, `int`, `uint`, `long`, `ulong`, `char`, `string`, or an *enum-type*, then that is the governing type of the `switch` statement. Otherwise, exactly one user-defined implicit conversion operator (§13.4) shall exist from the type of the switch expression or a base type of this type to one of the following possible governing types: `sbyte`, `byte`, `short`, `ushort`, `int`, `uint`, `long`, `ulong`, `char`, `string`. If no such implicit conversion operator exists, or if more than one such implicit conversion operator exists, a compile-time error occurs.

> ### Switching on a string
>
> Switching on strings can be implemented efficiently in several ways.
>
> On the CLI, one can rely on string interning. The CLI keeps an internal hash table of string constants, and since the case labels are constants they are placed in the assembly metadata by the C# compiler and are interned by the CLI. To evaluate the switch, the governing expression is evaluated and the resulting string is interned, producing a reference. Then a sequence of fast reference comparisons suffices to select the correct branch. At the time of writing, this is approach taken by the Mono C# compiler.

The current Microsoft C# compiler takes another approach when compiling a switch statement with many branches: It builds a hash dictionary mapping the case labels to integers,
and then uses the standard implementation of dense integer switches to select the branch corresponding to that integer. Interestingly, this approach does not rely on CLI semantics.

Switching on nullables...

At the time of writing, the Microsoft C# 2.0 compiler accepts the following program, which
switches on a `char?`, a nullable type:

```
void SwitchOnNullable(char? value)
{
  switch (value)
  {
    case 'z':
      Console.WriteLine("z");
      break;
    case null:
      Console.WriteLine("null");
      break;
    default:
      Console.WriteLine("default");
      break;
  }
}

void DemoInvalidCode()
{
  SwitchOnNullable('z');   // selects the 'z' branch
  SwitchOnNullable(null);  // selects the null branch
  SwitchOnNullable('w');   // selects the default branch
}
```

The Standard does not support switching on nullables; for the preceding code to be compliant,
there would have to be an implicit conversion from `char?` to `char`, which there is not.

Unfortunately, the behavior is also nonconforming as it appears that no warning is ever issued
and the conformance requirements (§2) specify:

Conforming implementations are required to diagnose programs that use extensions that are
ill formed according to this International Standard. Having done so, however, they can compile
and execute such programs.

The Microsoft C# 2.0 compiler behavior is intentional, though documentation is sparse, and it
has emerged that Microsoft did intend to bring this to the Standardization Committee for consideration; however, by mistake this never happened. It is likely they will bring it in future, but
we cannot say when or what the outcome might be.

At the time of writing this annotation, the Mono C# compiler followed the Standard and
rejected the preceding program. However, see the following annotation written some time
later.

Unfortunately, due to the lack of a warning, a program may be unwittingly non-Standard.

> **Et tu, Mono?**
>
> The Mono C# compiler now also supports switching on nullables starting with version 1.1.16. We were not aware of this feature until someone submitted a bug report about it, but being compatible with Microsoft is very important to us.
>
> *Martin Baulig*

The constant expression of each `case` label shall denote a value of a type that is implicitly convertible (§13.1) to the governing type of the `switch` statement. A compile-time error occurs if two or more `case` labels in the same `switch` statement specify the same constant value.

There can be at most one `default` label in a switch statement.

A `switch` statement is executed as follows:

- The switch expression is evaluated and converted to the governing type.
- If one of the constants specified in a `case` label in the same `switch` statement is equal to the value of the switch expression, control is transferred to the statement list following the matched `case` label.
- If none of the constants specified in `case` labels in the same `switch` statement is equal to the value of the switch expression, and if a `default` label is present, control is transferred to the statement list following the `default` label.
- If none of the constants specified in `case` labels in the same `switch` statement is equal to the value of the switch expression, and if no `default` label is present, control is transferred to the end point of the `switch` statement.

If the end point of the statement list of a switch section is reachable, a compile-time error occurs. This is known as the "no fall through" rule. [*Example*: The example

```
switch (i)
{
case 0:
  CaseZero();
  break;
case 1:
  CaseOne();
  break;
default:
  CaseOthers();
  break;
}
```

is valid because no switch section has a reachable end point. Unlike C and C++, execution of a switch section is not permitted to "fall through" to the next switch section, and the example

```
switch (i)
{
case 0:
  CaseZero();
case 1:
  CaseZeroOrOne();
default:
  CaseAny();
}
```

results in a compile-time error. When execution of a switch section is to be followed by execution of another switch section, an explicit `goto case` or `goto default` statement shall be used:

```
switch (i)
{
case 0:
  CaseZero();
  goto case 1;
case 1:
  CaseZeroOrOne();
  goto default;
default:
  CaseAny();
  break;
}
```

end example]

Multiple labels are permitted in a *switch-section*. [*Example*: The example

```
switch (i)
{
case 0:
  CaseZero();
  break;
case 1:
  CaseOne();
  break;
case 2:
default:
  CaseTwo();
  break;
}
```

is valid. The example does not violate the "no fall through" rule because the labels `case 2:` and `default:` are part of the same *switch-section. end example*]

[*Note*: The "no fall through" rule prevents a common class of bugs that occur in C and C++ when `break` statements are accidentally omitted. In addition, because of this rule, the switch sections of a `switch` statement can be arbitrarily rearranged without affecting the behavior of the statement. For example, the sections of the `switch` statement above can be reversed without affecting the behavior of the statement:

```
switch (i)
{
default:
  CaseAny();
  break;
case 1:
  CaseZeroOrOne();
  goto default;
case 0:
  CaseZero();
  goto case 1;
}
```

end note]

Independent, within limits

The "no fall through" rule makes each switch section independent but it does *not* make it into a local declaration space. Therefore, the scope of a declaration in a switch section is the whole of the *switch-block*. However, the definite assignment status of a variable is determined independently for each switch section (§12.3.3.6).

In other statements, such as `if` and `while`, a body is often a *block* and hence a local declaration space.

The scope of declarations introduced in a switch section can be limited to just that section by enclosing it in braces, `{` and `}`, so that it becomes a *block*. For example, consider:

```
int x;
...
switch(x)
{
  case 1:
    int z;       // scope of z is whole of switch-block

    z = 4;
    ...
    break;
  case 2:
    {
      int w;     // scope of w is this switch section

      w = z;     // invalid, z not definitely assigned
      z = x;     // valid, z in scope
      ...
      break;
    }
  case 3:
    z = x;       // valid, z in scope
    w = x;       // invalid, w not in scope
    ...
    break;
  case 4:
    {
      ...
    }
    break;       // break must be inside switch block
                 // but can be outside block
}
```

[*Note*: The statement list of a switch section typically ends in a `break`, `goto case`, or `goto default` statement, but any construct that renders the end point of the statement list unreachable is permitted. For example, a `while` statement controlled by the Boolean expression `true` is known to never reach its end point. Likewise, a `throw` or `return` statement always transfers control elsewhere and never reaches its end point. Thus, the following example is valid:

```
switch (i)
{
case 0:
  while (true) F();
```

```
case 1:
  throw new ArgumentException();
case 2:
  return;
}
```

end note]

[*Example*: The governing type of a `switch` statement can be the type `string`. For example:

```
void DoCommand(string command)
{
  switch (command.ToLower())
  {
  case "run":
    DoRun();
    break;
  case "save":
    DoSave();
    break;
  case "quit":
    DoQuit();
    break;
  default:
    InvalidCommand(command);
    break;
  }
}
```

end example]

[*Note*: Like the string equality operators (§14.9.7), the `switch` statement is case sensitive and will execute a given switch section only if the switch expression string exactly matches a `case` label constant. *end note*]

When the governing type of a `switch` statement is `string`, the value `null` is permitted as a case label constant.

The *statement-list*s of a *switch-block* can contain declaration statements (§15.5). The scope of a local variable or constant declared in a switch block is the switch block.

Within a switch block, the meaning of a name used in an expression context shall always be the same (§14.5.2.1).

The statement list of a given switch section is reachable if the `switch` statement is reachable and at least one of the following is true:

- The switch expression is a non-constant value.
- The switch expression is a constant value that matches a `case` label in the switch section.
- The switch expression is a constant value that doesn't match any `case` label, and the switch section contains the `default` label.
- A switch label of the switch section is referenced by a reachable `goto case` or `goto default` statement.

The end point of a `switch` statement is reachable if at least one of the following is true:

- The `switch` statement contains a reachable `break` statement that exits the `switch` statement.

- The `switch` statement is reachable, the switch expression is a non-constant value, and no `default` label is present.
- The `switch` statement is reachable, the switch expression is a constant value that doesn't match any `case` label, and no `default` label is present.

Switch section reordering

Insisting that the end point of the statement list of a switch section is not reachable (even for the `default` section) allows the switch sections to be reordered easily and is an example of the C# design guideline that declaration order should not be significant.

Bad switch in a bad switch

On January 15, 1990, a bug in switching equipment caused millions of American citizens to lose their phone service. This bug was traced to a C code fragment exhibiting an inadvertent switch-case fall-though.

15.8 Iteration statements

Iteration statements repeatedly execute an embedded statement.

> *iteration-statement:*
>   *while-statement*
>   *do-statement*
>   *for-statement*
>   *foreach-statement*

15.8.1 The while statement

The `while` statement conditionally executes an embedded statement zero or more times.

> *while-statement:*
>   `while` (*boolean-expression*) *embedded-statement*

A `while` statement is executed as follows:

- The *boolean-expression* (§14.17) is evaluated.
- If the Boolean expression yields `true`, control is transferred to the embedded statement. When and if control reaches the end point of the embedded statement (possibly from execution of a `continue` statement), control is transferred to the beginning of the `while` statement.
- If the Boolean expression yields `false`, control is transferred to the end point of the `while` statement.

Within the embedded statement of a `while` statement, a `break` statement (§15.9.1) can be used to transfer control to the end point of the `while` statement (thus ending iteration of the embedded statement), and a `continue` statement (§15.9.2) can be used to transfer control to the end point of the embedded statement (thus performing another iteration of the `while` statement).

The embedded statement of a `while` statement is reachable if the `while` statement is reachable and the Boolean expression does not have the constant value `false`.

The end point of a `while` statement is reachable if at least one of the following is true:

- The `while` statement contains a reachable `break` statement that exits the `while` statement.
- The `while` statement is reachable and the Boolean expression does not have the constant value `true`.

15.8.2 The do statement

The `do` statement conditionally executes an embedded statement one or more times.

> *do-statement:*
>   do *embedded-statement* while (*boolean-expression*) ;

A `do` statement is executed as follows:

- Control is transferred to the embedded statement.
- When and if control reaches the end point of the embedded statement (possibly from execution of a `continue` statement), the *boolean-expression* (§14.17) is evaluated. If the Boolean expression yields `true`, control is transferred to the beginning of the `do` statement. Otherwise, control is transferred to the end point of the `do` statement.

Within the embedded statement of a `do` statement, a `break` statement (§15.9.1) can be used to transfer control to the end point of the `do` statement (thus ending iteration of the embedded statement), and a `continue` statement (§15.9.2) can be used to transfer control to the end point of the embedded statement (thus performing another iteration of the `do` statement).

The embedded statement of a `do` statement is reachable if the `do` statement is reachable.

The end point of a `do` statement is reachable if at least one of the following is true:

- The `do` statement contains a reachable `break` statement that exits the `do` statement.
- The end point of the embedded statement is reachable and the Boolean expression does not have the constant value `true`.

15.8.3 The for statement

The `for` statement evaluates a sequence of initialization expressions and then, while a condition is true, repeatedly executes an embedded statement and evaluates a sequence of iteration expressions.

> *for-statement:*
>   for (*for-initializer*$_{opt}$; *for-condition*$_{opt}$; *for-iterator*$_{opt}$)
>   *embedded-statement*
>
> *for-initializer:*
>   *local-variable-declaration*
>   *statement-expression-list*
>
> *for-condition:*
>   *boolean-expression*
>
> *for-iterator:*
>   *statement-expression-list*

```
statement-expression-list:
    statement-expression
    statement-expression-list  ,  statement-expression
```

The *for-initializer*, if present, consists of either a *local-variable-declaration* (§15.5.1) or a list of *statement-expression*s (§15.6) separated by commas. The scope of a local variable declared by a *for-initializer* starts at the *local-variable-declarator* for the variable and extends to the end of the embedded statement. The scope includes the *for-condition* and the *for-iterator*.

The *for-condition*, if present, shall be a *boolean-expression* (§14.17).

The *for-iterator*, if present, consists of a list of *statement-expression*s (§15.6) separated by commas.

A `for` statement is executed as follows:

- If a *for-initializer* is present, the variable initializers or statement expressions are executed in the order they are written. This step is only performed once.
- If a *for-condition* is present, it is evaluated.
- If the *for-condition* is not present or if the evaluation yields `true`, control is transferred to the embedded statement. When and if control reaches the end point of the embedded statement (possibly from execution of a `continue` statement), the expressions of the *for-iterator*, if any, are evaluated in sequence, and then another iteration is performed, starting with evaluation of the *for-condition* in the step above.
- If the *for-condition* is present and the evaluation yields `false`, control is transferred to the end point of the `for` statement.

Iteration count not fixed

Following languages such as C and Java, the C# definition of the `for` statement is very general and does not guarantee a fixed number of iterations. For example, consider:

```
for (int i = 0; i < 10; i++)
{
    Console.WriteLine(i);
    i += i % 2 == 0 ? 3 : -1;
}
```

This loop iterates just three times (with `i` being 0, 4, 8, and 12).

In fact, a `for` construct is just syntactic sugar for this `while` construct:

```
{
    for-initializer;
    while( for-condition )
    {
        embedded-statement;
        for-iterator
    }
}
```

Here the outermost block is to restrict the scope of any variables declared in the *for-initializer*.

The `for` statement is an interesting contrast to the `foreach` statement (§15.8.4); the latter disallows assignment to its controlling variable, yet changing it would not alter the number of iterations performed.

Unlike some languages (for example, Ada), C# does not provide any simple iteration construct that guarantees to loop exactly *n* times. However, by using a suitable collection type with the `foreach` statement (§15.8.4), a fixed iteration count loop can be realized. One approach is shown in §8.18.

Within the embedded statement of a `for` statement, a `break` statement (§15.9.1) can be used to transfer control to the end point of the `for` statement (thus ending iteration of the embedded statement), and a `continue` statement (§15.9.2) can be used to transfer control to the end point of the embedded statement (thus executing another iteration of the `for` statement).

The embedded statement of a `for` statement is reachable if one of the following is true:

- The `for` statement is reachable and no *for-condition* is present.
- The `for` statement is reachable and a *for-condition* is present and does not have the constant value `false`.

The end point of a `for` statement is reachable if at least one of the following is true:

- The `for` statement contains a reachable `break` statement that exits the `for` statement.
- The `for` statement is reachable and a *for-condition* is present and does not have the constant value `true`.

15.8.4 The foreach statement

The `foreach` statement enumerates the elements of a collection, executing an embedded statement for each element of the collection.

> *foreach-statement:*
>   `foreach` (*type identifier* `in` *expression*) *embedded-statement*

The *type* and *identifier* of a `foreach` statement declare the **iteration variable** of the statement. The iteration variable corresponds to a read-only local variable with a scope that extends over the embedded statement. During execution of a `foreach` statement, the iteration variable represents the collection element for which an iteration is currently being performed. A compile-time error occurs if the embedded statement attempts to modify the iteration variable (via assignment or the `++` and `--` operators) or pass the iteration variable as a `ref` or `out` parameter.

The compile-time processing of a foreach statement first determines the **collection type**, **enumerator type** and **element type** of the expression. This determination proceeds as follows:

- If the type `X` of *expression* is an array type then there is an implicit reference conversion from `X` to the `System.Collections.IEnumerable` interface (since `System.Array` implements this interface). The **collection type** is the `System.Collections.IEnumerable` interface, the **enumerator type** is the `System.Collections.IEnumerator` interface and the **element type** is the element type of the array type `X`.
- Otherwise, determine whether the type `X` has an appropriate `GetEnumerator` method:
  - Perform member lookup on the type `X` with identifier `GetEnumerator` and no type arguments. If the member lookup does not produce a match, or it produces an ambiguity, or produces a match that is not a method group, check for an enumerable interface as described below. It is recommended that a warning be issued if member lookup produces anything except a method group or no match.
  - Perform overload resolution using the resulting method group and an empty argument list. If overload resolution results in no applicable methods, results in an ambiguity, or results in a single best method but that method is either static or not public, check for an enumerable interface as described below. It is recommended that a warning be issued if overload resolution produces anything except an unambiguous public instance method or no applicable methods.
  - If the return type `E` of the `GetEnumerator` method is not a class, struct or interface type, an error is produced and no further steps are taken.

o   Member lookup is performed on E with the identifier `Current` and no type arguments. If the member lookup produces no match, the result is an error, or the result is anything except a public instance property that permits reading, an error is produced and no further steps are taken.

o   Member lookup is performed on E with the identifier `MoveNext` and no type arguments. If the member lookup produces no match, the result is an error, or the result is anything except a method group, an error is produced and no further steps are taken.

o   Overload resolution is performed on the method group with an empty argument list. If overload resolution results in no applicable methods, results in an ambiguity, or results in a single best method but that method is either static or not public, or its return type is not `bool`, an error is produced and no further steps are taken.

o   The **collection type** is X, the **enumerator type** is E, and the **element type** is the type of the `Current` property.

• Otherwise, check for an enumerable interface:

o   If there is exactly one type T such that there is an implicit conversion from X to the interface `System.Collections.Generic.IEnumerable<T>`, then the **collection type** is this interface, the **enumerator type** is the interface `System.Collections.Generic.IEnumerator<T>`, and the **element type** is T.

o   Otherwise, if there is more than one such type T, then an error is produced and no further steps are taken.

o   Otherwise, if there is an implicit conversion from X to the `System.Collections.IEnumerable` interface, then the **collection type** is this interface, the **enumerator type** is the interface `System.Collections.IEnumerator`, and the **element type** is `object`.

o   Otherwise, an error is produced and no further steps are taken.

GetEnumerator() selection

The preceding rules for selecting `GetEnumerator()` mean that any noninterface or implicit interface member will be selected in preference to an explicitly implemented interface member (§20.4.1). This behavior may be used by a type to provide one `GetEnumerator()`, which is used by the `foreach` statement and direct calls, and another that is used when the type is cast to `IEnumerable`/`IEnumerable<T>`. This might be done for efficiency (perceived, see annotations on §18).

For example, the CLI Standard Library class `System.Collections.Generic.Dictionary<TKey,TValue>` provides two methods:

```
public System.Collections.Generic.Dictionary.Enumerator
                                      GetEnumerator();


IEnumerator<KeyValuePair<TKey, TValue>>
      IEnumerable<KeyValuePair<TKey, TValue>>.GetEnumerator();
```

where `System.Collections.Generic.Dictionary.Enumerator` is a struct type; `IEnumerator<KeyValuePair<TKey, TValue>>` is, of course, a reference type.

The above steps, if successful, unambiguously produce a collection type C, enumerator type E and element type T. A foreach statement of the form

```
foreach (V v in x) embedded-statement
```

is then expanded to:

```
{
  E e = ((C)(x)).GetEnumerator();
  try
  {
    V v;
    while (e.MoveNext())
    {
      v = (V)(T)e.Current;
      embedded-statement
    }
  }
  finally
  {
    ... // Dispose e
  }
}
```

The variable e is not visible to or accessible to the expression x or the embedded statement or any other source code of the program. The variable v is read-only in the embedded statement. If there is not an explicit conversion (§13.2) from T (the element type) to V (the *type* in the foreach statement), an error is produced and no further steps are taken. [*Note*: If x has the value null, a System.NullReferenceException is thrown at run-time. *end note*]

Why is the iteration variable read-only?

The preceding expansion of foreach shows that allowing changes to the iteration variable (v) would not alter the number of iterations made, and each iteration would begin with the iteration variable correctly set to the next value. However, the iteration variable is read-only. Why?

This behavior is in contrast to the for statement (§15.8.4), where assignment to the loop variable does alter the iteration behavior and *is* allowed.

One explanation for the read-only semantics is that with the other three C# looping constructs, namely while (§15.8.1), do (§15.8.2), and for (§15.8.3), assignment to a variable controlling the iteration can alter the iteration count. However, given the expansion of foreach, assignment to the iteration variable would not alter the iteration count, so allowing such an assignment might be misleading.

Another plausible explanation is that when foreach is used to iterate over a collection such as an arraylist, one might be tempted to think that assignment to the iteration variable would replace the current item in the collection (which it does not).

It is interesting to note that other languages, for example, Ada, disallow assignment to the loop variable in for statements, while yet others, such as Java 1.5, allow assignment in foreach statements.

Subtle change due to anonymous methods

Before anonymous methods (§14.5.15) were added to C#, it did not matter whether the declaration (V v) was inside or outside the while loop. Indeed, the previous edition of the Standard had the declaration of v inside the loop, but that would not give the semantics that the designers intended for an anonymous method in the *embedded-statement* that captures variable v. The intended semantics were that each anonymous method created in the loop would capture the same instance of v, but with the declaration inside the loop each would capture a different instance. This would prevent the desirable optimization of allocating a single anonymous method object and sharing it among all iterations of the loop (see second annotation on §14.5.15).

When this was discovered, the declaration of v was moved outside the loop for this C# 2.0 standard. With anonymous methods, small differences matter. That this choice may not be the one expected by all developers is evidenced by Paolo Molaro's annotation on §14.5.15.3.1.

The body of the finally block is constructed according to the following steps:

- If there is an implicit conversion from E to the System.IDisposable interface, then the finally clause is expanded to the semantic equivalent of:

```
finally
{
   ((System.IDisposable)e).Dispose();
}
```

except that if e is a value type, or a type parameter instantiated to a value type, then the cast of e to System.IDisposable shall not cause boxing to occur.

- Otherwise, if E is a sealed type, the finally clause is expanded to an empty block:

```
finally
{
}
```

- Otherwise, the finally clause is expanded to:

```
finally
{
   System.IDisposable d = e as System.IDisposable;
   if (d != null) d.Dispose();
}
```

The local d is not visible to or accessible to any user code. In particular, it does not conflict with any other variable whose scope includes the finally block.

The order in which foreach traverses the elements of an array, is as follows: For single-dimensional arrays elements are traversed in increasing index order, starting with index 0 and ending with index Length − 1. For multi-dimensional arrays, elements are traversed such that the indices of the rightmost dimension are increased first, then the next left dimension, and so on to the left.

[*Example*: The following example prints out each value in a two-dimensional array, in element order:

```
using System;

class Test
{
  static void Main()
  {
    int[,] values =
    {
      {1, 2, 3, 4},
      {5, 6, 7, 8}
    };
```

```
      foreach (int elementValue in values)
        Console.Write("{0} ", elementValue);
      Console.WriteLine();
    }
  }
```

The output produced is as follows:

```
  1 2 3 4 5 6 7 8
```

end example]

Implications of MoveNext()

The order in which elements are processed by `foreach` derives from the behavior of `Move-Next()`. All the types in the Standard Library (both C# and CLI) enumerate in the obvious order. For example, a `string` is enumerated from the first to last character.

If `MoveNext()` throws an exception then the `foreach` will fail. Any `MoveNext()` from an `IEnumerator` or `IEnumerator<T>` instance *must*, according to the interface contract, throw an exception if the collection being enumerated is modified (elements being added, removed, or reordered). It is therefore not recommended to use the `foreach` statement on a collection that may be modified, by the current or another thread, before the statement completes.

However, both the Microsoft and Mono compilers current at the time of writing do *not* throw exceptions if an array being enumerated is modified and may not do so for some other types. This is nonconformant and should not be relied upon.

Iteration variable: read-only != readonly

The iteration variable corresponds to a read-only local variable. This is interesting because you cannot declare true `readonly` local variables, and read-only local variables appear to be treated differently from `readonly` fields. For example, calling a method on a `readonly` value type field causes the method to be called on a *copy* of the field (see annotation in §14.5.4). By contrast, this wording does not require such copying of the iteration variable, but it is unclear whether it would be wrong for an implementation to do so. The same question arises for the resource variable in a `using` statement (§15.13).

Neither the Microsoft implementation nor the Mono implementation of C# creates a copy when calling a method on a read-only value type iteration variable. Therefore, they treat read-only iteration variables and `readonly` fields differently, as illustrated by this program:

```
struct S
{
  public S(int value)
  {
    this.value = value;
  }

  public override string ToString()
  {
    return value.ToString();
  }

  public void Assign(S rhs)
  {
```

```
      this = rhs;
    }

    private int value;
}

class Eg
{
  public static readonly S field = new S();

  public static void Main()
  {
    foreach (S s in new S[ 1] )
    {
      System.Console.WriteLine(s);  // 0
      s.Assign(new S(42));
      System.Console.WriteLine(s);  // 42
    }

    System.Console.WriteLine(field); // 0
    field.Assign(new S(42));
    System.Console.WriteLine(field); // 0
  }
}
```

The lack of clarity in the Standard on this issue is unfortunate.

15.9 Jump statements

Jump statements unconditionally transfer control.

jump-statement:
  break-statement
  continue-statement
  goto-statement
  return-statement
  throw-statement

The location to which a jump statement transfers control is called the ***target*** of the jump statement.

When a jump statement occurs within a block, and the target of that jump statement is outside that block, the jump statement is said to ***exit*** the block. While a jump statement can transfer control out of a block, it can never transfer control into a block.

Execution of jump statements is complicated by the presence of intervening `try` statements. In the absence of such `try` statements, a jump statement unconditionally transfers control from the jump statement to its target. In the presence of such intervening `try` statements, execution is more complex. If the jump statement exits one or more `try` blocks with associated `finally` blocks, control is initially transferred to the `finally` block of the innermost `try` statement. When and if control reaches the end point of a `finally` block, control is transferred to the `finally` block of the next enclosing `try` statement. This process is repeated until the `finally` blocks of all intervening `try` statements have been executed.

[*Example*: In the following code

```
using System;

class Test
{
  static void Main()
  {
    while (true)
    {
      try
      {
        try
        {
          Console.WriteLine("Before break");
          break;
        }
        finally
        {
          Console.WriteLine("Innermost finally block");
        }
      }
      finally
      {
        Console.WriteLine("Outermost finally block");
      }
      Console.WriteLine("After break");
    }
  }
}
```

the finally blocks associated with two try statements are executed before control is transferred to the target of the jump statement.

The output produced is as follows:

```
Before break
Innermost finally block
Outermost finally block
After break
```

end example]

15.9.1 The break statement

The breakstatement exits the nearest enclosing switch, while, do, for, or foreach statement.

> *break-statement:*
>   break   ;

The target of a break statement is the end point of the nearest enclosing switch, while, do, for, or foreach statement. If a break statement is not enclosed by a switch, while, do, for, or foreach statement, a compile-time error occurs.

When multiple switch, while, do, for, or foreach statements are nested within each other, a break statement applies only to the innermost statement. To transfer control across multiple nesting levels, a goto statement (§15.9.3) shall be used.

A break statement cannot exit a finally block (§15.10). When a break statement occurs within a finally block, the target of the break statement shall be within the same finally block; otherwise a compile-time error occurs.

A break statement is executed as follows:

- If the break statement exits one or more try blocks with associated finally blocks, control is initially transferred to the finally block of the innermost try statement. When and if control reaches the end point of a finally block, control is transferred to the finally block of the next enclosing try statement. This process is repeated until the finally blocks of all intervening try statements have been executed.
- Control is transferred to the target of the break statement.

Because a break statement unconditionally transfers control elsewhere, the end point of a break statement is never reachable.

15.9.2 The continue statement

The continue statement starts a new iteration of the nearest enclosing while, do, for, or foreach statement.

> *continue-statement:*
>   continue ;

The target of a continue statement is the end point of the embedded statement of the nearest enclosing while, do, for, or foreach statement. If a continue statement is not enclosed by a while, do, for, or foreach statement, a compile-time error occurs.

When multiple while, do, for, or foreach statements are nested within each other, a continue statement applies only to the innermost statement. To transfer control across multiple nesting levels, a goto statement (§15.9.3) shall be used.

A continue statement cannot exit a finally block (§15.10). When a continue statement occurs within a finally block, the target of the continue statement shall be within the same finally block; otherwise a compile-time error occurs.

A continue statement is executed as follows:

- If the continue statement exits one or more try blocks with associated finally blocks, control is initially transferred to the finally block of the innermost try statement. When and if control reaches the end point of a finally block, control is transferred to the finally block of the next enclosing try statement. This process is repeated until the finally blocks of all intervening try statements have been executed.
- Control is transferred to the target of the continue statement.

Because a continue statement unconditionally transfers control elsewhere, the end point of a continue statement is never reachable.

15.9.3 The goto statement

The goto statement transfers control to a statement that is marked by a label.

> *goto-statement:*
>   goto *identifier* ;
>   goto case *constant-expression* ;
>   goto default ;

The target of a `goto` *identifier* statement is the labeled statement with the given label. If a label with the given name does not exist in the current function member, or if the `goto` statement is not within the scope of the label, a compile-time error occurs. [*Note:* This rule permits the use of a `goto` statement to transfer control *out of* a nested scope, but not *into* a nested scope. In the example

```
using System;

class Test
{
  static void Main(string[ ] args)
  {
    string[,] table =
    {
      {"red", "blue", "green"},
      {"Monday", "Wednesday", "Friday"}
    };

    foreach (string str in args)
    {
      int row, colm;
      for (row = 0; row <= 1; ++row)
        for (colm = 0; colm <= 2; ++colm)
          if (str == table[row,colm] )
            goto done;

      Console.WriteLine("{0} not found", str);
      continue;
    done:
      Console.WriteLine("Found {0} at [{1}][{2}] ", str, row, colm);
    }
  }
}
```

a `goto` statement is used to transfer control out of a nested scope. *end note*]

The target of a `goto case` statement is the statement list in the immediately enclosing switch statement (§15.7.2) which contains a `case` label with the given constant value. If the `goto case` statement is not enclosed by a `switch` statement, if the *constant-expression* is not implicitly convertible (§13.1) to the governing type of the nearest enclosing `switch` statement, or if the nearest enclosing `switch` statement does not contain a `case` label with the given constant value, a compile-time error occurs.

The target of a `goto default` statement is the statement list in the immediately enclosing switch statement (§15.7.2), which contains a `default` label. If the `goto default` statement is not enclosed by a `switch` statement, or if the nearest enclosing `switch` statement does not contain a `default` label, a compile-time error occurs.

A `goto` statement cannot exit a `finally` block (§15.10). When a `goto` statement occurs within a `finally` block, the target of the `goto` statement shall be within the same `finally` block, or otherwise a compile-time error occurs.

A `goto` statement is executed as follows:

- If the `goto` statement exits one or more `try` blocks with associated `finally` blocks, control is initially transferred to the `finally` block of the innermost `try` statement. When and if control reaches the end point of a `finally` block, control is transferred to the `finally` block of the next enclosing `try` statement. This process is repeated until the `finally` blocks of all intervening `try` statements have been executed.

- Control is transferred to the target of the `goto` statement.

Because a `goto` statement unconditionally transfers control elsewhere, the end point of a `goto` statement is never reachable.

15.9.4 The return statement

The `return` statement returns control to the caller of the function member in which the `return` statement appears.

> *return-statement:*
>   return *expression$_{opt}$*   ;

A `return` statement with no expression can be used only in a function member that does not compute a value; that is, a method with the return type `void`, the `set` accessor of a property or indexer, the add and remove accessors of an event, an instance constructor, static constructor, or a finalizer.

A `return` statement with an expression can only be used in a function member that computes a value, that is, a method with a non-void return type, the `get` accessor of a property or indexer, or a user-defined operator. An implicit conversion (§13.1) shall exist from the type of the expression to the return type of the containing function member.

It is a compile-time error for a `return` statement to appear in a `finally` block (§15.10).

A `return` statement is executed as follows:

- If the `return` statement specifies an expression, the expression is evaluated and the resulting value is converted to the return type of the containing function member by an implicit conversion. The result of the conversion becomes the value returned to the caller.
- If the `return` statement is enclosed by one or more `try` blocks with associated `finally` blocks, control is initially transferred to the `finally` block of the innermost `try` statement. When and if control reaches the end point of a `finally` block, control is transferred to the `finally` block of the next enclosing `try` statement. This process is repeated until the `finally` blocks of all enclosing `try` statements have been executed.
- Control is returned to the caller of the containing function member.

Because a `return` statement unconditionally transfers control elsewhere, the end point of a `return` statement is never reachable.

15.9.5 The throw statement

The `throw` statement throws an exception.

> *throw-statement:*
>   throw *expression$_{opt}$*   ;

A `throw` statement with an expression throws the value produced by evaluating the expression. The expression shall denote a value of the class type `System.Exception` or of a class type that derives from `System.Exception`. If evaluation of the expression produces `null`, a `System.NullReferenceException` is thrown instead.

null → NullReferenceException

As a consequence of the preceding rule, a thrown exception is always non-null. Hence, a C#-generated exception caught by `catch` is also always non-null. This is exactly as in the Java programming language.

Plug-in style exception handling

The ability to rethrow an exception means common exception handling functionality can be captured in a method and reused just like any other common piece of code. Many programmers seem to be unaware of this possibility. For example:

```
using System;

public delegate void Action();
public delegate void ExceptionHandler(Exception error);

public class Demo
{
   ...
  private void Execute(Action action, ExceptionHandler handler)
  {
    try
    {
      action();
    }
    catch (Exception error)
    {
      handler(error);
    }
  }

  private void ManagedExceptionHandler(Exception error)
  {
    if (error is SpecificException)
    {
      // reusable specific error handling code
      // that would otherwise have to be
      // repeated in each catch handler
    }
    else
    {
      throw error;
    }
  }
}
```

The `throw` statement can be used with an expression whose type is given by a type parameter (§25.1.1) only if that type parameter has `System.Exception` (or a subclass thereof) as its effective base class (§25.7).

A `throw` statement with no expression can be used only in a `catch` block, in which case, that statement re-throws the exception that is currently being handled by that `catch` block.

Because a `throw` statement unconditionally transfers control elsewhere, the end point of a `throw` statement is never reachable.

When an exception is thrown, control is transferred to the first `catch` clause in an enclosing `try` statement that can handle the exception. The process that takes place from the point of the exception being thrown to the point of transferring control to a suitable exception handler is known as **exception propagation**. Propagation of an exception consists of repeatedly evaluating the following steps until a `catch` clause that matches the exception is found. In this description, the **throw point** is initially the location at which the exception is thrown.

- In the current function member, each `try` statement that encloses the throw point is examined. For each statement S, starting with the innermost `try` statement and ending with the outermost `try` statement, the following steps are evaluated:
    - If the `try` block of S encloses the throw point and if S has one or more `catch` clauses, the `catch` clauses are examined in order of appearance to locate a suitable handler for the exception. The first `catch` clause that specifies the exception type or a base type of the exception type is considered a match. A general `catch` (§15.10) clause is considered a match for any exception type. If a matching `catch` clause is located, the exception propagation is completed by transferring control to the block of that `catch` clause.
    - Otherwise, if the `try` block or a `catch` block of S encloses the throw point and if S has a `finally` block, control is transferred to the `finally` block. If the `finally` block throws another exception, processing of the current exception is terminated. Otherwise, when control reaches the end point of the `finally` block, processing of the current exception is continued.
- If an exception handler was not located in the current function member invocation, the function member invocation is terminated. The steps above are then repeated for the caller of the function member with a throw point corresponding to the statement from which the function member was invoked.
- If the exception processing terminates all function member invocations in the current thread, indicating that the thread has no handler for the exception, then the thread is itself terminated. The impact of such termination is implementation-defined.

Spot the difference

Note: This annotation discusses something that is not part of Standard C#—the exception stack trace—and applies to code executed using the current Microsoft and Mono C# systems. However, we expect the issue will be of interest to many readers.

What is the difference between these two code fragments?

```
catch (Exception caught)
{
  ...
  throw caught;
}


catch (Exception)
{
  ...
```

```
    throw;
  }
```

The answer is that currently on the CLR (but not on Mono):

- `throw caught`: This drops the original stack trace associated with exception object referred to by caught and creates a brand new stack trace rooted at the throw statement.
- `throw`: The original stack trace remains in place.

15.10 The try statement

The `try` statement provides a mechanism for catching exceptions that occur during execution of a block. Furthermore, the `try` statement provides the ability to specify a block of code that is always executed when control leaves the `try` statement.

try-statement:
  `try` *block* *catch-clauses*
  `try` *block* *catch-clauses$_{opt}$* *finally-clause*

catch-clauses:
  specific-catch-clauses
  specific-catch-clauses$_{opt}$ *general-catch-clause*

specific-catch-clauses:
  specific-catch-clause
  specific-catch-clauses *specific-catch-clause*

specific-catch-clause:
  `catch` (*class-type* *identifier$_{opt}$*) *block*

general-catch-clause:
  `catch` *block*

finally-clause:
  `finally` *block*

There are three possible forms of `try` statements:

- A `try` block followed by one or more `catch` blocks.
- A `try` block followed by a `finally` block.
- A `try` block followed by one or more `catch` blocks followed by a `finally` block.

When a `catch` clause specifies a *class-type*, the type shall be `System.Exception` or a type that derives from `System.Exception`.

When a `catch` clause specifies both a *class-type* and an *identifier*, an **exception variable** of the given name and type is declared. The exception variable corresponds to a local variable with a scope that extends over the `catch` block. During execution of the `catch` block, the exception variable represents the exception currently being handled. For purposes of definite assignment checking, the exception variable is considered definitely assigned in its entire scope.

Unless a `catch` clause includes an exception variable name, it is impossible to access the exception object in the `catch` block.

The type named in a catch clause can be a type parameter only if that type parameter (§25.1.1) has `System.Exception` (or a subclass thereof) as its effective base class (§25.7).

A `catch` clause that specifies neither an exception type nor an exception variable name is called a general `catch` clause. A `try` statement can only have one general `catch` clause, and, if one is present, it shall be the last `catch` clause.

[*Note*: Some environments, especially those supporting multiple languages, might support exceptions that are not representable as an object derived from `System.Exception`, although such an exception could never be generated by C# code. In such an environment, a general catch clause might be used to catch such an exception. Thus, a general catch clause is semantically different from one that specifies the type `System.Exception`, in that the former might also catch exceptions from other languages. *end note*]

Possible security vulnerability

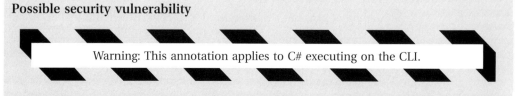

Warning: This annotation applies to C# executing on the CLI.

Many C# programmers appear to be unaware of the `catch { ...}` syntax, probably because they assume `catch (Exception error) { ...}` will catch everything. However, the CLI is one of the environments mentioned in the preceding note. Calling code written in other languages, or interop into unmanaged code, might result in an exception not derived from `System.Exception`. A programmer unaware of this can introduce a security vulnerability:

```
try
{
  ...
}
catch (Exception error)
{
  // Cleanup code. Could result in security issue if not run.
  // Ooops. What if the exception does not derive from System.Exception...
  // Should use a general catch { ...} clause
}
```

To help address this, CLR 2.0 and Mono (but not Standard CLI) will optionally wrap all thrown objects that do not derive from `System.Exception` inside a new exception type that does: `System.Runtime.CompilerServices.RuntimeWrappedException`.

By default, the Microsoft and Mono C# compilers opt into the new wrapped exception model.

```
try
{
  ...
}
catch (Exception error)
{
  ...
}
catch
{
  // new compiler warning emitted, as this is now unreachable code
}
```

On the CLR and Mono you can control this behavior at a per-assembly level using `System.Runtime.CompilerServices.RuntimeCompatibilityAttribute`.

In order to locate a handler for an exception, `catch` clauses are examined in lexical order. A compile-time error occurs if a `catch` clause specifies a type that is the same as, or is derived from, a type that was specified in an earlier `catch` clause for the same `try`. [*Note*: Without this restriction, it would be possible to write unreachable `catch` clauses. *end note*]

Within a `catch` block, a `throw` statement (§15.9.5) with no expression can be used to re-throw the exception that was caught by the `catch` block. Assignments to an exception variable do not alter the exception that is re-thrown.

Variety is the spice of life

People have asked why the variable introduced in a catch clause is not read-only. After all, the variables introduced by `foreach` (§15.8.4) and `using` (§15.13) statements are.

Just as the iteration variable in `foreach` is read-only because it dispels any doubt whether the items of a collection can be updated by assigning to that variable, it could be a good idea to make the exception variable read-only to dispel any doubt about which exception is thrown by the rethrow statement `throw;` (15.9.5) after an assignment to the exception variable. In a similar vein, there is no fixed count iteration statement and the variable in the `for` (§15.8.3) is assignable, which is not so in every language.

In short, C# is inconsistent, but then who is not occasionally?

Why is the exception variable name optional?

The names of method parameters are compulsory, yet the name of the exception variable is optional. One reason for this is the ability to rethrow an exception:

```
catch (Exception)
{
    //recover local resources
    throw;
}
```

Forcing the exception variable to be named in this case would result in an unused variable warning.

[*Example*: In the following code

```
using System;

class Test
{
  static void F()
  {
    try
    {
      G();
    }
    catch (Exception e)
    {
      Console.WriteLine("Exception in F: " + e.Message);
      e = new Exception("F");
      throw;        // re-throw
    }
  }
}
```

```
static void G()
{
  throw new Exception("G");
}

static void Main()
{
  try
  {
    F();
  }
  catch (Exception e)
  {
    Console.WriteLine("Exception in Main: " + e.Message);
  }
}
}
```

the method F catches an exception, writes some diagnostic information to the console, alters the exception variable, and re-throws the exception. The exception that is re-thrown is the original exception, so the output produced is:

```
Exception in F: G
Exception in Main: G
```

If the first catch block had thrown e instead of rethrowing the current exception, the output produced would be as follows:

```
Exception in F: G
Exception in Main: F
```

end example]

It is a compile-time error for a break, continue, or goto statement to transfer control out of a finally block. When a break, continue, or goto statement occurs in a finally block, the target of the statement shall be within the same finally block, or otherwise a compile-time error occurs.

It is a compile-time error for a return statement to occur in a finally block.

Rationale: Why is jumping out of a finally block forbidden?

The preceding restrictions ensure that the finally block can be encapsulated in a separate method, which might be useful when compiling C# to a non-CLI platform. Encapsulating and naming the code in the finally block may be necessary to avoid code duplication; a method is an obvious device for such encapsulation.

A try statement is executed as follows:

- Control is transferred to the try block.
- When and if control reaches the end point of the try block:
  - o If the try statement has a finally block, the finally block is executed.
  - o Control is transferred to the end point of the try statement.
- If an exception is propagated to the try statement during execution of the try block:

- o The catch clauses, if any, are examined in order of appearance to locate a suitable handler for the exception. The first catch clause that specifies the exception type or a base type of the exception type is considered a match. A general catch clause is considered a match for any exception type. If a matching catch clause is located:
  - If the matching catch clause declares an exception variable, the exception object is assigned to the exception variable.
  - Control is transferred to the matching catch block.
  - When and if control reaches the end point of the catch block:
    - o If the try statement has a finally block, the finally block is executed.
    - o Control is transferred to the end point of the try statement.
  - If an exception is propagated to the try statement during execution of the catch block:
    - o If the try statement has a finally block, the finally block is executed.
    - o The exception is propagated to the next enclosing try statement.
- o If the try statement has no catch clauses or if no catch clause matches the exception:
  - If the try statement has a finally block, the finally block is executed.
  - The exception is propagated to the next enclosing try statement.

The statements of a finally block are always executed when control leaves a try statement. This is true whether the control transfer occurs as a result of normal execution, as a result of executing a break, continue, goto, or return statement, or as a result of propagating an exception out of the try statement.

If an exception is thrown during execution of a finally block, the exception is propagated to the next enclosing try statement. If another exception was in the process of being propagated, that exception is lost. The process of propagating an exception is discussed further in the description of the throw statement (§15.9.5).

The try block of a try statement is reachable if the try statement is reachable.

A catch block of a try statement is reachable if the try statement is reachable.

The finally block of a try statement is reachable if the try statement is reachable.

The end point of a try statement is reachable if both of the following are true:

- The end point of the try block is reachable or the end point of at least one catch block is reachable.
- If a finally block is present, the end point of the finally block is reachable.

Unstoppable exceptions?

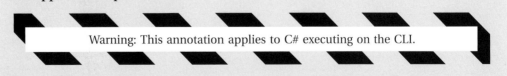

Warning: This annotation applies to C# executing on the CLI.

By default a ThreadAbortException from the CLI namespace System.Threading will automatically be rethrown by the CLI at the end of its catch block. To try to prevent this automatic rethrow you can call Thread.ResetAbort (which needs appropriate permissions).

```
try
{
  ...
}
catch (ThreadAbortException error)
{
  ...
}
// By default control does not get to this line
```

Note that `ThreadAbortException` is not only part of the C# Standard Library described in Annex D, but also part of the CLI Standard Library. See annotation at beginning of §10.1.

Sometimes other code runs before finally

Warning: This annotation applies to C# executing on the CLI that is being called by other CLI code that uses CLI's 'filter blocks.' The example uses Microsoft's VB.NET language, but would apply to any language using CLI filter blocks. None of this is part of Standard C#, but we expect the issue will be of interest to many readers.

As `finally` blocks are usually used for clean-up purposes, the prospect of code from another class being run (invisibly) before the finally block is an alarming one. However, that is possible in some environments, such as the CLI. Consider the following C# and VB.NET code for Microsoft's CLR, where the VB.NET code uses an exception filter. First the C# code:

```
// Library.cs:
using System;

public class Library
{
  public static void Foo()
  {
    try
    {
      Console.WriteLine ("In the C# try block");
      throw new Exception();
    }
    finally
    {
      Console.WriteLine ("In the C# finally block");
    }
  }
}
```

and the VB.NET code:

```
//Test.vb:
Imports System
```

```
Class Test

    Shared Sub Main()
        Try
            Library.Foo()
        Catch e As Exception When CatchTest()
            Console.WriteLine ("In VB.NET Catch")
        End Try
    End Sub

    Shared Function CatchTest() As Boolean
        Console.WriteLine ("In VB.NET CatchTest")
        Return True
    End Function

End Class
```

Compiling these two classes and running together on Microsoft's CLR produces the output:

```
In the C# try block
In VB.NET CatchTest
In the C# finally block
In VB.NET Catch
```

This behavior comes from the CLI's algorithm for handling exceptions:

1. First the call stack is traversed to find the first catch handler that can handle the exception. This traversal necessarily involves executing the filters on filter blocks.
2. If a catch handler is found, a second traversal is made to execute any finally blocks and then the catch handler is invoked.
3. If a catch handler is not found, the CLI aborts the program *possibly without executing the finally blocks.*

Consider the possibility of a try block acquiring some resource, obtaining some particular privileged resource, being very careful over the calls it makes, and then releasing the resource in the finally block. A rogue piece of code using an exception filter may be able to make use of this resource before it is released. Worrying indeed.

Jon Skeet

15.11 The checked and unchecked statements

The checked and unchecked statements are used to control the ***overflow-checking context*** for integral-type arithmetic operations and conversions.

checked-statement:
   checked   *block*

unchecked-statement:
   unchecked   *block*

The checked statement causes all expressions in the *block* to be evaluated in a checked context, and the unchecked statement causes all expressions in the *block* to be evaluated in an unchecked context.

Nested un/checking?

A checked statement/expression can itself contain an unchecked statement/expression (and vice versa). For example, consider the code fragment:

```
checked
{
  int value = F();
  unchecked
  {
    value = value * value * value * value * value * value;
  }
  value = unchecked(checked(F() * G()) + 42);
}
```

The preceding paragraph is not completely clear on this point. A more precise wording would be, "The checked statement causes all expressions in the *block* to be evaluated in a checked context, unless contained in a nested unchecked statement or unchecked expression," and similarly for unchecked.

The precise meaning of checked and unchecked is covered in §14.5.1 and associated annotations.

Issues like this highlight how difficult it is to be precise.

The checked and uncheckedstatements are precisely equivalent to the checked and unchecked operators (§14.5.13), except that they operate on blocks instead of expressions.

15.12 The lock statement

The lock statement obtains the mutual-exclusion lock for a given object, executes a statement, and then releases the lock.

> *lock-statement:*
>   lock (*expression*)   *embedded-statement*

The compile time type of the expression of a lock statement shall be a *reference-type* or a type parameter (§25.1.1) known to be a reference type. It is a compile-time error for the compile time type of the expression to denote a *value-type*.

A lock statement of the form

```
lock (x) ...
```

is precisely equivalent to:

```
object obj = x;

System.Threading.Monitor.Enter(obj);
try
{
  ...
}
finally
{
  System.Threading.Monitor.Exit(obj);
}
```

[*Example*:

```
class Cache
{
  public void Add(object x)
  {
    lock (key)
    {
      ...
    }
  }

  public void Remove(object x)
  {
    lock (key)
    {
      ...
    }
  }

  private readonly object key = new object();
}
```

end example]

Lock thread safety?

There is a *potential* weak point in any code that acquires a resource, uses it inside a try block, and then releases it in a finally block (to ensure exception safety). For example, consider:

```
Resource r = null;
r = o.Acquire();
// ...weak-point is here...
try
{
  ...
}
finally
{
  if (r != null)
    r.Release();
}
```

The problem is that an exception could occur after the resource has been acquired but before the try block has been entered, thus bypassing the resource release in the finally block. This may be unlikely, but between a compiler's latitude in code generation and concurrent execution it *is* possible (and on the CLI an asynchronous ThreadAbortException *can* trigger this problem). This code pattern is equivalent to the expansion of the lock statement; consequently, the call to Monitor.Exit *might not occur*.

It is tempting to think you can solve this problem by moving the r = o.Acquire() inside the try block, but you cannot; all that does is move the weak point:

```
Resource r = null;
try
{
  r = /* weak-point is now here */ o.Acquire();
}
```

```
    finally
    {
      if (r != null)
        r.Release();
    }
```

The Standard does *not* require a compiler to address this. However, the `lock` statement, in addition to conveniently encapsulating a common coding pattern, provides a "hook" to enable a compiler to do so. At the time of writing, the Microsoft and Mono compilers do *not* completely address this issue.

A coding pattern that is recommended is to move the assignment inside the acquiring method by utilizing an out parameter—that is, redesigning `Acquire()` above replacing the assignment with:

```
    o.Acquire(out r);
```

This replaces multiple assignments, one at each call site, with one, inside the callee. While it does *not* solve the problem, which is simply relocated, but it does allow it to be addressed in just one location. A given implementation might provide access to features outside Standard C# and CLI that help address this issue.

Lock safety

The lock statement names the locked expression only once. If you explicitly call `Monitor.Enter/Exit` you must pass a reference to the *same* object to both `Enter` and `Exit`. This is one reason to prefer readonly variables to hold references used for locking.

A built-in safety feature of the lock statement is that it can only lock a reference-type expression. Consider:

```
    bool key = false;
    lock (key)          // Compile-time error
    {
      ...
    }
```

This does not compile. In contrast, `Monitor.Enter` and `Monitor.Exit` accept an object parameter and thus will happily box a value-type argument! For example:

```
    bool key = false;
    Monitor.Enter(key);    // Locks a boxed copy of key. Ooops
    try
    {
      ...
    }
    finally
    {
      Monitor.Exit(key);  // Attempts to unlock another boxed copy, oops...
    }
```

This compiles and produces a runtime error (attempt to unlock a not-locked object).

15.13 The using statement

The `using` statement obtains one or more resources, executes a statement, and then disposes of the resource.

using-statement:
   using (*resource-acquisition*)   *embedded-statement*

resource-acquisition:
  local-variable-declaration
  expression

A ***resource*** is a class or struct that implements the System.IDisposable interface. The System.IDisposable interface includes a single parameterless method named Dispose. Code that is using a resource can call Dispose to indicate that the resource is no longer needed. If Dispose is not called, then automatic disposal eventually occurs as a consequence of garbage collection (assuming the finalizer of the resource type calls Dispose or otherwise performs the equivalent actions).

Rationale: designing for nonmemory resources

Garbage collection deallocates unused memory resources automatically, so C# programmers need not concern themselves with memory management. If an object needs to perform certain actions prior to being deallocated, it may declare a finalizer method to be invoked by the garbage collector. Objects that allocate nonmemory resources can use finalizers to free those resources, thus ensuring that they will not be retained indefinitely. However, the timing of garbage collection is indeterminate, so finalizers are not suitable when timely or deterministic deallocation is important.

A file handle is a nonmemory resource for which timely release is desirable. While the handle is open, the file may be locked on disk, and nonrelease of the handle will prevent others from opening the file. Contrast this with memory, where the timing of the release of memory cannot have any semantic effect (other than performance). Garbage collection is the right model for memory resources, but not for nonmemory resources.

The C# design team spent a lot of time investigating how language support could make resource handling code less bug prone. One alternative considered, modeled after the C++ language, was to add a new kind of type whose finalizer would be invoked when a reference to the object went out of scope. The tracking of scope would be achieved by allocating these new resource objects on the stack, which had several undesirable consequences. First, the object designer would need to pick the resource allocation model of the object at design time. Secondly, this in turn would encourage a bifurcated framework design. For example, one would soon need both a heap allocated File class and a stack allocated File resource struct. This did not seem like the right approach.

The using statement model allows framework designers to provide deterministic finalization, to be exploited by users of the resource object. It allows framework designers to design only a single class for each resource type. The using statement's most significant strength is that it gives a well known and terse idiom for writing code that handles resources correctly, even in the presence of exceptions. Without the using statement, programmers would rarely write exception-safe resource handling code.

Consider this example:

```
using (File fileRead = File.OpenRead("source.txt"))
{
  using (File fileWrite = File.OpenWrite("dest.txt"))
  {
    ...
  }
}
```

Without the `using` statement, the alternative is to use nested `try`/`finally` statements:

```
File fileRead = null;
try
{
  fileRead = File.OpenRead("source.txt"));
  File fileWrite = null;
  try
  {
    fileWrite = File.OpenWrite("dest.txt")
    {
      ...
    }
  }
  finally
  {
    if (fileWrite != null) fileWrite.Dispose();
  }
}
finally
{
  if (fileRead != null) fileRead.Dispose();
}
```

Experience with other languages has shown that the nested `try`/`finally` pattern is too cumbersome for programmers to adopt in regular usage.

Peter Hallam

Local variables declared in a *resource-acquisition* are read-only, and shall include an initializer. A compile-time error occurs if the embedded statement attempts to modify these local variables (via assignment or the ++ and -- operators) or pass them as `ref` or `out` parameters.

A `using` statement is translated into three parts: acquisition, usage, and disposal. Usage of the resource is implicitly enclosed in a `try` statement that includes a `finally` clause. This `finally` clause disposes of the resource. If a `null` resource is acquired, then no call to `Dispose` is made, and no exception is thrown.

A `using` statement of the form

```
using (expression) embedded-statement
```

is equivalent to a using statement of the form:

```
using (ResourceType resource = expression) embedded-statement
```

where `ResourceType` is the type of the *expression* and the `resource` variable is not visible to or accessible from any source code of the program.

A `using` statement of the form

```
using (ResourceType resource = expression) embedded-statement
```

corresponds to the expansion:

```
{
  ResourceType resource = expression;
  try
```

```
  {
    embedded-statement
  }
  finally
  {
    ... // Dispose of resource
  }
}
```

The `resource` variable is read-only in the embedded statement.

The precise form of the finally block is determined as follows:

- If there is not an implicit conversion from `ResourceType` to the `System.IDisposable` interface, then a compile-time error is produced.
- Otherwise, if `ResourceType` is a non-nullable value type or a type parameter with the value type constraint (§25.7), the finally clause is expanded to the semantic equivalent of:

```
finally
{
    ((System.IDisposable)resource).Dispose();
}
```

except that casting `resource` to `System.IDisposable` shall not cause boxing to occur.

- Otherwise, the finally clause is expanded to:

```
finally
{
    if (resource != null) ((System.IDisposable)resource).Dispose();
}
```

When a *resource-acquisition* takes the form of a *local-variable-declaration*, it is possible to acquire multiple resources of a given type. A `using` statement of the form

```
using (ResourceType r1 = e1, r2 = e2, ..., rN = eN) statement
```

is precisely equivalent to a sequence of nested `using` statements:

```
using (ResourceType r1 = e1)
  using (ResourceType r2 = e2)
    ...
      using (ResourceType rN = eN)
        statement
```

[*Example*: The example below creates a file named `log.txt` and writes two lines of text to the file. The example then opens that same file for reading and copies the contained lines of text to the console.

```
using System;
using System.IO;

class Test
{
  static void Main()
  {
    using (TextWriter w = File.CreateText("log.txt"))
```

```
      {
        w.WriteLine("This is line one");
        w.WriteLine("This is line two");
      }

      using (TextReader r = File.OpenText("log.txt"))
      {
        string s;
        while ((s = r.ReadLine()) != null)
        {
          Console.WriteLine(s);
        }
      }
    }
  }
}
```

Since the `TextWriter` and `TextReader` classes implement the `IDisposable` interface, the example can use `using` statements to ensure that the underlying file is properly closed following the write or read operations. *end example*]

Redux: One implementation's treasure is another's garbage

An annotation on §10.9 highlights that an object referenced by a local variable may be garbage collected before the end of the block in which the local variable is declared if the C# implementation can determine that the variable is no longer used.

It is a common design for classes that allocate resources to both implement `IDisposable` and arrange for finalization to free the resource. As the annotation on §10.9 demonstrates, relying on the finalizer is most unwise as it may result in premature freeing, or prolonged ownership, of the resource. Consider the following simple rewrite of the example in §10.9:

```
class Waste { ...}                      // as in §10.9

class KeepAround : IDisposable
{
  public KeepAround()
  {
    // allocate resource
  }

  public void Dispose()
  {
    // free resource if needed
  }

  ~KeepAround()
  {
    Dispose();
  }
}

void Test()
{
  KeepAround ka = new KeepAround();  // assign to local
```

```
        for (int i = 0; i < 100; i++)        // generate garbage
        {
          Waste two = new Waste();
        }
      }
```

Storing the instance of `KeepAround` in local variable `ka` does **not** guarantee that it will not be garbage collected until some time after `Test()` has finished. To ensure that the `KeepAround` instance remains allocated, a `using` statement may be used:

```
    void Test()
    {
      using(KeepAround ka = new KeepAround())
      {
        for (int i = 0; i < 100; i++)  // generate garbage
        {
          Waste two = new Waste();
        }
      }
    }
```

With this change we precisely define the period during which the resource is allocated. The lesson from this example is simple: It is far better to explicitly release resources than to rely on finalization. The latter should be reserved for cleaning up objects whose time of death is noncritical.

Note: Microsoft's CLR (not standard CLI) `System.Threading.Mutex` class for creating system-wide mutexes both implements `IDisposable` and has a finalizer that releases the mutex resource. It is therefore an example of a class susceptible to this issue.

15.14 The yield statement

The `yield` statement is used in an iterator block (§26.1) to yield a value to the enumerator object or to signal the end of the iteration.

> *yield-statement:*
>   `yield  return` *expression* `;`
>   `yield  break` `;`

To ensure compatibility with existing programs, `yield` is not a keyword; `yield` has special meaning only when it is used immediately before a `return` or `break` keyword. In other contexts, `yield` can be used as an identifier.

The are several restrictions on where a `yield` statement can appear, as described in the following.

- It is a compile-time error for a `yield` statement (of either form) to appear outside a *method-body, operator-body,* or *accessor-body*.
- It is a compile-time error for a `yield` statement (of either form) to appear inside an anonymous method.
- It is a compile-time error for a `yield` statement (of either form) to appear in the `finally` clause of a `try` statement.
- It is a compile-time error for a `yield return` statement to appear anywhere in a `try` statement that contains *catch-clauses*.

[*Example*: The following example shows some valid and invalid uses of `yield` statements.

```
delegate IEnumerable<int> D();

IEnumerator<int> GetEnumerator()
{
  try
  {
    yield return 1;     // Ok
    yield break;        // Ok
  }
  finally
  {
    yield return 2;     // Error, yield in finally
    yield break;        // Error, yield in finally
  }

  try
  {
    yield return 3;     // Error, yield return in try...catch
    yield break;        // Ok
  }
  catch
  {
    yield return 4;     // Error, yield return in try...catch
    yield break;        // Ok
  }

  D d = delegate {
    yield return 5;     // Error, yield in an anonymous method
  };
}

int MyMethod()
{
  yield return 1;       // Error, wrong return type for an iterator
}
```

end example]

An implicit conversion (§13.1) shall exist from the type of the expression in the `yield return` statement to the yield type (§26.1.3) of the iterator block.

A `yield return` statement is executed as follows:

- The expression given in the statement is evaluated, implicitly converted to the yield type, and assigned to the `Current` property of the enumerator object.
- Execution of the iterator block is suspended. If the `yield return` statement is within one or more `try` blocks, the associated `finally` blocks are *not* executed at this time.
- The `MoveNext` method of the enumerator object returns `true` to its caller, indicating that the enumerator object successfully advanced to the next item.

The next call to the enumerator object's `MoveNext` method resumes execution of the iterator block from where it was last suspended, namely at the end point of the `yield return` statement that caused the suspension.

A `yield break` statement is executed as follows:

- If the `yield break` statement is enclosed by one or more `try` blocks with associated `finally` blocks, control is initially transferred to the `finally` block of the innermost `try` statement. When and if control reaches the end point of a `finally` block, control is transferred to the `finally` block of the next enclosing `try` statement. This process is repeated until the `finally` blocks of all enclosing `try` statements have been executed.
- Control is returned to the caller of the iterator block. This is either the `MoveNext` method or `Dispose` method of the enumerator object.

Because a `yield break` statement unconditionally transfers control elsewhere, the end point of a `yield break` statement is never reachable.

---

yield syntax?

An early candidate for the yield statement syntax was:

> *yield-statement:*
>   yield *expression* ;
>   yield break ;

This is arguably the most natural syntax but requires introducing yield as a bona-fide new keyword. (For example, `yield(42)` could be a function call, whereas in the preceding syntax yield is a keyword and (42) is a redundantly parenthesized expression.) When C# 2.0 was being designed, it was envisaged some new features would be introduced using contextual keywords (such as "where") but others would inevitably require new keywords. The plan for these new keywords was to provide a conversion utility based on the @ keyword escape mechanism (for example, yield to @yield). However, every new feature except yield could be easily introduced using contextual keywords. This created pressure to find an alternative contextual keyword solution for the yield statement. The final syntax is:

> *yield-statement:*
>   yield return *expression* ;
>   yield break ;

Note that in both cases yield is followed by a true keyword. Thus, a C# 2.0 compiler can also compile all C# 1.0 programs and the need for a conversion tool disappeared.

16 Namespaces

C# programs are organized using namespaces. Namespaces are used both as an "internal" organization system for a program, and as an "external" organization system—a way of presenting program elements that are exposed to other programs.

Using directives (§16.3) are provided to facilitate the use of namespaces.

16.1 Compilation units

A *compilation-unit* defines the overall structure of a source file. A compilation unit consists of zero or more *extern-alias-directive*s followed by zero or more *using-directive*s followed by zero or more *global-attributes* followed by zero or more *namespace-member-declaration*s.

> *compilation-unit:*
>   *extern-alias-directives*_{opt} *using-directives*_{opt} *global-attributes*_{opt}
>   *namespace-member-declarations*_{opt}

A C# program consists of one or more compilation units, each contained in a separate source file. When a C# program is compiled, all of the compilation units are processed together. Thus, compilation units can depend on each other, possibly in a circular fashion.

> **Compilation-unit misnomer**
>
> The name "compilation unit" is somewhat of a misnomer, since they are *not* the units that the compiler processes. As noted, the compiler processes many compilation units together. The name comes from the C language standard, where the compiler really did process a single source file at a time.
>
> *Peter Golde*

The *extern-alias-directives* of a compilation unit affect the *using-directives*, *global-attributes* and *namespace-member-declarations* of that compilation unit, but have no effect on other compilation units.

The *using-directives* of a compilation unit affect the *global-attributes* and *namespace-member-declarations* of that compilation unit, but have no effect on other compilation units.

The *global-attributes* (§24) of a compilation unit permit the specification of attributes for the target assembly. Assemblies act as physical containers for types.

The *namespace-member-declarations* of each compilation unit of a program contribute members to a single declaration space called the global namespace. [*Example*:

File `A.cs`:

```
class A {}
```

File `B.cs`:

```
class B {}
```

The two compilation units contribute to the single global namespace, in this case declaring two classes with the fully qualified names A and B. Because the two compilation units contribute to the same declaration space, it would have been an error if each contained a declaration of a member with the same name. *end example*]

Class libraries

A class library (§4) is an assembly (§4) containing one or more compilation units previously compiled. When a class library is made available to a compilation by some external mechanism not defined in this specification, its members are added to the global namespace and may be referenced by constructs in the compilation unit(s) being compiled. No `using` statement is required to make the members of the class library available.

The presence of a class library during compilation affects name resolution and the meaning of *using-directives*. Since the members of a class library are automatically added to the global namespace, simply changing which class libraries are specified in a compilation can change the meaning of that compilation. This is covered in an annotation on §16.4.2.

This appears to never be directly specified in the normative text of the Standard, but is covered in the informative clause §8.12.

16.2 Namespace declarations

A *namespace-declaration* consists of the keyword `namespace`, followed by a namespace name and body, optionally followed by a semicolon.

> *namespace-declaration:*
>   `namespace` *qualified-identifier* *namespace-body* `;` $_{opt}$
>
> *qualified-identifier:*
>   *identifier*
>   *qualified-identifier* `.` *identifier*
>
> *namespace-body:*
>   `{` *extern-alias-directives*$_{opt}$ *using-directives*$_{opt}$ *namespace-member-*
>   *declarations*$_{opt}$ `}`

A *namespace-declaration* can occur as a top-level declaration in a *compilation-unit* or as a member declaration within another *namespace-declaration*. When a *namespace-declaration* occurs as a top-level declaration in a *compilation-unit*, the namespace becomes a member of the global namespace. When a *namespace-declaration* occurs within another *namespace-declaration*, the inner namespace becomes a member of the outer namespace. In either case, the name of a namespace shall be unique within the containing namespace.

Namespaces are implicitly `public` and the declaration of a namespace cannot include any access modifiers.

Within a *namespace-body*, the optional *using-directives* import the names of other namespaces and types, allowing them to be referenced directly instead of through qualified names. The optional *namespace-member-declarations* contribute members to the declaration space of the namespace. All *extern-alias-directives* shall appear before any *using-directives* and all *extern-alias-directives* and *using-directives* shall appear before any member declarations.

The *qualified-identifier* of a *namespace-declaration* can be a single identifier or a sequence of identifiers separated by "`.`" tokens. The latter form permits a program to define a nested namespace without lexically nesting several namespace declarations. [*Example*:

```
namespace N1.N2
{
  class A { }

  class B { }
}
```

is semantically equivalent to

```
namespace N1
{
  namespace N2
  {
    class A { }

    class B { }
  }
}
```

end example]

Namespaces are open-ended, and two namespace declarations with the same fully qualified name (§10.8.2) contribute to the same declaration space (§10.3). [*Example*: In the following code

```
namespace N1.N2
{
  class A { }
}

namespace N1.N2
{
  class B { }
}
```

the two namespace declarations above contribute to the same declaration space, in this case declaring two classes with the fully qualified names N1.N2.A and N1.N2.B. Because the two declarations contribute to the same declaration space, it would have been an error if each contained a declaration of a member with the same name. *end example*]

Fully qualified names beginning with System. are reserved for use by the Standard Library (Annex D).

16.3 Extern alias directives

An *extern-alias-directive* introduces an identifier that serves as an alias for an externally defined namespace. The specification of the aliased namespace is external to the source code of the program.

> *extern-alias-directives:*
>   *extern-alias-directive*
>   *extern-alias-directives*   *extern-alias-directive*
>
> *extern-alias-directive:*
>   extern   alias   *identifier*   ;

The scope of an *extern-alias-directive* extends over the *using-directives, global-attributes* and *namespace-member-declarations* of its immediately containing *compilation-unit* or *namespace-body*. An *extern-alias-directive* contributes its name to the **alias declaration space** of the containing compilation unit or namespace body (§10.3) and not to the declaration space of the containing namespace.

Within a compilation unit or namespace body that contains an *extern-alias-directive*, the identifier introduced by the *extern-alias-directive* can be used to reference the aliased namespace. It is a compile-time error for the *identifier* to be the word `global`.

Within C# source code, a type is declared a member of a single namespace. However, a namespace hierarchy referenced by an extern alias may contain types that are also members of other namespaces. For example, if A and B are extern aliases, the names `A::X`, `B::C.Y` and `global::D.Z` may, depending on the external specification supported by the particular compiler, all refer to the same type.

> **Extern alias implied flexibility**
>
> The aliasing example might be confusing to some: How could `A::X`, `B::C.Y` and `global::D.Z` all refer to the same type?
>
> While A, `B::C` and `global::D` could all be aliases of the same *namespace*, the example also says that X, Y and Z may refer to the same *type*. However, within C#, though a *using-alias-directive* may be used to alias a type, that alias can only be accessed from within its enclosing compilation unit or namespace body.
>
> The example is intended to suggest that the external mechanism used for external aliases may include the ability to reference type aliases, such as those that may be introduced in C# by a *using-alias-directive* directive, from *outside* the enclosing namespace. That is, in the example, two or three of X, Y and Z would themselves be type aliases.

The alias introduced by an *extern-alias-directive* is very similar to the alias introduced by a *using-alias-directive*. See §16.4.1 for more detailed discussion of *extern-alias-directives* and *using-alias-directives*.

Like `get` and `set` in property accessors, `alias` is not a keyword (§9.4.3). The word `alias` only has special meaning when it immediately follows the `extern` keyword in an *extern-alias-directive*. [*Example*: In fact an `extern` alias could use the identifier `alias` as its name:

```
extern alias alias;
```

end example]

16.4 Using directives

Using directives facilitate the use of namespaces and types defined in other namespaces. *using-directives* impact the name resolution process of *namespace-or-type-name*s (§10.8) and *simple-name*s (§14.5.2), but unlike declarations, *using-directives* do not contribute new members to the underlying declaration spaces of the compilation units or namespaces within which they are used.

using-directives:
  using-directive
  using-directives   using-directive

using-directive:
  using-alias-directive
  using-namespace-directive

A *using-alias-directive* (§16.4.1) introduces an alias for a namespace or type.

A *using-namespace-directive* (§16.4.2) imports the type members of a namespace.

The scope of a *using-directive* extends over the *namespace-member-declarations* of its immediately containing compilation unit or namespace body. The scope of a *using-directive* specifically does not include its peer *using-directives*. Thus, peer *using-directives* do not affect each other, and the order in which they are written is insignificant. In contrast, the scope of an *extern-alias-directive* includes the *using-directives* defined in the same compilation unit or namespace body.

16.4.1 Using alias directives

A *using-alias-directive* introduces an identifier that serves as an alias for a namespace or type within the immediately enclosing compilation unit or namespace body.

using-alias-directive:
  using *identifier* = *namespace-or-type-name* ;

Within global attributes and member declarations in a compilation unit or namespace body that contains a *using-alias-directive*, the identifier introduced by the *using-alias-directive* can be used to reference the given namespace or type. [*Example*:

```
namespace N1.N2
{
  class A{}
}

namespace N3
{
  using A = N1.N2.A;

  class B: A{}
}
```

Above, within member declarations in the N3 namespace, A is an alias for N1.N2.A, and thus class N3.B derives from class N1.N2.A. The same effect can be obtained by creating an alias R for N1.N2 and then referencing R.A:

```
namespace N3
{
  using R = N1.N2;

  class B: R.A{}
}
```

end example]

Within using directives, global attributes and member declarations in a compilation unit or namespace body that contains an *extern-alias-directive*, the identifier introduced by the *extern-alias-directive* can be used to reference the associated namespace. [*Example*: For example:

```
namespace N1
{
  extern alias N2;

  class B: N2::A {}
}
```

Above, within member declarations in the N1 namespace, N2 is an alias for some namespace whose definition is external to the source code of the program. Class N1.B derives from class N2.A. The same effect can be obtained by creating an alias A for N2.A and then referencing A:

```
namespace N1
{
  extern alias N2;
  using A = N2::A;

  class B: A {}
}
```

end example]

An *extern-alias-directive* or *using-alias-directive* makes an alias available within a particular compilation unit or namespace body, but it does not contribute any new members to the underlying declaration space. In other words, an alias directive is not transitive, but, rather, affects only the compilation unit or namespace body in which it occurs. [*Example*: In the following code

```
namespace N3
{
  extern alias R1;
  using R2 = N1.N2;
}

namespace N3
{
  class B: R1::A, R2.I {}     // Error, R1 and R2 unknown
}
```

the scopes of the alias directives that introduce R1 and R2 only extend to member declarations in the namespace body in which they are contained, so R1 and R2 are unknown in the second namespace declaration. However, placing the alias directives in the containing compilation unit causes the alias to become available within both namespace declarations:

```
extern alias R1;
using R2 = N1.N2;

namespace N3
{
  class B: R1::A, R2.I {}
}

namespace N3
{
  class C: R1::A, R2.I {}
}
```

end example]

Each *extern-alias-directive* or *using-alias-directive* in a *compilation-unit* or *namespace-body* contributes a name to the **alias declaration space** (§10.3) of the immediately enclosing *compilation-unit* or *namespace-body*. The *identifier* of the alias directive shall be unique within the corresponding alias declaration space. The alias identifier need not be unique within the global declaration space or the declaration space of the corresponding namespace. [*Example*:

```
extern alias A;
extern alias B;

using A = N1.N2;    // Error: alias A already exists

class B {}          // Ok
```

The using alias named A causes an error since there is already an alias named A in the same compilation unit. The class named B does not conflict with the extern alias named B since these names are added to distinct declaration spaces. The former is added to the global declaration space and the latter is added to the alias declaration space for this compilation unit.

When an alias name matches the name of a member of a namespace, usage of either must be appropriately qualified:

```
namespace N1.N2
{
  class B {}
}

namespace N3
{
  class A {}
  class B : A {}
}

namespace N3
{
  using A = N1.N2;
  using B = N1.N2.B;

  class W : B {}      // Error: B is ambiguous
  class X : A.B {}    // Error: A is ambiguous
  class Y : A::B {}   // Ok: uses N1.N2.B
  class Z : N3.B {}   // Ok: uses N3.B
}
```

In the second namespace body for N3, unqualified use of B results in an error, since N3 contains a member named B and the namespace body that also declares an alias with name B; likewise for A. The class N3.B can be referenced as N3.B or global::N3.B. The alias A can be used in a *qualified-alias-member* (§16.7), such as A::B. The alias B is essentially useless. It cannot be used in a *qualified-alias-member* since only namespace aliases can be used in a *qualified-alias-member* and B aliases a type. *end example*]

Just like regular members, names introduced by alias directives are hidden by similarly named members in nested scopes. [*Example*: In the following code

```
using R = N1.N2;

namespace N3
{
  class R {}

  class B: R.A {}     // Error, R has no member A
}
```

the reference to `R.A` in the declaration of `B` causes a compile-time error because `R` refers to `N3.R`, not `N1.N2`. *end example*]

The order in which *extern-alias-directive*s are written has no significance. Likewise, the order in which *using-alias-directive*s are written has no significance, but all *using-alias-directive*s must come after all *extern-alias-directive*s in the same compilation unit or namespace body. Resolution of the *namespace-or-type-name* referenced by a *using-alias-directive* is not affected by the *using-alias-directive* itself or by other *using-directive*s in the immediately containing compilation unit or namespace body, but may be affected by *extern-alias-directive*s in the immediately containing compilation unit or namespace body. In other words, the *namespace-or-type-name* of a *using-alias-directive* is resolved as if the immediately containing compilation unit or namespace body had no *using-directive*s but has the correct set of *extern-alias-directive*s. [*Example*: In the following code

```
namespace N1.N2 {}

namespace N3
{
  extern alias E;

  using R1 = E::N;    // OK

  using R2 = N1;      // OK

  using R3 = N1.N2;   // OK

  using R4 = R2.N2;   // Error, R2 unknown
}
```

the last *using-alias-directive* results in a compile-time error because it is not affected by the previous *using-alias-directive*. The first *using-alias-directive* does not result in an error since the scope of the extern alias `E` includes the *using-alias-directive*. *end example*]

A *using-alias-directive* can create an alias for any namespace or type, including the namespace within which it appears and any namespace or type nested within that namespace.

Accessing a namespace or type through an alias yields exactly the same result as accessing that namespace or type through its declared name. [*Example*: Given

```
namespace N1.N2
{
  class A {}
}

namespace N3
{
  using R1 = N1;
  using R2 = N1.N2;
```

```
    class B
    {
      N1.N2.A a;      // refers to N1.N2.A
      R1.N2.A b;      // refers to N1.N2.A
      R2.A c;         // refers to N1.N2.A
    }
}
```

the names N1.N2.A, R1.N2.A, and R2.A are equivalent and all refer to the class whose fully qualified name is N1.N2.A. *end example*]

Although each part of a partial type (§17.1.4) is declared within the same namespace, the parts are typically written within different namespace declarations. Thus, different extern alias directives and using directives can be present for each part. When interpreting simple names (§14.5.2) within one part, only the extern alias directives and using directives of the namespace bodies and compilation unit enclosing that part are considered. This may result in the same identifier having different meanings in different parts. [*Example*:

```
    namespace N
    {
      using List = System.Collections.ArrayList;

      partial class A
      {
        List x;       // x has type System.Collections.ArrayList
      }
    }

    namespace N
    {
      using List = Widgets.LinkedList;

      partial class A
      {
        List y;      // y has type Widgets.LinkedList
      }
    }
```

end example]

Using alias constraints

The right-hand side of a using alias must be a *namespace-or-type-name*. This means you cannot write:

```
    using Integer = int; // compile-time error
```

Instead, you have to write:

```
    using Integer = System.Int32; // ok
```

This is one of the few places in C# where a *predefined-type* keyword (e.g., int) and its equivalent type-name (e.g., System.Int32) are *not* interchangeable (another is inside a string during reflection). You also cannot create an alias for an array type or a pointer type:

```
using Array = Wibble[] ; // compile-time error
using Pointer = Wibble*; // compile-time error
```

Using alias reordering

An identifier introduced by a using alias directive *cannot* be used in sibling using directives. This design is a consequence of the C# principle that declaration order should not be significant (reordering sibling using directives never affects their meanings).

```
using S = System;
using Integer = S.Int32; // compile-time error
```

However, you *can* use aliases from "outer" using directives. For example:

```
using Type1 = Name1.Name2.Type1;
using Type2 = Name1.Name2.Type2;

namespace Annotation
{
  using C = A.B.C<Type1,Type2>; // ok, can use outer Type1 and Type2
  ...
}
```

Another example of declaration order not being significant is the ability to create an alias for a lexically following type:

```
using Self = Point;

public struct Point
{
  ...
  public static bool operator==(Self lhs, Self rhs)
  {
    ...
  }
  public static bool operator!=(Self lhs, Self rhs)
  {
    ...
  }
}
```

16.4.2 Using namespace directives

A *using-namespace-directive* imports the types contained in a namespace into the immediately enclosing compilation unit or namespace body, enabling the identifier of each type to be used without qualification.

> *using-namespace-directive:*
>   using *namespace-name* ;

Within member declarations in a compilation unit or namespace body that contains a *using-namespace-directive*, the types contained in the given namespace can be referenced directly. [*Example*:

```
namespace N1.N2
{
  class A{}
}

namespace N3
{
  using N1.N2;

  class B: A{}
}
```

Above, within member declarations in the N3 namespace, the type members of N1.N2 are directly available, and thus class N3.B derives from class N1.N2.A. *end example*]

A *using-namespace-directive* imports the types contained in the given namespace, but specifically does not import nested namespaces. [*Example*: In the following code

```
namespace N1.N2
{
  class A{}
}

namespace N3
{
  using N1;

  class B: N2.A{}    // Error, N2 unknown
}
```

the *using-namespace-directive* imports the types contained in N1, but not the namespaces nested in N1. Thus, the reference to N2.A in the declaration of B results in a compile-time error because no members named N2 are in scope. *end example*]

Unlike a *using-alias-directive*, a *using-namespace-directive* can import types whose identifiers are already defined within the enclosing compilation unit or namespace body. In effect, names imported by a *using-namespace-directive* are hidden by similarly named members in the enclosing compilation unit or namespace body. [*Example*:

```
namespace N1.N2
{
  class A{}

  class B{}
}

namespace N3
{
  using N1.N2;

  class A{}
}
```

Here, within member declarations in the N3 namespace, A refers to N3.A rather than N1.N2.A. *end example*]

Ouch, it bit me!

Yes, this annotation is inspired by real life events....

The hiding of identifiers introduced by a *using-namespace-directive* can be counterintuitive. For example, consider the type One.Two stored in the file "One_Two.cs":

```
namespace One
{
  public class Two
  {
    public static void M()
    {

      System.Console.WriteLine ("One.Two.M");
    }
  }
}
```

and the class Ouch.Program, stored in the file "Ouch.cs," which uses it:

```
using One;

namespace Ouch
{
  class Program
  {
    static void Main()
    {
      Two.M();
    }
  }
}
```

Compiling the first class into an external assembly, and then compiling the second supplying that external assembly, produces the expected result (the Mono compiler is used in this example):

```
$ gmcs -t:library -out:One.dll One_Two.cs
$ gmcs Ouch.cs -r:One.dll
$ mono Ouch.exe
One.Two.M
$
```

However, adding a second, as yet unused library to the compilation produces a different result:

```
$ gmcs Ouch.cs -r:One.dll -r:Pain.dll
Ouch.cs(9,13): error CS0234: The type or namespace name 'M'

does not exist in the namespace 'Two'.
Are you missing an assembly reference?
Compilation failed: 1 error(s), 0 warnings
$
```

What was placed in "Pain.dll" to cause the compilation to fail? The answer is surprisingly innocuous:

```
namespace Two
{
  public class Four
  {
    public static void N()
    {
      System.Console.WriteLine("Two.Four.N");
    }
  }
}
```

The namespace Two is placed into the global namespace (§16.1, §8.14) and hides the type Two introduced by the using One statement. This might be counterintuitive to a user's expectation that names introduced by a using statement might prevail.

Though the example here is contrived, the problem, unfortunately, is real. External libraries can be large and contain many namespaces and types, many of which a particular user may never need or even know about. If one of those unknown namespaces or types just happens to have the same name as a type introduced by a using statement, then the problem can occur.

In C# v1 there was no easy solution to this problem. Dropping the using statement and using a fully qualified name might also result in a clash as there was no way to distinguish between fully qualified and relative names, the latter ones taking priority.

In C# v2, the new *qualified-alias-member* (§16.7) form using global::*identifier* can be used as a unique reference to any type.

There is no simple solution to this issue; using statements do improve readability. Employing the *qualified-alias-member* form for every nonlocal reference would rapidly reduce readability. Selecting obscure namespace and type names is certainly not to be recommended. So the advice is to wait until it bites, then deal with it. It can only occur at compile time, not at runtime after your product has shipped.

See also the annotation on §10.8.

When more than one namespace imported by *using-namespace-directive*s in the same compilation unit or namespace body contain types by the same name, references to that name are considered ambiguous. [*Example*: In the following code

```
namespace N1
{
  class A {}
}

namespace N2
{
  class A {}
}

namespace N3
{
  using N1;

  using N2;

  class B: A {}        // Error, A is ambiguous
}
```

both N1 and N2 contain a member A, and because N3 imports both, referencing A in N3 is a compile-time error. In this situation, the conflict can be resolved through qualification of references to A, or by introducing a *using-alias-directive* that picks a particular A. For example:

```
namespace N3
{
  using N1;

  using N2;

  using A = N1.A;

  class B: A{}          // A means N1.A
}
```

end example]

Like a *using-alias-directive*, a *using-namespace-directive* does not contribute any new members to the underlying declaration space of the namespace, but, rather, affects only the compilation unit or namespace body in which it appears.

The *namespace-name* referenced by a *using-namespace-directive* is resolved in the same way as the *namespace-or-type-name* referenced by a *using-alias-directive*. Thus, *using-namespace-directive*s in the same compilation unit or namespace body do not affect each other and can be written in any order.

Intercepting calls

This annotation is related to the previous one, this time showing a potential benefit. By careful design and judicious use of using directives it is possible to intercept calls. This could be useful, for example, in debugging situations. Consider the following program fragment:

```
using System;

namespace LogOutput
{
  public class Console
  {
    public static void WriteLine(string s)
    {
      // log the output
      ...
      // now do normal output
      System.Console.WriteLine(s.Replace('e', 'E'));
    }

    // Other members of Console...
    ...
  }
}

namespace UsurpDemo
{
  // using LogOutput;  // uncomment to log output

  public class Demo
```

```
  {
    public void Run()
    {
      Console.WriteLine("Hello there!");
    }
  }
}
```

Here the class `LogOutput` redefines `Console` so that calls can be intercepted and logged. When the `using` directive in `UsurpDemo` is commented out, execution proceeds as normal. Remove the comment and all calls to `WriteLine` are intercepted.

We cannot rule out that there exist malicious uses of this idea. Forewarned is forearmed.

16.5 Namespace members

A *namespace-member-declaration* is either a *namespace-declaration* (§16.2) or a *type-declaration* (§16.6).

> *namespace-member-declarations:*
>   *namespace-member-declaration*
>   *namespace-member-declarations*   *namespace-member-declaration*
>
> *namespace-member-declaration:*
>   *namespace-declaration*
>   *type-declaration*

A compilation unit or a namespace body can contain *namespace-member-declarations*, and such declarations contribute new members to the underlying declaration space of the containing compilation unit or namespace body.

16.6 Type declarations

A *type-declaration* is a *class-declaration* (§17.1), a *struct-declaration* (§18.1), an *interface-declaration* (§20.1), an *enum-declaration* (§21.1), or a *delegate-declaration* (§22.1).

> *type-declaration:*
>   *class-declaration*
>   *struct-declaration*
>   *interface-declaration*
>   *enum-declaration*
>   *delegate-declaration*

A *type-declaration* can occur as a top-level declaration in a compilation unit or as a member declaration within a namespace, class, or struct.

When a type declaration for a type `T` occurs as a top-level declaration in a compilation unit, the fully qualified name (§10.8.2) of the type declaration is the same as the unqualified name of the declaration (§10.8.1). When a type declaration for a type `T` occurs within a namespace, class, or struct, the fully qualified name (§10.8.2) of the type declaration is `S.N`, where `S` is the fully qualified name of the containing namespace or type declaration, and `N` is the unqualified name of the declaration (§10.8.1).

A type declared within a class or struct is called a nested type (§17.2.6).

The permitted access modifiers and the default access for a type declaration depend on the context in which the declaration takes place (§10.5.1):

- Types declared in compilation units or namespace declarations can have `public` or `internal` access. The default is `internal` access.
- Types declared in classes can have `public`, `protected internal`, `protected`, `internal`, or `private` access. The default is `private` access.
- Types declared in structs can have `public`, `internal`, or `private` access. The default is `private` access.

16.7 Qualified alias member

A *qualified-alias-member* provides explicit access to the global namespace and to extern or using aliases that are potentially hidden by other entities.

> *qualified-alias-member:*
>   *identifier* :: *identifier* *type-argument-list*$_{opt}$

A *qualified-alias-member* can be used as a *namespace-or-type-name* (§10.8) or as the left operand in a *member-access* (§14.5.4).

A *qualified-alias-member* consists of two identifiers, referred to as the left-hand and right-hand identifiers, separated by the :: token and optionally followed by a *type-argument-list*. When the left-hand identifier is `global` then the global namespace is searched for the right-hand identifier. For any other left-hand identifier, that identifier is looked up as an extern or using alias (§16.3 and §16.4.1). A compile-time error occurs if there is no such alias or the alias references a type. If the alias references a namespace then that namespace is searched for the right-hand identifier.

A *qualified-alias-member* has one of two forms:

- `A::B<G`$_1$`, ..., G`$_N$`>`, where `A` and `B` represent identifiers, and `<G`$_1$`, ..., G`$_N$`>` is a type argument list. (`N` is always at least one.)
- `A::B`, where `A` and `B` represent identifiers. (In this case, `N` is considered to be zero.)

Using this notation, the meaning of a *qualified-alias-member* is determined as follows:

- If `A` is the identifier `global`, then the global namespace is searched for `B`:
  - If the global namespace contains a namespace named `B` and `N` is zero, then the *qualified-alias-member* refers to that namespace.
  - Otherwise, if the global namespace contains a non-generic type named `B` and `N` is zero, then the *qualified-alias-member* refers to that type.
  - Otherwise, if the global namespace contains a type named `B` that has `N` type parameters, then the *qualified-alias-member* refers to that type constructed with the given type arguments.
  - Otherwise, the *qualified-alias-member* is undefined and a compile-time error occurs.
- Otherwise, starting with the namespace declaration (§16.2) immediately containing the *qualified-alias-member* (if any), continuing with each enclosing namespace declaration (if any), and ending with the compilation unit containing the *qualified-alias-member*, the following steps are evaluated until an entity is located:

- ○ If the namespace declaration or compilation unit contains a *using-alias-directive* that associates A with a type, then the *qualified-alias-member* is undefined and a compile-time error occurs.
- ○ Otherwise, if the namespace declaration or compilation unit contains an *extern-alias-directive* or *using-alias-directive* that associates A with a namespace, then:
  - • If the namespace associated with A contains a namespace named B and N is zero, then the *qualified-alias-member* refers to that namespace.
  - • Otherwise, if the namespace associated with A contains a non-generic type named B and N is zero, then the *qualified-alias-member* refers to that type.
  - • Otherwise, if the namespace associated with A contains a type named B that has N type parameters, then the *qualified-alias-member* refers to that type constructed with the given type arguments.
  - • Otherwise, the *qualified-alias-member* is undefined and a compile-time error occurs.
- • Otherwise, the *qualified-alias-member* is undefined and a compile-time error occurs.

[*Example*: In the code:

```
using S = System.Net.Sockets;

class A
{
  public static int x;
}

class C
{
  public void F(int A, object S)
  {
    // Use global::A.x instead of A.x
    global::A.x += A;

    // Use S::Socket instead of S.Socket
    S::Socket s = S as S::Socket;
  }
}
```

the class A is referenced with global::A and the type System.Net.Sockets.Socket is referenced with S::Socket. Using A.x and S.Socket instead would have caused compile-time errors because A and S would have resolved to the parameters. *end example*]

[*Note*: The identifier global has special meaning only when used as the left-hand identifier of a *qualified-alias-name*. It is not a keyword and it is not itself an alias. In the code:

```
class A{}

class C
{
  global.A x;  // Error: global is not defined
  global::A y; // Valid: References A in the global namespace
}
```

using global.A causes a compile-time error since there is no entity named global in scope. If some entity named global were in scope, then global in global.A would have resolved to that entity.

Using `global` as the left-hand identifier of a *qualified-alias-member* always causes a lookup in the global namespace, even if there is a using alias named `global`. [*Example*: In the code:

```
using global = MyGlobalTypes;

class A {}

class C
{
  global.A x;  // Valid: References MyGlobalTypes.A
  global::A y; // Valid: References A in the global namespace
}
```

`global.A` resolves to `MyGlobalTypes.A` and `global::A` resolves to class `A` in the global namespace. *end note*]

17 Classes

A class is a data structure that can contain data members (constants and fields), function members (methods, properties, events, indexers, operators, instance constructors, finalizers, and static constructors), and nested types. Class types support inheritance, a mechanism whereby a ***derived class*** can extend and specialize a ***base class***.

17.1 Class declarations

A *class-declaration* is a *type-declaration* (§16.6) that declares a new class.

> *class-declaration:*
>   *attributes*_{opt} *class-modifiers*_{opt} partial_{opt} class *identifier*
>   *type-parameter-list*_{opt} *class-base*_{opt} *type-parameter-constraints-clauses*_{opt}
>   *class-body* ;_{opt}

A *class-declaration* consists of an optional set of *attributes* (§24), followed by an optional set of *class-modifiers* (§17.1.1), followed by an optional partial modifier (§17.1.4), followed by the keyword class and an *identifier* that names the class, followed by an optional *type-parameter-list* (§25.1.1), followed by an optional *class-base* specification (§17.1.2), followed by an optional *type-parameter-constraints-clauses* (§25.7), followed by a *class-body* (§17.1.3), optionally followed by a semicolon.

A class declaration shall not supply a *type-parameter-constraints-clauses* unless it also supplies a *type-parameter-list*.

A class declaration that supplies a *type-parameter-list* is a generic class declaration (§25.1).

Trailing semicolons

The optional trailing semicolon allowed at the end of a class, struct, enum, interface, and namespace declaration serves no purpose and exists solely for the benefit of programmers used to languages (such as C++) that require or allow trailing semicolons. Note, however, that a trailing semicolon is *not* permitted after a method or accessor block:

```
class Typo
{
  public Typo()
  {
  } ; // compile time error
}
```

17.1.1 Class modifiers

A *class-declaration* can optionally include a sequence of class modifiers:

> *class-modifiers:*
>   *class-modifier*
>   *class-modifiers* *class-modifier*
>
> *class-modifier:*
>   new
>   public
>   protected
>   internal

```
private
abstract
sealed
static
```

It is a compile-time error for the same modifier to appear multiple times in a class declaration.

The `new` modifier is permitted on nested classes. It specifies that the class hides an inherited member by the same name, as described in §17.2.2. It is a compile-time error for the `new` modifier to appear on a class declaration that is not a nested class declaration.

The `public`, `protected`, `internal`, and `private` modifiers control the accessibility of the class. Depending on the context in which the class declaration occurs, some of these modifiers might not be permitted (§10.5.1).

When a partial type declaration (§17.1.4) includes an accessibility specification (via the `public`, `protected`, `internal`, and `private` modifiers), that specification shall agree with all other parts that include an accessibility specification. If no part of a partial type includes an accessibility specification, the type is given the appropriate default accessibility (§10.5.1).

The `abstract`, `sealed`, and `static` modifiers are discussed in the following subclauses.

17.1.1.1 Abstract classes

The `abstract` modifier is used to indicate that a class is incomplete and that it is intended to be used only as a base class. An ***abstract class*** differs from a ***non-abstract class*** in the following ways:

- An abstract class cannot be instantiated directly, and it is a compile-time error to use the `new` operator on an abstract class. While it is possible to have variables and values whose compile-time types are abstract, such variables and values will necessarily either be `null` or contain references to instances of non-abstract classes derived from the abstract types.
- An abstract class is permitted (but not required) to contain abstract members.
- An abstract class cannot be sealed.

When a non-abstract class is derived from an abstract class, the non-abstract class shall include actual implementations of all inherited abstract members, thereby overriding those abstract members. [*Example*: In the following code

```
abstract class A
{
  public abstract void F();
}

abstract class B: A
{
  public void G() {}
}

class C: B
{
  public override void F()
  {
    // actual implementation of F
  }
}
```

the abstract class A introduces an abstract method F. Class B introduces an additional method G, but since it doesn't provide an implementation of F, B shall also be declared abstract. Class C overrides F and provides an actual implementation. Since there are no abstract members in C, C is permitted (but not required) to be non-abstract. *end example*]

If one or more parts of a partial type declaration (§17.1.4) of a class include the `abstract` modifier, the class is abstract. Otherwise, the class is non-abstract.

abstract + override == redundant?

As with any other class, an abstract class implementing an interface (§20.4.5) must declare how it "implements" each of the interface members it inherits:

```
interface IPlayable
{
  void Play();
}

abstract class CommonPlayable : IPlayable
{
    // error, does not declare Play()
}
```

In contrast, an abstract class extending another abstract class does *not* need to redeclare its "implements" of the abstract base members it inherits:

```
abstract class CommonPlayable : IPlayable
{
  public abstract void Play();
}

abstract class Allowed : CommonPlayable
{
}

abstract class AlsoAllowed : CommonPlayable
{
  public abstract override void Play(); // not required
}
```

Of course, a nonabstract class extending an abstract class must implement any abstract base members it inherits.

abstract + override != redundant

The abstract + override modifier combination is for unusual situations where an abstract method overrides a *non-abstract* base class method:

```
class ConcretePlayable : IPlayable
{
  public virtual void Play()
  {
    ...
  }
}
```

```
     abstract class AllowedButUnusual : ConcretePlayable
     {
       public abstract override void Play();
     }
```

17.1.1.2 Sealed classes

The sealed modifier is used to prevent derivation from a class. A compile-time error occurs if a sealed class is specified as the base class of another class.

A sealed class cannot also be an abstract class.

[*Note*: The sealed modifier is primarily used to prevent unintended derivation, but it also enables certain run-time optimizations. In particular, because a sealed class is known never to have any derived classes, it is possible to transform virtual function member invocations on sealed class instances into non-virtual invocations. *end note*]

If one or more parts of a partial type declaration (§17.1.4) of a class include the sealed modifier, the class is sealed. Otherwise, the class is unsealed.

17.1.1.3 Static classes

When a class declaration includes a static modifier, the class being declared is said to be a *static class*.

A static class declaration is subject to the following restrictions:

- A static class shall not include a sealed or abstract modifier. (However, since a static class cannot be instantiated or derived from, it behaves as if it were both sealed and abstract.)
- A static class shall not include a *class-base* specification (§17.1.2) and cannot explicitly specify a base class or a list of implemented interfaces. A static class implicitly inherits from type object.
- A static class shall not contain any operators.
- A static class shall not have members with protected or protected internal declared accessibility.
- A static class shall only contain static members (§17.2.5). [*Note*: constants and nested types are classified as static members. *end note*]

[*Example*:

```
using System.Diagnostics;
public static class Precondition
{
  public sealed class Exception: System.ApplicationException
  {
    public Exception(string message) : base(message) {}
  }

  [Conditional("CHECK_PRECONDITIONS")]
  public static void Required(bool condition, string description)
  {
    if (!condition)
    {
      throw new Exception(description);
    }
  }
}
```

end example]

A static class has no instance constructors. It is not possible to declare an instance constructor in a static class, and no default instance constructor (§17.10.4) is provided for a static class.

The members of a static class are not implicitly made static; except for constants and nested types, member declarations that are intended to be static shall explicitly include a `static` modifier. When a class is nested within a static outer class, the nested class is not a static class unless it explicitly includes a `static` modifier.

A *namespace-or-type-name* (§10.8) is permitted to reference a static class if

- The *namespace-or-type-name* is the `T` in a *namespace-or-type-name* of the form `T.I`, or
- The *namespace-or-type-name* is the `T` in a *typeof-expression* (§14.5.11) of the form `typeof (T)`.

A *primary-expression* (§14.5) is permitted to reference a static class if

- The *primary-expression* is the `E` in a *member-access* (§14.5.4) of the form `E.I`.

In any other context, it is a compile-time error to reference a static class. [*Note*: For example, it is an error for a static class to be used as a base class, a constituent type (§17.2.4) of a member, a generic type argument, or a type parameter constraint. Likewise, a static class cannot be used in an array type, a pointer type, a `new` expression, a cast expression, an `is` expression, an `as` expression, a `sizeof` expression, or a default value expression. *end note*]

If one or more parts of a partial type declaration (§17.1.4) of a class include the `static` modifier, the class is static. Otherwise, the class is not static.

Some bugs lead to features

In the Version 1 implementation of the Microsoft CLI, the `System.Environment` class contained a nonstatic property called `HasShutdownStarted`:

```
namespace System
{
  public sealed class Environment
  {
    ...
    public bool HasShutdownStarted // ???
    {
      get { ...}
    }
    ...
    private Environment()
    {
    }
  }
}
```

This property could never be accessed since the class is sealed and its constructor is private! (All the other properties in `System.Environment` are static.)

A similar example is the `HttpVersion` class, which contains only two static fields but has a public constructor:

```
namespace System
{
  public class HttpVersion
```

```
{
  public HttpVersion() // ???
  { ...
  }

  public static readonly Version Version10 = 1.0;
  public static readonly Version Version11 = 1.1;
}
}
```

These unfortunate accidents served a useful purpose—they fostered the idea of a non-instantiable class that can only have static members, that is, the notion of static class described in this clause.

17.1.2 Class base specification

A class declaration can include a *class-base* specification, which defines the direct base class of the class and the interfaces (§20) implemented by the class.

> *class-base:*
> :   *class-type*
> :   *interface-type-list*
> :   *class-type* , *interface-type-list*
>
> *interface-type-list:*
>   *interface-type*
>   *interface-type-list* , *interface-type*

Positional inheritance notation

C# uses a positional notation to distinguish between the base classes and the implemented interfaces of a class. This is one example where C# followed the C++ syntactic style, favoring brevity over explicitness, in contrast to Java, which uses `extends` for base class and `implements` for implemented interfaces.

If a C# class has a direct base class *and* implements one or more interfaces, the base class *must* come first.

```
class ExampleA : BaseClass, InterfaceA // correct
{ ...
}

class ExampleB : InterfaceA, BaseClass // compile time error
{ ...
}
```

The use of positional notation is one reason the C# (and CLI) naming guidelines recommend a leading I for interface names, a last vestige of Hungarian notation. This is unfortunate, creating unintended and awkward consequences. For example, all interface names clump together under "I" in documentation indexes.

In making this choice, C# may appear to waver between brevity, as in this case, and explicitness, as in the switch statement (§15.7.2).

However, C# uses the colon (:) also to specify constraints on type parameters (§25.7), and for this purpose it is preferable to have only one symbol. The constraint on a type parameter may be a class, an interface, or another type parameter, and having to distinguish these three cases with different keywords would be awkward and restrictive. The Java designers chose to use only `extends` in type parameter constraints, which indeed has led some developers to wrongly conclude that in Java one can constrain a type parameter with a class but not with an interface or another type parameter.

17.1.2.1 Base classes

When a *class-type* is included in the *class-base*, it specifies the direct base class of the class being declared. If a non-partial class declaration has no *class-base*, or if the *class-base* lists only interface types, the direct base class is `object`. When a partial class declaration includes a base class specification, that base class specification shall reference the same type as all other parts of that partial type that include a base class specification. If no part of a partial class includes a base class specification, the base class is `object`. A class inherits members from its direct base class, as described in §17.2.1.

[*Example*: In the following code

```
class A {}

class B: A {}
```

class `A` is said to be the direct base class of `B`, and `B` is said to be derived from `A`. Since `A` does not explicitly specify a direct base class, its direct base class is implicitly `object`. *end example*]

The base class specified in a class declaration can be a constructed class type (§25.5). A base class cannot be a type parameter on its own, though it can involve the type parameters that are in scope. [*Example*:

```
class Extend<V>: V {}       // Error, type parameter used as base class

class C<V>: Base<V[ ]> {}    // Ok
```

end example]

The direct base class (and any type arguments) of a class type shall be at least as accessible as the class type itself (§10.5.4). For example, it is a compile-time error for a `public` class to derive from a `private` or `internal` class.

The direct base class of a class type shall not be any of the following types: `System.Array`, `System.Delegate`, `System.Enum`, or `System.ValueType`.

The base classes of a class are the direct base class and its base classes (after substituting type arguments for type parameters in constructed generic types). In other words, the set of base classes is the transitive closure of the direct base class relationship. [*Note*: Referring to the example above, the base classes of `B` are `A` and `object`. *end note*]

Except for class `object`, every class has exactly one direct base class. The `object` class has no direct base class and is the ultimate base class of all other classes.

When a class `B` derives from a class `A`, it is a compile-time error for `A` to depend on `B`. A class *directly depends on* its direct base class (if any) and ***directly depends on*** the class within which it is immediately nested (if any). Given this definition, the complete set of classes upon which a class depends is the transitive closure of the *directly depends on* relationship.

[*Example*: The example

```
class A: B { }

class B: C { }

class C: A { }
```

is in error because the classes circularly depend on themselves. Likewise, the example

```
class A: B.C { }

class B: A
{
    public class C { }
}
```

results in a compile-time error because A depends on B.C (its direct base class), which depends on B (its immediately enclosing class), which circularly depends on A. *end example*]

A class does not depend on the classes that are nested within it. [*Example*: In the following code

```
class A
{
    class B: A { }
}
```

B depends on A (because A is both its direct base class and its immediately enclosing class), but A does not depend on B (since B is neither a base class nor an enclosing class of A). Thus, the example is valid. *end example*]

It is not possible to derive from a sealed class. [*Example*: In the following code

```
sealed class A { }

class B: A { }        // Error, cannot derive from a sealed class
```

class B results in a compile-time error because it attempts to derive from the sealed class A. *end example*]

17.1.2.2 Interface implementations

A *class-base* specification can include a list of interface types, in which case the class is said to implement the given interface types.

The set of interfaces for a type declared in multiple parts (§17.1.4) is the union of the interfaces specified on each part. A particular interface can only be named once on each part, but multiple parts can name the same base interface(s). There shall only be one implementation of each member of any given interface. [*Example*: In the following:

```
partial class C: IA, IB {...}

partial class C: IC {...}

partial class C: IA, IB {...}
```

the set of base interfaces for class C is IA, IB, and IC. *end example*]

Typically, each part provides an implementation of the interface(s) declared on that part; however, this is not a requirement. A part can provide the implementation for an interface declared on a different part. [*Example*:

```
partial class X
{
  int IComparable.CompareTo(object o) {...}
}

partial class X: IComparable
{
  ...
}
```

end example]

The base interfaces specified in a class declaration can be constructed interface types (§25.5). A base interface cannot be a type parameter on its own, though it can involve the type parameters that are in scope. [*Example*: The following code illustrates how a class can implement and extend constructed types:

```
class C<U, V> {}

interface I1<V> {}

class D: C<string, int>, I1<string> {}
```

class E<T>: C<int, T>, I1<T> {}

end example]

Interface implementations are discussed further in §20.4.

17.1.3 Class body
The *class-body* of a class defines the members of that class.

> *class-body:*
>   {   *class-member-declarations*_{opt}   }

17.1.4 Partial declarations

Divide and confuse...

Partial declarations, which may be for classes (§17.1, §25.1), structs (§18.1, §25.2), or interfaces (§20.1, §25.3), allow a single declaration to be split into one or more parts within one file or across multiple files. Partial declarations are not a mechanism for separate compilation: All parts of a partial declaration must be provided to the compiler at the same time—and the onus is on the programmer to do this as the compiler has no way of checking.

As stated in §8.7.13, partial declarations allow a declaration too large to fit in one file to be split, and may assist in the situation where one part of a declaration is to be generated by a tool while another part is handwritten.

Each part of a partial declaration forms part of a single declaration space (§10.3). The textual order of declarations within a declaration space is usually not significant, so the order of declarations with different parts of a partial declaration is not significant. However, the textual order of field declarations is important as it determines the order of initialization. For partial declarations the only guarantee provided is that a field declared in one part will be initialized before any declared textually later *in the same part* (§10.3, §17.4.5); it is therefore permissible for the initialization of fields in different parts to be interleaved.

Different parts of a partial declaration may be in the scope of different *extern-alias-directives* (§16.3) and *using-directives* (§16.4), so a name may have different meanings in different parts. This means that care must be taken if a declaration in one part is moved to another part.

If two or more parts of a partial declaration each have an accessibility modifier (`public`, `protected`, `private`, or `internal`), then those accessibility modifiers must be identical. If an accessibility modifier is applied to any part, then that is the accessibility of the combined declaration.

The `abstract` (§17.1.1.1), `sealed` (§17.1.1.2), `static` (§17.1.1.3), and `new` (§17.2.2) modifiers only need to be applied to one, or more, parts of a partial declaration to be applied to all of them.

However, if the `unsafe` (§27.1) modifier is applied to one (or more) parts of a partial declaration, the modifier only applies to that part (or parts).

Only one part of a partial declaration needs to have a base class specified for it to be the base class of all parts. If more than one part has a base class, they must all resolve (allowing for any aliases in scope) to the same class (§17.1.2.1). The interfaces implemented by a partial declaration are the union of those declared on each of its parts (§17.1.2.2).

The attributes attached to a partial declaration is the combination of the attributes attached to any part; duplicates are allowed (§24.2).

Generic partial declarations (§25.1, §25.2, §25.3) must have the same number of type parameters, with the same names in the same order (§25.1.1). If any part has constraints (§25.7), then the constraints apply to the combined declaration. If two or more parts have constraints those constraints must be equivalent (§25.7).

So in summary, when considering code defined in one part of a partial declaration, *it may not be readily apparent*:

- what modifiers are applied to the enclosing declaration;
- what the base class is;
- what interfaces are being implemented;
- what attributes are attached to the enclosing declaration;
- what other declarations are defined in the same declaration space;
- what constraints are in force on type parameters; and
- whether a name in the current part has the same meaning as the same name in another part.

Recommendation: Use partial declarations only after careful consideration, and when doing so use comments liberally to provide clarity on the preceding points.

But sometimes useful

Partial declarations were invented primarily to simplify the integration of handwritten code and machine-generated code, such as class declarations autogenerated from a database schema. But partial declarations are useful in other contexts too. One example is where existing C# 1.0 code must continue to work, and there is also a need to build upon it using C# 2.0 features. When extending the existing classes it may be a lot cleaner to put the new code into a separate file and use partial declarations, rather than having large numbers of lines of code inside `#if` conditionals. When using partial declarations, only minor parts (such as the `partial` keyword itself) need to be enclosed in `#if` conditionals.

For example, consider a C# 1.0 class `CustomObject`, which is to be extended using C# 2.0 features while maintaining the ability to compile the original version. The C# 1.0 code for the class is placed in the file `customobject_cs1.cs` with a conditional partial declaration:

```
#if TARGET_V2
partial
#endif
public class CustomObject { ...}
```

The extension of class `CustomObject`, which uses C# 2.0 features, is placed in the file `customobject_cs2.cs` and contains code without any version-specific `#if` conditionals:

```
// extra for C# 2.0
partial public class CustomObject { ...}
```

The code in `customobject_cs1.cs` must also contain `#if` conditionals around uses of members defined in `customobject_cs2.cs`.

To compile the code for C# 1.0 the compiler call would be something like (using Mono):

```
gmcs customobject_cs1.cs ...
```

To compile for C# 2.0 the command would be:

```
gmcs -d:TARGET_V2 customobject_cs1.cs customobject_cs2.cs ...
```

We used partial classes to evolve Mono's C# compiler from a 1.0 compiler to a 2.0 compiler while maintaining a single code base. When generics support was added to the compiler, we tried to keep the differences between the 1.0 and 2.0 compiler versions to a minimum—so instead of having half of our static `TypeManager` class inside `#if` conditionals, a partial class was used with all the 2.0 code in a separate file.

Martin Baulig

The modifier `partial` is used when defining a class, struct, or interface type in multiple parts. Like `get` and `set` in property accessors, `partial` is not a keyword. `partial` shall appear immediately before one of the keywords `class`, `struct`, or `interface`.

Each part of a ***partial type*** declaration shall include a `partial` modifier and shall be declared in the same namespace or containing type as the other parts. The `partial` modifier indicates that additional parts of the type declaration might exist elsewhere, but the existence of such additional parts is not a requirement; it is valid for the only declaration of a type to include the `partial` modifier.

All parts of a partial type shall be compiled together such that the parts can be merged at compile-time. Partial types specifically do not allow already compiled types to be extended.

Nested types can be declared in multiple parts by using the `partial` modifier. Typically, the containing type is declared using `partial` as well, and each part of the nested type is declared in a different part of the containing type.

[*Example*: The following partial class is implemented in two parts, which reside in different source files. The first part is machine generated by a database-mapping tool while the second part is manually authored:

```
public partial class Customer
{
  private int id;
  private string name;
  private string address;
  private List<Order> orders;
```

```
        public Customer()
        {
           ...
        }
    }

    public partial class Customer
    {
      public void SubmitOrder(Order orderSubmitted)
      {
        orders.Add(orderSubmitted);
      }

      public bool HasOutstandingOrders()
      {
        return orders.Count > 0;
      }
    }
```

When the two parts above are compiled together, the resulting code behaves as if the class had been written as a single unit, as follows:

```
    public class Customer
    {
      private int id;
      private string name;
      private string address;
      private List<Order> orders;

      public Customer()
      {
         ...
      }

      public void SubmitOrder(Order orderSubmitted)
      {
        orders.Add(orderSubmitted);
      }

      public bool HasOutstandingOrders()
      {
        return orders.Count > 0;
      }
    }
```

end example]

The handling of attributes specified on the type or type parameters of different parts of a partial declaration is discussed in §24.2

17.2 Class members

The members of a class consist of the members introduced by its *class-member-declaration*s and the members inherited from the direct base class.

class-member-declarations:
  class-member-declaration
  class-member-declarations   class-member-declaration

class-member-declaration:
  constant-declaration
  field-declaration
  method-declaration
  property-declaration
  event-declaration
  indexer-declaration
  operator-declaration
  constructor-declaration
  finalizer-declaration
  static-constructor-declaration
  type-declaration

The members of a class are divided into the following categories:

- Constants, which represent constant values associated with that class (§17.3).
- Fields, which are the variables of that class (§17.4).
- Methods, both non-generic and generic, which implement the computations and actions that can be performed by that class (§17.5, §25.6).
- Properties, which define named characteristics and the actions associated with reading and writing those characteristics (§17.6).
- Events, which define notifications that can be generated by that class (§17.7).
- Indexers, which permit instances of that class to be indexed in the same way as arrays (§17.8).
- Operators, which define the expression operators that can be applied to instances of that class (§17.9).
- Instance constructors, which implement the actions required to initialize instances of that class (§17.10)
- Finalizers, which implement the actions to be performed before instances of that class are permanently discarded (§17.12).
- Static constructors, which implement the actions required to initialize that class itself (§17.11).
- Types, which represent the types that are local to that class (§16.6).

Members that can contain executable code are collectively known as the *function members* of the class. The function members of a class are the methods, properties, events, indexers, operators, instance constructors, finalizers, and static constructors of that class.

A *class-declaration* creates a new declaration space (§10.3), and the *type-parameters* and the *class-member-declarations* immediately contained by the *class-declaration* introduce new members into this declaration space. The following rules apply to *class-member-declarations*:

- Instance constructors, finalizers, and static constructors shall have the same name as the immediately enclosing class. All other members shall have names that differ from the name of the immediately enclosing class.

Minor Java difference

In Java a constructor and a method *can* share the same name. Java employs the *use context* of a name to distinguish between package, type, method, and field/variable names. However, using the same identifier for different entities "is discouraged as a matter of style" and if Java's naming conventions are followed, conflicts should be rare.

The CLI also employs use context to distinguish between methods, fields, nested types, properties, and events.

C# could have made a similar choice to Java and the CLI, but did not. There is, of course, no absolute "right" choice.

- The name of a type parameter in the *type-parameter-list* of a class declaration shall differ from the names of all other type parameters in the same *type-parameter-list* and shall differ from the name of the class and the names of all members of the class.
- The name of a type shall differ from the names of all non-type members declared in the same class. If two or more type declarations share the same fully qualified name, the declarations shall have the partial modifier (§17.1.4) and these declarations combine to define a single type. [*Note*: Since the fully qualified name of a type declaration encodes the number of type parameters, two distinct types may share the same name as long as they have different number of type parameters. *end note*]
- The name of a constant, field, property, or event shall differ from the names of all other members declared in the same class.
- The name of a method shall differ from the names of all other non-methods declared in the same class. In addition, the signature (§10.6) of a method shall differ from the signatures of all other methods declared in the same class, and two methods declared in the same class shall not have signatures that differ solely by `ref` and `out`.
- The signature of an instance constructor shall differ from the signatures of all other instance constructors declared in the same class, and two constructors declared in the same class shall not have signatures that differ solely by `ref` and `out`.
- The signature of an indexer shall differ from the signatures of all other indexers declared in the same class.
- The signature of an operator shall differ from the signatures of all other operators declared in the same class.

The inherited members of a class (§17.2.1) are not part of the declaration space of a class. [*Note*: Thus, a derived class is allowed to declare a member with the same name or signature as an inherited member (which in effect hides the inherited member). *end note*]

The set of members of a type declared in multiple parts (§17.1.4) is the union of the members declared in each part. The bodies of all parts of the type declaration share the same declaration space (§10.3), and the scope of each member (§10.7) extends to the bodies of all the parts. The accessibility domain of any member always includes all the parts of the enclosing type; a `private` member declared in one part is freely accessible from another part. It is a compile-time error to declare the same member in more than one part of the type, unless that member is a type having the `partial` modifier. [*Example*:

```
partial class A
{
    int x;                  // Error, cannot declare x more than once
```

```
    partial class Inner    // Ok, Inner is a partial type
    {
      int y;
    }
  }

  partial class A
  {
    int x;                 // Error, cannot declare x more than once

    partial class Inner    // Ok, Inner is a partial type
    {
      int z;
    }
  }
```

end example]

The ordering of members within a type declared in multiple parts is undefined. [*Note*: Although the ordering of members within a type is not significant to C# code, it may be significant when interfacing with other languages and environments. *end note*]

17.2.1 Inheritance

A class **inherits** the members of its direct base class. Inheritance means that a class implicitly contains all members of its direct base class, except for the instance constructors, finalizers, and static constructors of the base class. Some important aspects of inheritance are:

- Inheritance is transitive. If C is derived from B, and B is derived from A, then C inherits the members declared in A as well as the members declared in B.
- A derived class *extends* its direct base class. A derived class can add new members to those it inherits, but it cannot remove the definition of an inherited member.
- Instance constructors, finalizers, and static constructors are not inherited, but all other members are, regardless of their declared accessibility (§10.5). However, depending on their declared accessibility, inherited members might not be accessible in a derived class.
- A derived class can **hide** (§10.7.1.2) inherited members by declaring new members with the same name or signature. However, hiding an inherited member does not remove that member—it merely means that member will not be found by member lookup within the derived class.
- An instance of a class contains a set of all instance fields declared in the class and its base classes, and an implicit conversion (§13.1.4) exists from a derived class type to any of its base class types. Thus, a reference to an instance of some derived class can be treated as a reference to an instance of any of its base classes.
- A class can declare virtual methods, properties, indexers, and events, and derived classes can override the implementation of these function members. This enables classes to exhibit polymorphic behavior wherein the actions performed by a function member invocation varies depending on the run-time type of the instance through which that function member is invoked.
- Members inherited from a constructed generic type are inherited after type substitution. That is, any constituent types in the member have the base class declaration's type parameters replaced with the corresponding type arguments used in the *class-base* specification.

[*Example*: In the example:

```
class A<S>
{
  public S field;
}

class B<T> : A<T[ ]>
{
  // inherited: public T[ ] field;
  public A<T> Meth(T t) {...}
}

class C : B<string>
{
  // inherited: public string[ ] field;
  // inherited: public A<string> Meth(string t);
}
```

class B<T> inherits member `field` from A<S> after type parameter S is replaced with the type argument T[ ]. Similarly, class C inherits the members of B<T> (including the inherited member `field`) after type parameter T is replaced with the type argument `string`. *end example*]

17.2.2 The new modifier

A *class-member-declaration* is permitted to declare a member with the same name or signature as an inherited member. When this occurs, the derived class member is said to **hide** the base class member. See §10.7.1.2 for a precise specification of when a member hides an inherited member.

An inherited member M is considered to be **available** if M is accessible and there is no other inherited accessible member N that already hides M.

Hiding an available inherited member is not considered an error, but it does cause the compiler to issue a warning. To suppress the warning, the declaration of the derived class member can include a `new` modifier to indicate that the derived member is intended to hide the base member. If one or more parts of a partial declaration §17.1.4) of a nested type include the `new` modifier, no warning is issued if the nested type hides an available inherited member.

If a `new` modifier is included in a declaration that doesn't hide an available inherited member, a warning to that effect is issued.

17.2.3 Access modifiers

A *class-member-declaration* can have any one of the five possible kinds of declared accessibility (§10.5.1): `public`, `protected internal`, `protected`, `internal`, or `private`. Except for the `protected internal` combination, it is a compile-time error to specify more than one access modifier. When a *class-member-declaration* does not include any access modifiers, `private` is assumed.

Absent modifier != default modifier

Destructors, static constructors, and explicit interface implementations are not allowed access modifiers but their access is *not* private:

- Destructors and static constructors cannot be called directly; they are invoked automatically as required by the semantics.
- Explicit interface implementations can only be called explicitly via the interface and have public (albeit indirect) accessibility.

- All other members (such as fields) without an explicit access modifier default to `private` and are accessible to the declaring type.

An alternative would have been to have no default accessibility, so every member must explicitly declare its accessibility. However, this option was not taken and is one of the few times C# favors brevity over explicitness.

17.2.4 Constituent types

Types that are used in the declaration of a member are called the ***constituent types*** of that member. Possible constituent types are the type of a constant, field, property, event, or indexer, the return type of a method or operator, and the parameter types of a method, indexer, operator, or instance constructor. The constituent types of a member shall be at least as accessible as that member itself (§10.5.4).

17.2.5 Static and instance members

Members of a class are either ***static members*** or ***instance members***. [*Note*: Generally speaking, it is useful to think of static members as belonging to classes and instance members as belonging to objects (instances of classes). *end note*]

When a field, method, property, event, operator, or constructor declaration includes a `static` modifier, it declares a static member. In addition, a constant or type declaration implicitly declares a static member. Static members have the following characteristics:

- When a static member is referenced in a *member-access* (§14.5.4) of the form `E.M`, `E` shall denote a type that has a member `M`. It is a compile-time error for `E` to denote an instance.

No access to static members through instance expressions

In contrast to C#, both C++ and Java allow a static member to be accessed using the syntax of an instance method call.

The restriction is welcome on readability grounds. For instance, the following is perfectly valid in Java, but rather misleading:

```
Thread t = new Thread(someRunnableImplementation);
t.start();
t.sleep(5000);
```

This appears to make the new thread sleep for 5 seconds—but in fact it makes the current thread sleep for 5 seconds. `Thread.sleep` is a static method, but this is obscured by the code. Fortunately, some Java IDEs have options to be stricter than the Java Language Specification itself. It is good that there is no need for "extra" voluntary restrictions like this in C#.

Jon Skeet

- A static field in a non-generic class identifies exactly one storage location. No matter how many instances of a non-generic class are created, there is only ever one copy of a static field. Each distinct closed constructed type (§25.5.2) has its own set of static fields, regardless of the number of instances of the closed constructed type.
- A static function member (method, property, event, operator, or constructor) does not operate on a specific instance, and it is a compile-time error to refer to `this` in such a function member.

When a field, method, property, event, indexer, constructor, or finalizer declaration does not include a `static` modifier, it declares an instance member. (An instance member is sometimes called a non-static member.) Instance members have the following characteristics:

- When an instance member is referenced in a *member-access* (§14.5.4) of the form E.M, E shall denote an instance of a type that has a member M. It is a compile-time error for E to denote a type.
- Every instance of a class contains a separate set of all instance fields of the class.
- An instance function member (method, property, indexer, event, instance constructor, or finalizer) operates on a given instance of the class, and this instance can be accessed as `this` (§14.5.7).

[*Example*: The following example illustrates the rules for accessing static and instance members:

```
class Test
{
  int x;
  static int y;

  void F()
  {
    x = 1;      // Ok, same as this.x = 1
    y = 1;      // Ok, same as Test.y = 1
  }

  static void G()
  {
    x = 1;      // Error, cannot access this.x
    y = 1;      // Ok, same as Test.y = 1
  }

  static void Main()
  {
    Test t = new Test();
    t.x = 1;      // Ok
    t.y = 1;      // Error, cannot access static member through instance
    Test.x = 1; // Error, cannot access instance member through type
    Test.y = 1; // Ok
  }
}
```

The F method shows that in an instance function member, a *simple-name* (§14.5.2) can be used to access both instance members and static members. The G method shows that in a static function member, it is a compile-time error to access an instance member through a *simple-name*. The Main method shows that in a *member-access* (§14.5.4), instance members shall be accessed through instances, and static members shall be accessed through types. *end example*]

Rationale: instance method call semantics

The semantics for both class/struct and interface calls to instance methods (method, property, indexer, event) in C# are designed to work on, but they are not the same as, the CLI.

In the CLI an instance method call can either be nonvirtual, in which case the method is located via the class/struct type given in the call instruction, or virtual, in which case the method is located via the runtime type of the object instance. A virtual method can be called either way (subject to certain restrictions for security, not important to this discussion), which surfaces in the C# semantics of base access (§14.5.8).

Whichever way a method is called on the CLI, in the actual call the method is specified by its signature (name and parameter types) *and* the class that contains its original declaration. For a virtual method and call the actual implementation used may be from a derived class or struct if the instance is of a derived type. For example, given:

- virtual method V is declared and implemented in class J;
- class K derives from J and provides an overriding implementation of V;
- class L derives from K,

then:

- a virtual call of J.V on an instance of L executes the implementation K.V.

These semantics are reflected in C# *except* that the name of the declaring type is *not* part of the method call syntax. A C# compiler compiling for the CLI must determine the declaring type according to the semantics of C# and emit the appropriate CLI call.

On the CLI, a derived class can declare a new instance method (virtual or nonvirtual) with the same name as an instance method in a base class. This causes no confusion for the CLI, as method calls include the name of the declaring type, so the two methods can be distinguished. For example, given:

- instance method V is declared and implemented in class J;
- class K derives from J and also declares and implements an instance method V;
- class L derives from K,

then:

- on an instance of L a call of K.V executes the method declared by K;
- while a call of J.V executes the method declared by J.

C# semantics differ here. When class K introduces a new method V, it *hides* the version in the base class (§17.2.2, §17.5.3). To call the hidden method J.V the L instance must first be cast to J. The important difference is that on the CLI no cast takes place. It is not a change of type that allows the J.V method to be invoked, but the fact that an instance of class L has two different V methods. A CLI C# compiler must translate from the casting model of C# to the multiple method model of the CLI.

Finally, on the CLI a class implements all of the interfaces that it declares, all those any base class declares, and all those any of these declared interfaces specify as required, transitively. All these implementations are per type; a derived class has its own implementation of each interface implemented by its base classes. The interfaces available depend solely on the run time type of an instance; casting to a base class does not make the base class's implementation of an interface available. For example, given:

- interface F declares method V;
- interface G declares method W;
- class J declares a method V and implements interface F;
- class K derives from J, declares a method W, and implements interface G; and
- class L derives from K declares a method V and implements interface F,

then:

- An instance of K implements interface F with F.V mapping to J.V, and implements interface G with G.W mapping to K.W; and
- An instance of L implements interface F with F.V mapping to L.V, and implements interface G with G.W mapping to K.W.
- Even if an instance of L is cast to K or J this does not change the actual run time type. If the resultant reference is cast to F or G, the mappings to L.V and K.W still apply.

The C# semantics mirror the CLI in this case, which is why casting to a base class does not change the interface mapping (§20.4.4), whereas it can change the virtual method mapping (§17.5.3).

17.2.6 Nested types

A type declared within a class or struct is called a ***nested type***. A type that is declared within a compilation unit or namespace is called a ***non-nested type***. [*Example*: In the following example:

```
using System;

class A
{
  class B
  {
    static void F()
    {
      Console.WriteLine("A.B.F");
    }
  }
}
```

class B is a nested type because it is declared within class A, and class A is a non-nested type because it is declared within a compilation unit. *end example*]

Delegates and enums are types too

The phrase "nested types" usually evokes images of classes, structs, and interfaces. But delegate types and enum types can also be declared inside other types, and then are nested types too. But since they do not have members whose accessibility needs to be considered, they are sometimes not thought about in this way. In terms of accessibility, delegates and enums are like field and method members.

It is easy to miss that a delegate type declaration is a nested type as it looks more like a cross between a field and a method declaration than it looks like other type declarations.

```
public class Wibble
{
  // Nested type declaration:
  public delegate void FluxHandler(object sender,
                                   FluxEventArgs args);

  ...
}
```

Jon Skeet

17.2.6.1 Fully qualified name

The fully qualified name (§10.8.2) for a nested type declaration is S.N where S is the fully qualified name of the type declaration in which type N is declared and N is the unqualified name (§10.8.1) of the nested type declaration (including any *generic-dimension-specifier* (§14.5.11).

17.2.6.2 Declared accessibility

Non-nested types can have public or internal declared accessibility and they have internal declared accessibility by default. Nested types can have these forms of declared accessibility too, plus one or more additional forms of declared accessibility, depending on whether the containing type is a class or struct:

- A nested type that is declared in a class can have any of five forms of declared accessibility (public, protected internal, protected, internal, or private) and, like other class members, defaults to private declared accessibility.
- A nested type that is declared in a struct can have any of three forms of declared accessibility (public, internal, or private) and, like other struct members, defaults to private declared accessibility.

[*Example*: The example

```
public class List
{
  // Private data structure
  private class Node
  {
    public object Data;
    public Node Next;
    public Node(object data, Node next)
    {
      this.Data = data;
      this.Next = next;
    }
  }

  private Node first = null;
  private Node last = null;

  // Public interface
  public void AddToFront(object o) {...}
  public void AddToBack(object o) {...}
  public object RemoveFromFront() {...}
  public object AddToFront() {...}
  public int Count { get {...} }
}
```

declares a private nested class Node. *end example*]

17.2.6.3 Hiding

A nested type can hide (§10.7.1.1) a base member. The new modifier (§17.2.2) is permitted on nested type declarations so that hiding can be expressed explicitly. [*Example*: The example

```
using System;

class Base
```

```
{
  public static void M()
  {
    Console.WriteLine("Base.M");
  }
}

class Derived: Base
{
  new public class M
  {
    public static void F()
    {
      Console.WriteLine("Derived.M.F");
    }
  }
}

class Test
{
  static void Main()
  {
    Derived.M.F();
  }
}
```

shows a nested class M that hides the method M defined in Base. *end example*]

17.2.6.4 this access

A nested type and its containing type do not have a special relationship with regard to *this-access* (§14.5.7). Specifically, this within a nested type cannot be used to refer to instance members of the containing type. In cases where a nested type needs access to the instance members of its containing type, access can be provided by providing the this for the instance of the containing type as a constructor argument for the nested type. [*Example*: The following example

```
using System;

class C
{
  int i = 123;
  public void F()
  {
    Nested n = new Nested(this);
    n.G();
  }

  public class Nested
  {
    C this_c;
    public Nested(C c)
    {
      this_c = c;
    }
```

```
      public void G()
      {
        Console.WriteLine(this_c.i);
      }
    }
  }
}

class Test
{
  static void Main()
  {
    C c = new C();
    c.F();
  }
}
```

shows this technique. An instance of C creates an instance of Nested, and passes its own this to Nested's constructor in order to provide subsequent access to C's instance members. *end example*]

Simulating Java-style inner classes

The preceding technique—a nested class that holds a reference to an instance of the enclosing class—is the obvious way to simulate a Java inner class in C#. Here is a Java declaration corresponding to the preceding C# code. Note that the C reference implicitly held by the inner class Nested can be accessed using the Java syntax C.this:

```
// Java code

class C
{
  private int i = 123;
  public void F()
  {
    Nested n = new Nested();
    n.G();
  }

  public class Nested        // Inner class!
  {
    public void G()
    {
      System.out.println(C.this.i);
    }
  }
}

class Test
{
  public static void main(String[ ] args)
  {
    C c = new C();
    c.F();
  }
}
```

A Java static member class is the same as a C# member class. A Java inner class is a nonstatic member class, or a local class declared in an instance method; in any case it holds a reference to an instance of the enclosing class(es). The term "inner class" should not be used about a static member class.

Implementation aside:

The CLI, the virtual machine usually targeted by C# compilers, has direct support for nested classes. However, the JVM, the virtual machine usually targeted by Java compilers, does not. Therefore, when targeting the JVM, a Java compiler must implement the nested class semantics explicitly. Typically, a nested class such as the one shown here is compiled to a separate class, possibly named `C$Nested`, that has no particular relation to the enclosing class `C`. To allow this separate class to access the private members of the enclosing class, the Java compiler adds public accessor methods to the enclosing class. This incurs a small runtime overhead on each access to a field of the enclosing class. Paradoxically, this means that, for this particular feature, the CLI may be a better target than the JVM for a Java compiler.

17.2.6.5 Access to private and protected members of the containing type

A nested type has access to all of the members that are accessible to its containing type, including members of the containing type that have private and protected declared accessibility. [*Example*: The example

```
using System;

class C
{
  private static void F()
  {
    Console.WriteLine("C.F");
  }
  public class Nested
  {
    public static void G()
    {
      F();
    }
  }
}

class Test
{
  static void Main()
  {
    C.Nested.G();
  }
}
```

shows a class `C` that contains a nested class `Nested`. Within `Nested`, the method `G` calls the static method `F` defined in `C`, and `F` has private declared accessibility. *end example*]

Access clarification

The statement that "a nested type has access to all of the members that are accessible to its containing type" at first appears to contradict the preceding clause (§17.2.6.4). What the statement means is that code in the nested type:

a. *can* access static members of the enclosing type, *and*

b. *can* access instance members of the enclosing type via an explicit instance reference, *but*

c. *cannot* access instance members via an implicit instance reference, *and*

d. *cannot* refer explicitly to an instance reference (`this`) for the enclosing type (as there might not even be an instance to refer to).

For all intents and purposes, code in the nested class is static relative to the enclosing type: The context in which that code executes does not provide a reference to an instance of the enclosing type.

Older C++ difference

In the 1998 C++ ISO standard, members of a nested class had *no* special access to members of an enclosing class. However, this was the subject of C++ Defect Report 45, which says a nested member is a member and as such has the same access rights as any other member. Therefore, more recent C++ Standards stipulate that members of a nested class do have special access to the members of the enclosing class. That is, C# and C++ (and Java) now agree on this point.

A nested type also can access protected members defined in a base type of its containing type. [*Example*: In the following code

```
using System;

class Base
{
  protected void F()
  {
    Console.WriteLine("Base.F");
  }
}

class Derived: Base
{
  public class Nested
  {
    public void G()
    {
      Derived d = new Derived();
      d.F();     // ok
    }
  }
}

class Test
{
  static void Main()
  {
```

```
       Derived.Nested n = new Derived.Nested();
       n.G();
    }
  }
```

the nested class `Derived.Nested` accesses the protected method `F` defined in `Derived`'s base class, `Base`, by calling through an instance of `Derived`. *end example*]

17.2.7 Reserved member names

To facilitate the underlying C# runtime implementation, for each source member declaration that is a property, event, or indexer, the implementation shall reserve two method signatures based on the kind of the member declaration, its name, and its type (§17.2.7.1, §17.2.7.2, §17.2.7.3). It is a compile-time error for a program to declare a member whose signature matches a signature reserved by a member declared in the same scope, even if the underlying runtime implementation does not make use of these reservations.

The reserved names do not introduce declarations, thus they do not participate in member lookup. However, a declaration's associated reserved method signatures do participate in inheritance (§17.2.1), and can be hidden with the new modifier (§17.2.2).

[*Note*: The reservation of these names serves three purposes:

1. To allow the underlying implementation to use an ordinary identifier as a method name for get or set access to the C# language feature.
2. To allow other languages to inter-operate using an ordinary identifier as a method name for get or set access to the C# language feature.
3. To help ensure that the source accepted by one conforming compiler is accepted by another, by making the specifics of reserved member names consistent across all C# implementations.

end note]

The declaration of a finalizer (§17.12) also causes a signature to be reserved (§17.2.7.4).

17.2.7.1 Member names reserved for properties

For a property `P` (§17.6) of type `T`, the following signatures are reserved:

```
T get_P();
void set_P(T value);
```

Both signatures are reserved, even if the property is read-only or write-only.

Neutral, but not agnostic

These two signatures are reserved to allow easy implementation on the CLI, and reveal how that platform implements properties. There is, however, *no* requirement on a C# implementation to follow this implementation model provided that when implementing a property `P` in a given type `T`:

- The model chosen does not reserve other valid C# member signatures in `T` unless they conform to the requirements of reserved names defined in §9.4.2.
- The preceding two signatures derived from `P` are reserved in `T`, even if unused by the implementation model. That is, no other methods may be declared using those signatures.

Incidentally, if `get_P` and `set_P` had been named `get__P` and `set__P` with double under-scores, then the names would have been reserved ones (§9.4.2) and this clause of the specification would not have been needed.

[*Example*: In the following code

```
using System;

class A
{
  public int P
  {
    get { return 123; }
  }
}

class B: A
{
  new public int get_P()
  {
    return 456;
  }
  new public void set_P(int value)
  {
  }
}

class Test
{
  static void Main()
  {
    B b = new B();
    A a = b;
    Console.WriteLine(a.P);
    Console.WriteLine(b.P);
    Console.WriteLine(b.get_P());
  }
}
```

a class `A` defines a read-only property `P`, thus reserving signatures for `get_P` and `set_P` methods. A class `B` derives from `A` and hides both of these reserved signatures. The example produces the output:

```
123
123
456
```

end example]

The meaning of "reserved"

Though the Standard states clearly that declaring a property results in two signatures being "reserved," the definition of this term given in §17.2.7 is a little woolly. What is the rationale for signatures not participating in member lookup but participating in inheritance? We can say what is **not** intended: Overriding a reserved signature is not an intended way to alter the behavior or semantics of a property. As the preceding annotation makes clear, an implementation need not use such a signature for anything, so overriding one is meaningless.

The preceding example, like all examples in the Standard, is *informative*, and although it does indeed produce the stated output on the current Microsoft and Mono compilers, both compilers issue a warning.

Furthermore, the two compilers do not always agree when dealing with combinations where A.P is nonvirtual or virtual and the method B.get_P() is qualified with new, override or neither of these. However, in all cases where B contains a property P, the two compilers do agree with each other and with the standard C# rules governing virtual, new, and override.

It is unfortunate that the Standard does not define "reserved" more precisely and includes an example, even though informative, which is ill-defined. However, if "reserved" is taken to mean "*inaccessible and must not be used, hidden or overridden in the defining or any derived class*" then no problems will result.

17.2.7.2 Member names reserved for events
For an event E (§17.7) of delegate type T, the following signatures are reserved:

```
void add_E(T handler);
void remove_E(T handler);
```

17.2.7.3 Member names reserved for indexers
For an indexer (§17.8) of type T with parameter-list L, the following signatures are reserved:

```
T get_Item(L);
void set_Item(L, T value);
```

Both signatures are reserved, even if the indexer is read-only or write-only.

Indexer names on CLI

On the CLI, the System.Runtime.CompilerServices.IndexerName attribute can be applied to an indexer to specify its CLI name. At that point, it appears that the current Microsoft and Mono C# compilers reserve names of the form get_X and set_X, where X is the indexer name. An example that compiles due to this, which should not compile due to the preceding clause (i.e., is non-conforming) is:

```
using System.Runtime.CompilerServices;

class Test
{
  [ IndexerName("Fred")]
  public int this[ int x]
  {
    get { return x; }
  }

  public int get_Item(int x)
  {
    return 5;
  }
}
```

Without the attribute, compilation fails as expected. See also the annotation on §17.2.7.1.

> *Note:* The C# Standard makes no statement about how indexers should be compiled for any given platform; that is a compiler issue. The current Microsoft and Mono compilers targeting the CLI both compile a C# indexer into a CLI indexer called `Item`.
>
> *Jon Skeet*

17.2.7.4 Member names reserved for finalizers

For a class containing a finalizer (§17.12), the following signature is reserved:

```
void Finalize();
```

17.3 Constants

A ***constant*** is a class member that represents a constant value: a value that can be computed at compile-time. A *constant-declaration* introduces one or more constants of a given type.

> The phrase "can be computed" means "can and *shall* be computed"; see §14.16.

constant-declaration:
  attributes_{opt} *constant-modifiers_{opt}* `const` *type* *constant-declarators* ;

constant-modifiers:
  constant-modifier
  constant-modifiers *constant-modifier*

constant-modifier:
  `new`
  `public`
  `protected`
  `internal`
  `private`

constant-declarators:
  constant-declarator
  constant-declarators , *constant-declarator*

constant-declarator:
  identifier = *constant-expression*

A *constant-declaration* can include a set of *attributes* (§24), a `new` modifier (§17.2.2), and a valid combination of the four access modifiers (§17.2.3). The attributes and modifiers apply to all of the members declared by the *constant-declaration*. Even though constants are considered static members, a *constant-declaration* neither requires nor allows a `static` modifier. It is an error for the same modifier to appear multiple times in a constant declaration.

> ### Constant references do not trigger static initialization
>
> The value of a constant is obtained at compile-time (§17.4.2.2) and is not a runtime access to a static member of a type. Therefore, using a constant does not trigger the initialization of static fields (§17.4.5.1) or static constructors (§17.11 and §18.3.10).

The *type* of a *constant-declaration* specifies the type of the members introduced by the declaration. The type is followed by a list of *constant-declarators*, each of which introduces a new member. A *constant-declarator* consists of an *identifier* that names the member, followed by an "=" token, followed by a *constant-expression* (§14.16) that gives the value of the member.

The *type* specified in a constant declaration shall be sbyte, byte, short, ushort, int, uint, long, ulong, char, float, double, decimal, bool, string, an *enum-type*, or a *reference-type*. Each *constant-expression* shall yield a value of the target type or of a type that can be converted to the target type by an implicit conversion (§13.1).

The *type* of a constant shall be at least as accessible as the constant itself (§10.5.4).

The value of a constant is obtained in an expression using a *simple-name* (§14.5.2) or a *member-access* (§14.5.4).

A constant can itself participate in a *constant-expression*. Thus, a constant can be used in any construct that requires a *constant-expression*. [*Note*: Examples of such constructs include case labels, goto case statements, enum member declarations, attributes, and other constant declarations. *end note*]

[*Note*: As described in §14.16, a *constant-expression* is an expression that can be fully evaluated at compile-time. Since the only way to create a non-null value of a *reference-type* other than string is to apply the new operator, and since the new operator is not permitted in a *constant-expression*, the only possible value for constants of *reference-types* other than string is null. *end note*]

Having nothing might be useful

There is at least one use for declaring constants of *reference-types*, other than string. Consider the following:

```
class Wibble { ...}

class Details
{
   public void Dump(Wibble wb) { ...}
   public void Dump(object o) { ...}
}
```

Calling Dump with a null constant will produce an ambiguous error at compile time. One way to resolve this is with a cast; another is with a null constant:

```
const Wibble nullWibble = null;

Dump(nullWibble);       // ok, invokes Dump(Wibble wb)
Dump((Wibble)null);     // ok, also invokes Dump(Wibble wb)
Dump(null);             // compile-time error, cannot determine
                        // correct Dump() to invoke
```

Typed nulls might be useful to help resolve overloading or in some uses of generics; however, code that uses them might be clearer if redesigned not to require them.

When a symbolic name for a constant value is desired, but when the type of that value is not permitted in a constant declaration, or when the value cannot be computed at compile-time by a *constant-expression*, a readonly field (§17.4.2) can be used instead. [*Note*: The versioning semantics of const and readonly differ (§17.4.2.2). *end-note*]

A constant declaration that declares multiple constants is equivalent to multiple declarations of single constants with the same attributes, modifiers, and type. [*Example*:

```
class A
{
   public const double X = 1.0, Y = 2.0, Z = 3.0;
}
```

is equivalent to

```
class A
{
   public const double X = 1.0;
   public const double Y = 2.0;
   public const double Z = 3.0;
}
```

end example]

Constants are permitted to depend on other constants within the same program as long as the dependencies are not of a circular nature. The compiler automatically arranges to evaluate the constant declarations in the appropriate order. [*Example*: In the following code

```
class A
{
   public const int X = B.Z + 1;
   public const int Y = 10;
}

class B
{
   public const int Z = A.Y + 1;
}
```

the compiler first evaluates A.Y, then evaluates B.Z, and finally evaluates A.X, producing the values 10, 11, and 12. *end example*] Constant declarations can depend on constants from other programs, but such dependencies are only possible in one direction. [*Example*: Referring to the example above, if A and B were declared in separate programs, it would be possible for A.X to depend on B.Z, but B.Z could then not simultaneously depend on A.Y. *end example*]

17.4 Fields

A *field* is a member that represents a variable associated with an object or class. A *field-declaration* introduces one or more fields of a given type.

> *field-declaration:*
>   *attributes*$_{opt}$ *field-modifiers*$_{opt}$ *type* *variable-declarators* ;
>
> *field-modifiers:*
>   *field-modifier*
>   *field-modifiers* *field-modifier*
>
> *field-modifier:*
>   new
>   public
>   protected

```
        internal
        private
        static
        readonly
        volatile
```

variable-declarators:
  variable-declarator
  variable-declarators , *variable-declarator*

variable-declarator:
  identifier
  identifier = *variable-initializer*

variable-initializer:
  expression
  array-initializer

A *field-declaration* can include a set of *attributes* (§24), a `new` modifier (§17.2.2), a valid combination of the four access modifiers (§17.2.3), and a `static` modifier (§17.4.1). In addition, a *field-declaration* can include a `readonly` modifier (§17.4.2) or a `volatile` modifier (§17.4.3), but not both. The attributes and modifiers apply to all of the members declared by the *field-declaration*. It is an error for the same modifier to appear multiple times in a *field declaration*.

The *type* of a *field-declaration* specifies the type of the members introduced by the declaration. The type is followed by a list of *variable-declarators*, each of which introduces a new member. A *variable-declarator* consists of an *identifier* that names that member, optionally followed by an "=" token and a *variable-initializer* (§17.4.5) that gives the initial value of that member.

The *type* of a field shall be at least as accessible as the field itself (§10.5.4).

The value of a field is obtained in an expression using a *simple-name* (§14.5.2), a *member-access* (§14.5.4), a *this-access* (§14.5.7), or a *base-access* (§14.5.8). The value of a non-readonly field is modified using an *assignment* (§14.14). The value of a non-readonly field can be both obtained and modified using postfix increment and decrement operators (§14.5.9) and prefix increment and decrement operators (§14.6.5).

A field declaration that declares multiple fields is equivalent to multiple declarations of single fields with the same attributes, modifiers, and type. [*Example*:

```
class A
{
   public static int X = 1, Y, Z = 100;
}
```

is equivalent to

```
class A
{
   public static int X = 1;
   public static int Y;
   public static int Z = 100;
}
```

end example]

17.4.1 Static and instance fields

When a field declaration includes a `static` modifier, the fields introduced by the declaration are **static fields**. When no `static` modifier is present, the fields introduced by the declaration are **instance fields**. Static fields and instance fields are two of the several kinds of variables (§12) supported by C#, and at times they are referred to as **static variables** and **instance variables**, respectively.

As explained in §17.2.5, each instance of a class contains a complete set of the instance fields of the class, while there is only one set of static fields for each non-generic class or closed constructed type, regardless of the number of instances of the class or closed constructed type.

17.4.2 Readonly fields

When a *field-declaration* includes a `readonly` modifier, the fields introduced by the declaration are **readonly fields**. Direct assignments to readonly fields can only occur as part of that declaration or in an instance constructor or static constructor in the same class. (A readonly field can be assigned to multiple times in these contexts.) Specifically, direct assignments to a `readonly` field are permitted only in the following contexts:

- In the *variable-declarator* that introduces the field (by including a *variable-initializer* in the declaration).
- For an instance field, in the instance constructors of the class that contains the field declaration; for a static field, in the static constructor of the class that contains the field declaration. These are also the only contexts in which it is valid to pass a `readonly` field as an `out` or `ref` parameter.

Attempting to assign to a `readonly` field or pass it as an `out` or `ref` parameter in any other context is a compile-time error.

Readonly yet modifiable

Note that only the field itself is not modifiable. If the `readonly` field has reference type and refers to an object, that object may still be modifiable. For instance, a `readonly` field that refers to a `System.Collections.IList` object will not prevent that list's contents from being modified; items may be added and removed.

When the `readonly` field has value type, the field's value is truly unmodifiable.

Jon Skeet

17.4.2.1 Using static readonly fields for constants

A `static readonly` field is useful when a symbolic name for a constant value is desired, but when the type of the value is not permitted in a `const` declaration, or when the value cannot be computed at compile-time. [*Example*: In the following code

```
public class Color
{
  public static readonly Color Black = new Color(0, 0, 0);
  public static readonly Color White = new Color(255, 255, 255);
  public static readonly Color Red = new Color(255, 0, 0);
  public static readonly Color Green = new Color(0, 255, 0);
  public static readonly Color Blue = new Color(0, 0, 255);
```

```
    private byte red, green, blue;

    public Color(byte r, byte g, byte b)
    {
      red = r;
      green = g;
      blue = b;
    }
  }
```

the `Black`, `White`, `Red`, `Green`, and `Blue` members cannot be declared as `const` members because their values cannot be computed at compile-time. However, declaring them `static readonly` instead has much the same effect. *end example*]

17.4.2.2 Versioning of constants and static readonly fields

Constants and readonly fields have different binary versioning semantics. When an expression references a constant, the value of the constant is obtained at compile-time, but when an expression references a readonly field, the value of the field is not obtained until run-time. [*Example*: Consider an application that consists of two separate programs:

```
namespace Program1
{
  public class Utils
  {
    public static readonly int X = 1;
  }
}
```

and

```
using System;

namespace Program2
{
  class Test
  {
    static void Main()
    {
      Console.WriteLine(Program1.Utils.X);
    }
  }
}
```

The `Program1` and `Program2` namespaces denote two programs that are compiled separately. Because `Program1.Utils.X` is declared as a static readonly field, the value output by the `Console.WriteLine` statement is not known at compile-time, but rather is obtained at run-time. Thus, if the value of `X` is changed and `Program1` is recompiled, the `Console.WriteLine` statement will output the new value even if `Program2` isn't recompiled. However, had `X` been a constant, the value of `X` would have been obtained at the time `Program2` was compiled, and would remain unaffected by changes in `Program1` until `Program2` is recompiled. *end example*]

17.4.3 Volatile fields

When a *field-declaration* includes a `volatile` modifier, the fields introduced by that declaration are ***volatile fields***. For non-volatile fields, optimization techniques that reorder instructions can lead to unexpected and unpredictable results in multi-threaded programs that access fields without synchronization such as that provided by the *lock-statement* (§15.12). These optimizations can be performed by the compiler, by the runtime system, or by hardware. For volatile fields, such reordering optimizations are restricted:

- A read of a volatile field is called a ***volatile read***. A volatile read has "acquire semantics"; that is, it is guaranteed to occur prior to any references to memory that occur after it in the instruction sequence.
- A write of a volatile field is called a ***volatile write***. A volatile write has "release semantics"; that is, it is guaranteed to happen after any memory references prior to the write instruction in the instruction sequence.

These restrictions ensure that all threads will observe volatile writes performed by any other thread in the order in which they were performed. A conforming implementation is not required to provide a single total ordering of volatile writes as seen from all threads of execution. The type of a volatile field shall be one of the following:

- A *reference-type*.
- A *type-parameter* that is known to be a reference type (§25.7).
- The type `byte`, `sbyte`, `short`, `ushort`, `int`, `uint`, `char`, `float`, or `bool`.
- An *enum-type* having an enum base type of `byte`, `sbyte`, `short`, `ushort`, `int`, or `uint`.

Evolution of volatile

The semantics of volatile have evolved over time, with (currently) C/C++ using one model, and C#/Java 1.5 using an extended one.

In C (and C++), the volatile qualifier enables the control of the order in which reads and writes must be visible externally, and no read or write may be optimized away, even if it appears to the program to be unnecessary, because something external to the program may be reading or writing the location. These semantics support operations such as memory-mapped I/O, and indeed the C Standard uses a memory-mapped real-time clock as an example. As only the ordering of reads and writes to volatile qualified variables is guaranteed, these semantics are less useful in a multithreaded environment. These same semantics are used by early versions of Java.

The semantics used in C# and Java 1.5 extend the ordering as described by introducing the "acquire" and "release" models for nonvolatile reads and writes. This enables a volatile variable to be used to guarantee that one thread sees the writes made by another to a *nonvolatile* variable. The following example demonstrates this.

The semantics of volatile in C#/Java 1.5 extend that of C/C++. Proposals have been made that the semantics of C/C++ should be changed to include acquire/release semantics or to provide interthread guarantees in other ways. Whether these proposals will be adopted in future versions of the C/C++ Language Standards is unknown, but some implementations of C/C++ have already extended volatile with acquire/release semantics. Also note that the CLI provides a `MemoryBarrier()` mechanism, which has semantics different from volatile.

[*Example*: The example

```
using System;
using System.Threading;

class Test
{
    public static int result;
    public static volatile bool finished;
```

```
    static void Thread2()
    {
      result = 143;
      finished = true;
    }

    static void Main()
    {
      finished = false;
      // Run Thread2() in a new thread
      new Thread(new ThreadStart(Thread2)).Start();
      // Wait for Thread2 to signal that it has a result by setting
      // finished to true.
      for (;;)
      {
        if (finished)
        {
          Console.WriteLine("result = {0} ", result);
          return;
        }
      }
    }
  }
```

produces the output:

```
    result = 143
```

In this example, the method `Main` starts a new thread that runs the method `Thread2`. This method stores a value into a non-volatile field called `result`, then stores `true` in the volatile field `finished`. The main thread waits for the field `finished` to be set to `true`, then reads the field `result`. Since `finished` has been declared `volatile`, the main thread shall read the value 143 from the field `result`. If the field `finished` had not been declared `volatile`, then it would be permissible for the store to `result` to be visible to the main thread *after* the store to `finished`, and hence for the main thread to read the value 0 from the field `result`. Declaring `finished` as a `volatile` field prevents any such inconsistency. *end example]*

Unrealistic optimism redux

A volatile field may be passed as a reference or output parameter. However, as covered in §14.4.1, it "may not" be treated as volatile under these circumstances.

In practice the phrase "may not" is unrealistically optimistic; in all likelihood, the reference or output parameter *will not* be treated as volatile. Consider the following change to the preceding example:

```
    static void Worker(out bool done)
    {
      result = 143;
      done = true;
    }

    static void Thread2()
    {
      Worker(out finished);
    }
```

Here the "work" formerly done by `Thread2` is placed into `Worker` with the completion flag being passed as an `out` parameter.

In general, a method such as `Worker` could be called from many locations and a compiler cannot determine whether the `out` parameter refers to a normal or a `volatile` field; all the compiler has is an undistinguished reference. The type system of C# (and others, including C++, Java, and Ada 95) cannot express that a reference or output parameter refers to a field that "*may or may not be*" volatile, and a runtime mechanism for such parameters to indicate whether the callee passed a volatile field would impose an unacceptable burden on implementations.

Therefore, unless the platform supports tagging a reference as volatile, it is extremely unlikely that a volatile field passed as a reference or output parameter will be treated as volatile in the callee. To our knowledge none of the implementations current at the time of writing do so, and it would probably take computer hardware architectural changes before compiler writers even consider supporting such semantics.

17.4.4 Field initialization

The initial value of a field, whether it be a static field or an instance field, is the default value (§12.2) of the field's type. It is not possible to observe the value of a field before this default initialization has occurred, and a field is thus never "uninitialized". [*Example*: The example

```
using System;

class Test
{
  static bool b;
  int i;

  static void Main()
  {
    Test t = new Test();
    Console.WriteLine("b = {0} , i = {1} ", b, t.i);
  }
}
```

produces the output

```
b = False, i = 0
```

because `b` and `i` are both automatically initialized to default values. *end example*]

17.4.5 Variable initializers

Field declarations can include *variable-initializer*s. For static fields, variable initializers correspond to assignment statements that are executed during class initialization. For instance fields, variable initializers correspond to assignment statements that are executed when an instance of the class is created.

[*Example*: The example

```
using System;

class Test
{
  static double x = Math.Sqrt(2.0);
```

```
    int i = 100;
    string s = "Hello";

    static void Main ()
    {
      Test a = new Test ();
      Console.WriteLine ("x = {0} , i = {1} , s = {2} ", x, a.i, a.s);
    }
  }
```

produces the output

```
    x = 1.4142135623731, i = 100, s = Hello
```

because an assignment to x occurs when static field initializers execute and assignments to i and s occur when the instance field initializers execute. *end example*]

The default value initialization described in §17.4.4 occurs for all fields, including fields that have variable initializers. Thus, when a class is initialized, all static fields in that class are first initialized to their default values, and then the static field initializers are executed in textual order. Likewise, when an instance of a class is created, all instance fields in that instance are first initialized to their default values, and then the instance field initializers are executed in textual order. When there are field declarations in multiple partial type declarations for the same type, the order of the parts is unspecified. However, within each part the field initializers are executed in order.

It is possible for static fields with variable initializers to be observed in their default value state. [*Example*: However, this is strongly discouraged as a matter of style. The example

```
    using System;

    class Test
    {
      static int a = b + 1;
      static int b = a + 1;

      static void Main ()
      {
        Console.WriteLine ("a = {0} , b = {1} ", a, b);
      }
    }
```

exhibits this behavior. Despite the circular definitions of a and b, the program is valid. It results in the output

```
    a = 1, b = 2
```

because the static fields a and b are initialized to 0 (the default value for int) before their initializers are executed. When the initializer for a runs, the value of b is zero, and so a is initialized to 1. When the initializer for b runs, the value of a is already 1, and so b is initialized to 2. *end example*]

17.4.5.1 Static field initialization

The static field variable initializers of a class declaration correspond to a sequence of assignments that are executed in the textual order in which they appear in the class declaration. If a static constructor (§17.11) exists in the class, execution of the static field initializers occurs immediately prior to executing that static constructor. Otherwise, the static field initializers are executed at an implementation-dependent time prior to the first use of a static field of that class. [*Example*: The example

```
using System;

class Test
{
  static void Main()
  {
    Console.WriteLine("{0} {1} ", B.Y, A.X);
  }

  public static int F(string s)
  {
    Console.WriteLine(s);
    return 1;
  }
}

class A
{
  public static int X = Test.F("Init A");
}

class B
{
  public static int Y = Test.F("Init B");
}
```

might produce either the output:

```
Init A
Init B
1 1
```

or the output:

```
Init B
Init A
1 1
```

because the execution of X's initializer and Y's initializer could occur in either order; they are only constrained to occur before the references to those fields. However, in the example:

```
using System;

class Test
{
  static void Main()
  {
    Console.WriteLine("{0} {1} ", B.Y, A.X);
  }

  public static int F(string s)
  {
    Console.WriteLine(s);
    return 1;
  }
}
```

```
class A
{
  static A () { }
  public static int X = Test.F ("Init A");
}

class B
{
  static B () { }
  public static int Y = Test.F ("Init B");
}
```

the output shall be:

```
Init B
Init A
1 1
```

because the rules for when static constructors execute provide that B's static constructor (and hence B's static field initializers) shall run before A's static constructor and field initializers. *end example*]

Static fields may never be initialized

Consider a class that has no static constructor (§17.11). If no static methods of the class are called, and only instance methods that do not reference static fields are called, then the class's static fields will not be initialized. However, if a static constructor is added, even one whose body is empty, then as soon as an instance of the class is created, all static fields will be initialized, whether they are ever referenced or not.

Recommendation: Assume only that all static fields *may* be initialized at some point, and *will* be prior to use. Do not use static field initialization to produce effects other the assignment of values to fields. Although the rules are well defined, small changes can affect whether and when the static fields in a class get initialized.

Initialization is different when there is a static constructor (§17.11) and for value types (§18.3.10). Also, throwing exceptions from initialization is ill advised (§23.3). See those clauses and associated annotations for details.

17.4.5.2 Instance field initialization

The instance field variable initializers of a class correspond to a sequence of assignments that are executed immediately upon entry to any one of the instance constructors (§17.10.2) of that class. The variable initializers are executed in the textual order in which they appear in the class declaration. The class instance creation and initialization process is described further in §17.10.

A variable initializer for an instance field cannot reference the instance being created. Thus, it is a compile-time error to reference `this` in a variable initializer, as it is a compile-time error for a variable initializer to reference any instance member through a *simple-name*. [*Example*: In the following code

```
class A
{
  int x = 1;
  int y = x + 1;   // Error, reference to instance member of this
}
```

the variable initializer for y results in a compile-time error because it references a member of the instance being created. *end example*]

Rationale: why field initializers cannot reference instance fields

One reason for the preceding restriction is that field initializers are executed before the direct base class constructor (§17.10.3). Hence, if a field initializer could refer to `this` or to other instance fields, it could refer to base class fields whose initializers have not yet been executed. That could be very confusing and risky because representation invariants of the base class might not have been established yet.

The restriction is not found in Java, because in Java the direct base class constructor, and hence the base class field initializers, are executed before the derived class's field initializers.

The problems with Java's approach and the rationale for C#'s approach are discussed in the annotation on §17.10.3.

Unable to create inner objects

The rule about not referring to instance members can be frustrating at times. To give a concrete example, I have a locking library designed to avoid deadlocks—a lock can have an "inner" lock and an "outer" lock that must not be acquired after the inner one. It would be nice to be able to initialize this as:

```
class Example
{
    OrderedLock inner = new OrderedLock("Inner");
    OrderedLock outer = new OrderedLock("Outer").SetInnerLock(inner);
}
```

but this rule disallows it. (The `SetInnerLock` method has been designed to return the outer lock for precisely this kind of use.) Instead, the inner lock has to be set in the constructor. Note that the rule does not apply for static initializers, and that Java only disallows references to member variables that come later in the class definition.

Of course, in C# one can perform all instance field initializations in the constructor(s), but separating field declaration from field initialization increases the risk that a newly added field is left uninitialized. It also underscores the importance of using constructor initializers so that field initialization code has to be written and maintained in only one place.

Jon Skeet

17.5 Methods

A ***method*** is a member that implements a computation or action that can be performed by an object or class. Methods are declared using *method-declaration*s:

> *method-declaration:*
>   *method-header   method-body*
>
> *method-header:*
>   *attributes_{opt}   method-modifiers_{opt}   return-type   member-name*
>   *type-parameter-list_{opt}*
>   (*formal-parameter-list_{opt}*)   *type-parameter-constraints-clauses_{opt}*

method-modifiers:
  method-modifier
  method-modifiers   *method-modifier*

method-modifier:
  `new`
  `public`
  `protected`
  `internal`
  `private`
  `static`
  `virtual`
  `sealed`
  `override`
  `abstract`
  `extern`

return-type:
  type
  `void`

member-name:
  identifier
  interface-type   .   *identifier*

method-body:
  block
  ;

The *member-name* specifies the name of the method. Unless the method is an explicit interface member implementation (§20.4.1), the *member-name* is simply an *identifier*. For an explicit interface member implementation, the *member-name* consists of an *interface-type* followed by a " . " and an *identifier*.

A *method-declaration* can include a set of *attributes* (§24) and a valid combination of the four access modifiers (§17.2.3), the `new` (§17.2.2), `static` (§17.5.2), `virtual` (§17.5.3), `override` (§17.5.4), `sealed` (§17.5.5), `abstract` (§17.5.6), and `extern` (§17.5.7) modifiers.

A declaration has a valid combination of modifiers if all of the following are true:

- The declaration includes a valid combination of access modifiers (§17.2.3).
- The declaration does not include the same modifier multiple times.
- The declaration includes at most one of the following modifiers: `static`, `virtual`, and `override`.
- The declaration includes at most one of the following modifiers: `new` and `override`.
- If the declaration includes the `abstract` modifier, then the declaration does not include any of the following modifiers: `static`, `virtual`, `sealed`, or `extern`.
- If the declaration includes the `private` modifier, then the declaration does not include any of the following modifiers: `virtual`, `override`, or `abstract`.
- If the declaration includes the `sealed` modifier, then the declaration also includes the `override` modifier.

- If the declaration is an explicit interface member implementation (indicated by a *member-name* including an *interface-type*, §20.4.1), then the declaration includes no modifiers other than possibly the `extern` modifier.

The *return-type* of a method declaration specifies the type of the value computed and returned by the method. The *return-type* is `void` if the method does not return a value.

The optional *type-parameter-list* specifies the type parameters for a generic method. The optional *type-parameter-constraints-clauses* specify the constraints for the type parameters. A *method-declaration* shall not have *type-parameter-constraints-clauses* unless it also has a *type-parameter-list*. A *method-declaration* for an explicit interface member implementation shall not have any *type-parameter-constraints-clauses*. A generic *method-declaration* for an explicit interface member implementation inherits any constraints from the constraints on the interface method. Similarly, a method declaration with the `override` modifier shall not have any *type-parameter-constraints-clauses* and the constraints of the method's type parameters are inherited from the virtual method being overridden. Generic methods are fully specified in §25.6.

The optional *formal-parameter-list* specifies the parameters of the method (§17.5.1).

The *return-type* and each of the types referenced in the *formal-parameter-list* of a method shall be at least as accessible as the method itself (§10.5.4).

For `abstract` and `extern` methods, the *method-body* consists simply of a semicolon. For all other methods, the *method-body* consists of a *block*, which specifies the statements to execute when the method is invoked.

The name, the number of type parameters, and the formal parameter list of a method define the signature (§10.6) of the method. Specifically, the signature of a method consists of its name, the number of its type parameters, and the number, *parameter-modifiers*, and types of its formal parameters. The return type is not part of a method's signature, nor are the names of the formal parameters, the names of the type parameters, or the constraints. When a formal parameter type references a type parameter of the method, the ordinal position of the type parameter (not the name of the type parameter) is used for type equivalence.

The name of a method shall differ from the names of all other non-methods declared in the same class. In addition, the signature of a method shall differ from the signatures of all other methods declared in the same class, and two methods declared in the same class shall not have signatures that differ solely by `ref` and `out`.

Why no throw specifications?

In some languages, notably the Java programming language, a method `F` that may throw an `ArgumentException` is declared as follows:

```
void F(...) throws ArgumentException { ...}
```

The `throws` clause specifies the exceptions the method may throw. (Java programmers will know that certain common exceptions need not be included, but this is not relevant to the discussion here). C# deliberately omits such throw specifications and there is certainly healthy debate on the issue in general.

In C# there are a number of reasons given for the choice. A significant technical reason is that in a language that has function values/pointers (such as C#'s delegates), a very expressive type system is needed to make throw specifications sufficiently flexible. For example, consider the C# method `CallFromTo` that calls a delegate `f`, where that delegate may throw exceptions:

```
public void CallFromTo(IntFunction f, int from, int to)
{
   if (from > to)
```

```
        throw new ArgumentException("Invalid range");
    for (int i = from; i <= to; i++)
        f(i);
}
public delegate void IntFunction(int x);
```

It follows that if the method must have a throw specification, then the delegate type `IntFunction` must also describe the exceptions that the delegate can throw. One could imagine adding this information to C#'s delegate types, but it would reduce the generality and utility of delegate types; for example, rules would be required for matching throw specifications when creating an instance of a delegate type.

This problem is experienced already with Java's anonymous inner classes, but in that case, method declarations in interfaces can carry the Java throws clause.

Moreover, one quickly arrives at the desire to say "method `CallFromTo` can throw `ArgumentException` plus all those exceptions that could be thrown by delegate `f` of type `IntFunction`." (This cannot be expressed in Java's type system.) While such generic type-and-effect systems have been proposed, they have not yet been proven in mainstream programming languages, and would add considerable complexity to the language.

Another reason given for not requiring throw specifications in C# is issues with versioning, which becomes more difficult when throw specifications are required. For example, once a method had been published with a given throw specification, no new exception could be added to that specification without breaking every client. Either a client would be missing a catch clause for the new exception or would need to have its throw specification amended.

A distinction between checked exceptions (those that must be declared in throw specifications) and unchecked exceptions (those that need not) is usually made in languages that require throw specifications. [*Note: The terms checked/unchecked here do not relate to the constructs of the same name in C#.*] In making the decision whether to employ a checked or unchecked exception, a class author must judge whether a given exception can occur throughout a given program and whether recovery from the exception is possible in client code. See, for instance, Bloch's *Effective Java*, Chapter 8. The C# designers felt that that would be a difficult decision to make, because it depends primarily on the (unknown) client code.

However, it is interesting to note that the designers of Spec#, an extension of C# that supports design by contract, have found it necessary to introduce throw specifications in the language. Basically, one cannot prove that a method preserves an object representation invariant if any method call that it performs can prevent it from executing to completion.

The debate will undoubtedly continue.

17.5.1 Method parameters

The parameters of a method, if any, are declared by the method's *formal-parameter-list*.

formal-parameter-list:
  fixed-parameters
  fixed-parameters , parameter-array
  parameter-array

fixed-parameters:
  fixed-parameter
  fixed-parameters , fixed-parameter

fixed-parameter:
  attributes$_{opt}$ parameter-modifier$_{opt}$ type identifier

parameter-modifier:
  ref
  out

parameter-array:
  attributes$_{opt}$ params *array-type identifier*

The formal parameter list consists of one or more comma-separated parameters of which only the last can be a *parameter-array*.

A *fixed-parameter* consists of an optional set of *attributes* (§24), an optional ref or out modifier, a *type*, and an *identifier*. Each *fixed-parameter* declares a parameter of the given type with the given name.

A *parameter-array* consists of an optional set of *attributes* (§24), a params modifier, an *array-type*, and an *identifier*. A parameter array declares a single parameter of the given array type with the given name. The *array-type* of a parameter array shall be a single-dimensional array type (§19.1). In a method invocation, a parameter array permits either a single argument of the given array type to be specified, or it permits zero or more arguments of the array element type to be specified. Parameter arrays are described further in §17.5.1.4.

A method declaration creates a separate declaration space (§10.3) for type parameters, formal parameters, local variables, and local constants. Names are introduced into this declaration space by the type parameter list and formal parameter list of the method and by local variable declarations and by local constant declarations in the *block* of the method. It is an error for two members of a method declaration space to have the same name. It is an error for the method declaration space and the local variable declaration space of a nested declaration space to contain elements with the same name.

A method invocation (§14.5.5.1) creates a copy, specific to that invocation, of the formal parameters and local variables of the method, and the argument list of the invocation assigns values or variable references to the newly created formal parameters. Within the *block* of a method, formal parameters can be referenced by their identifiers in *simple-name* expressions (§14.5.2).

There are four kinds of formal parameters:

- Value parameters, which are declared without any modifiers.
- Reference parameters, which are declared with the ref modifier.
- Output parameters, which are declared with the out modifier.
- Parameter arrays, which are declared with the params modifier.

[*Note*: As described in §10.6, the ref and out modifiers are part of a method's signature, but the params modifier is not. *end note*]

17.5.1.1 Value parameters

A parameter declared with no modifiers is a value parameter. A value parameter corresponds to a local variable that gets its initial value from the corresponding argument supplied in the method invocation.

When a formal parameter is a value parameter, the corresponding argument in a method invocation shall be an expression of a type that is implicitly convertible (§13.1) to the formal parameter type.

A method is permitted to assign new values to a value parameter. Such assignments only affect the local storage location represented by the value parameter—they have no effect on the actual argument given in the method invocation.

17.5.1.2 Reference parameters

A parameter declared with a `ref` modifier is a reference parameter. Unlike a value parameter, a reference parameter does not create a new storage location. Instead, a reference parameter represents the same storage location as the variable given as the argument in the method invocation.

When a formal parameter is a reference parameter, the corresponding argument in a method invocation shall consist of the keyword `ref` followed by a *variable-reference* (§12.3.3.27) of the same type as the formal parameter. A variable shall be definitely assigned before it can be passed as a reference parameter.

A round peg in a square hole...

The `ref`/`out` argument must be the *same* type as the `ref`/`out` parameter. This is in contrast to a value argument, which need not be the same type as the value parameter (as long as there is an implicit conversion). Why is this? Consider the following example:

```
class Example
{
  static void F(out long v)
  {
    v = 42;
  }
  static void Main()
  {
    int intValue;
    F(out intValue); // compile-time error
    long longValue;
    F(out longValue); // ok
  }
}
```

If the call `F(out intValue)` were permitted, the assignment inside `F` would write a 64-bit `long` to the storage location aliased by `v`. This would cause memory corruption since the storage location aliased by `v` would be `intValue`, which is a 32-bit `int`.

In contrast, it is worth noting that VB.NET does allow the equivalent of the preceding example when its *Option Strict* is not on. In VB.NET it is implemented by copying the value of the variable into a local variable of type `object`, passing that by reference, then attempting to cast back afterwards. That changes the semantics significantly—it is pass-by-value-result semantics rather than pass-by-reference. In particular, it means the changes are not visible at the caller until the method completes, and there is no aliasing of arguments. For example, consider the following VB.NET code:

```
Module Example

  Class Aliasing
    Public Shared intField As Integer

    Public Function Assign1(ByRef loc As Long) As Boolean
      loc = 42
      Return intField = 42
    End Function

    Public Function Assign2(ByRef loc As Integer) As Boolean
      loc = 42
```

```
            Return intField = 42
        End Function
    End Class

    Sub Main()
        Dim a As Aliasing = New Aliasing

        Dim ans1 As Boolean = a.Assign1(Aliasing.intField)
                            ' intField = 42, ans1 = False
        Dim ans2 As Boolean = a.Assign2(Aliasing.intField)
                            ' intField = 42, ans2 = True

    End Sub

End Module
```

The call to `Assign1` sets `intField` to `42` and yet returns `False` for the comparison due to the use of call-by-value-result. This might be surprising. The equivalent program in C# is invalid. (Notes for C# programmers: `shared` is equivalent to C#'s `static`; the single quote character begins an endline comment.)

VB.NET takes the same approach when passing properties by reference: The property is fetched into a local variable, the local variable is passed by reference, and then the property is set from the local variable afterwards. Again, this is not really what one would expect from pass-by-reference semantics.

Within a method, a reference parameter is always considered definitely assigned.

[*Example*: The example

```csharp
using System;

class Test
{
    static void Swap(ref int x, ref int y)
    {
        int temp = x;
        x = y;
        y = temp;
    }

    static void Main()
    {
        int i = 1, j = 2;
        Swap(ref i, ref j);
        Console.WriteLine("i = {0}, j = {1} ", i, j);
    }
}
```

produces the output

```
i = 2, j = 1
```

For the invocation of `Swap` in `Main`, x represents i and y represents j. Thus, the invocation has the effect of swapping the values of i and j. *end example*]

In a method that takes reference parameters, it is possible for multiple names to represent the same storage location. [*Example*: In the following code

```
class A
{
  string s;

  void F(ref string a, ref string b)
  {
    s = "One";
    a = "Two";
    b = "Three";
  }

  void G()
  {
    F(ref s, ref s);
  }
}
```

the invocation of F in G passes a reference to s for both a and b. Thus, for that invocation, the names s, a, and b all refer to the same storage location, and the three assignments all modify the instance field s. *end example*]

17.5.1.3 Output parameters

A parameter declared with an out modifier is an output parameter. Similar to a reference parameter, an output parameter does not create a new storage location. Instead, an output parameter represents the same storage location as the variable given as the argument in the method invocation.

When a formal parameter is an output parameter, the corresponding argument in a method invocation shall consist of the keyword out followed by a *variable-reference* (§12.3.3.27) of the same type as the formal parameter. A variable need not be definitely assigned before it can be passed as an output parameter, but following an invocation where a variable was passed as an output parameter, the variable is considered definitely assigned.

Within a method, just like a local variable, an output parameter is initially considered unassigned and shall be definitely assigned before its value is used.

Every output parameter of a method shall be definitely assigned before the method returns.

Output parameters are typically used in methods that produce multiple return values. [*Example*:

```
using System;

class Test
{
  static void SplitPath(string path, out string dir, out string name)
  {
    int i = path.Length;
    while (i > 0)
    {
      char ch = path[i - 1];
      if (ch == '\\' || ch == '/' || ch == ':') break;
      i--;
    }
```

```
      dir = path.Substring(0, i);
      name = path.Substring(i);
   }

   static void Main()
   {
      string dir, name;
      SplitPath(@"c:\Windows\System\hello.txt", out dir, out name);
      Console.WriteLine(dir);
      Console.WriteLine(name);
   }
}
```

The example produces the output:

```
c:\Windows\System\
hello.txt
```

Note that the `dir` and `name` variables can be unassigned before they are passed to `SplitPath`, and that they are considered definitely assigned following the call. *end example*]

17.5.1.4 Parameter arrays

A parameter declared with a `params` modifier is a parameter array. If a formal parameter list includes a parameter array, it shall be the last parameter in the list and it shall be of a single-dimensional array type. [*Example*: The types `string[ ]` and `string[ ][ ,]` can be used as the type of a parameter array, but the type `string[ ,]` can not. *end example*] It is not possible to combine the `params` modifier with the modifiers `ref` and `out`.

A parameter array permits arguments to be specified in one of two ways in a method invocation:

- The argument given for a parameter array can be a single expression that is implicitly convertible (§13.1) to the parameter array type. In this case, the parameter array acts precisely like a value parameter.
- Alternatively, the invocation can specify zero or more arguments for the parameter array, where each argument is an expression that is implicitly convertible (§13.1) to the element type of the parameter array. In this case, the invocation creates an instance of the parameter array type with a length corresponding to the number of arguments, initializes the elements of the array instance with the given argument values, and uses the newly created array instance as the actual argument.

Except for allowing a variable number of arguments in an invocation, a parameter array is precisely equivalent to a value parameter (§17.5.1.1) of the same type.

[*Example*: The example

```
using System;

class Test
{
   static void F(params int[] args)
   {
      Console.Write("Array contains {0} elements:", args.Length);
      foreach (int i in args)
         Console.Write(" {0} ", i);
      Console.WriteLine();
   }
```

```
static void Main()
{
  int[] arr = {1, 2, 3};
  F(arr);
  F(10, 20, 30, 40);
  F();
}
}
```

produces the output

```
Array contains 3 elements: 1 2 3
Array contains 4 elements: 10 20 30 40
Array contains 0 elements:
```

The first invocation of F simply passes the array arr as a value parameter. The second invocation of F automatically creates a four-element int[ ] with the given element values and passes that array instance as a value parameter. Likewise, the third invocation of F creates a zero-element int[ ] and passes that instance as a value parameter. The second and third invocations are precisely equivalent to writing:

```
F(new int[] {10, 20, 30, 40});
F(new int[] {});
```

end example]

Params arrays can be null

In particular, note that a params array *can* be null:

```
class Test
{
  static void F(params int[] args)
  {
    if (args != null)
    {
      ...
    }
  }

  static void Main()
  {
    F();       // equivalent to F(new int[] {});
    F(null); // no array passed, args will be null
  }
}
```

When performing overload resolution, a method with a parameter array might be applicable, either in its normal form or in its expanded form (§14.4.2.1). The expanded form of a method is available only if the normal form of the method is not applicable and only if a method with the same signature as the expanded form is not already declared in the same type.

[*Example*: The example

```
using System;

class Test
{
  static void F(params object[] a)
  {
    Console.WriteLine("F(object[])");
  }

  static void F()
  {
    Console.WriteLine("F()");
  }

  static void F(object a0, object a1)
  {
    Console.WriteLine("F(object,object)");
  }

  static void Main()
  {
    F();
    F(1);
    F(1, 2);
    F(1, 2, 3);
    F(1, 2, 3, 4);
  }
}
```

produces the output

```
F();
F(object[]);
F(object,object);
F(object[]);
F(object[]);
```

In the example, two of the possible expanded forms of the method with a parameter array are already included in the class as regular methods. These expanded forms are therefore not considered when performing overload resolution, and the first and third method invocations thus select the regular methods. When a class declares a method with a parameter array, it is not uncommon to also include some of the expanded forms as regular methods. By doing so, it is possible to avoid the allocation of an array instance that occurs when an expanded form of a method with a parameter array is invoked. *end example*]

When the type of a parameter array is object[], a potential ambiguity arises between the normal form of the method and the expanded form for a single object parameter. The reason for the ambiguity is that an object[] is itself implicitly convertible to type object. The ambiguity presents no problem, however, since it can be resolved by inserting a cast if needed.

[*Example*: The example

```
using System;

class Test
```

```
{
  static void F(params object[] args)
  {
    foreach (object o in args)
    {
      Console.Write(o.GetType().FullName);
      Console.Write(" ");
    }
    Console.WriteLine();
  }

  static void Main()
  {
    object[] a = {1, "Hello", 123.456};
    object o = a;
    F(a);
    F((object)a);
    F(o);
    F((object[])o);
  }
}
```

produces the output

```
System.Int32 System.String System.Double
System.Object[]
System.Object[]
System.Int32 System.String System.Double
```

In the first and last invocations of F, the normal form of F is applicable because an implicit conversion exists from the argument type to the parameter type (both are of type object[ ]). Thus, overload resolution selects the normal form of F, and the argument is passed as a regular value parameter. In the second and third invocations, the normal form of F is not applicable because no implicit conversion exists from the argument type to the parameter type (type object cannot be implicitly converted to type object[ ]). However, the expanded form of F is applicable, so it is selected by overload resolution. As a result, a one-element object[ ] is created by the invocation, and the single element of the array is initialized with the given argument value (which itself is a reference to an object[ ]). *end example*]

Is the params keyword needed?

When a method includes the params in its signature, it is giving a caller the right to have the language do something automatically that the caller can do "longhand" anyway. For example, consider:

```
class Demo
{
  void M(string msg, params int[] args) { ...}

  public void Variations()
  {
    int[] myArray = ...;
    ...
```

```
        M("null array", null);          // only one way
        M("existing array", myArray);  // only one way

        M("Direct: empty array", new int[0] );
        M("Params: empty array");

        M("Direct: multiple", new int[] { 42, 51 });
        M("Params: multiple", 42, 51);
    }
}
```

The first call to M passes a null value and the second one passes a pre-existing array value. There is only one way to pass these values; the presence of the params in the callee has no effect.

The next four calls are made up of two pairs, the first pair passing an empty array and the second pair passing a multi-element array. In each pair the first call shows what a caller must do if the callee does not include the params keyword (but *may* do even if params is present). The second call in each pair shows what the caller may do if the callee does specify params (but *need not* do). A C# compiler will probably produce *exactly* the same code for each pair of calls and both the current Microsoft and Mono compilers do so.

The presence of params has to be considered during overload resolution (§14.4.2) and type inference for generic methods (§25.6.4).

C# *could* have been designed without the params keyword, and all calls allowed to behave as if it were present—having the keyword does not allow anything to be achieved that cannot be without it. Would there be any disadvantages to this approach?

Consider a method Liberal that has a few overloads, including this one:

```
    void Liberal(params object[] args)
```

This overload of method Liberal takes zero or more arguments of *any* type. This means that any call to Liberal is valid. Programmers are alerted to this by the keyword params in the declaration. If the keyword were *not* required, the programmer might be surprised to find that static checking of his method calls had essentially been turned off.

The params keyword is an example of where the C# design has favored explicitness over brevity; there is specific method call behavior that is explicitly indicated on the method declaration.

17.5.2 Static and instance methods

When a method declaration includes a static modifier, that method is said to be a static method. When no static modifier is present, the method is said to be an instance method.

A static method does not operate on a specific instance, and it is a compile-time error to refer to this in a static method.

An instance method operates on a given instance of a class, and that instance can be accessed as this (§14.5.7).

The differences between static and instance members are discussed further in §17.2.5.

17.5.3 Virtual methods

When an instance method declaration includes a virtual modifier, that method is said to be a **virtual method**. When no virtual modifier is present, the method is said to be a **non-virtual method**.

Instance methods are nonvirtual by default

By default, instance methods are *not* virtual. This is the same as C++, but different from Small-talk, Java, and Eiffel, where instance methods are virtual by default.

The C# designers give several reasons for this choice, two of which stand out: *performance* and *versioning*. The performance argument centers on the cost of dynamic dispatch. The version-ing argument is that the introduction of new methods in a base class, a common version change, is riskier when virtual methods are involved. For example, a method in a derived class may find itself unexpectedly overriding a newly introduced method in a base class.

In supporting the choice it is also argued that although it is tempting to declare every method as virtual on the grounds that someone, somewhere, might someday want to override it, this is not good practice. Good design should be restrictive and grounded in a context, not vaguely speculative.

Counter-arguments obviously exist to those put forward by the C# designers, especially from the Smalltalk, Java, and Eiffel camps. In the case of C#, specific counter-arguments to the per-formance and versioning cases have been proposed. First, in modern JIT-based virtual execu-tion environments such as the CLI-platform, performance may be less of an issue because there is some amount of overhead in all calls anyway—for example, to determine whether the method has been JIT'ed yet, or whether the JIT'ed code has been collected—and hence the method needs to be re-JIT'ed. Secondly, C#'s choice to require explicit overriding would appear to mitigate against the accidental overriding of newly introduced base class methods and thus counter the versioning argument.

It is interesting to note that the C# rationale could equally well apply to classes. A sealed class indicates a closing of the design, preventing future classes from deriving from it; a nonsealed class indicates an open-ended design, allowing future classes to derive from it. By default, C# classes are *not* sealed and this default is perhaps surprising given the opposite default for methods.

It has also been argued that unsealed classes present a possible security risk since an attacker could potentially subclass them and thus inject malicious code. In this case the C# choice to default to nonvirtual methods would appear to reduce the risk, without the need to also default to sealed classes, as overriding is not possible by default.

In retrospect, it might have been better to make classes sealed by default, or introduce an `unsealed` keyword and insist that all (nonabstract) classes must be explicitly declared as sealed or unsealed.

The implementation of a non-virtual method is invariant: The implementation is the same whether the method is invoked on an instance of the class in which it is declared or an instance of a derived class. In contrast, the implementation of a virtual method can be superseded by derived classes. The process of superseding the implementation of an inherited virtual method is known as ***overriding*** that method (§17.5.4).

In a virtual method invocation, the ***run-time type*** of the instance for which that invocation takes place determines the actual method implementation to invoke. In a non-virtual method invoca-tion, the ***compile-time type*** of the instance is the determining factor. In precise terms, when a method named N is invoked with an argument list A on an instance with a compile-time type C and a run-time type R (where R is either C or a class derived from C), the invocation is processed as follows:

- First, overload resolution is applied to C, N, and A, to select a specific method M from the set of methods declared in and inherited by C. This is described in §14.5.5.1.
- Then, if M is a non-virtual method, M is invoked.

- Otherwise, M is a virtual method, and the most derived implementation of M with respect to R is invoked.

For every virtual method declared in or inherited by a class, there exists a **_most derived implementation_** of the method with respect to that class. The most derived implementation of a virtual method M with respect to a class R is determined as follows:

- If R contains the introducing virtual declaration of M, then this is the most derived implementation of M.
- Otherwise, if R contains an override of M, then this is the most derived implementation of M with respect to R.
- Otherwise, the most derived implementation of M with respect to R is the same as the most derived implementation of M with respect to the direct base class of R.

Non-virtual calling of virtual methods

In addition to virtual method invocation based on run-time type, called a **_virtual call_**, it is also possible to invoke a virtual method based on compile-time type, called a **_non-virtual call_**. This occurs when a base access (§14.5.8) is used to identify a virtual method. In this case the most derived method with respect to the direct base class of the class containing the base access is determined at compile time and a direct, non-virtual call to the virtual method used.

[*Example*: The following example illustrates the differences between virtual and non-virtual methods:

```
using System;

class A
{
  public void F() { Console.WriteLine("A.F"); }
  public virtual void G() { Console.WriteLine("A.G"); }
}

class B: A
{
  new public void F() { Console.WriteLine("B.F"); }
  public override void G() { Console.WriteLine("B.G"); }
}

class Test
{
  static void Main()
  {
    B b = new B();
    A a = b;
    a.F();
    b.F();
    a.G();
    b.G();
  }
}
```

In the example, A introduces a non-virtual method F and a virtual method G. The class B introduces a *new* non-virtual method F, thus *hiding* the inherited F; it also *overrides* the inherited method G. The example produces the output:

```
A.F
B.F
B.G
B.G
```

Notice that the statement `a.G()` invokes `B.G`, not `A.G`. This is because the run-time type of the instance (which is `B`), not the compile-time type of the instance (which is `A`), determines the actual method implementation to invoke. *end example*]

Because methods are allowed to hide inherited methods, it is possible for a class to contain several virtual methods with the same signature. This does not present an ambiguity problem, since all but the most derived method are hidden. [*Example*: In the following code

```
using System;

class A
{
  public virtual void F() { Console.WriteLine ("A.F"); }
}

class B: A
{
  public override void F() { Console.WriteLine ("B.F"); }
}

class C: B
{
  new public virtual void F() { Console.WriteLine ("C.F"); }
}

class D: C
{
  public override void F() { Console.WriteLine ("D.F"); }
}

class Test
{
  static void Main()
  {
    D d = new D();
    A a = d;
    B b = d;
    C c = d;
    a.F();
    b.F();
    c.F();
    d.F();
  }
}
```

the `C` and `D` classes contain two virtual methods with the same signature: The one introduced by `A` and the one introduced by `C`. The method introduced by `C` hides the method inherited from `A`. Thus, the override declaration in `D` overrides the method introduced by `C`, and it is not possible for `D` to override the method introduced by `A`. The example produces the output:

```
B.F
B.F
D.F
D.F
```

Note that it is possible to invoke the hidden virtual method by accessing an instance of D through a less derived type in which the method is not hidden. *end example*]

Invocation by compile-time and run-time type

Previously it is stated that the *run-time* type of the instance for which that invocation takes place determines the actual method implementation to invoke in a virtual method invocation. However, the preceding example demonstrating the use of new to introduce a new method with the same name hiding the existing one (§10.7.1.2) shows that the process is actually slightly more involved:

1. The *compile-time* type of the instance is first used to determine the virtual method to invoke. In the preceding example for the calls a.F() and b.F(), this is A.F, and for c.F() and d.F(), this is C.F.

2. Then the *run-time* type of the instance is used to select the most derived implementation of the method determined in the previous step. For example, for the call a.F() the first step selects A.F. The most derived implementation of A.F with respect to the run-time of a, which is D, is B.F.

17.5.4 Override methods

When an instance method declaration includes an override modifier, the method is said to be an **override method**. An override method overrides an inherited virtual method with the same signature. Whereas a virtual method declaration *introduces* a new method, an override method declaration *specializes* an existing inherited virtual method by providing a new implementation of that method.

The method overridden by an override declaration is known as the **overridden base method**. For an override method M declared in a class C, the overridden base method is determined by examining each base class of C, starting with the direct base class of C and continuing with each successive direct base class, until an accessible method with the same signature as M is located. For the purposes of locating the overridden base method, a method is considered accessible if it is public, if it is protected, if it is protected internal, or if it is internal and declared in the same program as C.

A compile-time error occurs unless all of the following are true for an override declaration:

- An overridden base method can be located as described above.
- The overridden base method is a virtual, abstract, or override method. In other words, the overridden base method cannot be static or non-virtual.
- The overridden base method is not a sealed method.
- The override declaration and the overridden base method have the same return type.
- The override declaration and the overridden base method have the same declared accessibility. In other words, an override declaration cannot change the accessibility of the virtual method.

An override declaration can access the overridden base method using a *base-access* (§14.5.8). [*Example*: In the following code

```
class A
{
  int x;

  public virtual void PrintFields()
  {
    Console.WriteLine("x = {0} ", x);
  }
}

class B: A
{
  int y;

  public override void PrintFields()
  {
    base.PrintFields();
    Console.WriteLine("y = {0} ", y);
  }
}
```

the base.PrintFields() invocation in B invokes the PrintFields method declared in A. A
base-access disables the virtual invocation mechanism and simply treats the base method as a
non-virtual method. Had the invocation in B been written ((A)this).PrintFields(), it
would recursively invoke the PrintFields method declared in B, not the one declared in A,
since PrintFields is virtual and the run-time type of ((A)this) is B. *end example*]

Only by including an override modifier can a method override another method. In all other
cases, a method with the same signature as an inherited method simply hides the inherited
method. [*Example*: In the following code

```
class A
{
  public virtual void F() {}
}

class B: A
{
  public virtual void F() {}    // Warning, hiding inherited F()
}
```

the F method in B does not include an override modifier and therefore does not override the F
method in A. Rather, the F method in B hides the method in A, and a warning is reported because
the declaration does not include a new modifier. *end example*]

[*Example*: In the following code

```
class A
{
  public virtual void F() {}
}

class B: A
{
  new private void F() {}      // Hides A.F within B
}
```

```
class C: B
{
  public override void F() {}   // Ok, overrides A.F
}
```

the F method in B hides the virtual F method inherited from A. Since the new F in B has private access, its scope only includes the class body of B and does not extend to C. Therefore, the declaration of F in C is permitted to override the F inherited from A. *end example*]

17.5.5 Sealed methods

When an instance method declaration includes a `sealed` modifier, that method is said to be a **sealed method**. A sealed method overrides an inherited virtual method with the same signature. A sealed method shall also be marked with the `override` modifier. Use of the `sealed` modifier prevents a derived class from further overriding the method.

[*Example*: The example

```
using System;
class A
{
  public virtual void F()
  {
    Console.WriteLine("A.F");
  }

  public virtual void G()
  {
    Console.WriteLine("A.G");
  }
}

class B: A
{
  public sealed override void F()
  {
    Console.WriteLine("B.F");
  }

  public override void G()
  {
    Console.WriteLine("B.G");
  }
}

class C: B
{
  public override void G()
  {
    Console.WriteLine("C.G");
  }
}
```

the class B provides two override methods: an F method that has the `sealed` modifier and a G method that does not. B's use of the `sealed` modifier prevents C from further overriding F. *end example*]

17.5.6 Abstract methods

When an instance method declaration includes an abstract modifier, that method is said to be an *abstract method*. Although an abstract method is implicitly also a virtual method, it cannot have the modifier virtual.

An abstract method declaration introduces a new virtual method but does not provide an implementation of that method. Instead, non-abstract derived classes are required to provide their own implementation by overriding that method. Because an abstract method provides no actual implementation, the *method-body* of an abstract method simply consists of a semicolon.

Abstract method declarations are only permitted in abstract classes (§17.1.1.1).

[*Example*: In the following code

```
public abstract class Shape
{
  public abstract void Paint(Graphics g, Rectangle r);
}

public class Ellipse: Shape
{
  public override void Paint(Graphics g, Rectangle r)
  {
    g.DrawEllipse(r);
  }
}

public class Box: Shape
{
  public override void Paint(Graphics g, Rectangle r)
  {
    g.DrawRect(r);
  }
}
```

the Shape class defines the abstract notion of a geometrical shape object that can paint itself. The Paint method is abstract because there is no meaningful default implementation. The Ellipse and Box classes are concrete Shape implementations. Because these classes are non-abstract, they are required to override the Paint method and provide an actual implementation. *end example*]

It is a compile-time error for a *base-access* (§14.5.8) to reference an abstract method. [*Example*: In the following code

```
abstract class A
{
  public abstract void F();
}

class B: A
{
  public override void F()
  {
    base.F();            // Error, base.F is abstract
  }
}
```

a compile-time error is reported for the `base.F()` invocation because it references an abstract method. *end example*]

An abstract method declaration is permitted to override a virtual method. This allows an abstract class to force re-implementation of the method in derived classes, and makes the original implementation of the method unavailable. [*Example*: In the following code

```
using System;

class A
{
  public virtual void F()
  {
    Console.WriteLine("A.F");
  }
}

abstract class B: A
{
  public abstract override void F();
}

class C: B
{
  public override void F()
  {
    Console.WriteLine("C.F");
  }
}
```

class A declares a virtual method, class B overrides this method with an abstract method, and class C overrides that abstract method to provide its own implementation. *end example*]

17.5.7 External methods

When a method declaration includes an `extern` modifier, the method is said to be an ***external method***. External methods are implemented externally, typically using a language other than C#. Because an external method declaration provides no actual implementation, the *method-body* of an external method simply consists of a semicolon.

The mechanism by which linkage to an external method is achieved, is implementation-defined.

[*Example*: The following example demonstrates the use of the `extern` modifier in combination with a `DllImport` attribute that specifies the name of the external library in which the method is implemented:

```
using System.Text;
using System.Security.Permissions;
using System.Runtime.InteropServices;

class Path
{
  [DllImport("kernel32", SetLastError=true)]
  static extern bool CreateDirectory(string name, SecurityAttribute sa);

  [DllImport("kernel32", SetLastError=true)]
  static extern bool RemoveDirectory(string name);
```

```
        [DllImport("kernel32", SetLastError=true)]
        static extern int GetCurrentDirectory(int bufSize, StringBuilder buf);

        [DllImport("kernel32", SetLastError=true)]
        static extern bool SetCurrentDirectory(string name);
    }
```

end example]

17.5.8 Method body

The *method-body* of a method declaration consists of either a *block* or a semicolon.

Abstract and external method declarations do not provide a method implementation, so their method bodies simply consist of a semicolon. For any other method, the method body is a block (§15.2) that contains the statements to execute when that method is invoked.

When the return type of a method is void, return statements (§15.9.4) in that method's body are not permitted to specify an expression. If execution of the method body of a void method completes normally (that is, control flows off the end of the method body), that method simply returns to its caller.

When the return type of a method is not void, each return statement in that method body shall specify an expression of a type that is implicitly convertible to the return type. The endpoint of the method body of a value-returning method shall not be reachable. In other words, in a value-returning method, control is not permitted to flow off the end of the method body.

Foreign bodies

With the introduction in C# 2.0 of anonymous methods (§14.5.15), a method body can now lexically contain other method bodies. The preceding paragraphs do not recursively include return statements in any such nested method bodies.

[*Example*: In the following code

```
    class A
    {
      public int F() {}       // Error, return value required

      public int G()
      {
        return 1;
      }

      public int H(bool b)
      {
        if (b)
        {
          return 1;
        }
        else
        {
          return 0;
        }
      }
    }
```

the value-returning F method results in a compile-time error because control can flow off the end of the method body. The G and H methods are correct because all possible execution paths end in a return statement that specifies a return value. *end example*]

17.5.9 Method overloading
The method overload resolution rules are described in §14.4.2.

17.6 Properties

A *property* is a member that provides access to a characteristic of an object or a class. Examples of properties include the length of a string, the size of a font, the caption of a window, the name of a customer, and so on. Properties are a natural extension of fields—both are named members with associated types, and the syntax for accessing fields and properties is the same. However, unlike fields, properties do not denote storage locations. Instead, properties have *accessors* that specify the statements to be executed when their values are read or written. Properties thus provide a mechanism for associating actions with the reading and writing of an object's characteristics; furthermore, they permit such characteristics to be computed.

Properties are declared using *property-declaration*s:

> *property-declaration:*
>   *attributes_opt property-modifiers_opt type member-name* { *accessor-declarations* }
>
> *property-modifiers:*
>   *property-modifier*
>   *property-modifiers property-modifier*
>
> *property-modifier:*
>   new
>   public
>   protected
>   internal
>   private
>   static
>   virtual
>   sealed
>   override
>   abstract
>   extern

A *property-declaration* can include a set of *attributes* (§24) and a valid combination of the four access modifiers (§17.2.3), the new (§17.2.2), static (§17.6.1), virtual (§17.5.3, §17.6.3), override (§17.5.4, §17.6.3), sealed (§17.5.5), abstract (§17.5.6, §17.6.3), and extern modifiers.

Property declarations are subject to the same rules as method declarations (§17.5) with regard to valid combinations of modifiers.

The *type* of a property declaration specifies the type of the property introduced by the declaration, and the *member-name* specifies the name of the property. Unless the property is an explicit interface member implementation, the *member-name* is simply an *identifier*. For an explicit interface member implementation (§20.4.1), the *member-name* consists of an *interface-type* followed by a "." and an *identifier*.

The *type* of a property shall be at least as accessible as the property itself (§10.5.4).

The *accessor-declarations*, which shall be enclosed in "{ " and "} " tokens, declare the accessors (§17.6.2) of the property. The accessors specify the executable statements associated with reading and writing the property.

Even though the syntax for accessing a property is the same as that for a field, a property is not classified as a variable. Thus, it is not possible to pass a property as a `ref` or `out` argument.

A property cannot be a ref or out parameter

If a read-write property—one supporting both `get` and `set` accessors (§17.6.2)—could be used as a `ref` (or `out`) argument, then it would have to be passed as a pair of get and set methods. This is completely different from the usual implementation of `ref` argument passing, which passes just the address of the `ref` argument. Since a method with a `ref` parameter could be called in one place with an ordinary variable argument and another place with a property argument, the `ref` parameter passing mechanism would have to be the most general one—a pair of get and set functions—which would imply a considerable loss of efficiency in the ordinary case of a variable being passed as a `ref` argument.

Hence, if the language allowed a property (or indexer) as `ref` or `out` argument, the efficiency of all `ref` or `out` parameter passing would suffer.

The accessors of a property cannot be named

One workaround to the limitation described by the previous annotation is to pass the property's get and set accessors explicitly as delegates. For example, if we want to pass a property of type `int` to a method `M`, we could first define two delegate types and a suitable version of the method:

```
delegate int GetP();
delegate void SetP(int x);

void M(GetP getP, SetP setP)
{
  setP(getP() * 7);
  setP(getP() * 8);
}
```

Then we can pass the property `o.P` to `M` using two anonymous methods of type `GetP` and `SetP`:

```
M(delegate { return o.P; }, delegate(int value) { o.P = value; });
```

This is rather cumbersome. Part of the reason is that, whereas there is an implicit conversion from any method to a suitable delegate type, there is not even a way to mention the get and set accessors of a property (or indexer), and thus the two wrapper delegates are required. One could imagine a syntax such as `o.P.get` to name the get accessor of property `o.P`, but that would be ambiguous if the type of `o.P` has a member (such as a field) called `get`.

However, this technique cannot be used to pass the accessors of a property from inside a struct type declaration. Namely, an anonymous method expression must not capture the `this` reference of a struct (§14.5.15.2).

When a property declaration includes an `extern` modifier, the property is said to be an ***external property***. Because an external property declaration provides no actual implementation, each of its *accessor-declarations* consists of a semicolon.

17.6.1 Static and instance properties

When a property declaration includes a `static` modifier, the property is said to be a ***static property***. When no `static` modifier is present, the property is said to be an ***instance property***.

A static property is not associated with a specific instance, and it is a compile-time error to refer to `this` in the accessors of a static property.

An instance property is associated with a given instance of a class, and that instance can be accessed as `this` (§14.5.7) in the accessors of that property.

The differences between static and instance members are discussed further in §17.2.5.

17.6.2 Accessors

The *accessor-declarations* of a property specify the executable statements associated with reading and writing that property.

> *accessor-declarations:*
>   *get-accessor-declaration*   *set-accessor-declaration$_{opt}$*
>   *set-accessor-declaration*   *get-accessor-declaration$_{opt}$*
>
> *get-accessor-declaration:*
>   *attributes$_{opt}$*   *accessor-modifier$_{opt}$*   `get`   *accessor-body*
>
> *set-accessor-declaration:*
>   *attributes$_{opt}$*   *accessor-modifier$_{opt}$*   `set`   *accessor-body*
>
> *accessor-modifier:*
>   `protected`
>   `internal`
>   `private`
>   `protected internal`
>   `internal protected`
>
> *accessor-body:*
>   *block*
>   `;`

The accessor declarations consist of a *get-accessor-declaration*, a *set-accessor-declaration*, or both. Each accessor declaration consists of the token `get` or `set` followed by an *accessor-body*. For `abstract` and `extern` properties, the *accessor-body* for each accessor specified is simply a semi-colon. For the accessors of any non-abstract, non-extern property, the *accessor-body* is a *block* that specifies the statements to be executed when the corresponding accessor is invoked.

A `get` accessor corresponds to a parameterless method with a return value of the property type. Except as the target of an assignment, when a property is referenced in an expression, the `get` accessor of the property is invoked to compute the value of the property (§14.1.1). The body of a `get` accessor shall conform to the rules for value-returning methods described in §17.5.8. In particular, all `return` statements in the body of a `get` accessor shall specify an expression that is implicitly convertible to the property type. Furthermore, the endpoint of a `get` accessor shall not be reachable.

A `set` accessor corresponds to a method with a single value parameter of the property type and a `void` return type. The implicit parameter of a `set` accessor is always named `value`. When a property is referenced as the target of an assignment (§14.14), or as the operand of ++ or -- (§14.5.9, §14.6.5), the `set` accessor is invoked with an argument that provides the new value

(§14.14.1). The body of a set accessor shall conform to the rules for void methods described in §17.5.8. In particular, return statements in the set accessor body are not permitted to specify an expression. Since a set accessor implicitly has a parameter named value, it is a compile-time error for a local variable declaration or a local constant declaration in a set accessor to have that name.

More foreign bodies

With the introduction in C# 2.0 of anonymous methods (§14.5.15), an accessor body can now lexically contain method bodies. The preceding paragraphs do not recursively include return statements in any such contained method bodies.

Value hiding in an accessor

In a set accessor, and also the add and remove accessors for events (§17.7.2), the simple name value is just a parameter; its being implicitly declared (and some code editors high-lighting it like a keyword) does not change this. Therefore, writing value on the left-hand side of an assignment is allowed, which might be surprising. For example, consider:

```
class Buggy
{
  private int value;

  public int Property
  {
    set                    // implicit declaration: public void set(int value);
    {
      value = value;  // oops!
    }
  }
}
```

If you want the left-hand side of the assignment to refer to the private field, you have to use the this keyword:

```
class ABitBetter
{
  private int value;

  public int Property
  {
    set
    {
      this.value = value;
    }
  }
}
```

Note: Writing @value = value would just result in the same self-assignment to the value parameter.

Based on the presence or absence of the `get` and `set` accessors, a property is classified as follows:

- A property that includes both a `get` accessor and a `set` accessor is said to be a ***read-write*** property.
- A property that has only a `get` accessor is said to be a ***read-only*** property. It is a compile-time error for a read-only property to be the target of an assignment.
- A property that has only a `set` accessor is said to be a ***write-only*** property. Except as the target of a simple assignment, it is a compile-time error to reference a write-only property in an expression. [*Note*: The pre- and postfix ++ and -- operators and compound assignment operators cannot be applied to write-only properties, since these operators read the old value of their operand before they write the new one. *end note*]

The use of *accessor-modifier*s is governed by the following restrictions:

- An *accessor-modifier* cannot be used in an interface or in an explicit interface member implementation.
- For a property or indexer that has no `override` modifier, an *accessor-modifier* is permitted only if the property or indexer has both a `get` and `set` accessor, and then is permitted only on one of those accessors.
- For a property or indexer that includes an `override` modifier, the *accessor-modifier* of an accessor shall match the *accessor-modifier*, if any, of the accessor being overridden.
- The *accessor-modifier* shall declare an accessibility that is strictly more restrictive than the declared accessibility of the property or indexer itself. To be precise:
  - If the property or indexer has a declared accessibility of `public`, any *accessor-modifier* can be used.
  - If the property or indexer has a declared accessibility of `protected internal`, the *accessor-modifier* can be `internal`, `protected`, or `private`.
  - If the property or indexer has a declared accessibility of `internal` or `protected`, the *accessor-modifier* shall be `private`.
  - If the property or indexer has a declared accessibility of `private`, no *accessor-modifier* shall be used.

If an accessor has an *accessor-modifier*, the accessibility domain (§10.5.2) of the accessor is determined using the declared accessibility of the *accessor-modifier*. If an accessor does not have an *accessor-modifier*, the accessibility domain of the accessor is determined from the declared accessibility of the property or indexer.

[*Example*: In the following code

```
public class Button: Control
{
  private string caption;

  public string Caption
  {
    get
    {
      return caption;
    }
    set
    {
      if (caption != value)
```

```
        {
          caption = value;
          Repaint();
        }
      }
    }

    public override void Paint(Graphics g, Rectangle r)
    {
      // Painting code goes here
    }
  }
```

the `Button` control declares a public `Caption` property. The `get` accessor of the `Caption` property returns the string stored in the private `caption` field. The `set` accessor checks if the new value is different from the current value, and if so, it stores the new value and repaints the control. Properties often follow the pattern shown above: The `get` accessor simply returns a value stored in a private field, and the `set` accessor modifies that private field and then performs any additional actions required to update fully the state of the object.

Given the `Button` class above, the following is an example of use of the `Caption` property:

```
Button okButton = new Button();
okButton.Caption = "OK";        // Invokes set accessor
string s = okButton.Caption;    // Invokes get accessor
```

Here, the `set` accessor is invoked by assigning a value to the property, and the `get` accessor is invoked by referencing the property in an expression. *end example*]

The `get` and `set` accessors of a property are not distinct members, and it is not possible to declare the accessors of a property separately. [*Example*: The example

```
class A
{
  private string name;

  public string Name        // Error, duplicate member name
  {
    get { return name; }
  }

  public string Name        // Error, duplicate member name
  {
    set { name = value; }
  }
}
```

does not declare a single read-write property. Rather, it declares two properties with the same name, one read-only and one write-only. Since two members declared in the same class cannot have the same name, the example causes a compile-time error to occur. *end example*]

When a derived class declares a property by the same name as an inherited property, the derived property hides the inherited property with respect to both reading and writing. [*Example*: In the following code

```
class A
{
  public int P
```

```
      {
         set {...}
      }
   }

   class B: A
   {
     new public int P
     {
        get {...}
     }
   }
```

the P property in B hides the P property in A with respect to both reading and writing. Thus, in the statements

```
   B b = new B();
   b.P = 1;        // Error, B.P is read-only
   ((A)b).P = 1;   // Ok, reference to A.P
```

the assignment to b.P causes a compile-time error to be reported, since the read-only P property in B hides the write-only P property in A. Note, however, that a cast can be used to access the hidden P property. *end example*]

Unlike public fields, properties provide a separation between an object's internal state and its public interface. [*Example*: Consider the following:

```
   class Label
   {
     private int x, y;
     private string caption;

     public Label(int x, int y, string caption)
     {
        this.x = x;
        this.y = y;
        this.caption = caption;
     }

     public int X
     {
        get { return x; }
     }

     public int Y
     {
        get { return y; }
     }

     public Point Location
     {
        get { return new Point(x, y); }
     }

     public string Caption
```

```
  {
    get { return caption; }
  }
}
```

Here, the `Label` class uses two `int` fields, `x` and `y`, to store its location. The location is publicly exposed both as an `X` and a `Y` property and as a `Location` property of type `Point`. If, in a future version of `Label`, it becomes more convenient to store the location as a `Point` internally, the change can be made without affecting the public interface of the class:

```
class Label
{
  private Point location;
  private string caption;

  public Label(int x, int y, string caption)
  {
    this.location = new Point(x, y);
    this.caption = caption;
  }

  public int X
  {
    get { return location.x; }
  }

  public int Y
  {
    get { return location.y; }
  }

  public Point Location
  {
    get { return location; }
  }

  public string Caption
  {
    get { return caption; }
  }
}
```

Had `x` and `y` instead been `public readonly` fields, it would have been impossible to make such a change to the `Label` class. *end example*]

[*Note*: Exposing state through properties is not necessarily any less efficient than exposing fields directly. In particular, when a property is non-virtual and contains only a small amount of code, the execution environment might replace calls to accessors with the actual code of the accessors. This process is known as ***inlining***, and it makes property access as efficient as field access, yet preserves the increased flexibility of properties. *end note*]

[*Example*: Since invoking a `get` accessor is conceptually equivalent to reading the value of a field, it is considered bad programming style for `get` accessors to have observable side-effects. In the example

```
class Counter
{
  private int next;

  public int Next
  {
    get { return next++; }
  }
}
```

the value of the `Next` property depends on the number of times the property has previously been accessed. Thus, accessing the property produces an observable side effect, and the property should be implemented as a method instead. *end example*]

[*Note*: The "no side-effects" convention for `get` accessors doesn't mean that `get` accessors should always be written simply to return values stored in fields. Indeed, `get` accessors often compute the value of a property by accessing multiple fields or invoking methods. However, a properly designed `get` accessor performs no actions that cause observable changes in the state of the object. *end note*]

Properties can be used to delay initialization of a resource until the moment it is first referenced. [*Example*:

```
using System.IO;

public class Console
{
  private static TextReader reader;
  private static TextWriter writer;
  private static TextWriter error;

  public static TextReader In
  {
    get
    {
      if (reader == null)
      {
        reader = new StreamReader(Console.OpenStandardInput());
      }
      return reader;
    }
  }

  public static TextWriter Out
  {
    get
    {
      if (writer == null)
      {
        writer = new StreamWriter(Console.OpenStandardOutput());
      }
      return writer;
```

```
      }
    }

    public static TextWriter Error
    {
      get
      {
        if (error == null)
        {
          error = new StreamWriter(Console.OpenStandardError());
        }
        return error;
      }
    }
    ...
}
```

The `Console` class contains three properties, `In`, `Out`, and `Error`, that represent the standard input, output, and error devices, respectively. By exposing these members as properties, the `Console` class can delay their initialization until they are actually used. For example, upon first referencing the `Out` property, as in

```
Console.Out.WriteLine("hello, world");
```

the underlying `TextWriter` for the output device is created. However, if the application makes no reference to the `In` and `Error` properties, then no objects are created for those devices. *end example*]

The presence of an *accessor-modifier* never affects member lookup (§14.3) or overload resolution (§14.4.2). The modifiers on the property or indexer always determine which property or indexer is bound to, regardless of the context of the access.

Once a particular property or indexer has been selected, the accessibility domains of the specific accessors involved are used to determine if that usage is valid:

- If the usage is as a value (§14.1.1), the `get` accessor shall exist and be accessible.
- If the usage is as the target of a simple assignment (§14.14.1), the `set` accessor shall exist and be accessible.
- If the usage is as the target of compound assignment (§14.14.2), or as the target of the `++` or `--` operators (§14.5.9, §14.6.5), both the `get` accessors and the `set` accessor shall exist and be accessible.

[*Example*: In the following example, the property `A.Text` is hidden by the property `B.Text`, even in contexts where only the `set` accessor is called. In contrast, the property `B.Count` is not accessible to class `M`, so the accessible property `A.Count` is used instead.

```
class A
{
  public string Text
  {
    get { return "hello"; }
    set { }
  }

  public int Count
  {
    get { return 5; }
```

```
      set { }
    }
  }

  class B: A
  {
    private string text = "goodbye";
    private int count = 0;

    new public string Text
    {
      get { return text; }
      protected set { text = value; }
    }

    new protected int Count
    {
      get { return count; }
      set { count = value; }
    }
  }

  class M
  {
    static void Main()
    {
      B b = new B();
      b.Count = 12;        // Calls A.Count set accessor
      int i = b.Count;     // Calls A.Count get accessor
      b.Text = "howdy";    // Error, B.Text set accessor not accessible
      string s = b.Text;   // Calls B.Text get accessor
    }
  }
```

end example]

An accessor that is used to implement an interface cannot have an *accessor-modifier*. However, if only one accessor is used to implement an interface, the other accessor can be declared with an *accessor-modifier*. [*Example*:

```
  public interface I
  {
    string Prop { get; }
  }

  public class C: I
  {
    public string Prop
    {
      get { return "April"; } // Shall not have a modifier here
      internal set {...}      // Ok, because I.Prop has no set accessor
    }
  }
```

end example]

> **The most frequently requested new feature**
>
> In the first version of the C# standard, the get and set accessors of a property were required to have the same accessibility. The ability to declare them with different accessibilities (for example, a `public` get accessor combined with an `internal` set accessor) was one of the most frequently requested features.
>
> *Peter Hallam*

17.6.3 Virtual, sealed, override, and abstract accessors

A `virtual` property declaration specifies that the accessors of the property are virtual. The `virtual` modifier applies to all non-private accessors of a property. When an accessor of a `virtual` property has the `private` *accessor-modifier*, the `private` accessor is implicitly not virtual.

An `abstract` property declaration specifies that the accessors of the property are virtual, but does not provide an actual implementation of the accessors. Instead, non-abstract derived classes are required to provide their own implementation for the accessors by overriding the property. Because an accessor for an abstract property declaration provides no actual implementation, its *accessor-body* simply consists of a semicolon. An abstract property shall not have a `private` accessor.

A property declaration that includes both the `abstract` and `override` modifiers specifies that the property is abstract and overrides a base property. The accessors of such a property are also abstract.

Abstract property declarations are only permitted in abstract classes (§17.1.1.1). The accessors of an inherited virtual property can be overridden in a derived class by including a property declaration that specifies an `override` directive. This is known as an ***overriding property declaration***. An overriding property declaration does not declare a new property. Instead, it simply specializes the implementations of the accessors of an existing virtual property.

An overriding property declaration shall specify the exact same accessibility modifiers, type, and name as the inherited property. If the inherited property has only a single accessor (i.e., if the inherited property is read-only or write-only), the overriding property shall include only that accessor. If the inherited property includes both accessors (i.e., if the inherited property is read-write), the overriding property can include either a single accessor or both accessors. If one of the inherited accessors is not accessible to the overriding type, the overriding property shall not include that accessor. In addition, the declared accessibility of the accessors shall match that of the overridden accessors. [*Example*:

```
public class B
{
  public virtual int P
  {
    protected set {...}
    get {...}
  }
  public virtual int Q
  {
    private set {...}          // not virtual
    get {...}
  }
}
```

```
public class D: B
{
  public override int P
  {
    protected set {...}      // Must specify protected here
    get {...}                // Must not have a modifier here
  }
  public override int Q
  {
    private set {...}        // Error: inherited set is not accessible
    get {...}                // Must not have a modifier here
  }
}
```

end example]

An overriding property declaration can include the `sealed` modifier. Use of this modifier prevents a derived class from further overriding the property. The accessors of a sealed property are also sealed.

Except for differences in declaration and invocation syntax, virtual, sealed, override, and abstract accessors behave exactly like virtual, sealed, override and abstract methods. Specifically, the rules described in §17.5.3, §17.5.4, §17.5.5, and §17.5.6 apply as if accessors were methods of a corresponding form:

- A `get` accessor corresponds to a parameterless method with a return value of the property type and the same modifiers as the containing property.
- A `set` accessor corresponds to a method with a single value parameter of the property type, a `void` return type, and the same modifiers as the containing property.

[*Example*: In the following code

```
abstract class A
{
  int y;

  public virtual int X
  {
    get { return 0; }
  }

  public virtual int Y
  {
    get { return y; }
    set { y = value; }
  }

  public abstract int Z { get; set; }
}
```

X is a virtual read-only property, Y is a virtual read-write property, and Z is an abstract read-write property. Because Z is abstract, the containing class A shall also be declared abstract.

A class that derives from A is show below:

```
class B: A
{
  int z;

  public override int X
  {
    get { return base.X + 1; }
  }

  public override int Y
  {
    set { base.Y = value < 0? 0: value; }
  }

  public override int Z
  {
    get { return z; }
    set { z = value; }
  }
}
```

Here, the declarations of X, Y, and Z are overriding property declarations. Each property declaration exactly matches the accessibility modifiers, type, and name of the corresponding inherited property. The get accessor of X and the set accessor of Y use the base keyword to access the inherited accessors. The declaration of Z overrides both abstract accessors—thus, there are no outstanding abstract function members in B, and B is permitted to be a non-abstract class. *end example*]

17.7 Events

An **event** is a member that enables an object or class to provide notifications. Clients can attach executable code for events by supplying **event handlers**.

Events are declared using *event-declaration*s:

event-declaration:
   attributes$_{opt}$ *event-modifiers*$_{opt}$ event *type* *variable-declarators* ;
   attributes$_{opt}$ *event-modifiers*$_{opt}$ event *type* *member-name*
     { *event-accessor-declarations* }

event-modifiers:
  event-modifier
  event-modifiers *event-modifier*

event-modifier:
  new
  public
  protected
  internal
  private
  static
  virtual
  sealed
  override

```
abstract
extern
```

event-accessor-declarations:
   add-accessor-declaration   remove-accessor-declaration
   remove-accessor-declaration   add-accessor-declaration

add-accessor-declaration:
   attributes$_{opt}$ `add` *block*

remove-accessor-declaration:
   attributes$_{opt}$ `remove` *block*

An *event-declaration* can include a set of *attributes* (§24) and a valid combination of the four access modifiers (§17.2.3), the `new` (§17.2.2), `static` (§17.5.2, §17.7.3), `virtual` (§17.5.3, §17.7.4), `override` (§17.5.4, §17.7.4), `sealed` (§17.5.5), `abstract` (§17.5.6, §17.7.4), and `extern` modifiers.

Event declarations are subject to the same rules as method declarations (§17.5) with regard to valid combinations of modifiers.

The *type* of an event declaration shall be a *delegate-type* (§11.2), and that *delegate-type* shall be at least as accessible as the event itself (§10.5.4).

An event declaration can include *event-accessor-declaration*s. However, if it does not, for non-extern, non-abstract events, the compiler shall supply them automatically (§17.7.1); for extern events, the accessors are provided externally.

An event declaration that omits *event-accessor-declaration*s defines one or more events—one for each of the *variable-declarator*s. The attributes and modifiers apply to all of the members declared by such an *event-declaration*.

It is a compile-time error for an *event-declaration* to include both the `abstract` modifier and *variable-initializer*s or brace-delimited *event-accessor-declaration*s.

When an event declaration includes an `extern` modifier, the event is said to be an **external event**. Because an external event declaration provides no actual implementation, it is an error for it to include both the `extern` modifier and *event-accessor-declaration*s.

An event can be used as the left-hand operand of the += and -= operators. These operators are used, respectively, to attach event handlers to, or to remove event handlers from an event, and the access modifiers of the event control the contexts in which such operations are permitted.

The only operations that are permitted on an event by code that is outside the type in which that event is declared, are += and -=. Therefore, while such code can add and remove handlers for an event, it cannot directly obtain or modify the underlying list of event handlers. In an operation of the form x += y or x -= y, when x is an event and the reference takes place outside the type that contains the declaration of x, the result of the operation has type `void` (as opposed to having the type of x, with the value of x after the assignment). This rule prohibits external code from indirectly examining the underlying delegate of an event.

Externally, events are write-only

The preceding wording is a little loose, but take note of "permitted *on*." Outside of the declaring type, an event can only occur on the *left-hand* side of += and -= operators; they are not permitted on the right-hand side of these operators.

[*Example*: The following example shows how event handlers are attached to instances of the Button class:

```
public delegate void EventHandler(object sender, EventArgs e);

public class Button: Control
{
  public event EventHandler Click;
}

public class LoginDialog: Form
{
  Button OkButton;
  Button CancelButton;

  public LoginDialog()
  {
    OkButton = new Button(...);
    OkButton.Click += OkButtonClick;
    CancelButton = new Button(...);
    CancelButton.Click += CancelButtonClick;
  }

  void OkButtonClick(object sender, EventArgs e)
  {
    // Handle OkButton.Click event
  }

  void CancelButtonClick(object sender, EventArgs e)
  {
    // Handle CancelButton.Click event
  }
}
```

Here, the LoginDialog instance constructor creates two Button instances and attaches event handlers to the Click events. *end example*]

17.7.1 Field-like events
Within the program text of the class or struct that contains the declaration of an event, certain events can be used like fields. To be used in this way, an event shall not be abstract or extern, and shall not explicitly include *event-accessor-declaration*s. Such an event can be used in any context that permits a field. The field contains a delegate (§22), which refers to the list of event handlers that have been added to the event. If no event handlers have been added, the field contains null.

[*Example*: In the following code

```
public delegate void EventHandler(object sender, EventArgs e);

public class Button: Control
{
  public event EventHandler Click;

  protected void OnClick(EventArgs e)
  {
```

```
      EventHandler toRaise = Click;
      if (toRaise != null)
        toRaise(this, e);
   }

   public void Reset()
   {
      Click = null;
   }
}
```

`Click` is used as a field within the `Button` class. As the example demonstrates, the field can be examined, modified, and used in delegate invocation expressions. The `OnClick` method in the `Button` class "raises" the `Click` event. The notion of raising an event is precisely equivalent to invoking the delegate represented by the event—thus, there are no special language constructs for raising events. Note that the delegate invocation is preceded by a check that ensures the delegate is non-null and that the check is made on a local copy to ensure thread safety.

Do-nothing delegate

Another way to ensure thread safety is to initialize the event field to a "do nothing" delegate rather than null (the Null Object Pattern). For example:

```
public delegate void EventHandler(object sender, EventArgs e);

public class Button: Control
{
   public event EventHandler Click = delegate {};

   protected void OnClick(EventArgs e)
   {
      Click(this, e);
   }
}
```

However, this is not quite 100% safe; two anonymous delegate expressions that both do nothing are semantically identical and thus could compare equal (§14.9.8) and hence could be removed:

```
Button ok = new Button();
ok.Click -= delegate {};
// ok.Click could now be null
```

In order to make the Null Object pattern safe, the do-nothing delegate must never compare equal with another delegate. The annotation in §14.9.8 explains how to ensure this.

Outside the declaration of the `Button` class, the `Click` member can only be used on the left-hand side of the += and -= operators, as in

```
b.Click += new EventHandler(...);
```

which appends a delegate to the invocation list of the `Click` event, and

```
b.Click -= new EventHandler(...);
```

which removes a delegate from the invocation list of the `Click` event. *end example*]

Event −= vs. +=

Specifically, `b.Click -= new EventHandler(obj.Callback)` removes the most recently added occurrence of a delegate wrapping `obj.Callback` from the invocation list of the `Click` event (this is specified by `operator-` for delegate types, §14.7.5). Thus, `+=` followed by `-=` is an identity.

When compiling a field-like event, the compiler automatically creates storage to hold the delegate, and creates accessors for the event that add or remove event handlers to the delegate field. In order to be thread-safe:

- The addition and removal operations on all instance events of a class shall be done while holding the lock (§15.12) on an object uniquely associated with the containing object (`this`). [*Note*: For example, the unique object may be the containing object itself, or a hidden instance field. *end note*]
- The addition and removal operations on all static events of a class shall be done while holding the lock (§15.12) on an object uniquely associated with the containing class. [*Note*: For example, the unique object may be the type object (§14.5.11) for the containing class, or a hidden static field. *end note*]

[*Note*: Thus, instance event declarations of the form:

```
class X
{
  public event D Ev1;
  public event D Ev2;
}
```

could be compiled to:

```
class X
{
  public event D Ev1
  {
    add
    {
      lock(this) { __ev1 = __ev1 + value; }
    }

    remove
    {
      lock(this) { __ev1 = __ev1 - value; }
    }
  }

  public event D Ev2
  {
    add
    {
      lock(this) { __ev2 = __ev2 + value; }
    }
    remove
    {
      lock(this) { __ev2 = __ev2 - value; }
```

```
      }
    }

    private D __ev1;  // field to hold a delegate
    private D __ev2;  // field to hold a delegate
  }
```

or to:

```
  class X
  {
    public event D Ev1
    {
      add
      {
        lock(__key) { __ev1 = __ev1 + value; }
      }

      remove
      {
        lock(__key) { __ev1 = __ev1 - value; }
      }
    }

    public event D Ev2
    {
      add
      {
        lock(__key) { __ev2 = __ev2 + value; }
      }

      remove
      {
        lock(__key) { __ev2 = __ev2 - value; }
      }
    }

    private D __ev1;  // field to hold a delegate
    private D __ev2;  // field to hold a delegate
    private readonly object __key = new object();
  }
```

Similarly, static event declarations of the form:

```
  class X
  {
    public static event D Ev1;
    public static event D Ev2;
  }
```

could be compiled to:

```
  class X
  {
    public static event D Ev1
    {
```

```
      add
      {
         lock(typeof(X)) { __ev1 = __ev1 + value; }
      }

      remove
      {
         lock(typeof(X)) { __ev1 = __ev1 - value; }
      }
   }

   public static event D Ev2
   {
      add
      {
         lock(typeof(X)) { __ev2 = __ev2 + value; }
      }

      remove
      {
         lock(typeof(X)) { __ev2 = __ev2 - value; }
      }
   }

   private static D __ev1; // field to hold a delegate
   private static D __ev2; // field to hold a delegate
}
```

or to:

```
class X
{
   public static event D Ev1
   {
      add
      {
         lock(__key) { __ev1 = __ev1 + value; }
      }

      remove
      {
         lock(__key) { __ev1 = __ev1 - value; }
      }
   }

   public static event D Ev2
   {
      add
      {
         lock(__key) { __ev2 = __ev2 + value; }
      }

      remove
      {
         lock(__key) { __ev2 = __ev2 - value; }
```

```
        }
    }

    private static D __ev1; // field to hold a delegate
    private static D __ev2; // field to hold a delegate
    private static readonly object __key = new object();
}
```

Within class X, references to Ev1 and Ev2 are compiled to reference the hidden fields __ev1 and __ev2 instead. The names __ev1 and __ev2 are arbitrary; the hidden fields could have any name or no name at all. *end note*]

[*Note*: Access to a field-like event contained within a struct type is not thread-safe. *end note*]

Non-thread-safe struct events

The Standard specifies the locking semantics for events inside a `class` but *not* for events inside a `struct`.

```
public struct UnSpecified
{
    public event EventHandler Click; // locking?
    ...
}
```

The committee considered making struct event fields implicitly lock in the same manner as class event fields. The obvious solution is to specify a translation identical to the hidden field for classes:

```
public struct OneOption
{
    ...
    public event EventHandler Click
    {
        add
        {
            lock(__key)
            {
                __ev += value;
            }
        }
        remove
        {
            lock(__key)
            {
                __ev -= value;
            }
        }
    }
    private EventHandler __ev;
    private readonly object __key = new object(); // nope...
}
```

The problem with this is that struct instance fields cannot be initialized at their point of declaration, so the last line is invalid. Without such initialization, the struct's default constructor (which always exists) would set the hidden __key field to null and not to a new object instance. Therefore, this translation would not work without changing the semantics of C#.

Another possibility considered was to use a hidden *static* lock. For example:

```
public struct AnotherOption
{
  ...
  public event EventHandler Click
  {
    add
    {
      lock(__key)
      {
        __ev += value;
      }
    }
    remove
    {
      lock(__key)
      {
        __ev -= value;
      }
    }
  }
  private EventHandler __ev;
  private static readonly object __key = new object();
}
```

This was rejected on the grounds that locking would then be type-wide and not per instance as for classes.

There is, of course, no impediment to programmers implementing locking semantics for struct event fields; it is simply that it is not provided implicitly as for class event fields.

17.7.2 Event accessors

[*Note*: Event declarations typically omit *event-accessor-declaration*s, as in the `Button` example above. One situation for doing so involves the case in which the storage cost of one field per event is not acceptable. In such cases, a class can include *event-accessor-declaration*s and use a private mechanism for storing the list of event handlers. Similarly, in cases where the handling of an event requires access to external resources, event accessors can be used to manage these resources. *end note*]

The *event-accessor-declaration*s of an event specify the executable statements associated with adding and removing event handlers.

The accessor declarations consist of an *add-accessor-declaration* and a *remove-accessor-declaration*. Each accessor declaration consists of the token `add` or `remove` followed by a *block*. The *block* associated with an *add-accessor-declaration* specifies the statements to execute when an event handler is added, and the *block* associated with a *remove-accessor-declaration* specifies the statements to execute when an event handler is removed.

Each *add-accessor-declaration* and *remove-accessor-declaration* corresponds to a method with a single value parameter of the event type, and a `void` return type. The implicit parameter of an event accessor is named `value`. When an event is used in an event assignment, the appropriate event accessor is used. Specifically, if the assignment operator is += then the add accessor is used, and if the assignment operator is -= then the remove accessor is used. In either case, the right-hand operand of the assignment operator is used as the argument to the event accessor. The block of an *add-accessor-declaration* or a *remove-accessor-declaration* shall conform to the rules for `void` methods described in §17.5.8. In particular, `return` statements in such a block are not permitted to specify an expression.

Since an event accessor implicitly has a parameter named `value`, it is a compile-time error for a local variable or constant declared in an event accessor to have that name.

[*Example*: In the following code

```
class Control: Component
{
  // Unique keys for events
  static readonly object mouseDownEventKey = new object();
  static readonly object mouseUpEventKey = new object();

  // Return event handler associated with key
  protected Delegate GetEventHandler(object key) {...}

  // Add event handler associated with key
  protected void AddEventHandler(object key, Delegate handler) {...}

  // Remove event handler associated with key
  protected void RemoveEventHandler(object key, Delegate handler) {...}

  // MouseDown event
  public event MouseEventHandler MouseDown
  {
    add { AddEventHandler(mouseDownEventKey, value); }
    remove { RemoveEventHandler(mouseDownEventKey, value); }
  }

  // MouseUp event
  public event MouseEventHandler MouseUp
  {
    add { AddEventHandler(mouseUpEventKey, value); }
    remove { RemoveEventHandler(mouseUpEventKey, value); }
  }

  // Invoke the MouseUp event
  protected void OnMouseUp(MouseEventArgs args)
  {
    MouseEventHandler handler;
    handler = (MouseEventHandler)GetEventHandler(mouseUpEventKey);
    if (handler != null)
      handler(this, args);
  }
}
```

the `Control` class implements an internal storage mechanism for events. The `AddEventHandler` method associates a delegate value with a key, the `GetEventHandler` method returns the delegate currently associated with a key, and the `RemoveEventHandler` method removes a delegate as an event handler for the specified event. Presumably, the underlying storage mechanism is designed such that there is no cost for associating a `null` delegate value with a key, and thus unhandled events consume no storage. *end example*]

> **Custom event handler semantics**
>
> When compiling an event, the compiler automatically creates storage to hold a delegate and creates thread-safe accessors that add or remove event handlers to the delegate (§17.7.1). When user-defined accessors are provided, they must handle both the storage (which need not be a delegate) of event handlers and thread safety (if required, and implemented any way desired). In short, the precise semantics and implementation are entirely at the programmer's discretion.

17.7.3 Static and instance events

When an event declaration includes a `static` modifier, the event is said to be a ***static event***. When no `static` modifier is present, the event is said to be an ***instance event***.

A static event is not associated with a specific instance, and it is a compile-time error to refer to `this` in the accessors of a static event.

An instance event is associated with a given instance of a class, and this instance can be accessed as `this` (§14.5.7) in the accessors of that event.

When an event is referenced in a *member-access* (§14.5.4) of the form E.M, if M is a static event, E shall denote a type, and if M is an instance event, E shall denote an instance.

The differences between static and instance members are discussed further in §17.2.5.

17.7.4 Virtual, sealed, override, and abstract accessors

A `virtual` event declaration specifies that the accessors of that event are virtual. The `virtual` modifier applies to both accessors of an event.

An `abstract` event declaration specifies that the accessors of the event are virtual, but does not provide an actual implementation of the accessors. Instead, non-abstract derived classes are required to provide their own implementation for the accessors by overriding the event. Because an accessor for an abstract event declaration provides no actual implementation, its *accessor-body* simply consists of a semicolon.

An event declaration that includes both the `abstract` and `override` modifiers specifies that the event is abstract and overrides a base event. The accessors of such an event are also abstract.

Abstract event declarations are only permitted in abstract classes (§17.1.1.1).

The accessors of an inherited virtual event can be overridden in a derived class by including an event declaration that specifies an `override` modifier. This is known as an ***overriding event declaration***. An overriding event declaration does not declare a new event. Instead, it simply specializes the implementations of the accessors of an existing virtual event.

An overriding event declaration shall specify the exact same accessibility modifiers, type, and name as the overridden event.

An overriding event declaration can include the `sealed` modifier. Use of this modifier prevents a derived class from further overriding the event. The accessors of a sealed event are also sealed.

It is a compile-time error for an overriding event declaration to include a `new` modifier.

Except for differences in declaration and invocation syntax, virtual, sealed, override, and abstract accessors behave exactly like virtual, sealed, override and abstract methods. Specifically, the rules described in §17.5.3, §17.5.4, §17.5.5, and §17.5.6 apply as if accessors were methods of a corresponding form. Each accessor corresponds to a method with a single value parameter of the event type, a `void` return type, and the same modifiers as the containing event.

17.8 Indexers

An ***indexer*** is a member that enables an object to be indexed similar to an array. Indexers are declared using *indexer-declaration*s:

> *indexer-declaration:*
>   *attributes_{opt}* *indexer-modifiers_{opt}* *indexer-declarator* { *accessor-declarations* }

> *indexer-modifiers:*
>   *indexer-modifier*
>   *indexer-modifiers* *indexer-modifier*

> *indexer-modifier:*
>   new
>   public
>   protected
>   internal
>   private
>   virtual
>   sealed
>   override
>   abstract
>   extern

> *indexer-declarator:*
>   *type* this [*formal-parameter-list*]
>   *type* *interface-type* . this [*formal-parameter-list*]

An *indexer-declaration* can include a set of *attributes* (§24) and a valid combination of the four access modifiers (§17.2.3), the new (§17.2.2), virtual (§17.5.3), override (§17.5.4), sealed (§17.5.5), abstract (§17.5.6), and extern (§17.5.7) modifiers.

Indexer declarations are subject to the same rules as method declarations (§17.5) with regard to valid combinations of modifiers, with the one exception being that the static modifier is not permitted on an indexer declaration.

The modifiers virtual, override, and abstract are mutually exclusive except in one case. The abstract and override modifiers can be used together so that an abstract indexer can override a virtual one.

The *type* of an indexer declaration specifies the element type of the indexer introduced by the declaration. Unless the indexer is an explicit interface member implementation, the *type* is followed by the keyword this. For an explicit interface member implementation, the *type* is followed by an *interface-type*, a ".", and the keyword this. Unlike other members, indexers do not have user-defined names.

The *formal-parameter-list* specifies the parameters of the indexer. The formal parameter list of an indexer corresponds to that of a method (§17.5.1), except that at least one parameter shall be specified, and that the ref and out parameter modifiers are not permitted.

The *type* of an indexer and each of the types referenced in the *formal-parameter-list* shall be at least as accessible as the indexer itself (§10.5.4).

The *accessor-declarations* (§17.6.2), which shall be enclosed in "{ " and "} " tokens, declare the accessors of the indexer. The accessors specify the executable statements associated with reading and writing indexer elements.

Even though the syntax for accessing an indexer element is the same as that for an array element, an indexer element is not classified as a variable. Thus, it is not possible to pass an indexer element as a `ref` or `out` argument.

The *formal-parameter-list* of an indexer defines the signature (§10.6) of the indexer. Specifically, the signature of an indexer consists of the number and types of its formal parameters. The element type and names of the formal parameters are not part of an indexer's signature.

The signature of an indexer shall differ from the signatures of all other indexers declared in the same class.

Indexers and properties are very similar in concept, but differ in the following ways:

- A property is identified by its name, whereas an indexer is identified by its signature.
- A property is accessed through a *simple-name* (§14.5.2) or a *member-access* (§14.5.4), whereas an indexer element is accessed through an *element-access* (§14.5.6.2).
- A property can be a `static` member, whereas an indexer is always an instance member.

No static indexers

There is no conceptual difficulty in providing static indexers on a type, but the committee never seriously considered incorporating them in the Standard. Why is lost in the mists of time, but we can offer an insight into Microsoft's viewpoint. In a public discussion group where this came up, Eric Gunnerson stated:

> *Indexers are intended as a way to make your instance behave as if it was an array, and static indexers are outside of that usage. They could be added, but we'd have to be convinced that their utility was worth the additional complexity.*

The obvious counterargument is: Why should a class not be allowed to behave like a static array? There is also the orthogonality argument: C# has static types (classes), methods, properties, and fields, so why not indexers?

Since one could simply use a static method instead of a static indexer, the lack of static indexers does not limit C#'s expressiveness, it just impacts its "look and feel." It is interesting to note that VB.NET, effectively a cousin to C#, does provide static indexers. Neither language is "right" or "wrong" in an absolute sense; having or not having static indexers is a matter of choice, orthogonality (VB.NET), or minimalist (C#).

- A `get` accessor of a property corresponds to a method with no parameters, whereas a `get` accessor of an indexer corresponds to a method with the same formal parameter list as the indexer.
- A `set` accessor of a property corresponds to a method with a single parameter named `value`, whereas a `set` accessor of an indexer corresponds to a method with the same formal parameter list as the indexer, plus an additional parameter named `value`.
- It is a compile-time error for an indexer accessor to declare a local variable or local constant with the same name as an indexer parameter.
- In an overriding property declaration, the inherited property is accessed using the syntax `base.P`, where P is the property name. In an overriding indexer declaration, the inherited indexer is accessed using the syntax `base[E]`, where E is a comma-separated list of expressions.

Aside from these differences, all rules defined in §17.6.2 and §17.6.3 apply to indexer accessors as well as to property accessors.

When an indexer declaration includes an `extern` modifier, the indexer is said to be an ***external indexer***. Because an external indexer declaration provides no actual implementation, each of its *accessor-declarations* consists of a semicolon.

[*Example*: The example below declares a `BitArray` class that implements an indexer for accessing the individual bits in the bit array.

```
using System;

class BitArray
{
  int[ ] bits;
  int length;

  public BitArray(int length)
  {
    if (length < 0) throw new ArgumentException();
    bits = new int[((length - 1) >> 5) + 1];
    this.length = length;
  }

  public int Length
  {
    get { return length; }
  }

  public bool this[int index]
  {
    get
    {
      if (index < 0 || index >= length)
      {
        throw new IndexOutOfRangeException();
      }
      return (bits[index >> 5] & 1 << index) != 0;
    }

    set
    {
      if (index < 0 || index >= length)
      {
        throw new IndexOutOfRangeException();
      }
      if (value)
      {
        bits[index >> 5] |= 1 << index;
      }
      else
      {
        bits[index >> 5] &= ~(1 << index);
      }
    }
  }
}
```

An instance of the `BitArray` class consumes substantially less memory than a corresponding `bool[]` (since each value of the former occupies only one bit instead of the latter's one byte), but it permits the same operations as a `bool[]`.

The following `CountPrimes` class uses a `BitArray` and the classical "sieve" algorithm to compute the number of primes between 2 and a given maximum:

```
class CountPrimes
{
  static int Count(int max)
  {
    BitArray flags = new BitArray(max + 1);
    int count = 0;
    for (int i = 2; i <= max; i++)
    {
      if (!flags[i])
      {
        for (int j = i * 2; j <= max; j += i) flags[j] = true;
        count++;
      }
    }
    return count;
  }

  static void Main(string[] args)
  {
    int max = int.Parse(args[0]);
    int count = Count(max);
    Console.WriteLine("Found {0} primes between 2 and {1} ", count, max);
  }
}
```

Note that the syntax for accessing elements of the `BitArray` is precisely the same as for a `bool[]`. *end example*]

[*Example*: The following example shows a 26 x 10 grid class that has an indexer with two parameters. The first parameter is required to be an upper- or lowercase letter in the range A–Z, and the second is required to be an integer in the range 0–9.

```
using System;

class Grid
{
  const int NumRows = 26;
  const int NumCols = 10;
  int[,] cells = new int[NumRows, NumCols];

  public int this[char c, int colm]
  {
    get
    {
      c = Char.ToUpper(c);
      if (c < 'A' || c > 'Z')
      {
        throw new ArgumentException();
      }
```

```
      if (colm < 0 || colm >= NumCols)
      {
        throw new IndexOutOfRangeException();
      }
      return cells[c - 'A', colm];
    }

  set
  {
    c = Char.ToUpper(c);
    if (c < 'A' || c > 'Z')
    {
      throw new ArgumentException();
    }
    if (colm < 0 || colm >= NumCols)
    {
      throw new IndexOutOfRangeException();
    }
    cells[c - 'A', colm] = value;
  }
}
}
```

end example]

Named indexers

C# does not support named indexers. This can be frustrating—for example, they would offer a handy way of providing read-only access to an array held in a class. However, with a little effort it is possible to fake named indexers:

```
Example eg = new Example();
string word = eg.Word[ 42] ;

class Example
{
  ...
  public NamedReadOnlyIndexer<string> Word
  {
    get
    {
      return new NamedReadOnlyIndexer<string>(words);
    }
  }

  private string[] words;
}

struct NamedReadOnlyIndexer<T>
{
  public NamedReadOnlyIndexer(T[] values)
  {
    this.values = values;
  }
```

```
      public T this[int at]
      {
        get
        {
          return values[at] ;
        }
      }

      private readonly T[ ] values;
}
```

As with static indexers (see preceding annotation), the question has been asked why C# does not support named indexers. The answer is the same as well: It is a choice, and VB.NET chose to do so while C# chose not to. Neither choice is "right" or "wrong" in any absolute sense. While discussion forums on the net appear to have more voices calling for named indexers in C# than call for static indexers, people do not appear to be claiming they use VB.NET "because C# lacks static/named indexers."

17.8.1 Indexer overloading
The indexer overload resolution rules are described in §14.4.2.

17.9 Operators

An ***operator*** is a member that defines the meaning of an expression operator that can be applied to instances of the class. Operators are declared using *operator-declaration*s:

operator-declaration:
   attributes$_{opt}$ *operator-modifiers*   *operator-declarator*   *operator-body*

operator-modifiers:
   operator-modifier
   operator-modifiers   *operator-modifier*

operator-modifier:
   `public`
   `static`
   `extern`

operator-declarator:
   unary-operator-declarator
   binary-operator-declarator
   conversion-operator-declarator

unary-operator-declarator:
   type   `operator`   *overloadable-unary-operator*   `(`   *type*   *identifier*   `)`

overloadable-unary-operator: one of
   `+   -   !   ~   ++   --   true   false`

binary-operator-declarator:
   type   `operator`   *overloadable-binary-operator*
      `(`   *type*   *identifier*   `,`   *type*   *identifier*   `)`

overloadable-binary-operator: one of
```
+    –    *   /   %
&    |    ^
<<   right-shift
==   !=   >   <   >=   <=
```

conversion-operator-declarator:
```
implicit  operator  type  (  type  identifier  )
explicit  operator  type  (  type  identifier  )
```

operator-body:
  block
  ;

There are three categories of overloadable operators: Unary operators (§17.9.1), binary operators (§17.9.2), and conversion operators (§17.9.3).

When an operator declaration includes an `extern` modifier, the operator is said to be an **external operator**. Because an external operator provides no actual implementation, its *operator-body* consists of a semi-colon. For all other operators, the *operator-body* consists of a *block*, which specifies the statements to execute when the operator is invoked. The *block* of an operator shall conform to the rules for value-returning methods described in §17.5.8.

The following rules apply to all operator declarations:

- An operator declaration shall include both a `public` and a `static` modifier.
- The parameter(s) of an operator shall be value parameters. It is a compile-time error for an operator declaration to specify `ref` or `out` parameters.
- The signature of an operator (§17.9.1, §17.9.2, §17.9.3) shall differ from the signatures of all other operators declared in the same class.
- All types referenced in an operator declaration shall be at least as accessible as the operator itself (§10.5.4).
- It is an error for the same modifier to appear multiple times in an operator declaration.

Each operator category imposes additional restrictions, as described in the following subclauses.

Like other members, operators declared in a base class are inherited by derived classes. Because operator declarations always require the class or struct in which the operator is declared to participate in the signature of the operator, it is not possible for an operator declared in a derived class to hide an operator declared in a base class. Thus, the `new` modifier is never required, and therefore never permitted, in an operator declaration.

Additional information on unary and binary operators can be found in §14.2.

Additional information on conversion operators can be found in §13.4.

The best laid plans of mice and men...

The preceding assertion that one operator cannot hide another is misleading; it is possible for operators in two different types to have the same signature, and if the two types are related by inheritance, then one does in a sense "hide" the other. However, though an operator is static, unlike other static method calls, the type is not given explicitly, so operator resolution is always required. This resolution process examines each type that is used as an operand to the operator, so "hiding" does not occur in the usual sense.

How this lack of clarity escaped all reviews is surprising, and might make an interesting annotation in its own right—especially as it was spotted and still not clarified, but here we will just explain what the situation really is!

Consider the program fragment:

```
class Alpha
{
    public static Alpha operator +(Alpha lhs, Beta rhs) { ...}
}

class Beta
{
    public static Beta operator +(Alpha lhs, Beta rhs) { ...}
}
```

Neither of these operators "hides" the other; no inheritance is involved (indeed, `Alpha` and `Beta` could both be structs). However, if `Beta` were derived from `Alpha`, and inheritance comes into play, it would make *no difference* to this particular example.

Now consider the expression:

```
new Alpha() + new Beta()
```

Which operator, if any, is called?

Operator overload resolution (§14.2.4) first determines the set of candidate operators (§14.2.5). In this case the set consists of both `Alpha.operator+` and `Beta.operator+`.

Next, the usual method overload resolution (§14.4.2) rules are applied and which, if any, member of the set is the *better function member* (§14.4.2.2) is determined. In this case neither operator is better than the other, as they have identical signatures, so the expression is ambiguous and a compile-time error occurs.

The usual advice applies; use overloading with care.

Bedfellows: operators and structs

Operators are formally specified in the classes clause but have a stronger affinity to `struct` values than `class` objects:

- Operators must be static. This means operators are never virtual and thus cannot be polymorphic. This matches the implicitly sealed nature of structs.
- Operator parameters must be passed by value; they cannot be passed using the `ref` or `out` (or `params`) keywords. This matches the implicit nature of structs—they represent values.
- Classes that do implement operators (such as `string` and any `delegate` type) tend to be sealed and immutable, and in many respects behave like values.
- Conversion operators that convert to a base class are not allowed. This again matches the nature of structs (since structs never have a base class).

Of course, declaring operators in classes is not wrong and, as noted, several prominent classes do declare operators. The key guideline is that operators should have no side effects on their operands. For example, `lhs == rhs` should have no effect on `lhs` or `rhs`.

17.9.1 Unary operators

The following rules apply to unary operator declarations, where `T` denotes the class or struct type that contains the operator declaration:

- A unary +, -, !, or ~ operator shall take a single parameter of type T or T? and can return any type.
- A unary ++ or -- operator shall take a single parameter of type T or T? and shall return the same type.
- A unary true or false operator shall take a single parameter of type T or T? and shall return type bool.

The signature of a unary operator consists of the operator token (+, -, !, ~, ++, --, true, or false) and the type of the single formal parameter. The return type is not part of a unary operator's signature, nor is the name of the formal parameter.

The true and false unary operators require pair-wise declaration. A compile-time error occurs if a class declares one of these operators without also declaring the other. The true and false operators are described further in §14.17.

[*Example*: The following example shows an implementation and subsequent usage of operator++ for an integer vector class:

```
public class IntVector
{
  public int Length {...}            // read-only property
  public int this[int index] {...}   // read-write indexer
  public IntVector(int vectorLength) {...}
  public static IntVector operator++(IntVector iv)
  {
    IntVector temp = new IntVector(iv.Length);
    for (int i = 0; i < iv.Length; ++i)
      temp[i] = iv[i] + 1;
    return temp;
  }
}

class Test
{
  static void Main()
  {
    IntVector iv1 = new IntVector(4);   // vector of 4x0
    IntVector iv2;

    iv2 = iv1++;   // iv2 contains 4x0, iv1 contains 4x1
    iv2 = ++iv1;   // iv2 contains 4x2, iv1 contains 4x2
  }
}
```

Note how the operator method returns the value produced by adding 1 to the operand, just like the postfix increment and decrement operators (§14.5.9), and the prefix increment and decrement operators (§14.6.5). Unlike in C++, this method need not, and, in fact, should not, modify the value of its operand directly. *end example*]

17.9.2 Binary operators
The following rules apply to binary operator declarations, where T denotes the class or struct type that contains the operator declaration:

- A binary non-shift operator must take two parameters, at least one of which must have type T or T?, and can return any type.

- A binary << or >> operator (§14.8) must take two parameters, the first of which must have type T or T? and the second of which must have type int or int?, and can return any type.

The signature of a binary operator consists of the operator token (+, -, *, /, %, &, |, ^, <<, *right-shift*, ==, !=, >, <, >=, or <=) and the types of the two formal parameters. The return type and the names of the formal parameters are not part of a binary operator's signature.

Certain binary operators require pair-wise declaration. For every declaration of either operator of a pair, there shall be a matching declaration of the other operator of the pair. Two operator declarations match when they have the same return type and the same type for each parameter. The following operators require pair-wise declaration:

- operator == and operator !=
- operator > and operator <
- operator >= and operator <=

17.9.3 Conversion operators

A conversion operator declaration introduces a ***user-defined conversion operator*** (§13.4), which augments the pre-defined implicit and explicit conversions.

A conversion operator declaration that includes the implicit keyword introduces a user-defined implicit conversion operator. Implicit conversions can occur in a variety of situations, including function member invocations, cast expressions, and assignments. This is described further in §13.1.

A conversion operator declaration that includes the explicit keyword introduces a user-defined explicit conversion operator. Explicit conversions can occur in cast expressions, and are described further in §13.2.

A conversion operator converts from a source type, indicated by the parameter type of the conversion operator, to a target type, indicated by the return type of the conversion operator. A class or struct is permitted to declare a conversion from a source type S to a target type T only if all of the following are true, where S0 and T0 are the types that result from removing the trailing ? modifiers, if any, from S and T:

- S0 and T0 are different types.
- Either S0 or T0 is the class or struct type in which the operator declaration takes place.
- Neither S0 nor T0 is an *interface-type.*
- Excluding user-defined conversions, a conversion does not exist from S to T or from T to S.

From the second rule it follows that a conversion operator shall convert either to or from the class or struct type in which the operator is declared. [*Example*: It is possible for a class or struct type C to define a conversion from C to int and from int to C, but not from int to bool. *end example*]

It is not possible to redefine a pre-defined conversion. Thus, conversion operators are not allowed to convert from or to object because implicit and explicit conversions already exist between object and all other types. Likewise, neither the source nor the target types of a conversion can be a base type of the other, since a conversion would then already exist.

User-defined conversions are not allowed to convert from or to *interface-type*s. In particular, this restriction ensures that no user-defined transformations occur when converting to an *interface-type*, and that a conversion to an *interface-type* succeeds only if the object being converted actually implements the specified *interface-type.*

Indirect implicit conversion to an interface

The preceding rules do *not* prevent a class (or struct) from declaring a conversion to another type that implements an interface. For example, consider:

```
interface IFoo { ...}

class FooImpl : IFoo { ...}

class Convertible
{
  public static implicit operator FooImpl(Convertible from)
  {
    return new FooImpl(from);
  }
}
```

Here, there is user-defined implicit conversion from Convertible to FooImpl and a standard implicit conversion from FooImpl to IFoo. Therefore (§13.1.8), there is an implicit conversion from Convertible to IFoo. For example:

```
class App
{
  public static void Main()
  {
    Convertible c = new Convertible();
    IFoo i = c; // user conversion followed by standard conversion
  }
}
```

Although permitted by the Standard, the current Microsoft C# compiler does *not* accept the assignment "IFoo i = c;". The current Mono compiler does accept the code. With Microsoft's current compiler you may write the conversion *explicitly*:

```
    Convertible c = new Convertible();
    IFoo i = (FooImpl)c;
```

This will, of course, also work with the Mono compiler.

The signature of a conversion operator consists of the source type and the target type. (This is the only form of member for which the return type participates in the signature.) The implicit or explicit classification of a conversion operator is not part of the operator's signature. Thus, a class or struct cannot declare both an implicit and an explicit conversion operator with the same source and target types.

[*Note*: In general, user-defined implicit conversions should be designed to never throw exceptions and never lose information. If a user-defined conversion can give rise to exceptions (for example, because the source argument is out of range) or loss of information (such as discarding high-order bits), then that conversion should be defined as an explicit conversion. *end note*]

[*Example*: In the following code

```
using System;

public struct Digit
{
  byte value;
```

```
   public Digit(int value)
   {
     if (value < 0 || value > 9) throw new ArgumentException();
     this.value = value;
   }

   public static implicit operator byte(Digit d)
   {
     return d.value;
   }

   public static explicit operator Digit(int n)
   {
     return new Digit(n);
   }
}
```

the conversion operator from `Digit` to `byte` is implicit because it never throws exceptions or loses information, but the conversion operator from `int` to `Digit` is explicit since `Digit` can only represent a subset of the possible values of an `int`. *end example*]

17.10 Instance constructors

An ***instance constructor*** is a member that implements the actions required to initialize an instance of a class. Instance constructors are declared using *constructor-declaration*s:

> *constructor-declaration:*
>   *attributes_{opt}   constructor-modifiers_{opt}   constructor-declarator   constructor-body*

> *constructor-modifiers:*
>   *constructor-modifier*
>   *constructor-modifiers   constructor-modifier*

> *constructor-modifier:*
>   public
>   protected
>   internal
>   private
>   extern

> *constructor-declarator:*
>   *identifier   (formal-parameter-list_{opt}   )   constructor-initializer_{opt}*

> *constructor-initializer:*
>   :   base   (*argument-list _{opt}*   )
>   :   this   (*argument-list _{opt}*   )

> *constructor-body:*
>   *block*
>   ;

A *constructor-declaration* can include a set of *attributes* (§24), a valid combination of the four access modifiers (§17.2.3), and an `extern` (§17.5.7) modifier. A constructor declaration is not permitted to include the same modifier multiple times.

The *identifier* of a *constructor-declarator* shall name the class in which the instance constructor is declared. If any other name is specified, a compile-time error occurs.

The optional *formal-parameter-list* of an instance constructor is subject to the same rules as the *formal-parameter-list* of a method (§17.5). The formal parameter list defines the signature (§10.6) of an instance constructor and governs the process whereby overload resolution (§14.4.2) selects a particular instance constructor in an invocation.

Each of the types referenced in the *formal-parameter-list* of an instance constructor shall be at least as accessible as the constructor itself (§10.5.4).

The optional *constructor-initializer* specifies another instance constructor to invoke before executing the statements given in the *constructor-body* of this instance constructor. This is described further in §17.10.1.

When a constructor declaration includes an `extern` modifier, the constructor is said to be an **external constructor**.

Because an external constructor declaration provides no actual implementation, its *constructor-body* consists of a semicolon. For all other constructors, the *constructor-body* consists of a *block*, which specifies the statements to initialize a new instance of the class. This corresponds exactly to the *block* of an instance method with a `void` return type (§17.5.8).

Instance constructors are not inherited. Thus, a class has no instance constructors other than those actually declared in the class. If a class contains no instance constructor declarations, a default instance constructor is automatically provided (§17.10.4).

Instance constructors are invoked by *object-creation-expression*s (§14.5.10.1) and through *constructor-initializer*s.

17.10.1 Constructor initializers

All instance constructors (except those for class `object`) implicitly include an invocation of another instance constructor immediately before the *constructor-body*. The constructor to implicitly invoke is determined by the *constructor-initializer*:

- An instance constructor initializer of the form `base` (*argument-list$_{opt}$*) causes an instance constructor from the direct base class to be invoked. That constructor is selected using *argument-list* and the overload resolution rules of §14.4.2. The set of candidate instance constructors consists of all accessible instance constructors declared in the direct base class, or the default constructor (§17.10.4), if no instance constructors are declared in the direct base class. If this set is empty, or if a single best instance constructor cannot be identified, a compile-time error occurs.

- An instance constructor initializer of the form `this` (*argument-list$_{opt}$*) causes an instance constructor from the class itself to be invoked. The constructor is selected using *argument-list* and the overload resolution rules of §14.4.2. The set of candidate instance constructors consists of all accessible instance constructors declared in the class itself. If that set is empty, or if a single best instance constructor cannot be identified, a compile-time error occurs. If an instance constructor declaration includes a constructor initializer that invokes the constructor itself, a compile-time error occurs.

Infinite recursion not erroneous

The last sentence only defines self-recursion as erroneous. Consider the following:

```
class C
{
  public C(bool b) : this(false) {}    // invalid - self recursive

  public C() : this(42) {}             // ok but wrong - mutual
  public C(int value) : this() {}      // recursion isn't disallowed
                                       // but will of course fail

}
```

Mutual recursion, between two or more constructors, is not defined to be erroneous but will of course fail—just as any unlimited recursion will.

Why does the Standard declare self-recursion to be erroneous, without doing so for mutual recursion? Self-recursion is easily detected, and requiring implementations to report it provides a benefit at low cost. Mutual recursion is more costly to detect, and the benefit of making it erroneous was presumably not felt to balance the cost imposed on implementations. This, of course, is a design choice with no "right" answer. Not all languages define self-recursion to be erroneous, and a C# implementation is free to report invalid mutual recursion.

If an instance constructor has no constructor initializer, a constructor initializer of the form `base` `()` is implicitly provided. [*Note*: Thus, an instance constructor declaration of the form

```
C(...) {...}
```

is exactly equivalent to

```
C(...) : base() {...}
```

end note]

The scope of the parameters given by the *formal-parameter-list* of an instance constructor declaration includes the constructor initializer of that declaration. Thus, a constructor initializer is permitted to access the parameters of the constructor. [*Example*:

```
class A
{
public A(int x, int y) {}
}

class B: A
{
public B(int x, int y) : base(x + y, x - y) {}
}
```

end example]

An instance constructor initializer cannot access the instance being created. Therefore it is a compile-time error to reference `this` in an argument expression of the constructor initializer, as it is a compile-time error for an argument expression to reference any instance member through a *simple-name*.

17.10.2 Instance variable initializers

When an instance constructor has no constructor initializer, or it has a constructor initializer of the form `base(...)`, that constructor implicitly performs the initializations specified by the *variable-initializer*s of the instance fields declared in its class. This corresponds to a sequence of assignments that are executed immediately upon entry to the constructor and before the implicit invocation of the direct base class constructor. The variable initializers are executed in the textual order in which they appear in the class declaration (§17.4.5).

17.10.3 Constructor execution

Variable initializers are transformed into assignment statements, and these assignment statements are executed *before* the invocation of the base class instance constructor. This ordering ensures that all instance fields are initialized by their variable initializers before *any* statements that have access to that instance are executed. [*Example*:

```
using System;

class A
{
  public A()
  {
    PrintFields();
  }

  public virtual void PrintFields() {}
}

class B: A
{
  int x = 1;
  int y;

  public B()
  {
    y = -1;
  }

  public override void PrintFields()
  {
    Console.WriteLine("x = {0} , y = {1} ", x, y);
  }
}
```

When `new B()` is used to create an instance of B, the following output is produced:

```
x = 1, y = 0
```

The value of `x` is 1 because the variable initializer is executed before the base class instance constructor is invoked. However, the value of `y` is 0 (the default value of an `int`) because the assignment to `y` is not executed until after the base class constructor returns.

It is useful to think of instance variable initializers and constructor initializers as statements that are automatically inserted before the *constructor-body*. The example

```
using System;
using System.Collections;

class A
{
  int x = 1, y = -1, count;
```

```
    public A()
    {
      count = 0;
    }

    public A(int n)
    {
      count = n;
    }
}

class B: A
{
    double sqrt2 = Math.Sqrt(2.0);
    ArrayList items = new ArrayList(100);
    int max;

    public B(): this(100)
    {
      items.Add("default");
    }

    public B(int n): base(n - 1)
    {
      max = n;
    }
}
```

contains several variable initializers; it also contains constructor initializers of both forms (base and this). The example corresponds to the code shown below, where each comment indicates an automatically inserted statement (the syntax used for the automatically inserted constructor invocations isn't valid, but merely serves to illustrate the mechanism).

```
    using System.Collections;

    class A
    {
      int x, y, count;

      public A()
      {
        x = 1;                      // Variable initializer
        y = -1;                     // Variable initializer
        object();                   // Invoke object() constructor
        count = 0;
      }

      public A(int n)
      {
        x = 1;                      // Variable initializer
        y = -1;                     // Variable initializer
```

```
        object();                        // Invoke object() constructor
        count = n;
      }
    }

    class B: A
    {
      double sqrt2;
      ArrayList items;
      int max;

      public B(): this(100)
      {
        B(100);                          // Invoke B(int) constructor
        items.Add("default");
      }

      public B(int n): base(n - 1)
      {
        sqrt2 = Math.Sqrt(2.0);          // Variable initializer
        items = new ArrayList(100);      // Variable initializer
        A(n - 1);                        // Invoke A(int) constructor
        max = n;
      }
    }
```

end example]

Rationale: field initialization before base constructor invocation

There is a good reason for C#'s executing field initializers before the constructor initializer, and hence before the base class constructor and base class field initializers. Namely, if the constructor initializer were executed before instance field initializers, then virtual methods in the base class which are overridden in the derived class can be called before referred-to fields in the derived class have been initialized, as shown by the following Java example. This may cause subtle bugs or throw exceptions, for instance, if an instance field appears to be initialized to a collection and the derived method attempts to add an item to that collection—while in reality the field is still `null`:

```
// Java code

class Base
{
  public Base()
  {
    Before();
  }

  public void Before() {}    // virtual by default in Java
}

class Derived extends Base
{
  private ArrayList<Derived> instances = new ArrayList<Derived>();
```

```
        public void Before()        // override by default in Java
        {
          instances.add(this);
        }
    }
```

The author of class `Derived` would reason that his code is safe, for surely the `instances` field will be initialized to hold an `ArrayList` before anybody attempts to add an item to it? But this is not true, because the base class constructor can call method `Before`, which would throw a NullReferenceException.

The initialization order used by C# avoids this problem, but at a price: Instance field initializers are not allowed to refer to `this`, or to other instance fields. See annotation on §17.5.4.2.

In either language, one should not call a virtual method (even indirectly) from a constructor. It leads to subtle code, and possibly to surprises as shown here.

17.10.4 Default constructors

If a class contains no instance constructor declarations, a default instance constructor is automatically provided. That default constructor simply invokes the parameterless constructor of the direct base class. If the direct base class does not have an accessible parameterless instance constructor, a compile-time error occurs. If the class is abstract then the declared accessibility for the default constructor is protected. Otherwise, the declared accessibility for the default constructor is public. [*Note*: Thus, the default constructor is always of the form

```
    protected C(): base() {}
```

or

```
    public C(): base() {}
```

where `C` is the name of the class. *end note*]

[*Example*: In the following code

```
    class Message
    {
      object sender;
      string text;
    }
```

a default constructor is provided because the class contains no instance constructor declarations. Thus, the example is precisely equivalent to

```
    class Message
    {
      object sender;
      string text;

      public Message(): base() {}
    }
```

end example]

17.10.5 Private constructors

When a class declares only private instance constructors, it is not possible for other classes (that are not nested in the class) to derive from that class or to create instances of that class. [*Example*:

Private instance constructors can be used to restrict instantiation of the class to a prescribed set of instances. For example:

```
public class Color
{
  private byte val;

  private Color(byte val) { this.val = val; }
  public static readonly Color Red = new Color(0);
  public static readonly Color Green = new Color(1);
  public static readonly Color Blue = new Color(2);

}
```

Since `Color`'s constructor is private, there will never be more than three instances of the `Color` class, namely the ones stored in the static fields and returned by the static properties. *end example]*

At least one instance constructor shall be declared to suppress the automatic generation of a default constructor.

17.10.6 Optional instance constructor parameters

[*Note*: The `this(...)` form of constructor initializer is commonly used in conjunction with overloading to implement optional instance constructor parameters. In the example

```
class Text
{
  public Text() : this(0, 0, null) {}
  public Text(int x, int y) : this(x, y, null) {}
  public Text(int x, int y, string s)
  {
    // Actual constructor implementation
  }
}
```

the first two instance constructors merely provide the default values for the missing arguments. Both use a `this(...)` constructor initializer to invoke the third instance constructor, which actually does the work of initializing the new instance. The effect is that of optional constructor parameters:

```
Text t1 = new Text();           // Same as Text(0, 0, null)
Text t2 = new Text(5, 10);      // Same as Text(5, 10, null)
Text t3 = new Text(5, 20, "Hello");
```

end note]

17.11 Static constructors

A ***static constructor*** is a member that implements the actions required to initialize a class. Static constructors are declared using *static-constructor-declarations*:

static-constructor-declaration:
  attributes_{opt} *static-constructor-modifiers* *identifier* ( ) *static-constructor-body*

static-constructor-modifiers:
  extern_{opt} static
  static extern_{opt}

```
static-constructor-body:
    block
    ;
```

A *static-constructor-declaration* can include a set of *attributes* (§24) and an `extern` modifier (§17.5.7).

The *identifier* of a *static-constructor-declaration* shall name the class in which the static constructor is declared. If any other name is specified, a compile-time error occurs.

When a static constructor declaration includes an `extern` modifier, the static constructor is said to be an **external static constructor**. Because an external static constructor declaration provides no actual implementation, its *static-constructor-body* consists of a semicolon. For all other static constructor declarations, the *static-constructor-body* consists of a *block*, which specifies the statements to execute in order to initialize the class. This corresponds exactly to the *method-body* of a static method with a `void` return type (§17.5.8).

Static constructors are not inherited, and cannot be called directly.

No access specifier; no parameter

Static constructors and finalizers share an inability to be declared with access specifiers or parameters:

```
class Example
{
  private static Example(int nope) // compile-time errors
  {
  }
  public ~Example(int nope)        // compile-time errors
  {
  }
}
```

These restrictions are simply reflections of the constraint that these members cannot be called directly from user-code.

The static constructor for a non-generic class executes at most once in a given application domain. The static constructor for a generic class declaration executes at most once for each closed constructed type constructed from the class declaration (§25.1.5). The execution of a static constructor is triggered by the first of the following events to occur within an application domain:

- An instance of the class is created.
- Any of the static members of the class are referenced.

Trigger one, trigger all

The instance constructor of a derived class invokes, directly or indirectly, the instance constructor of its direct base class (§17.10.1). Therefore, creating an instance of derived class also triggers a static constructor of the direct base class, and so on up the class hierarchy.

For example, consider:

```
using System;

class Test
{
```

```
      static void Main()
      {
        B b = new B();
      }
    }

  class A
  {
    public A()
    {
      Console.WriteLine("Create an instance of A");
    }

    static A()
    {
      Console.WriteLine("Init A");
    }
  }

  class B : A
  {
    public B()
    {
      Console.WriteLine("Create an instance of B");
    }

    static B()
    {
      Console.WriteLine("Init B");
    }
  }
```

This produces the output:

```
  Init B
  Init A
  Create an instance of A
  Create an instance of B
```

because the constructor initializer `base()` implicitly provided for B's instance constructor (§17.10.1) triggers the execution of A's instance constructor, which in turn requires A's static constructor to be run.

Nicu Georgian Fruja

Constants are not "referenced"

A constant (§17.3) is processed at compile-time (§17.4.2.2) and is not a runtime reference to a static member. Therefore, using a constant does not trigger execution of a static constructor.

Which static constructor is triggered?

A reference to a static may only directly trigger the execution of a static constructor in the class in which the static is declared. Although the static fields and methods declared by a base class are also considered members of a derived class (§10.4.4), they are not "of the [derived] class." Therefore, referencing them via the derived class does not trigger the execution of any static constructor of the derived class.

For example, consider:

```
using System;

class Test
{
  static void Main()
  {
    Console.WriteLine("B.X = {0}", B.X);
  }
}

class A
{
  public static int X;
  static A()
  {
    Console.WriteLine("Init A");
  }
}

class B : A
{
  static B()
  {
    Console.WriteLine("Init B");
  }
}
```

This produces the output:

```
Init A
B.X = 0
```

since B.X's reference triggers only the execution of the static constructor whose class declares the field B.X, (i.e., A).

Nicu Georgian Fruja

If a class contains the Main method (§10.1) in which execution begins, the static constructor for that class executes before the Main method is called. If a class contains any static fields with initializers, those initializers are executed in textual order immediately prior to executing the static constructor (§17.4.5).

[*Example*: The example

```
using System;

class Test
{
  static void Main()
  {
```

```
        A.F();
        B.F();
      }
    }

    class A
    {
      static A()
      {
        Console.WriteLine("Init A");
      }
      public static void F()
      {
        Console.WriteLine("A.F");
      }
    }

    class B
    {
      static B()
      {
        Console.WriteLine("Init B");
      }
      public static void F()
      {
        Console.WriteLine("B.F");
      }
    }
```

shall produce the output:

```
    Init A
    A.F
    Init B
    B.F
```

because the execution of A's static constructor is triggered by the call to A.F, and the execution of B's static constructor is triggered by the call to B.F. *end example*]

It is possible to construct circular dependencies that allow static fields with variable initializers to be observed in their default value state.

[*Example*: The example

```
    using System;

    class A
    {
      public static int X;
      static A() { X = B.Y + 1;}
    }

    class B
    {
      public static int Y = A.X + 1;
```

```
static B() {}
static void Main()
{
  Console.WriteLine("X = {0} , Y = {1} ", A.X, B.Y);
}
}
```

produces the output

```
X = 1, Y = 2
```

To execute the Main method, the system first runs the initializer for B.Y, prior to class B's static constructor. Y's initializer causes A's static constructor to be run because the value of A.X is referenced. The static constructor of A in turn proceeds to compute the value of X, and in doing so fetches the default value of Y, which is zero. A.X is thus initialized to 1. The process of running A's static field initializers and static constructor then completes, returning to the calculation of the initial value of Y, the result of which becomes 2. *end example*]

Indeterminately deterministic

Though the rules for when static constructors are called are well defined and deterministic, writing code which relies upon these rules is not recommended. For example, consider this minor variation of the preceding example:

```
class A
{
  public static int X;
  static A() { X = B.Y + 1; }
}

class B
{
  public static int Y = A.X + 1;
  static B() {}
}

class C
{
  static void Main()
  {
    int x = A.X;
    int y = B.Y;
    Console.WriteLine("X = {0} , Y = {1} ", x, y);
  }
}
```

This outputs:

```
X = 2, Y = 1
```

However, make the seemingly innocuous change of swapping the declaration order:

```
int y = B.Y;
int x = A.X;
```

and the output becomes:

```
X = 1, Y = 2
```

Further, as reliance on when a static constructor is executed is discouraged, throwing an exception from one is ill advised at best. This topic is covered §23.3 and associated annotations.

Recommendations:

- Only use static constructors to initialize static fields and not to produce other (side) effects.
- Avoid dependency cycles between static initializers and constructors.
- Assume only that all static fields *may* be initialized at some point, and *will* be prior to use. Simply moving an initialization from a constructor to a field initializer can change when, and if, it occurs.
- Avoid throwing an exception from a static constructor or static field initialization.

Initialization is different when there are only static field initializers (§17.4.5.1) and for value types (§18.3.10); see those clauses and associated annotations for details.

17.12 Finalizers

[*Note*: In the previous version of this standard, what is now referred to as a "finalizer" was called a "destructor". Experience has shown that the term "destructor" caused confusion and often resulted to incorrect expectations, especially to programmers knowing C++. In C++, a destructor is called in a determinate manner, whereas, in C#, a finalizer is not. To get determinate behavior from C#, one should use `Dispose`. *end note*]

C++ destructors versus C# finalizers

C++ destructors are determinate in the sense that they are run at known points in time, in a known order, and from a known thread. They are thus semantically *very* different from C# finalizers, which are run at unknown points in time, in an unknown order, from an unknown thread, and at the discretion of the garbage collector.

A *finalizer* is a member that implements the actions required to finalize an instance of a class. A finalizer is declared using a *finalizer-declaration*:

> *finalizer-declaration:*
>   *attributes*_{opt} `extern`_{opt} ~ *identifier* ( ) *finalizer-body*

> *finalizer-body:*
>   *block*
>   *;*

A *finalizer-declaration* can include a set of *attributes* (§24).

The *identifier* of a *finalizer-declarator* shall name the class in which the finalizer is declared. If any other name is specified, a compile-time error occurs.

When a finalizer declaration includes an `extern` modifier, the finalizer is said to be an ***external finalizer***. Because an external finalizer declaration provides no actual implementation, its *finalizer-body* consists of a semicolon. For all other finalizers, the *finalizer-body* consists of a *block*, which specifies the statements to execute in order to finalize an instance of the class. A *finalizer-body* corresponds exactly to the *method-body* of an instance method with a `void` return type (§17.5.8).

Finalizers are not inherited. Thus, a class has no finalizers other than the one that can be declared in that class.

[*Note*: Since a finalizer is required to have no parameters, it cannot be overloaded, so a class can have, at most, one finalizer. *end note*]

Finalizers are invoked automatically, and cannot be invoked explicitly. An instance becomes eligible for finalization when it is no longer possible for any code to use that instance. Execution of the finalizer for the instance can occur at any time after the instance becomes eligible for finalization (§10.9). When an instance is finalized, the finalizers in that instance's inheritance chain are called, in order, from most derived to least derived. [*Example*: The output of the example

```
using System;

class A
{
  ~A()
  {
    Console.WriteLine("A's finalizer");
  }
}

class B: A
{
  ~B()
  {
    Console.WriteLine("B's finalizer");
  }
}

class Test
{
  static void Main()
  {
    B b = new B();
    b = null;
    GC.Collect();
    GC.WaitForPendingFinalizers();
  }
}
```

is

```
B's finalizer
A's finalizer
```

since finalizers in an inheritance chain are called in order, from most derived to least derived. *end example*]

[*Note*: If an uncaught exception is thrown, it is unspecified whether the base class finalizer is called (§23.3). *end note*]

Thwarting a finalizer

The preceding note would appear to provide an opportunity to thwart the execution of a finalizer. Despite any indications to the contrary, a finalizer is not an overridable virtual method; finalizers are not inherited (§10.4), and when an object is finalized any finalizers declared in its base classes are invoked in order. On application termination, the finalizers of all objects that have not been garbage collected are called (§10.2).

However, it is undefined whether any base class finalizers will be called if an uncaught exception is thrown (§23.3), thus theoretically providing a way to prevent the finalizer of a particular non-sealed class from executing by deriving from it and writing a finalizer which throws. For example, consider the following change to B from the preceding example:

```
class B : A
{
  ~B()
  {
    Console.WriteLine("B's finalizer");
    throw new Exception("Attempt to thwart execution of ~A()");
  }
}
```

The Standard allows for the execution of ~A() to not occur when finalizing an instance of B. But what will happen with the exception (§23.3) is undefined, so exploiting this technique to thwart the execution of a finalizer is unreliable.

Both the current Microsoft and Mono C# systems execute base class finalizers in this situation, so this technique cannot be exploited at all on those systems.

Note that an uncaught exception thrown from a finalizer may result in application termination, which in turn results in finalization of all non-garbage-collected objects, one of which might throw an uncaught exception...the death throes could take a while.

Thwarting a finalizer on the CLI

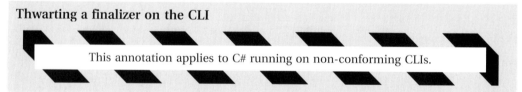

This annotation applies to C# running on non-conforming CLIs.

When C# is compiled to the CLI, the obvious mechanism for implementing a finalizer is to adopt the CLI finalization mechanism and override the method virtual void System. Object.Finalize(). On the CLI any override of this method must invoke its base class finalizer (i.e., in C#-ese base.Finalize()), and this is the only case where CLI application code calls the finalizer. The CLI garbage collector takes care of invoking the finalizer.

The current Microsoft and Novell C# systems running on the CLR and Mono use this CLI finalization mechanism and follow the requirements; in particular, they ensure that the base class finalizer is called.

However, there is a window of opportunity for rogue types:

1. A non-C# CLI type extends a C# type.
2. That type overrides System.Object.Finalize but violates the CLI requirement to call the base Finalize.
3. The particular CLI does not enforce the CLI requirement.

Unfortunately, it is believed that the current versions of Microsoft's CLR and Novell's Mono do not enforce the CLI requirement to call the base class finalizer, so on those systems the C# (and CLI) semantics are not guaranteed.

CLI programmers can, if the language they are using allows it (i.e., CIL does), partially work around this nonconformance by sealing their override of System.Object.Finalize. While this ensures the finalizer will be called, it is rather draconian as it prevents any derived classes from having finalizers.

It has been suggested that C# could support this workaround by allowing a class to specify that no derived class shall define a finalizer, maybe by overloading the meaning of `sealed` keyword (it would be an overloaded meaning as C# finalizers are not virtual). However, it is not known that the committee ever considered any such proposal.

Finalizer issues

The Standard does not specify which thread will execute a finalizer. An object may be accessed by several threads, and the thread last referencing an object may not be the thread that created the object, so an object may not have an obvious "home" thread. For this reason it is left to the implementation on which thread to execute the finalizers, which could be a thread created for internal use by the implementation or one created by user code. In most circumstances this makes no difference, but programmers need to be aware of it in special cases.

Finalizers in Microsoft's and Mono's implementation are invoked on a separate thread, not from the thread that created the object. This is a source of problems when the finalizer is used to release resources that are not controlled by the execution environment (unmanaged resources).

Hence, it is preferable that classes utilizing unmanaged resources explicitly expose the `IDis-posable` interface and encourage users of the API to call the `Dispose` method when the resources are no longer in use, instead of depending on the finalizer to be executed.

Miguel de Icaza

Final deadlock

As the previous annotation explains, an implementation is free to execute a finalizer on a thread of its choosing.

However, implementations should take great care to protect themselves from rogue finalizers. Conceivably, if finalizers are executed on the garbage collector thread, then a single finalizer that waits indefinitely for a lock may bring the garbage collector and hence all allocation to a halt. Similarly, if all finalizers are executed on a special finalizer thread, then a single finalizer that blocks may halt all other finalizers and so halt the reclamation of unreferenced objects needing finalization. Both these situations could potentially deadlock an application.

To avoid any potential problems programmers should, if possible, avoid taking locks in finalizers, directly or indirectly.

A C# implementation can implement finalizers by overriding the virtual method `Finalize` on `System.Object`. However, C# programs are not permitted to override this method or call it (or overrides of it) directly. [*Example*: For instance, the program

```
class A
{
  protected override void Finalize() {}  // error
  public void F()
  {
```

```
        this.Finalize();    // error
    }
}
```

contains two errors. *end example*]

The compiler behaves as if `System.Object.Finalize`, and overrides of it, does not exist at all. [*Example*: Thus, this program:

```
class A
{
  void Finalize() {}    // permitted
}
```

is valid and the method shown hides `System.Object`'s `Finalize` method, without requiring the `new` modifier. *end example*]

Erroneous details

The previous two paragraphs and code examples should not be part of the Standard. They describe something in CLI terms and specific to a particular compiler that is covered normatively elsewhere in the Standard, and the text here is more misleading than illuminating.

The name and signature of `Finalize` is reserved (§17.2.7.4) and no attempt should be made to define, override, or call it. For further details, see clause §17.2.7, its subclauses, and the associated annotations.

For a discussion of the behavior when an exception is thrown from a finalizer, see §23.3.

18 Structs

Structs are similar to classes in that they represent data structures that can contain data members and function members. However, unlike classes, structs are value types and do not require heap allocation. A variable of a struct type directly contains the data of the struct, whereas a variable of a class type contains a reference to the data, the latter known as an object.

Freedom of allocation

The Standard states that value types "do not *require* heap allocation" but does not forbid it or recommend an alternative. However, it does specify the semantics of value types, such as copy-on-assignment.

The most conventional choice for an implementation would be to use stack allocation for local variables and method parameters of value type, and indeed all implementations available at the time of writing do so.

However, where should, for example, a static field of value type be stored? Stack allocation seems less suitable: Which stack frame would be used? It is left to the implementor to decide what is most appropriate on the target platform, and the two major implementations current at the time of writing have handled this differently. It is important to note that this implementation choice *does not* impact the C# programmer and need be of no concern to him.

"Heap" allocation required

The freedom of allocation is curtailed in the presence of local variable capture by anonymous methods (§14.5.15.3.1). If a local variable is captured, its lifetime may have to be extended beyond that of the current method activation, and that usually precludes stack allocation. The standard approach is to "box" captured local variables into an instance, allocated on the heap, of a compiler-generated class.

Furthermore, this boxing of captured struct variables does not change their value type semantics. In particular, invocation of an interface method on a struct will still result in the struct being boxed (§14.4.3.1). In other words, the captured struct will be copied from the compiler-generated heap object into another heap object.

[*Note*: Structs are particularly useful for small data structures that have value semantics. Complex numbers, points in a coordinate system, or key-value pairs in a dictionary are all good examples of structs. Key to these data structures is that they have few data members, that they do not require use of inheritance or referential identity, and that they can be conveniently implemented using value semantics where assignment copies the value instead of the reference. *end note*]

As described in §11.1.4, the simple types provided by C#, such as `int`, `double`, and `bool`, are, in fact, all struct types. Just as these predefined types are structs, it is also possible to use structs and operator overloading to implement new "primitive" types in the C# language.

Union City blues

> Warning: This annotation applies to C# executing on Microsoft's CLR and Novell's Mono; it uses features that are not part of Standard CLI and attributes that are not part of Standard C#. The code subverts the C# type system and is potentially type unsafe (see the annotation "Danger, UXB!") and should therefore only be used when absolutely required.

The CLR [StructLayout(LayoutKind.Explicit)] and [FieldOffset(0)] attributes can combine to define a struct (or class) where every field is overlaid at offset zero — the equivalent of an untagged C-like union. The memory size of Union is therefore just the maximum of each individual field size. For example:

```
using System.Runtime.InteropServices;

[ StructLayout (LayoutKind.Explicit)]
public struct Union
{
  public Union(A a)
  {
    this = new Union();
    this.a = a;
  }

  public Union(B b)
  {
    this = new Union();
    this.b = b;
  }

  public Union(C c)
  {
    this = new Union();
    this.c = c;
  }

  ...

  [ FieldOffset(0)]
  private readonly A a;

  [ FieldOffset(0)]
  private readonly B b;

  [ FieldOffset(0)]
  private readonly C c;
}
```

As far as the C# compiler is concerned, the Union contains three distinct fields. C#'s definite assignment rules require every struct constructor to initialize every field. The assignment to `this` satisfies this requirement by overwriting the whole structure with a default-initialized instance of `Union`. The subsequent assignment then stores a particular value in the `Union`.

Premature optimization

Warning: This annotation applies to C# executing on Microsoft's CLR and Novell's Mono; it uses features that are not part of Standard CLI and attributes that are not part of Standard C#. The code subverts the C# type system and is potentially type unsafe (see the annotation "Danger, UXB!") and should therefore only be used when absolutely required.

Considering the example in the previous annotation, if you attempt to write a property to type check access as follows:

```
[ StructLayout (LayoutKind.Explicit)]
struct Union
{
   ...
   public A A
   {
      get
      {
         if (a is A)
            return a;
         else
            throw new ...;
      }
   }

   [ FieldOffset (0)]
   private readonly A a;
   ...
}
```

then it does not work...

The compiler believes that field `a` is of type `A`, as it knows nothing about `[ StructLayout (LayoutKind.Explicit)]`, and therefore optimizes the test `(a is A)` to be just `(a != null)`. However, as shown, this is wrong in this case. You can write the test like this:

```
[ StructLayout (LayoutKind.Explicit)]
struct Union
{
   ...
   public A A
   {
      get
      {
         if (a.GetType() == typeof(A))
            return a;
         else
            throw new ...;
```

```
      }
    }

    [ FieldOffset(0)]
    private readonly A a;

    ...
  }
```

This shows that compiler optimizations that are reasonable in a reasonable world are not in an unreasonable one. You have been warned.

Danger, UXB!

> Warning: This annotation applies to C# executing on Microsoft's CLR and Novell's Mono; it uses features that are not part of Standard CLI and attributes that are not part of Standard C#. The code subverts the C# type system.

The previous annotation relies on using the CLR's `StructLayout` attribute. The very existence of this attribute blows a humongous hole in the type safety of C#; **it is not part of Standard C#**. Here is an example of what can go terribly wrong. First, we start with a simple class with a `private readonly` field:

```
    sealed class SecureClient
    {
      private readonly string passKey;

      internal SecureClient(string key)
      {
        passKey = key;
      }

      public void ShowPassKey()
      {
        Console.WriteLine(passKey);
      }
    }
```

Introduce a hacker and a paper wall:

```
    class Hacker
    {
      public uint Violate;
    }

    [ StructLayout(LayoutKind.Explicit)]
    struct PaperWall
    {
      public PaperWall(object v)
      {
        this = new PaperWall();
```

```
        this.victim = v;
    }

    [FieldOffset(0)]
    private readonly object victim;

    [FieldOffset(0)]
    public readonly Hacker Memory;
}
```

Finally, put these together and launch an attack:

```
class Danger
{
    static void Invade()
    {
        SecureClient sc = new SecureClient("key");

        PaperWall u = new PaperWall(sc);   // Place the victim inside the
                                           // paper wall

        sc.ShowPassKey();                  // Prints "key"
        u.Memory.Violate = 0xC0DEDEAD;     // Hack the private readonly field
        sc.ShowPassKey();                  // Kaboom!
    }
}
```

Under Microsoft and Mono C#, this compiles, passes *peverify*, and blows up—in this particular case with an invalid access exception (Microsoft) or a null violation (Mono), which is a little better than crashing the computer—just.

The code contains a major type violation; an instance of `PaperWall` is initialized with an instance of the `SecureClient` class, which is then referenced as though it were in fact an instance of the `Hacker` class.

Having gained access to the `SecureClient` instance as though it were an instance of `Hacker`, we stuff the unsigned 32-bit integer 0xC0DEDEAD into the `private readonly string` field `passKey`. This has serious consequences: We have converted an integer into a heap address! How much garbage is written into the output buffer before `Console.WriteLine` causes a memory violation is anybody's guess.

If instead of using the manufactured heap address for read access it is used for write access, the potential consequences are much greater. The exploit could also be used to replace the supposedly inaccessible `passKey` with one known by the attacker.

We have just one piece of advice: *Any code that uses `StructLayout`, or any assembly that references `StructLayout`, should be deemed to have the type safety of assembler, and trusted accordingly.* We reiterate: This is **not part of Standard C#**.

18.1 Struct declarations

A *struct-declaration* is a *type-declaration* (§16.6) that declares a new struct:

> *struct-declaration:*
>   *attributes*$_{opt}$ *struct-modifiers*$_{opt}$ partial$_{opt}$ struct *identifier*
>   *type-parameter-list*$_{opt}$
>   *struct-interfaces*$_{opt}$ *type-parameter-constraints-clauses*$_{opt}$ *struct-body* ;$_{opt}$

A *struct-declaration* consists of an optional set of *attributes* (§24), followed by an optional set of *struct-modifiers* (§18.1.1), followed by an optional `partial` modifier (§17.1.4), followed by the keyword `struct` and an *identifier* that names the struct, followed by an optional *type-parameter-list* (§25.1.1), followed by an optional *struct-interfaces* specification (§18.1.2), followed by an optional *type-parameter-constraints-clauses* (§25.7), followed by a *struct-body* (§18.1.3), optionally followed by a semicolon.

A struct declaration shall not supply a *type-parameter-constraints-clauses* unless it also supplies a *type-parameter-list*.

A struct declaration that supplies a *type-parameter-list* is a generic struct declaration (§25.2).

18.1.1 Struct modifiers
A *struct-declaration* can optionally include a sequence of struct modifiers:

> *struct-modifiers:*
>   *struct-modifier*
>   *struct-modifiers*   *struct-modifier*

> *struct-modifier:*
>   `new`
>   `public`
>   `protected`
>   `internal`
>   `private`

It is a compile-time error for the same modifier to appear multiple times in a struct declaration.

The modifiers of a struct declaration have the same meaning as those of a class declaration (§17.1.1).

18.1.2 Struct interfaces
A struct declaration can include a *struct-interfaces* specification, in which case the struct is said to implement the given interface types.

> *struct-interfaces:*
>   :   *interface-type-list*

The handling of interfaces on multiple parts of a partial struct declaration (§17.1.4) are discussed further in §17.1.2.2.

Interface implementations are discussed further in §20.4.

18.1.3 Struct body
The *struct-body* of a struct defines the members of the struct.

> *struct-body:*
>   {   *struct-member-declarations*$_{opt}$ }

18.2 Struct members
The members of a struct consist of the members introduced by its *struct-member-declarations* and the members inherited from the type `System.ValueType`.

struct-member-declarations:
  struct-member-declaration
  struct-member-declarations   *struct-member-declaration*

struct-member-declaration:
  constant-declaration
  field-declaration
  method-declaration
  property-declaration
  event-declaration
  indexer-declaration
  operator-declaration
  constructor-declaration
  static-constructor-declaration
  type-declaration

All kinds of *class-member-declaration*s except *finalizer-declaration* are also *struct-member-declaration*s. Except for the differences noted in §18.3, the descriptions of class members provided in §17.2 through §17.11 apply to struct members as well.

18.3 Class and struct differences

readonly value-type fields

A `readonly` field *cannot* change regardless of the type of the field. However, the mechanism by which a `readonly` field upholds this guarantee might be surprising when the field is a `struct`. Given the following:

```
struct Mile
{
  ...
  public void Add(Mile rhs)
  {
    value += rhs.value;
  }

  private int value;
}
```

consider the `distance.Add(more)` call in this fragment:

```
class Gotcha
{
  ...
  public void Ouch(Mile more)
  {
    distance.Add(more); // ? :-(
  }

  private readonly Mile distance;
}
```

Crucially, `distance` is an instance of a `struct` and is declared a `readonly` field. This creates a conflict: `distance.Add(more)` apparently modifies `distance.value` but `distance` is declared `readonly` so `distance.value` cannot change. How can this be? The answer is that `Add(more)` is called on a *copy* of `distance`!

The lesson from this probably unexpected behavior is that value types are best used for immutable types and that new values are best created using operators, or returned as method results. For example, consider:

```
struct Mile
{
  public Mile(int value)
  {
    this.value = value;
  }
  ...
  public static Mile operator+(Mile lhs, Mile rhs)
  {
    return new Mile(lhs.value + rhs.value);
  }

  private readonly int value;
}
```

In this design, `operator+` can be applied to any `Mile` values, readonly or otherwise; if an attempt is made to assign the result to a readonly field, a compile-time error will always be produced, thus reducing the chances of an unwelcome surprise.

18.3.1 Value semantics

Structs are value types (§11.1) and are said to have value semantics. Classes, on the other hand, are reference types (§11.2) and are said to have reference semantics.

A variable of a struct type directly contains the data of the struct, whereas a variable of a class type contains a reference to the data, the latter known as an object.

With classes, it is possible for two variables to reference the same object, and thus possible for operations on one variable to affect the object referenced by the other variable. With structs, the variables each have their own copy of the data, and it is not possible for operations on one to affect the other. Furthermore, because structs are not reference types, it is not possible for values of a struct type to be `null`.

[*Example*: Given the declaration

```
struct Point
{
  public int x, y;

  public Point(int x, int y)
  {
    this.x = x;
    this.y = y;
  }
}
```

the code fragment

```
Point a = new Point(10, 10);
Point b = a;

a.x = 100;
System.Console.WriteLine(b.x);
```

outputs the value 10. The assignment of a to b creates a copy of the value, and b is thus unaffected by the assignment to a.x. Had Point instead been declared as a class, the output would be 100 because a and b would reference the same object. *end example*]

Struct layout cycles

To determine the size and layout of an instance of some type S, one must determine the size and layout of its instance fields. When an instance field has reference type, we know that the field can be represented by a reference of a fixed size. However, when the instance field has struct type, one must recursively determine the size and layout of instances of that struct type. If, furthermore, the instance field has the same type S as the enclosing type, we have an infinite regress, also called a cycle in the struct layout, which must be rejected by the compiler. Such cycles can also occur between two or more types. Note that if the field is static, there is no problem, because a static field does not contribute to the size and layout of instances.

Hence, the following struct declaration Sc is illegal because of a layout cycle, whereas struct declaration Sa has no layout cycle and is legal. Moreover, class declaration C is legal because the only field in a C instance is a reference, which has fixed size. The struct declarations Sf and Sg form a cycle involving two struct types and therefore are illegal:

```
struct Sc
{
   Sc s;        // Illegal: struct layout cycle
}

struct Sa
{
   static Sa s; // Legal: no instance fields and hence no cycle
}

class C
{
   C s;         // Legal: one instance field, a reference
}

struct Sf      // ⎫
{              // |
  int x;       // |
  Sg g;        // |
}              // |
               // ⎬ Illegal: Sf <-> Sg struct cycle
struct Sg      // |
{              // |
  int y;       // |
  Sf f;        // |
}              // ⎭
```

The CLI specification Ecma-335 section II.13 defines the precise requirements on structure declarations, using the notion of an acyclic finite flattening graph. This algorithm is applicable to C#, regardless of whether it is hosted on the CLI or not.

Struct equality contracts

Programmers expect to be able to compare values using == and !=, so a good rule of thumb is that a struct should provide these operators. There is an expectation that equality (and relational) operators never throw an exception. In the following code fragment note that the expressions lhs.Equals, other.x and other.y are safe because Point is a value type, so lhs and other cannot be null. If Point were a class, this would not be true and the expressions could throw a NullReferenceException.

```
struct Point
{
  private int x, y;
  ...
  public static operator==(Point lhs, Point rhs)
  {
    return lhs.Equals(rhs);
  }

  public static operator!=(Point lhs, Point rhs)
  {
    return !lhs.Equals(rhs);
  }

  private bool Equals(Point other)
  {
    return x == other.x && y == other.y;
  }
}
```

All values can be boxed, so another rule of thumb is that structs should also override object.Equals. Most programmers also expect certain behavior from the Equals method and there is even a formal contract governing object.Equals—one part of which is that it must not throw an exception (see the annotation on §14.9). This is why the (Point)other cast is guarded (using a short-circuiting && operator) by an is operator dynamic type test in the following code fragment:

```
struct Point
{
  private int x, y;
  ...
  public override bool Equals(object other)
  {
    return other is Point && Equals((Point) other);
  }

  private bool Equals(Point other)
  {
    return x == other.x && y == other.y;
  }
}
```

It's not a good idea to implement the `==` and `!=` operators by forwarding to the `Equals (Object)` override as this causes needless boxing and needless type testing:

```
struct Point
{
  private int x, y;
  ...
  public static operator==(Point lhs, Point rhs)
  {
    return lhs.Equals(rhs); // don't do this
  }

  public override bool Equals(object other)
  {
    ...
  }
}
```

On the other hand, to avoid code duplication, `==` may well be defined in terms of the `Equals (Point)` override, or vice versa, without incurring extra runtime type checks or boxings.

18.3.2 Inheritance

All struct types implicitly inherit from `System.ValueType`, which, in turn, inherits from class `object`. A struct declaration can specify a list of implemented interfaces, but it is not possible for a struct declaration to specify a base class.

Struct types are never abstract and are always implicitly sealed. The `abstract` and `sealed` modifiers are therefore not permitted in a struct declaration.

Since inheritance isn't supported for structs, the declared accessibility of a struct member cannot be `protected` or `protected internal`.

Function members in a struct cannot be `abstract` or `virtual`, and the `override` modifier is allowed only to override methods inherited from the type `System.ValueType`.

18.3.3 Assignment

Assignment to a variable of a struct type creates a *copy* of the value being assigned. This differs from assignment to a variable of a class type, which copies the reference but not the object identified by the reference.

Similar to an assignment, when a struct is passed as a value parameter or returned as the result of a function member, a copy of the struct is created. A struct can be passed by reference to a function member using a `ref` or `out` parameter.

When a property or indexer of a struct is the target of an assignment, the instance expression associated with the property or indexer access shall be classified as a variable. If the instance expression is classified as a value, a compile-time error occurs. This is described in further detail in §14.14.1.

18.3.4 Default values

As described in §12.2, several kinds of variables are automatically initialized to their default value when they are created. For variables of class types and other reference types, this default value is `null`. However, since structs are value types that cannot be `null`, the default value of a struct is the value produced by setting all value type fields to their default value and all reference type fields to `null`.

[*Example*: Referring to the `Point` struct declared above, the example

```
Point[] a = new Point[100];
```

initializes each `Point` in the array to the value produced by setting the `x` and `y` fields to zero. *end example*]

The default value of a struct corresponds to the value returned by the default constructor of the struct (§11.1.1). Unlike a class, a struct is not permitted to declare a parameterless instance constructor. Instead, every struct implicitly has a parameterless instance constructor, which always returns the value that results from setting all value type fields to their default value and all reference type fields to `null`.

[*Note*: Structs should be designed to consider the default initialization state a valid state. In the example

```
using System;

struct KeyValuePair
{
  string key;
  string value;

  public KeyValuePair(string key, string value)
  {
    if (key == null || value == null) throw new ArgumentException();
    this.key = key;
    this.value = value;
  }
}
```

the user-defined instance constructor protects against null values only where it is explicitly called. In cases where a `KeyValuePair` variable is subject to default value initialization, the `key` and `value` fields will be null, and the struct should be prepared to handle this state. *end note*]

Why do structs always have a default constructor?

Consider if the rules were different and it was possible to create a struct that did *not* have a public parameterless instance constructor, as in:

```
struct Point
{
  private Point() // hypothetical
  { ...
  }
}
```

How would the `Point` values in an array of `Point`s be initialized?

```
Point[] locations = new Point[16];
```

Or even a simple `Point` variable?

```
Point centre;
```

Note: By design C# does not require a compiler to produce a distinct default constructor for every value type. However, that is an issue for compiler writers; to the programmer, all that is required is that an implementation behave as if every value type has its own default constructor.

18.3.5 Boxing and unboxing

A value of a class type can be converted to type `object` or to an interface type that is implemented by the class simply by treating the reference as another type at compile-time. Likewise, a value of type `object` or a value of an interface type can be converted back to a class type without changing the reference (but, of course, a run-time type check is required in this case).

Since structs are not reference types, these operations are implemented differently for struct types. When a value of a struct type is converted to type `object` or to an interface type that is implemented by the struct, a boxing operation takes place. Likewise, when a value of type `object` or a value of an interface type is converted back to a struct type, an unboxing operation takes place. A key difference from the same operations on class types is that boxing and unboxing *copies* the struct value either into or out of the boxed instance. [*Note*: Thus, following a boxing or unboxing operation, changes made to the unboxed struct are not reflected in the boxed struct. *end note*]

For further details on boxing and unboxing, see §11.3.

18.3.6 Meaning of this

Within an instance constructor or instance function member of a class, `this` is classified as a value. Thus, while `this` can be used to refer to the instance for which the function member was invoked, it is not possible to assign to `this` in a function member of a class.

Within an instance constructor of a struct, `this` corresponds to an `out` parameter of the struct type, and within an instance function member of a struct, `this` corresponds to a `ref` parameter of the struct type. In both cases, `this` is classified as a variable, and it is possible to modify the entire struct for which the function member was invoked by assigning to `this` or by passing `this` as a `ref` or `out` parameter.

18.3.7 Field initializers

As described in §18.3.4, the default value of a struct consists of the value that results from setting all value type fields to their default value and all reference type fields to `null`. For this reason, a struct does not permit instance field declarations to include variable initializers. [*Example*: As such, the following example results in one or more compile-time errors:

```
struct Point
{
  public int x = 1; // Error, initializer not permitted
  public int y = 1; // Error, initializer not permitted
}
```

end example]

This restriction applies only to instance fields. Static fields of a struct are permitted to include variable initializers.

18.3.8 Constructors

Unlike a class, a struct is not permitted to declare a parameterless instance constructor. Instead, every struct implicitly has a parameterless instance constructor, which always returns the value that results from setting all value type fields to their default value and all reference type fields to null (§11.1.1). A struct can declare instance constructors having parameters. [*Example*:

```
struct Point
{
  int x, y;

  public Point(int x, int y)
  {
    this.x = x;
    this.y = y;
  }
}
```

Given the above declaration, the statements

```
Point p1 = new Point();
Point p2 = new Point(0, 0);
```

both create a Point with x and y initialized to zero. *end example*]

A struct instance constructor is not permitted to include a constructor initializer of the form base (*argument-list$_{opt}$*).

The this variable of a struct instance constructor corresponds to an out parameter of the struct type, and similar to an out parameter, this shall be definitely assigned (§12.3) at every location where the constructor returns. [*Example*: Consider the instance constructor implementation below:

```
struct Point
{
  int x, y;

  public int X
  {
    set { x = value; }
  }

  public int Y
  {
    set { y = value; }
  }

  public Point(int x, int y)
  {
    X = x;     // error, this is not yet definitely assigned
    Y = y;     // error, this is not yet definitely assigned
  }
}
```

No instance member function (including the set accessors for the properties X and Y) can be called until all fields of the struct being constructed have been definitely assigned. Note, however, that if Point were a class instead of a struct, the instance constructor implementation would be permitted.

end example]

Definite assignment inside a struct constructor

Though the preceding example fails to compile, it is simple to make it valid. The default constructor (§11.1.2) of a value type results in all fields being definitely assigned; within a value type constructor an assignment to `this` (§18.3.6) enables all fields to be set. Combine these and the example can be made valid by incorporating a call to the default constructor inside the user constructor as follows:

```
struct Point
{
  ...
  public Point(int x, int y)
  {
    this = new Point(); // <-- - this statement added
    X = x;
    Y = y;
  }
}
```

An example using this technique may be found in an annotation to §18.

Non–dynamic allocation using new

The `new` keyword is strongly associated with the dynamic creation of objects (e.g., in C++ and Java). Programmers are often surprised to discover that a `struct` constructor call *must* be accompanied by the `new` keyword:

```
struct Point{}
F(Point());             // compile time error
F(new Point());         // ok
Point p1 = Point();     // compile time error
Point p2 = new Point(); // ok
```

However, a uniform struct/class syntax greatly simplifies generic code (which, of course, sometimes does not know whether the type is a struct or a class).

18.3.9 Finalizers

A struct is not permitted to declare a finalizer.

Why no ~S() in struct type S?

The idea of permitting the declaration of `~S()` in a struct type `S` was considered early in C#'s life. Like a C++ style destructor, it could de-initialize a value in a deterministic manner when it went out of scope, whether normally or because of an exception. However, that path was not taken; instead the `using` statement was introduced (§15.13). Since struct instances are usually not allocated on the heap and not managed by the garbage collector, C# style (nondeterministic) finalizers are not natural for structs.

18.3.10 Static constructors

Static constructors for structs follow most of the same rules as for classes. The execution of a static constructor for a struct is triggered by the first of the following events to occur within an application domain:

- An instance member of the struct is referenced.
- A static member of the struct is referenced.
- An explicitly declared constructor of the struct is called.

[*Note*: The creation of default values (§18.3.4) of struct types does not trigger the static constructor. (An example of this is the initial value of elements in an array.) *end note*]

Static constructor roulette

As discussed in annotations on static field initialization (§17.4.5.1) and static constructors in classes (§17.11), writing code that relies on the ordering and triggers for static initialization in classes is very ill advised. Small changes to code can affect whether a static field is initialized at all, and the deterministic rules can be almost indeterminable. Also, throwing exceptions from initialization is unwise (§23.3). The recommendation for classes is to code assuming a static field will be initialized at some point before use, and may or may not be otherwise.

For value types this recommendation is even stronger as, at the time of writing, there is a lack of consensus on what the rules should be and standards and implementations differ. Given this lack of consensus, knowing exactly what each requires/does is unimportant; only what may be relied upon in all cases is important. However, for completeness, we included the current situation; some readers may wish to skip to the discussion and recommendations at the end.

The design of C# is influenced by the CLI, and the main implementations of C# currently run on implementations of the CLI. This is how the standards and implementations currently behave in regard to the execution of static constructors on value types:

a. The C# Standard requires execution only when the first of the following occurs:

- An instance member of the struct is referenced.
- A static member of the struct is referenced.
- An explicitly declared constructor of the struct is called.

b. The CLI Standard requires execution only when the first of the following occurs:

- A static member of the struct is referenced.
- An explicitly declared constructor of the struct is called.

The CLI does *not* allow execution when an instance member is referenced. Note that, unlike for classes, an instance member of a value type can be referenced without any constructor executing because the default constructor is not explicitly declared.

c. Experiments suggest that the current Microsoft C# compiler executing on the CLR and the current Novell compiler executing on Mono actually trigger the static constructor at the first of the following:

- An instance *method* of the struct is referenced.
- A static member of the struct is referenced.
- An explicitly declared constructor of the struct is called.

Note that in triggering on instance method reference the CLR and Mono fail to conform to the CLI Standard, and in not triggering on instance field access both compilers fail to conform to the C# Standard!

d. Experiments suggest that the current Microsoft C# compiler executing on the NGEN implementation conforms to the CLI Standard and not to the C# Standard.

Our experiments may not be exhaustive, and compilers and runtimes may change, so the reported behavior should not be relied upon.

Clearly the current situation is unfortunate; however, adhering to the same advice given for classes will ensure your code behaves predictably according to the Standard on all current implementations we have tested, whether classes or structs are involved, and whether static constructors or just static field initializers are used.

Recommendations:

- Only use static constructors to initialize static fields and not to produce other (side) effects.
- Avoid dependency cycles between static initializers and constructors.
- Assume only that all static fields *may* be initialized at some point, and *will* be prior to use. Simply moving an initialization from a constructor to a field initializer can change when, or if, it occurs.
- Do not throw exceptions from static constructors or static field initializers.

19 Arrays

An array is a data structure that contains a number of variables that are accessed through computed indices. The variables contained in an array, also called the ***elements*** of the array, are all of the same type, and this type is called the ***element type*** of the array.

An array has a rank that determines the number of indices associated with each array element. The rank of an array is also referred to as the dimensions of the array. An array with a rank of one is called a ***single-dimensional array.*** An array with a rank greater than one is called a ***multi-dimensional array.*** Specific sized multi-dimensional arrays are often referred to as two-dimensional arrays, three-dimensional arrays, and so on. Each dimension of an array has an associated length that is an integral number greater than or equal to zero. The dimension lengths are not part of the type of the array, but rather are established when an instance of the array type is created at run-time. The length of a dimension determines the valid range of indices for that dimension: For a dimension of length N, indices can range from 0 to N − 1 inclusive. The total number of elements in an array is the product of the lengths of each dimension in the array. If one or more of the dimensions of an array have a length of zero, the array is said to be empty.

The element type of an array can be any type, including an array type.

19.1 Array types

An array type is written as a *non-array-type* followed by one or more *rank-specifier*s:

> *array-type:*
>   *non-array-type   rank-specifiers*
>
> *non-array-type:*
>   *value-type*
>   *class-type*
>   *interface-type*
>   *delegate-type*
>   *type-parameter*
>
> *rank-specifiers:*
>   *rank-specifier*
>   *rank-specifiers   rank-specifier*
>
> *rank-specifier:*
>   [*dim-separators_{opt}*   ]
>
> *dim-separators:*
>   ,
>   *dim-separators*   ,

A *non-array-type* is any *type* that is not itself an *array-type*.

The rank of an array type is given by the leftmost *rank-specifier* in the *array-type*: A *rank-specifier* indicates that the array is an array with a rank of one plus the number of "," tokens in the *rank-specifier*.

The element type of an array type is the type that results from deleting the leftmost *rank-specifier*:

- An array type of the form T[R] is an array with rank R and a non-array element type T.

- An array type of the form T[R] [R₁] ...[Rₙ] is an array with rank R and an element type T [R₁] ...[Rₙ] .

In effect, the *rank-specifier*s are read from left to right *before* the final non-array element type. [*Example*: The type int[ ] [,,] [,] is a single-dimensional array of three-dimensional arrays of two-dimensional arrays of int. *end example*]

At run-time, a value of an array type can be null or a reference to an instance of that array type or a covariant array type, as described in §19.5.

19.1.1 The System.Array type

The type System.Array is the abstract base type of all array types. An implicit reference conversion (§13.1.4) exists from any array type to System.Array and to any interface type implemented by System.Array. An explicit reference conversion (§13.2.3) exists from System.Array and any interface type implemented by System.Array to any array type. System.Array is not itself an *array-type*. Rather, it is a *class-type* from which all *array-type*s are derived.

At run-time, a value of type System.Array can be null or a reference to an instance of any array type.

19.2 Array creation

Array instances are created explicitly by *array-creation-expression*s (§14.5.10.2) or by field or local variable declarations that include an *array-initializer* (§19.7). Array instances can also be created implicitly by invoking a method in its expanded form (§14.4.1).

When an array instance is created, the rank and length of each dimension are established and then remain constant for the entire lifetime of the instance. In other words, it is not possible to change the rank of an existing array instance, nor is it possible to resize its dimensions.

An array instance is always of an array type. The System.Array type is an abstract type that cannot be instantiated.

Elements of arrays created by *array-creation-expression*s are always initialized to their default value (§12.2).

19.3 Array element access

Array elements are accessed using *element-access* expressions (§14.5.6.1) of the form A[I₁, I₂, ..., Iₙ] , where A is an expression of an array type and each Iₓ is an expression of type int, uint, long, ulong, or of a type that can be implicitly converted to one or more of these types. The result of an array element access is a variable, namely the array element selected by the indices.

The elements of an array can be enumerated using a foreach statement (§15.8.4).

foreach: simpler and faster

Writing a foreach statement is simpler than writing a for statement and could also be much faster at runtime. For example, the Microsoft C# compiler compiles a foreach statement iterating through a locally declared one-dimensional array variable into a specific CIL pattern. The Microsoft CLR JIT recognizes this pattern and is able to optimize away the bounds check when presenting each array element.

19.4 Array members

Every array type inherits the members declared by the `System.Array` type.

Arrays and vectors on the CLI

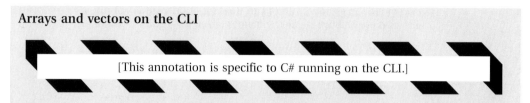

[This annotation is specific to C# running on the CLI.]

Note, however, that not every instance of a class derived from `System.Array` is an instance of an array type. This is due to the restriction that array types are zero based, whereas instances of classes derived from `System.Array` *may* have lower bounds other than zero. These can be created using `System.Array.CreateInstance`.

Interestingly enough, though, a multidimensional array with nonzero lower bounds can be used as an array type. This is due to the distinction used in the CLI between an `array` (which may have multiple dimensions and nonzero lower bounds) and a `vector` (which is always single dimensional and must have a lower bound of zero). It is not hard to see that vectors are more efficient for access than arrays. Single-dimensional C# array types correspond with CLI vectors, whereas multi-dimensional C# array types correspond with CLI arrays. Here is some code that demonstrates that:

```
using System;

class Test
{
  static void Main()
  {
    // Creates an array with a single dimension, and
    // a lower bound of zero. In other words, a "normal" array.
    // The first parameter gives the type, the second
    // gives the length for each dimension, and the third
    // gives the lower bound for each dimension.
    Array first = Array.CreateInstance(typeof(string),
                                       new int[] { 10},
                                       new int[] { 0} );

    Console.WriteLine("first is a string[]? {0}",
                      first is string[] );

    // Creates an array with a single dimension, and
    // a lower bound of one.
    Array second = Array.CreateInstance(typeof(string),
                                        new int[] { 10},
                                        new int[] { 1} );

    Console.WriteLine("second is a string[]? {0}",
                      second is string[] );

    // Creates an array with two dimensions, and
    // lower bounds of three for each dimension.
```

```
            Array third = Array.CreateInstance(typeof(string),
                                new int[] { 10, 10},
                                new int[] { 3, 3} );

            Console.WriteLine("third is a string[ ,]? { 0} ",
                            third is string[ ,] );

        }
    }
```

The output from both the current Microsoft and Mono implementations is:

```
    first is a string[ ]? True
    second is a string[ ]? False
    third is a string[,]? True
```

Jon Skeet

19.5 Array covariance

For any two *reference-type*s A and B, if an implicit reference conversion (§13.1.4) or explicit reference conversion (§13.2.3) exists from A to B, then the same reference conversion also exists from the array type A[R] to the array type B[R] , where R is any given *rank-specifier* (but the same for both array types). This relationship is known as ***array covariance***. Array covariance, in particular, means that a value of an array type A[R] might actually be a reference to an instance of an array type B[R] , provided an implicit reference conversion exists from B to A.

Because of array covariance, assignments to elements of reference type arrays include a run-time check which ensures that the value being assigned to the array element is actually of a permitted type (§14.14.1). [*Example*:

```
    class Test
    {
      static void Fill(object[] array, int index, int count, object value)
      {
        for (int i = index; i < index + count; i++) array[i] = value;
      }

      static void Main()
      {
        string[] strings = new string[100] ;
        Fill(strings, 0, 100, "Undefined");
        Fill(strings, 0, 10, null);
        Fill(strings, 90, 10, 0);
      }
    }
```

The assignment to array[i] in the Fill method implicitly includes a run-time check, which ensures that the object referenced by value is either null or an instance of a type that is compatible with the actual element type of array. In Main, the first two invocations of Fill succeed, but the third invocation causes a System.ArrayTypeMismatchException to be thrown upon executing the first assignment to array[i] . The exception occurs because a boxed int cannot be stored in a string array. *end example*]

Array covariance specifically does not extend to arrays of *value-type*s. For example, no conversion exists that permits an int[ ] to be treated as an object[ ].

19.6 Arrays and the generic IList interface

A one-dimensional array S[ ] implements the interface System.Collections.Generic. IList<S> (IList<S> for short) and its base interfaces. Accordingly, there is an implicit conversion from S[ ] to IList<S> and its base interfaces. In addition, if there is an implicit reference conversion from S to T then S[ ] implements IList<T> and there is an implicit reference conversion from S[ ] to IList<T> and its base interfaces (§13.1.4). If there is an explicit reference conversion from S to T then there is an explicit reference conversion from S[ ] to IList<T> and its base interfaces (§13.2.3). [*Example*: For example:

```
using System.Collections.Generic;

class Test
{
  static void Main()
  {
    string[] sa = new string[5];
    object[] oa1 = new object[5];
    object[] oa2 = sa;

    IList<string> lst1 = sa;  // OK
    IList<string> lst2 = oa1; // Error - need cast
    IList<object> lst3 = sa;  // OK
    IList<object> lst4 = oa1; // OK

    IList<string> lst5 = (IList<string>)oa1; // Exception
    IList<string> lst6 = (IList<string>)oa2; // OK
  }
}
```

The assignment lst2 = oa1 generates a compile-time error since the conversion from object[ ] to IList<string> is an explicit conversion, not implicit. The cast (IList<string>)oa1 will cause an exception to be thrown at runtime since oa1 references an object[ ] and not a string[ ]. However the cast (IList<string>)oa2 will not cause an exception to be thrown since oa2 references a string[ ]. *end example*]

Whenever there is an implicit or explicit reference conversion from S[ ] to IList<T>, there is also an explicit reference conversion from IList<T> and its base interfaces to S[ ] (§13.2.3).

When an array type S[ ] implements IList<T>, some of the members of the implemented interface may throw exceptions. The precise behavior of the implementation of the interface is beyond the scope of this specification.

19.7 Array initializers

Array initializers can be specified in field declarations (§17.4), local variable declarations (§15.5.1), and array creation expressions (§14.5.10.2):

> *array-initializer:*
>   {   *variable-initializer-list_{opt}*   }
>   {   *variable-initializer-list*   ,   }

variable-initializer-list:
  variable-initializer
  variable-initializer-list , variable-initializer

variable-initializer:
  expression
  array-initializer

An array initializer consists of a sequence of variable initializers, enclosed by "{ "and "} " tokens and separated by "," tokens. Each variable initializer is an expression or, in the case of a multi-dimensional array, a nested array initializer.

The context in which an array initializer is used determines the type of the array being initialized. In an array creation expression, the array type immediately precedes the initializer. In a field or variable declaration, the array type is the type of the field or variable being declared. When an array initializer is used in a field or variable declaration, [*Example*:

```
int[ ] a = {0, 2, 4, 6, 8} ;
```

end example] it is simply shorthand for an equivalent array creation expression: [*Example*:

```
int[ ] a = new int[ ] {0, 2, 4, 6, 8} ;
```

end example]

For a single-dimensional array, the array initializer shall consist of a sequence of expressions that are assignment compatible with the element type of the array. The expressions initialize array elements in increasing order, starting with the element at index zero. The number of expressions in the array initializer determines the length of the array instance being created. [*Example*: The array initializer above creates an `int[ ]` instance of length 5 and then initializes the instance with the following values:

```
a[0] = 0; a[1] = 2; a[2] = 4; a[3] = 6; a[4] = 8;
```

end example]

For a multi-dimensional array, the array initializer shall have as many levels of nesting as there are dimensions in the array. The outermost nesting level corresponds to the leftmost dimension and the innermost nesting level corresponds to the rightmost dimension. The length of each dimension of the array is determined by the number of elements at the corresponding nesting level in the array initializer. For each nested array initializer, the number of elements shall be the same as the other array initializers at the same level. [*Example*: The example:

```
int[,] b = {{0, 1} , {2, 3} , {4, 5} , {6, 7} , {8, 9} } ;
```

creates a two-dimensional array with a length of five for the leftmost dimension and a length of two for the rightmost dimension:

```
int[,] b = new int[5, 2] ;
```

and then initializes the array instance with the following values:

```
b[0, 0] = 0; b[0, 1] = 1;
b[1, 0] = 2; b[1, 1] = 3;
b[2, 0] = 4; b[2, 1] = 5;
b[3, 0] = 6; b[3, 1] = 7;
b[4, 0] = 8; b[4, 1] = 9;
```

end example]

When an array creation expression includes both explicit dimension lengths and an array initializer, the lengths shall be constant expressions and the number of elements at each nesting level shall match the corresponding dimension length. [*Example*: Here are some examples:

```
int i = 3;
int[ ]  x = new int[3] {0, 1, 2} ;      // OK
int[ ]  y = new int[i] {0, 1, 2} ;      // Error, i not a constant
int[ ]  z = new int[3] {0, 1, 2, 3} ;  // Error, length/initializer mismatch
```

Here, the initializer for y results in a compile-time error because the dimension length expression is not a constant, and the initializer for z results in a compile-time error because the length and the number of elements in the initializer do not agree. *end example*]

[*Note*: Like Standard C++, C# allows a trailing comma at the end of an *array-initializer*. This syntax provides flexibility in adding or deleting members from such a list, and simplifies machine generation of such lists. *end note*]

Brace depth must equal array dimension

However, unlike Standard C++, C# does *not* add braces to match the dimension:

```
int[ ,] whacky = new int[ 1,1] { 0 } ;    // compile-time error
```

```
int[ ,] whacky = new int[ 1,1] {{ 0 }} ; // ok
```

20 Interfaces

An interface defines a contract. A class or struct that implements an interface shall adhere to its contract. An interface can inherit from multiple base interfaces, and a class or struct can implement multiple interfaces.

Interfaces can contain methods, properties, events, and indexers. The interface itself does not provide implementations for the members that it declares. The interface merely specifies the members that shall be supplied by classes or interfaces that implement the interface.

20.1 Interface declarations

An *interface-declaration* is a *type-declaration* (§16.6) that declares a new interface type.

> *interface-declaration:*
>   *attributes$_{opt}$ interface-modifiers$_{opt}$* partial$_{opt}$ interface *identifier*
>   *type-parameter-list$_{opt}$*
>   *interface-base$_{opt}$ type-parameter-constraints-clauses$_{opt}$ interface-body* ;$_{opt}$

An *interface-declaration* consists of an optional set of *attributes* (§24), followed by an optional set of *interface-modifiers* (§20.1.1), followed by an optional partial modifier (§17.1.4), followed by the keyword interface and an *identifier* that names the interface, followed by an optional *type-parameter-list* (§25.1.1), followed by an optional *interface-base* specification (§20.1.2), followed by an optional *type-parameter-constraints-clauses* (§25.7), followed by an *interface-body* (§20.1.3), optionally followed by a semicolon.

An interface declaration shall not supply a *type-parameter-constraints-clauses* unless it also supplies a *type-parameter-list*.

An interface declaration that supplies a *type-parameter-list* is a generic interface declaration (§25.3).

> **Partial interfaces?**
>
> Originally, the committee planned to allow only partial structs and classes. However, for consistency, partial interfaces were also allowed. Partial interfaces are unusual but there are scenarios where they could prove useful. For example, it is possible to imagine two developers working on a class where both developers provide a partial class and its partial interface.
>
> ```
> //developer1
> partial interface ISplittable{ ...}
> partial class Widget : ISplittable{ ...}
>
> //developer2
> partial interface ISplittable{ ...}
> partial class Widget : ISplittable{ ...}
> ```

20.1.1 Interface modifiers

An *interface-declaration* can optionally include a sequence of interface modifiers:

> *interface-modifiers:*
>   *interface-modifier*
>   *interface-modifiers interface-modifier*

> *interface-modifier:*
>   new

```
public
protected
internal
private
```

It is a compile-time error for the same modifier to appear multiple times in an interface declaration.

The `new` modifier is only permitted on nested interfaces. It specifies that the interface hides an inherited member by the same name, as described in §17.2.2.

The `public`, `protected`, `internal`, and `private` modifiers control the accessibility of the interface. Depending on the context in which the interface declaration occurs, only some of these modifiers might be permitted (§10.5.1). When a partial type declaration (§17.1.4) includes an accessibility specification (via the `public`, `protected`, `internal`, and `private` modifiers), the rules in §17.1.1 apply.

20.1.2 Base interfaces

An interface can inherit from one or more interfaces, which are called the ***explicit base interfaces*** of the interface. When an interface has one or more explicit base interfaces, then in the declaration of that interface, the interface identifier is followed by a colon and a comma-separated list of base interfaces.

interface-base:
   :   *interface-type-list*

The explicit base interfaces can be constructed interface types (§25.5). A base interface cannot be a type parameter on its own, though it can involve the type parameters that are in scope.

The explicit base interfaces (and any type arguments) of an interface shall be at least as accessible as the interface itself (§10.5.4). [*Note*: For example, it is a compile-time error to specify a `private` or `internal` interface in the *interface-base* of a `public` interface. *end note*]

It is a compile-time error for an interface to directly or indirectly inherit from itself.

The ***base interfaces*** of an interface are the explicit base interfaces and their base interfaces (after substituting type arguments for type parameters in constructed generic types). In other words, the set of base interfaces is the complete transitive closure of the explicit base interfaces, their explicit base interfaces, and so on. An interface inherits all members of its base interfaces. [*Example*: In the following code

```
interface IControl
{
  void Paint();
}

interface ITextBox: IControl
{
  void SetText(string text);
}

interface IListBox: IControl
{
  void SetItems(string[] items);
}

interface IComboBox: ITextBox, IListBox {}
```

the base interfaces of `IComboBox` are `IControl`, `ITextBox`, and `IListBox`. In other words, the `IComboBox` interface above inherits members `SetText` and `SetItems` as well as `Paint`. *end example*]

Different inheritance

Due to the different natures of interfaces and classes, the word "inheritance" has a different meaning for interfaces and classes.

An interface does not provide any member implementations; it only specifies that, to fulfill its contract, a class must provide certain declarations and implementations (the latter allowing that a non-abstract derived class may provide that implementation if the class providing the interface is abstract).

Therefore, when an interface "inherits" another, it is stating the requirement that any class implementing the interface must also implement the inherited interface. The base interfaces are the set of interfaces that must also be implemented to meet the interface contract.

Note that if C# had taken the Java approach of distinguishing base classes from implemented interfaces, as discussed in the annotation on §17.1.2, then the meaning here would also have been clearer.

Members inherited from a constructed generic type are inherited after type substitution. That is, any constituent types in the member have the base class declaration's type parameters replaced with the corresponding type arguments used in the *class-base* specification. [*Example*: In the following code

```
interface IBase<T>
{
  T[] Combine(T a, T b);
}

interface IDerived : IBase<string[,]>
{
  // Inherited: string[][,] Combine(string[,] a, string[,] b);
}
```

the interface `IDerived` inherits the `Combine` method after the type parameter `T` is replaced with `string[,]`. *end example*]

A class or struct that implements an interface also implicitly implements all of the interface's base interfaces.

The handling of interfaces on multiple parts of a partial interface declaration (§17.1.4) are discussed further in §17.1.2.2.

20.1.3 Interface body
The *interface-body* of an interface defines the members of the interface.

> *interface-body:*
>   {   *interface-member-declarations*$_{opt}$ }

20.2 Interface members
The members of an interface are the members inherited from the base interfaces and the members declared by the interface itself.

interface-member-declarations:
   interface-member-declaration
   interface-member-declarations   *interface-member-declaration*

interface-member-declaration:
   interface-method-declaration
   interface-property-declaration
   interface-event-declaration
   interface-indexer-declaration

An interface declaration can declare zero or more members. The members of an interface shall be methods, properties, events, or indexers. An interface cannot contain constants, fields, operators, instance constructors, finalizers, or types, nor can an interface contain static members of any kind.

All interface members implicitly have public access. It is a compile-time error for interface member declarations to include any modifiers. In particular, interface members cannot be declared with the modifiers `abstract`, `public`, `protected`, `internal`, `private`, `virtual`, `override`, or `static`.

[*Example*: The example

```
public delegate void StringListEventHandler(IStringList sender,
  ListEventArgs e);

public interface IStringList
{
  void Add(string s);

  int Count { get; }

  event StringListEventHandler Changed;

  string this[int index] { get; set; }
}
```

declares an interface that contains one each of the possible kinds of members: A method, a property, an event, and an indexer. *end example*]

An *interface-declaration* creates a new declaration space (§10.3), and the type parameters and *interface-member-declarations* immediately contained by the *interface-declaration* introduce new members into this declaration space. The following rules apply to *interface-member-declaration*s:

- The name of a type parameter in the *type-parameter-list* of an interface declaration shall differ from the names of all other type parameters in the same *type-parameter-list* and shall differ from the names of all members of the interface.
- The name of a method shall differ from the names of all properties and events declared in the same interface. In addition, the signature (§10.6) of a method shall differ from the signatures of all other methods declared in the same interface, and two methods declared in the same interface shall not have signatures that differ solely by `ref` and `out`.
- The name of a property or event shall differ from the names of all other members declared in the same interface.
- The signature of an indexer shall differ from the signatures of all other indexers declared in the same interface.

The inherited members of an interface are specifically not part of the declaration space of the interface. Thus, an interface is allowed to declare a member with the same name or signature as an inherited member. When this occurs, the derived interface member is said to *hide* the base interface member. Hiding an inherited member is not considered an error, but it does cause the compiler to issue a warning. To suppress the warning, the declaration of the derived interface member shall include a `new` modifier to indicate that the derived member is intended to hide the base member. This topic is discussed further in §10.7.1.2.

If a `new` modifier is included in a declaration that doesn't hide an inherited member, a warning is issued to that effect. This warning is suppressed by removing the `new` modifier.

[*Note*: The members in class `object` are not, strictly speaking, members of any interface (§20.2). However, the members in class `object` are available via member lookup in any interface type (§14.3). *end note*]

For a discussion about members of an interface declared in multiple parts (§17.1.4), see §17.2.

20.2.1 Interface methods

Interface methods are declared using *interface-method-declaration*s:

> *interface-method-declaration:*
>   *attributes*_{opt} `new`_{opt} *return-type*   *identifier*   *type-parameter-list*_{opt}
>   (*formal-parameter-list*_{opt}   )   *type-parameter-constraints-clauses*_{opt}   ;

The *attributes*, *return-type*, *identifier*, and *formal-parameter-list* of an interface method declaration have the same meaning as those of a method declaration in a class (§17.5). An interface method declaration is not permitted to specify a method body; therefore, the declaration always ends with a semicolon. An *interface-method-declaration* shall not have *type-parameter-constraints-clauses* unless it also has a *type-parameter-list*.

20.2.2 Interface properties

Interface properties are declared using *interface-property-declaration*s:

> *interface-property-declaration:*
>   *attributes*_{opt} `new`_{opt} *type*   *identifier*   {   *interface-accessors*   }
>
> *interface-accessors:*
>   *attributes*_{opt} `get` ;
>   *attributes*_{opt} `set` ;
>   *attributes*_{opt} `get` ;   *attributes*_{opt} `set` ;
>   *attributes*_{opt} `set` ;   *attributes*_{opt} `get` ;

The *attributes*, *type*, and *identifier* of an interface property declaration have the same meaning as those of a property declaration in a class (§17.6).

The accessors of an interface property declaration correspond to the accessors of a class property declaration (§17.6.2), except that the accessor body shall always be a semicolon. Thus, the accessors simply indicate whether the property is read-write, read-only, or write-only.

20.2.3 Interface events

Interface events are declared using *interface-event-declaration*s:

> *interface-event-declaration:*
>   *attributes*_{opt} `new`_{opt} `event`   *type*   *identifier*   ;

The *attributes*, *type*, and *identifier* of an interface event declaration have the same meaning as those of an event declaration in a class (§17.7).

20.2.4 Interface indexers

Interface indexers are declared using *interface-indexer-declaration*s:

> *interface-indexer-declaration:*
>   *attributes$_{opt}$* new$_{opt}$ *type* this [*formal-parameter-list*]
>   { *interface-accessors* }

The *attributes*, *type*, and *formal-parameter-list* of an interface indexer declaration have the same meaning as those of an indexer declaration in a class (§17.8).

The accessors of an interface indexer declaration correspond to the accessors of a class indexer declaration (§17.8), except that the accessor body shall always be a semicolon. Thus, the accessors simply indicate whether the indexer is read-write, read-only, or write-only.

20.2.5 Interface member access

Interface members are accessed through member access (§14.5.4) and indexer access (§14.5.6.2) expressions of the form I.M and I[A] , where I is an expression having an interface type, M is a method, property, or event of that interface type, and A is an indexer argument list.

For interfaces that are strictly single-inheritance (each interface in the inheritance chain has exactly zero or one direct base interface), the effects of the member lookup (§14.3), method invocation (§14.5.5.1), and indexer access (§14.5.6.2) rules are same as for classes and structs: More derived members hide less derived members with the same name or signature. However, for multiple-inheritance interfaces, ambiguities can occur when two or more unrelated base interfaces declare members with the same name or signature. This subclause shows several examples of such situations. In all cases, explicit casts can be used to resolve the ambiguities.

[*Example*: In the following code

```
interface IList
{
  int Count { get; set; }
}

interface ICounter
{
  void Count(int i);
}

interface IListCounter: IList, ICounter {}

class C
{
  void Test(IListCounter x)
  {
    x.Count(1);               // Error
    x.Count = 1;              // Error
    ((IList)x).Count = 1;     // Ok, invokes IList.Count.set
    ((ICounter)x).Count(1);   // Ok, invokes ICounter.Count
  }
}
```

the first two statements cause compile-time errors because the member lookup (§14.3) of `Count` in `IListCounter` is ambiguous. As illustrated by the example, the ambiguity is resolved by casting `x` to the appropriate base interface type. Such casts have no run-time costs—they merely consist of viewing the instance as a less derived type at compile-time. *end example*]

[*Example*: In the following code

```
interface IInteger
{
  void Add(int i);
}

interface IDouble
{
  void Add(double d);
}

interface INumber: IInteger, IDouble {}

class C
{
  void Test(INumber n)
  {
    n.Add(1);                // Error, both Add methods are applicable
    n.Add(1.0);              // Ok, only IDouble.Add is applicable
    ((IInteger)n).Add(1);    // Ok, only IInteger.Add is a candidate
    ((IDouble)n).Add(1);     // Ok, only IDouble.Add is a candidate
  }
}
```

the invocation `n.Add(1)` is ambiguous because a method invocation (§14.5.5.1) requires all overloaded candidate methods to be declared in the same type. However, the invocation `n.Add (1.0)` is permitted because only `IDouble.Add` is applicable. When explicit casts are inserted, there is only one candidate method, and thus no ambiguity. *end example*]

[*Example*: In the following code

```
interface IBase
{
  void F(int i);
}

interface ILeft: IBase
{
  new void F(int i);
}

interface IRight: IBase
{
  void G();
}

interface IDerived: ILeft, IRight {}
```

```
class A
{
  void Test (IDerived d)
  {
    d.F(1);              // Invokes ILeft.F
    ((IBase)d).F(1);     // Invokes IBase.F
    ((ILeft)d).F(1);     // Invokes ILeft.F
    ((IRight)d).F(1);    // Invokes IBase.F
  }
}
```

the `IBase.F` member is hidden by the `ILeft.F` member. The invocation `d.F(1)` thus selects `ILeft.F`, even though `IBase.F` appears to not be hidden in the access path that leads through `IRight`.

The intuitive rule for hiding in multiple-inheritance interfaces is simply this: If a member is hidden in any access path, it is hidden in all access paths. Because the access path from `IDerived` to `ILeft` to `IBase` hides `IBase.F`, the member is also hidden in the access path from `IDerived` to `IRight` to `IBase`. *end example*]

20.3 Fully qualified interface member names

An interface member is sometimes referred to by a ***qualified interface member name***. A qualified interface member name consists of a name identifying the interface in which the member is declared, followed by a dot, followed by the name of the member. [*Example*: Given the declarations

```
interface IControl
{
  void Paint();
}

interface ITextBox: IControl
{
  void SetText(string text);
}
```

a qualified interface member name for `Paint` is `IControl.Paint` and a qualified interface member name for `SetText` is `ITextBox.SetText`. In the example above, it is not possible to refer to `Paint` as `ITextBox.Paint`. *end example*]

When an interface is part of a namespace, a qualified interface member name can include the namespace name. [*Example*:

```
namespace System
{
  public interface ICloneable
  {
    object Clone();
  }
}
```

Within the `System` namespace, both `ICloneable.Clone` and `System.ICloneable.Clone` are qualified interface member names for the `Clone` method. *end example*]

20.4 Interface implementations

Interfaces can be implemented by classes and structs. To indicate that a class or struct implements an interface, the interface is included in the base class list of the class or struct. [*Example*:

```
interface ICloneable
{
  object Clone();
}

interface IComparable
{
  int CompareTo(object other);
}

class ListEntry: ICloneable, IComparable
{
  public object Clone() {...}

  public int CompareTo(object other) {...}
}
```

end example]

A class or struct that implements an interface also implicitly implements all of the interface's base interfaces. This is true even if the class or struct doesn't explicitly list all base interfaces in the base class list. [*Example*:

```
interface IControl
{
  void Paint();
}

interface ITextBox: IControl
{
  void SetText(string text);
}

class TextBox: ITextBox
{
  public void Paint() {...}

  public void SetText(string text) {...}
}
```

Here, class `TextBox` implements both `IControl` and `ITextBox`. *end example*]

Interfaces implemented through the base class

A class or struct also inherits all interfaces implemented by its base classes (§20.4.3).

Nicu Georgian Fruja

20.4.1 Explicit interface member implementations

For purposes of implementing interfaces, a class or struct can declare ***explicit interface member implementations***. An explicit interface member implementation is a method, property, event, or indexer declaration that references a qualified interface member name. [*Example*:

```
interface ICloneable
{
  object Clone();
}

interface IComparable
{
  int CompareTo(object other);
}

class ListEntry: ICloneable, IComparable
{
  object ICloneable.Clone() {...}

  int IComparable.CompareTo(object other) {...}
}
```

Here, `ICloneable.Clone` and `IComparable.CompareTo` are explicit interface member implementations. *end example*]

[*Example*: In some cases, the name of an interface member might not be appropriate for the implementing class, in which case, the interface member can be implemented using explicit interface member implementation. A class implementing a file abstraction, for example, would likely implement a `Close` member function that has the effect of releasing the file resource, and implement the `Dispose` method of the `IDisposable` interface using explicit interface member implementation:

```
interface IDisposable
{
  void Dispose();
}

class MyFile: IDisposable
{
  void IDisposable.Dispose()
  {
    Close();
  }

  public void Close()
  {
    // Do what's necessary to close the file
    System.GC.SuppressFinalize(this);
  }
}
```

end example]

It is not possible to access an explicit interface member implementation through a qualified interface member name in a method invocation, property access, event access, or indexer access.

An explicit interface member implementation can only be accessed through an interface instance, and is in that case referenced simply by its member name.

It is a compile-time error for an explicit interface member implementation to include any modifiers other than `extern` (§17.5). It is a compile-time error for an explicit interface method implementation to include *type-parameter-constraints-clauses*. The constraints for a generic explicit interface method implementation are inherited from the interface method.

> ### Excess accessors not allowed in explicit interface member implementation
>
> The Standard omits to specify that an interface contract for a property or indexer that has only a `get` accessor *or* a `set` accessor, but not both, cannot be met by an explicit interface member implementation that has both a `get` accessor *and* a `set` accessor:
>
> ```
> public interface I
> {
>   string Prop { get; }
> }
>
> public class C: I
> {
>   string I.Prop
>   {
>     get { return "April"; }
>     set { /* unreachable! */ }
>   }
> }
> ```
>
> The current Microsoft and Mono compilers both correctly issue a compile-time error in this situation.

Explicit interface member implementations have different accessibility characteristics than other members. Because explicit interface member implementations are never accessible through a qualified interface member name in a method invocation or a property access, they are in a sense private. However, since they can be accessed through an interface instance, they are in a sense also public.

Explicit interface member implementations serve two primary purposes:

- Because explicit interface member implementations are not accessible through class or struct instances, they allow interface implementations to be excluded from the public interface of a class or struct. This is particularly useful when a class or struct implements an internal interface that is of no interest to a consumer of that class or struct.
- Explicit interface member implementations allow disambiguation of interface members with the same signature. Without explicit interface member implementations it would be impossible for a class or struct to have different implementations of interface members with the same signature and return type, as would it be impossible for a class or struct to have any implementation at all of interface members with the same signature but with different return types.

For an explicit interface member implementation to be valid, the class or struct shall name an interface in its base class list that contains a member whose containing type, name, type, number of type parameters, and parameter types exactly match those of the explicit interface member implementation. If an interface function member has a parameter array, the corresponding parameter of an associated explicit interface member implementation is allowed, but not required, to have the `params` modifier. If the interface function member does not have a parameter array then an associated explicit interface member implementation shall not have a parameter array. [*Example*: Thus, in the following class

```
class Shape: ICloneable
{
  object ICloneable.Clone() {...}

  int IComparable.CompareTo(object other) {...}   // invalid
}
```

the declaration of `IComparable.CompareTo` results in a compile-time error because `IComparable` is not listed in the base class list of `Shape` and is not a base interface of `ICloneable`. Likewise, in the declarations

```
class Shape: ICloneable
{
  object ICloneable.Clone() {...}
}

class Ellipse: Shape
{
  object ICloneable.Clone() {...}  // invalid
}
```

the declaration of `ICloneable.Clone` in `Ellipse` results in a compile-time error because `ICloneable` is not explicitly listed in the base class list of `Ellipse`. *end example*]

The qualified interface member name of explicit interface member implementation shall reference the interface in which the member was declared. [*Example*: Thus, in the declarations

```
interface IControl
{
  void Paint();
}

interface ITextBox: IControl
{
  void SetText(string text);
}

class TextBox: ITextBox
{
  void IControl.Paint() {...}

  void ITextBox.SetText(string text) {...}
}
```

the explicit interface member implementation of `Paint` shall be written as `IControl.Paint` and not as `ITextBox.Paint`. *end example*]

Simulating return type covariance

A struct or class is allowed both an explicit interface implementation and a member with the same name. For example:

```
namespace System
{
  public sealed class Picture : ICloneable
  {
    ...
    object ICloneable.Clone()
    {
      return Clone();

    }

    public Picture Clone()
    {
      ...
    }
  }
}
```

This can be used to simulate return type covariance:

- At the interface level, the return type is the more general type (in this case, `object`)
- At the class level, the return type is the more specific type (in this case, `Picture`)

The explicit implementation is directly inaccessible (even to itself) so the call to `Clone()` inside `ICloneable.Clone()` is safe and does not cause recursion.

[*Note:* Covariance is supported for arrays (§19.5), and both covariance and contravariance are supported when creating delegates (§14.5.10.3, §22.1).]

params oddity

As mentioned in the preceding clause, in an explicit interface, implementation of a `params` keyword is redundant but allowed:

```
interface I
{
  void Method(params int[] values);
}
class C : I
{
  void I.Method(params int[] values) // ?!
  {
    ...
  }
}
```

The purpose of the `params` is to tell the compiler that a *call* to `Method` can take any number of `int` arguments. But `Method` can only be called through the interface type, so it is sufficient (and necessary) that the `params` modifier appears in the interface.

20.4.2 Interface mapping

A class or struct shall provide implementations of all members of the interfaces that are listed in the base class list of the class or struct. The process of locating implementations of interface members in an implementing class or struct is known as ***interface mapping***.

Interface mapping for a class or struct C locates an implementation for each member of each interface specified in the base class list of C. The implementation of a particular interface member I.M, where I is the interface in which the member M is declared, is determined by examining each class or struct S, starting with C and repeating for each successive base class of C, until a match is located:

- If S contains a declaration of an explicit interface member implementation that matches I and M, then this member is the implementation of I.M.
- Otherwise, if S contains a declaration of a non-static public member that matches M, then this member is the implementation of I.M.

A compile-time error occurs if implementations cannot be located for all members of all interfaces specified in the base class list of C. The members of an interface include those members that are inherited from base interfaces.

Members of a constructed interface type are considered to have any type parameters replaced with the corresponding type arguments as specified in §25.5.4. [*Example*: For example, given the generic interface declaration:

```
interface I<T>
{
  T F(int x, T[,] y);
  T this[int y] { get; }
}
```

the constructed interface I<string[]> has the members:

```
string[] F(int x, string[,][] y);
string[] this[int y] { get; }
```

end example]

For purposes of interface mapping, a class or struct member A matches an interface member B when:

- A and B are methods, and the name, type, and formal parameter lists of A and B are identical.
- A and B are properties, the name and type of A and B are identical, and A has the same accessors as B (A is permitted to have additional accessors if it is not an explicit interface member implementation).
- A and B are events, and the name and type of A and B are identical.
- A and B are indexers, the type and formal parameter lists of A and B are identical, and A has the same accessors as B (A is permitted to have additional accessors if it is not an explicit interface member implementation).

Notable implications of the interface-mapping algorithm are:

- Explicit interface member implementations take precedence over other members in the same class or struct when determining the class or struct member that implements an interface member.
- Neither non-public nor static members participate in interface mapping.

[*Example*: In the following code

```
interface ICloneable
{
  object Clone();
}
```

```
class C: ICloneable
{
  object ICloneable.Clone() {...}

  public object Clone() {...}
}
```

the `ICloneable.Clone` member of `C` becomes the implementation of `Clone` in `ICloneable` because explicit interface member implementations take precedence over other members. *end example*]

Morphing non-virtual methods

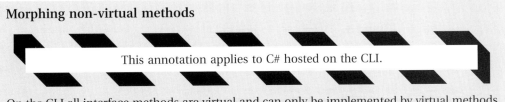

This annotation applies to C# hosted on the CLI.

On the CLI all interface methods are virtual and can only be implemented by virtual methods. To support implementation of interfaces by non-virtual instance methods, as required by the Standard, CLI C# compilers morph non-virtual instance methods used for interfaces into `sealed virtual` ones. This change has no impact on the C# programmer.

If a class or struct implements two or more interfaces containing a member with the same name, type, and parameter types, it is possible to map each of those interface members onto a single class or struct member. [*Example*:

```
interface IControl
{
  void Paint();
}

interface IForm
{
  void Paint();
}

class Page: IControl, IForm
{
  public void Paint() {...}
}
```

Here, the `Paint` methods of both `IControl` and `IForm` are mapped onto the `Paint` method in `Page`. It is of course also possible to have separate explicit interface member implementations for the two methods. *end example*]

If a class or struct implements an interface that contains hidden members, then some members shall necessarily be implemented through explicit interface member implementations. [*Example*:

```
interface IBase
{
  int P { get; }
}
```

```
interface IDerived: IBase
{
  new int P();
}
```

An implementation of this interface would require at least one explicit interface member implementation, and would take one of the following forms

```
class C: IDerived
{
  int IBase.P { get {...} }

  int IDerived.P() {...}
}

class C: IDerived
{
  public int P { get {...} }

  int IDerived.P() {...}
}

class C: IDerived
{
  int IBase.P { get {...} }

  public int P() {...}
}
```

end example]

Inaccurate assertion

The preceding assertion is inaccurate. It is true only if the hidden and non-hidden members are of different kinds (method, property, etc.) or different signatures. Interface mapping allows a single member to satisfy both hidden and non-hidden interface members of the same kind and signature. For example, consider:

```
interface IBase
{
  int P();
}

interface IDerived : IBase
{
  new int P();
}

class C : IDerived
{
  public int P()
  {
    return 42;
  }
}
```

Here `IDerived.P` hides `IBase.P`. However, as they are both methods and have the same signature, interface mapping selects `C.P` for both.

This behavior comes from the fact that interfaces do not derive from other interfaces, but can only specify that other interfaces must also be implemented (§20.1.2). Therefore, the previous example can be rewritten almost equivalently as:

```
interface IBase
{
   int P();
}

interface IDerived
{
   new int P();
}

class C : IDerived, IBase
{
   public int P()
   {
      return 42;
   }
}
```

[*Note:* It is only "almost" equivalent, as in this version there is no requirement that if `IDerived` is implemented then so too must `IBase` be.]

This version is clearly valid by the preceding clause, and `P()` is mapped to both interfaces.

When a class implements multiple interfaces that have the same base interface, there can be only one implementation of the base interface. [*Example*: In the following code

```
interface IControl
{
   void Paint();
}

interface ITextBox: IControl
{
   void SetText(string text);
}

interface IListBox: IControl
{
   void SetItems(string[] items);
}

class ComboBox: IControl, ITextBox, IListBox
{
   void IControl.Paint() {...}

   void ITextBox.SetText(string text) {...}

   void IListBox.SetItems(string[] items) {...} }
```

it is not possible to have separate implementations for the IControl named in the base class list, the IControl inherited by ITextBox, and the IControl inherited by IListBox. Indeed, there is no notion of a separate identity for these interfaces. Rather, the implementations of ITextBox and IListBox share the same implementation of IControl, and ComboBox is simply considered to implement three interfaces, IControl, ITextBox, and IListBox. *end example*]

The members of a base class participate in interface mapping. [*Example*: In the following code

```
interface Interface1
{
  void F();
}

class Class1
{
  public void F() {}

  public void G() {}
}

class Class2: Class1, Interface1
{
  new public void G() {}
}
```

the method F in Class1 is used in Class2's implementation of Interface1. *end example*]

20.4.3 Interface implementation inheritance
A class inherits all interface implementations provided by its base classes.

Erratum?

The previous sentence should technically say, "A class *or struct* inherits all interface implementations provided by its base classes." However, this would only make a difference if System.ValueType or System.Object were to implement any interfaces. They currently do not, so this little mistake has no current impact unless a particular implementation adds its own interfaces (which would be conforming according to §4).

Meaning of "implements"

The interfaces implemented by a type *include* those implemented by its base classes. The preceding statement that a type "inherits all interface implementations" means that the type's implementation of an interface inherited from a base class uses the same mapping (§20.4.2) as the direct base class implementation, unless one or more interface members are re-implemented (§20.4.4) by the type. See the annotation on §17.2.5 for more details.

One particular implication of this definition is that there exists an implicit conversion (§13.1.4) from a type to every interface mentioned directly by the type, by any of its base classes, and by any of those interfaces, transitively.

Without explicitly **re-implementing** an interface, a derived class cannot alter the interface mappings it inherits from its base classes. [*Example*: In the declarations

```
interface IControl
{
  void Paint();
}

class Control: IControl
{
  public void Paint() {...}
}

class TextBox: Control
{
  new public void Paint() {...}
}
```

the `Paint` method in `TextBox` hides the `Paint` method in `Control`, but it does not alter the mapping of `Control.Paint` onto `IControl.Paint`, and calls to `Paint` through class instances and interface instances will have the following effects

```
Control c = new Control();
TextBox t = new TextBox();
IControl ic = c;
IControl it = t;
c.Paint();      // invokes Control.Paint();
t.Paint();      // invokes TextBox.Paint();
ic.Paint();     // invokes Control.Paint();
it.Paint();     // invokes Control.Paint();
```

end example]

However, when an interface method is mapped onto a virtual method in a class, it is possible for derived classes to override the virtual method and alter the implementation of the interface. [*Example*: Rewriting the declarations above to

```
interface IControl
{
  void Paint();
}

class Control: IControl
{
  public virtual void Paint() {...}
}

class TextBox: Control
{
  public override void Paint() {...}
}
```

the following effects will now be observed

```
Control c = new Control();
TextBox t = new TextBox();
IControl ic = c;
IControl it = t;
c.Paint();      // invokes Control.Paint();
```

```
t.Paint();      // invokes TextBox.Paint();
ic.Paint();     // invokes Control.Paint();
it.Paint();     // invokes TextBox.Paint();
```

end example]

Since explicit interface member implementations cannot be declared virtual, it is not possible to override an explicit interface member implementation. However, it is perfectly valid for an explicit interface member implementation to call another method, and that other method can be declared virtual to allow derived classes to override it. [*Example*:

```
interface IControl
{
  void Paint();
}

class Control: IControl
{
  void IControl.Paint() { PaintControl(); }

  protected virtual void PaintControl() {...}
}

class TextBox: Control
{
  protected override void PaintControl() {...}
}
```

Here, classes derived from `Control` can specialize the implementation of `IControl.Paint` by overriding the `PaintControl` method. *end example*]

20.4.4 Interface re-implementation

A class that inherits an interface implementation is permitted to ***re-implement*** the interface by including it in the base class list.

A re-implementation of an interface follows exactly the same interface mapping rules as an initial implementation of an interface. Thus, the inherited interface mapping has no effect whatsoever on the interface mapping established for the re-implementation of the interface. [*Example*: In the declarations

```
interface IControl
{
  void Paint();
}

class Control: IControl
{
  void IControl.Paint() {...}
}

class MyControl: Control, IControl
{
  public void Paint() {}
}
```

the fact that `Control` maps `IControl.Paint` onto `Control.IControl.Paint` doesn't affect the re-implementation in `MyControl`, which maps `IControl.Paint` onto `MyControl.Paint`. *end example*]

Original implementation inaccessible

As discussed in §17.5.3 and associated annotation, if a member implementation in a base class is hidden by a `new` one in a derived class, then the hidden implementation may still be invoked via an instance of the derived class by first casting to the base class.

Given this, it might be assumed that, if an interface is re-implemented by a derived class, then casting to a base class and then to the interface may gain access to the hidden implementation. However, this is not the case. Consider the code fragment:

```
interface IMsg
{
  void Msg();
}

class Base : IMsg
{
  public virtual void Msg()
  {
    Console.WriteLine("Base.Msg");
  }
}

class Derived : Base, IMsg
{
  new public virtual void Msg()
  {
    Console.WriteLine("Derived.Msg");
  }
}

...

void Test()
{
  Derived d = new Derived();
  IMsg ia = d;
  Base b = d;
  IMsg ib = b;

  d.Msg();    // Derived.Msg
  ia.Msg();   // Derived.Msg
  b.Msg();    // Base.Msg
  ib.Msg();   // Derived.Msg not Base.Msg which is
              // implementation of IMsg on Base

}
```

Here casting d to b of type `Base` and then invoking the virtual method `Msg` obtains the version defined in `Base` due to the `new` in `Derived` (§17.5.3).

However, casting b to ib of type `IMsg` does *not* get the original implementation of `IMsg` by `Base` but the re-implementation by `Derived`.

This apparent difference between instance method implementation/new instance method on the one hand, and interface implementation/re-implementation on the other hand, may be surprising to some but follows a logical design; see the annotation on §17.2.5.

Inherited public member declarations and inherited explicit interface member declarations participate in the interface mapping process for re-implemented interfaces. [*Example*:

```
interface IMethods
{
  void F();
  void G();
  void H();
  void I();
}

class Base: IMethods
{
  void IMethods.F() {}
  void IMethods.G() {}
  public void H() {}
  public void I() {}
}

class Derived: Base, IMethods
{
  public void F() {}
  void IMethods.H() {}
}
```

Here, the implementation of `IMethods` in `Derived` maps the interface methods onto `Derived.F`, `Base.IMethods.G`, `Derived.IMethods.H`, and `Base.I`. *end example*]

When a class implements an interface, it implicitly also implements all that interface's base interfaces. Likewise, a re-implementation of an interface is also implicitly a re-implementation of all of the interface's base interfaces. [*Example*:

```
interface IBase
{
  void F();
}

interface IDerived: IBase
{
  void G();
}

class C: IDerived
{
  void IBase.F() {...}

  void IDerived.G() {...}
}

class D: C, IDerived
{
  public void F() {...}

  public void G() {...} }
```

Here, the re-implementation of `IDerived` also re-implements `IBase`, mapping `IBase.F` onto `D. F`. *end example*]

20.4.5 Abstract classes and interfaces

Like a non-abstract class, an abstract class shall provide implementations of all members of the interfaces that are listed in the base class list of the class. However, an abstract class is permitted to map interface methods onto abstract methods. [*Example*:

```
interface IMethods
{
  void F();
  void G();
}

abstract class C: IMethods
{
  public abstract void F();
  public abstract void G();
}
```

Here, the implementation of `IMethods` maps `F` and `G` onto abstract methods, which shall be overridden in non-abstract classes that derive from `C`. *end example*]

Explicit interface member implementations cannot be abstract, but explicit interface member implementations are of course permitted to call abstract methods. [*Example*:

```
interface IMethods
{
  void F();
  void G();
}

abstract class C: IMethods
{
  void IMethods.F() { FF(); }
  void IMethods.G() { GG(); }
  protected abstract void FF();
  protected abstract void GG();
}
```

Here, non-abstract classes that derive from `C` would be required to override `FF` and `GG`, thus providing the actual implementation of `IMethods`. *end example*]

Abstract class interface alternatives

Programmers sometimes want to create an abstract class that provides the implementation of only *some* of an interface's operations. However, as they quickly learn, an abstract declaration must be provided for every unimplemented member:

```
public interface ICollection
{
  int Count { get; }
  bool IsEmpty { get; }

  ...
}
```

```
public abstract class CommonCollection : ICollection
{
  // compile-time error: no implementation of Count property
  public bool IsEmpty
  {
    get
    {
      return this.Count == 0;
    }
  }
}
```

The abstract class must provide an explicit abstract method for *every* "unimplemented" interface operation:

```
public abstract class CommonCollection : ICollection
{
  ...
  public abstract int Count { get; } // now okay

  public bool IsEmpty
  {
    get
    {
      return this.Count == 0;
    }
  }
}
```

However, there is an alternative. Rather than implementing the interface, the abstract class can introduce an abstract property (Self in the following example) that returns an object implementing the interface, and then implement the common behavior with reference to that object:

```
public abstract class CommonCollection
{
  public bool IsEmpty
  {
    get
    {
      return Self.Count == 0;
    }
  }
  ...
  protected abstract ICollection Self { get; }
}
```

Any concrete derived class must inherit from the abstract class and the interface and implement the abstract property Self so that it returns this:

```
public class Example : CommonCollection, ICollection
{
  ...
  public int Count
  {
    get
```

```
      {
        return wibbles.Count;
      }
    }

    protected override ICollection Self
    {
      get
      {
        return this;
      }
    }

    private readonly ArrayList wibbles;
  }
```
This is a variation of the Template Method Pattern.

21 Enums

An **enum type** is a distinct type that declares a set of named constants. [*Example*: The example

```
enum Color
{
  Red,
  Green,
  Blue
}
```

declares an enum type named `Color` with members `Red`, `Green`, and `Blue`. *end example*]

Enums are integral types

An **enum type** in C# declares a new distinct integral type that has the same range and number of values as one of the predefined integral types, called its **underlying type** (§21.1). The named constants are just a subset of the values of the enum. For example, `Color` has the underlying type `int` (this is the default; see §21.1) and there are another $2^{32}-3$ values of type `Color` that have no literal representation. However, when converted to a `string` using `ToString()`, values without a named constant are converted to their representation in the underlying type.

This behavior is different from languages such as Pascal, Ada, and Haskell, where the defined literals are the *only* valid values of an enumeration type. It is also different from the predefined enumerated types in C#, which include the integral, character, and Boolean types—all the values of these types have a literal representation.

This behavior has consequences. For example, enums support a subset of the arithmetic operators (§21.5), and these are one way to produce values that have no literal representation. It also means that care must be taken when doing comparisons:

```
Color cv;
...
switch (cv)
{
  case Color.Red:
    ...
    break;
  case Color.Green:
    ...
    break;
  case Color.Blue:
    ...
    break;
  default:
    // This *is* reachable
    ...
    break;
}
```

The `default` clause is reachable and should be included for correctness.

The behavior also allows the use of enums as sets with up to 8, 16, 32, or 64 members depending on the underlying type. To support this use, the bitwise logical operators (§21.5) can be used on enum types. For example, redefining `Color` allows other "colors" and tests for containment:

```
enum Color
{
    Red = 1,
    Green = 2,
    Blue = 4
}
...
Color cv;
const Color Yellow = Color.Red | Color.Green;
...
if ( (cv & Color.Red) != 0 )
{  // cv contains some red
    ...
}
```

It is reasonable to ask, given that enums in C# are just new names for existing integral types, why to use them at all? The answer is that they do assist program correctness as any conversions to and from the underlying type must be explicit. They also improve readability. However, if you require strong enums, where only the defined literals are valid, then you should not use C#'s enums but define your own types (see the annotation on §21.3 for one possible design).

21.1 Enum declarations

An enum declaration declares a new enum type. An enum declaration begins with the keyword enum, and defines the name, accessibility, underlying type, and members of the enum.

> *enum-declaration:*
>   *attributes*$_{opt}$ *enum-modifiers*$_{opt}$ enum *identifier enum-base*$_{opt}$
>   *enum-body*   ;$_{opt}$
>
> *enum-base:*
>   : *integral-type*
>
> *enum-body:*
>   { *enum-member-declarations*$_{opt}$ }
>   { *enum-member-declarations* , }

Each enum type has a corresponding integral type called the ***underlying type*** of the enum type. This underlying type shall be able to represent all the enumerator values defined in the enumeration. An enum declaration can explicitly declare an underlying type of byte, sbyte, short, ushort, int, uint, long or ulong. [*Note*: char cannot be used as an underlying type. *end note*] An enum declaration that does not explicitly declare an underlying type has an underlying type of int.

[*Example*: The example

```
enum Color: long
{
    Red,
    Green,
    Blue
}
```

declares an enum with an underlying type of `long`. *end example*] [*Note*: A developer might choose to use an underlying type of `long`, as in the example, to enable the use of values that are in the range of `long` but not in the range of `int`, or to preserve this option for the future. *end note*]

[*Note*: C# allows a trailing comma in an *enum-body*, just like it allows one in an *array-initializer* (§19.7). *end note*]

Why no char underlying type?

The committee considered letting `int` be the only underlying type for all enum types, but decided to allow other underlying types for several reasons:

- To support byte-sized enums, thus enabling a 75% space optimization for cases in which the number of enum values is small.
- To support interoperability with other platforms. On some platforms, the size of enums is 16 bits, which is equivalent to `short` in C#.
- To support 64-bit values. For example, 64-bit enums may be preferred for scenarios in which enum members are used to represent flags (that is, a bit set).

Having decided to support the four integral types `byte`, `short`, `int`, `long`, it seemed natural to also support the corresponding unsigned integral types `sbyte`, `ushort`, `uint`, and `ulong`. However, the `char` type not only represents a range of integral values, but also comes with additional semantics and its size is the same as `short`, so the committee decided not to allow it.

21.2 Enum modifiers

An *enum-declaration* can optionally include a sequence of enum modifiers:

> *enum-modifiers:*
>   *enum-modifier*
>   *enum-modifiers   enum-modifier*

> *enum-modifier:*
>   `new`
>   `public`
>   `protected`
>   `internal`
>   `private`

It is a compile-time error for the same modifier to appear multiple times in an enum declaration.

The modifiers of an enum declaration have the same meaning as those of a class declaration (§17.1.1). However, the `abstract` and `sealed` modifiers are not permitted in an enum declaration. Enums cannot be abstract and do not permit derivation.

21.3 Enum members

The body of an enum type declaration defines zero or more enum members, which are the named constants of the enum type. No two enum members can have the same name.

> *enum-member-declarations:*
>   *enum-member-declaration*
>   *enum-member-declarations   ,   enum-member-declaration*

```
enum-member-declaration:
    attributes_opt  identifier
    attributes_opt  identifier  =  constant-expression
```

Second-class citizens

An enum member is not a literal: Any reference to the member must be preceded by the enum type name and is classified as a member access (§14.5.4). This contrasts to languages with strong enums (e.g., Ada and Pascal), and even some with weak enums (e.g., C/C++) where the members are literals and can be referenced without being prefixed by the type name. Fortunately, it is also in contrast to the built-in enumeration types in C#; thus, not only is `bool.true` not required, but it is also invalid. Enums in C# are most definitely second-class citizens.

The reason behind C#'s use of member access semantics for enum members is simple: C# views an enum type as a value type with one static constant field per member. This is explained in the annotation "enum alternatives."

Each enum member has an associated constant value. The type of this value is the underlying type for the containing enum. The constant value for each enum member shall be in the range of the underlying type for the enum. [*Example*: The example

```
enum Color : uint
{
    Red = -1,
    Green = -2,
    Blue = -3
}
```

results in a compile-time error because the constant values −1, −2, and −3 are not in the range of the underlying integral type `uint`. *end example*]

Type of an enum member

It is important to remember there are two types related to each enum member:

- The type of the enum itself is the type of the containing enum declaration. For example, in the preceding (if it was correct), the type of `Color.Red` is `Color`.
- The type of the *constant-expression* associated with an enum member is the underlying type of the containing enum declaration. For example, in the preceding the underlying type of `Color.Red` is `uint`.

There is no implicit conversion between these two types; to move between them requires an explicit enum conversion (§13.2.2).

Multiple enum members can share the same associated value. [*Example*: The example

```
enum Color
{
    Red,
    Green,
    Blue,

    Max = Blue
}
```

shows an enum that has two enum members—`Blue` and `Max`—that have the same associated value. *end example*]

The associated value of an enum member is assigned either implicitly or explicitly. If the declaration of the enum member has a *constant-expression* initializer, the value of that constant expression, implicitly converted to the underlying type of the enum, is the associated value of the enum member. If the declaration of the enum member has no initializer, its associated value is set implicitly, as follows:

- If the enum member is the first enum member declared in the enum type, its associated value is zero.
- Otherwise, the associated value of the enum member is obtained by increasing the associated value of the textually preceding enum member by one. This increased value shall be within the range of values that can be represented by the underlying type.

[*Example*: The example

```
using System;

enum Color
{
  Red,
  Green = 10,
  Blue
}

class Test
{
  static void Main()
  {
    Console.WriteLine(StringFromColor(Color.Red));
    Console.WriteLine(StringFromColor(Color.Green));
    Console.WriteLine(StringFromColor(Color.Blue));
  }

  static string StringFromColor(Color c)
  {
    switch (c)
    {
      case Color.Red:
        return String.Format("Red = {0} ", (int) c);

      case Color.Green:
        return String.Format("Green = {0} ", (int) c);

      case Color.Blue:
        return String.Format("Blue = {0} ", (int) c);

      default:
        return "Invalid color";
    }
  }
}
```

prints out the enum member names and their associated values. The output is:

```
Red = 0
Green = 10
Blue = 11
```

for the following reasons:

- the enum member Red is automatically assigned the value zero (since it has no initializer and is the first enum member);
- the enum member Green is explicitly given the value 10;
- and the enum member Blue is automatically assigned the value one greater than the member that textually precedes it.

end example]

The associated value of an enum member shall not, directly or indirectly, use the value of its own associated enum member. Other than this circularity restriction, enum member initializers can freely refer to other enum member initializers, regardless of their textual position. Within an enum member initializer, values of other enum members are always treated as having the type of their underlying type, so that casts are not necessary when referring to other enum members.

[*Example*: The example

```
enum Circular
{
  A = B,
  B
}
```

results in a compile-time error because the declarations of A and B are circular. A depends on B explicitly, and B depends on A implicitly. *end example*]

Enum members are named and scoped in a manner exactly analogous to fields within classes. The scope of an enum member is the body of its containing enum type. Within that scope, enum members can be referred to by their simple name. From all other code, the name of an enum member shall be qualified with the name of its enum type. Enum members do not have any declared accessibility—an enum member is accessible if its containing enum type is accessible.

enum alternatives

An enum like this:

```
public enum Suit : int { Clubs, Diamonds, Hearts, Spades }
```

is defined to have the semantics equivalent to the following pseudo-C# struct:

```
public struct Suit : System.Enum
{
  private int value__;

  private Suit(int x)
  {
    value__ = x;
  }

  public static explicit operator Suit(int x)
  {
    return new Suit(x);
  }
}
```

```
      public static explicit operator int(Suit es)
      {
        return es.value__;
      }

      public const Suit Clubs     = (Suit)0;
      public const Suit Diamonds  = (Suit)1;
      public const Suit Hearts    = (Suit)2;
      public const Suit Spades    = (Suit)3;
  }
```

(Note: This is pseudo-C# as fields of user-defined `struct` type cannot be `const`ant. Also, C# disallows the use of `System.Enum` as a base class.)

An alternative transformation (considered by the committee) is as follows:

```
  public struct Suit : System.Enum
  {
    // as above, until...

    public static readonly Suit Clubs     = (Suit)0;
    public static readonly Suit Diamonds  = (Suit)1;
    public static readonly Suit Hearts    = (Suit)2;
    public static readonly Suit Spades    = (Suit)3;
  }
```

(Note: This is almost valid C# as fields of user-defined `struct` type can be `readonly`. However, it still uses `System.Enum` as a base class.)

These two translations differ due to the semantics of constants and readonly fields:

- The value of a `const` in C# is determined at compile time and incorporated into the compiled code (§17.4.2.2).
- The value of a `static readonly` in C# is determined at runtime and a compiler *must* produce code which retrieves the value.

The Standard chose the first transformation as its semantics, which allows a compiler to produce more efficient code, in particular for switch statements. It also happens to coincide with the semantics of enumerations on the CLI.

However, this choice means that if you change an enum you cannot simply recompile into a new component and rely on client components automatically picking up the new `enum` via versioning (see §17.4.2.2). The client components will need to be recompiled. In the preceding example this is not an issue since it is a safe bet packs of cards are not going to acquire a new suit any time soon. However, if you are expecting your `enum` to change and versioning is an issue, the readonly transformation, without the use of `System.Enum` as the base class, is worth considering as an alternative to using the built-in `enum` types.

Furthermore, if your application requires strong enums (see annotation on §21), then the second transformation can provide the needed semantics, as the explicit conversion operator from the underlying type to the enum can perform validity checking.

21.4 The System.Enum type

The type `System.Enum` is the abstract base class of all enum types (this is distinct and different from the underlying type of the enum type), and the members inherited from `System.Enum` are available in any enum type. A boxing conversion (§11.3.1) exists from any enum type to `System.Enum`, and an unboxing conversion (§11.3.2) exists from `System.Enum` to any enum type.

Note that `System.Enum` is not itself an *enum-type*. Rather, it is a *class-type* from which all *enum-types* are derived. The type `System.Enum` inherits from the type `System.ValueType` (§11.1.1), which, in turn, inherits from type `object`. At run-time, a value of type `System.Enum` can be `null` or a reference to a boxed value of any enum type.

21.5 Enum values and operations

Each enum type defines a distinct type; an explicit enumeration conversion (§13.2.2) is required to convert between an enum type and an integral type, or between two enum types. The set of values that an enum type can take on is not limited by its enum members. In particular, any value of the underlying type of an enum can be cast to the enum type, and is a distinct valid value of that enum type.

Enum members have the type of their containing enum type (except within other enum member initializers: see §21.3). The value of an enum member declared in enum type E with associated value v is (E) v.

The following operators can be used on values of enum types: ==, !=, <, >, <=, >= (§14.9.5), + (§14.7.4), – (§14.7.5), ^, &, | (§14.10.2), ~ (§14.6.4), ++, – – (§14.5.9 and §14.6.5), and `sizeof` (§27.5.4).

> **Operations on enums**
>
> The compound assignment (§14.14.2) versions of the binary operators also exist for enums.
>
> The operations fall into two groups: those that make sense when an enum is used to represent a set of distinct values, and those for enums used as flags (i.e., bit sets; see annotation "Enums are integral types" in §21).
>
> For distinct value enums, the operators (and meanings) are: < ("precedes"), > ("succeeds"), <=, >=, ++ ("successor"), – – ("predecessor"), + ("n[th] successor"), and – ("n[th] predecessor").
>
> For flag enums, the operators (and meanings) are: ^ ("symmetric difference"), & ("intersection"), | ("union"), and ~ ("complement"). Note that the difference between flag enum p and flag enum q is *not* found by p – q but by (p ^ q) & p. To determine whether p is a subset of q, one can use the expression (p & q) == p.

Every enum type automatically derives from the class `System.Enum` (which, in turn, derives from `System.ValueType` and `object`). Thus, inherited methods and properties of this class can be used on values of an enum type.

22 Delegates

[*Note*: Delegates enable scenarios that some other languages have addressed with function pointers. However, unlike function pointers, delegates are object-oriented and type-safe. A delegate encapsulates both an object instance and a method. *end note*]

A delegate declaration defines a class that is derived from the class `System.Delegate`. A delegate instance encapsulates one or more methods, each of which is referred to as a ***callable entity***. For instance methods, a callable entity consists of an instance and a method on that instance. For static methods, a callable entity consists of just a method. Given a delegate instance and an appropriate set of arguments, one can invoke all of that delegate instance's methods with that set of arguments.

[*Note*: An interesting and useful property of a delegate instance is that it does not know or care about the classes of the methods it encapsulates; all that matters is that those methods be consistent (§22.1) with the delegate's type. This makes delegates perfectly suited for "anonymous" invocation. *end note*]

22.1 Delegate declarations

A *delegate-declaration* is a *type-declaration* (§16.6) that declares a new delegate type.

> *delegate-declaration:*
>   *attributes*_{opt} *delegate-modifiers*_{opt} `delegate` *return-type* *identifier*
>   *type-parameter-list*_{opt}
>   (*formal-parameter-list*_{opt}) *type-parameter-constraints-clauses*_{opt} ;
>
> *delegate-modifiers:*
>   *delegate-modifier*
>   *delegate-modifiers* *delegate-modifier*
>
> *delegate-modifier:*
>   `new`
>   `public`
>   `protected`
>   `internal`
>   `private`

It is a compile-time error for the same modifier to appear multiple times in a delegate declaration.

A delegate declaration shall not supply a *type-parameter-constraints-clauses* unless it also supplies a *type-parameter-list*.

A delegate declaration that supplies a *type-parameter-list* is a generic delegate declaration (§25.4).

The `new` modifier is only permitted on delegates declared within another type, in which case it specifies that such a delegate hides an inherited member by the same name, as described in §17.2.2.

The `public`, `protected`, `internal`, and `private` modifiers control the accessibility of the delegate type. Depending on the context in which the delegate declaration occurs, some of these modifiers might not be permitted (§10.5.1).

The delegate's type name is *identifier*.

The optional *formal-parameter-list* specifies the parameters of the delegate, and *return-type* indicates the return type of the delegate. A method and a delegate type are **consistent** if the following are true:

- For each parameter of the method:
    - If the parameter has no `ref` or `out` modifier, then the corresponding parameter of the delegate type has no `ref` or `out` modifier and there is an identity conversion or implicit reference conversion from the corresponding delegate parameter type to the method parameter type.
    - If the parameter has a `ref` or `out` modifier, then the corresponding parameter of the delegate type has the same modifier and the corresponding delegate parameter type is the same as the method parameter type.
- There is an identity conversion or implicit reference conversion from the return type of the method to the return type of the delegate type.

This definition of consistency allows covariance in return type and contravariance in parameter types.

Delegate types in C# are name equivalent, not structurally equivalent. Specifically, two delegate types that have the same parameter lists and return type are considered different delegate types. [*Example*:

```
delegate int D1(int i, double d);

class A
{
  public static int M1(int a, double b) {...}
}

class B
{
  delegate int D2(int c, double d);
  public static int M1(int f, double g) {...}
  public static void M2(int k, double l) {...}
  public static int M3(int g) {...}
  public static void M4(int g) {...}

  delegate object D3(string s);
  public static object M5(string s) {...}
  public static int[] M6(object o) {...}
}
```

The delegate types `D1` and `D2` are both consistent with the methods `A.M1` and `B.M1`, since they have the same return type and parameter list; however, these delegate types are two different types, so they are not interchangeable. The delegate types `D1` and `D2` are not consistent with the methods `B.M2`, `B.M3`, and `B.M4`. The methods `B.M5` and `B.M6` are both consistent with delegate type `D3`. *end example*]

The only way to declare a delegate type is via a *delegate-declaration*. A delegate type is a reference type that is derived from `System.Delegate`. Delegate types are implicitly `sealed`, so it is not permissible to derive any type from a delegate type. It is also not permissible to derive a non-delegate class type from `System.Delegate`. `System.Delegate` is not itself a delegate type; it is a class type from which all delegate types are derived.

C# provides special syntax for delegate instantiation and invocation. Except for instantiation, any operation that can be applied to a class or class instance can also be applied to a delegate class or instance, respectively. In particular, it is possible to access members of the System.Delegate type via the usual member access syntax.

The set of methods encapsulated by a delegate instance is called an ***invocation list***. When a delegate instance is created (§22.2) from a single method, it encapsulates that method, and its invocation list contains only one entry. However, when two non-null delegate instances are combined, their invocation lists are concatenated—in the order left operand then right operand—to form a new invocation list, which contains two or more entries. An invocation list can never be empty.

Delegates are combined using the binary + (§14.7.4) and += operators (§14.14.2). A delegate can be removed from a combination of delegates, using the binary – (§14.7.5) and -= operators (§14.14.2). Delegates can be compared for equality (§14.9.8).

[*Example*: The following example shows the instantiation of a number of delegates, and their corresponding invocation lists:

```
delegate void D(int x);
class Test
{
  public static void M1(int i) {...}
  public static void M2(int i) {...}
}

class Demo
{
  static void Main() {
    D cd1 = new D(Test.M1); // M1
    D cd2 = new D(Test.M2); // M2
    D cd3 = cd1 + cd2;      // M1 + M2
    D cd4 = cd3 + cd1;      // M1 + M2 + M1
    D cd5 = cd4 + cd3;      // M1 + M2 + M1 + M1 + M2
  }
}
```

When cd1 and cd2 are instantiated, they each encapsulate one method. When cd3 is instantiated, it has an invocation list of two methods, M1 and M2, in that order. cd4's invocation list contains M1, M2, and M1, in that order. Finally, cd5's invocation list contains M1, M2, M1, M1, and M2, in that order.

For more examples of combining (as well as removing) delegates, see §22.3. *end example*]

22.2 Delegate instantiation

An instance of a delegate is created by a *delegate-creation-expression* (§14.5.10.3) or by an implicit conversion from an anonymous method or method group to a delegate type (§13.5 and §13.6). The newly created delegate instance then refers to one or more of:

- A static method.
- A target object (which cannot be null) and instance method.

When the argument of a *delegate-creation-expression* (§14.5.10.3) is a delegate instance the resulting delegate has the same invocation list as the argument, which may contain more than one entry.

[*Example*:

```
delegate void D(int x);
class Test
{
  public static void M1(int i) {...}
  public void M2(int i)     {...}
}

class Demo
{
  static void Main()
  {
    D cd1 = new D(Test.M1); // static method
    Test t = new Test();
    D cd2 = new D(t.M2);    // instance method
    D cd3 = new D(cd2);     // another delegate
  }
}
```

end example]

Once instantiated, delegate instances always refer to the same list of target objects and methods. [*Note*: Remember, when two delegates are combined, or one is removed from another, a new delegate results with its own invocation list; the invocation lists of the delegates combined or removed remain unchanged. *end note*]

Creation does not trigger static initialization

If a *delegate-creation-expression* (§14.5.10.3) references a static method, this does not trigger the execution of any static constructor (§17.11) of the class that declares the static method. There is no need to initialize the class as the static method is not invoked. For example, consider:

```
using System;

class Test
{
  static void Main()
  {
    D d;
    Console.WriteLine("Before delegate creation");
    d = new D(A.F);
    Console.WriteLine("Before delegate call");
    d();
    Console.WriteLine("After delegate call");
  }
}

delegate void D();

class A
{
  static A ()
  {
    Console.WriteLine("Init A");
  }
```

```
  public static void F()
  {
    Console.WriteLine("A.F called");
  }
}
```

The static constructor is not triggered until, and if, the delegate is invoked, so the output is:

```
Before delegate creation
Before delegate call
Init A
A.F called
After delegate call
```

Nicu Georgian Fruja

Delegates for value type instance methods

This clause refers to a "target object," and objects are reference types, so at first reading, it might be assumed that a delegate cannot refer to an instance method of a value type. However, C# strives to present a unified view of its type system (§11) and one short sentence in §14.4.3.1, *Invocations on boxed instances*, states that a method can be invoked on a boxed instance:

When the function member is invoked through a delegate.

So this clause is precise when it refers to "target object," remembering that value types are automatically boxed to produce an object when required (§11.3.1).

However, as hinted in §14.4.3.1, the results may be surprising. For example, consider the following program fragment:

```
delegate int Func(int x);

struct Storage
{
  public int store;

  public Storage(int v)
  {
    store = v;
  }

  public int ReadThenUpdate(int x)
  {
    int hold = store;
    store = x;
    return hold;
  }
}

void ConcreteBox()
{
  Storage val = new Storage(42);
```

```
Func f = new Func(val.ReadThenUpdate); // creates a boxed copy of val

int a = f(6);     // a = 42
int b = f(8);     // b = 6
val.store = 37;  // does not effect copy of val used by f
int c = f(b);     // c = 8

Console.WriteLine("a = {0}, b = {1}, c = {2}", a, b, c);
}
```

The delegate f refers to a boxed copy of val and not to val itself. Therefore, any changes to val.store are not visible to f, and vice-versa. When the method ConcreteBox is invoked, the output is:

```
a = 42, b = 6, c = 8
```

The C# pimpernel...

Without resorting to unsafe code (§27), the boxed copy of a value type used by a delegate is a very elusive creature. It is impossible to first create the box and then the delegate. Continuing with the previous example, consider the statements:

```
ValueType val_obj = val;                             // box val
Func f2 = new Func(val_obj.ReadThenUpdate); // compile-time error
```

The delegate creation is invalid as there is no ReadThenUpdate method on System. ValueType.

Within an instance method of a value type, this (§18.3.6) is a reference parameter (§12.1.5), so, continuing with our example, a method may be added to Storage:

```
struct Storage
{
  ...

  public Storage GetBoxContents()
  {
    return this;
  }
}
```

However, the method GetBoxContents() only returns a copy of the value inside the box, not the elusive box itself.

22.3 Delegate invocation

C# provides special syntax for invoking a delegate. When a non-null delegate instance whose invocation list contains one entry, is invoked, it invokes the one method with the same arguments it was given, and returns the same value as the referred to method. (See §14.5.5.2 for detailed information on delegate invocation.) If an exception occurs during the invocation of such a delegate, and that exception is not caught within the method that was invoked, the search for an exception catch clause continues in the method that called the delegate, as if that method had directly called the method to which that delegate referred.

Invocation of a delegate instance whose invocation list contains multiple entries, proceeds by invoking each of the methods in the invocation list, synchronously, in order. Each method so called is passed the same set of arguments as was given to the delegate instance. If such a delegate invocation includes reference parameters (§17.5.1.2), each method invocation will occur with a reference to the same variable; changes to that variable by one method in the invocation list will be visible to methods further down the invocation list. If the delegate invocation includes output parameters or a return value, their final value will come from the invocation of the last delegate in the list. If an exception occurs during processing of the invocation of such a delegate, and that exception is not caught within the method that was invoked, the search for an exception catch clause continues in the method that called the delegate, and any methods further down the invocation list are not invoked.

Attempting to invoke a delegate instance whose value is `null` results in an exception of type `System.NullReferenceException`.

[*Example*: The following example shows how to instantiate, combine, remove, and invoke delegates:

```
using System;

delegate void D(int x);
class Test
{
  public static void M1(int i)
  {
    Console.WriteLine("Test.M1: " + i);
  }

  public static void M2(int i)
  {
    Console.WriteLine("Test.M2: " + i);
  }

  public void M3(int i)
  {
    Console.WriteLine("Test.M3: " + i);
  }
}

class Demo
{
  static void Main() {
    D cd1 = new D(Test.M1);
    cd1(-1);   // call M1

    D cd2 = new D(Test.M2);
    cd2(-2);   // call M2

    D cd3 = cd1 + cd2;
    cd3(10);   // call M1 then M2

    cd3 += cd1;
    cd3(20);   // call M1, M2, then M1

    Test t = new Test();
    D cd4 = new D(t.M3);
```

```
            cd3 += cd4;
            cd3(30);    // call M1, M2, M1, then M3

            cd3 -= cd1; // remove last M1
            cd3(40);    // call M1, M2, then M3

            cd3 -= cd4;
            cd3(50);    // call M1 then M2

            cd3 -= cd2;
            cd3(60);    // call M1
            cd3 -= cd2; // impossible removal is benign
            cd3(60);    // call M1

            cd3 -= cd1; // cd3 is null
    //      cd3(70);    // System.NullReferenceException thrown
            cd3 -= cd1; // impossible removal is benign
        }
    }
```

As shown in the statement cd3 += cd1;, a method can be present in an invocation list multiple times. In this case, it is simply invoked once per occurrence. In an invocation list such as this, when that method is removed, the last occurrence in the invocation list is the one actually removed.

Immediately prior to the execution of the final statement, cd3 -= cd1;, the delegate cd3 is null. Attempting to subtract a delegate from null (or to subtract a non-existent delegate from a non-empty list) is not an error.

The output produced is:

```
    Test.M1: -1
    Test.M2: -2

    Test.M1: 10
    Test.M2: 10

    Test.M1: 20
    Test.M2: 20
    Test.M1: 20

    Test.M1: 30
    Test.M2: 30
    Test.M1: 30
    Test.M3: 30

    Test.M1: 40
    Test.M2: 40
    Test.M3: 40

    Test.M1: 50
    Test.M2: 50

    Test.M1: 60
    Test.M1: 60
```

end example]

23 Exceptions

Exceptions in C# provide a structured, uniform, and type-safe way of handling both system level and application-level error conditions. [*Note:* The exception mechanism in C# is quite similar to that of C++, with a few important differences:

- In C#, all exceptions shall be represented by an instance of a class type derived from `System.Exception`. In C++, any value of any type can be used to represent an exception.
- In C#, a finally block (§15.10) can be used to write termination code that executes in both normal execution and exceptional conditions. C++ has no equivalent construct.
- In C#, system-level exceptions such as overflow, divide-by-zero, and null dereferences have well defined exception classes and are on a par with application-level error conditions.

end note]

Exceptions not advised as control flow

Some might consider using exceptions as another form of flow-control—for example, as a way to provide a multilevel return that cancels a whole stack of method invocations. In general, this is not advised.

Throwing an exception is comparatively very slow—maybe 20,000 cpu cycles—on Microsoft's current CLR (and Mono is believed to behave similarly), and much slower than in most Standard ML implementations, for example. This suggests that:

1. A performance-conscious developer should make sure that exceptions are not thrown on frequent execution paths;
2. A performance-conscious library designer should always give clients an exception-free way to test whether something might fail—for example, the C5 library follows this guideline; and
3. The designers of CLI and C# did not intend exceptions to be used for control flow, the former for allowing them to be slow and the latter for adopting the CLI implementation.

The reason for the slowness? It is partly that when an exception is thrown on the CLI, a stack trace gets incorporated into the exception object. This suggests that one of the expected uses of exceptions was to assist debugging, in addition to their normal use to handle exceptional situations during normal program execution. Note that, in Java, the stack trace gets incorporated when the exception object is created, not thrown. This allows an optimization in Java when the stack trace is known to be ignored: Create the exception once and for all, and throw it where needed.

23.1 Causes of exceptions

Exceptions can be thrown in two different ways.

- A `throw` statement (§15.9.5) throws an exception immediately and unconditionally. Control never reaches the statement immediately following the `throw`.
- Certain exceptional conditions that arise during the processing of C# statements and expressions cause an exception in certain circumstances when the operation cannot be completed normally. [*Example*: An integer division operation (§14.7.2) throws a `System.DivideByZeroException` if the denominator is zero. *end example*] See §23.4 for a list of the various exceptions that can occur in this way.

Asynchronous exceptions

It is possible for exceptions to be generated by events outside the current thread of execution; such exceptions arrive asynchronously. The impact of this on execution is discussed in §10.10.

One particular asynchronous exception is the CLI's `ThreadAbortException`, which is discussed in an annotation in §10.1.

Unexpected exception

Exceptions that can arise during normal processing are not always explicitly listed in the Standard. For example, the `System.StackOverflowException` (§23.4) may be thrown when an attempt to invoke a function is made. However, the clause "Function member invocation" (§14.4.3) does not list this exception.

Similarly, when the Standard explicitly states that a specific exception will be thrown under certain circumstances, it is possible for a different exception to be thrown. For example, referring to the same function invocation clause (§14.4.3), we find that if an instance method invocation is attempted on a null object, then "a `System.NullReferenceException` is thrown and no further steps are executed." However, an exception is an object and therefore must be allocated, so it is possible that allocation may fail resulting in a `System.OutOfMemoryException` (§23.4) exception. The Standard does not require exceptions to be preallocated to avoid this, though an implementation might find it difficult to meet the Standard's requirements if it did not at least preallocate an instance of `System.OutOfMemoryException`.

The exceptions that might occur "unexpectedly" in this way are those from which recovery is usually hard and most programs would not normally be designed to catch them.

23.2 The System.Exception class

The `System.Exception` class is the base type of all exceptions. This class has a few notable properties that all exceptions share:

- `Message` is a read-only property of type `string` that contains a human-readable description of the reason for the exception.
- `InnerException` is a read-only property of type `Exception`. If its value is non-`null`, it refers to the exception that caused the current exception. (That is, the current exception was raised in a catch block handling the type `InnerException`.) Otherwise, its value is null, indicating that this exception was not caused by another exception. (The number of exception objects chained together in this manner can be arbitrary.)

The value of these properties can be specified in calls to the instance constructor for `System.Exception`.

Optional InnerException

The preceding paragraph does not state that an implementation *must*, or even *may*, set the `InnerException` property when an exception occurs during the execution of a `catch` block.

Every exception class listed in Annex D provides an instance constructor that allows setting of `InnerException` when the exception is *created*, not when it is *thrown*. If the underlying implementation were to set this property itself when an exception is thrown, it would replace any value set by the programmer at creation. At the time of writing, neither the Microsoft nor the Mono implementations set the `InnerException` when throwing an exception in a `catch` block. However, both do include the inner exception (if non-null) when formatting an exception using `ToString()` or when reporting an unhandled exception.

Therefore, the `InnerException` property cannot be relied upon to categorically determine that one exception was thrown as a result of handling another. This can only be assumed if all developers follow coding standards, typically using a pattern such as this:

```
try
{
    ...
}
catch (Exception error)
{
    ...
    throw new ApplicationException("Unrecoverable mess", error);
}
```

Given the definition of `InnerException`, the inability to rely on it might be surprising.

[*Note*: The Standard Library provides two types that inherit directly from `System.Exception`: `System.SystemException` and `System.ApplicationException`. These classes are provided as a means to differentiate between exceptions defined by the system versus exceptions defined by applications, respectively. As such, it is recommended that exception classes be derived from one of these classes as appropriate, rather than from `System.Exception` directly. *end note*]

A good idea in theory, but not in practice

The `ApplicationException` vs. `SystemException` distinction was a good idea in theory. However, in practice, for whatever reason, many programmers have not followed the guideline. The reality is that some exception classes derive straight from `System.Exception`, some system-related exception classes from `System.ApplicationException`, and some application-related exception classes from `System.SystemException`.

23.3 How exceptions are handled

Exceptions are handled by a `try` statement (§15.10).

When an exception occurs, the system searches for the nearest `catch` clause that can handle the exception, as determined by the run-time type of the exception. First, the current method is searched for a lexically enclosing `try` statement, and the associated `catch` clauses of the `try` statement are considered in order. If that fails, the method that called the current method is searched for a lexically enclosing `try` statement that encloses the point of the call to the current method. This search continues until a `catch` clause is found that can handle the current exception, by naming an exception class that is of the same class, or a base class, of the run-time type of the exception being thrown. A `catch` clause that doesn't name an exception class can handle any exception.

Once a matching `catch` clause is found, the system prepares to transfer control to the first statement of the `catch` clause. Before execution of the `catch` clause begins, the system first executes, in order, any `finally` clauses that were associated with `try` statements more nested that than the one that caught the exception.

If no matching catch clause is found, one of two things occurs:

- If the search for a matching `catch` clause reaches a static constructor (§17.11) or static field initializer, then a `System.TypeInitializationException` is thrown at the point that triggered the invocation of the static constructor. The inner exception of the `System.TypeInitializationException` contains the exception that was originally thrown.
- If the search for matching `catch` clauses reaches the code that initially started the thread, then execution of the thread is terminated. The impact of such termination is implementation-defined.

The behavior of uncaught exceptions that occur during finalizer execution is unspecified.

Here be dragons

The C# Standard does not specify what state a class or struct is in after `System.Type InitializationException` has been thrown. If you are using a compiler running on the CLI you are no better off as the CLI makes no guarantees either. Compound this with the indeterminate determinism of static constructors and static field initialization (see §17.4.5.1, §17.11, §18.3.10, and associated annotations), and attempting to catch and recover from a `System.TypeInitializationException` is courting disaster.

Recommendations:

- Avoid throwing any exceptions from static constructors or static field initializers if possible.
- If there are exceptions that might be thrown and can be handled, do so within the static constructor.
- Do not catch and attempt to recover from `System.TypeInitializationException`—abort gracefully.

23.4 Common exception classes

The following exceptions are thrown by certain C# operations.

`System.ArithmeticException`	A base class for exceptions that occur during arithmetic operations, such as `System.DivideByZeroException` and `System.OverflowException`.
`System.ArrayTypeMismatchException`	Thrown when a store into an array fails because the runtime type of the stored element is incompatible with the runtime type of the array.
`System.DivideByZeroException`	Thrown when an attempt to divide an integral value by zero occurs.
`System.IndexOutOfRangeException`	Thrown when an attempt to index an array via an index that is less than zero or outside the bounds of the array.
`System.InvalidCastException`	Thrown when an explicit conversion from a base type or interface to a derived type fails at run time.
`System.NullReferenceException`	Thrown when a `null` reference is used in a way that causes the referenced object to be required.
`System.OutOfMemoryException`	Thrown when an attempt to allocate memory (via `new`) fails.

System.OverflowException	Thrown when an arithmetic operation in a `checked` context overflows.
System.StackOverflowException	Thrown when the execution stack is exhausted by having too many pending method calls; typically indicative of very deep or unbounded recursion.
System.TypeInitializationException	Thrown when a static constructor throws an exception, and no `catch` clause exists to catch it.

Genteel exception classes?

The preceding table does not include all the exceptions thrown by C# operations. Those omitted are:

System.InvalidOperationException	Thrown when an attempt to obtain the `Value` property (or language operation which equates to this) of a nullable type is made and the `HasValue` is `false` (§11.4.1, §12.2, §13.7).
System.NotSupportedException	May be thrown by the `Reset` method of an enumerator object of an iterator (§26.2).

For exceptions thrown by types in the Standard Library, refer to Annex D.

24 Attributes

[*Note*: Much of the C# language enables the programmer to specify declarative information about the entities defined in the program. For example, the accessibility of a method in a class is specified by decorating it with the *method-modifiers* `public`, `protected`, `internal`, and `private`. *end note*]

C# enables programmers to invent new kinds of declarative information, called **attributes**. Programmers can then attach attributes to various program entities, and retrieve attribute information in a run-time environment. [*Note*: For instance, a framework might define a `HelpAttribute` attribute that can be placed on certain program entities (such as classes and methods) to provide a mapping from those program entities to their documentation. *end note*]

Attributes are defined through the declaration of attribute classes (§24.1), which can have positional and named parameters (§24.1.2). Attributes are associated with program entities using attribute specifications (§24.2), and can be retrieved at run-time as attribute instances (§24.3).

24.1 Attribute classes

A class that derives from the abstract class `System.Attribute`, whether directly or indirectly, is an **attribute class**. The declaration of an attribute class defines a new kind of attribute that can be placed on program entities. By convention, attribute classes are named with a suffix of `Attribute`. Uses of an attribute can either include or omit this suffix.

Suffix omission clarification

Uses of an attribute class *as an attribute specification* can either include or omit this suffix. However, in all other cases where the attribute class is referenced, the suffix must be included as it is part of the name. For example, consider the code fragment:

```
public class MyAttribute : Attribute {}

[My] // ok
class App
{
    void Example()
    {
        Type t1 = typeof(MyAttribute); // ok
        Type t2 = typeof(My);          // compile-time error
        ...
    }
}
```

In the `typeof` expression, the full name of the class is required.

A generic class declaration shall not use `System.Attribute` as a direct or indirect base class. [*Example*:

```
using System;

public class B : Attribute {}

public class C<T> : B {}   // Error – generic cannot be an attribute
```

end example]

24.1.1 Attribute usage

The attribute AttributeUsage (§24.4.1) is used to describe how an attribute class can be used.

AttributeUsage has a positional parameter (§24.1.2) that enables an attribute class to specify the kinds of declarations on which it can be used. [*Example*: The example

```
using System;

[AttributeUsage(AttributeTargets.Class
| AttributeTargets.Interface)]
public class SimpleAttribute: Attribute {}
```

defines an attribute class named SimpleAttribute that can be placed on *class-declaration*s and *interface-declaration*s only. The example

```
[Simple] class Class1 {...}

[Simple] interface Interface1 {...}
```

shows several uses of the Simple attribute. Although this attribute is defined with the name SimpleAttribute, when this attribute is used, the Attribute suffix can be omitted, resulting in the short name Simple. Thus, the example above is semantically equivalent to the following

```
[SimpleAttribute] class Class1 {...}

[SimpleAttribute] interface Interface1 {...}
```

end example]

AttributeUsage has a named parameter (§24.1.2), called AllowMultiple, which indicates whether the attribute can be specified more than once for a given entity. If AllowMultiple for an attribute class is true, then that class is a ***multi-use attribute class***, and can be specified more than once on an entity. If AllowMultiple for an attribute class is false or it is unspecified, then that class is a ***single-use attribute class***, and can be specified at most once on an entity.

[*Example*: The example

```
using System;

[AttributeUsage(AttributeTargets.Class, AllowMultiple = true)]
public class AuthorAttribute: Attribute
{
  public AuthorAttribute(string name)
  {
    this.name = name;
  }
  public string Name { get { return name;} }
  private string name;
}
```

defines a multi-use attribute class named AuthorAttribute. The example

```
[Author("Brian Kernighan"), Author("Dennis Ritchie")]
class Class1 {...}
```

shows a class declaration with two uses of the Author attribute. *end example*]

AttributeUsage has another named parameter (§24.1.2), called Inherited, which indicates whether the attribute, when specified on a base class, is also inherited by classes that derive from that base class. If Inherited for an attribute class is true, then that attribute is inherited. If

`Inherited` for an attribute class is false then that attribute is not inherited. If it is unspecified, its default value is true.

An attribute class `X` not having an `AttributeUsage` attribute attached to it, as in

```
using System;

class X: Attribute {...}
```

is equivalent to the following:

```
using System;

[AttributeUsage(AttributeTargets.All, AllowMultiple = false,
                                      Inherited = true)]
class X: Attribute {...}
```

24.1.2 Positional and named parameters

Attribute classes can have *positional parameters* and *named parameters*. Each public instance constructor for an attribute class defines a valid sequence of positional parameters for that attribute class. Each non-static public read-write field and property for an attribute class defines a named parameter for the attribute class. Both accessors of a property need to be public for the property to define a named parameter.

[*Example*: The example

```
using System;

[AttributeUsage(AttributeTargets.Class)]
public class HelpAttribute: Attribute
{

   public HelpAttribute(string url)  // url is a positional parameter
   {
      ...
   }

   public string Topic  // Topic is a named parameter
   {
      get {...}
      set {...}
   }

   public string Url { get {...} }
}
```

defines an attribute class named `HelpAttribute` that has one positional parameter (`string url`) and one named parameter (`string Topic`). Although it is non-static and public, the property `Url` does not define a named parameter, since it is not read-write.

This attribute class might be used as follows:

```
[Help("http://www.mycompany.com/.../Class1.htm")]
class Class1
{
}
```

```
[Help("http://www.mycompany.com/…/Misc.htm", Topic ="Class2")]
class Class2
{
}
```

end example]

24.1.3 Attribute parameter types

The types of positional and named parameters for an attribute class are limited to the ***attribute parameter types***, which are:

- One of the following types: `bool`, `byte`, `char`, `double`, `float`, `int`, `long`, `short`, `string`.
- The type `object`.
- The type `System.Type`.
- An enum type, provided it has public accessibility and the types in which it is nested (if any) also have public accessibility.
- Single-dimensional arrays of the above types.

24.2 Attribute specification

Attribute specification is the application of a previously defined attribute to a program entity. An attribute is a piece of additional declarative information that is specified for a program entity. Attributes can be specified at global scope (to specify attributes on the containing assembly) and for *type-declarations* (§16.6), *class-member-declarations* (§17.2), *struct-member-declarations* (§18.2), *interface-member-declarations* (§20.2), *enum-member-declarations* (§21.3), *accessor-declarations* (§17.6.2), *event-accessor-declarations* (§17.7), elements of *formal-parameter-lists* (§17.5.1), and elements of *type-parameter-lists* (§25.1.1).

Attributes are specified in ***attribute sections***. An attribute section consists of a pair of square brackets, which surround a comma-separated list of one or more attributes. The order in which attributes are specified in such a list, and the order in which sections attached to the same program entity are arranged, is not significant. For instance, the attribute specifications `[A][B]`, `[B][A]`, `[A, B]`, and `[B, A]` are equivalent.

> *global-attributes:*
>   *global-attribute-sections*
>
> *global-attribute-sections:*
>   *global-attribute-section*
>   *global-attribute-sections   global-attribute-section*
>
> *global-attribute-section:*
>   [*global-attribute-target-specifier   attribute-list*   ]
>   [*global-attribute-target-specifier   attribute-list   ,*   ]
>
> *global-attribute-target-specifier:*
>   *global-attribute-target*   :
>
> *global-attribute-target:*
>   *identifier*
>   *keyword*

attributes:
  attribute-sections

attribute-sections:
  attribute-section
  attribute-sections   attribute-section

attribute-section:
  [*attribute-target-specifier$_{opt}$ attribute-list*   ]
  [*attribute-target-specifier$_{opt}$ attribute-list*   ,   ]

attribute-target-specifier:
  attribute-target   :

attribute-target:
  identifier
  keyword

attribute-list:
  attribute
  attribute-list   ,   *attribute*

attribute:
  attribute-name   attribute-arguments$_{opt}$

attribute-name:
  type-name

attribute-arguments:
  (*positional-argument-list$_{opt}$*   )
  (*positional-argument-list*   ,   *named-argument-list*   )
  (*named-argument-list*   )

positional-argument-list:
  positional-argument
  positional-argument-list   ,   *positional-argument*

positional-argument:
  attribute-argument-expression

named-argument-list:
  named-argument
  named-argument-list   ,   *named-argument*

named-argument:
  identifier   =   *attribute-argument-expression*

attribute-argument-expression:
  expression

An attribute consists of an *attribute-name* and an optional list of positional and named arguments. The positional arguments (if any) precede the named arguments. A positional argument consists of an *attribute-argument-expression*; a named argument consists of a name, followed by an equal sign, followed by an *attribute-argument-expression*, which, together, are constrained by the same rules as simple assignment. The order of named arguments is not significant.

---

return vs. @return

The *global-attribute-target* and *attribute-target* non-terminals allow the use of a leading @ symbol. For example, you can use `return` or `@return`:

```
public class Example
{
  [@return:X()]
  public void Method()
  {
     ...
  }
}
```

Using `@return` helps to emphasize that this is not a normal return statement keyword. A code editor with color-syntax highlighting might well color `@return` as an identifier but be fooled into coloring `return` as a keyword.

[*Note*: For convenience, a trailing comma is allowed in a *global-attribute-section* and an *attribute-section*, just as one is allowed in an *array-initializer* (§19.7). *end note*]

The *attribute-name* identifies an attribute class. *type-name* shall refer to an attribute class. Otherwise, a compile-time error occurs. [*Example*: The example

```
class Class1 {}

[Class1] class Class2 {}   // Error
```

results in a compile-time error because it attempts to use `Class1` as an attribute class when `Class1` is not an attribute class. *end example*]

When an attribute is placed at the global level, a *global-attribute-target-specifier* is required. The only standardized *global-attribute-target* name is `assembly`. This target name shall only be used in the context of an assembly.

The only standardized *attribute-target* names are `event`, `field`, `method`, `param`, `property`, `return`, `type`, and `typevar`. These target names shall only be used in the following contexts:

- `event` — an event.
- `field` — a field. A field-like event (i.e., one without accessors) can also have an attribute with this target.
- `method` — a constructor, finalizer, method, operator, property get and set accessors, indexer get and set accessors, and event add and remove accessors. A field-like event (i.e., one without accessors) can also have an attribute with this target.
- `param` — a property set accessor, an indexer set accessor, event add and remove accessors, and a parameter in a constructor, method, and operator.
- `property` — a property and an indexer.
- `return` — a delegate, method, operator, property get accessor, and indexer get accessor.
- `type` — a delegate, class, struct, enum, and interface.
- `typevar` — a type parameter.

Certain contexts permit the specification of an attribute on more than one target. A program can explicitly specify the target by including an *attribute-target-specifier*. In the absence of an *attribute-target-specifier*, a reasonable default is applied, but an *attribute-target-specifier* can be used to affirm or override the default in certain ambiguous cases (or just to affirm the default in non-ambiguous cases). Thus, typically, *attribute-target-specifier*s can be omitted. The potentially ambiguous contexts are resolved as follows (using equality as defined in §9.4.2):

- An attribute specified on a delegate declaration can apply either to the delegate beingdeclared or to its return value. In the absence of an *attribute-target-specifier*, the attribute applies to the delegate. An *attribute-target* equal to `type` indicates that the attribute applies to the delegate; an *attribute-target* equal to `return` indicates that the attribute applies to the return value.

- An attribute specified on a method declaration can apply either to the method being declared or to its return value. In the absence of an *attribute-target-specifier*, the attribute applies to the method. An *attribute-target* equal to `method` indicates that the attribute applies to the method; an *attribute-target* equal to `return` indicates that the attribute applies to the return value.

- An attribute specified on an operator declaration can apply either to the operator being declared or to its return value. In the absence of an *attribute-target-specifier*, the attribute applies to the operator. An *attribute-target* equal to `method` indicates that the attribute applies to the operator; an *attribute-target* equal to `return` indicates that the attribute applies to the return value.

- An attribute specified on a get accessor declaration for a property or indexer declaration can apply either to the associated method or to its return value. In the absence of an *attribute-target-specifier*, the attribute applies to the method. An *attribute-target* equal to `method` indicates that the attribute applies to the method; an *attribute-target* equal to `return` indicates that the attribute applies to the return value.

- An attribute specified on a set accessor for a property or indexer declaration can apply either to the associated method or to its lone implicit parameter. In the absence of an *attribute-target-specifier*, the attribute applies to the method. An *attribute-target* equal to `method` indicates that the attribute applies to the method; an *attribute-target* equal to `param` indicates that the attribute applies to the parameter.

- An attribute specified on an event declaration that omits *event-accessor-declaration*s can apply to the event being declared, to the associated field (if the event is not abstract), or to the associated add and remove methods. In the absence of an *attribute-target-specifier*, the attribute applies to the event declaration. An *attribute-target* equal to `event` indicates that the attribute applies to the event; an *attribute-target* equal to `field` indicates that the attribute applies to the field; and an *attribute-target* equal to `method` indicates that the attribute applies to the methods.

- In the case of an event declaration that does not omit *event-accessor-declaration*s, an attribute specified on an add or remove accessor declaration for an event declaration can apply either to the associated method or to its lone parameter. In the absence of an *attribute-target-specifier*, the attribute applies to the method. An *attribute-target* equal to `method` indicates that the attribute applies to the method; an *attribute-target* equal to `param` indicates that the attribute applies to the parameter.

An implementation can accept other attribute target specifiers, the purposes of which are implementation-defined. However, an implementation that does not recognize such a target, shall issue a warning.

By convention, attribute classes are named with a suffix of `Attribute`. An *attribute-name* can either include or omit this suffix. Specifically, an *attribute-name* is resolved as follows:

- If the right-most identifier of the *attribute-name* is a verbatim identifier (§9.4.2), then the *attribute-name* is resolved as a *type-name* (§10.8). If the result is not a type derived from System.Attribute, a compile-time error occurs.
- Otherwise,
  - The *attribute-name* is resolved as a *type-name* (§10.8) except any errors are suppressed. If this resolution is successful and results in a type derived from System.Attribute then the type is the result of this step.
  - The characters Attribute are appended to the right-most identifier in the *attribute-name* and the resulting string of tokens is resolved as a *type-name* (§10.8) except any errors are suppressed. If this resolution is successful and results in a type derived from System.Attribute then the type is the result of this step.

If exactly one of the two steps above results in a type derived from System.Attribute, then that type is the result of the *attribute-name*. Otherwise a compile-time error occurs.

[*Example*: Informally, when attempting to resolve an *attribute-name*, if an attribute class is found both with and without the Attribute suffix, an ambiguity is present, and a compile-time error is issued. If the *attribute-name* is spelled such that its right-most *identifier* is a verbatim identifier (§9.4.2), then only an attribute without a suffix is matched, thus enabling such an ambiguity to be resolved. The example

```
using System;

[AttributeUsage(AttributeTargets.All)]
public class X: Attribute {}

[AttributeUsage(AttributeTargets.All)]
public class XAttribute: Attribute {}

[X]              // error: ambiguity
class Class1 {}

[XAttribute]     // refers to XAttribute
class Class2 {}

[@X]             // refers to X
class Class3 {}

[@XAttribute]    // refers to XAttribute
class Class4 {}
```

shows two attribute classes named X and XAttribute. The attribute reference [X] is ambiguous, since it could refer to either X or XAttribute. Using a verbatim identifier allows the exact intent to be specified in such rare cases. The attribute reference [XAttribute] is not ambiguous (although it would be if there were an attribute class named XAttributeAttribute!). If the declaration for class X is removed, then both attributes refer to the attribute class named XAttribute, as follows:

```
using System;

[AttributeUsage(AttributeTargets.All)]
public class XAttribute: Attribute {}
```

```
[X]                 // refers to XAttribute
class Class1 {}

[XAttribute]        // refers to XAttribute
class Class2 {}

[@X]                // error: no attribute named "X"
class Class3 {}
```

end example]

It is a compile-time error to use a single-use attribute class more than once on the same entity. [*Example*: The example

```
using System;

[AttributeUsage(AttributeTargets.Class)]
public class HelpStringAttribute: Attribute
{
  string value;

  public HelpStringAttribute(string value)
  {
    this.value = value;
  }

  public string Value { get {...} }
}

[HelpString("Description of Class1")]
[HelpString("Another description of Class1")]
public class Class1 {}
```

results in a compile-time error because it attempts to use `HelpString`, which is a single-use attribute class, more than once on the declaration of `Class1`. *end example*]

> **Specification omission**
>
> While the Standard explicitly says that a single-use attribute class cannot be used multiple times on the same target, it neglects to state that an attribute class X can be used only on the targets listed in the `AttributeUsage` attribute of X (§24.4.1). This requirement must have been omitted by mistake. Note that if there is no `AttributeUsage` attribute on X, then X can be used on all targets (§24.1.1).

An expression E is an *attribute-argument-expression* if all of the following statements are true:

- The type of E is an attribute parameter type (§24.1.3).
- At compile-time, the value of E can be resolved to one of the following:
  - A constant value.
  - A *typeof-expression* (§14.5.11) specifying a non-generic type, a closed constructed type (§25.5.2), or an unbound generic type (§25.5).
  - A one-dimensional array of *attribute-argument-expression*s.

[*Example*:

```
using System;

[AttributeUsage(AttributeTargets.Class)]
public class MyAttribute: Attribute
{
  public int P1
  {
    get {...}
    set {...}
  }

  public Type P2
  {
    get {...}
    set {...}
  }

  public object P3
  {
    get {...}
    set {...}
  }
}

[My(P1 = 1234, P3 = new int[]{1, 3, 5}, P2 = typeof(float))]
class MyClass {}

class C<T>
{
  [My(P2 = typeof(T))]       // Error – T not a closed type.
  int x1;

  [My(P2 = typeof(C<T>))]    // Error – C<T> not a closed type.
  int x2;

  [My(P2 = typeof(C<int>))]  // Ok
  int x3;

  [My(P2 = typeof(C<>))]     // Ok
  int x4;
}
```

end example]

Multiple declaration unclarity

The preceding examples all place an attribute on a *single* field in a single declaration. What is the meaning if *several* fields are introduced in the same declaration?

```
class Eg
{
  ...
  [ My(typeof(int))]
  int x1, x2, x3;
}
```

Unfortunately, the Standard is not as clear as it might be in this case. The intention is that if several fields are introduced in the same attributed declaration, then *all* the fields in the declaration are attributed (rather than just the first field in the list). Fortunately, the current Microsoft and Mono compiler writers understood the intention of the Standard's authors.

The attributes of a type declared in multiple parts are determined by combining, in an unspecified order, the attributes of each of its parts. If the same attribute is placed on multiple parts, it is equivalent to specifying that attribute multiple times on the type. [*Example*: The two parts:

```
[Attr1, Attr2("hello")]
partial class A{}

[Attr3, Attr2("goodbye")]
partial class A{}
```

are equivalent to the following single declaration:

```
[Attr1, Attr2("hello"), Attr3, Attr2("goodbye")]
class A{}
```

end example]

Attributes on type parameters combine in the same way.

24.3 Attribute instances

An ***attribute instance*** is an instance that represents an attribute at run-time. An attribute is defined with an attribute class, positional arguments, and named arguments. An attribute instance is an instance of the attribute class that is initialized with the positional and named arguments.

Retrieval of an attribute instance involves both compile-time and run-time processing, as described in the following subclauses.

24.3.1 Compilation of an attribute

The compilation of an *attribute* with attribute class T, *positional-argument-list* P, *named-argument-list* N, and specified on a program entity E is compiled into an assembly A via the following steps:

- Follow the compile-time processing steps for compiling an *object-creation-expression* of the form new T(P). These steps either result in a compile-time error, or determine an instance constructor on T that can be invoked at run-time. Call this instance constructor C.
- If C does not have public accessibility, then a compile-time error occurs.
- For each *named-argument* Arg in N:
  - Let Name be the *identifier* of the *named-argument* Arg.
  - Name shall identify a non-static read-write public field or property on T. If T has no such field or property, then a compile-time error occurs.
- Store the following information (for run-time instantiation of the attribute) in the assembly output by the compiler as a result of compiling the program containing the attribute: the attribute class T, the instance constructor C on T, the *positional-argument-list* P, the *named-argument-list* N, and the associated program entity E, with the values resolved completely at compile-time.

Constructor not called at compile-time

Note in particular that the constructor C is *not* called during the compile-time processing of an attribute. Instead, the constructor is called at each run-time instantiation of the attribute, as detailed in §24.3.2.

24.3.2 Run-time retrieval of an attribute instance

The attribute instance represented by T, C, P, and N, and associated with E can be retrieved at run-time from the assembly A using the following steps:

- Follow the run-time processing steps for executing an *object-creation-expression* of the form new T(P), using the instance constructor C and values as determined at compile-time. These steps either result in an exception, or produce an instance of T. Call this instance O.
- For each *named-argument* Arg in N, in order:
  - Let Name be the *identifier* of the *named-argument* Arg. If Name does not identify a non-static public read-write field or property on O, then an exception is thrown.
  - Let Value be the result of evaluating the *attribute-argument-expression* of Arg.
  - If Name identifies a field on O, then set this field to the value Value.
  - Otherwise, Name identifies a property on O. Set this property to the value Value.
  - The result is O, an instance of the attribute class T that has been initialized with the *positional-argument-list* P and the *named-argument-list* N.

[*Note*: The format for storing T, C, P, N (and associating it with E) in A and the mechanism to specify E and retrieve T, C, P, N from A (and hence how an attribute instance is obtained at run-time) is beyond the scope of this standard. *end note*]

[*Example*: In an implementation of the CLI, the Help attribute instances in the assembly created by compiling the example program in §24.1.2 can be retrieved with the following program:

```
using System;
using System.Reflection;

public sealed class InterrogateHelpUrls
{
  public static void Main(string[] args)
  {
    Type helpType = typeof(HelpAttribute);
    string assemblyName = args[0];
    foreach (Type t in Assembly.Load(assemblyName).GetTypes())
    {
      Console.WriteLine("Type : {0} ", t.ToString());
      HelpAttribute[] helpers =
        (HelpAttribute[])t.GetCustomAttributes(helpType, false);
      for (int at = 0; at != helpers.Length; at++)
      {
        Console.WriteLine("\tUrl : {0} ", helpers[at].Url);
      }
    }
  }
}
```

end example]

Reflection not part of C# standard

The preceding example showing the use of reflection to access attributes at runtime is *informative*. Reflection is also mentioned informatively in §14.5.11. Reflection is not part of the C# Standard, but it is part of the CLI Standard (Ecma-335).

24.4 Reserved attributes

The following attributes affect the language, as stated:

- `System.AttributeUsageAttribute` (§24.4.1), which is used to describe the ways in which an attribute class can be used.
- `System.Diagnostics.ConditionalAttribute` (§24.4.2), is a multi-use attribute class which is used to define conditional methods and conditional attribute classes. This attribute indicates a condition by testing a conditional compilation symbol.
- `System.ObsoleteAttribute` (§24.4.3), which is used to mark a member as obsolete.

24.4.1 The AttributeUsage attribute

The attribute `AttributeUsage` is used to describe the manner in which the attribute class can be used.

A class that is decorated with the `AttributeUsage` attribute shall derive from `System.Attribute`, either directly or indirectly. Otherwise, a compile-time error occurs.

[*Note*: For an example of using this attribute, see §24.1.1. *end note*]

AttributeUsage and partial compile-time checks

Specifying the `AttributeUsage` for an attribute class allows the compiler to discover ill-placed attributes. For instance, if the `Author` attribute in §24.1.1 were specified for a method, then the compiler could flag that attribute as ill placed, since the `AuthorAttribute` class has an `AttributeUsage` attribute specifying only classes as possible targets.

The targets that can be listed in an `AttributeUsage` specification are the elements of enum type `AttributeTargets`, shown in Annex D of this Standard. The attribute targets include: `Class`, `Struct`, and several others; no distinction is made between generic classes and non-generic classes. This means that the compile-time checks are only partial. Namely, some attributes are meaningful only on nongeneric classes and nongeneric struct types. One example is the `StructLayout` attribute from Microsoft's CLR and Novell's Mono (also used in an annotation on §18):

```
[ StructLayout (LayoutKind.Explicit)]
struct PaperWall<T>
{
  [ FieldOffset (0)]
  public int Left;

  [ FieldOffset (0)]
  public T Right;
}
```

This code will be accepted by the compiler but will fail at run-time with a `TypeLoadException`. There is no way to use the `AttributeUsage` specification to tell the compiler to reject this use of the `StructLayout` attribute.

24.4.2 The Conditional attribute

The attribute `Conditional` enables the definition of **conditional methods** and **conditional attribute classes**.

24.4.2.1 Conditional methods

A method decorated with the `Conditional` attribute is a conditional method. Each conditional method is thus associated with the conditional compilation symbols declared in its `Conditional` attributes. [*Example*:

```
using System.Diagnostics;
class Eg
{
  [Conditional("ALPHA")]
  [Conditional("BETA")]
  public static void M()
  {
     ...
  }
}
```

declares `Eg.M` as a conditional method associated with the two conditional compilation symbols `ALPHA` and `BETA`. *end example*]

A call to a conditional method is included if one or more of its associated conditional compilation symbols is defined at the point of call, otherwise the call is omitted.

A conditional method is subject to the following restrictions:

- The conditional method shall be a method in a *class-declaration* or *struct-declaration*. A compile-time error occurs if the `Conditional` attribute is specified on an interface method.
- The conditional method shall have a return type of `void`.
- The conditional method shall not have `out` parameters.
- The conditional method shall not be marked with the `override` modifier. A conditional method can be marked with the `virtual` modifier, however. Overrides of such a method are implicitly conditional, and shall not be explicitly marked with a `Conditional` attribute.
- The conditional method shall not be an implementation of an interface method. Otherwise, a compile-time error occurs.

In addition, a compile-time error occurs if a conditional method is used in a *delegate-creation-expression*.

Derived surprises

The conditional attribute on a virtual method is inherited by overrides of that method. This can lead to surprises because it is impossible to see from the declaration of an override method in a derived class that the method is conditional: One must look at the base class source (which may not be available) or documentation (which may not be complete).

Consider this apparently innocent class declaration with a field and an override method:

```
sealed class B : A
{
  public int X;
  public override void M()
  {
    X = 42;
  }
}
```

One may be puzzled to find that after executing B b = new B(); b.M(), the field b.X does *not* have the value 42. How can this be?

The reason might be that M is conditional in the base class, and the conditional compilation symbol not defined at the point of the b.M() call. It is entirely reasonable that an override method is conditional whenever the overridden method is. What is less pleasant is that there is no way to discover from the declaration of class B or method B.M() that the method is conditional.

[*Example*: The example

```
#define DEBUG

using System;
using System.Diagnostics;

class Class1
{
  [Conditional("DEBUG")]
  public static void M()
  {
    Console.WriteLine("Executed Class1.M");
  }
}

class Class2
{
  public static void Test()
  {
    Class1.M();
  }
}
```

declares Class1.M as a conditional method. Class2's Test method calls this method. Since the conditional compilation symbol DEBUG is defined, if Class2.Test is called, it will call M. If the symbol DEBUG had not been defined, then Class2.Test would not call Class1.M. *end example*]

It is important to understand that the inclusion or exclusion of a call to a conditional method is controlled by the conditional compilation symbols at the point of the call. [*Example*: In the following code

```
// Begin class1.cs

  using System;
  using System.Diagnostics;

  class Class1
  {
    [Conditional("DEBUG")]
    public static void F()
    {
      Console.WriteLine("Executed Class1.F");
    }
  }

// End class1.cs

// Begin class2.cs

  #define DEBUG

  class Class2
  {
    public static void G()
    {
      Class1.F();        // F is called
    }
  }

// End class2.cs

// Begin class3.cs

  #undef DEBUG

  class Class3
  {
    public static void H()
    {
      Class1.F();        // F is not called
    }
  }

// End class3.cs
```

the classes Class2 and Class3 each contain calls to the conditional method Class1.F, which is
conditional based on whether or not DEBUG is defined. Since this symbol is defined in the context
of Class2 but not Class3, the call to F in Class2 is included, while the call to F in Class3 is
omitted. *end example*]

The use of conditional methods in an inheritance chain can be confusing. Calls made to a conditional method through base, of the form base.M, are subject to the normal conditional
method call rules. [*Example*: In the following code

```
// Begin class1.cs

  using System;
  using System.Diagnostics;

  class Class1
  {
    [Conditional("DEBUG")]
    public virtual void M()
    {
      Console.WriteLine("Class1.M executed");
    }
  }

// End class1.cs

// Begin class2.cs

  using System;

  class Class2: Class1
  {
    public override void M()
    {
      Console.WriteLine("Class2.M executed");
      base.M();              // base.M is not called!
    }
  }

// End class2.cs

// Begin class3.cs

  #define DEBUG

  using System;

  class Class3
  {
    public static void Test()
    {
      Class2 c = new Class2();
      c.M();                 // M is called
    }
  }

// End class3.cs
```

Class2 includes a call to the M defined in its base class. This call is omitted because the base
method is conditional based on the presence of the symbol DEBUG, which is undefined. Thus,
the method writes to the console "Class2.M executed" only. Judicious use of *pp-declaration*s
can eliminate such problems. *end example*]

24.4.2.2 Conditional attribute classes

An attribute class (§24.1) decorated with one or more `Conditional` attributes is a ***conditional attribute class***. A conditional attribute class is thus associated with the conditional compilation symbols declared in its `Conditional` attributes.

[*Example*:

```
using System;
using System.Diagnostics;
[Conditional("ALPHA")]
[Conditional("BETA")]
public class TestAttribute : Attribute{}
```

declares `TestAttribute` as a conditional attribute class associated with the conditional compilations symbols `ALPHA` and `BETA`. *end example*]

Attribute specifications (§24.2) of a conditional attribute are included if one or more of its associated conditional compilation symbols is defined at the point of specification, otherwise the attribute specification is omitted.

It is important to note that the inclusion or exclusion of an attribute specification of a conditional attribute class is controlled by the conditional compilation symbols at the point of the specification. [*Example*: In the example

File `test.cs`:

```
using System;
using System.Diagnostics;

[Conditional("DEBUG")]
public class TestAttribute : Attribute{}
```

File `class1.cs`:

```
#define DEBUG

[Test]        // TestAttribute is specified
class Class1{}
```

File `class2.cs`:

```
#undef DEBUG

[Test]        // TestAttribute is not specified
class Class2{}
```

the classes `Class1` and `Class2` are each decorated with attribute `Test`, which is conditional based on whether or not `DEBUG` is defined. Since this symbol is defined in the context of `Class1` but not `Class2`, the specification of the `Test` attribute on `Class1` is included, while the specification of the `Test` attribute on `Class2` is omitted. *end example*]

24.4.3 The Obsolete attribute

The attribute `Obsolete` is used to mark types and members of types that should no longer be used.

If a program uses a type or member that is decorated with the `Obsolete` attribute, then the compiler shall issue a warning or error in order to alert the developer, so the offending code can be fixed. Specifically, the compiler shall issue a warning if no error parameter is provided, or if the error parameter is provided and has the value false. The compiler shall issue a compile-time error if the error parameter is specified and has the value true.

What error parameter?

The preceding paragraph refers to the "error parameter" without defining it. As specified in Annex D, the `Obsolete` attribute has three constructors:

```
public ObsoleteAttribute();
public ObsoleteAttribute(string message);
public ObsoleteAttribute(string message, bool error);
```

The first of these issues a standard warning message (whose wording is not specified in the C# Standard), the second issues a warning using the supplied text, and the third issues a warning or an error depending on the value of the `bool` parameter as specified earlier. See also the annotation on §9.4.4.1.

[*Example*: In the following code

```
[Obsolete("This class is obsolete; use class B instead")]
class A
{
  public void F() {}
}

class B
{
  public void F() {}
}

class Test
{
  static void Main()
  {
    A a = new A(); // warning
    a.F();
  } }
```

the class A is decorated with the `Obsolete` attribute. Each use of A in Main results in a warning that includes the specified message, "This class is obsolete; use class B instead." *end example*]

Really obsolete

Some compilers take liberties with the requirement to issue warnings if items are attributed with `Obsolete` to reduce the amount of noise. For example, consider:

```
[Obsolete]
class ObsoleteClass {}
```

```
[Obsolete]
class AlsoObsolete: ObsoleteClass {}
```

At least one compiler current at the time of writing does not warn that the base class of obsolete class, `AlsoObsolete`, is itself obsolete. Though this might technically be a non-conformance with the Standard, it is, I believe, entirely reasonable.

Marek Safar

25 Generics

Not separate, just pragmatic

Generics is probably the main "headline" new feature introduced in C# 2.0. There was some discussion whether the description of generics should be spread throughout the text of the Standard or be given in a separate chapter. Generics is not a new separate feature, but extends existing ones; for example, classes can now be abstracted over types. On the one hand, this is a simple idea; just like a method is a statement abstracted over values (the parameters of the method), a generic class is a class abstracted over types (the type parameters of the generic class). That suggests distributing the details over the Standard document. On the other hand, it is a large conceptual step for some readers, which suggests a separate chapter on generics.

In the end, the decision for this version of the Standard came down largely to pragmatics; it was easier to add a separate chapter correctly. Some of the other new features in C# are distributed and not separated out. Maybe in the next version the decision for generics will change.

C# generics compared to Ada, C++, Haskell, Java 1.5...

The C# generics support is built on a rich history but of course is not exactly the same as any of its ancestors or siblings.

Value parameters

C# only supports types as generic parameters. If you are used to Ada generics or C++ templates, where both types and values can be used as generic parameters, you can achieve the equivalent in C# using generic parameters and constructor arguments. For example, the Ada 95 package for a generic bounded buffer:

```
generic
   type Element is private;
   Maximum : Integer;
package BoundedBuffer is
   ...
end BoundedBuffer;
...
package FloatFifty = new BoundedBuffer(Float, 50);
```

and the similar C++ template:

```
template<typename Element, int Maximum> class BoundedBuffer
{
   ...
};
...
BoundedBuffer<float,50> * FloatFifty = new BoundedBuffer
                                       <float,50>();
```

can be realized in C# as:

```
class BoundedBuffer<Element>
{
  public readonly int Maximum;

  public BoundedBuffer(int max)
  {
    Maximum = max;
  }
```

```
   ...
}
...
BoundedBuffer<float> FloatFifty = new BoundedBuffer<float>(50);
```

Constraints and type checking

The constraint mechanisms of C# and Ada 95 are different. For example, the Ada 95 package:

```
generic
   type Float_Type is digits <>;
package Generic_Complex_Numbers is
   ...
end Generic_Complex_Numbers;
```

can only be instantiated with floating point types and has no equivalent in C#. However, C# constraints are quite powerful, as described later in §25.7, and allow things not possible in Ada 95.

C#, like Ada, Haskell, ML, and similar languages, type checks your generic classes at the point of declaration. Any subsequent use of the generic class, provided the generic parameters satisfy any constraints specified, cannot produce type errors.

This is very different to C++, where templates are not type-checked at declaration but only later when the template arguments are known. This means that C++ delays type error reporting to the point of use, a potential disadvantage. However, it does allow some C++ templates to be defined that would not be possible with declaration time type checking. For example, the preceding Ada type for complex numbers can be declared in C++ as follows:

```
template<typename Float_Type> class Generic_Complex_Numbers
{
   ... code that assumes Float_Type is indeed a floating point type ...
};
```

However, unlike in Ada, this type will not be checked until it is instantiated. If at instantiation an inappropriate type is given for `Float_Type` then an error will *probably* result, unless you are unlucky—in which case the code might compile and function incorrectly.

This feature of delayed-typechecking is used by the C++ STL to enable its classes to be applied to disparate types. If you use templates in this way in your own designs, you will need to change your approach when using C#.

Other languages

If you are coming from Haskell, ML, and similar languages, you will probably find C# generics restrictive, just as you would if using Ada 95 et al.

C# 2.0 and Java 1.5 generics are very similar in features. There is, however, one potentially significant difference; Java 1.5 is designed to run on a virtual machine that does not support generics directly, whereas C# 2.0 usually runs on a virtual machine that does. This may have performance implications and does impact the availability of type information at runtime. The *Java™ Language Specification, Third Edition* statement on this is:

The decision not to make all generic types reifiable *[available at runtime]* is one of the most crucial, and controversial design decisions involving the language's type system.

This could be read more than one way. Of course, the impact of this difference depends entirely on the application.

25.1 Generic class declarations

A generic class declaration is a declaration of a class that requires type arguments to be supplied in order to form runtime types.

[*Note*: A class declaration (§17.1), can optionally define type parameters and their associated constraints:

> *class-declaration:*
> > *attributes*_{opt} *class-modifiers*_{opt} `partial`_{opt} `class`_{opt} *identifier*
> > > *type-parameter-list*_{opt} *class-base*_{opt}
> > *type-parameter-constraints-clause*_{opt} *class-body* `;`_{opt}

A class declaration shall not supply *type-parameter-constraints-clauses* (§25.7) unless it also supplies a *type-parameter-list* (§25.1.1).

A class declaration that supplies a *type-parameter-list* is a generic class declaration. *end note*]

Any class nested inside a generic class declaration or a generic struct declaration (§25.2) is itself a generic class declaration, since type parameters for the containing type shall be supplied to create a constructed type.

Generic class declarations follow the same rules as non-generic class declarations except where noted. Generic class declarations can be nested inside non-generic class declarations.

> **No type parameters in constructor declarations, but type arguments in constructor invocations**
>
> Note that a constructor declaration `C(...) { ...}` never takes type parameters (§17.10), either within a nongeneric type declaration `B` or within a generic type declaration `C<T>`:
>
> ```
> class B
> {
>    public B<T>(T value) { ...}     // compile-time error
> }
> class C<T>
> {
>    public C<T>(T value) { ...}     // compile-time error
> }
> ```
>
> However, a call to a constructor in a generic type must always have type arguments, as in `new C<int>(...)`, because what follows the `new` operator is a constructed type (§14.5.10.1):
>
> ```
> new C<int>(42);          // OK
> new C(42);               // compile-time error
> ```
>
> In particular, type inference (§25.6.4) is only used for generic method calls, never in constructor invocations.
>
> One could imagine a different language design in which type arguments were inferred from given constructor arguments at object creation, but in a language with subtyping that is likely to produce unexpected and undesirable results.

A generic class is referenced using a constructed type (§25.5). [*Example*: Given the generic class declaration

```
class List<T> {}
```

some examples of constructed types are List<T>, List<int> and List<List<string>>. *end example*] A constructed type that uses one or more type parameters, such as List<T>, is called an ***open constructed type*** (§25.5). A constructed type that uses no type parameters, such as List<int>, is called a ***closed constructed type*** (§25.5).

Generic types can be "overloaded" on the number of type parameters; that is two type declarations within the same namespace or outer type declaration can use the same identifier as long as they have a different number of type parameters.

```
class C {}
class C<V> {}      // OK
struct C<U,V> {}   // OK
class C<A,B> {}    // Error, C with two type parameters defined twice
```

Overloading on number of type parameters

The overloading of type declarations on the number of type parameters allows a generic type to coexist with a nongeneric type of the same name. This is particularly useful when a legacy nongeneric type needs to be used alongside a new generic type. It also allows all members of a family of generic types to have the same name, as shown by the two families of generic delegate types in the §25.4 annotation.

The type lookup rules used during type name resolution (§10.8), simple name resolution (§14.5.2) and member access (§14.5.4) respect the number of type parameters.

The base interfaces of a generic class declaration shall satisfy the uniqueness rule described in §25.3.1.

25.1.1 Type parameters

Type parameters can be supplied in a class declaration. Each type parameter is a simple identifier that denotes a placeholder for a type argument supplied to create a constructed type. A type parameter is a formal placeholder for a type that will be supplied later. By contrast, a type argument (§25.5.1) is the runtime type that is substituted for the type parameter when a constructed type is created.

> *type-parameter-list:*
>   < *type-parameters* >
>
> *type-parameters:*
>   *attributes*$_{opt}$ *type-parameter*
>   *type-parameters* , *attributes*$_{opt}$ *type-parameter*
>
> *type-parameter:*
>   *identifier*

Each type parameter in a class declaration defines a name in the declaration space (§10.3) of that class. Thus, it cannot have the same name as another type parameter or a member declared in that class. A type parameter shall not have the same name as the type itself.

The scope (§10.7) of a type parameter on a class includes the *class-base, type-parameter-constraints-clauses,* and *class-body.* Unlike members of a class, this scope does not extend to derived classes. Within its scope, a type parameter can be used as a type.

Since a type parameter can be instantiated with many different runtime type arguments, type parameters have slightly different operations and restrictions than other types. [*Note*: These include the following:

- A type parameter cannot be used directly to declare a base class or interface (§17.1.2).
- The rules for member lookup on type parameters depend on the constraints, if any, applied to the type parameter. They are detailed in §25.7.2.
- The available conversions for a type parameter depend on the constraints, if any, applied to the type parameter. They are detailed in §25.7.4.
- The literal `null` cannot be converted to a value of a type given by a type parameter, except if the type parameter is known to be a reference type (§25.7.4). However, a default value expression (§14.5.14) can be used to generate the default value of a type parameter.

> **Null comparison despite no conversion**
>
> Note that you *can* use the `==` and `!=` operators to compare an *unconstrained* type parameter with `null` (§14.9.6).
>
> ```
> class Eg<T>
> {
>   public static void Comparison(T t)
>   {
>     if (t == null) // allowed
>     {
>       . . .
>     }
>   }
> }
> ```
>
> At runtime, if `T` is a non-nullable value type, then `(t == null)` will always be `false` and, similarly, `(t != null)` will always be `true`.
>
> However, `t` *cannot* even be compared to itself when `T` is unconstrained:
>
> ```
> class Eg<T>
> {
>   public static void Comparison(T t)
>   {
>     if (t == t) // compile-time error
>     {
>       . . .
>     }
>   }
> }
> ```

- A `new` expression (§14.5.10.1) can only be used with a type parameter if the type parameter is constrained by a *constructor-constraint* or the value type constraint (§25.7).
- A type parameter cannot be used anywhere within an attribute (§24.2).
- A type parameter cannot be used in a member access to identify a static member (§14.5.4), or in a type name to identify a nested type (§10.8).
- In unsafe code, a type parameter cannot be used as an *unmanaged-type* (§27.2).

end note]

As a type, type parameters are purely a compile-time construct. At run-time, each type parameter is bound to a run-time type that was specified by supplying a type argument to the generic type declaration. Thus, the type of a variable declared with a type parameter will, at run-time, be a closed constructed type (§25.5.2). The run-time execution of all statements and expressions involving type parameters uses the runtime type that was supplied as the type argument for that parameter.

25.1.2 The instance type

Each class declaration has an associated constructed type, the ***instance type***. For a generic class declaration, the instance type is formed by creating a constructed type (§25.5) from the type declaration, with each of the supplied type arguments being the corresponding type parameter. Since the instance type uses the type parameters, it can only be used where the type parameters are in scope; that is, inside the class declaration. The instance type is the type of `this` for code written inside the class declaration. For non-generic classes, the instance type is simply the declared class. [*Example*: The following shows several class declarations along with their instance types:

```
class A<T>              // instance type: A<T>
{
  class B{}             // instance type: A<T>.B
  class C<U> {}         // instance type: A<T>.C<U>
}
class D{}              // instance type: D
```

end example]

25.1.3 Members of generic classes

All members of a generic class can use type parameters from any enclosing class, either directly or as part of a constructed type. When a particular closed constructed type (§25.5.2) is used at run-time, each use of a type parameter is replaced with the runtime type argument supplied to the constructed type. [*Example*:

```
class C<V>
{
  public V F1;
  public C<V> F2 = null;

  public C(V x)
  {
    this.F1 = x;
    this.F2 = this;
  }
}

class Application
{
  static void Main()
  {
    C<int> x1 = new C<int>(1);
    Console.WriteLine(x1.F1);    // Prints 1

    C<double> x2 = new C<double>(3.1415);
    Console.WriteLine(x2.F1);    // Prints 3.1415
  }
}
```

end example]

Within instance function members, the type of `this` is the instance type (§25.1.2) of the containing declaration.

Apart from the use of type parameters as types, members in generic class declarations follow the same rules as members of non-generic classes. Additional rules that apply to particular kinds of members are discussed in the following subclauses.

25.1.4 Static fields in generic classes

A static variable in a generic class declaration is shared amongst all instances of the same closed constructed type (§25.5.2), but is not shared amongst instances of different closed constructed types. These rules apply regardless of whether the type of the static variable involves any type parameters or not.

[*Example*:

```
class C<V>
{
  static int count = 0;

  public C()
  {
    count++;
  }

  public static int Count
  {
    get { return count; }
  }
}

class Application
{
  static void Main()
  {
    C<int> x1 = new C<int>();
    Console.WriteLine(C<int>.Count);    // Prints 1

    C<double> x2 = new C<double>();
    Console.WriteLine(C<double>.Count); // Prints 1
    Console.WriteLine(C<int>.Count);    // Prints 1

    C<int> x3 = new C<int>();
    Console.WriteLine(C<int>.Count);    // Prints 2
  }
}
```

end example]

Non-identical twins

As noted in the annotation on §10.5.3, different type instantiations of the same generic type are *twins* and can access each other's nonpublic members. This language design choice follows that of Java and Visual Basic and suggests that type instantiation is viewed rather differently than derivation.

In contrast, however, different type instantiations do not share static fields; there is one set of static fields per type instantiation. This design choice follows Visual Basic but differs from Java, and suggests that in this case type instantiation is viewed similarly to derivation, in which each derived class has its own set of static fields.

The Java model may seem more consistent; a type instantiation defines the value of a type parameter but the class identity does not change, so naturally access is allowed to non-public members and there is one set of static fields. However, the Java approach disallows the use of type parameters in the types of static fields and static methods, as there is only one instance of each static field and it cannot have different types in different type instantiations.

The model used by C# does allow the use of type parameters for static fields and static methods, as there is a different static field per distinct class created by instantiation. However, these distinct classes have access to each other's nonpublic members, weakening encapsulation.

The model used by the CLI provides static fields per type instantiation and leaves each hosted language to decide whether access to nonpublic members of other type instantiations is allowed, so distinct statics and strong encapsulation are possible.

25.1.5 Static constructors in generic classes

A static constructor in a generic class is used to initialize static fields and to perform other initialization for each different closed constructed type that is created from that generic class declaration. The type parameters of the generic type declaration are in scope, and can be used, within the body of the static constructor.

A new closed constructed class type is initialized the first time that either:

- An instance of the closed constructed type is created.
- Any of the static members of the closed constructed type are referenced.

To initialize a new closed constructed class type, first a new set of static fields (§25.1.4) for that particular closed constructed type is created. Each of the static fields is initialized to its default value (§12.2). Next, the static field initializers (§17.4.5.1) are executed for those static fields. Finally, the static constructor is executed.

Because the static constructor is executed exactly once for each closed constructed class type, it is a convenient place to enforce run-time checks on the type parameter that cannot be checked at compile-time via constraints (§25.7). [*Example*: The following type uses a static constructor to enforce that the type argument is an enum:

```
class Gen<T> where T: struct
{
  static Gen()
  {
    if (!typeof(T).IsEnum)
    {
      throw new ArgumentException("T must be an enum");
    }
  }
}
```

end example]

25.1.6 Accessing protected members

[*Note*: The accessibility domain (§10.5.2) of a protected member declared in a generic class includes the program text of all class declarations derived from any type constructed from that generic class. In the example:

```
class C<T>
{
  protected static T x;
}
class D: C<string>
{
  static void Main()
  {
    C<int>.x = 5;
  }
}
```

The reference to protected member `C<int>.x` in `D` is valid even though the class `D` derives from `C<string>`.

end note]

Within a generic class declaration, access to inherited protected instance members (§10.5.3) is permitted through an instance of any class type constructed from the generic class. [*Example*: In the following code

```
class C<T>
{
  protected T x;
}

class D<T>: C<T>
{
  static void F()
  {
    D<T> dt = new D<T>();
    D<int> di = new D<int>();
    D<string> ds = new D<string>();
    dt.x = default(T);
    di.x = 123;
    ds.x = "test";
  }
}
```

the three assignments to `x` are permitted because they all take place through instances of class types constructed from the generic type. *end example*]

25.1.7 Overloading in generic classes

Methods, constructors, indexers, and operators within a generic class declaration can be overloaded. While signatures as declared must be unique, it is possible that substitution of type arguments results in identical signatures. In such a situation, overload resolution will pick the most specific one (§14.4.2.2).

Clarifications

The previous sentence might be written:

In such a situation, overload resolution will pick the most specific (§14.4.2.2) of the original signatures (before substitution of type arguments), if it exists, and otherwise report an error.

The following sentence might be written:

The following examples show overloads that are valid according to this rule and substitutions that would introduce ambiguities.

[*Example*: The following examples show overloads that are valid according to this rule:

```
interface I1<T> {...}

interface I2<T> {...}

class G1<U>
{
  long F1(U u) {...}              // Overload resolution for G<int>.F1
  int F1(int i) {...}            // will pick non-generic

  void F3(I1<U> a) {...}         // Valid overload
  void F3(I2<U> a) {...}
}

class G2<U, V>
{
  void F5(U u, V v) {...}         // Overload resolution for
                                  // G2<int, int> would
  void F5(V v, U u) {...}         // fail

  void F6(U u, I1<V> v) {...}     // Valid, overload resolution
                                  // on G2<I1<int>, int> in is ambiguous
  void F6(I1<V> v, U u) {...}

  void F7(U u1, I1<V> v2) {...}  // Valid overload
  void F7(V v1, U u2) {...}

  void F8(ref U u) {...}          // Valid overload
  void F8(out V v) {...}
}
```

end example]

25.1.8 Parameter array methods and type parameters

Type parameters can be used in the type of a parameter array. [*Example*: Given the declaration

```
class C<V>
{
  static void F(int x, int y, params V[] args) {...}
}
```

the following invocations of the expanded form of the method:

```
C<int>.F(10, 20);
```

```
C<object>.F(10, 20, 30, 40);
C<string>.F(10, 20, "hello", "goodbye");
```

correspond exactly to:

```
C<int>.F(10, 20, new int[] {});
C<object>.F(10, 20, new object[] {30, 40});
C<string>.F(10, 20, new string[] {"hello", "goodbye"} );
```

end example]

25.1.9 Overriding and generic classes

Function members in generic classes can override function members in base classes, as usual. When determining the overridden base member, the members of the base classes shall be determined by substituting type arguments, as described in §25.5.4. Once the members of the base classes are determined, the rules for overriding are the same as for non-generic classes.

[*Example*: The following example demonstrates how the overriding rules work in the presence of generics:

```
abstract class C<T>
{
  public virtual T F() {...}
  public virtual C<T> G() {...}
  public virtual void H(C<T> x) {...}
}

class D: C<string>
{
  public override string F() {...}         // Ok
  public override C<string> G() {...}      // Ok
  public override void H(C<int> x) {...} // Error, should be C<string>
}

class E<T, U>: C<U>
{
  public override U F() {...}              // Ok
  public override C<U> G() {...}           // Ok
  public override void H(C<T> x) {...}     // Error, should be C<U>
}
```

end example]

25.1.10 Operators in generic classes

Generic class declarations can define operators, following the same rules as non-generic class declarations. The instance type (§25.1.2) of the class declaration shall be used in the declaration of operators in a manner analogous to the normal rules for operators, as follows:

- A unary operator shall take a single parameter of the instance type. The unary ++ and -- operators shall return the instance type or a type derived from the instance type.
- At least one of the parameters of a binary operator shall be of the instance type.
- Either the parameter type or the return type of a conversion operator shall be of the instance type.

[*Example*: The following shows some examples of valid operator declarations in a generic class:

```
class X<T>
{
  public static X<T> operator ++(X<T> operand) {...}
  public static int operator * (X<T> op1, int op2) {...}
  public static explicit operator X<T>(T value) {...}
}
```

end example]

> ## No operators on constructed type
>
> Note that it is not possible to declare an operator in a generic type such that it works only on certain types constructed from the generic type. For instance, let Expr<R> be the type of expression of type R. Then one can declare a static method Add(lhs, rhs) to build an addition expression of type int from subexpressions of type int, but one cannot overload the (+) operator to do the same job:
>
> ```
> public abstract class Expr<R>
> {
>   public abstract R Eval();   // This expr evaluates to an R
>
>   public static
>   Expr<int> operator +(Expr<int> lhs, Expr<int> rhs) { ...}      // Error
>
>   public static Expr<int> Add(Expr<int> lhs, Expr<int> rhs) { ...} // Ok
> }
> ```
>
> Since the method declaration is perfectly legal and implementable, the operator declaration would seem to be implementable as well as useful.

For a conversion operator that converts from a source type S to a target type T, when the rules specified in 17.9.3 are applied, any type parameters associated with S or T are considered to be unique types that have no inheritance relationship with other types, and any constraints on those type parameters are ignored.

[*Example*: In the following code

```
class C<T> {...}

class D<T>: C<T>
{
  public static implicit operator C<int>(D<T> value) {...}    // Ok
  public static implicit operator C<string>(D<T> value) {...} // Ok
  public static implicit operator C<T>(D<T> value) {...}      // Error
}
```

the first two operator declarations are permitted because, for the purposes of §17.9.3, T, and int and string, respectively, are considered unique types with no relationship. However, the third operator is an error because C<T> is the base class of D<T>. *end example]*

It is possible to declare operators that, for some type arguments, specify conversions that already exist as pre-defined conversions. [*Example*: In the following code

```
struct Convertible<T>
{
  public static implicit operator Convertible<T>(T value) {...}
```

```
        public static explicit operator T(Convertible<T> value) {...}
    }
```

when type `object` is specified as a type argument for `T`, the second operator declares a conversion that already exists (an implicit, and therefore also an explicit, conversion exists from any type to type `object`). *end example*]

In cases where a pre-defined conversion exists between two types, any user-defined conversions between those types are ignored. Specifically:

- If a pre-defined implicit conversion (§13.1) exists from type `S` to type `T`, all user-defined conversions (implicit or explicit) from `S` to `T` are ignored.
- If a pre-defined explicit conversion (§13.2) exists from type `S` to type `T`, any user-defined explicit conversions from `S` to `T` are ignored. However, user-defined implicit conversions from `S` to `T` are still considered.

[*Example*: For all types but `object`, the operators declared by the `Convertible<T>` type above do not conflict with pre-defined conversions. For example:

```
void F(int i, Convertible<int> n)
{
  i = n;                          // Error
  i = (int)n;                     // User-defined explicit conversion
  n = i;                          // User-defined implicit conversion
  n = (Convertible<int>)i;        // User-defined implicit conversion
}
```

However, for type `object`, pre-defined conversions hide the user-defined conversions in all cases but one:

```
void F(object o, Convertible<object> n)
{
  o = n;                          // Pre-defined boxing conversion
  o = (object)n;                  // Pre-defined boxing conversion
  n = o;                          // User-defined implicit conversion
  n = (Convertible<object>)o;     // Pre-defined unboxing conversion
}
```

end example]

Ignored ambiguity

The behavior exhibited by the previous example might be surprising to some. If a particular substitution of type parameters in a generic type results in two or more members having the same signature (§10.6), then any attempt to reference the member results in an ambiguous overloading error (§25.1.7). However, if the ambiguity is between a user-defined conversion and a built-in conversion, the ambiguity is silently ignored and the built-in one used.

This is shown in the preceding examples. Here is an additional example; consider:

```
class C<T, U> {}

class D<T, U> : C<T, U>
{
  public static implicit operator C<U, T>(D<T, U> value)
  {
    // conversion involving re-structuring value
```

```
    ...
  }
}

...

D<int, char> dii = new D<int, char>();
C<char, int> cii = dii;          // user-defined
                                 // conversion, value restructured

D<int, int> dii = new D<int, int>();
C<int, int> cii = dii;           // built-in base type conversion,
                                 // value not restructured
```

where we assume the conversion from a D<T, U> to a C<T, U> involves some work. In the first use, that work will be done; in the second use, it will not. This could be surprising.

This annotation was suggested by queries raised by Toshiaki Kurokawa as part of the project to translate the Standard into Japanese.

25.1.11 Nested types in generic classes

A generic class declaration can contain nested type declarations. The type parameters of the enclosing class can be used within the nested types. A nested type declaration can contain additional type parameters that apply only to the nested type.

Every type declaration contained within a generic class declaration is implicitly a generic type declaration. When writing a reference to a type nested within a generic type, the containing constructed type, including its type arguments, shall be named. However, from within the outer class, the nested type can be used without qualification; the instance type of the outer class can be implicitly used when constructing the nested type. [*Example*: The following example shows three different correct ways to refer to a constructed type created from Inner; the first two are equivalent:

```
class Outer<T>
{
  class Inner<U>
  {
    public static void F(T t, U u) {...}
  }

  static void F(T t)
  {
    Outer<T>.Inner<string>.F(t, "abc");    // These two statements have
    Inner<string>.F(t, "abc");             // the same effect

    Outer<int>.Inner<string>.F(3, "abc");  // This type is different

    Outer.Inner<string>.F(t, "abc");       // Error, Outer needs type arg
  }
}
```

end example]

Although it is bad programming style, a type parameter in a nested type can hide a member or type parameter declared in the outer type. [*Example*:

```
    class Outer<T>
  {
    class Inner<T>    // Valid, hides Outer's T
    {
      public T t;      // Refers to Inner's T
    }
  }
```

end example]

Thinking generically: containers

In previous versions of C#, as in many object-oriented languages, the standard idiom for container types is to make them general purpose by defining them over the common root class, namely, `object` in C#. For example, a dequeue class might be declared as:

```
public class Dequeue
{
  private class Node
  {
    public Node next;
    public object val;
    public Node prev;
  }

  int count;  // number of items in dequeue
  Node join;  // dummy node linking dequeue into a ring

  public void Add(object newItem)
  {
    Node link = new Node();

    link.val = newItem;
    link.next = join;
    link.prev = join.prev;
    join.prev.next = link;
    join.prev = link;
    count++;
  }

  public object Remove() { ...}

  public void AddFront(object newItem) { ...}

  public object RemoveBack() { ...}

    ...
  }
```

and used as:

```
  PersonnelRecord pr_1, pr_2;
  Dequeue promotions;
  ...
  promotions.Add(pr_1);
  ...
```

```
    pr_2 = (PersonnelRecord)promotions.Remove();
```

While this idiom produces re-usable containers, it suffers from two drawbacks:

- The container is heterogeneous; values of different type may be added as every type derives from `object`; and consequently
- When an item is removed, a type check must be performed and a runtime exception thrown if a value removed has a different type.

Generic containers address both these drawbacks, allowing homogeneous collections of any particular type (and any of its subtypes) to be created without the need for type-checking on removal. To design containers generically, determine what items can be of *some* type; for every group of such items that should be of the same type, abstract the type out as a type parameter. This process will produce the most general, and hence most re-usable, type while providing the best compile-time type-checking. If this process is performed correctly on an existing general purpose container, then the only changes that will be required are replacing some type names with type parameter names; *if further changes are required then the type abstraction is incorrect.* For example, the Dequeue class may be redefined generically as:

```
public class Dequeue<Item>
{
  private class Node
  {
    public Node next;
    public Item val;
    public Node prev;
  }

  ...

  public void Add(Item newItem)
  {
    Node link = new Node();

    link.val = newItem;
    link.next = join;
    link.prev = join.prev;
    join.prev.next = link;
    join.prev = link;
    count++;
  }

  public Item Remove() { ...}

  public void AddFront(Item newItem) { ...}

  public Item RemoveBack() { ...}

  ...
}
```

and used as:

```
PersonnelRecord pr_1, pr_2;
Dequeue<PersonnelRecord> promotions;
...
```

```
promotions.Add(pr_1);
...
pr_2 = promotions.Remove();
```

This version will do more compile-time type checking and produce better run-time code. Win–win.

25.2 Generic struct declarations

[*Note*: A struct declaration (§18.1), can optionally define type parameters and their associated constraints:

> *struct-declaration:*
>   *attributes*$_{opt}$ *struct-modifiers*$_{opt}$ partial$_{opt}$ struct *identifier*
>   *type-parameter-list*$_{opt}$ *struct-interfaces*$_{opt}$
>   *type-parameter-constraints-clauses*$_{opt}$ *struct-body* ;$_{opt}$

end note]

The rules for generic class declarations (§25.1 and its subclauses) apply equally to generic struct declarations, as do the exceptions noted in §18.3.

Infinite chains of constructed types

The storage size of a field of reference type can be determined irrespective of the type. For value types, the situation is the exact opposite: Without knowing the exact type of a field the storage size cannot be determined.

The fields of a type refer to other types and thereby form a network of inter-related types. Such a network may contain cycles except, as previously covered in an annotation on §18.3.1, there can be no cycle (including a cycle of length one, a type that references itself) containing only value types due to the need to determine (the finite) storage size.

When constructed types are involved, it becomes possible to construct infinite chains of types, and the number of inter-related types in a network can be infinite. If the types involved are all reference types this (maybe surprisingly) need not be a problem. However, if value types are involved, infinite chains can cause the same problems as cycles. For example, consider:

```
class B<U> { }

struct S<T>
{
  static T aField;
  static S<B<T>> s;    // Illegal: Infinite number of constructed types
}

class C<T>
{
  static C<B<T>> s;    // Legal: Only potentially infinite number
}
```

How much storage is required for the type S<T>? To determine this, the size of its static fields needs to be calculated; that is the size of a T field plus the size of an S<B<T>>, which in turn is the size of a B<T> field plus... *ad nauseam*. The size of S<T>'s static fields is infinite.

The type `C<T>` does not suffer from this problem because the size of its static field `s`, being a reference type, is known (and finite).

The same problem can occur with instance fields.

There is a degenerate case of the preceding example:

```
class B<U> {}

struct S<T>
{
   static S<B<T>> s;    // Illegal? Infinite number of constructed types
}
```

Here the storage size of the type `S<T>`'s static fields is zero. Should a compiler be able to deal with this degenerate case? It still involves an infinite number of types, and representing a type requires more than simply allocating storage for its fields. It is possible for a compiler to handle this particular case, but also quite reasonable if it does not. At the time of writing, Microsoft's C# 2.0 compiler rejects this program with a message about *cycle in the struct layout*, which is, strictly speaking, misleading. The Mono C# compiler accepts the program, but the resulting assembly crashes its runtime system with a segmentation fault.

25.3 Generic interface declarations

[*Note*: An interface declaration (§20.1), can optionally define type parameters and their associated constraints:

> *interface-declaration:*
>   *attributes*$_{opt}$ *interface-modifiers*$_{opt}$ `partial`$_{opt}$ `interface` *identifier*
>   *type-parameter-list*$_{opt}$ *interface-base*$_{opt}$
>   *type-parameter-constraints-clauses*$_{opt}$ *interface-body* `;`$_{opt}$

end note]

Except where noted below, generic interface declarations follow the same rules as non-generic interface declarations.

Each type parameter in an interface declaration defines a name in the declaration space (§10.3) of that interface. The scope (§10.7) of a type parameter on an interface includes the *interface-base*, *type-parameter-constraints-clauses*, and *interface-body*. Within its scope, a type parameter can be used as a type. The same restrictions apply to type parameters on interfaces as apply to type parameter on classes (§25.1.1).

25.3.1 Uniqueness of implemented interfaces

The interfaces implemented by a generic type declaration shall remain unique for all possible constructed types. Without this rule, it would be impossible to determine the correct method to call for certain constructed types. [*Example*: Suppose a generic class declaration were permitted to be written as follows:

```
interface I<T>
{
  void F();
}

class X<U, V>: I<U>, I<V>          // Error: I<U> and I<V> conflict
{
```

```
      void I<U>.F() {...}
      void I<V>.F() {...}
   }
```

Were this permitted, it would be impossible to determine which code to execute in the following case:

```
   I<int> x = new X<int,int>();
   x.F();
```

end example]

To determine if the interface list of a generic type declaration is valid, the following steps are performed:

- Let L be the list of interfaces directly specified in a generic class, struct, or interface declaration C.
- Add to L any base interfaces of the interfaces already in L.
- Remove any duplicates from L.
- If any possible constructed type created from C would, after type arguments are substituted into L, cause two interfaces in L to be identical, then the declaration of C is invalid. Constraint declarations are not considered when determining all possible constructed types.

[*Note*: In the class declaration X above, the interface list L consists of I<U> and I<V>. The declaration is invalid because any constructed type with U and V being the same type would cause these two interfaces to be identical types. *end note*]

[*Example*: It is possible for interfaces specified at different inheritance levels to unify:

```
   interface I<T>
   {
     void F();
   }

   class Base<U>: I<U>
   {
     void I<U>.F() {...}
   }

   class Derived<U, V>: Base<U>, I<V>  // Ok
   {
     void I<V>.F() {...}
   }
```

This code is valid even though Derived<U, V> implements both I<U> and I<V>. The code

```
   I<int> x = new Derived<int,int>();
   x.F();
```

invokes the method in Derived, since Derived<int, int> effectively re-implements I<int> (§20.4.4). *end example*]

25.3.2 Explicit interface member implementations

Explicit interface member implementations work with constructed interface types in essentially the same way as with simple interface types. As usual, an explicit interface member implementation shall be qualified by an *interface-type* indicating which interface is being implemented. This type can be a simple interface or a constructed interface [*Example*:

```
interface IList<ElementType>
{
  ElementType[] GetElements();
}

interface IDictionary<KeyType,ElementType>
{
  ElementType this[KeyType key] { get; }
  void Add(KeyType key, ElementType value);
}

class List<ElementType>: IList<ElementType>,
                         IDictionary<int,ElementType>
{
  ElementType[] IList<ElementType>.GetElements() {...}

  // Return the element at index
  ElementType IDictionary<int,ElementType>.this[int index] {...}

  // Add value at the index
  void IDictionary<int,ElementType>.Add(int index, ElementType value)
    {...}
}
```

end example]

25.4 Generic delegate declarations

[*Note*: A delegate declaration (§22.1), can optionally define type parameters and their associated constraints:

> *delegate-declaration:*
>> *attributes_{opt}*   *delegate-modifiers_{opt}*   delegate   *return-type*   *identifier*
>>> *type-parameter-list_{opt}*
>>> (*formal-parameter-list_{opt}*   )   *type-parameter-constraints-clauses_{opt}*   ;

end note]

Generic delegate declarations follow the same rules as non-generic delegate declarations, except where noted below. Each type parameter in a generic delegate declaration defines a name in a special declaration space (§10.3) that is associated with that delegate declaration. The scope (§10.7) of a type parameter in a delegate declaration includes the *return-type*, *formal-parameter-list*, and *type-parameter-constraints-clauses*.

Like other generic type declarations, type arguments shall be given to create a constructed delegate type. The parameter types and return type of a constructed delegate type are created by substituting, for each type parameter in the delegate declaration, the corresponding type argument of the constructed delegate type. The resulting return type and parameter types are used in determining what methods are consistent (§22.1) with a constructed delegate type. [*Example*:

```
delegate bool Predicate<T>(T value);

class X
```

```
    {
      static void Main()
      {
        Predicate<int> p1 =
          delegate(int i)
          {
            ...
          };

        Predicate<string> p2 =
          delegate(string s)
          {
            ...
          };
      }
    }
```

end example]

Generic function types

Function types can be defined by a family of generic delegate types; here are the first few members of the family:

```
public delegate A Function<A>();                    // type void → A
public delegate B Function<A, B>(A argA);           // type A → B
public delegate C Function<A, B, C>(A argA, B argB); // type A × B → C
...
```

These declarations are useful as types of delegates and anonymous methods, as illustrated in an annotation in §14.5.15.5. All the function types can be given the same name (Function) because C# permits overloading generic types on the number of type parameters. Since void is not a legal type argument for a type parameter, you also need a parallel family Action of types of functions that do not return a result:

```
public delegate void Action();                      // type void → void
public delegate void Action<A>(A argA);             // type A → void
public delegate void Action<A, B>(A argA, B argB);  // type A × B → void
...
```

These types are so useful they have been defined in a technical report, Ecma TR-89/ISO TR-25438, accompanying the CLI Standard (they were unfortunately submitted too late to be considered for inclusion in the main Standard but deemed important enough to require a TR). However, they are not CLI specific. Indeed, they are written in Standard C# and are available in source form from http://kahu.zoot.net.nz/ecma.

25.5 Constructed types

A generic type declaration, by itself, denotes an **unbound generic type** that is used as a "blue-print" to form many different types, by way of applying **type arguments**. The type arguments are written within angle brackets (< and >) immediately following the name of the generic type declaration. A type that is named with at least one type argument is called a **constructed type**. A constructed type can be used in most places in the language in which a type name can appear. An unbound generic type can only be used within a *typeof-expression* (§14.5.11).

Constructed types can also be used in expressions as simple names (§14.5.2) or when accessing a member (§14.5.4).

When a *namespace-or-type-name* is evaluated, only generic types with the correct number of type parameters are considered. Thus, it is possible to use the same identifier to identify different types, as long as the types have different numbers of type parameters. This is useful when mixing generic and non-generic classes in the same program. [*Example*:

```
namespace Widgets
{
  class Queue {...}
  class Queue<ElementType> {...}
}

namespace MyApplication
{
  using Widgets;

  class X
  {
    Queue q1;          //Non-generic Widgets.Queue
    Queue<int> q2;   // Generic Widgets.Queue
  }
}
```

end example]

The detailed rules for name lookup in the *namespace-or-typename* productions is described in §10.8. The resolution of ambiguities in these productions is described in §9.2.3.

A *type-name* might identify a constructed type even though it doesn't specify type parameters directly. This can occur where a type is nested within a generic class declaration, and the instance type of the containing declaration is implicitly used for name lookup (§25.1.11). [*Example*:

```
class Outer<T>
{
  public class Inner {...}
  public Inner i;        // Type of i is Outer<T>.Inner
}
```

end example]

[*Note*: In unsafe code, a constructed type shall not be used as an *unmanaged-type* (25.2). *end note*]

25.5.1 Type arguments
Each argument in a type argument list is simply a *type*.

> *type-argument-list:*
>   <   *type-arguments*   >
>
> *type-arguments:*
>   *type-argument*
>   *type-arguments*   ,   *type-argument*
>
> *type-argument:*
>   *type*

Type arguments can be constructed types or type parameters. [*Note*: In unsafe code (§27), a *type-argument* shall not be a *pointer-type*. *end note*] Each type argument shall satisfy any constraints on the corresponding type parameter (§25.7.1).

25.5.2 Open and closed types

All types can be classified as ***open types*** or ***closed types***. An open type is a type that involves type parameters. More specifically:

- A type parameter defines an open type.
- An array type is an open type if and only if its element type is an open type.
- A constructed type is an open type if and only if one or more of its type arguments is an open type. A constructed nested type is an open type if and only if one or more of its type arguments or the type arguments of its containing type(s) is an open type.

A closed type is a type that is not an open type.

At run-time, all of the code within a generic type declaration is executed in the context of a closed constructed type that was created by applying type arguments to the generic declaration. Each type parameter within the generic type is bound to a particular run-time type. The run-time processing of all statements and expressions always occurs with closed types, and open types occur only during compile-time processing.

Each closed constructed type has its own set of static variables, which are not shared with any other closed constructed types. Since an open type does not exist at run-time, there are no static variables associated with an open type. Two closed constructed types are the same type if they are constructed from the same unbound generic type, and their corresponding type arguments are the same type.

25.5.3 Base classes and interfaces of a constructed type

A constructed class type has a direct base class, just like a simple class type. If the generic class declaration does not specify a base class, the base class is `object`. If a base class is specified in the generic class declaration, the base class of the constructed type is obtained by substituting, for each *type-parameter* in the base class declaration, the corresponding *type-argument* of the constructed type. [*Example*: Given the generic class declarations

```
class B<U,V> {...}

class G<T> : B<string,T[]> {...}
```

the base class of the constructed type G<int> would be B<string,int[]>. *end example*]

Similarly, constructed class, struct, and interface types have a set of explicit base interfaces. The explicit base interfaces are formed by taking the explicit base interface declarations on the generic type declaration, and substituting, for each *type-parameter* in the base interface declaration, the corresponding *type-argument* of the constructed type.

The set of all base classes and base interfaces for a type is formed, as usual, by recursively getting the base classes and interfaces of the immediate base classes and interfaces. [*Example*: Given the generic class declarations:

```
class A {...}

class B<T> : A {...}

class C<T> : B<IComparable<T>> {...}
```

```
class D<T>: C<T[ ]>{...}
```

the base classes of D<int> are C<int[ ]>, B<IComparable<int[ ]>>, A, and object. *end example*]

25.5.4 Members of a constructed type

The non-inherited members of a constructed type are obtained by substituting, for each *type-parameter* in the member declaration, the corresponding *type-argument* of the constructed type. The substitution process is based on the semantic meaning of type declarations, and is not simply textual substitution.

[*Example*: Given the generic class declaration

```
class Gen<T,U>
{
  public T[,] a;

  public void G(int i, T t, Gen<U,T> gt) {...}

  public U Prop { get {...} set {...} }

  public int H(double d) {...}
}
```

the constructed type Gen<int[ ],IComparable<string>> has the following members:

```
public int[,][ ] a;

public void G(int i, int[ ] t, Gen<IComparable<string>,int[ ]> gt) {...}

public IComparable<string> Prop { get {...} set {...} }

public int H(double d) {...}
```

The type of the member a in the generic class declaration Gen is "two-dimensional array of T", so the type of the member a in the constructed type above is "two-dimensional array of one-dimensional array of int", or int[,][ ]. *end example*]

The inherited members of a constructed type are obtained in a similar way. First, all the members of the immediate base class are determined. If the base class is itself a constructed type, this might involve a recursive application of the current rule. Then, each of the inherited members is transformed by substituting, for each *type-parameter* in the member declaration, the corresponding *type-argument* of the constructed type. [*Example*:

```
class B<U>
{
  public U F(long index) {...}
}

class D<T>: B<T[ ]>
{
  public T G(string s) {...}
}
```

In the above example, the constructed type D<int> has a non-inherited member public int G(string s) obtained by substituting the type argument int for the type parameter T. D<int> also has an inherited member from the class declaration B. This inherited member is determined by first determining the members of the constructed type B<T[ ]> by substituting T[ ] for U, yielding `public T[ ] F(long index)`. Then, the type argument `int` is substituted for the type parameter T, yielding the inherited member `public int[ ] F(long index)`. *end example*]

25.5.5 Accessibility of a constructed type

A constructed type $C<T_1, \ldots, T_N>$ is accessible when all of its components C, $T_1, \ldots, T_N$ are accessible. More precisely, the accessibility domain for a constructed type is the intersection of the accessibility domain of the unbound generic type and the accessibility domains of the type arguments.

25.5.6 Conversions

Constructed types follow the same conversion rules (§13) as do non-generic types. When applying these rules, the base classes and interfaces of constructed types shall be determined as described in §25.5.3.

No special conversions exist between constructed reference types other than those described in §13. In particular, unlike array types, constructed reference types do not permit co-variant conversions (§19.5). This means that a type List<B> has no conversion (either implicit or explicit) to List<A> even if B is derived from A. Likewise, no conversion exists from List<B> to List<object>.

[*Note*: The rationale for this is simple: if a conversion to List<A> is permitted, then apparently, one can store values of type A into the list. However, this would break the invariant that every object in a list of type List<B> is always a value of type B, or else unexpected failures can occur when assigning into collection classes. *end note*]

[*Example*: The behavior of conversions and runtime type checks is illustrated below:

```
class A{...}

class B: A{...}

class Collection{...}

class List<T>: Collection{...}

class Test
{
  void F()
  {
    List<A> listA = new List<A>();
    List<B> listB = new List<B>();

    Collection c1 = listA;        // Ok, List<A> is a Collection
    Collection c2 = listB;        // Ok, List<B> is a Collection

    List<A> a1 = listB;           // Error, no implicit conversion
    List<A> a2 = (List<A>)listB;  // Error, no explicit conversion
  }
}
```

end example]

25.5.7 Using alias directives

Using aliases can name a closed constructed type, but shall not name a generic type declaration without supplying type arguments. [*Example*:

```
namespace N1
{
  class A<T>
  {
    class B {}
  }
}

namespace N2
{
  using W = N1.A;          // Error, cannot name generic type

  using X = N1.A.B;        // Error, cannot name generic type

  using Y = N1.A<int>;   // Ok, can name closed constructed type
}
```

end example]

Aliases do not take type parameters

Note that a `using` alias cannot take type parameters, although that could be most useful:

```
using Renamer<T> = Dictionary<List<T>, T>;
```

This could be made a purely abbreviatory device with structural equivalence of types, as for other `using` aliases. Allowing it would probably not cause any conceptual or practical problems.

25.6 Generic methods

A generic method is a method whose declaration includes a type-parameter-list (§17.5 and §20.2.1). Generic methods can be declared inside class, struct, or interface declarations, which can themselves, be either generic or non-generic. If a generic method is declared inside a generic type declaration, the body of the method can refer to both the type parameters of the method, and the type parameters of the containing declaration.

The *type-parameter-list* and *type-parameter-constraints-clauses* of a generic method declaration have the same syntax and purpose as in a generic type declaration. The method's *type-parameters* are in scope throughout the *method-declaration*, and can be used to form types throughout that scope in *return-type*, *method-body*, and *type-parameter-constraints-clauses* but not in *attributes*.

The name of a method type parameter cannot be the same as the name of an ordinary parameter in the same method.

[*Example*: The following example finds the first element in an array, if any, that satisfies the given test delegate. (Generic delegates are described in §25.4.)

```
public delegate bool Test<T>(T item);

public class Finder
{
```

```
        public static T Find<T>(T[ ] items, Test<T> test)
        {
          foreach (T item in items)
          {
            if (test(item))
              return item;
          }
          throw new InvalidOperationException("Item not found");
        }
      }
```

end example]

25.6.1 Generic method signatures

For the purposes of signature comparisons any *type-parameter-constraints-clauses* are ignored, as are the names of the method's *type-parameter*s, but the number of generic type parameters is relevant, as are the ordinal positions of type-parameters in left-to-right ordering (§10.6). [*Example*: The following example shows how method signatures are affected by this rule:

```
    class A{ }

    class B{ }

    interface IX
    {
      T F1<T>(T[ ] a, int i);      // Error, both declarations have the same
      void F1<U>(U[ ] a, int i);   // signature because return type and type
                                   // parameter names are not significant

      void F2<T>(int x);           // Ok, the number of type parameters is
      void F2(int x);              // part of the signature

      void F3<T>(T t) where T: A;  // Error, constraints are not
      void F3<T>(T t) where T: B;  // considered in signatures
    }
```

end example]

25.6.2 Virtual generic methods

Generic methods can be declared using the `abstract`, `virtual`, and `override` modifiers. The signature matching rules described in §10.6 are used when matching methods for overriding or interface implementation. When a generic method overrides a generic method declared in a base class, or is an explicit interface member implementation of a method in a base interface, the method shall not specify any *type-parameter-constraints-clauses*. In these cases, the type parameters of the method inherit constraints from the method being overridden or implemented. [*Example*:

```
    abstract class Base
    {
      public abstract T F<T,U>(T t, U u) where U : T;

      public abstract T G<T>(T t) where T: IComparable;
    }
```

```
interface I
{
  bool M<T>(T a, T b) where T : class;
}

class Derived: Base, I
{

  public override X F<X,Y>(X x, Y y)    // Ok
  {
    // The implicit constraint Y : X is inherited
    // so y is implicitly convertible to type X.
    return y;
  }

  public override T G<T>(T t)
    where T: IComparable    // Error - constraints not allowed
  {...}

  bool I.M<U>(U a, U b)
  {
    // The implicit constraint U : class is inherited
    // so a and b can be compared using the reference type
    // equality operators.
    return a == b;
  }
}
```

The override of F is valid because type parameter names are permitted to differ. Within Derived.F, the type parameter Y implicitly has the constraint Y : X as inherited from Base.F. The override of G is invalid because overrides are not permitted to specify type parameter constraints. The explicit method implementation I.M in Derived implicitly inherits the U : class constraint from the interface method. *end example*]

When a generic method implicitly implements an interface method, the constraints given for each method type parameter shall be equivalent in both declarations (after any interface type parameters are replaced with the appropriate type arguments), where method type parameters are identified by ordinal positions, left to right. [*Example*:

```
interface I<A, B, C>
{
  void F<T>(T t) where T : A;
  void G<T>(T t) where T : B;
  void H<T>(T t) where T : C;
}

class Cls : I<object,Cls,string>
{
  public void F<T>(T t) {...}                // Ok
  public void G<T>(T t) where T : Cls {...}  // Ok
  public void H<T>(T t) where T : string {...} // Error
}
```

The method Cls.F<T> implicitly implements I<object,Cls,string>.F<T>. In this case, Cls.F<T> is not required (nor permitted) to specify the constraint T : object since object is an implicit constraint on all type parameters. The method `Cls.G<T>` implicitly implements `I<object,Cls,string>.G<T>` because the constraints match those in the interface, after the interface type parameters are replaced with the corresponding type arguments. The constraint for method `Cls.H<T>` is an error since sealed types (string in this case) cannot be used as constraints. Omitting the constraint would also be an error since constraints of implicit interface method implementations are required to match. Thus, it's impossible to implicitly implement `I<object,Cls,string>.H<T>`. This interface method needs to be implemented using an explicit interface member implementation:

```
class Cls : I<object,Cls,string>
{
  ...
  public void H<U>(U u) where U : class {...}
  void I<object,Cls,string>.H<T>(T t)
  {
    string s = t;  // Ok
    H<T>(t);
  }
}
```

In this example, the explicit interface member implementation invokes a public method having strictly weaker constraints. Note that the assignment from `t` to `s` is valid since `T` inherits a constraint of `T : string`, even though this constraint is not expressible in source code. *end example*]

25.6.3 Calling generic methods

A generic method invocation can explicitly specify a type argument list, or it can omit the type argument list and rely on type inference to determine the type arguments. The exact compile-time processing of a method invocation, including a generic method invocation, is described in §14.5.5.1. When a generic method is invoked without a type argument list, type inference takes place as described in §25.6.4.

[*Example*: The following example shows how overload resolution occurs after type inference and after type arguments are substituted into the parameter list:

```
class Test
{
  static void F<T>(int x, T y)
  {
    Console.WriteLine("one");
  }

  static void F<T>(T x, long y)
  {
    Console.WriteLine("two");
  }

  static void Main()
  {
    F<int>(5, 324);     // Ok, prints "one"
    F<byte>(5, 324);    // Ok, prints "two"
    F<double>(5, 324);  // Error, ambiguous

    F(5, 324);          // Ok, prints "one"
    F(5, 324L);         // Error, ambiguous
```

```
      }
    }
```

end example]

Polymorphic recursion

A polymorphic method M<U> may call itself recursively with a different type argument than U, as shown:

```
struct S<T> {}

class PolymorphicRecursion
{
  static void M<U> (int i, U s)
  {
    if (i > 0)
      M<S<U>> (i-1, new S<U> ());
  }
}
```

Calling M<double>(N, 3.14) will create N different constructed types from generic struct S<T>. This is disallowed in some functional languages that otherwise support generic (parametric polymorphic) functions. In C# it is permitted by this Standard, and is supported by both Microsoft's and Mono's current compilers, which construct types as needed at run-time. Given the strong theoretical background of the original designers of C# generics, it is clear that this was a conscious design decision. Polymorphic recursion usefully permits method Eval on type Expr<bool> to call method Eval on type Expr<int>, as would happen in an interpreter for arithmetic/logical expressions with comparison operators.

Further examples can be found among Peter Sestoft's generic C# sample programs, at http://www.itu.dk/people/sestoft/gcsharp/.

25.6.4 Inference of type arguments

When a generic method is called without specifying type arguments, a *type inference* process attempts to infer type arguments for the call. The presence of type inference allows a more convenient syntax to be used for calling a generic method, and allows the programmer to avoid specifying redundant type information. [*Example*: Given the method declaration:

```
class Chooser
{
  static Random rand = new Random();

  public static T Choose<T> (T first, T second)
  {
    return (rand.Next(2) == 0) ? first : second;
  }
}
```

it is possible to invoke the Choose method without explicitly specifying a type argument:

```
int i = Chooser.Choose(5, 213);              // Calls Choose<int>

string s = Chooser.Choose("foo", "bar");     // Calls Choose<string>
```

Through type inference, the type arguments `int` and `string` are determined from the arguments to the method. *end example*]

Type inference occurs as part of the compile-time processing of a method invocation (§14.5.5.1) and takes place before the overload resolution step of the invocation. When a particular method group is specified in a method invocation, and no type arguments are specified as part of the method invocation, type inference is applied to each generic method in the method group. If type inference succeeds, then the inferred type arguments are used to determine the types of arguments for subsequent overload resolution. If overload resolution chooses a generic method as the one to invoke, then the inferred type arguments are used as the runtime type arguments for the invocation. If type inference for a particular method fails, that method does not participate in overload resolution. The failure of type inference, in and of itself, does not cause a compile-time error. However, it often leads to a compile-time error when overload resolution then fails to find any applicable methods.

If the supplied number of arguments is different from the number of parameters in the method, then inference immediately fails. Otherwise, type inference first occurs independently for each regular argument that is supplied to the method. Assume this argument has type A, and the corresponding parameter has type P. Type inferences are produced by relating the types A and P according to the following steps:

- Nothing is inferred from the argument (but type inference succeeds) if any of the following are true:
    - P does not involve any method type parameters.
    - The argument has the null type (§11.2.7).
    - The argument is an anonymous method.
    - The argument is a method group.
- If P is an array type, and A is an array type of the same rank, then replace A and P, respectively, with the element types of A and P, and repeat this step.
- If P is an array type, and A is an instantiation of `IList<>`, `ICollection<>`, or `IEnumerable<>`, then replace A and P, respectively, with the element types of A and P, and repeat this step.
- If P is an array type, and A is not an array type of the same rank, or an instantiation of `IList<>`, `ICollection<>`, or `IEnumerable<>`, then type inference fails for the generic method.
- If P is a method type parameter, then type inference succeeds for this argument, and A is the type inferred for that type parameter.
- Otherwise, P shall be a constructed type. If, for each method type parameter M_X that occurs in P, exactly one type T_X can be determined such that replacing each M_X with each T_X produces a type to which A is convertible by a standard implicit conversion, then inferencing succeeds for this argument, and each T_X is the type inferred for each M_X. Method type parameter constraints, if any, are ignored for the purpose of type inference. If, for a given M_X, no T_X exists, or more than one T_X exists, then type inference fails for the generic method (a situation where more than one T_X exists can only occur if P is a generic interface type and A implements multiple constructed versions of that interface).

Specification bug

Mads Torgersen spotted some mistakes in the preceding specification: *Bullets three and four above have A and P swapped. Arrays convert to the interfaces, not the other way around.*
To clarify:

- The type `IList<>` has base interfaces `ICollection<>` and `IEnumerable<>` (Annex D). All three are constructed types.
- Standard implicit conversions exist for any array type to `IList<>`, and for any interface to its base interfaces (§13.1.4).
- Therefore, in the case where P is either `IList<>`, `ICollection<>`, or `IEnumerable<>` and A is an array type, then A is implicitly converted to the appropriate interface and the rules in the last bullet are applied.

If all of the method arguments are processed successfully by the above algorithm, then all inferences that were produced from the arguments are pooled. Type inference is said to have succeeded for the given generic method and argument list if both of the following are true:

- Each type parameter of the method had a type argument inferred for it (in short, the set of inferences is **complete**).
- For each type parameter, all of the inferences for that type parameter infer the same type argument (in short, the set of inferences is **consistent**).

If the generic method was declared with a parameter array (§17.5.1.4), then type inference is first performed against the method in its normal form. If type inference succeeds, and the resultant method is applicable, then the method is eligible for overload resolution in its normal form. Otherwise, type inference is performed against the method in its expanded form (§14.4.2.1).

Parameter arrays

The treatment of parameter arrays, which parallels their handling in overload resolution, means that the following program will work:

```
private static readonly Random rnd = new Random();

public static T Choose<T>(params T[] from)
{
    return from[ rnd.Next(from.Length)];
}

public static void Main()
{
    Console.WriteLine(Choose(7, 9, 13));
    Console.WriteLine(Choose("Oslo", "Honolulu"));
    string[] keywords = {"abstract", "as", "base", "bool"};
    Console.WriteLine(Choose(keywords));
}
```

Type inference will succeed for the first two calls to `Choose` because of the rule just before this annotation, thanks to the `params` modifier. If it did not, then the subsequent overload resolution would not find the expanded form (§14.4.2.1) of the `Choose` method. Type inference will succeed for the last call because of the ordinary type inference rules (second bullet in the first bullet list), essentially as if there were no `params` modifier.

25.6.5 Using a generic method with a delegate

An instance of a delegate can be created that refers to a generic method declaration. The exact compile-time processing of a delegate creation expression, including a delegate creation expression that refers to a generic method, is described in §14.5.10.3.

The type arguments used when invoking a generic method through a delegate are determined when the delegate is instantiated. The type arguments can be given explicitly via a *type-argument-list*, or determined by type inference (§25.6.4). If type inference is used, the parameter types of the delegate are used as argument types in the inference process. The return type of the delegate is *not* used for inference. [*Example*: The following example shows both ways of supplying a type argument to a delegate instantiation expression:

```
delegate int D(string s, int i);

delegate int E();

class X
{
  public static T F<T>(string s, T t) {...}

  public static T G<T>() {...}

  static void Main()
  {
    D d1 = new D(F<int>);    // Ok, type argument given explicitly
    D d2 = new D(F);         // Ok, int inferred as type argument

    E e1 = new E(G<int>);    // Ok, type argument given explicitly
    E e2 = new E(G);         // Error, cannot infer from return type
  }
}
```

be given, as in `new D<int>(...)` and `new E<int>(...)`. This is because the `new` operator must be followed by a type (§14.5.10.1), which in this case is a constructed delegate type. The type arguments on the constructors do not affect type inference for the generic method's type arguments:

```
delegate U D<U>(string s, U i);

delegate U E<U>();

class X
{
  public static T F<T>(string s, T t) { return default(T); }

  public static T G<T>() { return default(T); }

  static void Main()
  {
    D<int> d12 = F<int>;               // Ok, type argument given explicitly
    D<int> d22 = F;                    // Ok, int inferred as type argument
    E<int> e12 = G<int>;               // Ok, type argument given explicitly
    E<int> e22 = G;                    // Error, cannot infer from
                                       //        return type
    D<int> d11 = new D<int>(F<int>); // Ok, type argument given explicitly
    D<int> d21 = new D<int>(F);        // Ok, int inferred as type argument
    E<int> e11 = new E<int>(G<int>); // Ok, type argument given explicitly
    E<int> e21 = new E<int>(G);        // Error, cannot infer from
                                       //        return type
  }
}
```

end example]

Whenever a generic method is used to create delegate instance, type arguments are given or inferred when the delegate instance is created, and a *type-argument-list* shall not be supplied when the delegate is invoked (22.3).

25.6.6 No generic properties, events, indexers, operators, constructors, or finalizers

Properties, events, indexers, operators, constructors, and finalizers shall not themselves have type parameters (although they can occur in generic types, and use the type parameters from an enclosing type).

Rationale: no generic constructors, operators, properties, or indexers

A constructor, operator, property, or indexer declared within a generic class can use the type parameters of the class, but type parameters on these constructors themselves are disallowed. Here, I give the rationale for these decisions.

Generic constructors are not provided. To see why, consider this program fragment:

```
public class List<T>
{
  public List<TSubtype>(IEnumerable<TSubtype> collection)
  [public T this <T> [int index]
```

```
        where TSubtype : T { ...}
    }
```

Unfortunately, there is no good syntax to call this constructor as two sets of generic arguments are required, which is not particularly readable:

```
    List<string> stringList;
    List<object> newList = new List<object><string>(stringList);
                                                 // very ugly
```

A more serious problem is that because types can be overloaded on the number of type parameters, such constructor calls could be ambiguous:

```
    Foo(new List<string>())
```

Is that a call to the nongeneric constructor for a generic type List<T> taking one argument? Or is it a call to a generic constructor on a nongeneric type List? Requiring the use of an empty type parameter list <> to enable disambiguation would be ugly.

Generic operators are not provided. They would suffer from a similar problem. A generic operator declaration would look something like this:

```
    class C
    {
      public static operator + <T> (T t, C c) { ...}
      ...
    }
```

Now consider this calling code:

```
    C c1, c2;
    ...
    x = c1 + c2; // where to put the type argument?
```

Adding a type argument list here would be potentially confusing and ugly. Type inference would *have* to be used, where it is optional elsewhere.

Generic properties are not provided. Consider this example:

```
    class Program
    {
      public T Value<T>
      {
        get { ...}
      }
    }
```

The property Value would have to be accessed like this:

```
    Program p;
    int i = p.Value<int>;
```

Properties can be thought of as a way to encapsulate a field and add behavior to field accesses, so generic properties do not make much sense, just as generic fields do not.

Generic indexers are not provided. Consider:

```
    class Program
    {
      public T this<T>[ int index]
```

```
   {
     get{}
   }
 }
```

Such an indexer would have to be accessed like this:

```
Program p;
int i = p<int>[ 5] ;
```

Generic indexers would suffer from the same problems as generic properties. Also, the accessing syntax would be confusing. One might assume that p is an object that is generic and requires type arguments, when in fact it is the indexer on p, which requires type arguments.

Peter Hallam

25.7 Constraints

Generic type and method declarations can optionally specify type parameter constraints by including a *type-parameter-constraints-clauses* in the declaration.

> *type-parameter-constraints-clauses:*
>   *type-parameter-constraints-clause*
>   *type-parameter-constraints-clauses   type-parameter-constraints-clause*
>
> *type-parameter-constraints-clause:*
>   where *type-parameter : type-parameter-constraints*
>
> *type-parameter-constraints:*
>   *primary-constraint*
>   *secondary-constraints*
>   *constructor-constraint*
>   *primary-constraint   ,   secondary-constraints*
>   *primary-constraint   ,   constructor-constraint*
>   *secondary-constraints   ,   constructor-constraint*
>   *primary-constraint   ,   secondary-constraints   ,   constructor-constraint*
>
> *primary-constraint:*
>   *class-type*
>   class
>   struct
>
> *secondary-constraints:*
>   *interface-type*
>   *type-parameter*
>   *secondary-constraints   ,   interface-type*
>   *secondary-constraints   ,   type-parameter*
>
> *constructor-constraint:*
>   new   (   )

Each *type-parameter-constraints-clause* consists of the token where, followed by the name of a type parameter, followed by a colon and the list of constraints for that type parameter. There shall be at most one `where` clause for each type parameter, and the `where` clauses can be listed in any order. The `where` token is not a keyword.

The list of constraints given in a `where` clause can include any of the following components, in this order: a single primary constraint, one or more secondary constraints, and the constructor constraint, `new()`.

A primary constraint can be a class type or the ***reference type constraint*** `class` or the ***value type constraint*** `struct`. A secondary constraint can be a *type-parameter* or *interface-type*.

The reference type constraint specifies that a type argument used for the type parameter must be a reference type (§25.7.1). Any class type, interface type, delegate type, array type, or type parameter ***known to be a reference type*** (as defined below) satisfies this constraint.

The value type constraint specifies that a type argument used for the type parameter must be a value type (§25.7.1). Any non-nullable struct type, enum type, or type parameter having the value type constraint satisfies this constraint. A type parameter having the value type constraint shall not also have the *constructor-constraint*. The `System.Nullable<T>` type specifies the non-nullable value type constraint for `T`. Thus, recursively constructed types of the forms `T??` and `Nullable<Nullable<T>>` are prohibited.

> ### No nullable constraint
>
> C# treats nullable types, which are value types, as a third category distinct from both value and reference types. However, this is not a "first-class" category (§11.4.1), as a type parameter may be constrained to be a reference type or to be a non-nullable value type, but there is no way to constrain it to be a nullable value type.
>
> This lack of orthogonality is unfortunate.

Pointer types are never allowed to be type arguments so they are not considered to satisfy the reference type or value type constraints.

If a constraint is a class type, an interface type, or a type parameter, that type specifies a minimal "base type" that every type argument used for that type parameter shall support. Whenever a constructed type or generic method is used, the type argument is checked against the constraints on the type parameter at compile-time. The type argument supplied shall derive from or implement all of the constraints given for that type parameter.

A *class-type* constraint shall satisfy the following rules:

- The type shall be a class type.
- The type shall not be `sealed`.
- The type shall not be one of the following types: `System.Array`, `System.Delegate`, `System.Enum`, or `System.ValueType`.
- The type shall not be `object`. [*Note*: Since all types derive from `object`, such a constraint would have no effect if it were permitted. *end note*]
- At most one constraint for a given type parameter can be a class type.

A type specified as an *interface-type* constraint shall satisfy the following rules:

- The type shall be an interface type.
- A type shall not be specified more than once in a given `where` clause.

In either case, the constraint can involve any of the type parameters of the associated type or method declaration as part of a constructed type, and can involve the type being declared.

Any class or interface type specified as a type parameter constraint shall be at least as accessible (§10.5.4) as the generic type or method being declared.

A type specified as a *type-parameter* constraint shall satisfy the following rules:

- The type shall be a type parameter.
- A type shall not be specified more than once in a given `where` clause.

In addition, there shall be no cycles in the dependency graph of type parameters, where dependency is a transitive relation defined by:

- If a type parameter `T` is used as a constraint for type parameter `S` then `S` *depends on* `T`.
- If a type parameter `S` depends on a type parameter `T` and `T` depends on a type parameter `U` then `S` *depends on* `U`.

Given this relation, it is a compile-time error for a type parameter to depend on itself (directly or indirectly).

Any constraints must be consistent among dependent type parameters. If type parameter `S` depends on type parameter `T` then:

- `T` must not have the value type constraint. Otherwise, `T` is effectively sealed so `S` would be forced to be the same type as `T`, eliminating the need for two type parameters.
- If `S` has the value type constraint then `T` must not have a *class-type* constraint.
- If `S` has a class-type constraint `A` and `T` has a class-type constraint `B` then there must be an identity conversion or implicit reference conversion from `A` to `B` or an implicit reference conversion from `B` to `A`.
- If `S` also depends on type parameter `U` and `U` has a *class-type* constraint `A` and `T` has a *class-type* constraint `B` then there must be an identity conversion or implicit reference conversion from `A` to `B` or an implicit reference conversion from `B` to `A`.

It is valid for `S` to have the value type constraint and `T` to have the reference type constraint. Effectively this limits `T` to the types `System.Object`, `System.ValueType`, `System.Enum` and any interface type.

Using constraints to simulate Java wildcard types

In the Java programming language, constructed types can involve so-called wildcard type arguments, denoted by a question mark (`?`), which compensates to some extent for the lack of covariance and contravariance. In C# there are no wildcards, but the same effect can sometimes be achieved by using extra type parameters and suitable constraints on them.

For instance, the class `java.util.Collections` contains this generic method:

```
static <T> int binarySearch(List<? extends Comparable <? super T>> list,
                            T key)
```

The method's type says that it can be used to search for a key of type `T` in a list whose element type is a subtype of some type that implements `Comparable` of some supertype of `T`. This can be translated into C# by adding two extra type parameters `S` and `U` and constraining them as follows:

```
public static int BinarySearch<T,U,S>(List<S> list, T key)
  where T : U
  where S : IComparable<U>
```

So the list's elements must have some type `S` that implements `IComparable<U>`, where `U` is some supertype of `T`.

> Incidentally, back in 2004 this declaration would crash a prominent beta 1 compiler, so apparently this use of constraints had not been foreseen, but in beta 2 and the release version it works fine.
>
> Code like this may impress your boss and confuse your colleagues.

If the `where` clause for a type parameter includes a constructor constraint (which has the form `new()`), it is possible to use the `new` operator to create instances of the type (§14.5.10.1). Any type argument used for a type parameter with a constructor constraint shall have a public parameterless constructor (this includes all value types) or be a type parameter having the value type constraint or constructor constraint (see §25.7.1 for details).

[*Example*: The following are examples of constraints:

```
interface IPrintable
{
  void Print();
}

interface IComparable<T>
{
  int CompareTo(T value);
}

interface IKeyProvider<T>
{

  T GetKey();
}

class Printer<T> where T: IPrintable {...}

class SortedList<T> where T: IComparable<T> {...}

class Dictionary<K, V>
  where K: IComparable<K>
  where V: IPrintable, IKeyProvider<K>, new()
{
  ...
}
```

The following example is in error because it causes a circularity in the dependency graph of the type parameters:

```
class Circular<S, T>
  where S: T
  where T: S    // Error - circularity in dependency graph
{...}
```

The following examples illustrate additional invalid situations:

```
class Sealed<S, T>
  where S: T
  where T: struct  // Error - T is sealed
{...}

class A {...}
```

```
class B {...}

class Incompat<S, T>
  where S: A, T
  where T: B // Error - incompatible class-type constraints
{...}

class StructWithClass<S, T, U>
  where S: struct, T
  where T: U
  where U: A // Error - A incompatible with struct
{...}
```

end example]

The ***effective base class*** of a type parameter T is defined as follows:

- If T has no primary constraints or type parameter constraints, its effective base class is object.
- If T has the value type constraint, its effective base class is System.ValueType.
- If T has the reference type constraint, but no *type-parameter* constraints, its effective base class is object.
- If T has a *class-type* constraint C but no *type-parameter* constraints, its effective base class is C.
- If T has no primary constraints but has one or more *type-parameter* constraints, its effective base class is the most encompassed type (§13.4.2) in the set of effective base classes of its *type-parameter* constraints. The consistency rules ensure that such a most encompassed type exists.
- If T has both a *class-type* constraint and one or more *type-parameter* constraints, its effective base class is the most encompassed type (§13.4.2) in the set consisting of the *class-type* constraint of T and the effective base classes of its *type-parameter* constraints. The consistency rules ensure that such a most encompassed type exists.
- If T has both a reference type constraint and one or more *type-parameter* constraints, its effective base class is the most encompassed type (§13.4.2) in the set consisting of the effective base classes of its *type-parameter* constraints. The consistency rules ensure that such a most encompassed type exists.

Ineffective base class?

C# employs static type checking and this extends to determining the effective base class of a type parameter. Instantiating a type parameter with some type does *not* alter the effective base class. For example:

```
public class Alpha<T>
{
  public virtual T M<U>(U arg) where U : T
  {
    return arg;
  }
}
```

Here type parameter T is not constrained, so its effective base class is object. Type parameter U is constrained to type parameter T, so its effective base class is also object. Now consider the following class derived from Alpha:

```
public class Beta : Alpha<int>
{
  public override int M<X>(X arg)
  {
    // return arg;   // invalid, X's effective base class is object
       return 42;    // OK
  }
}
```

It might be assumed that the instantiation Alpha<int> constrains T, and hence also X in the override of method M, to be int; see §25.6.2. However, this is not the case. While the return type of method M must be given as int, the method parameter arg is *not* compatible with int.

However, if instead of instantiating the base class we make the derived class generic:

```
public class Beta<T> : Alpha<T>
{
  public override T M<X>(X arg)
  {
     return arg; // OK
  }
}
```

then X and T do have the same effective base class and arg *is* compatible with T.

Thus, overriding the method M in class Beta with a body identical to its definition in class Alpha is invalid *if and only if* the parameter to the Alpha base class specification is a closed type. In other words, providing a more specific type disallows an assignment that is type-correct! This is potentially confusing.

The ***effective interface set*** of a type parameter T is defined as follows:

- If T has no *secondary-constraints*, its effective interface set is empty.
- If T has *interface-type* constraints but no *type-parameter* constraints, its effective interface set is its set of *interface-type* constraints.
- If T has no *interface-type* constraints but has *type-parameter* constraints, its effective interface set is the union of the effective interface sets of its *type-parameter* constraints.
- If T has both *interface-type* constraints and *type-parameter* constraints, its effective interface set is the union of its set of *interface-type* constraints and the effective interface sets of its *type-parameter* constraints.

A type parameter is ***known to be a reference type*** if

- it has the reference type constraint, or
- its effective base class is not object or System.ValueType.

Values of a constrained type parameter type can be used to access the instance members implied by the constraints. [*Example*: In the following code

```
interface IPrintable
{
  void Print();
}

class Printer<T> where T: IPrintable
{
  void PrintOne(T x)
  {
    x.Print();
  }
}
```

the methods of IPrintable can be invoked directly on x because T is constrained to always implement IPrintable. *end example*]

Two generic partial type declarations (in the same program) contribute to the same unbound generic type if they have the same fully qualified name (which includes the number of type parameters) (§10.3). Two such partial type declarations shall specify the same name for each type parameter, in order.

When a partial generic type declaration includes constraints, the constraints shall agree with all other parts that include constraints. Specifically, each part that includes constraints shall have constraints for the same set of type parameters, and for each type parameter, the sets of primary, secondary, and constructor constraints shall be equivalent. Two sets of constraints are equivalent if they contain the same members. If no part of a partial generic type specifies type parameter constraints, the type parameters are considered unconstrained. [*Example*:

```
partial class Map<K,V>
  where K: IComparable<K>
  where V: IKeyProvider<K>, new()
{
  ...
}

partial class Map<K,V>
  where V: IKeyProvider<K>, new()
  where K: IComparable<K>
{
  ...
}

partial class Map<K,V>
{
  ...
}
```

is correct because those parts that include constraints (the first two) effectively specify the same set of primary, secondary, and constructor constraints for the same set of type parameters, respectively. *end example*]

No "numeric" constraints

Though the constraint mechanism is quite powerful, it has one notable omission: It is not possible to constrain an argument to be a numeric type. For example, consider this fragment of a class for double-precision complex numbers:

```
public struct ComplexDouble
{
    double re;
    double im;

    public static ComplexDouble operator+(ComplexDouble l,
                                          ComplexDouble r)
    {
        return new ComplexDouble(l.re + r.re, l.im + r.im);
    }
    ...
}
```

A single-precision complex number class would be rather similar:

```
public struct ComplexFloat
{
    float re;
    float im;

    public static ComplexFloat operator+(ComplexFloat l
                                         ComplexFloat r)
    {
        return new ComplexFloat(l.re + r.re, l.im + r.im);
    }
    ...
}
```

A natural expectation is that generics would assist here, for example, in *pseudo* C#:

```
public struct Complex<T> where T : floating_point_type
{
    T re;
    T im;

    public static Complex<T> operator+(Complex<T> l, Complex<T> r)
    {
        return new Complex<T>(l.re + r.re, l.im + r.im);
    }


    ...
}
```

However, there is no constraint for *floating_point_type* in C#.

C++ provides a `Complex<>` template, though without constraining the type parameter–as is the C++ way. Ada provides constraints for discrete numeric, real numeric, and general numeric types along with a generic package for complex numbers. Haskell provides similar features, etc.

The purposes of a floating point constraint on type parameter `T` include: to prevent instantiation with meaningless type arguments, such as string, and to allow infix operators (+, *, -, /, ...) to be used on arguments of type `T`.

It would be possible to use interfaces in C# (e.g., `IFloatingPoint`) to achieve much of what specific numeric constraints would. However, compiler (or JIT) involvement would still be required to transform operator calls to inline instructions. All built-in types would need to implement such introduced interfaces, just as when generics were introduced these types had interfaces such as `IComparable<>` added to them.

The lack of numeric type constraints in C# may limit the use of generics in numerical work. On the other hand, at least if the constraint as opposed to the interface option were selected, this feature would raise further design questions concerning numeric promotion, implicit conversions, and overloading resolution similar to, but not the same as, issues the other constraints raised.

25.7.1 Satisfying constraints

Whenever a constructed type or generic method is referenced, the supplied type arguments are checked against the type parameter constraints declared on the generic type or method. For each `where` clause, the type argument `A` that corresponds to the named type parameter is checked against each constraint as follows:

- If the constraint is a class type, an interface type, or a type parameter, let `C` represent that constraint with the supplied type arguments substituted for any type parameters that appear in the constraint. To satisfy the constraint, it shall be the case that type `A` is convertible to type `C` by one of the following:
  - An identity conversion (§13.1.1)
  - An implicit reference conversion (§13.1.4)
  - A boxing conversion (§13.1.5), provided that type `A` is a non-nullable value type
  - An implicit reference, boxing, or type parameter conversion from a type parameter `A` to `C` (§25.7.4).
- If the constraint is the reference type constraint, the type `A` must satisfy one of the following:
  - `A` is an interface type, class type, delegate type or array type. [*Note*: Note that `System.ValueType` and `System.Enum` are reference types so satisfy this constraint. *end note*]
  - `A` is a type parameter that is known to be a reference type (§25.7).
- If the constraint is the value type constraint, the type `A` must satisfy one of the following:
  - `A` is a non-nullable struct type or enum type. [*Note*: Note that `System.ValueType` and `System.Enum` are reference types so do not satisfy this constraint. *end note*]
  - `A` is a type parameter having the value type constraint (§25.7).
- If the constraint is the constructor constraint `new()`, the type argument `A` shall not be `abstract` and shall have a public parameterless constructor. This is satisfied if one of the following is true:
  - `A` is a value type, since all value types have a public default constructor (§11.1.2).
  - `A` is a type parameter having the constructor constraint (§25.7).
  - `A` is a type parameter having the value type constraint (§25.7).
  - `A` is a class that is not `abstract`, `A` contains an explicitly declared public constructor with no parameters.
  - `A` is not `abstract` and has a default constructor (§17.10.4).

A compile-time error occurs if one or more of a type parameter's constraints are not satisfied by the given type arguments.

Since type parameters are not inherited, constraints are never inherited either. [*Example*: In the code below, `D` needs to specify the constraint on its type parameter `T`, so that `T` satisfies the constraint imposed by the base class `B<T>`. In contrast, class `E` need not specify a constraint, because `List<T>` implements `IEnumerable` for any `T`.

```
class B<T> where T: IEnumerable {...}
```

```
class D<T>: B<T> where T: IEnumerable {...}

class E<T>: B<List<T>> {...}
```

end example]

25.7.2 Member lookup on type parameters

The results of member lookup in a type given by a type parameter T depends on the constraints, if any, specified for T. If T has no *class-type*, *interface-type* or *type-parameter* constraints, then member lookup on T returns the same set of members as member lookup on object. Otherwise, the first stage of member lookup (§14.3) considers all the members in the effective base class of T and all the members in each interface in the effective interface set of T. After performing the first stage of member lookup for each of theses types, the results are combined, and then hidden members are removed from the combined results.

Before the advent of generics, member lookup always returned either a set of members declared solely in classes, or a set of members declared solely in interfaces and possibly the type object. Member lookup on type parameters changes this somewhat. When a type parameter has both an effective base class other than object and a non-empty effective interface set, member lookup can return a set of members, some of which were declared in a class, and others of which were declared in an interface. The following additional rules handle this case.

- As specified in §14.3, during member lookup, members declared in a class other than object hide members declared in interfaces.
- During overload resolution of methods (§14.5.5.1) and indexers (§14.5.6.2), if any applicable member was declared in a class other than object, all members declared in an interface are removed from the set of considered members.

These rules only have effect when doing binding on a type parameter with both an effective base class other than object and a non-empty effective interface set. [*Note*: Informally, members defined in a class type constraint are preferred over members in an interface constraint. *end note*]

25.7.3 Type parameters and boxing

When a struct type overrides a virtual method inherited from System.Object (such as Equals, GetHashCode, or ToString), invocation of the virtual method through an instance of the struct type doesn't cause boxing to occur. This is true even when the struct is used as a type parameter and the invocation occurs through an instance of the type parameter type. [*Example*:

```
using System;

struct Counter
{
  int value;

  public override string ToString()
  {
    value++;
    return value.ToString();
  }
}

class Program
```

```
{
  static void Test<T>() where T: new()
  {
    T x = new T();
    Console.WriteLine(x.ToString());
    Console.WriteLine(x.ToString());
    Console.WriteLine(x.ToString());
  }

  static void Main()
  {
    Test<Counter>();
  }
}
```

The output of the program is:

```
1
2
3
```

Although it is bad style for `ToString` to have side effects, the example demonstrates that no boxing occurred for the three invocations of `x.ToString()`. *end example*]

Similarly, boxing never implicitly occurs when accessing a member on a constrained type parameter. [*Example*: Suppose an interface `ICounter` contains a method `Increment`, which can be used to modify a value. If `ICounter` is used as a constraint, the implementation of the `Increment` method is called with a reference to the variable that `Increment` was called on, never a boxed copy. This behavior is different from the non-generic case. When making a call to an interface implementation on a struct type the argument is always boxed.

```
using System;

interface ICounter
{
  void Increment();
}

struct Counter: ICounter
{
  int value;

  public override string ToString()
  {
    return value.ToString();
  }

  void ICounter.Increment()
  {
    value++;
  }
}

class Program
{
  static void Test<T>() where T: ICounter, new()
```

```
  {
    T x = new T();
    Console.WriteLine(x);
    x.Increment();              // Modify x
    Console.WriteLine(x);
    ((ICounter)x).Increment();   // Modify boxed copy of x
    Console.WriteLine(x);
  }

  static void Main()
  {
    Test<Counter>();
  }
}
```

The first call to Increment modifies the value in the variable x. This is not equivalent to the second call to Increment, which modifies the value in a boxed copy of x. Thus, the output of the program is:

```
0
1
1
```

end example]

No cast, no box

The statement, "This behavior is different from the nongeneric case," might be misconstrued. It is only in calls to interface methods where the variable is cast to the interface type that boxing occurs, and such a cast is required if the method is explicitly implemented—as in the preceding example. Direct calls to non explicit interface methods do not involve boxing. For example, the following produces exactly the same output:

```
struct Counter2 : ICounter
{
  int value;

  public override string ToString()
  {
    return value.ToString();
  }

  public void Increment()
  {
    value++;
  }
}

class Program
{
  static void Test()
  {
    Counter2 x = new Counter2();
    Console.WriteLine(x);
    x.Increment();                 // Modify x
```

```
        Console.WriteLine(x);
        ((ICounter)x).Increment();  // Modify boxed copy of x
        Console.WriteLine(x);
    }

    static void Main()
    {
        Test<Counter>();
        Test();
    }
}
```

The difference with generics is that *explicitly implemented* interface methods are called without boxing if the type parameter is constrained to implement the interface.

Inherited constraints

An `override` method inherits the type parameter constraints of the method it overrides (§25.6.2). Consider the following:

```
public abstract class Leaf<Visitor>
{
    public abstract void Accept<Concrete>(Concrete cv)
        where Concrete : Visitor;
}

public interface ILeafVisitor
{
    void Visit(LeafA visited);
    void Visit(LeafB visited);
}

public sealed class LeafA : Leaf<ILeafVisitor>
{
    public override void Accept<Concrete>(Concrete cv)
    {
        cv.Visit(this);                    // never boxes
        (cv as ILeafVisitor).Visit(this); // always boxes
    }
}
```

The method `Accept<Concrete>` in derived class `LeafA` appears to have no constraint on its type parameter `Concrete`, but it does: the one inherited from the abstract method it overrides. Therefore, even when `Concrete` is instantiated with a struct type, no boxing is performed in the call `cv.Visit(this)` due to the constraint that `Concrete` implements `ILeafVisitor`.

25.7.4 Conversions involving type parameters

The conversions that are allowed on a type parameter `T` depend on the constraints specified for `T` and are detailed in §13.

The conversion rules do not permit a direct explicit conversion from an unconstrained type parameter to an arbitrary non-interface type, which might be surprising. The reason for this rule is to prevent confusion and make the semantics of such conversions clear. [*Example*: Consider the following declaration:

```
class X<T>
{
  public static long F(T t)
  {
    return (long)t;      // Error, explicit conversion not permitted
  }
}
```

If the direct explicit conversion of `t` to `long` were permitted, one might easily expect that `X<int>.F(7)` would return 7L. However, it would not, because the standard numeric conversions are only considered when the types are known to be numeric at compile time. In order to make the semantics clear, the above example should be written:

```
class X<T>
{
  public static long F(T t)
  {
    return (long)(object)t;   // OK, conversions permitted
  }
}
```

This code will now compile but executing `X<int>.F(7)` would then throw an exception at runtime, since a boxed `int` cannot be converted directly to a `long`.

end example]

Thinking generically: algorithms

An earlier annotation (§25.1.11) introduced *generic containers*, which require one to know nothing about the type of the values they contain.

A *generic algorithm* is one that works for any type, provided the type supports certain operations. The prototypical generic algorithm is sorting; any collection of items can be sorted provided there exists an ordering operation over the collection's item type.

In earlier versions of C#, as in some other languages such as Java, generic algorithms could be specified using interfaces to define the set of operations supported by a type. For example, a function `Mid` to compute the middle value of three values may be written in C# as follows:

```
static IComparable Mid(IComparable a, IComparable b, IComparable c)
{
  if (a.CompareTo(b) < 0)
  {
    if (c.CompareTo(a) <= 0)
      return a;
    if (c.CompareTo(b) < 0)
      return c;
    else
      return b;
  }
  else
  {
    if (c.CompareTo(b) <= 0)
      return b;
    if (c.CompareTo(a) < 0)
      return c;
    else
```

```
            return a;
    }
}
```

This example uses the CLI standard interface `IComparable`, which specifies the `CompareTo` method. Note that the return type must also be `IComparable`; the identity of the type that meets the interface is lost. This means that when the method is used, a cast is required:

```
double x, y, z, ans;
...
ans = (double)Mid(x, y, z);
```

The need to include the cast might be viewed as a minor inconvenience; however, there is a more significant problem. The following also compiles and it is not until runtime that an error is reported:

```
double x, ans;
char y;
bool z;
...
ans = (double)Mid(x, y, z);
```

The problem here is that all of the types `double`, `char`, and `bool` implement `IComparable`, and it is not until the `CompareTo` method is evaluated at run-time that the type mismatch is discovered when the cast fails.

Using generics with constraints addresses the preceding problems because the identity of the type implementing the interface is not lost. In C# 2.0 the `Mid` method can be written, using the new CLI standard interface `IComparable<T>` as:

```
static T Mid<T>(T a, T b, T c) where T : IComparable<T>
{
  if (a.CompareTo(b) < 0)
  {
    if (c.CompareTo(a) <= 0)
      return a;
    if (c.CompareTo(b) < 0)
      return c;
    else
      return b;
  }
  else
  {
    if (c.CompareTo(b) <= 0)
      return b;
    if (c.CompareTo(a) < 0)
      return c;
    else
      return a;
  }
}
```

Note that as with generic containers only type names need to be changed, the algorithm code itself remains the same. Compared to the preceding nongeneric version, this specifies that the three parameters must all be of the *same* type and that the return is also of this type, so both the need for a cast and the risk of runtime type errors are removed:

```
double x, y, z, ans;
char v;
bool w;
...
ans = Mid(x, y, z);   // OK
ans = Mid(x, v, w);   // Compile-time type error
```

(The type argument to generic method Mid can be omitted thanks to type inference; §25.6.4.)

The constrained generic version of Mid also avoids the boxing and virtual call overhead (§25.7.3) that the nongeneric interface-based method incurs when called on value types.

26 Iterators

Growing pains

Iterators, as with anonymous methods (§14.5.15), change the nature of C#. A small code fragment may produce large amounts of code behind the scenes (§26.4), and small changes to code can result in significant changes in the size and/or performance of the compiled output. In other words, C# has become a "higher level" programming language.

An *iterator* is a means of implementing a function member whose return type is an enumerator interface or enumerable interface. The function member returns the ordered sequence of values as yielded by the iterator.

[*Example*: The following Stack<T> class implements its GetEnumerator method using an iterator. The iterator enumerates the elements of the stack in top to bottom order.

```
using System.Collections.Generic;

public class Stack<T>: IEnumerable<T>
{
  T[ ] items;
  int count;

  public void Push(T data) {...}

  public T Pop() {...}

  public IEnumerator<T> GetEnumerator()
  {
    for (int i = count - 1; i >= 0; --i)
    {
      yield return items[i];
    }
  }
}
```

Iterators are implemented using yield statements, which can only be used in methods whose return type is an enumerator interface. The presence of the GetEnumerator method makes Stack<T> an enumerable type, allowing instances of Stack<T> to be used in a foreach statement. The following example pushes the values 0 through 9 onto an integer stack and then uses a foreach loop to display the values in top to bottom order.

```
using System;

class Test
{
  static void Main()
  {
    Stack<int> s = new Stack<int>();
    for (int i = 0; i < 10; i++) s.Push(i);
    foreach (int i in s) Console.Write("{0} ", i);
    Console.WriteLine();
  }
}
```

The output of the example is:

```
9 8 7 6 5 4 3 2 1 0
```

end example]

Coroutines allowed?

Some readers may wonder, especially given the name of `yield`, whether iterators are implemented using coroutines. As shown in §26.4 iterators *may* be implemented by state machines, and indeed this is the method used by the Microsoft and Mono compilers at the time of writing (although the two compilers do not produce identical machines).

However, examining the `Tree` examples in §26.4 indicates that coroutines would *not* be a good choice for implementing iterators.

To see this, first consider how a coroutine-based tree iterator might be written by hand. The algorithm is to walk over the tree and "yield" each element as it is encountered. This mirrors the visitor-style enumerator shown in §14.5.15.3.1; the only difference is that the latter applies a delegate to each element while the former yields it. Coroutine (and visitor) enumerators work well because the state that needs to be maintained while traversing a structure is handled using the normal method call stack.

Compare this to the iterator style and in particular the "How many iterators does it take to enumerate?" annotation on §26.1.4. This shows that the C# iterator model produces a design where multiple iterators are combined to iterate over a complex structure; the state is not merged with the normal method activation but maintained as a flock of iterator objects. While each iterator could be implemented using a coroutine, nothing would be gained by doing so; a flock of objects/coroutines would still be required.

This is not to say that a handwritten coroutine-based iterator would not be a good choice for a particular application. With their similarity to visitor style enumerators, the annotation "Enumerating a data structure: iterators, handwritten enumerator, or visitor style?" on §26.1.4 tells us the exact opposite.

26.1 Iterator blocks

An ***iterator block*** is a *block* (§15.2) that yields an ordered sequence of values. An iterator block is distinguished from a normal statement block by the presence of one or more `yield` statements (§15.14).

- The `yield return` statement produces the next value of the iteration.
- The `yield break` statement indicates that the iteration is complete.

An iterator block can be used as a *method-body* (§17.5), *operator-body* (§17.9), or *accessor-body* (§17.6.2) as long as the return type of the corresponding function member is one of the enumerator interfaces (§26.1.1) or one of the enumerable interfaces (§26.1.2).

Iterator blocks are not a distinct element in the C# grammar. They are restricted in several ways and have a major effect on the semantics of a function member declaration; however, grammatically, they are just blocks.

When a function member is implemented using an iterator block, it is a compile-time error for the formal parameter list of the function member to specify any `ref` or `out` parameters.

It is a compile-time error for a `return` statement to appear in an iterator block (but `yield return` statements are permitted).

It is a compile-time error for an iterator block to contain an unsafe context (§27.1). An iterator block always defines a safe context, even when its declaration is nested in an unsafe context.

26.1.1 Enumerator interfaces

The *enumerator interfaces* are the non-generic interface System.Collections.IEnumerator and all instantiations of the generic interface System.Collections.Generic. IEnumerator<T>. For the sake of brevity, these interfaces are referenced in this specification as IEnumerator and IEnumerator<T>, respectively.

26.1.2 Enumerable interfaces

The *enumerable interfaces* are the non-generic interface System.Collections.IEnumerable and all instantiations of the generic interface System.Collections.Generic. IEnumerable<T>. For the sake of brevity, these interfaces are referenced in this specification as IEnumerable and IEnumerable<T>, respectively.

26.1.3 Yield type

An iterator block produces a sequence of values, all of the same type. This type is called the *yield type* of the iterator block.

- The yield type of an iterator block used to implement a function member that returns IEnumerator or IEnumerable is object.
- The yield type of an iterator block used to implement a function member that returns IEnumerator<T> or IEnumerable<T> is T.

26.1.4 This access

Within an iterator block of an instance member of a class, the expression this is classified as a value. The type of the value is the class within which the usage occurs, and the value is a reference to the object for which the member was invoked.

Within an iterator block of an instance member of a struct, the expression this is classified as a variable. The type of the variable is the struct within which the usage occurs. The variable represents a *copy* of the struct for which the member was invoked. The this variable in an iterator block of an instance member of a struct behaves exactly the same as a *value* parameter of the struct type. [*Note*: This is different than in a non-iterator function member body. *end note*]

> **How many iterators does it take to enumerate?**
>
> An iterator is the result of a single *block*. This means that iteration of a nonlinear data structure will probably involve multiple iterator instances. The cost of this needs to be considered when deciding whether to use an iterator block.
>
> For example, our nonlinear Tree type introduced in §14.5.15.3.1 can be extended to be enumerable as follows:
>
> ```
> public class Tree<T> : IEnumerable<T>  // interface added
> {
>                                         // Nested type for tree nodes
>   class Node : IEnumerable<T>           // interface added
>   {
>     /* as before... */
>                                         // Yield based enumerator
>     public IEnumerator<T> GetEnumerator()
>     {
> ```

```
      if (Left != null)
        foreach(T item in Left)
          yield return item;

      yield return Item;

      if (Right != null)
        foreach(T item in Right)
          yield return item;
    }

    System.Collections.IEnumerator System.Collections.
                              IEnumerable.GetEnumerator()
    {
      return GetEnumerator();
    }
  }

  /* as before... */

  // Simple enumerator for empty tree
  private IEnumerator<T> nullEnumerator()
  {
    yield break;
  }

  // Yield based enumerator
  public IEnumerator<T> GetEnumerator()
  {
    return root == null ? nullEnumerator() : root.GetEnumerator();
  }

  System.Collections.IEnumerator System.Collections.
                            IEnumerable.GetEnumerator()
  {
    return GetEnumerator();
  }
}
```

The code for `GetEnumerator` is straightforward, which is one advantage of iterator blocks, and is rather similar to that of the existing visitor `ForEach` method (§14.5.15.3.1). However, every "recursion" into a subtree involves the creation of a new iterator object that yields its result one item at a time to the calling iterator, which in turn yields them to its caller, and so on.

For the particular nonlinear data structure used here, a full enumeration of a structure containing N items will result in the creation of N iterator objects, and the number live at the same time is bounded only by the depth of the data structure. This is potentially a large amount of object creation and subsequent garbage generation.

The visitor enumeration introduced in §14.5.15.3.1 does not have this problem, but does require the use of delegates.

Enumerating a data structure: iterators, handwritten enumerator, or visitor style?

The obvious question that arises is, which coding style is best? There is no "right" answer to this, but here is one comparison.

First, we add a handwritten enumerator to our `Tree` class:

```csharp
public class Tree<T> : IEnumerable<T>
{
  // Nested type for tree nodes
  class Node : IEnumerable<T>
  {
    /* as before... */
  }

  /* as before... */

  public IEnumerator<T> GetCustomEnumerator()
  {
    return new TreeEnumerator(this);
  }

  // Custom enumerator, not yield based
  // Current is not cached, Reset supported
  // Internal state uses standard Stack
  class TreeEnumerator : IEnumerator<T>
  {
    Stack<Node> trail;   // trail of nodes to current
    Tree<T> myTree;      // Tree we're enumerating
    long initialCount;   // Initial count of items in tree

    public TreeEnumerator(Tree<T> myTree)
    {
      this.myTree = myTree;
      Reset();
    }

    public void Reset()
    {
      trail = new Stack<Node>();
      initialCount = myTree.count;
      if (myTree.root != null)
      {
        Node dummy = new Node();
        dummy.Right = myTree.root;
        trail.Push(dummy);
      }
    }

    public T Current
    {
      get
      {
        if (trail.Count == 0)
          throw new InvalidOperationException();
```

```
      else
        return trail.Peek().Item;
    }
  }

  object System.Collections.IEnumerator.Current
  {
    get { return Current; }
  }

  // MoveNext
  public bool MoveNext()
  {
    // Tree changed?
    if (initialCount != myTree.count)
      throw new InvalidOperationException();

    if (trail.Count > 0)
    {
      Node current = trail.Pop();
      if (current.Right != null)       // If current has a Right sibling
      {
        Node cursor = current.Right;   // then move Right...
        do
        {
          trail.Push(cursor);          // and all the way down
          cursor = cursor.Left;        // it's Left siblings
        } while (cursor != null);

        return true;
      }
      else
        return trail.Count > 0;        // otherwise previous node in
    }                                  // trail is next, if it exists
    else
      return false;                    // nothing remaining in trail
  }

  public void Dispose() {}
  }
}
```

For a nonlinear data structure, producing the handwritten enumerator is obviously more complicated than writing an iterator or the visitor enumerator. What is interesting is the relative performance of the three kinds of enumeration.

To examine this we ran a simple experiment using a data set of 54,940 given names:

```
public enum GenderKind { Male, Female };

public struct GivenName
{
  public string Name;
  public GenderKind Gender;
  public int Rank;
```

```
    public float Freq;

    /* methods... */
}
```

Using each kind of enumerator, the average length of the female names was computed 500 times and the *relative* performance of each enumeration calculated. The current Mono C# compiler produced a yield-based iterator that executed on average *15 times slower* than the handwritten iterator, which in turn executed on average *1.6 times slower* than the visitor enumerator. For the current Microsoft compiler, the results were *24 times slower* and *1.8 times slower*, respectively. No measurements of garbage produced were taken, but the yield-based iterator produces the most, the handwritten less, and the visitor enumerator the least.

Note that the codes to *write* yield-based iterators (see preceding) and visitor-style enumerators (see §14.5.15.3.1) is very similar. The *style* of use is different. Yield-based iterators are typically used in loops, while visitor enumerators are called with anonymous methods using local variable capture. However, the code is rather similar:

```
// Compute the average length of names of the given gender in the db
// Use the yield iterator to walk the db
static int YieldAverageLength(Tree<GivenName> db, GenderKind
                                                     gender)
{
  int total = 0;
  int count = 0;

  foreach (GivenName gn in db)
  {
    if (gn.Gender == gender)
    {
      total += gn.Name.Length;
      count++;
    }
  }

  return count != 0 ? total / count : -1;
}

// As above but use the visitor pattern and an anonymous delegate
// which updates local state
static int ForEachAverageLength(Tree<GivenName> db, GenderKind
                                                       gender)
{
  int total = 0;
  int count = 0;

  db.ForEach( delegate(GivenName gn)
        {
          if (gn.Gender == gender)
          {
            total += gn.Name.Length;
```

```
            count++;
        }
    }
);

return count != 0 ? total / count : -1;
}
```

This experiment shows that, using current compilers, yield-based iterators are significantly slower than the visitor-style enumerators and produce more garbage, for our given names data set. In another situation the difference may not be so great. The two styles have similar definitions and use and C# supports both well; the choice is yours.

26.2 Enumerator objects

When a function member returning an enumerator interface type is implemented using an iterator block, invoking the function member does not immediately execute the code in the iterator block. Instead, an ***enumerator object*** is created and returned. This object encapsulates the code specified in the iterator block, and execution of the code in the iterator block occurs when the enumerator object's MoveNext method is invoked. An enumerator object has the following characteristics:

- It implements IEnumerator and IEnumerator<T>, where T is the yield type of the iterator block.
- It implements System.IDisposable.
- It is initialized with a copy of the argument values (if any) and instance value passed to the function member.
- It has four potential states, ***before***, ***running***, ***suspended***, and ***after***, and is initially in the ***before*** state.

An enumerator object is typically an instance of a compiler-generated enumerator class that encapsulates the code in the iterator block and implements the enumerator interfaces, but other methods of implementation are possible. If an enumerator type is generated by the compiler, that class shall be nested, directly or indirectly, in the type containing the function member, it shall have private accessibility, and it shall have a name reserved for compiler use (§9.4.2).

An enumerator object can implement more interfaces than those specified above.

The following subclauses describe the exact behavior of the MoveNext, Current, and Dispose members of the IEnumerable and IEnumerable<T> interface implementations provided by an enumerator object.

Enumerator objects do not support the IEnumerator.Reset method. Invoking this method causes a System.NotSupportedException to be thrown.

Iterators, finally, lock and using

The following clauses define how an iterator block is "unwound" into MoveNext() (§26.2.1) and Dispose() (§26.2.3) methods and when any contained finally blocks are executed.

The lock (§15.12) and using (§15.13) statements are defined in terms of try/finally (§15.10) and any reference to the execution of finally blocks in the definition of iterators also applies to the completion actions of lock (§15.12) and using.

Obscure iterator and finally/lock/using interaction

An iterator block is different from other blocks in that it may be *suspended* and later *resumed*. The sequence of execution of the contents—that is, of an iterator block—is equivalent to that which would result if the suspend/resume operations never occurred, as if, say, `yield` statements passed the values to a method for processing.

However, iterators need not run to completion. That is, there is no requirement that `MoveNext()` *must* be called until it returns `false` or that `Dispose()` must be called. Therefore, if a `yield return` occurs inside a `try`, `lock`, or `using`, it is possible that these statements never complete and that the associated *completion code* (`finally`, lock release, resource dispose) is not executed. Consider the following program fragment:

```
public IEnumerable<string> LineIterator(string filename)
{
  TextReader reader = null;
  try
  {
    reader = new StreamReader(filename);
    String line;
    while ((line = reader.ReadLine()) != null)
      yield return line;
  }
  finally
  {
    reader.Close();
  }
}

public void Demo(string filename)
{
  IEnumerable<String> eble = lineIterator(filename);
  IEnumerator<String> etor = eble.GetEnumerator();
  for (int i = 0; i < 5 && etor.MoveNext(); i++)
    Console.WriteLine(etor.Current);
}
```

Clearly, the intention of the author of `LineIterator` was that the file reader will be closed when no longer needed. This would normally be expressed with a `using` statement, which has an implicit `finally` clause, but this example uses `try` to make the `finally` clause explicit.

If the method `Demo()` is passed the name of a file with fewer than five lines then:

- the `while` in `LineIterator` will exit;
- the iterator will execute the `finally` block closing the file; and
- `MoveNext()` will return `false`.

However, if the file passed to `Demo()` has five or more lines, then:

- the `while` never terminates;
- `MoveNext()` never executes the `finally` and returns `false`; and
- the file is *never* closed.

The `Dispose()` method would execute the `finally`, but it is never called in this example.

A compiler could possibly address this problem by implementing a finalizer (§17.12) in the generated iterator class, but there is *no* requirement that it do so. Further, in at least the case of `lock`, using a finalizer that executes at an indeterminate time may well be inappropriate (but probably better than not releasing the lock at all). Using a finalizer would also raise the issue of handling exceptions, as `Dispose()` could throw. None of the compilers current at the time of writing use finalizers in their iterator implementations.

Summary: If an iterator contains `finally`, `lock`, or `using`, the usual guarantees do not apply and the completion code may not be executed. The Standard does not address how this issue should be handled and current implementations do not do so.

Recommendation: If your enumerator design requires the use of `finally`, `using`, or `lock`, then using an iterator is not advised. For annotations covering alternative approaches that might be appropriate, see §14.5.15.3.1 and §26.1.4.

Notes:

- The common use case of an iterator, the `foreach` statement (§15.8.4), calls the `Dispose()` method; in this case any completion code will be executed.
- In a similar manner it is possible on the CLI to create a situation when using threads (see annotation on §10.1) such that `finally` blocks may not be executed, locks released, or resources disposed.

Raja Harinath

26.2.1 The MoveNext method

The `MoveNext` method of an enumerator object encapsulates the code of an iterator block. Invoking the `MoveNext` method executes code in the iterator block and sets the `Current` property of the enumerator object as appropriate. The precise action performed by `MoveNext` depends on the state of the enumerator object when `MoveNext` is invoked:

- If the state of the enumerator object is ***before***, invoking `MoveNext`:
  - ○ Changes the state to ***running***.
  - ○ Initializes the parameters (including `this`) of the iterator block to the argument values and instance value saved when the enumerator object was initialized.
  - ○ Executes the iterator block from the beginning until execution is interrupted (as described below).
- If the state of the enumerator object is ***running***, the result of invoking `MoveNext` is unspecified.
- If the state of the enumerator object is ***suspended***, invoking `MoveNext`:
  - ○ Changes the state to ***running***.
  - ○ Restores the values of all local variables and parameters (including `this`) to the values saved when execution of the iterator block was last suspended. (Note that the contents of any objects referenced by these variables might have changed since the previous call to `MoveNext`.)
  - ○ Resumes execution of the iterator block immediately following the `yield return` statement that caused the suspension of execution, and continues until execution is interrupted (as described below).
- If the state of the enumerator object is ***after***, invoking `MoveNext` returns `false`.

When `MoveNext` executes the iterator block, execution can be interrupted in four ways: By a `yield return` statement, by a `yield break` statement, by encountering the end of the iterator block, or by an exception being thrown and propagated out of the iterator block.

- When a `yield return` statement is encountered (§15.14):
    - The expression given in the statement is evaluated, implicitly converted to the yield type, and assigned to the `Current` property of the enumerator object.
    - Execution of the iterator body is suspended. The values of all local variables and parameters (including `this`) are saved, as is the location of this `yield return` statement. If the `yield return` statement is within one or more `try` blocks, the associated `finally` blocks are *not* executed at this time.
    - The state of the enumerator object is changed to ***suspended***.
    - The `MoveNext` method returns `true` to its caller, indicating that the iteration successfully advanced to the next value.
- When a `yield break` statement is encountered (§15.14):
    - If the `yield break` statement is within one or more `try` blocks, the associated `finally` blocks are executed.
    - The state of the enumerator object is changed to ***after***.
    - The `MoveNext` method returns `false` to its caller, indicating that the iteration is complete.
- When the end of the iterator body is encountered:
    - The state of the enumerator object is changed to ***after***.
    - The `MoveNext` method returns `false` to its caller, indicating that the iteration is complete.
- When an exception is thrown and propagated out of the iterator block:
    - Appropriate `finally` blocks in the iterator body will have been executed by the exception propagation.
    - The state of the enumerator object is changed to ***after***.
    - The exception propagation continues to the caller of the `MoveNext` method.

Implicit yield break at end of iterator block

It follows from the second and third bullets that when the end of an iterator block is reachable, having a `yield break` statement there is equivalent to not having one.

26.2.2 The Current property

An enumerator object's `Current` property is affected by `yield return` statements in the iterator block.

When an enumerator object is in the ***suspended*** state, the value of `Current` is the value set by the previous call to `MoveNext`. When an enumerator object is in the ***before***, ***running***, or ***after*** states, the result of accessing `Current` is unspecified.

For an iterator block with a yield type other than `object`, the result of accessing `Current` through the enumerator object's `IEnumerable` implementation corresponds to accessing `Current` through the enumerator object's `IEnumerator<T>` implementation and casting the result to `object`.

26.2.3 The Dispose method

The `Dispose` method is used to clean up the iteration by bringing the enumerator object to the ***after*** state.

- If the state of the enumerator object is ***before***, invoking `Dispose` changes the state to ***after***.

- If the state of the enumerator object is ***running***, the result of invoking `Dispose` is unspecified.
- If the state of the enumerator object is ***suspended***, invoking `Dispose`:
  - Changes the state to ***running***.
  - Executes any finally blocks as if the last executed `yield return` statement were a `yield break` statement. If this causes an exception to be thrown and propagated out of the iterator body, the state of the enumerator object is set to ***after*** and the exception is propagated to the caller of the `Dispose` method.
  - Changes the state to ***after***.
- If the state of the enumerator object is ***after***, invoking `Dispose` has no affect.

26.3 Enumerable objects

When a function member returning an enumerable interface type is implemented using an iterator block, invoking the function member does not immediately execute the code in the iterator block. Instead, an ***enumerable object*** is created and returned. The enumerable object's `GetEnumerator` method returns an enumerator object that encapsulates the code specified in the iterator block, and execution of the code in the iterator block occurs when the enumerator object's `MoveNext` method is invoked. An enumerable object has the following characteristics:

- It implements `IEnumerable` and `IEnumerable<T>`, where `T` is the yield type of the iterator block.
- It is initialized with a copy of the argument values (if any) and instance value passed to the function member.

An enumerable object is typically an instance of a compiler-generated enumerable class that encapsulates the code in the iterator block and implements the enumerable interfaces, but other methods of implementation are possible. If an enumerable class is generated by the compiler, that class shall be nested, directly or indirectly, in the class containing the function member, it shall have private accessibility, and it shall have a name reserved for compiler use (§9.4.2).

[*Note*: An enumerable object can implement more interfaces than those specified above. In particular, an enumerable object can also implement `IEnumerator` and `IEnumerator<T>`, enabling it to serve as both an enumerable and an enumerator. In that type of implementation, the first time an enumerable object's `GetEnumerator` method is invoked, the enumerable object itself is returned. Subsequent invocations of the enumerable object's `GetEnumerator`, if any, return a copy of the enumerable object. Thus, each returned enumerator has its own state, and changes in one enumerator will not affect another. *end note*]

26.3.1 The GetEnumerator method

An enumerable object provides an implementation of the `GetEnumerator` methods of the `IEnumerable` and `IEnumerable<T>` interfaces. The two `GetEnumerator` methods share a common implementation that acquires and returns an available enumerator object. The enumerator object is initialized with the argument values and instance value saved when the enumerable object was initialized, but otherwise the enumerator object functions as described in §26.2.

26.4 Implementation example

[*Note*: This section describes a possible implementation of iterators in terms of standard C# constructs. The implementation described here is by no means a mandated implementation or the only one possible.

The following Stack<T> class implements its GetEnumerator method using an iterator. The iterator enumerates the elements of the stack in top to bottom order.

```
using System;
using System.Collections;
using System.Collections.Generic;

class Stack<T>: IEnumerable<T>
{
  T[] items;
  int count;

  public void Push(T item)
  {
    if (items == null)
    {
      items = new T[4];
    }
    else if (items.Length == count)
    {
      T[] newItems = new T[count * 2];
      Array.Copy(items, 0, newItems, 0, count);
      items = newItems;
    }
    items[count++] = item;
  }

  public T Pop()
  {
    T result = items[--count];
    items[count] = default(T);
    return result;
  }

  public IEnumerator<T> GetEnumerator()
  {
    for (int i = count - 1; i >= 0; --i) yield return items[i];
  }
}
```

The GetEnumerator method can be translated into an instantiation of a compiler-generated enumerator class that encapsulates the code in the iterator block, as shown in the following.

```
class Stack<T>: IEnumerable<T>
{
  ...

  public IEnumerator<T> GetEnumerator()
  {
```

```
      return new __Enumerator1(this);
}

class __Enumerator1: IEnumerator<T>, IEnumerator
{
  int __state;
  T __current;
  Stack<T> __this;
  int i;

  public __Enumerator1(Stack<T> __this)
  {
    this.__this = __this;
  }

  public T Current
  {
    get { return __current; }
  }

  object IEnumerator.Current
  {
    get { return __current; }
  }

  public bool MoveNext()
  {
    switch (__state)
    {
      case 1: goto __state1;
      case 2: goto __state2;
    }
    i = __this.count - 1;
  __loop:
    if (i < 0) goto __state2;
    __current = __this.items[i];
    __state = 1;
    return true;
  __state1:
    --i;
    goto __loop;
  __state2:
    __state = 2;
    return false;
  }

  public void Dispose()
  {
    __state = 2;
  }


  void IEnumerator.Reset()
  {
```

```
      throw new NotSupportedException();
    }
  }
}
```

In the preceding translation, the code in the iterator block is turned into a state machine and placed in the `MoveNext` method of the enumerator class. Furthermore, the local variable `i` is turned into a field in the enumerator object so it can continue to exist across invocations of `MoveNext`.

The following example prints a simple multiplication table of the integers 1 through 10. The `FromTo` method in the example returns an enumerable object and is implemented using an iterator.

```csharp
using System;
using System.Collections.Generic;

class Test
{
  static IEnumerable<int> FromTo(int from, int to)
  {
    while (from <= to) yield return from++;
  }

  static void Main()
  {
    IEnumerable<int> e = FromTo(1, 10);
    foreach (int x in e)
    {
      foreach (int y in e)
      {
        Console.Write("{0,3} ", x * y);
      }
      Console.WriteLine();
    }
  }
}
```

The `FromTo` method can be translated into an instantiation of a compiler-generated enumerable class that encapsulates the code in the iterator block, as shown in the following.

```csharp
using System;
using System.Threading;
using System.Collections;
using System.Collections.Generic;

class Test
{
  ...

  static IEnumerable<int> FromTo(int from, int to)
  {
    return new __Enumerable1(from, to);
  }
```

```csharp
class __Enumerable1:
  IEnumerable<int>, IEnumerable,
  IEnumerator<int>, IEnumerator
{
  int __state;
  int __current;
  int __from;
  int from;
  int to;
  int i;

  public __Enumerable1(int __from, int to)
  {
    this.__from = __from;
    this.to = to;
  }

  public IEnumerator<int> GetEnumerator()
  {
    __Enumerable1 result = this;
    if (Interlocked.CompareExchange(ref __state, 1, 0) != 0)
    {
      result = new __Enumerable1(__from, to);
      result.__state = 1;
    }
    result.from = result.__from;
    return result;
  }

  IEnumerator IEnumerable.GetEnumerator()
  {
    return (IEnumerator)GetEnumerator();
  }

  public int Current
  {
    get { return __current; }
  }

  object IEnumerator.Current
  {
    get { return __current; }
  }

  public bool MoveNext()
  {
    switch (__state)
    {
    case 1:
      if (from > to) goto case 2;
      __current = from++;
      __state = 1;
      return true;
```

```
      case 2:
        __state = 2;
        return false;
      default:
        throw new InvalidOperationException();
    }
  }

  public void Dispose()
  {
    __state = 2;
  }

  void IEnumerator.Reset()
  {
    throw new NotSupportedException();
  }
  }
}
```

The enumerable class implements both the enumerable interfaces and the enumerator interfaces, enabling it to serve as both an enumerable and an enumerator. The first time the GetEnumerator method is invoked, the enumerable object itself is returned. Subsequent invocations of the enumerable object's GetEnumerator, if any, return a copy of the enumerable object. Thus, each returned enumerator has its own state and changes in one enumerator will not affect another. The Interlocked.CompareExchange method is used to ensure thread-safe operation.

The from and to parameters are turned into fields in the enumerable class. Because from is modified in the iterator block, an additional __from field is introduced to hold the initial value given to from in each enumerator.

The MoveNext method throws an InvalidOperationException if it is called when __state is 0. This protects against use of the enumerable object as an enumerator object without first calling GetEnumerator.

The following example shows a simple tree class. The Tree<T> class implements its GetEnumerator method using an iterator. The iterator enumerates the elements of the tree in infix order.

```
using System;
using System.Collections.Generic;

class Tree<T>: IEnumerable<T>
{
  T value;
  Tree<T> left;
  Tree<T> right;

  public Tree(T value, Tree<T> left, Tree<T> right)
  {
    this.value = value;
    this.left = left;
    this.right = right;
  }
```

```
    public IEnumerator<T> GetEnumerator()
    {
      if (left != null) foreach (T x in left) yield return x;
      yield return value;
      if (right != null) foreach (T x in right) yield return x;
    }
}

class Program
{
  static Tree<T> MakeTree<T>(T[ ] items, int left, int right)
  {
    if (left > right) return null;
    int i = (left + right) / 2;
    return new Tree<T>(items[i],
            MakeTree(items, left, i - 1),
            MakeTree(items, i + 1, right));
  }

  static Tree<T> MakeTree<T>(params T[ ] items)
  {
    return MakeTree(items, 0, items.Length - 1);
  }

  // The output of the program is:
  // 1 2 3 4 5 6 7 8 9
  // Mon Tue Wed Thu Fri Sat Sun
  //

  static void Main()
  {
    Tree<int> ints = MakeTree(1, 2, 3, 4, 5, 6, 7, 8, 9);
    foreach (int i in ints) Console.Write("{0} ", i);
    Console.WriteLine();

    Tree<string> strings = MakeTree("Mon", "Tue", "Wed", "Thu",
                                    "Fri", "Sat", "Sun");
    foreach (string s in strings) Console.Write("{0} ", s);
    Console.WriteLine();
  }
}
```

The GetEnumerator method can be translated into an instantiation of a compiler-generated enumerator class that encapsulates the code in the iterator block, as shown in the following.

```
class Tree<T> : IEnumerable<T>
{
  ...
  public IEnumerator<T> GetEnumerator()
  {
    return new __Enumerator1(this);
  }

  sealed class __Enumerator1 : IEnumerator<T>, IEnumerator
```

```csharp
{
  Node<T> __this;
  IEnumerator<T> __left, __right;
  int __state;
  T __current;

  public __Enumerator1(Node<T> __this) { this.__this = __this; }

  public T Current { get { return __current; } }

  public bool MoveNext()
  {
    try
    {
      switch (__state)
      {

      case 0:
        __state = -1;
        if (__this.left == null) goto __yield_value;
        __left = __this.left.GetEnumerator();
        goto case 1;

      case 1:
        __state = -2;
        if (!__left.MoveNext()) goto __left_dispose;
        __current = __left.Current;
        __state = 1;
        return true;

      __left_dispose:
        __state = -1;
        __left.Dispose();

      __yield_value:
        __current = __this.value;
        __state = 2;
        return true;

      case 2:
        __state = -1;
        if (__this.right == null) goto __end;
        __right = __this.right.GetEnumerator();
        goto case 3;

      case 3:
        __state = -3;
        if (!__right.MoveNext()) goto __right_dispose;
        __current = __right.Current;
        __state = 3;
        return true;

      __right_dispose:
        __state = -1;
```

```
          __right.Dispose();

        __end:
          __state = 4;
          break;

      }
    } finally
    {
      if (__state < 0) Dispose();
    }
    return false;
  }

  public void Dispose()
  {
    try
    {
      switch (__state)
      {

      case 1:
      case -2:
        __left.Dispose();
        break;

      case 3:
      case -3:
        __right.Dispose();
        break;

      }
    } finally
    {
      __state = 4;
    }
  }

  object IEnumerator.Current { get { return Current; } }

  void IEnumerator.Reset()
  {
    throw new NotSupportedException();
  }
  }
}
```

The compiler-generated temporaries used in the foreach statements are lifted into the __left and __right fields of the enumerator object. The __state field of the enumerator object is carefully updated so that the correct Dispose() method will be called correctly if an exception is thrown. Note that it is not possible to write the translated code with simple foreach statements. *end note*]

Anecdote: iterator blocks, generic parameters, and a bug

The previous implementation sketch helps understand a bug found in an early compiler. The following generic class C<T> contains an iterator block in which an object o is cast to the generic type parameter T, which must be a reference type (§14.9.11). Therefore, the generic parameter has a class constraint:

```
class C<T> where T : class
{
   public IEnumerable<T> M(object o)
   {
      T x = o as T;
      for (;;)
         yield return x;
   }
}
```

Clearly, the class generated for the iterator block should have generic parameter T. Unfortunately, an early (2004) version of Microsoft's compiler neglected to copy the class constraint to the type parameter of the generated class. As a consequence, the bytecode failed at runtime. The point is that the implementation of yield outlined earlier shows through in the bug.

For the same reason, it was easy to find a workaround; just replace the statement T x = o as T by the following, which does not require T to be a reference type:

```
T x = o is T ? (T)o : null;
```

27 Unsafe code

An implementation that does not support unsafe code is required to diagnose any usage of the keyword `unsafe`.

The remainder of this clause, including all of its subclauses, is conditionally normative.

[*Note*: The core C# language, as defined in the preceding clauses, differs notably from C and C++ in its omission of pointers as a data type. Instead, C# provides references and the ability to create objects that are managed by a garbage collector. This design, coupled with other features, makes C# a much safer language than C or C++. In the core C #language, it is simply not possible to have an uninitialized variable, a "dangling" pointer, or an expression that indexes an array beyond its bounds. Whole categories of bugs that routinely plague C and C++ programs are thus eliminated.

While practically every pointer type construct in C or C++ has a reference type counterpart in C#, nonetheless, there are situations where access to pointer types becomes a necessity. For example, interfacing with the underlying operating system, accessing a memory-mapped device, or implementing a time-critical algorithm might not be possible or practical without access to pointers. To address this need, C# provides the ability to write ***unsafe code***.

In unsafe code, it is possible to declare and operate on pointers, to perform conversions between pointers and integral types, to take the address of variables, and so forth. In a sense, writing unsafe code is much like writing C code within a C# program.

Unsafe code is in fact a "safe" feature from the perspective of both developers and users. Unsafe code shall be clearly marked with the modifier `unsafe`, so developers can't possibly use unsafe features accidentally, and the execution engine works to ensure that unsafe code cannot be executed in an untrusted environment. *end note*]

27.1 Unsafe contexts

The unsafe features of C# are available only in unsafe contexts. An unsafe context is introduced by including an `unsafe` modifier in the declaration of a type or member, or by employing an *unsafe-statement*:

- A declaration of a class, struct, interface, or delegate can include an `unsafe` modifier, in which case, the extent of that *type-declaration* is considered an unsafe context. [*Note*: If the *type-declaration* is partial, only that part is an unsafe context. *end note*]
- A declaration of a field, method, property, event, indexer, operator, instance constructor, finalizer, or static constructor can include an `unsafe` modifier, in which case, the entire textual extent of that member declaration is considered an unsafe context.
- An *unsafe-statement* enables the use of an unsafe context within a *block*. The entire textual extent of the associated *block* is considered an unsafe context.

The associated grammar extensions are shown below. For brevity, ellipses (...) are used to represent productions that appear in preceding clauses.

class-modifier:
  ...
  `unsafe`

struct-modifier:
  ...
  `unsafe`

interface-modifier:
 ...
 unsafe

delegate-modifier:
 ...
 unsafe

field-modifier:
 ...
 unsafe

method-modifier:
 ...
 unsafe

property-modifier:
 ...
 unsafe

event-modifier:
 ...
 unsafe

indexer-modifier:
 ...
 unsafe

operator-modifier:
 ...
 unsafe

constructor-modifier:
 ...
 unsafe

finalizer-declaration:
 attributes$_{opt}$ extern$_{opt}$ unsafe$_{opt}$ ~ *identifier* ( ) *finalizer-body*
 attributes$_{opt}$ unsafe$_{opt}$ extern$_{opt}$ ~ *identifier* ( ) *finalizer-body*

static-constructor-modifiers:
 extern$_{opt}$ unsafe$_{opt}$ static
 unsafe$_{opt}$ extern$_{opt}$ static
 extern$_{opt}$ static unsafe$_{opt}$
 unsafe$_{opt}$ static extern$_{opt}$
 static extern$_{opt}$ unsafe$_{opt}$
 static unsafe$_{opt}$ extern$_{opt}$

embedded-statement:
 ...
 unsafe-statement

unsafe-statement:
   unsafe   *block*

[*Example*: In the following code

```
public unsafe struct Node
{
  public int Value;
  public Node* Left;
  public Node* Right;
}
```

the `unsafe` modifier specified in the struct declaration causes the entire textual extent of the struct declaration to become an unsafe context. Thus, it is possible to declare the `Left` and `Right` fields to be of a pointer type. The example above could also be written

```
public struct Node
{
  public int Value;
  public unsafe Node* Left;
  public unsafe Node* Right;
}
```

Here, the `unsafe` modifiers in the field declarations cause those declarations to be considered unsafe contexts. *end example*]

Other than establishing an unsafe context, thus permitting the use of pointer types, the `unsafe` modifier has no effect on a type or a member. [*Example*: In the following code

```
public class A
{
  public unsafe virtual void F()
  {
    char* p;
    ...
  }
}

public class B: A
{
  public override void F()
  {
    base.F();
    ...
  }
}
```

the `unsafe` modifier on the `F` method in `A` simply causes the textual extent of `F` to become an unsafe context in which the unsafe features of the language can be used. In the override of `F` in `B`, there is no need to re-specify the `unsafe` modifier—unless, of course, the `F` method in `B` itself needs access to unsafe features.

The situation is slightly different when a pointer type is part of the method's signature

```
public unsafe class A
{
  public virtual void F(char* p) {...}
}
```

```
public class B: A
{
  public unsafe override void F(char* p) {...}
}
```

Here, because F's signature includes a pointer type, it can only be written in an unsafe context. However, the unsafe context can be introduced by either making the entire class unsafe, as is the case in A, or by including an `unsafe` modifier in the method declaration, as is the case in B. *end example*]

When the `unsafe` modifier is used on a partial type declaration (§17.1.4), only that particular part is considered an unsafe context.

27.2 Pointer types

In an unsafe context, a *type* (§11) can be a *pointer-type* as well as a *value-type*, a *reference-type*, or a *type-parameter*.

> *type:*
>   *value-type*
>   *reference-type*
>   *type-parameter*
>   *pointer-type*

A *pointer-type* is written as an *unmanaged-type* or the keyword `void`, followed by a `*` token:

> *pointer-type:*
>   *unmanaged-type*   `*`
>   `void`   `*`
>
> *unmanaged-type:*
>   *type*

The type specified before the `*` in a pointer type is called the **referent type** of the pointer type. It represents the type of the variable to which a value of the pointer type points.

Unlike references (values of reference types), pointers are not tracked by the garbage collector—the garbage collector has no knowledge of pointers and the data to which they point. For this reason a pointer is not permitted to point to a reference or to a struct that contains references, and the referent type of a pointer shall be an *unmanaged-type*.

An *unmanaged-type* is any type that isn't a *reference-type*, a *type-parameter*, or a generic *struct-type* and contains no fields whose type is not an *unmanaged-type*. In other words, an *unmanaged-type* is one of the following:

- `sbyte`, `byte`, `short`, `ushort`, `int`, `uint`, `long`, `ulong`, `char`, `float`, `double`, `decimal`, or `bool`.
- Any *enum-type*.
- Any *pointer-type*.
- Any non-generic user-defined *struct-type* that contains fields of *unmanaged-type*s only.

[*Note*: Constructed types and *type-parameter*s are never *unmanaged-type*s. *end note*]

The intuitive rule for mixing of pointers and references is that referents of references (objects) are permitted to contain pointers, but referents of pointers are not permitted to contain references.

[*Example*: Some examples of pointer types are given in the table below:

Example	Description
byte*	Pointer to byte
char*	Pointer to char
int**	Pointer to pointer to int
int*[]	Single-dimensional array of pointers to int
void*	Pointer to unknown type

end example]

Missing grammar rule

As can be seen from the preceding examples, arrays of pointers are supported. However, the grammar additions are not sufficient to allow this. An addition must also be made to *non-array-type* (§19.1) to include *pointer-type*:

   non-array-type:
     value-type
     class-type
     interface-type
     delegate-type
     type-parameter
     pointer-type

The Novell and Microsoft compilers current at the time of writing correctly support arrays of pointers as intended.

For a given implementation, all pointer types shall have the same size and representation.

[*Note*: Unlike C and C++, when multiple pointers are declared in the same declaration, in C# the * is written along with the underlying type only, not as a prefix punctuator on each pointer name. For example:

```
int* pi, pj;   // NOT as int *pi, *pj;
```

end note]

The value of a pointer having type T* represents the address of a variable of type T. The pointer indirection operator * (§27.5.1) can be used to access this variable. [*Example*: Given a variable P of type int*, the expression *P denotes the int variable found at the address contained in P. *end example*]

Like an object reference, a pointer can be null. Applying the indirection operator to a null pointer results in implementation-defined behavior. A pointer with value null is represented by all-bits-zero.

The void* type represents a pointer to an unknown type. Because the referent type is unknown, the indirection operator cannot be applied to a pointer of type void*, nor can any arithmetic be performed on such a pointer. However, a pointer of type void* can be cast to any other pointer type (and vice versa) and compared to values of other pointer types.

Pointer types are a separate category of types. Unlike reference types and value types, pointer types do not inherit from object and no conversions exist between pointer types and object. In particular, boxing and unboxing (§11.3) are not supported for pointers. However, conversions are permitted between different pointer types and between pointer types and the integral types. This is described in §27.4.

A *pointer-type* can be used as the type of a volatile field (§17.4.3).

Volatile pointers

The preceding paragraph means that the field holding the pointer can be volatile, rather than that the type pointed to is volatile. What is pointed to *may* also be volatile, but this cannot be determined because taking the address of a volatile field does not produce a "pointer to volatile" (§27.5.4).

A confusing C# vs. C/C++ syntax difference

When declaring a volatile pointer, the C# and C/C++ languages use the same tokens but in a different order, which can be just a mite confusing for people switching between the languages. For example, consider the C# declaration:

```
volatile int * widgetCSharp;      // This is C# code!
```

This declares a volatile field `widgetCSharp` of type `int *`.

C/C++ code declaring a volatile field of the same type would be written:

```
int * volatile widgetCPlusPlus;  // This is C/C++ code!
```

Apart from the change in the field name, this C/C++ declaration is equivalent to the preceding C# one.

To compound matters, the preceding C# token sequence is also valid in C/C++ but means something different. But our job is not to explain the complexities of C/C++ declarations—whole books could be written on that!

[*Note*: Although pointers can be passed as `ref` or `out` parameters, doing so can cause undefined behavior, since the pointer might well be set to point to a local variable that no longer exists when the called method returns, or the fixed object to which it used to point, is no longer fixed. For example:

```
using System;

class Test
{
  static int value = 20;

  unsafe static void F(out int* pi1, ref int* pi2)
  {
    int i = 10;
    pi1 = &i;
    fixed (int* pj = &value)
    {
      ...
      pi2 = pj;
    }
  }

  static void Main()
  {
```

```
      int i = 10;
      unsafe
      {
        int* px1;
        int* px2 = &i;
        F(out px1, ref px2);
        Console.WriteLine("*px1 = {0} , *px2 = {1} ",
          *px1, *px2);  // undefined behavior
      }
    }
  }
```

end note]

A method can return a value of some type, and that type can be a pointer. [*Example*: When given a pointer to a contiguous sequence of `int`s, that sequence's element count, and some other `int` value, the following method returns the address of that value in that sequence, if a match occurs; otherwise it returns `null`:

```
unsafe static int* Find(int* pi, int size, int value)
{
  for (int i = 0; i < size; ++i)
  {
    if (*pi == value)
    {
      return pi;
    }
    ++pi;
  }
  return null;
}
```

end example]

In an unsafe context, several constructs are available for operating on pointers:

- The unary `*` operator can be used to perform pointer indirection (§27.5.1).
- The `->` operator can be used to access a member of a struct through a pointer (§27.5.2).
- The `[ ]` operator can be used to index a pointer (§27.5.3).
- The unary `&` operator can be used to obtain the address of a variable (§27.5.4).
- The `++` and `--` operators can be used to increment and decrement pointers (§27.5.5).
- The binary `+` and `-` operators can be used to perform pointer arithmetic (§27.5.6).
- The `==`, `!=`, `<`, `>`, `<=`, and `>=` operators can be used to compare pointers (§27.5.7).
- The `stackalloc` operator can be used to allocate memory from the call stack (§27.7).
- The `fixed` statement can be used to temporarily fix a variable so its address can be obtained (§27.6).

27.3 Fixed and moveable variables

The address-of operator (§27.5.4) and the `fixed` statement (§27.6) divide variables into two categories: *Fixed variables* and *moveable variables*.

Fixed variables reside in storage locations that are unaffected by operation of the garbage collector. (Examples of fixed variables include local variables, value parameters, and variables created by dereferencing pointers.) On the other hand, moveable variables reside in storage locations that are subject to relocation or disposal by the garbage collector. (Examples of moveable variables include fields in objects and elements of arrays.)

The & operator (§27.5.4) permits the address of a fixed variable to be obtained without restrictions. However, because a moveable variable is subject to relocation or disposal by the garbage collector, the address of a moveable variable can only be obtained using a `fixed` statement (§27.6), and that address remains valid only for the duration of that `fixed` statement.

In precise terms, a fixed variable is one of the following:

- A variable resulting from a *simple-name* (§14.5.2) that refers to a local variable or a value parameter, as long as the variable is not captured by an anonymous method (§14.5.15.3.1).
- A variable resulting from a *member-access* (§14.5.4) of the form V.I, where V is a fixed variable of a *struct-type*.
- A variable resulting from a *pointer-indirection-expression* (§27.5.1) of the form * P, a *pointer-member-access* (§27.5.2) of the form P->I, or a *pointer-element-access* (§27.5.3) of the form P[E].

All other variables are classified as moveable variables.

A static field is classified as a moveable variable. Also, a `ref` or `out` parameter is classified as a moveable variable, even if the argument given for the parameter is a fixed variable. Finally, a variable produced by dereferencing a pointer is always classified as a fixed variable.

27.4 Pointer conversions

In an unsafe context, the set of available implicit conversions (§13.1) is extended to include the following implicit pointer conversions:

- From any *pointer-type* to the type void*.
- From the null type (§11.2.7) to any *pointer-type*.

Additionally, in an unsafe context, the set of available explicit conversions (§13.2) is extended to include the following explicit pointer conversions:

- From any *pointer-type* to any other *pointer-type*.
- From sbyte, byte, short, ushort, int, uint, long, or ulong to any *pointer-type*.
- From any *pointer-type* to sbyte, byte, short, ushort, int, uint, long, or ulong.

Finally, in an unsafe context, the set of standard implicit conversions (§13.3.1) includes the following pointer conversion:

- From any *pointer-type* to the type void*.

Conversions between two pointer types never change the actual pointer value. In other words, a conversion from one pointer type to another has no effect on the underlying address given by the pointer.

When one pointer type is converted to another, if the resulting pointer is not correctly aligned for the pointed-to type, the behavior is undefined if the result is dereferenced. In general, the concept "correctly aligned" is transitive: if a pointer to type A is correctly aligned for a pointer to type B, which, in turn, is correctly aligned for a pointer to type C, then a pointer to type A is correctly aligned for a pointer to type C. [*Example*: Consider the following case in which a variable having one type is accessed via a pointer to a different type:

```
char c = 'A';
char* pc = &c;
void* pv = pc;
```

```
int* pi = (int*)pv;
int i = *pi;      // undefined
*pi = 123456;     // undefined
```

end example]

When a pointer type is converted to a pointer to `byte`, the result points to the lowest addressed byte of the variable. Successive increments of the result, up to the size of the variable, yield pointers to the remaining bytes of that variable. [*Example*: The following method displays each of the eight bytes in a `double` as a hexadecimal value:

```
using System;

class Test
{
  static void Main()
  {
    double d = 123.456e23;
    unsafe
    {
      byte* pb = (byte*)&d;
      for (int i = 0; i < sizeof(double); ++i)
        Console.Write(" {0,2:X}", (uint)(*pb++));
      Console.WriteLine();
    }
  }
}
```

Of course, the output produced depends on byte ordering. *end example*]

Mappings between pointers and integers are implementation-defined. [*Note*: However, on 32- and 64-bit CPU architectures with a linear address space, conversions of pointers to or from integral types typically behave exactly like conversions of `uint` or `ulong` values, respectively, to or from those integral types. *end note*]

27.5 Pointers in expressions

In an unsafe context, an expression can yield a result of a pointer type, but outside an unsafe context, it is a compile-time error for an expression to be of a pointer type. In precise terms, outside an unsafe context a compile-time error occurs if any *simple-name* (§14.5.2), *member-access* (§14.5.4), *invocation-expression* (§14.5.5), or *element-access* (§14.5.6) is of a pointer type.

The *primary-no-array-creation-expression* (§14.5) productions permit the following additional construct:

> *primary-no-array-creation-expression:*
>   *...*
>   *sizeof-expression*

In an unsafe context, the *primary-no-array-creation-expression* (§14.5) and *unary-expression* (§14.6) productions permit the following additional constructs:

> *primary-no-array-creation-expression:*
>   *...*
>   *pointer-member-access*
>   *pointer-element-access*

unary-expression:
> ...
> *pointer-indirection-expression*
> *addressof-expression*

These constructs are described in the following subclauses.

There are also several predefined unary and binary operators for pointers. When applying unary or binary operator overload resolution, if none of the actual operands is a pointer type, then any predefined unary or binary operator with a pointer parameter type is removed from consideration.

[*Note*: The precedence and associativity of the unsafe operators is implied by the grammar. *end note*]

27.5.1 Pointer indirection

A *pointer-indirection-expression* consists of an asterisk (`*`) followed by a *unary-expression*.

> *pointer-indirection-expression:*
> `*`   *unary-expression*

The unary `*` operator denotes pointer indirection and is used to obtain the variable to which a pointer points. The result of evaluating `*P`, where `P` is an expression of a pointer type `T*`, is a variable of type `T`. It is a compile-time error to apply the unary `*` operator to an expression of type `void*` or to an expression that isn't of a pointer type.

The effect of applying the unary `*` operator to a `null` pointer is implementation-defined. In particular, there is no guarantee that this operation throws a `System.NullReferenceException`.

If an invalid value has been assigned to the pointer, the behavior of the unary `*` operator is undefined. [*Note*: Among the invalid values for dereferencing a pointer by the unary `*` operator are an address inappropriately aligned for the type pointed to (see example in §27.4), and the address of a variable after the end of its lifetime. *end note*]

For purposes of definite assignment analysis, a variable produced by evaluating an expression of the form `*P` is considered initially assigned (§12.3.1).

27.5.2 Pointer member access

A *pointer-member-access* consists of a *primary-expression*, followed by a "`->`" token, followed by an *identifier*.

> *pointer-member-access:*
> *primary-expression*   `->`   *identifier*   *type-argument-list*_{opt}

In a pointer member access of the form `P->I`, `P` shall be an expression of a pointer type other than `void*`, and `I` shall denote an accessible member of the type to which `P` points.

A pointer member access of the form `P->I` is evaluated exactly as `(*P).I`. For a description of the pointer indirection operator (`*`), see §27.5.1. For a description of the member access operator (`.`), see §14.5.4.

[*Example*: In the following code

```
struct Point
{
  public int x;
  public int y;
```

```
  public override string ToString()
  {
    return "(" + x + "," + y + ")";
  }
}

using System;

class Test
{
  static void Main()
  {
    Point point;
    unsafe
    {
      Point* p = &point;
      p->x = 10;
      p->y = 20;
      Console.WriteLine(p->ToString());
    }
  }
}
```

the -> operator is used to access fields and invoke a method of a struct through a pointer. Because the operation P->I is precisely equivalent to (*P).I, the Main method could equally well have been written:

```
using System;

class Test
{
  static void Main()
  {
    Point point;
    unsafe
    {
      Point* p = &point;
      (*p).x = 10;
      (*p).y = 20;
      Console.WriteLine((*p).ToString());
    }
  }
}
```

end example]

27.5.3 Pointer element access
A *pointer-element-access* consists of a *primary-no-array-creation-expression* followed by an expression enclosed in "[" and "] ".

> *pointer-element-access:*
>   *primary-no-array-creation-expression* [*expression*   ]

In a pointer element access of the form P[E] , P shall be an expression of a pointer type other than void*, and E shall be an expression of a type that can be implicitly converted to int, uint, long, or ulong.

A pointer element access of the form P[E] is evaluated exactly as * (P + E). For a description of the pointer indirection operator (*), see §27.5.1. For a description of the pointer addition operator (+), see §27.5.6.

[*Example*: In the following code

```
class Test
{
  static void Main()
  {
    unsafe
    {
      char* p = stackalloc char[256];
      for (int i = 0; i < 256; i++) p[i] = (char)i;
    }
  }
}
```

a pointer element access is used to initialize the character buffer in a for loop. Because the operation P[E] is precisely equivalent to * (P + E), the example could equally well have been written:

```
class Test
{
  static void Main()
  {
    unsafe
    {
      char* p = stackalloc char[256];
      for (int i = 0; i < 256; i++) * (p + i) = (char)i;
    }
  }
}
```

end example]

The pointer element access operator does not check for out-of-bounds errors and the behavior when accessing an out-of-bounds element is undefined. [*Note*: This is the same as C and C++. *end note*]

27.5.4 The address-of operator

An *addressof-expression* consists of an ampersand (&) followed by a *unary-expression*.

> *addressof-expression:*
>   &   *unary-expression*

Given an expression E which is of a type T and is classified as a fixed variable (§27.3), the construct &E computes the address of the variable given by E. The type of the result is T* and is classified as a value. A compile-time error occurs if E is not classified as a variable, if E is a read-only variable, or if E denotes a moveable variable. In the last case, a fixed statement (§27.6) can be used to temporarily "fix" the variable before obtaining its address.

> **No pointer-to-volatile**
> Note: Taking the address of a volatile field does not produce a pointer-to-volatile; see the annotation on §27.2 for further details.

The `&` operator does not require its argument to be definitely assigned, but following an `&` operation, the variable to which the operator is applied is considered definitely assigned in the execution path in which the operation occurs. It is the responsibility of the programmer to ensure that correct initialization of the variable actually does take place in this situation.

[*Example*: In the following code

```
using System;

class Test
{
  static void Main()
  {
    int i;
    unsafe
    {
      int* p = &i;
      *p = 123;
    }
    Console.WriteLine(i);
  }
}
```

`i` is considered definitely assigned following the `&i` operation used to initialize `p`. The assignment to `*p` in effect initializes `i`, but the inclusion of this initialization is the responsibility of the programmer, and no compile-time error would occur if the assignment were removed. *end example*]

[*Note*: The rules of definite assignment for the `&` operator exist such that redundant initialization of local variables can be avoided. For example, many external APIs take a pointer to a structure which is filled in by the API. Calls to such APIs typically pass the address of a local struct variable, and without the rule, redundant initialization of the struct variable would be required. *end note*]

[*Note*: As stated in §14.5.4, outside an instance constructor or static constructor for a struct or class that defines a readonly field, that field is considered a value, not a variable. As such, its address cannot be taken. Similarly, the address of a constant cannot be taken. *end note*]

When a local variable, value parameter, or parameter array is captured by an anonymous method (§14.5.15.3.1), that local variable, parameter, or parameter array is no longer considered to be a fixed variable (§27.3), but is instead considered to be a moveable variable. Thus it is an error for any `unsafe` code to take the address of a local variable, value parameter, or parameter array that has been captured by an anonymous method.

27.5.5 Pointer increment and decrement
In an unsafe context, the `++` and `--` operators (§14.5.9 and §14.6.5) can be applied to pointer variables of all types except `void*`. Thus, for every pointer type `T*`, the following operators are implicitly defined:

```
T* operator ++(T* x);
T* operator --(T* x);
```

The operators produce the same results as x+1 and x-1, respectively (§27.5.6). In other words, for a pointer variable of type T*, the ++ operator adds sizeof(T) to the address contained in the variable, and the -- operator subtracts sizeof(T) from the address contained in the variable.

If a pointer increment or decrement operation overflows the domain of the pointer type, the result is implementation-defined, but no exceptions are produced.

27.5.6 Pointer arithmetic

In an unsafe context, the + operator (§14.7.4) and - operator (§14.7.5) can be applied to values of all pointer types except void*. Thus, for every pointer type T*, the following operators are implicitly defined:

```
T* operator +(T* x, int y);
T* operator +(T* x, uint y);
T* operator +(T* x, long y);
T* operator +(T* x, ulong y);

T* operator +(int x, T* y);
T* operator +(uint x, T* y);
T* operator +(long x, T* y);
T* operator +(ulong x, T* y);

T* operator -(T* x, int y);
T* operator -(T* x, uint y);
T* operator -(T* x, long y);
T* operator -(T* x, ulong y);

long operator -(T* x, T* y);
```

Given an expression P of a pointer type T* and an expression N of type int, uint, long, or ulong, the expressions P + N and N + P compute the pointer value of type T* that results from adding N * sizeof(T) to the address given by P. Likewise, the expression P - N computes the pointer value of type T* that results from subtracting N * sizeof(T) from the address given by P.

Given two expressions, P and Q, of a pointer type T*, the expression P - Q computes the difference between the addresses given by P and Q and then divides that difference by sizeof(T). The type of the result is always long. In effect, P - Q is computed as ((long)(P) - (long)(Q)) / sizeof(T). [*Example*:

```
using System;

class Test
{
  static void Main()
  {
    unsafe
    {
      int* values = stackalloc int[20];

      int* p = &values[1];
      int* q = &values[15];
```

```
          Console.WriteLine ("p - q = {0} ", p - q);
          Console.WriteLine ("q - p = {0} ", q - p);
      }
    }
}
```

which produces the output:

```
p - q = -14
q - p = 14
```

end example]

If a pointer arithmetic operation overflows the domain of the pointer type, the result is truncated in an implementation-defined fashion, but no exceptions are produced.

27.5.7 Pointer comparison

In an unsafe context, the ==, !=, <, >, <=, and >= operators (§14.9) can be applied to values of all pointer types. The pointer comparison operators are:

```
bool operator == (void* x, void* y);
bool operator != (void* x, void* y);

bool operator < (void* x, void* y);
bool operator > (void* x, void* y);
bool operator <= (void* x, void* y);
bool operator >= (void* x, void* y);
```

Because an implicit conversion exists from any pointer type to the void* type, operands of any pointer type can be compared using these operators. The comparison operators compare the addresses given by the two operands as if they were unsigned integers.

27.5.8 The sizeof operator

The sizeof operator returns the number of 8-bit bytes occupied by a variable of a given type. The type specified as an operand to sizeof shall be an *unmanaged-type* (§27.2).

> *sizeof-expression:*
>   sizeof   (*unmanaged-type*   )

For the predefined types specified in §14.5.12 the sizeof operator yields a constant int value, and the *sizeof-expression* is allowed both inside and outside an unsafe context.

For all other types, the result of the sizeof operator is implementation-defined and is classified as an int value rather than an int constant, and the *sizeof-expression* shall be inside an unsafe context.

The order in which members are packed into a struct is unspecified.

For alignment purposes, there can be unnamed padding at the beginning of a struct, within a struct, and at the end of the struct. The contents of the bits used as padding are indeterminate.

When applied to an operand that has struct type, the result is the total number of bytes in a variable of that type, including any padding.

27.6 The fixed statement

In an unsafe context, the *embedded-statement* (§15) production permits an additional construct, the `fixed` statement, which is used to "fix" a moveable variable such that its address remains constant for the duration of the statement.

embedded-statement:
  …
  fixed-statement

fixed-statement:
  `fixed` (*pointer-type*   *fixed-pointer-declarators*)   *embedded-statement*

fixed-pointer-declarators:
  fixed-pointer-declarator
  fixed-pointer-declarators ,   *fixed-pointer-declarator*

fixed-pointer-declarator:
  identifier = *fixed-pointer-initializer*

fixed-pointer-initializer:
  & *variable-reference*
  expression

Each *fixed-pointer-declarator* declares a local variable of the given *pointer-type* and initializes that local variable with the address computed by the corresponding *fixed-pointer-initializer*. A local variable declared in a `fixed` statement is accessible in any *fixed-pointer-initializer*s occurring to the right of that variable's declaration, and in the *embedded-statement* of the `fixed` statement. A local variable declared by a `fixed` statement is considered read-only. A compile-time error occurs if the embedded statement attempts to modify this local variable (via assignment or the `++` and `--` operators) or pass it as a `ref` or `out` parameter.

It is an error to use a captured local variable (§14.5.15.3.1), value parameter, or parameter array in a *fixed-pointer-initializer*.

A *fixed-pointer-initializer* can be one of the following:

- The token "`&`" followed by a *variable-reference* (§12.4) to a moveable variable (§27.3) of an unmanaged type T, provided the type T* is implicitly convertible to the pointer type given in the `fixed` statement. In this case, the initializer computes the address of the given variable, and the variable is guaranteed to remain at a fixed address for the duration of the `fixed` statement.
- An expression of an *array-type* with elements of an unmanaged type T, provided the type T* is implicitly convertible to the pointer type given in the `fixed` statement. In this case, the initializer computes the address of the first element in the array, and the entire array is guaranteed to remain at a fixed address for the duration of the `fixed` statement. The behavior of the `fixed` statement is implementation-defined if the array expression is null or if the array has zero elements.
- An expression of type `string`, provided the type `char*` is implicitly convertible to the pointer type given in the `fixed` statement. In this case, the initializer computes the address of the first character in the string, and the entire string is guaranteed to remain at a fixed address for the duration of the `fixed` statement. The behavior of the `fixed` statement is implementation-defined if the string expression is null.

For each address computed by a *fixed-pointer-initializer* the `fixed` statement ensures that the variable referenced by the address is not subject to relocation or disposal by the garbage collector for the duration of the `fixed` statement. [*Example*: If the address computed by a *fixed-pointer-initializer* references a field of an object or an element of an array instance, the `fixed` statement guarantees that the containing object instance is not relocated or disposed of during the lifetime of the statement. *end example*]

It is the programmer's responsibility to ensure that pointers created by `fixed` statements do not survive beyond execution of those statements. [*Example*: When pointers created by `fixed` statements are passed to external APIs, it is the programmer's responsibility to ensure that the APIs retain no memory of these pointers. *end example*]

Fixed objects can cause fragmentation of the heap (because they can't be moved). For that reason, objects should be fixed only when necessary and then only for the shortest amount of time possible. [*Example*: The example

```
class Test
{
  static int x;
  int y;

  unsafe static void F(int* p)
  {
    *p = 1;
  }

  static void Main()
  {
    Test t = new Test();
    int[] a = new int[10];
    unsafe
    {
      fixed (int* p = &x) F(p);
      fixed (int* p = &t.y) F(p);
      fixed (int* p = &a[0]) F(p);
      fixed (int* p = a) F(p);
    }
  }
}
```

demonstrates several uses of the `fixed` statement. The first statement fixes and obtains the address of a static field, the second statement fixes and obtains the address of an instance field, and the third statement fixes and obtains the address of an array element. In each case, it would have been an error to use the regular `&` operator since the variables are all classified as moveable variables.

The third and fourth `fixed` statements in the example above produce identical results. In general, for an array instance a, specifying `&a[0]` in a `fixed` statement is the same as simply specifying a.

Here's another example of the `fixed` statement, this time using `string`:

```
class Test
{
  static string name = "xx";
```

```
unsafe static void F(char* p)
{
  for (int i = 0; p[i] != '\0'; ++i)
    Console.WriteLine(p[i]);
}

static void Main()
{
  unsafe
  {
    fixed (char* p = name) F(p);
    fixed (char* p = "xx") F(p);
  }
}
}
```

end example]

In an unsafe context, array elements of single-dimensional arrays are stored in increasing index order, starting with index 0 and ending with index Length − 1 For multi-dimensional arrays, array elements are stored such that the indices of the rightmost dimension are increased first, then the next left dimension, and so on to the left.

Within a fixed statement that obtains a pointer p to an array instance a, the pointer values ranging from p to p + a.Length − 1 represent addresses of the elements in the array. Likewise, the variables ranging from p[0] to p[a.Length − 1] represent the actual array elements. Given the way in which arrays are stored, we can treat an array of any dimension as though it were linear. [*Example*:

```
using System;

class Test
{
  static void Main()
  {
    int[,,] a = new int[2,3,4];

    unsafe
    {
      fixed (int* p = a)
      {
        for (int i = 0; i < a.Length; ++i)  // treat as linear
          p[i] = i;
      }
    }

    for (int i = 0; i < 2; ++i)
      for (int j = 0; j < 3; ++j)
      {
        for (int k = 0; k < 4; ++k)
          Console.Write("[{0},{1},{2}] = {3,2} ", i, j, k,
            a[i,j,k]);
        Console.WriteLine();
      }
  }
}
```

which produces the output:

```
[0,0,0]  =   0 [0,0,1]  =   1 [0,0,2]  =   2 [0,0,3]  =  3
[0,1,0]  =   4 [0,1,1]  =   5 [0,1,2]  =   6 [0,1,3]  =  7
[0,2,0]  =   8 [0,2,1]  =   9 [0,2,2]  = 10 [0,2,3]  = 11
[1,0,0]  = 12 [1,0,1]  = 13 [1,0,2]  = 14 [1,0,3]  = 15
[1,1,0]  = 16 [1,1,1]  = 17 [1,1,2]  = 18 [1,1,3]  = 19
[1,2,0]  = 20 [1,2,1]  = 21 [1,2,2]  = 22 [1,2,3]  = 23
```

end example]

[*Example*: In the following code

```
class Test
{
  unsafe static void Fill(int* p, int count, int value)
  {
    for (; count != 0; count--) *p++ = value;
  }

  static void Main()
  {
    int[] a = new int[100];
    unsafe
    {
      fixed (int* p = a) Fill(p, 100, -1);
    }
  }
}
```

a `fixed` statement is used to fix an array so its address can be passed to a method that takes a pointer. *end example*]

A `char*` value produced by fixing a non-null string instance always points to a null-terminated string. Within a fixed statement that obtains a pointer p to a string instance s, the pointer values ranging from p to p + s.Length – 1 represent addresses of the characters in the string, and the pointer value p + s.Length always points to a null character (the character with value '\0').

Modifying objects of managed type through fixed pointers can result in undefined behavior. [*Note*: For example, because strings are immutable, it is the programmer's responsibility to ensure that the characters referenced by a pointer to a fixed string are not modified. *end note*]

[*Note*: The automatic null-termination of strings is particularly convenient when calling external APIs that expect "C-style" strings. Note, however, that a string instance is permitted to contain null characters. If such null characters are present, the string will appear truncated when treated as a null-terminated `char*`. *end note*]

27.7 Stack allocation

In an unsafe context, a local variable declaration (§15.5.1) can include a stack allocation initializer, which allocates memory from the call stack.

> *local-variable-initializer:*
> *expression*
> *array-initializer*
> *stackalloc-initializer*

stackalloc-initializer:
    `stackalloc` *unmanaged-type* [*expression*]

The *unmanaged-type* indicates the type of the items that will be stored in the newly allocated location, and the *expression* indicates the number of these items. Taken together, these specify the required allocation size. Since the size of a stack allocation cannot be negative, it is a compile-time error to specify the number of items as a *constant-expression* that evaluates to a negative value.

A stack allocation initializer of the form `stackalloc T[E]` requires T to be an unmanaged type (§27.2) and E to be an expression convertible to type `int`. The construct allocates E * `sizeof` `(T)` bytes from the call stack and returns a pointer, of type T*, to the newly allocated block. If E is a negative value, then the behavior is undefined. If E is zero, then no allocation is made, and the pointer returned is implementation-defined. If there is not enough memory available to allocate a block of the given size, a `System.StackOverflowException` is thrown.

The content of the newly allocated memory is undefined.

Stack allocation initializers are not permitted in catch or finally blocks (§15.10).

[*Note*: There is no way to explicitly free memory allocated using `stackalloc`. *end note*] All stack-allocated memory blocks created during the execution of a function member are automatically discarded when that function member returns. [*Note*: This corresponds to the `alloca` function, an extension commonly found in C and C++ implementations. *end note*]

[*Example*: In the following code

```
using System;

class Test
{
  static string IntToString(int value)
  {
    int n = value >= 0 ? value : -value;
    unsafe
    {
      char* buffer = stackalloc char[16] ;
      char* p = buffer + 16;
      do
      {
        *--p = (char) (n % 10 + '0');
        n /= 10;
      } while (n != 0);
      if (value < 0) *--p = '-';
      return new string(p, 0, (int) (buffer + 16 - p));
    }
  }

  static void Main()
  {
    Console.WriteLine(IntToString(12345));
    Console.WriteLine(IntToString(-999));
  }
}
```

a `stackalloc` initializer is used in the `IntToString` method to allocate a buffer of 16 characters on the stack. The buffer is automatically discarded when the method returns. *end example*]

The programmer does not always come first

Stack allocation initializers are not permitted in catch or finally blocks, for example:

```
unsafe void F(int i)
{
  try
  {
    ...
  }
  finally
  {
    byte * bytes = stackalloc byte[42 + i];  // invalid
    ...
  }
}
```

The rationale for this restriction comes from a common implementation strategy for finally and catch blocks called "funclets." In this, the code in a catch or finally block is placed in a small function (the "funclet"), which is called from the main routine or the exception handling infrastructure, as appropriate. Because the funclet is in many ways a separate function, with its own stack frame, it is difficult for the funclet to allocate stack memory on the frame of its caller (F in the example) as this is a different function with its own stack frame.

There are ways around this in an implementation, but they are messy. For instance, the "local subroutines" used to implement finally blocks on the Java Virtual Machine (JVM) do share the enclosing method's stack frame, at the cost of seriously complicating bytecode verification. Conversely, the CLI design restricts stack allocation such that an implementation need not use local subroutines or other complex approaches.

Users can easily work around the limitation by simply placing the `stackalloc` in the surrounding code, instead of inside the catch or finally. The committee felt the utility of allowing a `stackalloc` inside a finally or catch is low, and it would be better to prohibit this rather than burden all implementations with this messiness.

27.8 Dynamic memory allocation

Except for the `stackalloc` operator, C# provides no predefined constructs for managing non-garbage collected memory. Such services are typically provided by supporting class libraries or imported directly from the underlying operating system. [*Example*: The `Memory` static class below illustrates how the heap functions of an underlying operating system might be accessed from C#:

```
using System;
using System.Runtime.InteropServices;
public unsafe static class Memory
{
  // Handle for the process heap. This handle is used in all calls to the
  // HeapXXX APIs in the methods below.
  static int ph = GetProcessHeap();
```

```
// Allocates a memory block of the given size. The allocated memory is
// automatically initialized to zero.
public static void* Alloc(int size)
{
  void* result = HeapAlloc(ph, HEAP_ZERO_MEMORY, size);
  if (result == null) throw new OutOfMemoryException();
  return result;
}

// Copies count bytes from src to dst. The source and destination
// blocks are permitted to overlap.
public static void Copy(void* src, void* dst, int count)
{
  byte* ps = (byte*)src;
  byte* pd = (byte*)dst;
  if (ps > pd)
  {
    for (; count != 0; count--) *pd++ = *ps++;
  }
  else if (ps < pd)
  {
    for (ps += count, pd += count; count != 0; count--) *--pd = *--
    ps;
  }
}

// Frees a memory block.
public static void Free(void* block)
{
  if (!HeapFree(ph, 0, block)) throw new InvalidOperationException();
}

// Re-allocates a memory block. If the reallocation request is for a
// larger size, the additional region of memory is automatically
// initialized to zero.
public static void* ReAlloc(void* block, int size)
{
  void* result = HeapReAlloc(ph, HEAP_ZERO_MEMORY, block, size);
  if (result == null) throw new OutOfMemoryException();
  return result;
}

// Returns the size of a memory block.
public static int SizeOf(void* block)
{
  int result = HeapSize(ph, 0, block);
  if (result == -1) throw new InvalidOperationException();
  return result;
}

// Heap API flags
const int HEAP_ZERO_MEMORY = 0x00000008;
// Heap API functions
[DllImport("kernel32")]
```

```
      static extern int GetProcessHeap();
      [DllImport("kernel32")]
      static extern void* HeapAlloc(int hHeap, int flags, int size);
      [DllImport("kernel32")]
      static extern bool HeapFree(int hHeap, int flags, void* block);
      [DllImport("kernel32")]
      static extern void* HeapReAlloc(int hHeap, int flags,
      void* block, int size);
      [DllImport("kernel32")]
      static extern int HeapSize(int hHeap, int flags, void* block);
   }
```

An example that uses the Memory class is given below:

```
   class Test
   {
     static void Main()
     {
       unsafe
       {
         byte* buffer = (byte*)Memory.Alloc(256);
         for (int i = 0; i < 256; i++) buffer[i] = (byte)i;
         byte[] array = new byte[256] ;
         fixed (byte* p = array) Memory.Copy(buffer, p, 256);
         Memory.Free(buffer);
         for (int i = 0; i < 256; i++) Console.WriteLine(array[i] );
       }
     }
   }
```

The example allocates 256 bytes of memory through Memory.Alloc and initializes the memory block with values increasing from 0 to 255. It then allocates a 256-element byte array and uses Memory.Copy to copy the contents of the memory block into the byte array. Finally, the memory block is freed using Memory.Free and the contents of the byte array are output on the console. *end example*]

End of conditionally normative text.

A Grammar

This clause is informative.

This annex contains summaries of the lexical and syntactic grammars found in the main document, and of the grammar extensions for unsafe code. Grammar productions appear here in the same order that they appear in the main document.

A.1 Lexical grammar

```
input::
  input-section_opt

input-section::
  input-section-part
  input-section  input-section-part

input-section-part::
  input-elements_opt  new-line
  pp-directive

input-elements::
  input-element
  input-elements  input-element

input-element::
  whitespace
  comment
  token
```

A.1.1 Line terminators

```
new-line::
  Carriage return character (U+000D)
  Line feed character (U+000A)
  Carriage return character (U+000D) followed by line feed character (U+000A)
  Next line character (U+2085)
  Line separator character (U+2028)
  Paragraph separator character (U+2029)
```

A.1.2 White space

```
whitespace::
  whitespace-characters

whitespace-characters::
  whitespace-character
  whitespace-characters  whitespace-character

whitespace-character::
  Any character with Unicode class Zs
  Horizontal tab character (U+0009)
```

        Vertical tab character (U+000B)
        Form feed character(U+000C)

A.1.3 Comments

comment::
  single-line-comment
  delimited-comment

single-line-comment::
  // *input-characters$_{opt}$*

input-characters::
  input-character
  input-characters input-character

input-character::
  Any Unicode character except a *new-line-character*

new-line-character::
  Carriage return character (U+000D)
  Line feed character (U+000A)
  Next line character (U+0085)
  Line separator character (U+2028)
  Paragraph separator character (U+2029)

delimited-comment::
  /* *delimited-comment-text$_{opt}$* *asterisks* /

delimited-comment-text::
  delimited-comment-section
  delimited-comment-text delimited-comment-section

delimited-comment-section::
  not-asterisk
  asterisks not-slash

asterisks::
  *
  asterisks *

not-asterisk::
  Any Unicode character except *

not-slash::
  Any Unicode character except /

A.1.4 Tokens

token::
  identifier
  keyword
  integer-literal

```
real-literal
character-literal
string-literal
operator-or-punctuator
```

A.1.5 Unicode escape sequences

```
unicode-escape-sequence::
 \u  hex-digit  hex-digit  hex-digit  hex-digit
 \U  hex-digit  hex-digit  hex-digit  hex-digit  hex-digit  hex-digit
                                                 hex-digit  hex-digit
```

A.1.6 Identifiers

```
identifier::
 available-identifier
 @  identifier-or-keyword
```

```
available-identifier::
 An identifier-or-keyword that is not a keyword
```

```
identifier-or-keyword::
 identifier-start-character   identifier-part-characters$_{opt}$
```

```
identifier-start-character::
 letter-character
 _ (the underscore character U+005F)
```

```
identifier-part-characters::
 identifier-part-character
 identifier-part-characters  identifier-part-character
```

```
identifier-part-character::
 letter-character
 decimal-digit-character
 connecting-character
 combining-character
 formatting-character
```

```
letter-character::
 A Unicode character of classes Lu, Ll, Lt, Lm, Lo, or Nl
 A unicode-escape-sequence representing a character of classes Lu, Ll, Lt,
                                                          Lm, Lo, or Nl
```

```
combining-character::
 A Unicode character of classes Mn or Mc
 A unicode-escape-sequence representing a character of classes Mn or Mc
```

```
decimal-digit-character::
 A Unicode character of the class Nd
 A unicode-escape-sequence representing a character of the class Nd
```

connecting-character::
  A Unicode character of the class Pc
  A *unicode-escape-sequence* representing a character of the class Pc

formatting-character::
  A Unicode character of the class Cf
  A *unicode-escape-sequence* representing a character of the class Cf

A.1.7 Keywords

keyword:: one of

abstract	as	base	bool	break
byte	case	catch	char	checked
class	const	continue	decimal	default
delegate	do	double	else	enum
event	explicit	extern	false	finally
fixed	float	for	foreach	goto
if	implicit	in	int	interface
internal	is	lock	long	namespace
new	null	object	operator	out
override	params	private	protected	public
readonly	ref	return	sbyte	sealed
short	sizeof	stackalloc	static	string
struct	switch	this	throw	true
try	typeof	uint	ulong	unchecked
unsafe	ushort	using	virtual	void
volatile	while			

A.1.8 Literals

literal::
  boolean-literal
  integer-literal
  real-literal
  character-literal
  string-literal
  null-literal

boolean-literal::
  true
  false

integer-literal::
  decimal-integer-literal
  hexadecimal-integer-literal

decimal-integer-literal::
  decimal-digits integer-type-suffix$_{opt}$

decimal-digits::
  decimal-digit
  decimal-digits decimal-digit

decimal-digit:: one of
  0 1 2 3 4 5 6 7 8 9

integer-type-suffix:: one of
  U u L l UL Ul uL ul LU Lu lU lu

hexadecimal-integer-literal::
  0x *hex-digits integer-type-suffix*$_{opt}$
  0X *hex-digits integer-type-suffix*$_{opt}$

hex-digits::
  hex-digit
  hex-digits hex-digit

hex-digit:: one of
  0 1 2 3 4 5 6 7 8 9 A B C D E F a b c d e f

real-literal::
  decimal-digits . decimal-digits exponent-part$_{opt}$ *real-type-suffix*$_{opt}$
  . decimal-digits exponent-part$_{opt}$ *real-type-suffix*$_{opt}$
  decimal-digits exponent-part real-type-suffix$_{opt}$
  decimal-digits real-type-suffix

exponent-part::
  e *sign*$_{opt}$ *decimal-digits*
  E *sign*$_{opt}$ *decimal-digits*

sign:: one of
  + -

real-type-suffix:: one of
  F f D d M m

character-literal::
  ' *character* '

character::
  single-character
  simple-escape-sequence
  hexadecimal-escape-sequence
  unicode-escape-sequence

single-character::
  Any character except ' (U+0027), \ (U+005C), and *new-line-character*

simple-escape-sequence:: one of
  \' \" \\ \0 \a \b \f \n \r \t \v

hexadecimal-escape-sequence::
  \x *hex-digit hex-digit*$_{opt}$ *hex-digit*$_{opt}$ *hex-digit*$_{opt}$

string-literal::
  regular-string-literal
  verbatim-string-literal

regular-string-literal::
  " *regular-string-literal-characters*_{opt} "

regular-string-literal-characters::
  regular-string-literal-character
  regular-string-literal-characters   regular-string-literal-character

regular-string-literal-character::
  single-regular-string-literal-character
  simple-escape-sequence
  hexadecimal-escape-sequence
  unicode-escape-sequence

single-regular-string-literal-character::
  Any character except " (U+0022), \ (U+005C), and *new-line-character*

verbatim-string-literal::
  @" *verbatim-string-literal-characters*_{opt} "

verbatim-string-literal-characters::
  verbatim-string-literal-character
  verbatim-string-literal-characters   verbatim-string-literal-character

verbatim-string-literal-character::
  single-verbatim-string-literal-character
  quote-escape-sequence

single-verbatim-string-literal-character::
  Any character except "

quote-escape-sequence::
  ""

null-literal::
  null

A.1.9 Operators and punctuators

operator-or-punctuator:: one of
  {   }   [   ]   (   )   .   ,   :   ;
  +   -   *   /   %   & | ^   !   ~
  =   <   >   ?   ??   ::   ++   --   && ||
  ->   ==   !=   <=   >=   +=   -=   *=   /=   %=
  &= |=   ^=   <<   <<=

right-shift::
  > >

right-shift-assignment::
  > >=

A.1.10 Pre-processing directives

```
pp-directive::
  pp-declaration
  pp-conditional
  pp-line
  pp-diagnostic
  pp-region
  pp-pragma

conditional-symbol::
  identifier
  Any keyword except true or false

pp-expression::
  whitespace_opt  pp-or-expression  whitespace_opt

pp-or-expression::
  pp-and-expression
  pp-or-expression  whitespace_opt  ||  whitespace_opt  pp-and-expression

pp-and-expression::
  pp-equality-expression
  pp-and-expression  whitespace_opt  &&  whitespace_opt
                            pp-equality-expression

pp-equality-expression::
  pp-unary-expression
  pp-equality-expression  whitespace_opt  ==  whitespace_opt
                                    pp-unary-expression
  pp-equality-expression  whitespace_opt  !=  whitespace_opt
                                    pp-unary-expression

pp-unary-expression::
  pp-primary-expression
  !  whitespace_opt  pp-unary-expression

pp-primary-expression::
  true
  false
  conditional-symbol
  (  whitespace_opt  pp-expression  whitespace_opt  )

pp-declaration::
  whitespace_opt  #  whitespace_opt  define  whitespace  conditional-symbol
                                                    pp-new-line
  whitespace_opt  #  whitespace_opt  undef  whitespace  conditional-symbol
                                                    pp-new-line

pp-new-line::
  whitespace_opt  single-line-comment_opt  new-line

pp-conditional::
  pp-if-section  pp-elif-sections_opt  pp-else-section_opt  pp-endif
```

```
pp-if-section::
  whitespace_opt # whitespace_opt if whitespace pp-expression
                                                       pp-new-line
      conditional-section_opt

pp-elif-sections::
  pp-elif-section
  pp-elif-sections pp-elif-section

pp-elif-section::
  whitespace_opt # whitespace_opt elif whitespace pp-expression
                                                       pp-new-line
      conditional-section_opt

pp-else-section::
  whitespace_opt # whitespace_opt else pp-new-line
                            conditional-section_opt

pp-endif::
  whitespace_opt # whitespace_opt endif pp-new-line

conditional-section::
  input-section
  skipped-section

skipped-section::
  skipped-section-part
  skipped-section skipped-section-part

skipped-section-part::
  whitespace_opt skipped-characters_opt new-line
  pp-directive

skipped-characters::
  not-number-sign input-characters_opt

not-number-sign::
  Any input-character except #

pp-line::
  whitespace_opt # whitespace_opt line whitespace line-indicator
                                                       pp-new-line

line-indicator::
  decimal-digits whitespace file-name
  decimal-digits
  identifier-or-keyword

file-name::
  " file-name-characters "
```

```
file-name-characters::
  file-name-character
  file-name-characters  file-name-character

file-name-character::
  Any character except " (U+0022), and new-line-character

pp-diagnostic::
  whitespace_opt  #  whitespace_opt  error  pp-message
  whitespace_opt  #  whitespace_opt  warning  pp-message

pp-message::
  new-line
  whitespace  input-characters_opt  new-line

pp-region::
  pp-start-region  conditional-section_opt  pp-end-region

pp-start-region::
  whitespace_opt  #  whitespace_opt  region  pp-message

pp-end-region::
  whitespace_opt  #  whitespace_opt  endregion  pp-message

pp-pragma:
  whitespace_opt  #  whitespace_opt  pragma  pp-pragma-text

pp-pragma-text:
  new-line
  whitespace  input-characters_opt  new-line
```

A.2 Syntactic grammar
A.2.1 Basic concepts

```
compilation-unit:
  extern-alias-directives_opt  using-directives_opt  global-attributes_opt
                                    namespace-member-declarations_opt

namespace-name:
  namespace-or-type-name

type-name:
  namespace-or-type-name

namespace-or-type-name:
  identifier  type-argument-list_opt
  qualified-alias-member
  namespace-or-type-name  .  identifier  type-argument-list_opt
```

A.2.2 Types

```
type:
  value-type
  reference-type
  type-parameter

value-type:
  struct-type
  enum-type

struct-type:
  type-name
  simple-type
  nullable-type

simple-type:
  numeric-type
  bool

numeric-type:
  integral-type
  floating-point-type
  decimal

integral-type:
  sbyte
  byte
  short
  ushort
  int
  uint
  long
  ulong
  char

floating-point-type:
  float
  double

enum-type:
  type-name

nullable-type:
  non-nullable-value-type  ?

non-nullable-value-type:
  enum-type
  type-name
  simple-type

reference-type:
  class-type
  interface-type
```

```
array-type
delegate-type

class-type:
  type-name
  object
  string

interface-type:
  type-name

array-type:
  non-array-type  rank-specifiers

non-array-type:
  value-type
  class-type
  interface-type
  delegate-type
  type-parameter

rank-specifiers:
  rank-specifier
  rank-specifiers  rank-specifier

rank-specifier:
  [  dim-separators_opt  ]

dim-separators:
  ,
  dim-separators  ,

delegate-type:
  type-name
```

A.2.3 Variables

```
variable-reference:
  expression
```

A.2.4 Expressions

```
argument-list:
  argument
  argument-list  ,  argument

argument:
  expression
  ref  variable-reference
  out  variable-reference
```

```
primary-expression:
  array-creation-expression
  primary-no-array-creation-expression

primary-no-array-creation-expression:
  literal
  simple-name
  parenthesized-expression
  member-access
  invocation-expression
  element-access
  this-access
  base-access
  post-increment-expression
  post-decrement-expression
  object-creation-expression
  delegate-creation-expression
  typeof-expression
  checked-expression
  unchecked-expression
  default-value-expression
  anonymous-method-expression

simple-name:
  identifier type-argument-listopt

parenthesized-expression:
  ( expression )

member-access:
  primary-expression . identifier type-argument-listopt
  predefined-type . identifier type-argument-listopt
  qualified-alias-member . identifier type-argument-listopt

predefined-type: one of
  bool   byte   char   decimal   double   float   int   long
  object   sbyte   short   string   uint   ulong   ushort

invocation-expression:
  primary-expression ( argument-listopt )

element-access:
  primary-no-array-creation-expression [ expression-list ]

expression-list:
  expression
  expression-list , expression

this-access:
  this

base-access:
  base . identifier type-argument-listopt
  base [ expression-list ]
```

post-increment-expression:
  primary-expression ++

post-decrement-expression:
  primary-expression --

object-creation-expression:
  new *type* (*argument-list*_{opt})

array-creation-expression:
  new *non-array-type* [*expression-list*] *rank-specifiers*_{opt}
                                        *array-initializer*_{opt}
  new *array-type* *array-initializer*

delegate-creation-expression:
  new *delegate-type* (*expression*)

typeof-expression:
  typeof (*type*)
  typeof (*unbound-type-name*)
  typeof (void)

unbound-type-name:
  identifier *generic-dimension-specifier*_{opt}
  identifier :: *identifier* *generic-dimension-specifier*_{opt}
  unbound-type-name . *identifier* *generic-dimension-specifier*_{opt}

generic-dimension-specifier:
  < *commas*_{opt} >

commas:
  ,
  commas ,

checked-expression:
  checked (*expression*)

unchecked-expression:
  unchecked (*expression*)

default-value-expression:
  default (*type*)

anonymous-method-expression:
  delegate *anonymous-method-signature*_{opt} *block*

anonymous-method-signature:
  (*anonymous-method-parameter-list*_{opt})

anonymous-method-parameter-list:
  anonymous-method-parameter
  anonymous-method-parameter-list , *anonymous-method-parameter*

```
anonymous-method-parameter:
  parameter-modifier_opt  type  identifier

unary-expression:
  primary-expression
  +  unary-expression
  -  unary-expression
  !  unary-expression
  ~  unary-expression
  pre-increment-expression
  pre-decrement-expression
  cast-expression

pre-increment-expression:
  ++  unary-expression

pre-decrement-expression:
  --  unary-expression

cast-expression:
  ( type )  unary-expression

multiplicative-expression:
  unary-expression
  multiplicative-expression  *  unary-expression
  multiplicative-expression  /  unary-expression
  multiplicative-expression  %  unary-expression

additive-expression:
  multiplicative-expression
  additive-expression  +  multiplicative-expression
  additive-expression  -  multiplicative-expression

shift-expression:
  additive-expression
  shift-expression  <<  additive-expression
  shift-expression  right-shift  additive-expression

relational-expression:
  shift-expression
  relational-expression  <   shift-expression
  relational-expression  >   shift-expression
  relational-expression  <=  shift-expression
  relational-expression  >=  shift-expression
  relational-expression  is  type
  relational-expression  as  type

equality-expression:
  relational-expression
  equality-expression  ==  relational-expression
  equality-expression  !=  relational-expression
```

```
and-expression:
  equality-expression
  and-expression  &  equality-expression

exclusive-or-expression:
  and-expression
  exclusive-or-expression  ^  and-expression

inclusive-or-expression:
  exclusive-or-expression
  inclusive-or-expression  |  exclusive-or-expression

conditional-and-expression:
  inclusive-or-expression
  conditional-and-expression  &&  inclusive-or-expression

conditional-or-expression:
  conditional-and-expression
  conditional-or-expression  ||  conditional-and-expression

null-coalescing-expression:
  conditional-or-expression
  conditional-or-expression  ??  null-coalescing-expression

conditional-expression:
  null-coalescing-expression
  null-coalescing-expression  ?  expression  :  expression

assignment:
  unary-expression  assignment-operator  expression

assignment-operator: one of
  =  +=  -=  *=  /=  %=  &=  |=  ^=  <<=  right-shift-assignment

expression:
  conditional-expression
  assignment

constant-expression:
  expression

boolean-expression:
  expression
```

A.2.5 Statements

```
statement:
  labeled-statement
  declaration-statement
  embedded-statement

embedded-statement:
  block
```

```
    empty-statement
    expression-statement
    selection-statement
    iteration-statement
    jump-statement
    try-statement
    checked-statement
    unchecked-statement
    lock-statement
    using-statement
    yield-statement

block:
  {  statement-list_opt }

statement-list:
  statement
  statement-list  statement

empty-statement:
  ;

labeled-statement:
  identifier : statement

declaration-statement:
  local-variable-declaration ;
  local-constant-declaration ;

local-variable-declaration:
  type local-variable-declarators

local-variable-declarators:
  local-variable-declarator
  local-variable-declarators , local-variable-declarator

local-variable-declarator:
  identifier
  identifier = local-variable-initializer

local-variable-initializer:
  expression
  array-initializer

local-constant-declaration:
  const type constant-declarators

constant-declarators:
  constant-declarator
  constant-declarators , constant-declarator

constant-declarator:
  identifier = constant-expression
```

```
expression-statement:
  statement-expression  ;

statement-expression:
  invocation-expression
  object-creation-expression
  assignment
  post-increment-expression
  post-decrement-expression
  pre-increment-expression
  pre-decrement-expression

selection-statement:
  if-statement
  switch-statement

if-statement:
  if  (  boolean-expression  )  embedded-statement
  if  (  boolean-expression  )  embedded-statement else
                                        embedded-statement

switch-statement:
  switch  (  expression  )  switch-block

switch-block:
  {  switch-sections_opt  }

switch-sections:
  switch-section
  switch-sections  switch-section

switch-section:
  switch-labels  statement-list

switch-labels:
  switch-label
  switch-labels  switch-label

switch-label:
  case  constant-expression  :
  default  :

iteration-statement:
  while-statement
  do-statement
  for-statement
  foreach-statement

while-statement:
  while  (  boolean-expression  )  embedded-statement

do-statement:
  do  embedded-statement  while  (  boolean-expression  )  ;
```

for-statement:
  for (*for-initializer*$_{opt}$; *for-condition*$_{opt}$; *for-iterator*$_{opt}$)
                                       embedded-statement

for-initializer:
  local-variable-declaration
  statement-expression-list

for-condition:
  boolean-expression

for-iterator:
  statement-expression-list

statement-expression-list:
  statement-expression
  statement-expression-list , *statement-expression*

foreach-statement:
  foreach (*type* *identifier* in *expression*) *embedded-statement*

jump-statement:
  break-statement
  continue-statement
  goto-statement
  return-statement
  throw-statement

break-statement:
  break ;

continue-statement:
  continue ;

goto-statement:
  goto *identifier* ;
  goto case *constant-expression* ;
  goto default ;

return-statement:
  return *expression*$_{opt}$;

throw-statement:
  throw *expression*$_{opt}$;

try-statement:
  try *block* *catch-clauses*
  try *block* *catch-clauses*$_{opt}$ *finally-clause*

catch-clauses:
  specific-catch-clauses
  specific-catch-clauses$_{opt}$ *general-catch-clause*

specific-catch-clauses:
  specific-catch-clause
  specific-catch-clauses *specific-catch-clause*

specific-catch-clause:
  catch (*class-type* *identifier*$_{opt}$) *block*

general-catch-clause:
  catch *block*

finally-clause:
  finally *block*

checked-statement:
  checked *block*

unchecked-statement:
  unchecked *block*

lock-statement:
  lock (*expression*) *embedded-statement*

using-statement:
  using (*resource-acquisition*) *embedded-statement*

resource-acquisition:
  local-variable-declaration
  expression

yield-statement:
  yield return *expression* ;
  yield break ;

namespace-declaration:
  namespace *qualified-identifier* *namespace-body* ;$_{opt}$

qualified-identifier:
  identifier
  qualified-identifier . *identifier*

namespace-body:
  { *extern-alias-directives*$_{opt}$ *using-directives*$_{opt}$
        namespace-member-declarations$_{opt}$ }

extern-alias-directives:
  extern-alias-directive
  extern-alias-directives *extern-alias-directive*

extern-alias-directive:
  extern alias *identifier* ;

```
using-directives:
  using-directive
  using-directives  using-directive

using-directive:
  using-alias-directive
  using-namespace-directive

using-alias-directive:
  using  identifier  =  namespace-or-type-name  ;

using-namespace-directive:
  using  namespace-name  ;

namespace-member-declarations:
  namespace-member-declaration
  namespace-member-declarations  namespace-member-declaration

namespace-member-declaration:
  namespace-declaration
  type-declaration

type-declaration:
  class-declaration
  struct-declaration
  interface-declaration
  enum-declaration
  delegate-declaration

qualified-alias-member:
  identifier  ::  identifier  type-argument-list_opt
```

A.2.6 Classes

```
class-declaration:
  attributes_opt  class-modifiers_opt  partial_opt  class  identifier
                                       type-parameter-list_opt
                                 class-base_opt  type-parameter-
                          constraints-clauses_opt  class-body  ;_opt

class-modifiers:
  class-modifier
  class-modifiers  class-modifier

class-modifier:
  new
  public
  protected
  internal
  private
  abstract
  sealed
  static
```

```
class-base:
  :  class-type
  :  interface-type-list
  :  class-type  ,  interface-type-list

interface-type-list:
  interface-type
  interface-type-list  ,  interface-type

class-body:
  {  class-member-declarations_opt  }

class-member-declarations:
  class-member-declaration
  class-member-declarations  class-member-declaration

class-member-declaration:
  constant-declaration
  field-declaration
  method-declaration
  property-declaration
  event-declaration
  indexer-declaration
  operator-declaration
  constructor-declaration
  finalizer-declaration
  static-constructor-declaration
  type-declaration

constant-declaration:
  attributes_opt  constant-modifiers_opt  const  type
                           constant-declarators  ;

constant-modifiers:
  constant-modifier
  constant-modifiers  constant-modifier

constant-modifier:
  new
  public
  protected
  internal
  private

constant-declarators:
  constant-declarator
  constant-declarators  ,  constant-declarator

constant-declarator:
  identifier  =  constant-expression

field-declaration:
  attributes_opt  field-modifiers_opt  type  variable-declarators  ;
```

field-modifiers:
  field-modifier
  field-modifiers field-modifier

field-modifier:
  new
  public
  protected
  internal
  private
  static
  readonly
  volatile

variable-declarators:
  variable-declarator
  variable-declarators , variable-declarator

variable-declarator:
  identifier
  identifier = variable-initializer

variable-initializer:
  expression
  array-initializer

method-declaration:
  method-header method-body

method-header:
  attributes$_{opt}$ method-modifiers$_{opt}$ return-type member-name
                             type-parameter-list$_{opt}$
                      (*formal-parameter-list$_{opt}$*)
                 type-parameter-constraints-clauses$_{opt}$

method-modifiers:
  method-modifier
  method-modifiers method-modifier

method-modifier:
  new
  public
  protected
  internal
  private
  static
  virtual
  sealed
  override
  abstract
  extern

```
return-type:
  type
  void

member-name:
  identifier
  interface-type  .  identifier

method-body:
  block
  ;

formal-parameter-list:
  fixed-parameters
  fixed-parameters  ,  parameter-array
  parameter-array

fixed-parameters:
  fixed-parameter
  fixed-parameters  ,  fixed-parameter

fixed-parameter:
  attributes_opt  parameter-modifier_opt  type  identifier

parameter-modifier:
  ref
  out

parameter-array:
  attributes_opt  params  array-type  identifier

property-declaration:
  attributes_opt  property-modifiers_opt  type  member-name
                       {  accessor-declarations  }

property-modifiers:
  property-modifier
  property-modifiers  property-modifier

property-modifier:
  new
  public
  protected
  internal
  private
  static
  virtual
  sealed
  override
  abstract
  extern
```

```
accessor-declarations:
  get-accessor-declaration  set-accessor-declaration_opt
  set-accessor-declaration  get-accessor-declaration_opt

get-accessor-declaration:
  attributes_opt  accessor-modifier_opt  get  accessor-body

set-accessor-declaration:
  attributes_opt  accessor-modifier_opt  set  accessor-body

accessor-modifier:
  protected
  internal
  private
  protected  internal
  internal  protected

accessor-body:
  block
  ;

event-declaration:
  attributes_opt  event-modifiers_opt  event  type  variable-declarators  ;
  attributes_opt  event-modifiers_opt  event  type  member-name
                                   {  event-accessor-declarations  }

event-modifiers:
  event-modifier
  event-modifiers  event-modifier

event-modifier:
  new
  public
  protected
  internal
  private
  static
  virtual
  sealed
  override
  abstract
  extern

event-accessor-declarations:
  add-accessor-declaration  remove-accessor-declaration
  remove-accessor-declaration  add-accessor-declaration

add-accessor-declaration:
  attributes_opt  add  block

remove-accessor-declaration:
  attributes_opt  remove  block
```

```
indexer-declaration:
  attributes_opt  indexer-modifiers_opt  indexer-declarator
                              {  accessor-declarations  }

indexer-modifiers:
  indexer-modifier
  indexer-modifiers  indexer-modifier

indexer-modifier:
  new
  public
  protected
  internal
  private
  virtual
  sealed
  override
  abstract
  extern

indexer-declarator:
  type  this  [  formal-parameter-list  ]
  type  interface-type  .  this  [  formal-parameter-list  ]

operator-declaration:
  attributes_opt  operator-modifiers  operator-declarator  operator-body

operator-modifiers:
  operator-modifier
  operator-modifiers  operator-modifier

operator-modifier:
  public
  static
  extern

operator-declarator:
  unary-operator-declarator
  binary-operator-declarator
  conversion-operator-declarator

unary-operator-declarator:
  type  operator  overloadable-unary-operator  (  type  identifier  )

overloadable-unary-operator: one of
  +  -  !  ~  ++  --  true  false

binary-operator-declarator:
  type  operator  overloadable-binary-operator  (  type  identifier  ,
                                                    type  identifier  )

overloadable-binary-operator: one of
  +  -  *  /  %
  &  |  ^
```

```
  <<  right-shift
  ==  !=  >  <  >=  <=

conversion-operator-declarator:
  implicit  operator  type  (  type  identifier  )
  explicit  operator  type  (  type  identifier  )

operator-body:
  block
  ;

constructor-declaration:
  attributes_opt  constructor-modifiers_opt  constructor-declarator
                                            constructor-body

constructor-modifiers:
  constructor-modifier
  constructor-modifiers  constructor-modifier

constructor-modifier:
  public
  protected
  internal
  private
  extern

constructor-declarator:
  identifier  (  formal-parameter-list_opt  )  constructor-initializer_opt

constructor-initializer:
  :  base  (  argument-list_opt  )
  :  this  (  argument-list_opt  )

constructor-body:
  block
  ;

static-constructor-declaration:
  attributes_opt  static-constructor-modifiers  identifier  (  )
                                    static-constructor-body

static-constructor-modifiers:
  extern_opt  static
  static  extern_opt

static-constructor-body:
  block
  ;

finalizer-declaration:
  attributes_opt  extern_opt  ~  identifier  (  )  finalizer-body
```

```
finalizer-body:
  block
  ;
```

A.2.7 Structs

```
struct-declaration:
  attributes_opt  struct-modifiers_opt  partial_opt  struct  identifier
                          type-parameter-list_opt  struct-interfaces_opt
                  type-parameter-constraints-clauses_opt  struct-body  ;_opt

struct-modifiers:
  struct-modifier
  struct-modifiers  struct-modifier

struct-modifier:
  new
  public
  protected
  internal
  private

struct-interfaces:
  :  interface-type-list

struct-body:
  {  struct-member-declarations_opt  }

struct-member-declarations:
  struct-member-declaration
  struct-member-declarations  struct-member-declaration

struct-member-declaration:
  constant-declaration
  field-declaration
  method-declaration
  property-declaration
  event-declaration
  indexer-declaration
  operator-declaration
  constructor-declaration
  static-constructor-declaration
  type-declaration
```

A.2.8 Arrays

```
array-type:
  non-array-type  rank-specifiers

non-array-type:
  value-type
  class-type
```

```
   interface-type
   delegate-type
   type-parameter

rank-specifiers:
  rank-specifier
  rank-specifiers  rank-specifier

rank-specifier:
 [  dim-separators_opt  ]

dim-separators:
 ,
  dim-separators ,

array-initializer:
  {  variable-initializer-list_opt }
  {  variable-initializer-list , }

variable-initializer-list:
  variable-initializer
  variable-initializer-list , variable-initializer

variable-initializer:
  expression
  array-initializer
```

A.2.9 Interfaces

```
interface-declaration:
   attributes_opt interface-modifiers_opt partial_opt interface identifier
                                   type-parameter-list_opt interface-base_opt
            type-parameter-constraints-clauses_opt interface-body ;_opt

interface-modifiers:
  interface-modifier
  interface-modifiers  interface-modifier

interface-modifier:
  new
  public
  protected
  internal
  private

interface-base:
  : interface-type-list

interface-body:
  { interface-member-declarations_opt }
```

```
interface-member-declarations:
  interface-member-declaration
  interface-member-declarations  interface-member-declaration

interface-member-declaration:
  interface-method-declaration
  interface-property-declaration
  interface-event-declaration
  interface-indexer-declaration

interface-method-declaration:
  attributes_opt new_opt return-type identifier type-parameter-list_opt
                               ( formal-parameter-list_opt )
                      type-parameter-constraints-clauses_opt ;

interface-property-declaration:
  attributes_opt new_opt type identifier { interface-accessors }

interface-accessors:
  attributes_opt get ;
  attributes_opt set ;
  attributes_opt get ;  attributes_opt set ;
  attributes_opt set ;  attributes_opt get ;

interface-event-declaration:
  attributes_opt new_opt event type identifier ;

interface-indexer-declaration:
  attributes_opt new_opt type this [ formal-parameter-list ]
                      { interface-accessors }
```

A.2.10 Enums

```
enum-declaration:
  attributes_opt enum-modifiers_opt enum identifier enum-base_opt
                                           enum-body ;_opt

enum-base:
  : integral-type

enum-body:
  { enum-member-declarations_opt }
  { enum-member-declarations , }

enum-modifiers:
  enum-modifier
  enum-modifiers enum-modifier

enum-modifier:
  new
  public
  protected
```

```
    internal
    private
```

enum-member-declarations:
  enum-member-declaration
  enum-member-declarations , *enum-member-declaration*

enum-member-declaration:
  attributes$_{opt}$ identifier
  attributes$_{opt}$ identifier = constant-expression

A.2.11 Delegates

delegate-declaration:
  attributes$_{opt}$ delegate-modifiers$_{opt}$ delegate return-type identifier
                type-parameter-list$_{opt}$ (formal-parameter-list$_{opt}$)
                       type-parameter-constraints- clauses$_{opt}$;

delegate-modifiers:
  delegate-modifier
  delegate-modifiers delegate-modifier

delegate-modifier:
  new
  public
  protected
  internal
  private

A.2.12 Attributes

global-attributes:
  global-attribute-sections

global-attribute-sections:
  global-attribute-section
  global-attribute-sections global-attribute-section

global-attribute-section:
  [*global-attribute-target-specifier attribute-list*]
  [*global-attribute-target-specifier attribute-list* ,]

global-attribute-target-specifier:
  global-attribute-target :

global-attribute-target:
  identifier
  keyword

attributes:
  attribute-sections

```
attribute-sections:
  attribute-section
  attribute-sections  attribute-section

attribute-section:
  [  attribute-target-specifier_opt  attribute-list  ]
  [  attribute-target-specifier_opt  attribute-list  ,  ]

attribute-target-specifier:
  attribute-target  :

attribute-target:
  identifier
  keyword

attribute-list:
  attribute
  attribute-list  ,  attribute

attribute:
  attribute-name  attribute-arguments_opt

attribute-name:
  type-name

attribute-arguments:
  (  positional-argument-list_opt  )
  (  positional-argument-list  ,  named-argument-list  )
  (  named-argument-list  )

positional-argument-list:
  positional-argument
  positional-argument-list  ,  positional-argument

positional-argument:
  attribute-argument-expression

named-argument-list:
  named-argument
  named-argument-list  ,  named-argument

named-argument:
  identifier  =  attribute-argument-expression

attribute-argument-expression:
  expression
```

A.2.13 Generics

```
type-parameter-list:
  <  type-parameters  >
```

```
type-parameters:
  attributes_opt  type-parameter
  type-parameters  ,  attributes_opt  type-parameter

type-parameter:
  identifier

type-argument-list:
  <  type-arguments  >

type-arguments:
  type-argument
  type-arguments  ,  type-argument

type-argument:
  type

type-parameter-constraints-clauses:
  type-parameter-constraints-clause
  type-parameter-constraints-clauses  type-parameter-constraints-clause

type-parameter-constraints-clause:
  where  type-parameter  :  type-parameter-constraints

type-parameter-constraints:
  primary-constraint
  secondary-constraints
  constructor-constraint
  primary-constraint  ,  secondary-constraints
  primary-constraint  ,  constructor-constraint
  secondary-constraints  ,  constructor-constraint
  primary-constraint  ,  secondary-constraints  ,  constructor-
constraint

primary-constraint:
  class-type
  class
  struct

secondary-constraints:
  interface-type
  type-parameter
  secondary-constraints  ,  interface-type
  secondary-constraints  ,  type-parameter

constructor-constraint:
  new  (  )
```

A.3 Grammar extensions for unsafe code

```
class-modifier:
  ...
  unsafe

struct-modifier:
  ...
  unsafe

interface-modifier:
  ...
  unsafe

delegate-modifier:
  ...
  unsafe

field-modifier:
  ...
  unsafe

method-modifier:
  ...
  unsafe

property-modifier:
  ...
  unsafe

event-modifier:
  ...
  unsafe

indexer-modifier:
  ...
  unsafe

operator-modifier:
  ...
  unsafe

constructor-modifier:
  ...
  unsafe
```

$finalizer\text{-}declaration:$
$\quad attributes_{opt}$ $extern_{opt}$ $unsafe_{opt}$ $\sim$ $identifier$ $(\ )$ $finalizer\text{-}body$
$\quad attributes_{opt}$ $unsafe_{opt}$ $extern_{opt}$ $\sim$ $identifier$ $(\ )$ $finalizer\text{-}body$

$static\text{-}constructor\text{-}modifiers:$
$\quad extern_{opt}$ $unsafe_{opt}$ $static$
$\quad unsafe_{opt}$ $extern_{opt}$ $static$
$\quad extern_{opt}$ $static$ $unsafe_{opt}$

```
    unsafe_opt  static   extern_opt
    static   extern_opt  unsafe_opt
    static   unsafe_opt  extern_opt
```

embedded-statement:
  ...
  unsafe-statement

unsafe-statement:
  unsafe *block*

type:
  value-type
  reference-type
  type-parameter
  pointer-type

pointer-type:
  unmanaged-type *
  void *

unmanaged-type:
  type

primary-no-array-creation-expression:
  sizeof-expression

primary-no-array-creation-expression:
  pointer-member-access
  pointer-element-access

unary-expression:
  pointer-indirection-expression
  addressof-expression

pointer-indirection-expression:
  * *unary-expression*

pointer-member-access:
  primary-expression -> *identifier* *type-argument-list*_opt

pointer-element-access:
  primary-no-array-creation-expression [*expression*]

addressof-expression:
  & *unary-expression*

sizeof-expression:
  sizeof (*unmanaged-type*)

embedded-statement:
  ...
  fixed-statement

```
fixed-statement:
  fixed ( pointer-type fixed-pointer-declarators )
                                  embedded-statement

fixed-pointer-declarators:
  fixed-pointer-declarator
  fixed-pointer-declarators , fixed-pointer-declarator

fixed-pointer-declarator:
  identifier = fixed-pointer-initializer

fixed-pointer-initializer:
  & variable-reference
  expression

local-variable-initializer:
  expression
  array-initializer
  stackalloc-initializer

stackalloc-initializer:
  stackalloc unmanaged-type [ expression ]
```

End of informative text.

B Portability issues

This clause is informative.

This annex collects some information about portability that appears in this International Standard.

B.1 Undefined behavior

A program that does not contain any occurrences of the unsafe modifier cannot exhibit any undefined behavior. The behavior is undefined in the following circumstances:

1. When dereferencing the result of converting one pointer type to another and the resulting pointer is not correctly aligned for the pointed-to type. (§27.4)
2. When the unary * operator is applied to a pointer containing an invalid value (§27.5.1).
3. When a pointer is subscripted to access an out-of-bounds element (§27.5.3).
4. Modifying objects of managed type through fixed pointers (§27.6).
5. The initial content of memory allocated by stackalloc (§27.7).
6. Attempting to allocate a negative number of items using stackalloc (§27.7).

B.2 Implementation-defined behavior

A conforming implementation is required to document its choice of behavior in each of the areas listed in this subclause. The following are implementation-defined:

1. The behavior when an identifier not in Normalization Form C is encountered. (§9.4.2)
2. The purpose of a *line-indicator* with an *identifier-or-keyword* whose value does not equal default. (§9.5.7)
3. The interpretation of the *input-characters* in the *pp-pragma-text* of a **#pragma** directive. (§9.5.8)
4. The values of any application parameters passed to Main by the host environment prior to application startup. (§10.1)
5. Whether a System.ArithmeticException (or a subclass thereof) is thrown or the overflow goes unreported with the resulting value being that of the left operand, when in an unchecked context and the left operand of an integer division is the maximum negative int or long value and the right operand is -1. (§14.7.2)
6. When a System.ArithmeticException (or a subclass thereof) is thrown when performing a decimal remainder operation. (§14.7.3)
7. The mechanism by which linkage to an external function is achieved. (§17.5.7)
8. The impact of thread termination when no matching catch clause is found for an exception and the code that initially started that thread is reached. (§23.3)
9. The purpose of attribute target specifiers other than those identified by this standard. (§24.2)
10. The mappings between pointers and integers. (§27.4)
11. The effect of applying the unary * operator to a null pointer. (§27.5.1)
12. The behavior when pointer arithmetic overflows the domain of the pointer type. (§27.5.5)
13. The result of the sizeof operator for non-pre-defined value types. (§27.5.8)
14. The behavior of the fixed statement if the array expression is null or if the array has zero elements. (§27.6)

15. The behavior of the fixed statement if the string expression is `null`. (§27.6)
16. The value returned when a stack allocation of size zero is made. (§27.7)

B.3 Unspecified behavior

1. The time at which the finalizer (if any) for an object is run, once that object has become eligible for finalization. (§10.9)
2. The value of the result when converting out-of-range values from `float` or `double` values to an integral type in an unchecked context. (§13.2.1)
3. The layout of arrays, except in an unsafe context. (§14.5.10.2)
4. Whether there is any way to execute the *block* of an anonymous method other than through evaluation and invocation of the *anonymous-method-expression*. (§14.5.15.2)
5. The invocation list of a delegate produced from an *anonymous-method-expression* contains a single entry. The exact target object and target method of the delegate are unspecified. (§14.5.15.4)
6. The exact timing of static field initialization. (§17.4.5.1)
7. The behavior of uncaught exceptions that occur during finalizer execution. (§23.3)
8. The attributes of a type declared in multiple parts are determined by combining, in an unspecified order, the attributes of each of its parts. (§24.2)
9. The order in which members are packed into a struct. (§27.5.8)
10. When an enumerator object is in the ***running*** state, the result of invoking `MoveNext` is unspecified (§26.2.1).
11. When an enumerator object is in the ***before***, ***running***, or ***after*** states, the result of accessing `Current` is unspecified. (§26.2.2)
12. When an enumerator object is in the ***running*** state, the result of invoking `Dispose` is unspecified. (§26.2.3)

B.4 Other Issues

1. The exact results of floating-point expression evaluation can vary from one implementation to another, because an implementation is permitted to evaluate such expressions using a greater range and/or precision than is required. (§11.1.6)
2. The CLI reserves certain signatures for compatibility with other programming languages. (§17.2.7)

End of informative text.

C Naming Guidelines

This annex is informative.

Information on this topic can be found at the following location:

http://msdn.microsoft.com/library/default.asp?url=/library/en-us/cpgenref/html/cpconnetfra-meworkdesignguidelines.asp

End of informative text.

Naming guideline summary

The capitalization guidelines can be summarized as:

- *non-public fields, parameters, variables*: use camel case
- *everything else*: use Pascal case

where:

- *Camel case*: the first letter of the identifier is lower case, the first letter of every subsequent "word" in the identifier is upper case. For example: camelCase.
- *Pascal case*: the first letter of the identifier is upper case, the first letter of every subsequent "word" in the identifier is upper case. For example: PascalCase.
- *Upper case*: all letters are upper case, recommended only for identifiers of one or two letters.

The naming guidelines can be summarized as:

- *events, methods*: use verbs or verb phrases
- *interfaces*: use nouns, adjectives, or noun/adjective phrases
- *everything else*: use nouns or noun phrases

Also, exception names should end in "Exception" and interface names should start with "I."

Note: the preceding URL is to Microsoft's general design guidelines, one of which is the naming guidelines. It is only the latter that the Standard informatively references. At the time of writing, the naming guideline itself can be found at:

http://msdn.microsoft.com/library/default.asp?url=/library/en-us/cpgenref/html/cpconna-mingguidelines.asp

Note: The naming guidelines only cover names that are (potentially) externally visible, so, for example, they do not provide guidance on the naming of local variables. However, we recommend the use of upper case for pre-processing symbols (§9.5.3).

D Standard Library

A conforming C# implementation shall provide a minimum set of types having specific semantics. These types and their members are listed here, in alphabetical order by namespace and type.
For a formal definition of these types and their members, refer to ISO/IEC 23271:2006 *Common
Language Infrastructure (CLI), Partition IV; Base Class Library (BCL), Extended Numerics Library,
and Extended Array Library*, which are included by reference in this International Standard.

Type names beginning with `System.` are intended for use by the Standard Library: Such names
not currently in use might be defined in a future version of this International Standard.

This text is informative.

The standard library is intended to be the minimum set of types and members required by a conforming C# implementation. As such, it contains only those members which are explicitly
required by the C# language specification.

It is expected that a conforming C# implementation will supply a significantly more extensive
library that enables useful programs to be written. For example, a conforming implementation
might extend this library by

- Adding namespaces.
- Adding types.
- Adding members to non-interface types.
- Having struct and class types implement additional interfaces.
- Adding attributes (other than the `ConditionalAttribute`) to existing types and
  members.

End of informative text.

```
namespace System
{
  public class ApplicationException : Exception
  {
    public ApplicationException();
    public ApplicationException(string message);
    public ApplicationException(string message, Exception
                                       innerException);
  }
}

namespace System
{
  public class ArgumentException : SystemException
  {
    public ArgumentException();
    public ArgumentException(string message);
    public ArgumentException(string message, Exception
                                   innerException);
  }
}

namespace System
{
  public class ArithmeticException : SystemException
```

```
    {
      public ArithmeticException();
      public ArithmeticException(string message);
      public ArithmeticException(string message, Exception
                                        innerException);
    }
}

namespace System
{
  public abstract class Array : IList, ICollection, IEnumerable
  {
    public int Length { get; }
    public int Rank { get; }
    public int GetLength(int dimension);
  }
}

namespace System
{
  public class ArrayTypeMismatchException : SystemException
  {
    public ArrayTypeMismatchException();
    public ArrayTypeMismatchException(string message);
    public ArrayTypeMismatchException(string message,
      Exception innerException);
  }
}

namespace System
{
  [AttributeUsageAttribute(AttributeTargets.All, Inherited = true,
    AllowMultiple = false)]
  public abstract class Attribute
  {
    protected Attribute();
  }
}

namespace System
{
  public enum AttributeTargets
  {
    Assembly = 1,
    Module = 2,
    Class = 4,
    Struct = 8,
    Enum = 16,
    Constructor = 32,
    Method = 64,
    Property = 128,
    Field = 256,
    Event = 512,
    Interface = 1024,
```

```
      Parameter = 2048,
      Delegate = 4096,
      ReturnValue = 8192,
      GenericParameter = 16384,
      All = 32767
  }
}

namespace System
{
  [AttributeUsageAttribute(AttributeTargets.Class, Inherited = true)]
  public sealed class AttributeUsageAttribute : Attribute
  {
    public AttributeUsageAttribute(AttributeTargets validOn);
    public bool AllowMultiple { get; set; }
    public bool Inherited { get; set; }
    public AttributeTargets ValidOn { get; }
  }
}

namespace System
{
  public struct Boolean
  {
  }
}

namespace System
{
  public struct Byte
  {
  }
}

namespace System
{
  public struct Char
  {
  }
}

namespace System
{
  public struct Decimal
  {
  }
}

namespace System
{
  public abstract class Delegate
  {
  }
}
```

```
namespace System
{
  public class DivideByZeroException : ArithmeticException
  {
    public DivideByZeroException();
    public DivideByZeroException(string message);
    public DivideByZeroException(string message, Exception
                                             innerException);
  }
}

namespace System
{
  public struct Double
  {
  }
}

namespace System
{
  public abstract class Enum : ValueType
  {
    protected Enum();
  }
}

namespace System
{
  public class Exception
  {
    public Exception();
    public Exception(string message);
    public Exception(string message, Exception innerException);
    public sealed Exception InnerException { get; }
    public virtual string Message { get; }
  }
}

namespace System
{
  public interface IDisposable
  {
    public void Dispose();
  }
}

namespace System
{
  public sealed class IndexOutOfRangeException : SystemException
  {
    public IndexOutOfRangeException();
    public IndexOutOfRangeException(string message);
    public IndexOutOfRangeException(string message,
```

```
        Exception innerException);
  }
}

namespace System
{
  public struct Int16
  {
  }
}

namespace System
{
  public struct Int32
  {
  }
}

namespace System
{
  public struct Int64
  {
  }
}

namespace System
{
  public class InvalidCastException : SystemException
  {
    public InvalidCastException();
    public InvalidCastException(string message);
    public InvalidCastException(string message, Exception
                                          innerException);
  }
}

namespace System
{
  public class InvalidOperationException : SystemException
  {
    public InvalidOperationException();
    public InvalidOperationException(string message);
    public InvalidOperationException(string message,
      Exception innerException);
  }
}

namespace System
{
  public abstract class MemberInfo
  {
    protected MemberInfo();
  }
}
```

```
namespace System
{
  public class NotSupportedException : SystemException
  {
    public NotSupportedException();
    public NotSupportedException(string message);
    public NotSupportedException(string message, Exception
                                      innerException);
  }
}

namespace System
{
  public struct Nullable<T>
  {
    public bool HasValue { get; }
    public T Value { get; }
  }
}

namespace System
{
  public class NullReferenceException : SystemException
  {
    public NullReferenceException();
    public NullReferenceException(string message);
    public NullReferenceException(string message, Exception
                                      innerException);
  }
}

namespace System
{
  public class Object
  {
    public Object();
    ~Object();
    public virtual bool Equals(object obj);
    public virtual int GetHashCode();
    public Type GetType();
    public virtual string ToString();
  }
}

namespace System
{
  [AttributeUsageAttribute(AttributeTargets.Class
      | AttributeTargets.Struct
      | AttributeTargets.Enum | AttributeTargets.Interface
      | AttributeTargets.Constructor | AttributeTargets.Method
      | AttributeTargets.Property | AttributeTargets.Field
      | AttributeTargets.Event | AttributeTargets.Delegate,
        Inherited = false)]
```

```csharp
      public sealed class ObsoleteAttribute : Attribute
      {
        public ObsoleteAttribute();
        public ObsoleteAttribute(string message);
        public ObsoleteAttribute(string message, bool error);
        public bool IsError { get; }
        public string Message { get; }
      }
    }

    namespace System
    {
      public class OutOfMemoryException : SystemException
      {
        public OutOfMemoryException();
        public OutOfMemoryException(string message);
        public OutOfMemoryException(string message, Exception
                                          innerException);
      }
    }

    namespace System
    {
      public class OverflowException : ArithmeticException
      {
        public OverflowException();
        public OverflowException(string message);
        public OverflowException(string message, Exception
                                          innerException);
      }
    }

    namespace System
    {
      public struct SByte
      {
      }
    }

    namespace System
    {
      public struct Single
      {
      }
    }

    namespace System
    {
      public sealed class StackOverflowException : SystemException
      {
        public StackOverflowException();
        public StackOverflowException(string message);
        public StackOverflowException(string message, Exception
                                          innerException);
```

```
    }
  }

  namespace System
  {
    public sealed class String : IEnumerable<Char>, IEnumerable
    {
      public int Length { get; }
      public char this[int index] { get; }
    }
  }

  namespace System
  {
    public class SystemException : Exception
    {
      public SystemException();
      public SystemException(string message);
      public SystemException(string message, Exception innerException);
    }
  }

  namespace System
  {
    public abstract class Type : MemberInfo
    {
    }
  }

  namespace System
  {
    public sealed class TypeInitializationException : SystemException
    {
      public TypeInitializationException(string fullTypeName,
        Exception innerException);
    }
  }

  namespace System
  {
    public struct UInt16
    {
    }
  }

  namespace System
  {
    public struct UInt32
    {
    }
  }

  namespace System
  {
```

```
    public struct UInt64
    {
    }
}

namespace System
{
  public abstract class ValueType
  {
    protected ValueType();
  }
}

namespace System.Collections
{
  public interface ICollection : IEnumerable
  {
    public int Count { get; }
    public bool IsSynchronized { get; }
    public object SyncRoot { get; }
    public void CopyTo(Array array, int index);
  }
}

namespace System.Collections
{
  public interface IEnumerable
  {
    public IEnumerator GetEnumerator();
  }
}

namespace System.Collections
{
  public interface IEnumerator
  {
    public object Current { get; }
    public bool MoveNext();
    public void Reset();
  }
}

namespace System.Collections
{
  public interface IList : ICollection, IEnumerable
  {
    public bool IsFixedSize { get; }
    public bool IsReadOnly { get; }
    public object this[int index] { get; set; }
    public int Add(object value);
    public void Clear();
    public bool Contains(object value);
    public int IndexOf(object value);
    public void Insert(int index, object value);
```

```
      public void Remove(object value);
      public void RemoveAt(int index);
  }
}

namespace System.Collections.Generic
{
  public interface ICollection<T> : IEnumerable<T>
  {
    public int Count { get; }
    public bool IsReadOnly { get; }
    public void Add(T item);
    public void Clear();
    public bool Contains(T item);
    public void CopyTo(T[] array, int arrayIndex);
    public bool Remove(T item);
  }
}

namespace System.Collections.Generic
{
  public interface IEnumerable<T> : IEnumerable
  {
    public IEnumerator<T> GetEnumerator();
  }
}

namespace System.Collections.Generic
{
  public interface IEnumerator<T> : IDisposable, IEnumerator
  {
    public T Current { get; }
  }
}

namespace System.Collections.Generic
{
  public interface IList<T> : ICollection<T>
  {
    public T this[int index] { get; set; }
    public int IndexOf(T item);
    public void Insert(int index, T item);
    public void RemoveAt(int index);
  }
}

namespace System.Diagnostics
{
  [AttributeUsageAttribute(AttributeTargets.Method
    | AttributeTargets.Class, AllowMultiple = true)]
  public sealed class ConditionalAttribute : Attribute
  {
    public ConditionalAttribute(string conditionString);
    public string ConditionString { get; }
```

```
    }
}

namespace System.Threading
{
  public static class Monitor
  {
    public static void Enter(object obj);
    public static void Exit(object obj);
  }
}
```

E Documentation Comments

This annex is informative.

C# provides a mechanism for programmers to document their code using a special comment syntax that contains XML text. Comments using such syntax are called ***documentation comments***. The XML generation tool is called the ***documentation generator***. (This generator could be, but need not be, the C# compiler itself.) The output produced by the documentation generator is called the ***documentation file***. A documentation file is used as input to a ***documentation viewer***, a tool intended to produce some sort of visual display of type information and its associated documentation.

A conforming C# compiler is not required to check the syntax of documentation comments; such comments are simply ordinary comments. A conforming compiler is permitted to do such checking, however.

This specification suggests a set of standard tags to be used in documentation comments. For C# implementations targeting the CLI, it also provides information about the documentation generator and the format of the documentation file. No information is provided about the documentation viewer.

E.1 Introduction

Comments having a special form can be used to direct a tool to produce XML from those comments and the source code elements, which they precede. Such comments are single-line comments of the form /// ... or delimited comments of the form /** ... */. They must immediately precede a user-defined type (such as a class, delegate, or interface) or a member (such as a field, event, property, or method) that they annotate. Attribute sections are considered part of declarations, so documentation comments must precede attributes applied to a type or member.

Syntax:

```
single-line-doc-comment::
  ///  input-characters_opt

delimited-doc-comment::
  /**  delimited-comment-characters_opt  */
```

In a *single-line-doc-comment*, if there is a *whitespace* character following the /// characters on each of the *single-line-doc-comments* adjacent to the current *single-line-doc-comment*, then that *whitespace* character is not included in the XML output.

In a *delimited-doc-comment*, if the first non-*whitespace* character on the second line is an *asterisk* and the same pattern of optional *whitespace* characters and an *asterisk* character is repeated at the beginning of each of the lines within the *delimited-doc-comment*, then the characters of the repeated pattern are not included in the XML output. The pattern can include *whitespace* characters after, as well as before, the *asterisk* character.

Example:

```
/**
 * <remarks>
 *  Class <c>Point</c> models a point in a two-dimensional plane.
 * </remarks>
 */
```

```
public class Point
{
  /// <remarks>Method <c>Draw</c> renders the point.</remarks>
  void Draw() { ... }
}
```

The text within documentation comments must be well formed according to the rules of XML
(http://www.w3.org/TR/REC-xml). If the XML is ill formed, a warning is generated and the documentation file will contain a comment saying that an error was encountered.

Although developers are free to create their own set of tags, a recommended set is defined in §E.2.
Some of the recommended tags have special meanings:

- The `<param>` tag is used to describe parameters. If such a tag is used, the documentation
  generator must verify that the specified parameter exists and that all parameters are
  described in documentation comments. If such verification fails, the documentation generator issues a warning.

- The `cref` attribute can be attached to any tag to provide a reference to a code element.
  The documentation generator must verify that this code element exists. If the verification
  fails, the documentation generator issues a warning. When looking for a name described
  in a `cref` attribute, the documentation generator must respect namespace visibility
  according to `using` statements appearing within the source code. For code elements that
  contain code that uses generics, the normal generics syntax, for instance `List<T>`, cannot
  be used because it produces invalid XML. Instead, curly braces can be used, such as `<see
  cref="List{ T} "/>`, or the normal XML escape syntax `<` and `>` for instance as in
  `List&lt;T&gt;`. Members of generic types are referred to as `List{ T} .Add(T)`. The variable `T` in `Add(T)` is bound by the type parameter `T` in `List{ T}`. Similarly, the parameter
  type `T` of the generic method `Sort{ T} (T[ ] )` is bound by the type-parameter `T`. In general,
  a generic method in a generic class is referred to as `C{ S} .F{ T} (S, List{ T} , U)`, here
  the parameter `S` is bound by the type parameter of the class `C{ S}` and the `T` in `List{ T}`
  is bound by the type parameter of the generic method `F{ T}`, the parameter type `U` is free.

- The `<summary>` tag is intended to be used by a documentation viewer to display additional information about a type or member.

Note carefully that the documentation file does not provide full information about the type and
members (for example, it does not contain any type information). To get such information about
a type or member, the documentation file must be used in conjunction with reflection on the
runtime type or member.

E.2 Recommended tags

The documentation generator must accept and process any tag that is valid according to the rules
of XML. The following tags provide commonly used functionality in user documentation. (Of
course, other tags are possible.)

Tag	Reference	Purpose
`<c>`	§E.2.1	Set text in a code-like font
`<code>`	§E.2.2	Set one or more lines of source code or program output
`<example>`	§E.2.3	Indicate an example
`<exception>`	§E.2.4	Identifies the exceptions a method can throw

`<list>`	§E.2.5	Create a list or table
`<para>`	§E.2.6	Permit structure to be added to text
`<param>`	§E.2.7	Describe a parameter for a method or constructor
`<paramref>`	§E.2.8	Identify that a word is a parameter name
`<permission>`	§E.2.9	Document the security accessibility of a member
`<remarks>`	§E.2.10	Describe a type
`<returns>`	§E.2.11	Describe the return value of a method
`<see>`	§E.2.12	Specify a link
`<seealso>`	§E.2.13	Generate a *See Also* entry
`<summary>`	§E.2.14	Describe a member of a type
`<typeparam>`	§E.2.15	Describe a type parameter for a generic type or method
`<typeparamref>`	§E.2.16	Identify that a word is a type parameter name
`<value>`	§E.2.17	Describe a property

E.2.1 <c>

This tag provides a mechanism to indicate that a fragment of text within a description should be set in a special font such as that used for a block of code. For lines of actual code, use `<code>` (§E.2.2).

Syntax:

```
<c>text to be set like code</c>
```

Example:

```
/// <remarks>
///  Class <c>Point</c> models a point in a two-dimensional plane.
/// </remarks>
public class Point
{
    ...
}
```

E.2.2 <code>

This tag is used to set one or more lines of source code or program output in some special font. For small code fragments in narrative, use `<c>` (§E.2.1).

Syntax:

```
<code>source code or program output</code>
```

Example:

```
/// <summary>
///  Changes the Point's location by the given x- and y-offsets.
/// </summary>
/// <example>
///  The following code:
///  <code>
///    Point p = new Point(3,5);
///    p.Translate(-1,3);
```

```
///   </code>
///   results in <c>p</c>'s having the value (2,8).
/// </example>
public void Translate(int xor, int yor)
{
   X += xor;
   Y += yor;
}
```

E.2.3 <example>

This tag allows example code within a comment, to specify how a method or other library member might be used. Ordinarily, this would also involve use of the tag <code> (§E.2.2) as well.

Syntax:

```
<example>description</example>
```

Example:

See <code> (§E.2.2) for an example.

E.2.4 <exception>

This tag provides a way to document the exceptions a method can throw.

Syntax:

```
<exception cref="member">description</exception>
```

where

member

> The name of a member. The documentation generator checks that the given member exists and translates member to the canonical element name in the documentation file.

description

> A description of the circumstances in which the exception is thrown.

Example:

```
public class DataBaseOperations
{
   /// <exception cref="MasterFileFormatCorruptException"> </exception>
   /// <exception cref="MasterFileLockedOpenException"></exception>
   public static void ReadRecord(int flag)
   {
      if (flag == 1)
         throw new MasterFileFormatCorruptException();
      else if (flag == 2)
         throw new MasterFileLockedOpenException();
         // …
   }
}
```

E.2.5 <list>

This tag is used to create a list or table of items. It can contain a `<listheader>` block to define the heading row of either a table or definition list. (When defining a table, only an entry for *term* in the heading need be supplied.)

Each item in the list is specified with an `<item>` block. When creating a definition list, both *term* and *description* must be specified. However, for a table, bulleted list, or numbered list, only *description* need be specified.

Syntax:

```
<list type="style">
  <listheader>
    <term>term</term>
    <description>description</description>
  </listheader>
  <item>
    <term>term</term>
    <description>description</description>
  </item>
    ...
  <item>
    <term>term</term>
    <description>description</description>
  </item>
</list>
```

where

style

> The style of the list. Must be `bullet`, `number`, or `table`.

term

> The term to define, whose definition is in `description`.

description

> Either an item in a bullet or numbered list, or the definition of a `term`.

Example:

```
public class MyClass
{
  /// <remarks>
  ///  Here is an example of a bulleted list:
  ///  <list type="bullet">
  ///    <item>
  ///      <description>First item.</description>
  ///    </item>
  ///    <item>
  ///      <description>Second item.</description>
  ///    </item>
  ///  </list>
  /// </remarks>
  public static void Main ()
  {
    ...
```

```
    }
  }
```

E.2.6 <para>

This tag is for use inside other tags, such as <remarks> (§E.2.10) or <returns> (§E.2.11), and permits structure to be added to text.

Syntax:

```
<para>content</para>
```

where

content

    The text of the paragraph.

Example:

```
/// <summary>
///  <para>
///    This is the entry point of the Point class testing program.
///  </para>
///  <para>
///    This program tests each method and operator, and is intended
///    to be run after any non-trivial maintenance has been performed
///    on the Point class.
///  </para>
/// </summary>
public static void Main()
{
    ...
}
```

E.2.7 <param>

This tag is used to describe a parameter for a method, constructor, or indexer.

Syntax:

```
<param name="name">description</param>
```

where

name

    The name of the parameter.

description

    A description of the parameter.

Example:

```
/// <summary>
///  This method changes the Point's location to the given coordinates.
/// </summary>
/// <param name="xor">The new x-coordinate.</param>
/// <param name="yor">The new y-coordinate.</param>
```

```
public void Move(int xor, int yor)
{
  X = xor;
  Y = yor;
}
```

E.2.8 <paramref>

This tag is used to indicate that a word is a parameter. The documentation file can be processed to format this parameter in some distinct way.

Syntax:

```
<paramref name="name"/>
```

where

name

> The name of the parameter.

Example:

```
/// <summary>
///  This constructor initializes the new Point to
///  (<paramref name="xor"/>,<paramref name="yor"/>).
/// </summary>
/// <param name="xor">The new Point's x-coordinate.</param>
/// <param name="yor">The new Point's y-coordinate.</param>
public Point(int xor, int yor)
{
  X = xor;
  Y = yor;
}
```

E.2.9 <permission>

This tag allows the security accessibility of a member to be documented.

Syntax:

```
<permission cref="member">description</permission>
```

where

member

> The name of a member. The documentation generator checks that the given code element exists and translates *member* to the canonical element name in the documentation file.

description

> A description of the access to the member.

Example:

```
/// <permission cref="System.Security.PermissionSet">
///  Everyone can access this method.
/// </permission>
public static void Test()
```

```
{
  ...
}
```

E.2.10 <remarks>

This tag is used to specify overview information about a type. Use `<summary>` (§E.2.14) to describe the members of a type.

Syntax:

```
<remarks>text</remarks>
```

where

text

> The text of the remarks.

Example:

```
/// <remarks>
///   Class <c>Point</c> models a point in a two-dimensional plane.
/// </remarks>
public class Point
{
  ...
}
```

E.2.11 <returns>

This tag is used to describe the return value of a method.

Syntax:

```
<returns>description</returns>
```

where

description

> A description of the return value.

Example:

```
/// <summary>
///   Report a Point's location as a string.
/// </summary>
/// <returns>
///   A string representing a Point's location, in the form (x,y),
///   without any leading, training, or embedded whitespace.
/// </returns>
public override string ToString()
{
  return "(" + X + "," + Y + ")";
}
```

E.2.12 <see>

This tag allows a link to be specified within text. Use `<seealso>` (§E.2.13) to indicate text that is to appear in a *See Also* subclause.

Syntax:

```
<see cref="member"/>
```

where

member

> The name of a member. The documentation generator checks that the given code element exists and passes *member* to the element name in the documentation file.

Example:

```
/// <summary>
///  This method changes the Point's location to the given coordinates.
///  Use the <see cref="Translate"/> method to apply a relative change.
/// </summary>
public void Move(int xor, int yor)
{
  X = xor;
  Y = yor;
}
/// <summary>
///  This method changes the Point's location by the given offsets.
///  Use the <see cref="Move"/> method to directly set the coordinates.
/// </summary>
public void Translate(int xor, int yor)
{
  X += xor;
  Y += yor;
}
```

E.2.13 <seealso>

This tag allows an entry to be generated for the *See Also* subclause. Use `<see>` (§E.2.12) to specify a link from within text.

Syntax:

```
<seealso cref="member"/>
```

where

member

> The name of a member. The documentation generator checks that the given code element exists and passes *member* to the element name in the documentation file.

Example:

```
/// <summary>
///  This method determines whether two Points have the same location.
/// </summary>
/// <seealso cref="operator =="/>
/// <seealso cref="operator !="/>
public override bool Equals(object o)
```

```
{
   ...
}
```

E.2.14 <summary>

This tag can be used to describe a member for a type. Use <remarks> (§E.2.10) to describe the type itself.

Syntax:

```
<summary>description</summary>
```

where

description

> A summary of the member.

Example:

```
/// <summary>
///  This constructor initializes the new Point to (0,0).
/// </summary>
public Point(): this(0,0)
{
}
```

E.2.15 <typeparam>

This tag is used to describe a type parameter for a generic type or method.

Syntax:

```
<typeparam name="name">description</typeparam>
```

where

name

> The name of the type parameter.

description

> A description of the parameter.

Example:

```
/// <summary>
///  This method creates a new array of arbitrary type.
/// </summary>
/// <typeparam name="T">The element type of the array</typeparam>
public static T[] MakeArray<T>(int n)
{
   return new T[n];
}
```

E.2.16 <typeparamref>

This tag is used to indicate that a word is a type parameter. The documentation file can be processed to format this parameter in some distinct way.

Syntax:

```
<typeparamref name="name"/>
```

where

name

    The name of the parameter.

Example:

```
/// <summary>
///  This method creates a new array of arbitrary type
///    <typeparamref name="T"/>
/// </summary>
/// <typeparam name="T">The element type of the array</typeparam>
public static T[ ] MakeArray<T>(int n)
{
   return new T[n] ;
}
```

E.2.17 <value>
This tag allows a property to be described.

Syntax:

```
<value>property description</value>
```

where

property description

    A description for the property.

Example:

```
/// <value>
///  The point's x-coordinate.
/// </value>
public int X
{
   get { return x; }
   set { x = value; }
}
```

E.3 Processing the documentation file

The following information is intended for C# implementations targeting the CLI.

The documentation generator generates an ID string for each element in the source code that is tagged with a documentation comment. This ID string uniquely identifies a source element. A documentation viewer can use an ID string to identify the corresponding metadata/reflection item to which the documentation applies.

The documentation file is not a hierarchical representation of the source code; rather, it is a flat list with a generated ID string for each element.

E.3.1 ID string format

The documentation generator observes the following rules when it generates the ID strings:

- No white space is placed in the string.
- The first part of the string identifies the kind of member being documented, via a single character followed by a colon. The following kinds of members are defined:

Character	Description
E	Event
F	Field
M	Method (including constructors, finalizers, and operators)
N	Namespace
P	Property (including indexers)
T	Type (such as class, delegate, enum, interface, and struct)
!	Error string; the rest of the string provides information about the error. For example, the documentation generator generates error information for links that cannot be resolved.

- The second part of the string is the fully qualified name of the element, starting at the root of the namespace. The name of the element, its enclosing type(s), and namespace are separated by periods. If the name of the item itself has periods, they are replaced by the NUMBER SIGN # (U+0023). (It is assumed that no element has this character in its name.)
- For methods and properties with arguments, the argument list follows, enclosed in parentheses. For those without arguments, the parentheses are omitted. The arguments are separated by commas. The encoding of each argument is the same as a CLI signature, as follows: Arguments are represented by their complete documentation name, which is based on their fully qualified name. For example, `int` becomes `System.Int32`, `string` becomes `System.String`, `object` becomes `System.Object`, and so on. Arguments that define generic type parameters have an appended grave accent character "`", followed by the number of type parameters; for example, `C`1`. For nested types, the number is based upon the of new type parameters on the nested type; for example, `C`1.NestedC`2`. Arguments having the `out` or `ref` modifier have an @ following their type name. Arguments passed by value or via `params` have no special notation. Arguments that are arrays are represented as [*lowerbound* : *size* , ... , *lowerbound* : *size*] where the number of commas is the rank less one, and the lower bounds and size of each dimension, if known, are represented in decimal. If a lower bound or size is not specified, it is omitted. If the lower bound and size for a particular dimension are omitted, the ":" is omitted as well. Jagged arrays are represented by one "[]" per level. Arguments that have pointer types other than void are represented using a * following the type name. A void pointer is represented using a type name of `System.Void`. Arguments that refer to generic type parameters on types are encoded using a single grave accent character "`" followed by the zero-based index of the type parameter. Arguments that use generic parameters on methods use double grave accent characters "`" followed by the zero-based index of the type-parameter instead of the single grave accent used for parameters on types. Arguments that refer to constructed generic types are encoded using the generic type followed by a comma-separated list of type arguments, enclosed by braces "{" and "}".

E.3.2 ID string examples

The following examples each show a fragment of C# code, along with the ID string produced from each source element capable of having a documentation comment:

- Types are represented using their fully qualified name.

```
enum Color { Red, Blue, Green }
namespace Acme
{
  interface IProcess { … }
  struct ValueType { … }
  class Widget: IProcess
  {
    public class NestedClass { … }
    public interface IMenuItem { … }
    public delegate void Del(int i);
    public enum Direction { North, South, East, West }
  }
  class MyList<T>
  {
    class Helper<U,V>{ … }
  }
}
```

```
"T:Color"
"T:Acme.IProcess"
"T:Acme.ValueType"
"T:Acme.Widget"
"T:Acme.Widget.NestedClass"
"T:Acme.Widget.IMenuItem"
"T:Acme.Widget.Del"
"T:Acme.Widget.Direction"
"T:Acme.MyList`1"
"T:Acme.MyList`1.Helper`2"
```

- Fields are represented by their fully qualified name.

```
namespace Acme
{
  struct ValueType
  {
    private int total;
  }
  class Widget: IProcess
  {
    public class NestedClass
    {
      private int value;
    }
    private string message;
    private static Color defaultColor;
    private const double PI = 3.14159;
    protected readonly double monthlyAverage;
    private long[] array1;
    private Widget[,] array2;
    private unsafe int *pCount;
```

```
        private unsafe float **ppValues;
    }
}

"F:Acme.ValueType.total"
"F:Acme.Widget.NestedClass.value"
"F:Acme.Widget.message"
"F:Acme.Widget.defaultColor"
"F:Acme.Widget.PI"
"F:Acme.Widget.monthlyAverage"
"F:Acme.Widget.array1"
"F:Acme.Widget.array2"
"F:Acme.Widget.pCount"
"F:Acme.Widget.ppValues"
```

- Constructors.

```
namespace Acme
{
  class Widget: IProcess
  {
    static Widget() { … }
    public Widget() { … }
    public Widget(string s) { … }
  }
}

"M:Acme.Widget.#cctor"
"M:Acme.Widget.#ctor"
"M:Acme.Widget.#ctor(System.String)"
```

- Finalizers.

```
namespace Acme
{
  class Widget: IProcess
  {

    ~Widget() { … }
  }
}

"M:Acme.Widget.Finalize"
```

- Methods.

```
namespace Acme
{
  struct ValueType
  {
    public void M(int i) { … }
  }
  class Widget: IProcess
```

```
{
  public class NestedClass
  {
    public void M(int i) { … }
  }
  public static void M0() { … }
  public void M1(char c, out float f, ref ValueType v) { … }
  public void M2(short[] x1, int[,] x2, long[][] x3) { … }

  public void M3(long[][] x3, Widget[][,,] x4) { … }
  public unsafe void M4(char *pc, Color **pf) { … }
  public unsafe void M5(void *pv, double *[][,] pd) { … }
  public void M6(int i, params object[] args) { … }
}
class MyList<T>
{
  public void Test(T t) { … }
}
class UseList
{
  public void Process(MyList<int> list) { … }
  public MyList<T> GetValues<T>(T value) { … }
}
}
```

```
"M:Acme.ValueType.M(System.Int32)"
"M:Acme.Widget.NestedClass.M(System.Int32)"
"M:Acme.Widget.M0"
"M:Acme.Widget.M1(System.Char,System.Single@,Acme.ValueType@)"
"M:Acme.Widget.M2(System.Int16[],System.Int32[0:,0:],
                                  System.Int64[][])"
"M:Acme.Widget.M3(System.Int64[][],Acme.Widget[0:,0:,0:][])"
"M:Acme.Widget.M4(System.Char*,Color**)"
"M:Acme.Widget.M5(System.Void*,System.Double*[0:,0:][])"
"M:Acme.Widget.M6(System.Int32,System.Object[])"
"M:Acme.MyList`1.Test(`0)"
"M:Acme.UseList.Process(Acme.MyList{System.Int32})"
"M:Acme.UseList.getValues`1(``0)"
```

- Properties and indexers.

```
namespace Acme
{
  class Widget: IProcess
  {
    public int Width {get { … } set { … }}
    public int this[int i] {get { … } set { … }}
    public int this[string s, int i] {get { … } set { … }}
  }
}
```

```
"P:Acme.Widget.Width"
"P:Acme.Widget.Item(System.Int32)"
"P:Acme.Widget.Item(System.String,System.Int32)"
```

- Events.

```
namespace Acme
{
  class Widget: IProcess
  {
    public event Del AnEvent;
  }
}
```

   "E:Acme.Widget.AnEvent"

- Unary operators.

```
namespace Acme
{
  class Widget: IProcess
  {
    public static Widget operator+(Widget x) { … }
  }
}
```

   "M:Acme.Widget.op_UnaryPlus(Acme.Widget)"

The complete set of unary operator function names used is as follows:
op_UnaryPlus, op_UnaryNegation, op_LogicalNot, op_OnesComplement,
op_Increment, op_Decrement, op_True, and op_False.

- Binary operators.

```
namespace Acme
{
  class Widget: IProcess
  {
    public static Widget operator+(Widget x1, Widget x2) { return x1; }
  }
}
```

   "M:Acme.Widget.op_Addition(Acme.Widget,Acme.Widget)"

The complete set of binary operator function names used is as follows:
op_Addition, op_Subtraction, op_Multiply, op_Division, op_Modulus,
op_BitwiseAnd, op_BitwiseOr, op_ExclusiveOr, op_LeftShift,
op_RightShift, op_Equality, op_Inequality, op_LessThan,
op_LessThanOrEqual, op_GreaterThan, and op_GreaterThanOrEqual.

- Conversion operators have a trailing "~" followed by the return type.

```
namespace Acme
{
  class Widget: IProcess
  {
```

```
      public static explicit operator int(Widget x) { … }
      public static implicit operator long(Widget x) { … }
  }
}
```

```
"M:Acme.Widget.op_Explicit(Acme.Widget)~System.Int32"
"M:Acme.Widget.op_Implicit(Acme.Widget)~System.Int64"
```

E.4 An example

E.4.1 C# source code

The following example shows the source code of a Point class:

```
namespace Graphics
{
/// <remarks>
///   Class <c>Point</c> models a point in a two-dimensional plane.
/// </remarks>
public class Point
{
  /// <summary>
  ///   Instance variable <c>x</c> represents the Point's x-coordinate.
  /// </summary>
  private int x;
  /// <summary>
  ///   Instance variable <c>y</c> represents the Point's y-coordinate.
  /// </summary>
  private int y;
  /// <value>
  ///   The Point's x-coordinate.
  /// </value>
  public int X
  {
    get { return x; }
    set { x = value; }
  }
  /// <value>
  ///   The Point's y-coordinate.
  /// </value>
  public int Y
  {
    get { return y; }
    set { y = value; }
  }
  /// <summary>
  ///   This constructor initializes the new Point to (0,0).
  /// </summary>
  public Point() : this(0,0) {}
  /// <summary>
  ///   This constructor initializes the new Point to
  ///   (<paramref name="xor"/>,<paramref name="yor"/>).
  /// </summary>
```

```
/// <param name="xor">The new Point's x-coordinate.</param>
/// <param name="yor">The new Point's y-coordinate.</param>
public Point(int xor, int yor)
{
  x = xor;
  y = yor;
}
/// <summary>
///  This method changes the point's location to the given
///  coordinates.
/// </summary>
/// <param name="xor">The new x-coordinate.</param>
/// <param name="yor">The new y-coordinate.</param>
/// <seealso cref="Translate"/>
public void Move(int xor, int yor)
{
  x = xor;
  y = yor;
}
/// <summary>
///  This method changes the point's location by the given
///  x- and y-offsets.
/// </summary>
/// <example>
///  The following code:
///  <code>
///    Point p = new Point(3,5);
///    p.Translate(-1,3);
///  </code>
///  results in <c>p</c>'s having the value (2,8).
/// </example>
/// <param name="xor">The relative x-offset.</param>
/// <param name="yor">The relative y-offset.</param>
/// <seealso cref="Move"/>
public void Translate(int xor, int yor)
{
  x += xor;
  y += yor;
}
/// <summary>
///  This method determines whether two Points have the same
///  location.


/// </summary>
/// <param name="o">
///  The object to be compared to the current object.
/// </param>
/// <returns>
///  True if the Points have the same location; otherwise, false.
/// </returns>
/// <seealso cref="operator =="/>
/// <seealso cref="operator !="/>
public override bool Equals(object o)
```

```
{
  Point p = o as Point;
  if (p == null) return false;
    return x == p.x && y == p.y;
}
/// <summary>
///  Computes the hash code for a Point.
/// </summary>
/// <returns>
///  A hash code computed from the x and y coordinates.
/// </returns>
public override int GetHashCode()
{
  return x ^ y;
}
/// <summary>
///  Report a point's location as a string.
/// </summary>
/// <returns>
///  A string representing a point's location, in the form (x,y),
///  without any leading, training, or embedded whitespace.
/// </returns>
public override string ToString()
{
  return "(" + x + "," + y + ")";
}
/// <summary>
///  This operator determines whether two Points have the same
///  location.
/// </summary>
/// <param name="p1">The first Point to be compared.</param>
/// <param name="p2">The second Point to be compared.</param>
/// <returns>
///  True if the Points have the same location; otherwise, false.
/// </returns>
/// <seealso cref="Equals"/>
/// <seealso cref="operator !="/>
public static bool operator ==(Point p1, Point p2)
{
  if ((object)p1 == null || (object)p2 == null) return false;
    return p1.x == p2.x && p1.y == p2.y;
}
/// <summary>
///  This operator determines whether two Points have the same
///  location.
/// </summary>
/// <param name="p1">The first Point to be compared.</param>
/// <param name="p2">The second Point to be compared.</param>
/// <returns>
///  True if the Points do not have the same location;
///  otherwise, false.
/// </returns>
/// <seealso cref="Equals"/>
/// <seealso cref="operator =="/>
```

```
public static bool operator !=(Point p1, Point p2)
{
  return !(p1 == p2);
}
/// <summary>
///   <para>
///     This is the entry point of the Point class testing program.
///   </para>
///   <para>
///     This program tests each method and operator, and is intended
///     to be run after any non-trivial maintenance has been performed
///     on the Point class.
///   </para>
/// </summary>
public static void Main()
{
  // class test code goes here
}
}
}
```

E.4.2 Resulting XML

Here is the output produced by one documentation generator when given the source code for class Point, shown above:

```xml
<?xml version="1.0"?>
<doc>
 <assembly>
  <name>Point</name>
 </assembly>
 <members>
  <member name="T:Graphics.Point">
   <remarks>
    Class <c>Point</c> models a point in a two-dimensional plane.
   </remarks>
  </member>
  <member name="F:Graphics.Point.x">
   <summary>
    Instance variable <c>x</c> represents the Point's x-coordinate.
   </summary>
  </member>
  <member name="F:Graphics.Point.y">
   <summary>
    Instance variable <c>y</c> represents the Point's y-coordinate.
   </summary>
  </member>
  <member name="M:Graphics.Point.#ctor">
   <summary>
    This constructor initializes the new Point to (0,0).
   </summary>
  </member>
  <member name="M:Graphics.Point.#ctor(System.Int32,System.Int32)">
```

```
  <summary>
   This constructor initializes the new Point to
   (<paramref name="xor"/>,<paramref name="yor"/>).
  </summary>
  <param name="xor">The new Point's x-coordinate.</param>
  <param name="yor">The new Point's y-coordinate.</param>
 </member>
 <member name="M:Graphics.Point.Move(System.Int32,System.Int32)">
  <summary>
   This method changes the point's location to the given
   coordinates.
  </summary>
  <param name="xor">The new x-coordinate.</param>
  <param name="yor">The new y-coordinate.</param>
  <seealso cref="M:Graphics.Point.Translate(System.Int32,
                                    System.Int32)"/>
 </member>
 <member name="M:Graphics.Point.Translate(System.Int32,
                                    System.Int32)">
  <summary>
   This method changes the point's location by the given
   x- and y-offsets.
  </summary>
  <example>
   The following code:
   <code>
    Point p = new Point(3,5);
    p.Translate(-1,3);
   </code>
   results in <c>p</c>'s having the value (2,8).
  </example>
  <param name="xor">The relative x-offset.</param>
  <param name="yor">The relative y-offset.</param>
  <seealso cref="M:Graphics.Point.Move(System.Int32,
                                    System.Int32)"/>
 </member>
 <member name="M:Graphics.Point.Equals(System.Object)">
  <summary>
   This method determines whether two Points have the same
   location.
  </summary>
  <param name="o">
   The object to be compared to the current object.
  </param>
  <returns>
   True if the Points have the same location; otherwise, false.
  </returns>
  <seealso cref="M:Graphics.Point.op_Equality(Graphics.Point,
                                    Graphics.Point)"/>
  <seealso cref="M:Graphics.Point.op_Inequality(Graphics.Point,
                                    Graphics.Point)"/>
 </member>
 <member name="M:Graphics.Point.GetHashCode">
  <summary>
```

```
     Computes the hash code for a Point.
    </summary>
    <returns>
     A hash code computed from the x and y coordinates.
    </returns>
   </member>
   <member name="M:Graphics.Point.ToString">
    <summary>
     Report a point's location as a string.
    </summary>
    <returns>
     A string representing a point's location, in the form (x,y),
     without any leading, training, or embedded whitespace.
    </returns>
   </member>
   <member name="M:Graphics.Point.op_Equality(Graphics.Point,
                                    Graphics.Point)">
    <summary>
     This operator determines whether two Points have the same
     location.
    </summary>
    <param name="p1">The first Point to be compared.</param>
    <param name="p2">The second Point to be compared.</param>
    <returns>
     True if the Points have the same location; otherwise, false.
    </returns>
    <seealso cref="M:Graphics.Point.Equals(System.Object)"/>
    <seealso cref="M:Graphics.Point.op_Inequality(Graphics.Point,
                                    Graphics.Point)"/>
   </member>
   <member name="M:Graphics.Point.op_Inequality(Graphics.Point,
                                    Graphics.Point)">
    <summary>
     This operator determines whether two Points have the same
     location.
    </summary>
    <param name="p1">The first Point to be compared.</param>
    <param name="p2">The second Point to be compared.</param>
    <returns>
     True if the Points do not have the same location;
     otherwise, false.
    </returns>
    <seealso cref="M:Graphics.Point.Equals(System.Object)"/>
    <seealso cref="M:Graphics.Point.op_Equality(Graphics.Point,Graphics.
Point)"/>
   </member>
   <member name="M:Graphics.Point.Main">
    <summary>
     <para>
      This is the entry point of the Point class testing program.
</para>
     <para>
      This program tests each method and operator, and is intended
      to be run after any non-trivial maintenance has been performed
```

```
            on the Point class.
</para>
     </summary>
    </member>
    <member name="P:Graphics.Point.X">
     <value>
      The Point's x-coordinate.
     </value>
    </member>
    <member name="P:Graphics.Point.Y">
     <value>
      The Point's y-coordinate.
     </value>
    </member>
   </members>
  </doc>
```

End of informative text.

F Bibliography

This annex is informative.

ANSI X3.274-1996, *Programming Language REXX*. (This document is useful in understanding floating-point decimal arithmetic rules.)

ISO 31-0:1992, Annex B (informative), *Guide to the rounding of numbers* (This document defines "banker's rounding.")

ISO/IEC 9899:1999, *Programming languages — C.*

ISO/IEC 14882:2003 *Programming languages — C++.*

End of informative text.

Index

Symbols

A

U